VISIT US AT

www.syngress.com

Syngress is committed to publishing high-quality books for IT Professionals and delivering those books in media and formats that fit the demands of our customers. We are also committed to extending the utility of the book you purchase via additional materials available from our Web site.

SOLUTIONS WEB SITE

To register your book, visit www.syngress.com/solutions. Once registered, you can access our solutions@syngress.com Web pages. There you may find an assortment of value-added features such as free e-books related to the topic of this book, URLs of related Web sites, FAQs from the book, corrections, and any updates from the author(s).

ULTIMATE CDs

Our Ultimate CD product line offers our readers budget-conscious compilations of some of our best-selling backlist titles in Adobe PDF form. These CDs are the perfect way to extend your reference library on key topics pertaining to your area of expertise, including Cisco Engineering, Microsoft Windows System Administration, CyberCrime Investigation, Open Source Security, and Firewall Configuration, to name a few.

DOWNLOADABLE E-BOOKS

For readers who can't wait for hard copy, we offer most of our titles in downloadable Adobe PDF form. These e-books are often available weeks before hard copies, and are priced affordably.

SYNGRESS OUTLET

Our outlet store at syngress.com features overstocked, out-of-print, or slightly hurt books at significant savings.

SITE LICENSING

Syngress has a well-established program for site licensing our e-books onto servers in corporations, educational institutions, and large organizations. Contact us at sales@syngress.com for more information.

CUSTOM PUBLISHING

Many organizations welcome the ability to combine parts of multiple Syngress books, as well as their own content, into a single volume for their own internal use. Contact us at sales@syngress.com for more information.

D1270376

SYNGRESS®

SYNGRESS®

How to Cheat at Configuring

Open Source Security Tools

Raven Alder

Josh Burke

Chad Keefer

Angela Orebaugh

Larry Pesce

Eric S. Seagren

KEY	SERIAL NUMBER
001	HJIRTCV764
002	PO9873D5FG
003	829KM8NJH2
004	BPOQ48722D
005	CVPLQ6WQ23
006	VBP965T5T5
007	HJJJ863WD3E
008	2987GVTWMK
009	629MP5SDJT
010	IMWQ295T6T

PUBLISHED BY
Syngress Publishing, Inc.
Elsevier, Inc.
30 Corporate Drive
Burlington, MA 01803

How to Cheat at Configuring Open Source Security Tools

Printed in the United States of America
1 2 3 4 5 6 7 8 9 0

ISBN-10: 1-59749-170-5
ISBN-13: 978-1-59749-170-9

Publisher: Amorette Pedersen   Acquisitions Editor: Andrew Williams
Page Layout and Art: Patricia Lupien   Cover Designer: Michael Kavish
Indexer: Richard Carlson

For information on rights, translations, and bulk sales, contact Matt Pedersen, Commercial Sales Director and Rights, at Syngress Publishing; email m.pedersen@syngress.com.

Contributing Authors

Raven Alder is a Senior Security Engineer for IOActive, a consulting firm specializing in network security design and implementation. She specializes in scalable enterprise-level security, with an emphasis on defense in depth. She designs large-scale firewall and IDS systems, and then performs vulnerability assessments and penetration tests to make sure they are performing optimally. In her copious spare time, she teaches network security for LinuxChix.org and checks cryptographic vulnerabilities for the Open Source Vulnerability Database. Raven lives in Seattle, WA. Raven was a contributor to *Nessus Network Auditing* (Syngress Publishing, ISBN: 1-931836-08-6).

Josh Burke (CISSP) is an independent information security consultant in Seattle, Washington. He has held positions in networking, systems, and security over the past seven years in the technology, financial, and media sectors. A graduate of the business school at the University of Washington, Josh concentrates on balancing technical and business needs for companies in the many areas of information security. He also promotes an inclusive, positive security philosophy for companies, which encourages communicating the merits and reasons for security policies, rather than educating only on what the policies forbid.

Josh is an expert in open-source security applications such as Snort, Ethereal, and Nessus. His research interests include improving the security and resilience of the Domain Name System (DNS) and the Network Time Protocol (NTP). He also enjoys reading about the mathematics and history of cryptography, but afterward often knows less about the subject than when he started.

Chad Keefer is the founder of Solirix, a computer network security company specializing in Information Assurance. Chad is a former developer of Sourcefire's RNA product team. Chad has over 13 years of industry experience in security, networking, and software engineering. He has worked extensively with the federal government and in a wide range of commercial industries to redefine and sharpen the current perception of security. He has also been a lead architect in this space, overseeing initiatives to redesign and build many security infrastructures. Chad holds a B.S. in Computer Science from the University of Maryland. He currently lives in Annapolis, MD with his wife and daughter.

Angela Orebaugh is an industry-recognized security technology visionary and scientist, with over 12 years hands-on experience. She currently performs leading-edge security consulting and works in research and development to advance the state of the art in information systems security. Angela currently participates in several security initiatives for the National Institute of Standards and Technology (NIST). She is the lead scientist for the National Vulnerability Database and author of several NIST Special Publications on security technologies. Angela has over a decade of experience in information technology, with a focus on perimeter defense, secure network design, vulnerability discovery, penetration testing, and intrusion detection systems. She has a Masters in Computer Science, and is currently pursuing her Ph.D. with a concentration in Information Security at George Mason University. Angela is the author of the Syngress best seller *Ethereal Packet Sniffing* (ISBN: 1932266828). She has also co-authored the *Snort Cookbook and Intrusion Prevention and Active Response: Deploying Network and Host IPS* (Syngress; ISBN: 193226647X). Angela is a researcher, writer, and speaker for SANS Institute and faculty for The Institute for Applied Network Security and George Mason University. Angela has a wealth of knowledge from industry, academia, and government from her consulting experience with prominent Fortune 500 companies, the Department of Defense, dot-com startups, and universities. She is a frequently invited speaker at a variety of conferences and security events.

Current research interests: intrusion detection, intrusion prevention, data mining, attacker profiling, user behavior analysis, network forensics

Larry Pesce (CCNA, GCFA Silver, GAWN Silver) is the Manager for Information Services Security at Care New England, a mid-sized healthcare organization in New England. In the last 13 years in the computer industry, Larry has become a jack of all trades; PC repair, Network Engineering, Web Design, Non-Linear Audio and Video production, and Computer Security. Larry is also gainfully employed as a Penetration Tester / Ethical Hacker with Defensive Intuition, a Rhode Island-based security consulting company. A graduate of Roger Williams University in Compute Information Systems, Larry is currently exploring his options for graduate education.

In addition to his industry experience, Larry is also a Security Evangelist for the PaulDotCom Security Weekly podcast at www.pauldotcom.com. Larry is currently completing a work with his PaulDotCom Security Weekly co-host, Paul Asadoorian on hacking the Linksys WRT54G. More of Larry's writing, guides, and rants can be found on his blog at www.haxorthematrix.com.

Eric S. Seagren (CISA, CISSP-ISSAP, SCNP, CCNA, CNE-4, MCP+I, MCSE-NT) has 10 years of experience in the computer industry, with the last eight years spent in the financial services industry working for a Fortune 100 company. Eric started his computer career working on Novell servers and performing general network troubleshooting for a small Houston-based company. Since he has been working in the financial services industry, his position and responsibilities have advanced steadily. His duties have included server administration, disaster recovery responsibilities, business continuity coordinator, Y2K remediation, network vulnerability assessment, and risk management responsibilities. He has spent the last few years as an IT architect and risk analyst, designing and evaluating secure, scalable, and redundant networks.

Eric has worked on several books as a contributing author or technical editor. These include *Hardening Network Security* (McGraw-Hill), *Hardening Network Infrastructure* (McGraw-Hill), *Hacking Exposed: Cisco Networks* (McGraw-Hill), *Configuring Check Point NGX VPN-1/FireWall-1* (Syngress), *Firewall Fundamentals* (Cisco Press), and *Designing and Building Enterprise DMZs* (Syngress). He has also received a CTM from Toastmasters of America.

Contents

## Chapter 1

Testing
and Auditing
Your Systems

Solutions in this chapter:

- **Taking Inventory**
- **Vulnerability Scanning**
- **OSSTMM**

☑ **Summary**

☑ **Solutions Fast Track**

☑ **Frequently Asked Questions**

Introduction

Sooner or later you will need to identify all the systems on your network. Despite the most stringent of usage policies, sometimes undocumented systems may be added to the network. Sometimes these systems are "test" systems that were never decommissioned. At other times you may find "rogue" systems whose mere presence on the network violates policy. There may be instances where the system is managed by a third party as part of a vendor's service offering. The value of a full network discovery is even more apparent if you are dealing with an environment that you are not familiar with, such as a newly acquired company, or if you are new to your position. If the network has few enough hosts, this task isn't much of a challenge. If the network is large, or spread across multiple locations, and visiting them all isn't practical, an automated discovery may be much more practical. We will look at some generic discovery/scanning tools, as well as some that are targeted at specific services.

After you have identified all the systems on your network, the next logical step is to determine the security posture of those systems. Several automated security scanning tools are available that can check for a large list of known vulnerabilities and can make this task easier. We will demonstrate the configuration and operation of some automated vulnerability scanners. We will also discuss the Microsoft Baseline Security Analyzer, which simply checks a Microsoft system and reports on any known security issues it finds. Finally, there are some formalized security testing methodologies that you can use to assess the security of a system, beyond simply running a vulnerability scanner.

Taking Inventory

In a perfect world, you would have 100 percent accurate and complete documentation encompassing every system that is connected to the corporate network. No one with access to the network would ever connect a system to the network without all the proper documentation and approvals to do so. Well, we all know "perfect" doesn't exist. Perhaps you have a specific reason to do the network discovery, or maybe not. A periodic discovery is a good idea anyway, even if you don't have any specific reason to do one. It can provide assurance that policies are being followed when you can successfully produce documented approval for all devices on your network. A host inventory can also demonstrate that your documentation matches the true state of the network and that routers and switches are where they are supposed to be. Given the fact that systems can be very hard to locate physically, especially given the increasingly smaller size of wireless access points, a network-based discovery is often more fruitful than a physical one.

Locating and Identifying Systems

There are two primary steps to performing a network inventory. The first step is simply to identify the existence of a system. There are a number of ways to do this; typically a combination of methods will result in the most accurate inventory. Pinging entire blocks of IP addresses will identify most systems. If the system is configured not to respond to a ping, however, it will of course be missed. This occurs most often when a personal firewall is running on the host that is blocking network pings. Even in cases where a system will not respond to a ping, the host is usually listening on *some* port. A more comprehensive TCP-based port scan will often reveal the presence of systems that a ping scan will not. Further, by capturing the initial output for each port you can often gather more information, which can be used to identify the listening software or host. For example, if you connect to

TCP port 21, and it responds with HTML headers, you could probably conclude that the system is running a Web server on the port normally used for FTP. You can inspect the DHCP scope on the DHCP servers in an attempt to identify a system that is not authorized to be on the network. Wireless systems can be identified relatively easily due to the fact that they must transmit a signal in order to communicate. Depending on the size of the network, you may even be able to take an inventory of the ports used on switches and routers, or for those with a lot of time on their hands, by cross-referencing the ARP tables of the switches with a list of known hosts. In 99% of the cases, however, a simple ping scan of all the network IP addresses combined with a TCP and UDP scan of a few key ports will provide a very good inventory of the hosts on the network.

TIP

A well-secured network will hinder exactly the types of inventory-building activities you will be performing. The same techniques that stop a hacker from mapping out your network will also hinder you as an admin. If you are not able to see the results you are expecting, remember that firewalls, VLANs, IPsec, and other security measures may skew your results.

After you have identified the systems that exist on your network, the next step is more time consuming: determining *where* the system is physically located. In some cases, maybe you don't need to, particularly if they are authorized systems, or if you can identify a means to contact the person responsible for the system in order to make the system "legal." If you do find a rogue system, however, you will want to see where it is located and perform other information-gathering steps in an attempt to get it removed from the network or complete the needed procedures for the system to have *authorized* access to the network. Sometimes this process is relatively simple, such as when the system is using a host-naming convention that tells you its location and maybe even the server role, such as DALLASWEB01.somecompany.com. In other cases you may need to use the IP address and *traceroute* to track down the physical location based on the subnet combined with a good network map (we'll go over an example in the next few paragraphs). In the case of a wireless system (host or access point), locating the rogue system can be particularly challenging.

Remember that a network device inventory is a living document. It will take time to perform an IP scan, track down any devices that you weren't familiar with, and verify network access approval or seek approval for all devices. By the time you're finished, it will probably be time to start the process over. Because the network is rarely a static entity, this type of discovery should be performed on a regular schedule. You may have local policies that dictate how frequently the discovery should be. If these policies are not present, you should develop a process and make it a part of your normal business operations. In this way, rogue systems can be located in a minimal amount of time and you can minimize any security risk that these systems may pose.

The contents of your inventory documentation will vary according to your needs, but there are some common elements. At a bare minimum you will want to know the IP address, host name, and contact information for the person(s) responsible for administering the device. You could get as detailed as including hardware specifications (manufacturer, model, memory, etc.), MAC address, administrative contacts, emergency contacts, operating system type and version, and much more.

Ultimately you will want to customize the documentation to your business needs. Perhaps deploying biometric authentication is a priority, in which case you might want to include a column indicating which devices have fingerprint scanners attached to them.

Nmap

Nmap is the most widely used general purpose network scanner. It is available from http://insecure.org/nmap/ for both Windows, Linux, MAC OS X, Sun Solaris, and several other operating systems. The operation of Nmap is largely the same whether you are running it on Windows on Linux. The most notable exception is that you will need the Windows packet capture driver, WinPcap, if you are running Nmap on Windows.

> **NOTE**
>
> The latest version of Nmap supports raw sockets, which means that if you are using Windows 2000, Windows XP, or Windows 2003 Server, you don't need the WinPcap drivers. For older versions of Windows you will still need WinPcap.

Nmap can scan for open ports using a variety of standardized TCP packet options, as well as using some of the options in non-standard ways. There are a large number of command-line options, which can sometimes appear confusing, but the Nmap documentation and support on the Internet are both very good. Periodically, a GUI front end will come and go, but currently there are no Windows front ends for Nmap being actively developed. NmapFE is a GUI front end for Linux and it is actively maintained by the creator of Nmap. The GUI has the benefit of enabling you to check boxes for various options instead of requiring you to know a more complex command-line syntax.

> **TIP**
>
> Be aware of the underlying network topology that you are working with. If you are scanning a host on the other side of a firewall it will likely severely alter your results. In some cases, even an ISP will filter out certain ports. Although this prevents those ports from being available over the Internet, they might still be available locally, and possibly still pose a security risk.

Assuming you have the Windows packet capture driver (WinPcap) installed and working properly, all that is needed to install Nmap on Windows is to extract the contents of the Zip download to a directory and run the Nmap executable. On Linux you can download and compile the source code, or install it as an RPM. When you run it with no options, you will see a lengthy help screen with a few examples. For the real treasure trove of helpful information, refer to the Nmap man page located at http://insecure.org/nmap/man/. If you are comfortable working on Linux or Windows, Nmap functions almost identically on either. There is, however, one difference that can be significant, which is speed. Nmap runs much faster on Linux than Windows. In a small network this may not be a consideration, but if you are scanning a large number of hosts, or ports, the difference in scan times can be significant.

Let's go through some examples of how you could make use of Nmap. Let's suppose you want to do an initial scan of your entire company network. If your company is using the private address space 192.168.0.0 or some portion thereof, you could scan the entire class B network, sending only a ping to see if the system is "alive" with the following command line.

```
nmap -v -sP 192.168.0.0/16
```

This would perform the most basic type of scan, which is a ping scan only, as specified by the use of the –sP option. You can see more information by using the –v option, which tells Nmap to be more verbose; in most cases you will find the extra information informative. This option can also be used multiple times for even more information, so –v, and –vv are both valid. Because it is fairly common for a personal firewall to block ping attempts, you may have better luck if you run the scan without the –sP option. If you don't specify a scan type, Nmap will default to a TCP SYN scan (same as –sS). The normal TCP *three-way* handshake consists of the initiating system sending a packet with the SYN bit set. The target host responds with a packet with the SYN and ACK bit set. The original system then sends an ACK packet back to the target. In this fashion a TCP session is established, which is followed by the desired communications. The SYN scan (-sS) will send the initial SYN packet, but when the target hose replies with a SYN ACK, Nmap never completes the three-way handshake to fully establish the session. This method is so fast and efficient that it is the default scanning method Nmap uses.

If you do not specify which TCP *ports* to scan, Nmap will scan all TCP ports defined in the *nmap-services* file, which at the time of this writing is 1680 of the most common ports. So let's suppose during your ping scan of the entire network a system was identified that you didn't recognize (192.168.1.106) and you want to find out more about it. After the ping scan you could perform an Nmap scan with no options and see which of the most commons ports are open. The output of *nmap 192.168.1.106*, being a typical single-host scan with no other options specified, is shown in Figure 1.1.

Figure 1.1 Nmap Results

```
C:\Apps\Nmap>nmap 192.168.1.106

Starting Nmap 4.11 ( http://www.insecure.org/nmap ) at 2006-09-17 14:54 Central
Standard Time
Interesting ports on 192.168.1.106:
Not shown: 1676 closed ports
PORT      STATE SERVICE
135/tcp   open  msrpc
139/tcp   open  netbios-ssn
445/tcp   open  microsoft-ds
5101/tcp open  admdog
MAC Address: 00:08:02:32:8A:4C (Compaq Computer)

Nmap finished: 1 IP address (1 host up) scanned in 2.172 seconds
```

From these results you can see that the system has TCP ports 135, 139, and 445 open, most likely indicating a Windows host. Just to confirm your suspicions, you could use Nmap's operating system fingerprinting feature. Any given system on the network was likely programmed slightly differently, resulting in slightly different ways of responding to network traffic. Nmap can use these subtle differences in responses (such as TCP ISN (initial sequence number) sampling, TCP options support and ordering, IPID (IP ID) sampling, and the initial window size) as clues and compare them to Nmap's nmap-os-fingerprint database. If it finds a match in the database, there is a good probability that the actual OS can accurately be identified. An example of the OS fingerprinting in action is shown in Figure 1.2 using the –O option.

Figure 1.2 Nmap OS Fingerprinting

```
I:\HackApps\Nmap>nmap 192.168.1.106 -O


Starting Nmap 4.11 ( http://www.insecure.org/nmap ) at 2006-09-17 15:00 Central
Standard Time
Interesting ports on 192.168.1.106:
Not shown: 1676 closed ports
PORT      STATE SERVICE
135/tcp   open  msrpc
139/tcp   open  netbios-ssn
445/tcp   open  microsoft-ds
5101/tcp  open  admdog
MAC Address: 00:08:02:32:8A:4C (Compaq Computer)
Device type: general purpose
Running: Microsoft Windows 2003/.NET|NT/2K/XP
OS details: Microsoft Windows 2003 Server or XP SP2


Nmap finished: 1 IP address (1 host up) scanned in 2.813 seconds
```

Nmap identified the system as either Windows 2003 Server or Windows XP with service pack 2. Further, you may notice that Nmap has identified the system as a Compaq based on the MAC address. With all this information you have a pretty good idea of what type of system this rogue PC is. The next step would likely be to find out where it is physically located. Assuming you don't recognize the subnet as belonging to a specific location, *traceroute* will use ICMP to try to trace each router between you and the target host. An example of *traceroute* output is shown in Figure 1.3.

Figure 1.3 Traceroute Output

```
I:\HackApps\Nmap>tracert 192.168.1.106


Tracing route to 192.168.1.106 over a maximum of 30 hops:
```

```
1      2 ms      2 ms      2 ms    192.168.102.1
2     11 ms     14 ms     10 ms    10.10.10.1
3     12 ms     10 ms     11 ms    router1.houston.your-co.com [10.10.20.1]
4     14 ms     12 ms     12 ms    router2.austin.your-co.com [10.10.30.1]
5     14 ms     10 ms     13 ms    router3.dallas.your-co.com [10.10.40.1]
6     20 ms     18 ms     17 ms    router4.orlando.your-co.com [192.168.2.1]
7     19 ms     20 ms     17 ms    192.168.1.106

Trace complete.
```

TIP

Different systems may have different commands to do the same thing. For example, on Windows systems the *traceroute* command is *tracert*, while on Linux systems it is *traceroute*.

I have edited the actual IP addresses and host names but you can try the *traceroute* command to a few hosts in your network. Because it is very common to include some indication of the geographic location in the naming convention for routers, often this will tell you where the host is located. In Figure 1.3, hop #6 would lead me to believe the host was in Orlando, Florida. Assuming you had a *managed* switch in Orlando, you could then Telnet to the switch (in this example a cisco 2900XL switch) and view the table of MAC addresses. Referring to our previous Nmap scan, we know the MAC address of our mystery system is 00:08:02:32:8A:4c, so we can use the following command to filter the MAC table to show only the MAC address we are interested in:

```
SWITCH#Show mac | incl 0008.0232.8A4C
0008.0232.8A4C        Dynamic          1      FastEthernet0/2
```

We could now provide an exact network port (port 2 on the switch) for someone who has local access to trace the cable and find the mystery machine. As you can see, Nmap has a lot of features. There are a large number of options that focus on avoiding IDS detection. There are many additional options that manipulate the TCP packets in far more unusual ways. Although these options aren't for everyone, even if you don't need to use these special options yourself, it is good to be familiar with them as a security professional. There are also options that specify the timeout period to be used when attempting to connect. The defaults are usually adequate, but you can use more aggressive timing if you want to speed up the scans. Although the Nmap man page is practically a necessity if you are going to be doing much scanning, Table 1.1 highlights some of the most useful command-line options, as a sort of tip sheet.

Table 1.1 Nmap Options

Option	Example	Notes
--exclude --excludefile	nmap 192.168.1.1-254 --exclude 192.168.1.106 nmap 192.168.1.1-254 --excludefile file1.txt	These are especially important when scanning large blocks of IP addresses so you can avoid certain critical servers.
-sP	nmap 192.168.1.1-254 -sP	Performs an ICMP ping scan only.
-sV	nmap 192.168.1.1-254 -sV	Attempt to determine service/version on open ports.
-sT	nmap 192.168.1.1-254 -sT	Performs TCP scan using 3-way handshake for each port
-p	nmap 192.168.1.106 -p135,136,137 nmap 192.168.1.106 -p U:514,T:514	Scan only the ports you specify, using TCP or UDP. U:<UDP ports>, T:<TCP ports>
-P0	nmap 192.168.1.1-254 -P0	Treat all hosts as online. Without this, Nmap will not scan the host if it fails to respond to a ping.
-O	nmap 192.168.1.1-254 -O	Perform OS detection.
-A	nmap 192.168.1.1-254 -A	Determine OS and Version info, same as -O and -sV
-oN <file>	nmap 192.168.1.1-254 -oN normal.txt	Sends the same output you would see on screen to a file.
-oX <file>	nmap 192.168.1.1-254 -oX XML.xml	Sends the output in XML format for web viewing.
-oG <file>	nmap 192.168.1.1-254 -oG grepable.txt	Sends the output in a more easily grep'ed format. Grep is the *nix command line filtering utility, similar in functionality to the Windows find utility.
-v or -vv	nmap 192.168.1.106 -v nmap 192.168.1.106 -vv	More verbose output providing more detail about what actions Nmap is performing.

Nmap is a good general purpose scanner that can perform a wide variety of scans. The available output formats can be very useful if you should need to provide reports of your scan results. You could even schedule a scan and have the output written to a file in XML, which you could then distribute via e-mail or view on a Web site. Figure 1.4 shows part of the XML output of a sample scan of 192.168.1.100.

Figure 1.4 Nmap XML Output

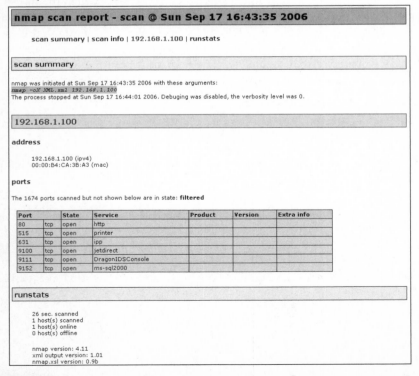

Super Scanner

Sometimes you want something simpler than Nmap, or maybe you want to use something that doesn't require the WinPcap drivers to be installed in order to run it on Windows. SuperScanner doesn't require the WinPcap drivers and doesn't even require a setup program. All you need to do is download the program from www.foundstone.com/resources/proddesc/superscan.htm, extract the executable from the Zip file, and run it. The latest version (version 4) will run on Windows 2000 and Windows XP. The main window is shown in Figure 1.5 with some results from systems it found.

Figure 1.5 SuperScan V4

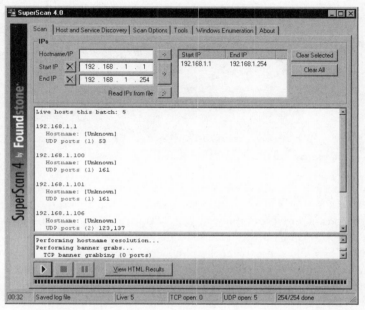

The operation of SuperScan is pretty straightforward. To scan a subnet, simply enter the starting and ending IP address and click the -> button to add it to the scanning queue. If you enter the same IP address and starting and ending IP, you can scan a single host. A third option is to click the -> button next to **Read IPs from file**, which will enable you to browse to a file that contains a list of IP addresses. After selecting the IPs or range of IPs to scan, click the start button at the bottom, which looks a lot like a traditional play button. The authors of the programs suggest using version 3 (shown in Figure 1.6) if version 4 doesn't work properly for you. I have included both versions because, while version 4 offers many more options, my experience has been that version 4 often returns no results after a scan while version 3 works much more reliably. One of the primary reasons to use V4 over V3 is that version 3 and earlier versions support scanning only a single class C network at a time. Version 4 also offers several additional features over version 3, specifically the capability to scan non-contiguous IP address ranges, additional control of some of the scanning parameters, and some special options aimed specifically at enumerating Windows hosts. As you can see, the improvements in version 4 are significant, so if version 4 does work for you, it would probably be the preferred version to use.

Figure 1.6 SuperScan V3

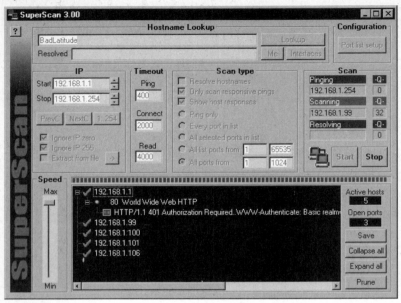

As you can see, the interfaces between version 3 and version 4 are substantially different. The button used to start the scan is actually a little more clearly labeled in versions prior to version four. When you click the start scan button, the scan will commence. The scan could take some time if you have a large number of hosts or ports to check. There will be a small plus next to systems that have open (i.e., listening) ports. You can expand the plus symbol and see a list of open ports. Expanding the next plus will show any responses the scanner received when connecting to that port.

SuperScan version 4 offers more control over the scanning options that are used, but the biggest difference between version 3 and version 4 is the enumeration options available for Windows hosts. Let's take a minute to talk about the Windows enumeration SuperScan 4 can do, and special purpose enumeration tools in general. A definition of enumerate is "to make a concise list of the relevant points." We can refine that definition to fit in a network security context as "building a list of objects or data points pertaining to a given network host." This could include things like running services and applications, file shares that are accessible, users and groups on a host, and so on. When it comes to Windows hosts, there is a lot of information gathering that you can do and lists that can be generated. For example, if you wanted to enumerate all the shared folders on a single host, you could use the following command:

```
net view \\192.168.1.108
Shared resources at \\192.168.1.108


Share name   Type   Used as   Comment
---------------------------------------------------------------------------
SharedDocs   Disk
The command completed successfully.
```

Many similar processes are automated for you by SuperScan. When you select the **Windows Enumeration** tab (shown in Figure 1.7), you are presented with various checks you can perform in the left pane. After you choose the option you wish to use, click **Enumerate** and the results will populate in the right pane.

Figure 1.7 Windows Enumeration V4

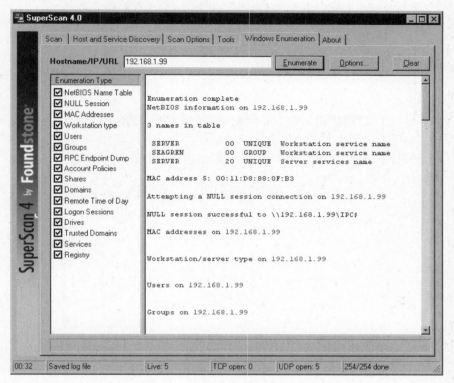

The process of enumerating the shares can be done for all hosts on the entire subnet instead of a single host by checking the **Shares** check box on the **Windows Enumeration** tab, and is just one of the enumeration options SuperScan can use. By default SuperScan will perform all of the enumeration using no credentials, but if you click **Options** on the **Windows Enumeration** tab, you can enter specific account information that should be used for the connections. The NetBIOS Name Table enumeration type is the same information you would get by using **nbtstat –A 192.168.1.108**. This shows the NetBIOS machine name (which can be different than the host name, though it rarely is), and the workgroup/domain the machine belongs to. Depending on how securely the system has been configured, you may be able to get a lot of information from these enumeration techniques. If the system is very secure you will get very little information. In general these checks carry little risk to the target system but as is always the case, if a service disruption is not acceptable, you should avoid running these types of checks because there is always *some* risk involved.

SuperScan has fewer features than Nmap with the exception of the Windows enumeration options, but it is easier to use, and does not require running a Setup Wizard, any registry entries, or special network drivers. Because SuperScan doesn't require any installation per se, and makes no changes to the registry, it can be very useful to have on a pen drive or shared network drive. This type of low-footprint tool can be very useful at times.

Angry IP Scanner

A final GUI scanner that is rapidly on the rise in popularity is Angry IP Scanner (www.angryziber.com/ipscan/). It lies somewhere between SuperScan 3 and 4 in functionality and does not require any installation. Angry IP Scanner also has the advantage that it does not need the WinPcap drivers. Although Angry IP Scanner uses a deceptively simple interface (shown in Figure 1.8), it packs a lot of features into its small file size.

Figure 1.8 Angry IP Scanner

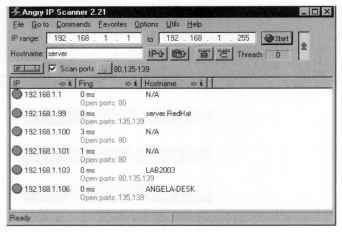

If you select an IP by highlighting it, and then navigate to Commands | Open Computer, you are presented with a list of handy Windows options such as In Explorer, Web Browser, Ping, Telnet, and Traceroute. There are two interesting features of Angry IP Scanner: it is an open source project and it is the only scanner covered that supports being run from the command line *in addition* to running from a GUI interface.

Scanline

If you happen to be looking for something even *more* lightweight, there is an excellent product available. Scanline, which is also available from Foundstone in their free tools section www.foundstone.com/resources/proddesc/scanline.htm, is a command-line-only TCP scanner. This can be especially valuable if you do not have remote GUI access to the system you want to scan *from*. If you have only command-line access, such as from an SSH session, Scanline would be a perfect fit. The usage of Scanline is pretty simple. Entering simply *sl* from the Scanline directory will result in the help screen shown in Figure 1.9.

Figure 1.9 Scanline Help

```
C:\Pers\Apps\Scanline>sl
ScanLine (TM) 1.01
Copyright (c) Foundstone, Inc. 2002
http://www.foundstone.com


sl [-?bhijnprsTUvz]
    [-cdgmq <n>]
    [-flLoO <file>]
    [-tu <n>[,<n>-<n>]]
    IP[,IP-IP]


 -?  - Shows this help text
 -b  - Get port banners
 -c  - Timeout for TCP and UDP attempts (ms). Default is 4000
 -d  - Delay between scans (ms). Default is 0
 -f  - Read IPs from file. Use "stdin" for stdin
 -g  - Bind to given local port
 -h  - Hide results for systems with no open ports
 -i  - For pinging use ICMP Timestamp Requests in addition to Echo Requests
 -j  - Don't output "------..." separator between IPs
 -l  - Read TCP ports from file
 -L  - Read UDP ports from file
 -m  - Bind to given local interface IP
 -n  - No port scanning - only pinging (unless you use -p)
 -o  - Output file (overwrite)
 -O  - Output file (append)
 -p  - Do not ping hosts before scanning
 -q  - Timeout for pings (ms). Default is 2000
 -r  - Resolve IP addresses to hostnames
 -s  - Output in comma separated format (csv)
 -t  - TCP port(s) to scan (a comma separated list of ports/ranges)
 -T  - Use internal list of TCP ports
 -u  - UDP port(s) to scan (a comma separated list of ports/ranges)
 -U  - Use internal list of UDP ports
 -v  - Verbose mode
 -z  - Randomize IP and port scan order


Example: sl -bht 80,100-200,443 10.0.0.1-200
```

```
This example would scan TCP ports 80, 100, 101...200 and 443 on all IP
addresses from 10.0.0.1 to 10.0.1.200 inclusive, grabbing banners
from those ports and hiding hosts that had no open ports.
```

The same scan we performed earlier of the 192.168.1.0 network could be performed with the following command line:

```
Sl 192.168.1.1-254 -n
```

The –n options tells Scanline to ping only and not to do a port scan. If you simply specify an IP address or range, with no other options, Scanline will scan its internal list of default ports. This behavior is the same as Nmap. The Scanline list of default ports currently includes the following ports.

```
UDP ports
7 9 11 53 67-69 111 123 135 137 138 161 191 192 256 260 407 445 500 514 520
1009 1024 1025 1027 1028 1030 1033 1034 1035 1037 1041 1058 1060 1091 1352
1434 1645 1646 1812 1813 1900 1978 2002 2049 2140 2161 2301 2365 2493 2631
2967 3179 3327 3456 4045 4156 4296 4469 4802 5631 5632 11487 31337
32768-32790 43981

TCP ports
7 9 11 13 15 19 21 22 23 25 43 49 53 66-68 70 79 80 81 88 89 98 109 110 111
113 118 119 135 139 143 150 156 179 256-259 264 389 396 427 443 445 457 465
512-515 524 540 563 587 593 636 691 799 900-901 1024-1031 1080 1100 1214
1243 1313 1352 1433 1494 1498 1521 1524-1525 1529 1541 1542 1720 1723 1745
1755 1813 1944 2000 2001 2003 2049 2080 2140 2301 2447 2766 2779 2869 2998
3128 3268 3300 3306 3372 3389 4000 4001 4002 4045 4321 4444 4665 4899 5000
5222 5556 5631 5632 5678 5800 5801 5802 5900 5901 6000 6112 6346 6347 6588
6666-6667 7000 7001 7002 7070 7100 7777 7947 8000 8001 8010 8080-8081 8100
8383 8888 9090 10000 12345 20034 27374 30821 32768-32790
```

The entire help file, or manual, is located on the same Foundstone page where you download Scanline. The sample output shown in Figure 1.10 shows the results of a simple scan using the following syntax: sl 192.168.1.115.

Figure 1.10 Scanline Results

```
C:\Pers\Apps\Scanline>sl 192.168.1.115
ScanLine (TM) 1.01
Copyright (c) Foundstone, Inc. 2002
http://www.foundstone.com


Scan of 1 IP started at Wed Aug 30 21:17:06 2006


-------------------------------------------------------------------------
192.168.1.115
Responded in 0 ms.
0 hops away
```

```
Responds with ICMP unreachable: Yes
TCP ports: 22 135 139 427 1025
UDP ports: 137 138 500


----------------------------------------------------------------


Scan finished at Wed Aug 30 21:17:14 2006


1 IP and 267 ports scanned in 0 hours 0 mins 8.34 secs
```

Special-Purpose Enumerators

The scanning utilities we have discussed have been general purpose scanners even if some included specialized enumeration techniques. Although SuperScan 4 includes some special Windows enumeration options, previous version of SuperScan, Nmap, and Scanline do not. In some cases you may want to scan for very specific responses. One example would be to scan for machines infected with the Back Orifice Trojan (BOPing) or to scan for SNMP-enabled devices (via SNScan). Nbtscan gathers NetBIOS information on a network for all devices. Both BOPing and SNScan are available from Foundstone, but there are many more examples of special purpose enumerators available on the Internet. The intended purpose of these special enumerating scanners may vary from legitimate security tools to scanning for systems to launch denial of service attacks from. As is always the case, use caution when downloading such tools from the Internet and research the source of the tool to ensure that you are not introducing a Trojan or virus into your environment. The general purpose scanners are *usually* intended for finding responsive systems and determining what ports they are listening on only.

Are You 0wned?

A Word of Caution

Perhaps you have been fortunate enough, or cautious enough, to never have downloaded any malicious software accidentally. One thing you will discover when searching for security software on the Internet is that it is precisely security software that is most often a security risk. Countless Internet sites like to offer up security tools to discover Trojans (or even more commonly, supposedly control the Trojans), to clean a virus, or otherwise protect you when in fact the programs you are downloading are infected with a virus, Trojan, or other malicious software. You must exercise extreme caution when scouring the Internet for security tools or you will become the next victim of unscrupulous people.

My advice is to only download your security tools from the major security researchers. In this way you can be fairly sure that the software will only do what it's

Continued

supposed to, without any hidden payload. There may be times when you simply cannot find what you are looking for from one of the most mainstream security sites, in these cases you may have to visit some less-well-known sites. In these instances I would recommend downloading the software to an isolated test system and only running the software after extensively testing it with a variety of anti-virus and anti-spyware programs. These steps should help minimize the chances of falling prey to malicious software.

Table 1.2 highlights the primary features of each scanner covered in this chapter.

Table 1.2 Scanner Features

Utility Feature Matrix					
	Nmap	Superscan Version 3	Superscan Version 4	Angry IP Scanner	Scanline
Command Line Support	✓	-	-	✓	✓
GUI Interface Support	-	✓	✓	✓	-
Non-Contiguous Target IP Ranges	✓	-	✓	-	-
Access to non-standard TCP scan types	✓	-	-	-	-
Special Purpose Enumeration	-	-	✓	✓	-
WinPcap Required	✓	-	-	-	-

Locating Wireless Systems

Some of the most difficult systems to locate are ones with no physical connection to the network, such as systems that rely on wireless connectivity. There are many reasons for doing a wireless site survey. If your company uses wireless technology you will probably want to learn what the effective network coverage is. Perhaps you don't want the building across the street to be able to use your wireless access point. On the flip side, you could perform a site survey to map out where your coverage is weak and needs to be redesigned. Or perhaps an employee has installed a wireless access point or repeater and such "rogue" devices are not permitted according to your company policy. If any of these are true you will want to identify that the device exists, and, if necessary, attempt to locate the physical device. Physically locating the system is more of an art than a science. A directional antenna and a little triangulation can help you get pretty close to a wireless device. A directional antenna can have as small as a 15-degree reception arc and when it comes to triangulating, the smaller the reception arc, the better.

The pastime of taking a laptop computer and driving around with a wireless network card and a wireless scanning utility such as NetStumbler is called *war driving*. This term is derived from an even older technique in which you use a modem to dial large blocks of telephone numbers to see if any computers answer the call, which is called *war dialing*. With the ever-increasing portability and wireless access points becoming so cheap and prolific, you no longer need a car to locate them. Simply walking around with your laptop looking for wireless signals has become known as *war walking*. There are Web sites, and groups of people, who make it a pastime to locate unsecured (i.e. publicly accessible) wireless access points and map them so that others will know where to find free wireless access. This is one such Web site www.wigle.net/gps/gps/Map/onlinemap/?state=TX&s=Show+State where if you zoom in enough, it shows the individual SSIDs of the wireless access point.

Also, see Chapter 7 for more information on wireless monitoring and intrusion detection.

Network Stumbler

NetStumbler, which is short for Network Stumbler (www.netstumbler.com), is a tool to detect wireless using 802.11a, 802.11b, and 802.11g. In addition to simply passively listening for indications of wireless devices, NetStumbler will send out various types of traffic in an attempt to solicit additional information from the device. In practice, NetStumbler is very easy to use. The only real concern is making sure you are using a wireless card that NetStumbler supports. Although there are no guarantees, typically sticking with cards that use the Lucent Orinoco chipset, or Cisco cards will provide good performance and compatible hardware. Senao also offers a higher power card with excellent sensitivity that I have used myself very successfully. Unfortunately, there is no comprehensive list of supported cards so a little research before buying can really pay off here. The NetStumbler site does contain some useful information on supported cards, though. When you start up NetStumbler you will see a screen similar to the one shown in Figure 1.11.

Figure 1.11 NetStumbler 802.11b

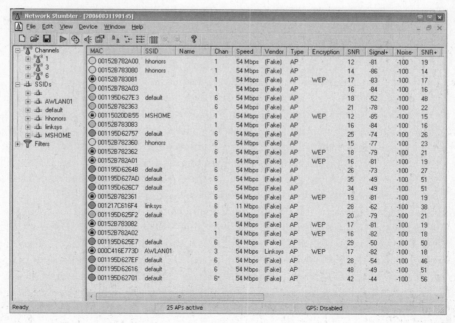

If everything is working properly, NetStumbler will start up in scanning mode and hopefully produce a list of detected devices. If you aren't getting any results and think you should be, navigate to **Device** at the top of the window and see if the proper network card is selected. You can change the selected card without stopping the scanning. The number of results you get will vary greatly depending on the quality of the wireless card and antenna you use.

A little research on the Internet can help you choose a good wireless network card. The Seattle Wireless (www.seattlewireless.net) Web site has many excellent articles that can help you make an informed decision. You will need to choose which wireless card to get, whether or not you want to use an external antenna (versus the standard built-in antennas) and if so, whether you want to use an omni-directional antenna or a directional one. If you are going to be trying to triangulate to find the devices in question, a directional antenna will make the job much easier. Also, remember when making your hardware selection that signal loss is the enemy, and for each connector between the antenna and the wireless device you are sacrificing some small amount of signal clarity. Because of this, having the proper connector on your antenna is preferable to using a "pigtail" as an adapter cable between the antenna and the wireless device.

TIP

When trying to triangulate the location of a given wireless device, bear in mind that wireless signals can be reflected off nearby objects, such as buildings. So you might get a stronger signal from a wireless access point in the room next door from the direction of the building across the street. This could happen if the walls between you and the wireless device were very well insulated and the building across the street was particularly well suited to reflecting the wireless signal.

Many wireless card manufacturers also offer a utility to monitor the signal strength of an access point. These will often show a graph of the signal strength and or signal quality. Their utilities generally require you to be associated with the access point in question, however, so their use as a war walking utility will be limited. NetStumbler packs a lot of information on its results page. The general quality of the signal is indicated by the color of the circle on the left (green is good, yellow not so good). The circles with a lock symbol indicate that the wireless device is using some form of encryption. The type of encryption is shown in the Encryption column. If NetStumbler detects an access point (green or yellow circle) but is no longer receiving any signal from the device, the circle will change to gray. The device could be gray due to ambient conditions such as whether causing a weak signal to no longer be detected, or the device could have been simply turned off.

The tree view (left-hand pane) of NetStumbler includes some handy ways to sort your results. The Channels entry can be expanded to list all the channels with signals on them. Each channel can be expanded again to see what devices are using those channels. This can be useful if you are getting interference from nearby devices on the same channel you are using. This will let you quickly see what other devices are using the same channel. The Filters entry also contains some handy ways to filter the results. One of the more useful filters is the Encryption Off, which, simply enough, shows a listing of all the devices that are *not* using encryption.

One feature you might find yourself searching for is a way to tell NetStumbler to connect to a given wireless device. Don't look too hard because NetStumbler does not include this feature. To connect to any of the access points you discover, you will need to use the operating system utilities or another software program. Boingo is one such program for Windows (www.boingo.com). While it is not at all full featured, and it is not very good at displaying accurate signal strength, you *can* highlight an AP and click Connect and it will attempt to connect for you. Another tool of note is Airsnort, which can be used to passively collect encrypted packets and eventually decrypt the keys used for wireless communications.

!WARNING

Remember to use sound judgment when dealing with wireless devices. After connecting, the owner of the device could be sniffing all of your traffic, looking for vulnerabilities to exploit, or blatantly attacking your system. Once connected, you should not make any additional connections through that wireless device or you could expose your credentials to whoever controls the access point. Even initiating an encrypted connection to a trusted device *through* the device would be ill advised because they could be acting as a man in the middle and intercept your credentials. None of these warnings even touch on the potential legal ramifications of using another's wireless bandwidth. The legality of such activities may vary from one locality to another. For this reason you should seek the legal guidance of your employer before connecting to an unknown wireless device.

Documentation

Documentation is frequently one of the most overlooked aspects of network engineering and design. Most people don't like to generate network diagrams and related documents. Many IT staff consider documentation a poor use of their time and would rather spend it doing "real" work. The fact is there are a lot of reasons why you need to have this documentation, and it is important that the documentation remain accurate and up to date. The types of documentation that is important will vary based on your specific business needs, but the following list represents some of the most important types of documentation from a security perspective.

- Network Topology Maps
- Access Request Forms
- Business Continuity and Disaster Recovery Plans
- IT Security Policies / Standards / Procedures

An additional consideration that applies to *all* your critical documentation is one of availability. If the network is unavailable and all your documentation is stored on a file server, you're going to have a hard time accessing the network documentation that you need to help repair the network. Many times individuals fail to account for this during an emergency and discover they cannot access their critical documentation. This could include not being able to access your business continuity plan, network diagrams, and other critical documents. Typically, copies of the documentation should be printed out and stored in a safe location offsite, possibly at the same location where you store your offsite data backups.

Network Topology Maps

Most people are probably familiar with network topology maps or network diagrams. The idea is to show a graphical representation of how the various network components are connected. Oftentimes this type of documentation is generated when the initial network is installed but it is not maintained like it should be. An *inaccurate* network map can actually cause more problems than not having one at all, because someone may assume things are configured one way, when in fact they are configured differently. Accurate network diagrams are critical. Their real value is apparent when there are problems and you need to troubleshoot the network. When you don't know how things are put together, any problem solving has to be preceded with an information-gathering exercise that only adds unneeded delays.

Or maybe the network is small enough that you know every device that is connected to it like you know the back of your hand, and you don't need a diagram. This might work adequately most of the time but if you ever have to bring in outside help, they probably *don't* know the network as well as you do, and now you have to pay for the consultant's time just to learn how things work, before they can even begin to do the work you actually hired them to do. In this situation the lack of accurate documentation is costing you or your company real dollars, not only to pay for the outside help to learn the lay of the land, but possibly in lost revenue while the solution is delayed. These costs can get outrageous quickly if you're not careful and these are the sort of things management will take notice of.

Yet another situation where quality documentation can really be valuable is for an audit. There are the obvious types of audits, Sarbanes-Oxley, SAS70, and related types of business audits. You might not be impacted by these types of regulations and requirements. There are other audit-like scenarios that may affect you. If you are looking to partner with another business entity in such as fashion that it will require network connectivity between the two entities, the other business partner will likely require documentation related to your network infrastructure. They will want to review it to make sure it is a secure configuration. If you cannot provide them with the documentation they requested it could impede the business venture, again causing a loss of revenue.

Okay, so I've harped on the value of good network maps enough. The next question is what exactly constitutes "good" network maps? At its most basic form, simply having all the important data in one place and it being accurate is all that is required. Beyond that, there are other characteristics that are nice to have, such as consistency. A consistent look and feel will go a long way for being able to quickly look at the diagram and understand the information it contains. This could mean a consistent set of icons or symbols, and consistent placement of key information, like who the document owner is, and version information. While different people generating the diagrams will have a stylistic impact on their work, if these get too disparate you can end up having a lot of difficulty sorting out one document from another.

You should also consider developing a stance on when it is appropriate to use logical diagrams or physical diagrams. Logical diagrams tend to be more high level and show the overall data flow and devices' general connectivity, while a physical diagram typically includes specifics on cables, ports, and so on. Each type of diagram has its place. A physical diagram is generally of more use when it comes time to troubleshoot a connectivity issue, while a logical diagram often is clearer for nontechnical staff, such as project managers and upper management. To some degree it may just come down to personal preferences; neither type is "wrong," and either or both types may be appropriate depending on your needs. When it comes to the aesthetics of documentation consistency will likely prove to be an asset. An example of the same diagram in both a logical and physical view is shown in Figure 1.12.

Figure 1.12 Logical and Physical Sample Diagram

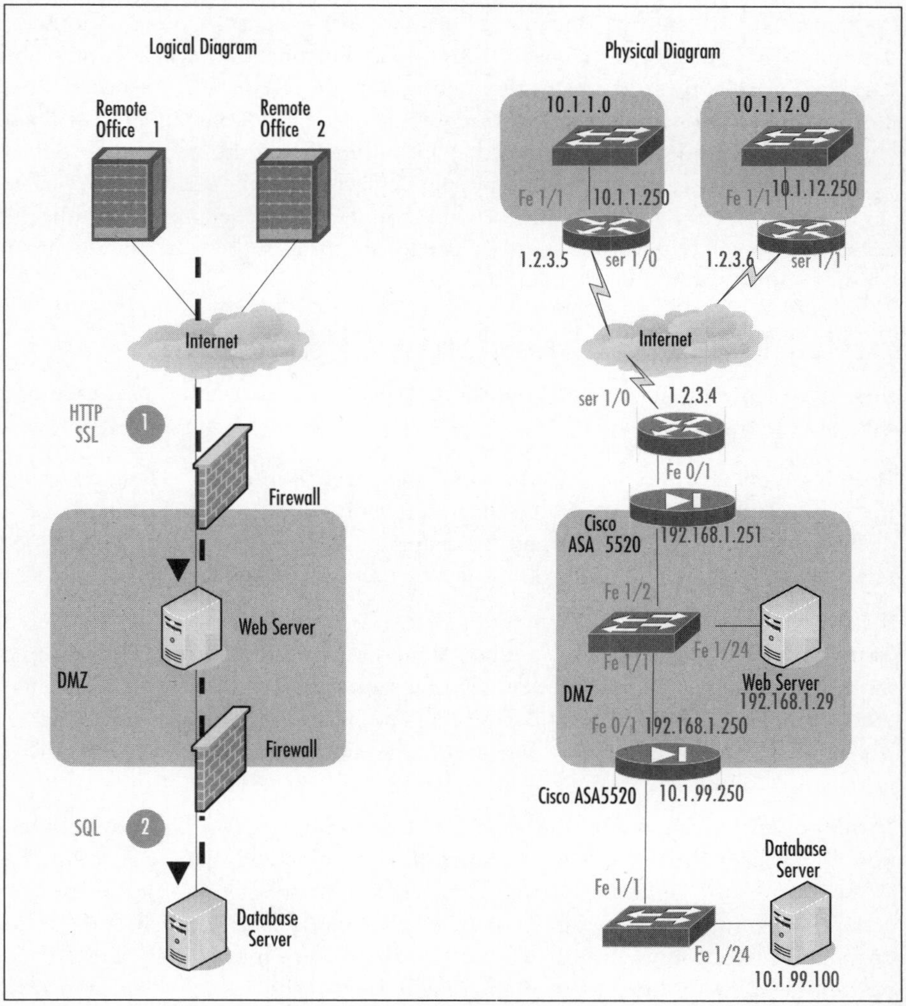

Access Request Forms

Another key piece of documentation is the access request form. You will want documentation to demonstrate that a user formally requested access to the network, or a particular network resource, such as a server. This documentation will also serve as a record for who approved the recourse, and for how long. This type of documentation will most often be useful for audits, to demonstrate which systems and users have approved access to use the network. This category can also include the signed IT security policy (which may be a requirement to approve network access). Either of these could be important if HR needs to follow up on a matter of network usage policy breach. As with the network diagrams, these types of documents could be useful for demonstrating best practices and instilling confidence in potential business partners.

Business Continuity and Disaster Recovery Plans

While not purely a network security document, there are many security considerations surrounding business continuity (BC) and disaster recovery (DR) plans. For one, they will typically contain a log of highly sensitive information in the plans themselves. For this reason, access to these documents should be limited to only those personnel who require access. This documentation will also serve as your first guide to walk through the processes that are outlined, and the infrastructure that is in place, and to look for any security risks. Oftentimes people neglect to secure their DR servers or leave backup tapes containing sensitive information laying around without securing them. In the end, this documentation will hopefully never be useful or needed, but if it is, these are the documents that can make or break a company after a disaster occurs.

IT Security Policies / Standards / Procedures

Because this subject is the cause of much confusion, it's worth summarizing what each of these types of documents should contain.

- **Policies** Policies are broad statements that are general in nature. These documents should not change often. For example, a policy statement could be "data classified as confidential or higher must be encrypted when traversing an untrusted network." These documents rarely contain sensitive information, and one company's policies will often look very much like another's.

- **Standards** These specify what method should be used to conform to policy. They are more specific than policies. An example of a standard would be "acceptable encryption protocols are 3DES, AES(128), and AES(256)." The information in standards may be useful to a hacker, such as what encryption you are using, but this information is typically of marginal value.

- **Procedures** Procedures are the most detailed documents. A procedure outlines exactly how to perform a given activity. These are very specific and include exact instructions such as "click here" or "run this program using these options." Because of the level of detail, procedures often make use of numbered steps and include specifics such as IP addresses and possible access accounts and passwords. While not every process will have procedures written for it, these documents often contain highly sensitive information and should be safeguarded appropriately.

Because some of the documentation in this category can contain sensitive information they should be handled with care. Processes need to be in place to ensure the information is available, and that the confidentiality of the data is maintained. The integrity of the data is sometimes overlooked but is of equal importance. Only authorized individuals should have access to modify this documentation.

Vulnerability Scanning

After locating all the hosts on your network, and hopefully removing or performing remediation on the unauthorized ones, you should determine the security status of all your systems. One of the most efficient ways of doing this is with an automated vulnerability scanner. These types of scanners typically work using varying levels of *invasiveness*. At the safest end of the spectrum, the devices only look for settings that *might* indicate a vulnerability, but they do not actually exploit the vulnerability. This approach can result in some false positives, but it is also the safest type of scanning because it caries the lowest risk of causing a service disruption on the target machine. At the opposite side of the spectrum, the scanner can actually attempt to exploit the vulnerability. Because many of the vulnerabilities are expressly designed to disrupt service, this type of scanning obviously carries a high risk along with it. It does, however, result in very few false positives and provide a very accurate indicator of the overall security of the system in question.

It's worth pointing out that a vulnerability scanner is just that, a scanner with no real intelligence. Some unscrupulous security companies will run the same scanner you can run for free, print the results and present it to their customer along with a bill. The vulnerability scanner has to depend on the human user to configure it intelligently. And even when something *is* found, it is a human that must make a judgment call as to whether or not that item is truly a risk in your current environment. In some cases, further investigation will be required to determine if the findings are valid and if they represent a true risk. What follows is a discussion of Nessus, one of, if not the, best of class free vulnerability scanners available today.

Nessus

Nessus has been around for a long time, since 1998, in fact. It is available for Linux, FreeBSD, Solaris, MAX OS X, and Windows (2000, XP, and 2003). The Windows product is currently listed as beta but it ran fine with no issues for me. You can download is from www.nessus.org/download/. While free, the most current version (Nessus 3) is no longer open source. The Nessus system is comprised of two components: a server and a client. The server process does the actual scanning, while the client is used to configure and run scans and to view the results of a scan. Nessus is a very feature-rich application, which can perform more than 10,000 different types of checks via downloadable plug-ins. The licensing is relatively generous, but there are some circumstances whereby you must purchase a license. In short, you can always scan your own personal systems but for scanning third-party networks some additional licensing will be needed. There are also license options for installing Nessus on an appliance to be provided to customers and for providing Nessus as an OEM product. For full details on the licensing of Nessus, refer to the licensing FAQ located here: http://nessus.org/plugins/index.php?view=faq.

You should periodically scan your hosts for vulnerabilities according to the requirements of your IT security policy. You should also perform a vulnerability scan any time significant changes are made to your network or hosts because this could inadvertently create a security risk, either due to human error or due to an interaction between the changes and the existing security controls. A significant change could include adding a new feature like enabling terminal services, performing an upgrade, or installing a new service pack. Basically, if significant changes have been made, you want to ensure that those changes haven't created a security vulnerability.

Running Nessus on Windows

The installation of Nessus is pretty straight forward. You will need to select the installation target directory and accept the license agreement. For an excellent reference on Nessus see *Nessus Network Auditing* (Syngress Publishing, 2004). With Nessus successfully installed, simply click the **Tenable Nessus** icon and you will see the startup screen as shown in Figure 1.13.

Figure 1.13 Windows Nessus

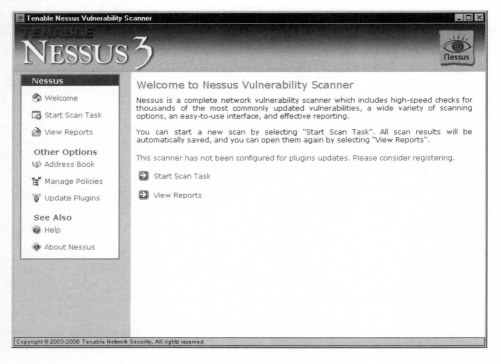

To begin, simply click **Start Scan Task** and then enter the target host to scan. You can enter a single IP address, a list of IP addresses separated by commas, a hostname, or even a network range. After entering the target(s), click **Next**. The next screen enables you to select the plug-ins you want to use. The default will be to run all plug-ins except the "dangerous" ones. The dangerous plug-ins are those that are more invasive and that run a higher risk of causing a service disruption. If you want more granular control over which specific plug-ins are executed, click **Manage Policies** (refer back to Figure 1.13). When you are satisfied with your plug-in selection, click **Next**. The next screen enables you to choose where to scan *from*. You can use the system you are on as a client, and instruct a different machine to do the actual scanning, or you can use the system you are on as both the client and the server, in which case it will perform the scan from the same system you configure the scan. After you have entered the information for the server to use, or left the default of **localhost**, click **Scan Now**.

Running all the plug-ins will take a little time to complete. After the scan has completed, your Web browser will open and display the results of the scan. A set of results from a default (that is, no dangerous plug-ins) scan of a Windows XP Professional system is shown in Figure 1.14.

Figure 1.14 Windows Nessus Results

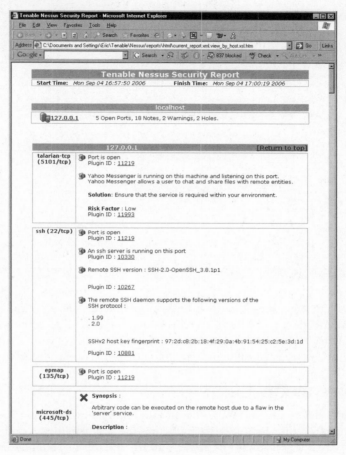

If you want more control of how the scan is performed, you can select **Manage Policies** in the left pane, and then click **Add a new policy** in the right pane. You will need to choose a name for the policy and click **OK**. After this is done, the policy will appear in the list. You can choose either **Edit Settings** or **Edit Plugins**. The settings option enables you to configure various parameters about the scan, such as whether or not the dangerous plug-ins should be used, credentials to use during the scan, ping options, etc. The **Edit Plugins** option is simply that, it enables you to pick and choose which plug-ins you want to use. The plug-in selection window has two panes, the one on the left is for a plug-in *family*, such as all plug-ins related to FTP, while the pane on the right lists the individual plug-ins within the selected family, as shown in Figure 1.15.

Figure 1.15 Nessus Plug-Ins (Windows)

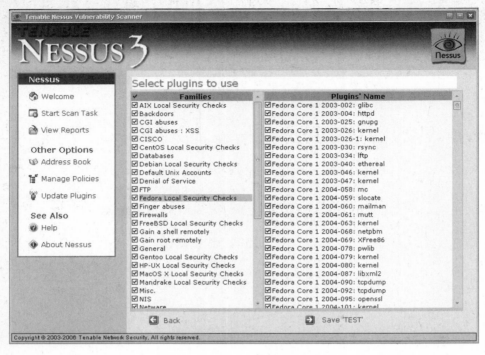

If you know you are using only Windows hosts, you could de-select entire families of plug-ins such as the highlighted Fedora Local Security Checks. Running these plug-ins when you know they will not be applicable to the system(s) being scanned will only increase your scan time, and in the case of the "dangerous" plug-ins, possibly increase the chances of causing a service disruption.

Running Nessus on Linux

Nessus operates a little differently on Linux than it does on Windows. On a Windows system, when you start Nessus, by default the client (which configures the scan parameters and views the scan results) is the same system that is doing the actual scan (the Nessus server). NessusWX is the Windows client that will enable you to connect to a remote Nessus server. In Linux, this does not have to be the case. The Nessus *server* process, *nessusd*, can be running on machine A, while you use the Nessus *client* on machine B to configure a scan against target host C. Machine A will then perform the scan and send the results to machine B for viewing. Because of this, the installation files for the client and server will need to be installed individually. This configuration provides additional flexibility in case you need to perform the scan from a different system than the client. One scenario where this could be useful is illustrated in Figure 1.16. In this case, there is a firewall between your Nessus client system and the target system, but there is no firewall between the Nessus server and the target you want to scan. If you were to use system B as the client and server, many of the checks that need to be performed would be blocked by the firewall, producing inaccurate results at best. With host B acting as a client only, and host A acting as the Nessus server, the firewall only needs to pass the Nessus client session (default TCP port 1241) and then the server could perform the checks on system C without the firewall interfering.

Figure 1.16 Nessus Client-Server Operation

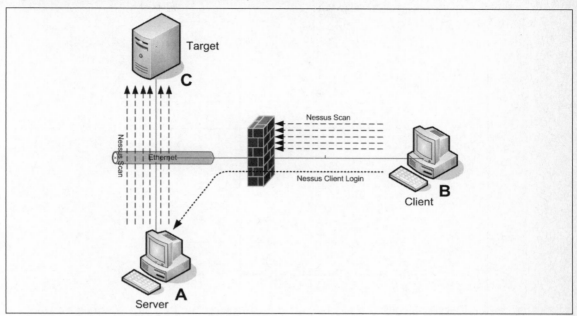

After the install is complete, you must create a user for the Nessus server. This is done by executing */opt/nessus/sbin/nessus-add-first-user*. Enter a username and then select the authentication method (the default is to use a password). If you selected password, enter the password twice for confirmation. You will then be asked to enter any user rules. The user rules serve to restrict what hosts this user can scan with Nessus. To permit a given user to scan any hosts in 192.168.1.0 and the Nessus client system they are using but nothing else, you would enter the following rules:

```
accept 192.168.1.0/24.
accept client_ip
default deny
```

See the man page for **nessus-adduser** for more detailed examples. Simply type **CTRL+D** to exit if you do not wish to apply any rules at this time, and then press **y** to verify your choices. After this is completed, enter **/opt/nessus/sbin/nessusd –D** to start the Nessus server daemon.

The Nessus client interface looks significantly different than it does on a Windows system, as shown in Figure 1.17. You will use the Nessus client to log in to the Nessus server even if both client and server happen to be on the same machine. Enter the Nessus user and password and click **Log in**. In the figure, the client and the server are the same system, this is why the **Nessusd Host** field contains the value **localhost**. You could also easily enter a remote hostname to use the Nessus server on a different system.

Figure 1.17 Linux Nessus Login Screen

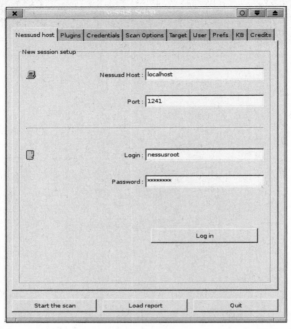

After you are logged in, you have access to several tabs. Select the Plugins tab to choose which types of checks to perform. Similar to the Windows interface, the top pane lists the plug-in family, and the bottom pane lists the individual plug-ins. Enable a given plug-in or plug-in family by placing a check next to them. At the time of this writing there were a total of more than 11,000 plug-ins as part of the default Nessus package. Use the Target tab to specify which machine(s) to scan. The Credentials tab is used to provide login information for SSH, SMB (Windows), and Kerberos. In some cases, Nessus will need to authenticate in order to perform some of the checks. The **Prefs** tab enables you to configure various options such as SNMP community strings, HTTP logins, scan verbosity, and many more variables. When you are satisfied with your choices, simply click the **Start the scan** button.

NOTE

Several types of checks will not be fully tested by default. These are types of scans that run a higher than normal risk of causing an undesirable response from the target host. This behavior is the same as the Windows Nessus, in that the more "dangerous" plug-ins are not used by default. To enable these plug-ins, you must remove the check next to **Safe Checks** on the **Scan Options** tab.

After the scan is completed, a report window should open with the results. The report window opens in a Nessus window, not in your Internet browser. The interface enables you to go from pane to pane and drill down into your results. By selecting the Subnet, you are presented with a list of hosts for that subnet in the Host pane. When you select a host, the Port pane populates and enables you to drill down on the results of a specific port. When you select a specific port you can then choose which results for that port you wish to see. The specific nature of the vulnerability will be explained in the largest pane in the lower right, as shown in Figure 1.18.

Figure 1.18 Linux Nessus Scan Results

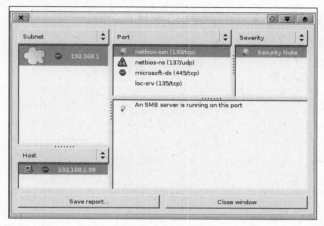

After having looked at the large number of plug-ins available, you can see that Nessus is a very powerful tool for determining what vulnerabilities your systems might have. With the large number of supported operating systems and ability to check for a wide range of vulnerabilities, Nessus is a valuable tool for testing the security of your systems. As is often the case, Nessus will run faster from a Linux system than it will from a Microsoft system, but if you don't need to scan many systems, the difference is probably not significant. The primary advantage to subscribing to Nessus is that you will receive updated plug-ins as soon as they are released. With the free "registered" version you are able to get the updated plug-ins seven days after the subscription users. If you choose not to register your Nessus software, you can get the updated plug-ins only with each new release of Nessus, so with the free version, there is some delay in getting the newest plug-ins. As a paying subscriber you can also configure scanning policies that Nessus will check; these policies can include a wide array of system settings. Even with these limitations, however, it is an excellent free vulnerability scanning tool.

X-Scan

Nessus isn't the only game in town when it comes to vulnerability scanning. There are many offerings but most of them are commercial products. Another free vulnerability scanner is X-Scan from www.xfocus.org/programs/200507/18.html. X-Scan is a Windows-only scanner that supports a couple of interesting features such as OS detection and weak password checking. Using X-Scan does not require an installation, all you have to do is decompress the files to a location of your choice and run the executable. The main window (with some scan results already populated) is shown in Figure 1.19.

Figure 1.19 X-Scan Results

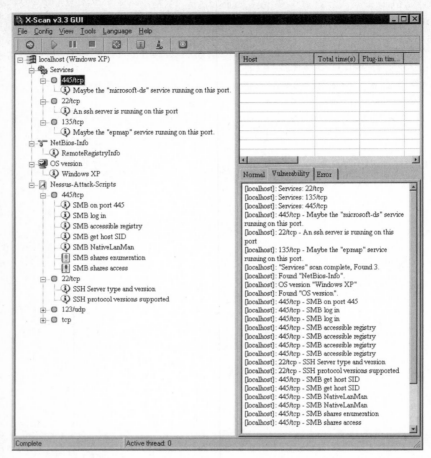

To perform a scan of the local host, you can simply click the green "play" triangle, or navigate to File | Start. If you want to scan a different host, navigate to Config | Scan Parameter. This will open the Config window. The left pane contains a hierarchy of configuration options. Select **Scan range** in the left pane and enter the target host(s) in the right pane in the **IP address range:** field. If you want to configure some of the checks that are specific to X-Scan, open the Config window and navigate to Global Options | Modules in the left pane. The center pane will display a list of modules, while the right pane explains what the module does. These modules include some OS fingerprinting and a large number of weak password checks.

By selecting Global options | Report in the left pane, you can choose what format to use for the scan report. The default is HTML, but you can also choose XMS or text file. If you select Global options | Others, you will find a couple of useful options. The default is to *Skip host when failed to get response*. By selecting Scan always, X-Scan will perform the scan even if the system is not responsive to a ping. This can be useful in cases where you know the target host will not respond to a ping but the system is up. You can also see that the default is for the OS fingerprinting to be performed by Nmap. The default list of ports can be edited by selecting Plug-in options | Port.

If you want to choose specific plug-ins to apply, navigate to Plug-in options | NASL. If the term NASL sounds familiar that's because it stands for *Nessus Attack Scripting Language*. X-Scan uses the same plug-ins that Nessus uses. The default is to select all plug-ins excluding the "destructive" ones, which in Nessus are called "dangerous." If you uncheck the Select all box, you can click Select at the top. The Select Scripts window enables you to choose which scripts to run in a familiar format, as shown in Figure 1.20.

Figure 1.20 X-Scan Script Selection

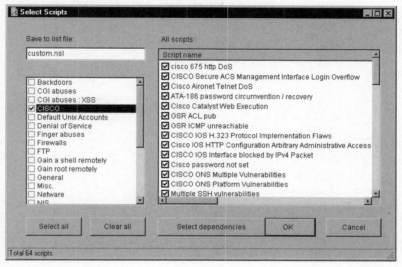

The left pane lists broad categories for the scripts, which is the same as the Nessus plug-in *family* lists. The right pane lists the individual scripts. After making your selection be sure to click **Select dependencies** so that any scripts that are needed to support the ones you selected are enabled. After you are satisfied with your selection, click **OK**. The **save to list file** field enables you to save your lists for future use. It might be useful to save a list that applies only to Windows hosts because many of these checks are for other types of systems. After making all your configuration changes, click **OK** and then run the scan. By default, X-scan will open your browser to view the report results when the scan is completed. A sample HTML report is shown in Figure 1.21.

Bear in mind you will need the WinPcap drivers installed in order to use X-Scan, though like many such utilities X-Scan will install WinPcap if you don't already have it installed. When it comes to the actual checks being performed, X-Scan uses the same Nessus plug-ins, but X-Scan also has the capability to perform some additional checks and OS fingerprinting. Like Nessus, X-Scan also supports command-line operations, which could be a plus depending on your environment. On the down side, X-Scan does not support the client-server architecture that Nessus does. If that type of functionality is needed, you could use some type of remote access functionality to run the scans from a system more appropriately located, but this would require third-party software. If this capability is needed, X-Scan may not be the best tool and Nessus might be a better fit.

Figure 1.21 X-Scan HTML Report

Microsoft Baseline Security Analyzer

The Microsoft Baseline Security Analyzer is a tool for checking the baseline security of supported Microsoft products. In this instance *baseline* means that the minimum security patches have been applied (MBSA uses the updater service to check patch levels) and the minimum security settings have been checked. The MSBS is not a general purpose vulnerability scanner like Nessus. MSBS is instead a way to check your Microsoft hosts for *weak* security settings, not necessarily vulnerabilities. The primary page for MBSA is www.microsoft.com/technet/security/tools/mbsahome.mspx. There are different versions of MBSA, each supporting different platforms. MBSA 1.2.1 is for users who have Office 2000 and Exchange 5.0 or 5.5. MBSA 2.0 supports Windows 2000 SP3 or later, Office XP, Exchange 2000, and SQL Server 2000 SP4 or later. A more complete listing of supported products can be found in the article located at http://support.microsoft.com/?scid=kb;en-us;895660. The older MSBA 1.2.1 supports only a limited set of software. You can use MBSA 1.2.1 combined with EST (Enterprise Scan Tool) to obtain fairly comprehensive scanning coverage of older legacy applications. The software is relatively small and lightweight, at less than 2 MB. The installation process is simple and quick. The MBSA interface, shown in Figure 1.22, is also very straightforward.

To scan a single computer, simply click **Scan a computer**, enter a computer name or IP address, and then click **Start Scan**. The scanner will report on any settings or options on the target that are suboptimal from a security standpoint. The results of a sample scan are shown in Figure 1.23.

The MBSA has marked a red "X" for any security issues it finds, including in this example not having all the disk partitions formatted as NTFS. NTFS is Microsoft's file system format that allows for configuration access controls on files and folders. Fat32 is an older Microsoft file system that has no file security.

Figure 1.22 Microsoft Baseline Security Analyzer

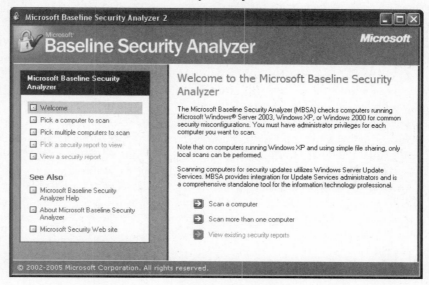

Figure 1.23 Microsoft Baseline Security Scanner Results

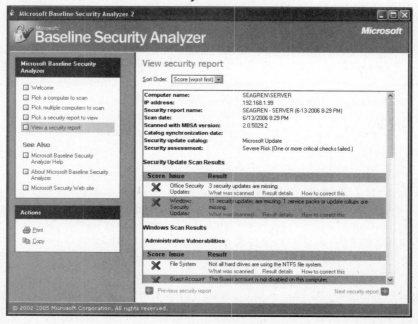

Be default, the scan results are stored in %USERPROFILE%\SecurityScans as .mbsa files. MBSA also includes a command-line version, called mbsacli.exe. There are several useful options that can be used on the command line. Basic usage would be *mbsacli /target 192.168.1.99*, for example. You could also use *mbsacli /r 192.168.1.1-192.168.1.254* to scan a range of IP addresses. If you omit the target completely, MBSA will default to the localhost as the target. By default, mbsacli this way produces text results directly to the console and creates an .mbsa report in the %USERPROFILE%\Security Scan\ directory. The text output can be redirected to a file, and while the output formatting *is* conducive to parsing the results programmatically, it is *not* a very good format for human viewing. Unfortunately, there isn't much out there to help you manipulate the findings. Microsoft does offer the Microsoft Office Visio 2003 Connector for the Microsoft Baseline Security Analyzer (MBSA) 2.0. This tool enables you to see the results in Visio when clicking on a Visio icon. You can download the Visio connector from www.microsoft.com/technet/security/tools/mbsavisio.mspx.

So let's suppose you wanted to test all your systems regularly using MBSA and report on critical updates that are not installed. You could use the command-line version and the job scheduler for the scheduling part. Then take your *text* output files and the *find* command, such as *find "Missing" <MBSAout.txt>*, to list all missing updates. You could further pipe this into *find* a second time to output only the missing critical updates with *find "Missing" <MBSAout.txt> | find "Critical"*. To summarize, MBSA is a very good tool but its most glaring weakness is the lack of a good reporting mechanism. If you have only a few systems to test, however, MBSA can be a very useful tool.

OSSTMM

Let's suppose that you can run vulnerability scanners and perform network discovery, but you want to take your security assessments to the next level. If you begin to think about all the security testing that *could* be done, covering such broad topics as wireless security, physical security, employee education, incident response, and much more, you might feel a bit overwhelmed. The task is so large that simply figuring out where to start could be difficult, and if you do that, there is always the possibility that you might miss something critical. The OSSTMM (Open Source Security Testing Methodology Manual) is exactly what it sounds like. This is a free manual on how to perform a security assessment. It is very detailed (version 2.0 is 120 pages) and can be downloaded from www.isecom.org/osstmm/. Even if you choose not to perform all the testing that is outlined in the manual, it is an invaluable resource to help guide you on proper testing procedures and practices.

In addition to covering such pre-testing tasks as defining scope of the testing and the rules of engagement, it breaks the actual areas to be tested down into sections and subsections called *modules*. Here are summaries of the sections covered.

- **Information Security** This broad category covers such tasks as scouring the Internet for publicly available information that can provide clues about non-public information. An example of such indirect disclosure would be a job posting that specifically requires experience with F5's BIGIP products, which would indirectly tell people what type of load balancers the company is using. It also covers the secure handling of confidential data, including personal data.

- **Process Security** This section includes testing verifying your procedures and attempting to gain unauthorized access via an e-mail or phone call, either through improper process (such as not verifying your identity before resetting an account) or while impersonating someone else. This section also includes luring authorized users to an external location (typically a virtual location such as a Web page) whereby their credentials can be compromised or other information gathered.

- **Internet Technology Security** This section focuses more on the underlying technologies, and examines such things as the network, packet loss, routes, and route control, ISP, and bandwidth of the target organization. This section is really where the build of security testing activity takes place. This section also includes performing a network survey and initial investigation via IP scanning and port scanning. Some indirect disclosure issues will also be touched upon here as you learn some things about the underlying network. The handling of confidential information will again be reviewed at the network level concerning encryption protocols and related technologies. This section also does the work of application vulnerability testing, route testing, access control testing, IDS testing, and testing of anti-Trojan and anti-virus systems. Finally, this section includes modules to address password cracking, denial of service testing, and a review of the organization's security policy.

- **Communication Security** This section includes testing the PBX and other communications methods such as voicemail, modems, and fax machines.

- **Wireless Security** Because of the complexity and expertise needed to thoroughly test wireless security, wireless has its own section in the OSSTMM. This section includes such esoteric modules as testing electromagnetic radiation (EMR), which can enable a person to read what appears on a CRT monitor from outside the building, based on the EMR that is projected beyond the display screen. It also covers the more mundane testing against the wireless network itself, including both 802.11x and Bluetooth networks. The broad category would even includes wireless headsets and the security of the conversations over them, wireless hand scanners (such as in a retail store), RFID devices, and other wireless/cordless devices.

- **Physical Security** This section includes evaluating perimeter security, security monitoring, and access controls methods, such as gates, doors and locks. It also includes alarm response (all types of alarms, including fire, environmental, and a security incident alarm). The geographical location and ramifications thereof are also reviewed in this section.

The end of the document contains multiple templates that can be used for your actual testing, such as a Firewall Analysis Template and a Password Cracking Template. These templates are not procedures but are rather the type of documentation you would include with your testing, detailing exactly what was tested and how. These templates can be valuable for both ensuring that you are documenting your testing adequately and helping ensure that you do not miss any vital steps, because many of the steps have explicit sections of the template to record the specifics.

The business model for the Institute for Security and Open Methodologies (ISECOM) is basically that they provide the OSSTMM for free. However, it is a peer-reviewed and updated document. As best practices change and the manual is updated, those changes are made available to "gold" and "silver" subscribers before the general public. Typically, the time delay for free access is a few months. Because this is a testing methodology, a few months' delay probably will not pose any significant problems for those who want the OSSTMM for free.

Summary

Taken as a whole, the tools and utilities covered in this chapter should empower you to locate the systems on your network using a variety of methods. The best of class utilities presented offer a broad spectrum of choices in complexity and features for discovery scanning. After all the systems are located, you can begin testing them with a vulnerability scanner to determine what their current security posture is. This enables you to build a complete and accurate picture of just how secure the systems are. The Microsoft Baseline Security Analyzer takes this one step further and reports on *weak* security settings for Microsoft operating systems, rather than vulnerabilities. All of this collectively gives you the information you need to complete the first step of securing your network, which is information gathering. Chapters 2 and 3 provide more detail on how to use this information to protect your perimeter and network resources.

Solutions Fast Track

Taking Inventory

☑ Taking an inventory of the devices on your network must be repeated regularly to ensure that the inventory remains accurate.

☑ Nmap has more features and option than any other free scanner. Familiarize yourself with not only the options you need to use, but also the ones you might encounter as a hacker attempts to collect information on your network.

☑ Because the various scanners have different strengths and weaknesses, you should familiarize yourself with all of them and choose the appropriate one for the task.

☑ Identifying that the wireless devices exist should be simple; it's determining the devices' physical location that is often difficult.

☑ To attempt to triangulate and locate the physical devices, you will need a scanner that displays an accurate signal strength and a directional antenna.

Vulnerability Scanning

☑ Be cognizant of the invasiveness of the scans you are running and of the risks that the scan poses to the target host(s).

☑ Consider the legal ramifications to any wireless activities you pursue and ensure you have adequate backing from your employer.

☑ MSBA is for Microsoft products only and reports on weak security settings, all of which do not necessarily represent a security vulnerability per se.

OSSTMM

☑ OSSTMM is a manual to guide you through the process of performing a security assessment using the peer-accepted best practices.

Frequently Asked Questions

The following Frequently Asked Questions, answered by the authors of this book, are designed to both measure your understanding of the concepts presented in this chapter and to assist you with real-life implementation of these concepts. To have your questions about this chapter answered by the author, browse to **www.syngress.com/solutions** and click on the **"Ask the Author"** form.

Q: Does a simple port scan pose any risk to my target hosts?

A: It definitely *can*. A simple ping scan to see which systems are alive shouldn't pose any risk, but a more involved port scan *might*. If the target host has significantly more resources than the target system, you could exhaust the resources of the target system and result in an inadvertent denial of service attack. Of even higher risk are some of Nmap's more unusual scanning options. Some of the specialized TCP flag manipulation scans carry a definite risk to the target host. Because the flag combinations can be illegal (according to the TCP specifications) the target host might not be coded well enough to handle them. Granted, in this day and age this shouldn't happen, but these types of scans still carry a risk.

Q: Why are wireless access points such a big security concern? Why should I care if my users want to use someone else's Internet bandwidth instead of mine?

A: There are many reasons. If a user who is connected to your corporate network also connects to an open wireless access point and his machine is attacked and compromised, the attacker has an open backdoor into your corporate network which probably bypasses all your firewalls and security measures. Even if you set aside all the security issues, the user in question now has an outside connection that you cannot easily monitor. You no longer have visibility if that user is trafficking in trade secrets or otherwise transmitting confidential information. When the user is using your company Internet connection, you have the capability to use an IDS, collect traffic statistics, take advantage of a firewall you control, and apply other security policies.

Q: Can I write my own custom "plug-ins" to perform special security checks using NASL?

A: You can. There is a large body of plug-ins already available and odds are good the check you're looking for is already available unless it is very customized. You can search the available plug-ins at http://nessus.org/plugins/index.php?view=search. The search results may include plug-ins that are not available yet except for the *direct feed* or *registered feed* customers. You can also create your own plug-ins from scratch and if they might be useful to others you can share them with the Nessus community. X-Scan will also enables you to create your own plug-ins and uses the same NASL plug-ins as Nessus.

## Chapter 2

Protecting Your Perimeter

Solutions in this chapter:

- **Firewall Types**
- **Firewall Architectures**
- **Implementing Firewalls**
- **Providing Secure Remote Access**

☑ **Summary**

☑ **Solutions Fast Track**

☑ **Frequently Asked Questions**

Introduction

When it comes to securing networks, the first items that come to mind are firewalls, which are the primary gatekeepers between an organization's internal network and the outside world. While a properly implemented firewall can be one of the most effective security tools in your arsenal, it shouldn't be the only tool. The adage "defense-in-depth" means that you should have multiple layers of security. Using a defense-in-depth configuration, if one component of your defense failed or was defeated, there would still be a variety of other fallbacks to protect your network. With the availability of increasingly affordable firewalls such as the popular Linksys cable/digital subscriber line (DSL) router, using the free firewall alternatives may not be as attractive for some. With a little effort, however, you will find the free alternatives are more configurable, allowing greater flexibility and control than the "home office" grade offerings.

This chapter focuses on securing your network perimeter. Remember that although the most common way to implement a firewall is between an internal network and the outside world (often the Internet), you should not limit yourself to placing firewalls only on the network edge. A firewall should be in any place you want to restrict the flow of traffic. With the current trend of security breaches originating from the inside of the network (often employees or ex-employees), companies are increasingly relying on firewalls to isolate and filter traffic between portions of the internal network.

This chapter reviews some basic firewall concepts and briefly discusses the different architectural ways to implement a firewall. The meat of this chapter discusses the installation and configuration of free firewalls to run on both Windows- and Linux-based systems. Finally, once the network edge has been adequately secured, we discuss how to create controlled, secure paths through the perimeter for remote connectivity, including administrative access or remote office/work from home scenarios.

Firewall Types

No discussion of firewalls would be complete without a discussion of the different types of firewalls. This is particularly true in this context, because it allows you to better understand exactly where in the spectrum the free firewall offerings lie. In the networking sense, a firewall is basically any component (software or hardware) that restricts the flow of network traffic. This is a sufficiently broad definition to allow for all of the various ways people have chosen to implement firewalls. Some firewalls are notoriously limited in capability and others are extremely easy to use.

Within the realm of firewalls there are many different ways to restrict network traffic. Most of these methods vary in the level of intelligence that is applied to the decision-making process. For example, to permit or deny traffic based on which network device is the sender or recipient, you would use a *packet-filtering firewall*. In reality, even the simplest packet filtering firewalls can typically make decisions based on the source Internet Protocol (IP) address, the destination IP address, and the source and/or destination port number. While this type of firewall may sound overly simplistic, consider if you have a server running a Web site for use on the Internet. In all likelihood, the only traffic that you need to allow to the server uses a destination port of Transmission Control Protocol (TCP) 80 or 443; thus, you could configure your firewall to permit only that traffic. These ports are used for HTTP and HTTPS, respectively Because the server is available for the Internet, you can't filter traffic based on the source address or source port, which will be different for each connection.

The primary drawback with a simple packet filter is that the packet filtering firewall has to rely on very primitive means to determine when traffic should be allowed (e.g., synchronous [SYN] or acknowledgement [ACK] bits being set). While this was adequate in the early days of the Internet when security was not as big of a concern, it won't work any more. It is trivial to set the bits on the packet using freely available software to make the traffic look like it is a reply to another connection. Thus the *stateful inspection firewall* was born of necessity. This type of firewall monitors all connections (inbound or outbound), and as the connection is permitted (based on the firewall's configured rules) it enters this connection into a table. When the reply to this connection comes back, even if the reply uses a port that the firewall was not previously configured to permit, it can intelligently realize the traffic is a response to a permitted session and permit the traffic.

Unfortunately, as the firewalls get better so do the methods hackers use to circumvent them. Suppose you have configured your firewall perfectly and there are no holes: every permitted port is one you expressly want to allow. Using the previous example, no traffic is allowed to the Web server except Web traffic. Sounds good, but the problem is, if the firewall is completely secure, the server might not be. Flaws in the Web server software could allow the attacker to send the server an HTTP request that is 10,000 characters long, overflowing the buffers and allowing the attacker to execute the code of his choice. The packets used to transport the 10,000-character HTTP request are all legal TCP packets as far as the firewall is concerned: therefore, it would permit them to pass through to the Web server. The next step in firewall evolution serves to combat this type of attack. These types of firewalls are *application gateways*, or layer 7 firewalls.

This type of firewall not only filters network traffic based on the standard network parameters, but they also understand the higher layer protocol information contained within the packet, in this example HTTP. The firewall itself knows what a legitimate HTTP request looks like and can filter out a malformed or malicious request even though, from a network perspective, it might otherwise be a permitted packet. There is a down side to this type of approach, which is that the firewall must be programmed with all the same intelligence needed to filter normal traffic, plus the firewall must fully understand the protocols it is inspecting. This means additional programming for any protocol you want the firewall to understand. Most of the major commercial application gateways offer support for the major protocols such as HTTP, File Transfer Protocol (FTP), and Simple Mail Transfer Protocol (SMTP).

With all of this information circulating in your head, you're probably wondering which type is available for free? Generally speaking, you can find many free varieties of firewalls that perform some type of stateful inspection. Application layer gateways are not readily available for free. In reality, few organizations have the funds to use application gateways extensively. One ramification of *not* using an application gateway is that you need to ensure that the service that is exposed to un-trusted traffic is configured as securely as possible and that the server itself is hardened against attack. Keeping the service patches up-to-date will help reduce the odds that an application-level attack will be successful.

Firewall Architectures

The most securely configured firewall in existence will not provide much protection if a network was not designed properly. For example, if the firewall was installed into an environment that allows an alternate network path that bypasses the firewall, the firewall would only be providing a false sense of security. This is an architectural error that would render the firewall useless. In short, where the firewall is implemented is every bit as important as how it is implemented. The first step to installing anything is always planning. What follows is a discussion of the most common firewall architectures, in increasing order of security. Remember, these sections are discussing firewall architectures independent of the firewall type. For example, you could use a packet-filtering firewall, a stateful inspection firewall, or an application gateway in any of the designs discussed in the next section.

Screened Subnet

A *screened subnet* is the simplest and most common firewall implementation. Most small businesses and homes use this type of firewall (see Figure 2.1). This design places the firewall on the edge of your network, dividing everything (from the firewall's point of view) into internal and external, with nothing in between.

Figure 2.1 Screened Subnet Firewall

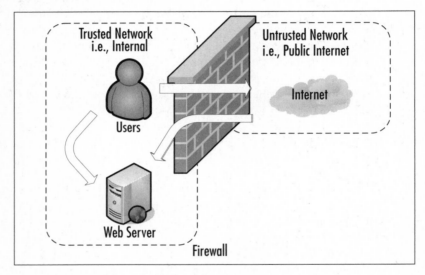

The screened subnet firewall (or *edge firewall*) is as straightforward as you can get. Internet users who need access to an internal server (e.g., Web, FTP, SMTP, and so on) must traverse the firewall to do so. Internal users needing access to those same servers would be able to access them directly. Internet traffic not destined for any Web-based server would be blocked at the firewall to prevent attacks on internal systems. All internal users must also traverse firewalls to access the Internet. This is the same type of firewall architecture you would have at home with a small network behind a Linksys router. This configuration has several advantages. The primary advantage is simplicity. With only two interfaces, the Access Control Lists (ACLs) (the filters that define the criteria for permitting or denying traffic) are much simpler.

Although this configuration is cost effective and simple to implement, it is not without it's drawbacks. In this arrangement, the hacker has several chances to penetrate your network. If he or she can find a security hole in the firewall, or if the firewall is improperly configured, he or she might be able to gain access to the internal network. Even if the firewall is executed flawlessly, the hacker has a second opportunity to gain access. If the hacker can compromise any available Web-based services and take control of the servers, he or she would then have an internal system from which to launch additional attacks. Finally, if the servers are critical to the business function, by allowing the internal users to access them without going through the firewall, you may loose some audit capability that the firewall might otherwise offer. By far the biggest security weakness in this configuration is that if you are exposing any Web-based services: the servers hosting those services will be attacked frequently, and a compromise of one of those servers may expose your entire network.

One-Legged

The one-legged demilitarized zone (DMZ) still has the advantage of cost, because you are building a DMZ using only a single firewall (see Figure 2.2). Commonly, the firewall interfaces are called Internal or Inside, External or Outside, and DMZ.

Figure 2.2 One-legged DMZ

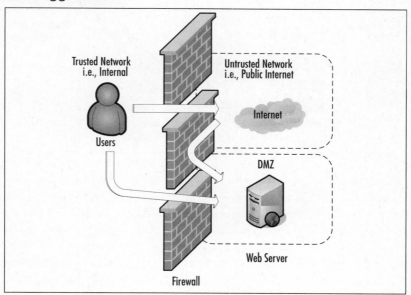

With this type of configuration you get to keep the low cost benefit, but add some isolation to your Internet-based servers. Internal users must traverse the firewall to access the servers or the Internet. External users must traverse the firewall to access the Web-based services. The real strength of this type of configuration is that if the servers that are hosting the Web-based services are compromised, the hacker still needs to contend with the firewall to continue attacking the internal network. As an added feature, because all users (internal or external) must traverse the firewall to access the Web-based servers, you may gain a higher degree of auditing from the firewall logs. If you wanted to provide even further isolation, assuming you have the available interfaces on the firewall, you could implement a separate DMZ for each Web-based server you needed.

The only real disadvantages to this configuration are complexity, and to a small degree, cost. As you add interfaces to the firewall, the configuration will become more complex. Not only does this complexity add to the time and labor for configuration and maintenance, it also increases the chance that an error could be made in the configuration. As you add interfaces there will often be additional costs associated with them. In most cases this cost will be minor and far less than an additional fire-wall, but with some high-speed interfaces, they can become very costly. Lastly, though many would consider it minor, with this configuration, if the firewall itself is defeated, the entire network is open to attack. Of course the solution to such paranoid thinking is costly.

True DMZ

The true DMZ is generally considered the most secure of firewall architectures. With this design, there is an external and internal firewall. Between the two is sandwiched any Internet accessible devices (see Figure 2.3).

Figure 2.3 True DMZ

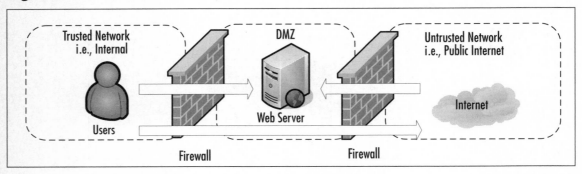

Internet traffic is only permitted to a server in the DMZ, and only on the port that server is listening on. For example, if you had a Web server in the DMZ and an FTP server in the DMZ, traffic with a destination port of 80 would only be permitted to the Web server. For users accessing the same servers, the same rules would apply. Internal users would have to have permission through both firewalls to access the Internet. Obviously, this type of design costs more, typically double, but that cost buys you increased security. In a true DMZ, if the Web server is compromised the hacker is still trapped between two firewalls. For those who want to go the extra mile, the inside and outside fire-walls can be of different types (say Cisco Private Internet Exchange [PIX] and Linux netfilter). In this way, a hacker that finds a security hole in one firewall is unlikely to be able to apply the same techniques to the other firewall.

With all of the basics out of the way, you will be in a better position to make informed decisions when it comes time to propose and implement a firewall solution for your network. Bear in mind, while this chapter covers the basics of firewalls, there are entire volumes (such as *Designing and Building Enterprise DMZs* by Syngress Publishing, 2006) that explore the topic of firewall architectures, DMZ design, and implementation.

> ## Tools & Traps...
>
> ### Accidents Happen
>
> I saw a corporate firewall/DMZ with a connection that allowed traffic to completely bypass their Internet firewall. I do not know why this happened, because the organization was not lacking properly trained networking professionals. These types of errors could occur because someone didn't analyze the implications of the changes adequately. Perhaps it was a "rush" to install some connectivity, or an emergency repair, or even a "temporary" fix. All of these things would indicate poor change control procedures. It is also possible that someone didn't realize the complete layout of the network when they made the connection in question, which could indicate inadequate network documentation among other things. In any case, these were trained professionals who should have known better, but accidents happen to the best of us.

Implementing Firewalls

When it comes to selecting a firewall there are a host of factors to consider. For commercial offerings there is the up front cost in addition to ongoing maintenance costs, which in comes cases can be considerable. For free offerings, however, one of the first considerations is what OS you want to run the firewall on. This will impact how it is managed, and while the capabilities of the firewalls are likely similar, the implementation details will be very different. Most firewalls (commercial and free) run on either Windows or Linux. Some commercial offerings run on their own base system (e.g., Cisco PIX). The underlying Linux system has been so heavily modified it is now considered proprietary. In the case of a Linux firewall, you also have the option of installing the firewall software on a Compact Disk – Read Only Memory (CD-ROM) or pen drive. These steps are discussed in more detail in the following sections, along with specific configuration examples for setting up a free firewall on both Linux and Windows.

Hardware versus Software Firewalls

Another consideration is whether the firewall decision-making logic is run as software that sits on top of another functional system, or if the firewall is a dedicated piece of hardware. In the case of a Cisco PIX firewall, the smallest models are the size of a small cigar box and there is no OS other than the PIX software. This is a dedicated hardware device used to perform the firewall function, also called a *firewall appliance*. The other alternative is that the firewall is not a dedicated box, but a software component. Many popular firewalls take this approach as well, such as a *checkpoint firewall* that can be installed on top of a Windows system. Of these two approaches, if you want a free solution the choice is made for you. I know of no free hardware-based firewalls, so you will be using a software firewall.

Configuring netfilter

When it comes to Linux-based firewalls, there is only one choice, which is netfilter. This is partially because it was the best option available for the longest time. Since version 2.4, however, netfilter has been built into the Linux kernel. Even many commercial firewalls are running a modified Linux OS with netfilter inside their own custom case. netfilter is the underlying software that makes up the built-in firewall on Linux systems. It is the netfilter component that reads the contents of the network packet and permit or deny network traffic. Many times people incorrectly refer to the firewall as iptables, or prior to that, ipchains. In fact, iptables is the software command that is used to configure the rules that netfilter uses to make decisions to permit or deny traffic and ipchains is the previous version of iptables. Even after you have settled on using Linux as your base OS for your firewall, there are some additional choices to make before you start any configuring.

Choosing a Linux Version

While all versions of Linux share some common characteristics, there will be differences. Depending on the specific Linux distribution, the differences could be significant and each distribution will likely offer some different sets of software packages. An excellent source of information on the different distributions is www.distrowatch.com. This site includes a brief summary of what the distribution is trying to accomplish, and includes links to the home page and download locations. Because there are so many free versions of Linux available, it doesn't cost anything but the time to download and install several different versions and see which one you like. In the following examples I use a base system of Fedora core 5, which is the free version of the Red Hat Enterprise Linux that many companies use. I chose this distribution because, being one of the oldest and most well-established Linux distributions, there is extensive support documentation available if you need it. If you just want to see if Linux is something you want to work with, try a live CD such as SLAX. When it comes to choosing the specific version of Linux you want to use, this decision must be made in parallel with choosing an installation media, because not all versions are supported on all media.

Choosing Installation Media

One of the more interesting features that Linux has over Windows is that it can be run from a variety of media. While windows is notoriously difficult to configure to run from a CD-ROM, there are Linux distributions that are capable of running off of a traditional hard disk install, CD-ROM, a Universal Serial Bus (USB) drive, or even a floppy disk. Each media type offers some security pros and cons, and not every distribution will be available on every media type. If you need the features of a specific distribution that doesn't come on the media you prefer, you may need to make a compromise. You will need to research the different media options and choose one that fits in your environment. We will review some of the pros and cons of each.

Full Install

The *full intall* is the traditional install to a system's hard disk. Much like Windows, you boot up an install CD and walk through a guided install process. Most of the Linux distributions installed on the hard disk offer graphical user interface (GUI) install programs that walk you through the installation steps. There is no great advantage to using this type of distribution other than that the size of the hard disk allows you to install a lot of extra software. For a firewall, you generally want to keep the software running to a minimum to enhance security, so this shouldn't be a very big consideration. This type of installation also has the advantage that it will be easy to modify and alter the configuration if needed.

On the down side, this type of installation has all of the same disadvantages of a Windows bastion host. Namely that the entire system is sitting on the hard drive and if a hacker manages to compromise the root account, they will be able to install a virus or Trojan on the system that can survive future reboots. This type of install isn't any better or worse than if you were using Windows for your bastion host OS. Despite these concerns, this is the most common type of Linux firewall installation and most versions of Linux install the firewall components by default. This means if you download a version of Linux you like and install it to a hard disk, you will have a firewall waiting to be configured when you're done.

TIP

In the event that you discover your firewall has been compromised, it is considered best practice to wipe the system clean and rebuild it from scratch. Unfortunately, unless you have some means of isolating *all* changes that were made, you cannot ensure that it is safe to leave the system operational. One of a hacker's first steps is often to install a back door so that they can easily gain access to the device in the future. These backdoors include techniques such as modifying various systems commands so that detecting the back door is difficult. For this reason, rather than risk leaving a system operational that may be compromised, a complete format and reinstall is recommended.

CD-ROM

While you can get windows running off of a bootable CD-ROM or live CD, it takes a lot more work than it does with Linux. There are many versions of Linux designed specifically to run from a CD-ROM, allowing you to turn virtually any machine into a firewall, router, or general-purpose PC. There is an obvious security advantage to having all of your configuration information on read-only media. Even if a hacker manages to compromise the system, all it takes is a reboot and it can be restored to its previous condition. The system can still fall victim to a virus or Trojan, but only until it is rebooted. Further, if the firewall system has a hardware failure such as a failed central processing unit (CPU), all you would need to do to restore your firewall would be to move the CD to a new system and reboot.

The primary advantage to a CD-ROM-based installation is also the primary disadvantage. If you burn the entire OS and configuration settings to a CD, any time you need to make adjustments you would need to burn a new CD-ROM. The cost of the CD media probably isn't an issue, but such a configuration may hinder your ability to remotely administer the system, which would be limited to making changes to the running configuration. Changes that remained after a reboot would require someone local to insert the CD-ROM containing the new configuration. If you needed to implement and test changes that required a reboot to take effect, this type of the setup would make things more difficult. Finally, due to simple space limitations on a CD-ROM, you may not be able to fit all of the needed software or functionality on a CD-ROM. That being said, if the firewall rules are relatively static and don't require frequent adjustment, a live CD could be a very attractive option.

USB Drive

If the space limitations are acceptable, a Linux-based firewall booting from a USB disk may offer the best compromise in security and flexibility. Having the operating systems and firewall software on a pen drive offers the same type of flexibility that a CD-ROM-based system provides, with increased storage capacity over that of a CD-ROM. If you purchase a USB disk that includes a physical write protect switch, you can make changes on the fly, like a live system, and then write protect the disk against modification when you are done. As the storage capacity of USB drive increases, you will be able to use a USB-based distribution that includes increasingly greater functionality. One key consideration with this type of media is that not all systems will support booting from a USB disk. While almost all newer systems support this option, many of the older systems that you may wish to install a free firewall on do not.

Floppy Disk

Although the functionality is typically very limited, there are many versions of Linux that can fit on a 3.5" floppy disk. The primary advantage of these distributions is their low resource requirements. Often, these systems only require 8 or 16 megabytes of memory and a 486 processor to function. The ability to toggle the write protect switch on the floppy can also provide a high degree of configuration flexibility and security. Considering the unreliable nature of floppy disks, it probably wouldn't be appropriate for use if an outage cannot be tolerated. At the very least you should have duplicate floppy disks available in the event of a failure. Another disadvantage to these is functionality. Generally, these floppy-based distributions are single-purpose devices and lack much in the way of functionality. Another consideration is that due to the space restrictions on a floppy disk, these floppy-based distributions are almost always command line only, with no GUI for configuration or management.

Linux Firewall Operation

Before diving into the specific commands used to configure the Linux firewall, we will cover some basic Linux firewall vocabulary and how the firewall operates. netfilter contains the firewall logic, and iptables is the program that is used to modify the rules that the firewall uses. (See the netfilter home page at www.netfilter.org/.) These rules (or ACLs) define the rules used to permit or deny packets and how to react to denied packets. The current iptables use both tables and chains. *Tables* are the blocks of processing where various actions are performed on the packets. Different tables process different chains. *Chains* are a set of rules (or ACLs). There are four built-in tables: *nat, mangle, filter,* and *raw,* each of which processes different chains (see Figure 2.4).

The following tables and chains are not listed in any particular order, as a given packet may be impacted by multiple tables and chains as it is processed. The primary built-in chains are INPUT, OUTPUT, and FORWARD. In addition to these, you can create your own user-defined chains. Capitalizing the names of the chains is a common convention, but is not required.

Figure 2.4 netfilter Tables and Chains

A brief summary of the roles the tables and chains play is included for reference.

- **Nat Table** This table is referenced with a packet that is used to create a new connection.
  - **PREROUTING** This chain is processed as soon as a packet is received and before any routing decisions are made.
  - **POSTROUTING** This chain is processed before a packet is sent to an interface but after any routing decisions have been made.
  - **OUTPUT** This chain is processed for packets generated locally.
- **Filter Table** This is the default table that is used when the iptables command is used to modify the rules and do not specify an alternate table. This is where the bulk of a firewall's processing is consumed.
  - **INPUT** This chain is processed for packets destined for the local system.
  - **FORWARD** This chain is processed for packets passing through the local system.
  - **OUTPUT** This chain is processed for packets generated by the local system.
- **Mangle Table** This table is used for any specialized packet alterations that are needed. Examples are performing Network Address Translation (NAT) or manipulating various bits within the packet.
  - **PREROUTING** This chain is processed on incoming packets before a routing decision is made.
  - **POSTROUTING** This chain is processed last before a packet is sent to an interface.
  - **OUTPUT** This chain is processed before a routing decision is made for packets generated locally.

- **INPUT** This chain is processed for packets destined for the local system.

- **FORWARD** This chain is processed for packets passing through the local system.

- **Raw Table** This table is primarily used for packets that are exempt from connection tracking, and if required, are called before any other netfilter table.

- **PREROUTING** This chain is processed as soon as a packet is received.

- **OUTPUT** This chain is processed for packets generated locally.

After you have reviewed all the various tables and chains, it's worth discussing the overall packet flow. The key to remember is that not all packets traverse all chains. To further muddy the waters, packets will traverse different chains depending on whether they are sourced from the netfilter host, destined for the netfilter host, or just passing through the netfilter host. Remember this will save you time when troubleshooting your firewall rules in the future. Refer to Figure 2.5 for a diagram depicting the packet flow through netfilter.

Figure 2.5 Netfilter Packet Flow

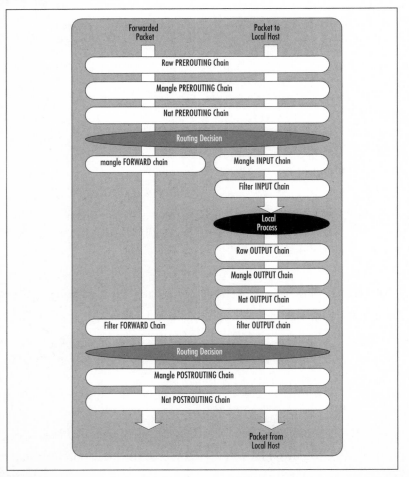

Targets are the actions that should be taken when a packet matches a given rule. A target is specified using the $-j$ <target> syntax (for jump). The primary targets used for a firewall are ACCEPT and DENY.

- **ACCEPT** The packet is accepted and processed by the rest of the TCP/IP stack.

- **DENY** The packet is dropped and no notice is given to the sender. While this does not honor the TCP/IP protocol specifications, it is considered the most secure option, because it denies a hacker useful information about the firewall. This behavior also has a negative side effect, which is if a system is trying to initiate a connection to a port that is blocked by a firewall, the connection attempt must time out before the initiating host gives up. If you use REJECT, the Internet Control Message Protocol (ICMP) port will allow the initiating system to abort the connection attempt immediately.

- **LOG** This allows you to perform kernel logging, which appears in the syslog log. Further options allow you to specify the log level and a descriptive prefix for the log entry.

- **RETURN** Processing continues in the previous chain at the rule just after the last rule processed in that chain.

- **QUEUE** This is a special target that will hold (or queue) a packet for processing by a userspace process.

Unlike some firewalls, netfilter allows you to apply multiple rulesets (chains) to the same interface. Although it may seem minor, this option creates a lot of powerful possibilities. For example, suppose you have an ACL and you want to permit all packets originating on the 192.168.1.0 network except those from 192.168.1.11, which is a host that a third-party uses and is not a completely trusted system. You want packets sourced from 192.168.1.11 with a destination port of 22, 25, 53, 80, and 443 to be permitted, while all other packets are blocked. (see Figure 2.6).

Figure 2.6 Cisco ACL

```
1 somerule
2 access-list 100 permit tcp host 192.168.1.11 any eq 22
3 access-list 100 permit tcp host 192.168.1.11 any eq 25
4 access-list 100 permit tcp host 192.168.1.11 any eq 53
5 access-list 100 permit tcp host 192.168.1.11 any eq 80
6 access-list 100 permit tcp host 192.168.1.11 any eq 443
7 access-list 100 deny ip host 192.168.1.11 any any
8 access-list 100 permit ip 192.168.1.0 255.255.255.0 any
9 somerule
```

In Figure 2.5, each line of the ACL is numbered for easy reference. The order of the rules is critical for proper operation of the firewall. Cisco processes each line in the ACL and compares the rule with the packet in question. If it finds a match, it performs the indicated action and then stops any further processing of the ACL. This means if you reversed the order of rules 7 and 8, all packets from 192.168.1.11 would be permitted. This type of arrangement also means that a packet with a source

IP address of 192.168.1.22 has to be compared against rules 2–7 before being accepted by rule # 8. With seven rules this will happen quickly, but if the ACL is lengthy this extra overhead could be CPU-intensive.

netfilter's ability to move through multiple chains for the same packet allows you to design your chains for greater efficiency (see Figure 2.7).

Figure 2.7 netfilter Chains

```
FORWARD Chain
     CUSTOM Chain

1 somerule
2 iptables -A FORWARD -p tcp -s 192.168.1.11 -j CUSTOM
      2.1 iptables -A CUSTOM -p tcp -s 192.168.1.11 --dport 22 -j ACCEPT
      2.2 iptables -A CUSTOM -p tcp -s 192.168.1.11 --dport 25 -j ACCEPT
      2.3 iptables -A CUSTOM -p tcp -s 192.168.1.11 --dport 53 -j ACCEPT
      2.4 iptables -A CUSTOM -p tcp -s 192.168.1.11 --dport 80 -j ACCEPT
      2.5 iptables -A CUSTOM -p tcp -s 192.168.1.11 --dport 443 -j ACCEPT
      2.6 iptables -A CUSTOM -p ip -s 192.168.1.11 -j DROP
      2.7 iptables -A CUSTOM -j RETURN
3 iptables -A FORWARD -p ip -s 192.168.1.0/24 -j ACCEPT
4 somerule
```

Using netfilter and iptables, you created rule # 2, which says that the source address is 192.168.1.11 for processing the CUSTOM chain. You can create the CUSTOM chain with the *iptables –N CUSTOM* command. Within the CUSTOM chain, you check for the five permitted destination ports (rules 2.1–2.5) and then reject everything else (rule 2.6). Rule # 2.7 has no matching criteria and will therefore match on any packet and instruct the packet to return to the FORWARD chain where processing can continue. FORWARD chain rule # 3 permits all other packets from the 192.168.1.0/24 network. This means that packets not sourced from 192.168.1.11 only have to be checked against rule # 2 and can then move through the chain(s) instead of being checked against all the rules. Figure 2.6 shows the flow of a packet through the rules. The actual rules as they would appear in iptables can be seen with the *iptables –L* command.

```
# iptables -L
Chain INPUT (policy DROP)
target     prot opt source            destination


Chain FORWARD (policy DROP)
target     prot opt source            destination
CUSTOM     tcp  --   192.168.1.11      anywhere
ACCEPT     tcp  --   192.168.1.0/24    anywhere


Chain OUTPUT (policy DROP)
target     prot opt source            destination
```

```
Chain CUSTOM (1 references)
target     prot opt source             destination
ACCEPT     tcp  --  192.168.1.11       anywhere            tcp dpt:ssh
ACCEPT     tcp  --  192.168.1.11       anywhere            tcp dpt:smtp
ACCEPT     tcp  --  192.168.1.11       anywhere            tcp dpt:domain
ACCEPT     tcp  --  192.168.1.11       anywhere            tcp dpt:http
ACCEPT     tcp  --  192.168.1.11       anywhere            tcp dpt:https
DROP       all  --  192.168.1.11       anywhere
RETURN     all  --  anywhere           anywhere
```

Another advantage is that because rule # 2 sent you to another chain, you can make certain assumptions that you wouldn't otherwise be able to. For example, in the CUSTOM chain you could replace

```
iptables -A CUSTOM -p tcp -s 192.168.1.11 --dport 22 -j ACCEPT
```

with

```
iptables -A CUSTOM --dport 22 -j ACCEPT.
```

This is because the packet would not be in the CUSTOM chain without matching the *–p tcp* and *–s* 192.168.1.11 (source IP address). If you want to tweak the CUSTOM chain even more, the RETURN target in rule # 2.7 isn't strictly required. If the packet reaches the end of a user-defined chain without having a match, it will RETURN to the previous chain by default. If a packet reaches the end of a built-in chain without a match, it will use the policy target (typically DROP). Now that you have a feel for the flexibility and power of iptables and netfilter, let's look at some practical configuration examples.

Configuration Examples

The next step is to demonstrate how to configure the netfilter firewall. This is a critical step, and the firewall should only be installed and configured after the underlying OS has been installed, updated, and hardened. These instructions assume you are working with an otherwise secure system and now need to configure the firewall functionality.

To make sure the firewall is enabled, you can run *chkconfig —list*, which lists all of the services and the run levels they are configured to start in. For example, you get the following output:

```
chkconfig --list | grep iptables
iptables    0:off    1:off    2:on    3:on    4:on    5:on    6:off
```

This output tells you that iptables will start in run levels 2–5. You can set it to run in run levels 2–5 by using the **chkconfig –level 2345 iptables on** command. If you are using a GUI window manager, you probably have another graphical application to see this information. For example, in Fedora Core 5, you can navigate to **System | Administration | Security Level and Firewall**, which opens the screen shown in Figure 2.8.

Figure 2.8 Fedora Core Firewall GUI

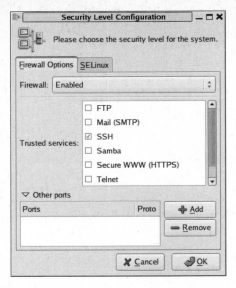

You can enable or disable the firewall by going to the **Firewall Options** tab and selecting **Enabled** or **Disabled**. This particular interface in Fedora Core 5 also allows you to perform limited configurations of the firewall rules (e.g., by checking the Trusted Service SSH, a rule would be added to allow inbound connections on TCP port 22). Because any graphical interface provided will likely vary from one distribution to another, we use the command line to configure the firewall.

Deleting Rules and Chains

With many Linux distributions, the netfilter firewall will become enabled, but with an empty ruleset. In others, it might come with the firewall enabled and a very liberal ruleset in place. Let's start configuring a Linux firewall by deleting any default rules that are present. You can use *iptables −L* (or *—list*) to list the current rules. An empty default ruleset should look like this:

```
iptables -L
Chain INPUT (policy ACCEPT)
Target     prot opt source              destination


Chain FORWARD (policy ACCEPT)
Target     prot opt source              destination


Chain OUTPUT (policy ACCEPT)
Target     prot opt source              destination
```

If there are any default rules present, they can be deleted using the *iptables −F* command. The *−F* option means to flush, which is equivalent to using *—flush*. This will clear all rules out of any existing chains. If distribution has any additional chains created beyond the default, you can delete a custom chain by using the *iptables −X customchain* command. Creating your own user-defined chain is accomplished using the *iptables −N customchain* command. In addition to the individual rules within a chain, the built-in chains have a default policy associated with them. This policy tells netfilter what to do if a packet reaches the end of the chain without finding a match. While the default policy is to ACCEPT, it is better to change this to DROP by using the −P option, which sets the default policy for that chain, as follows:

```
iptables -P INPUT DROP
iptables -P FORWARD DROP
iptables -P OUTPUT DROP
```

Permitting Traffic to and from the Firewall

Now that you have a clean slate and a default policy of DENY, the first thing you will want to do is make sure that management traffic is permitted to the firewall itself. This is done first, because once you have enabled the firewall with a default policy of DENY, you will not be able to manage the firewall remotely until you have configured the firewall rules to permit the management traffic. This traffic is processed against the INPUT chain, because the destination is the netfilter host itself. To allow secure shell (SSH) connections to the firewall, use the following command:

```
iptables -A INPUT -p tcp -s 192.168.99.0/24 --dport 22 -j ACCEPT
```

In this example, you are appending (-*A*) a rule to the INPUT chain to allow traffic from the 192.168.99.0/24 network to a destination port of TCP 22. With no other configurations, all other traffic through or to the firewall would be dropped. This will show up in the rule listing as follows:

```
iptables -L INPUT
Chain INPUT (policy DROP)
Target      prot opt source            destination
ACCEPT      tcp  --  192.168.99.0/24   anywhere              tcp dpt:ssh
```

Although the aforementioned rules will permit the inbound SSH session, there is currently no rule to permit the reply traffic for the SSH session. If you were to change the default policy for the OUTPUT chain to ACCEPT, this would permit the reply packet, but we will instead address this more securely in the next few examples.

If you also wanted to allow 192.168.99.99 access to the firewall with a destination of TCP port 80, you could use the same syntax with −*A* to append the rule, which would put the new rule for port 80 *after* the rule for port 22. You could also use −*I* for *insert*, as in the *iptables −I INPUT 1* **−p tcp** *−s 192.168.99.99 −−dport 80 −j ACCEPT* command. This would insert the new rule in the INPUT chain as rule # 1, meaning the rule for port 80 would come *before* the rule for port 22. Remember, this is still permitting only half of the conversation; you still need to permit the outbound reply packets. It is sometimes useful to list the chains with rule numbers using the *iptables −L −−line-numbers* command.

For outbound traffic (i.e., traffic generated by the firewall), you need to create rules in the OUTPUT chain. To enable syslog traffic from the firewall to a remote syslog server (192.168.1.99), you would enter the following:

```
iptables -A OUTPUT -p udp -d 192.168.1.99 --dport 514
```

This assumes you are using the default UDP syslog port of 514. Because syslog over UDP is a one-way conversation, you will not need to permit any inbound replies to the syslog traffic. The OUTPUT chain is where you need to permit replies for permitted traffic that you allowed inbound in the preceding examples. You could create rules to permit SSH and HTTP specifically, but there is also a way to permit all traffic that is a reply to a permitted session. You can enter

```
iptables -A OUTPUT -m state --state RELATED,ESTABLISHED -j ACCEPT
```

This will instruct netfilter to permit any outbound traffic that is part of an established session (ESTABLISHED). The RELATED keywork is similar, but is for traffic that is part of a different sessions, but where the sessions is related to an established session. Some protocols will open additional ports (such as FTP) as part of their normal behavior. For those that netfilter understands, it can see the request for the additional port and permit that new session.

TIP

iptables commands that manipulate the chains or rules themselves use uppercase letters:

```
    -A append, -D delete rule, -I insert, -R replace, -L list, -F flush, -N
new, -X delete chain
```

Lowercase options are used for specifying rule parameters:

```
    -s source address, -p protocol, -d destination address, -j jump, -i in-
interface, -o out-interface
```

Simulating the Windows Firewall

Now let's configure the firewall. The built-in firewall on Windows XP is enabled by default with service pack 2 or better. The standard configuration is to allow outbound connections from the host system, and deny inbound connections unless they are explicitly configured. The Windows firewall also allows any traffic that is a reply to traffic that the host originally generated outbound. After you execute the **iptables −F** command to flush out all of the previously configured rules, the following commands would configure the Linux host similarly:

```
iptables -P OUTPUT ACCEPT
iptables -P INPUT DROP
iptables -P FORWARD DROP
iptables -A INPUT -m state --state ESTABLISHED,RELATED -j ACCEPT
```

The —*state* extensions track the current status of the connections. By specifying ESTABLISHED or RELATED, the firewall allows packets that are part of a currently established session, or packets that are starting a new session, but where the session is related to an existing session (such as an FTP data session). If you were hosting a service on this system, such as a Web server, you would need to configure the INPUT chain appropriately. This configuration would afford any Linux system a minimum level of firewall security with virtually no impact to it's overall functionality.

Simulating a Home Network Router

With the basics of iptables configuration out of the way, let's tackle a more practical example. For a typical firewall, there is very little traffic destined *to* or *from* the firewall itself. In general, the only traffic that would fit this profile would be administrative sessions to configure the firewall itself. The vast majority of a firewall's traffic is passing through the firewall, and will thus be checked against the FORWARD chain. The following examples would configure the Linux firewall with the same access controls as a typical home network router such as a Linksys or Netgear router/firewall. This example assumes that 192.168.1.0/24 is the internal network on interface *eth0* and the external interface is *eth1*.

```
iptables -P OUTPUT ACCEPT

iptables -P INPUT DROP

iptables -P FORWARD DROP

iptables -A INPUT -p tcp -s 192.168.1.0/24 -i eth0 --dport 80 -j ACCEPT

iptables -A FORWARD -s 192.168.1.0/24 -i eth0 -o eth1 -j ACCEPT

iptables -A FORWARD -m state --state ESTABLISHED,RELATED -j ACCEPT
```

NOTE

Always remember that if you have configured the default policy for a chain to DROP (for example, iptables -P FORWARD DROP) that you will need to include an explicit rule to permit the return traffic. This can be done by using the following command:

```
iptables -A <CHAIN> -m state --state ESTABLISHED,RELATED -j ACCEPT
```

So if you wanted to permit the return traffic for a FORWARD chain, you would enter

```
iptables -A FORWARD -m state --state ESTABLISHED,RELATED -j ACCEPT
```

Many hours of troubleshooting Linux firewalls have been spent by overlooking a rule that permits the return traffic.

The INPUT chain allows port 80 to go to the firewall itself from the internal network. Many the home routers have a Web interface for configuring them, and while your configuration may not need this port open to the firewall, it is included here to help emphasize how the different chains are used. It is important to specify the input interface (using *–i*) so that the source IP cannot be spoofed by an external attacker. In this way, you ensure that even if a packet was generated with the proper source IP, if it came in on the outside interface (*eth1*) it would not match the rule and would thus not be permitted. The FORWARD rule allows any outbound traffic from the internal network to the external network. This configuration is simple to implement; however, the 192.168.1.0 IP range is a private IP range and is not routable on the Internet. Thus, this range wouldn't allow traffic from the internal network to the Internet quite yet. To make this Linux firewall a useful replacement for a home network router, you need to enable NAT, which allows all of the systems on your internal network to appear as a single IP address when communicating on the Internet.

Let's review NAT in it's various incarnations. In principle NAT is simple, but in a complex environment it can get confusing. As always, good documentation can help keep things straight. Basically, NAT means that the NAT device (in this case the Linux netfilter firewall) will change the IP address in a packet and retransmit that packet. Depending on your needs, you can alter the source IP address (source NAT [SNAT]), the destination IP address (destination NAT [DNAT]), or both (double NAT). For example, take a home router. The objective behind the NAT capability is to allow all of the internal hosts to communicate on the Internet using the single public IP provided by your Internet Service Provider (ISP). (In this case, SNAT is being used.) As each of the hosts on your private network make a connection to an Internet server, the firewall is altering the source address to look like the public IP from your ISP. By doing this, the return traffic can find it's way back to the firewall and be retranslated and sent to the originating host (see Figure 2.9).

Figure 2.9 SNAT

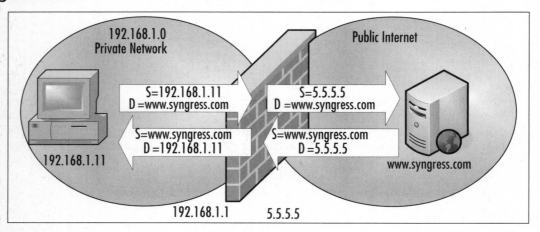

In Figure 2.9, the internal host has a private IP address of 192.168.1.11. The public address of the firewall is 5.5.5.5, which is provided by the ISP. If a host on the private network wants to make a connection to www.syngress.com using a Web browser, the connection is sent with source address 192.168.1.1 to a destination address of www.syngress.com. The firewall alters the source address to it's own public IP address of 5.5.5.5 and sends the packet on its way. When the server replies to destination 5.5.5.5, the firewall again edits the packet, this time inserting a new destination of 192.168.1.11. All of this takes place and is transparent to the 192.168.1.11 host and the www.syngress.com server. When multiple hosts are using SNAT, the firewall tracks which connections belong to which private hosts using the port numbers. While the destination port of the Web server remains static (typically port 80 for the Web), the source port is usually a random port above 1024. By tracking the source port, the firewall knows which address belongs to which session. In the event that two hosts attempt to use the same source port, the NAT device edits the source port of one of the connections and replaces it with another random source port. When the return traffic is received, it translates the source port back, just like it did for the IP address. Because this method of NAT relies heavily on using the source port number, it is sometimes referred to as port NAT (PNAT).

To add the SNAT functionality to the example firewall, use the following command:

```
iptables -t nat -A POSTROUTING -o eth1 -j SNAT --to-source 5.5.5.5
```

The *–t* option is used to specify the table we want to modify, and the *–A* option specifies that we are going to append this rule to the *POSTROUTING* chain. By specifying the outbound inter-face, we are ensuring that the SNAT only occurs as traffic leaves the private network, meaning only in the proper direction.

> ## NOTE
>
> SNAT can only be performed in the *nat* table. However, the rules for SNAT can only go in the *POSTROUTING* chain of the *nat* table. This means that any time you use SNAT, your rule will contain *–t nat –A POSTROUTING*.

The jump target SNAT is self explanatory. The *—to-source* option specifies what IP address we want to use as the new source address. SNAT assumes we have a static IP address to SNAT the out-going packets to. While this is likely the case in a corporate environment, a more appropriate solution to more closely mimic the configuration of a home router would be to use the *MASQUERADE* command:

```
iptables -t nat -A POSTROUTING -o eth1 -j MASQUERADE
```

The masquerade command does not require an IP specification, and will use the IP address of the firewall interface. You might be wondering why you wouldn't use the masquerade target all of the time instead of the SNAT target. Because the source IP is static, the SNAT target will cause the NAT calculations to be performed once for a given session. Subsequent packets belonging to that session are handled the same way as the first. With the masquerade target, each packet is checked for the source IP to use, which requires more overhead than with SNAT. This is why SNAT is preferable if you have a static source IP address, and masquerade is your only option if you do not have a static source IP address to use.

Additional Commands

By this point, you should have a relatively solid grasp of how to configure a Linux firewall. So far we have covered all of the core commands to permit and deny the traffic. Another useful command for your Linux firewall deals with logging packets. If you want to log everything passing through the firewall, use the **iptables –A FORWARD –j LOG** command. While simple, this would likely gen-erate an excessive amount of logging traffic. You also might want some additional control of how the logging occurs. There are some additional options to provide this functionality. Of particular note are the *—log-level* and *—log-prefix* options.

The *—log-level* option allows you to specify what logging level is used for the LOG rule. The effect this log level has depends on how you have your kernel logging configured (via syslog or syslog-ng). When you combine the custom logging level of iptables with the syslog configuration, you can have syslog act in any manner of ways based on the firewall logs, including sending e-mails for certain events. The *—log-prefix* option allows you to insert up to a 29-letter string in front of the log entry. This can be useful for troubleshooting purposes. Some examples of information you could place in log prefix would be the name of the chain that generated the log entry such as *iptables −A FORWARD −j LOG —log-prefix "from FORWARD chain."* (For more information on event logging, refer to Chapter 11, Network Reporting and Troubleshooting.)

> **NOTE**
>
> While a packet that matches an ACCEPT, DENY, or DROP rule will stop traversing any other chains, this is not true of packets that match a log rule. After matching the log rule, the packets continue through any appropriate chains to be processed. Keep this in mind, so that you can configure an additional rule and action for the packet if desired.

Now that you can create a working ruleset for netfilter, you will want to save it. There are two commands of note: one for saving the configurations and one for loading a saved configuration. You can use the **iptables–save** command to generate output that is the current active ruleset. By default, it will only generate the output to the stdout, meaning it will display in the console. To save this output, redirect it to a file. To redirect the current ruleset to a file called */etc/ruleset*, you would type **iptables–save > /etc/ruleset**. If you want to save the current packet counts and rule counts, use the **iptables–save −c > /etc/ruleset** command. Individual tables can be saved separately by specifying the −*t* option using the **iptables–save −t mangle > /etc/ruleset** command.

Restoring a ruleset is accomplished using the **iptables–restore** command. Like **iptables–save**, the restore function takes only two optional arguments. The −*c* option will cause iptables to load the saved packet and byte counts, overwriting the current count values. The default behavior when using *iptables-restore* is to flush the ruleset before loading the saved ruleset, thus all previous rules are lost. If you wish to override this behavior, you can use the **−n** option, in which case the rules will be added to the existing ruleset, and will only overwrite if there is a duplicate rule. You can use the **iptables–restore < /etc/ruleset** command to pipe the saved configuration to iptables–restore.

Command Summary

The following is a brief summary of the most useful iptables commands for easy reference, along with some examples to make the command usage more clear. Bear in mind this is not an exhaustive list of commands; it only represents the most important commands for configuring your firewall. For a complete list, refer to the iptables man page.

- −*A* appends a rule to a chain. *iptables −A INPUT −p icmp −j ACCEPT* will add the rule to permit ICMP at the bottom of the *INPUT* chain in the *FILTER* table.

- −*D* deletes a rule from a chain. *iptables −D INPUT −p icmp −j ACCEPT* will delete the matching rule from the *INPUT* chain. *iptables −D INPUT 3* will delete the third rule from the top in the *INPUT* chain.

- −*I* inserts a rule in a chain. *iptables −I INPUT 5 −p icmp −j ACCEPT* will insert this rule as the fifth rule in the *INPUT* chain

- *−R* replaces a rule in a chain. *iptables −R INPUT 4 −p icmp −j ACCEPT* will replace the fourth rule in the *INPUT* chain with this new rule.

- *−L* lists the rules. *iptables −L* will list all rules and *iptables −L INPUT* will list all rules in the *INPUT* chain only.

iptables −t nat −L

would list all the rules in the nat table only.

- *−F* will flush (delete) the rules. *iptables −F* will delete all rules in all chains. It will not delete chains, only the rules inside the chains.

- *−Z* will zero the packet and byte counters. *iptables −Z* will delete all of the counters. *iptables −Z FORWARD* will delete all of the counters in the *FORWARD* chain only.

- *−N* will create a new chain. *iptables −N CUSTOMCHAIN1* will create a new chain named *CUSTOMCHAIN1*.

- *−X* will delete a chain. *iptables −X CUSTOMCHAIN1* will delete the custom chain named *CUSTOMCHAIN1*.

- *−P* will change the policy for a chain. *iptables −P INPUT ACCEPT* will change the policy for the *INPUT* chain to *ACCEPT*

The policy for a chain does not need to be limited to *ACCEPT* or *DENY*; it could use a custom chain for a target, if desired.

Option Summary

- *−p* specifies the protocol to match (works with "!"). *iptables −A FORWARD −p tcp* will add a rule to match any TCP packet to the FORWARD chain. *iptables −A FORWARD −p ! tcp* will match any packet that was not TCP.

- *−s* specifies the source address to match (works with *!*). *iptables −A FORWARD −s 192.168.1.99* will match any packet with a source address of 192.168.1.99. *iptables −A FORWARD −s ! 192.168.1.99* will match any packet that did not have a source address of 192.168.1.99.

- *−d* specifies the destination address to match (works with *!*). *iptables −A FORWARD −d 192.168.1.99* will match any packet with a destination address of 192.168.1.99.

- *−i* specifies the network interface that the traffic was received on (works with *!*). *iptables −A FORWARD −i eth0* will match any packet entering the eth0 interface.

- *−j* specifies the target. *iptables −A FORWARD −p tcp −j DENY* would create a rule at the bottom of the *FORWARD* chain that will *DENY* any TCP packet.

- *−o* specifies the network interface that the traffic was sent out of (works with "!"). *iptables −A FORWARD −o eth1* would match any packet leaving on the *eth1* interface.

- *−t* specifies the table to manipulate. *iptables −t nat −A POSTROUTING −p tcp −j DENY* will add a rule to the bottom of the *POSTROUTING* chain in the NAT table, to *DENY* any TCP packet.

If you don't specify the *–t* option, iptables assumes you are working with the filter table.

- *–v* specifies to be verbose. *iptables –L –v* lists all of the rules and includes packet counts per chain and per rule.

- *—line-numbers* specifies that the rule list should be numbered:

    ```
    iptables -L --line-numbers
    ```

    This option makes it easier to know what number to use for the commands that take a rule number as an argument, such as *insert*, *delete*, *replace*, and so on.

- *-m* will match packets based on certain protocol-specific criteria. Because the match options are protocol specific, *-p* (*tcp/udp/icmp*) must be used with *–m*. Some common examples include:

    - *-m —sport* allows you to match packets based on the TCP or User Datagram Protocol (UDP) source port.

    - *-m —dport* allows you to match packets based on the TCP or UDP destination port.

    - *-m multiport* allows you to match packets based on multiple port numbers within the same rule. *iptables –A FORWARD –p tcp -m multiport —dport 22,25,53 –j DROP* would *DROP* any TCP packet with a destination port of 22, 25, or 53.

    - *-m state —state* will allow you to match packets based on the state of the connection. *iptables –A FORWARD –p tcp –m state —state NEW –j LOG* would *LOG* any TCP packets that were being used to initiate a new connection.

There are four recognized states*: NEW, ESTABLISHED, RELATED*, and *INVALID* netfilter and iptables give you powerful packet filtering and manipulation capabilities for free. With Linux distributions available for free download, a firewall is within any company's reach. Because of this, deploying firewalls internally to protect highly sensitive systems or data is becoming increasingly viable. If you want to obtain a Linux firewall without having to install Linux, try any of the many live CDs that are available. Some excellent choices are be Knoppix or Slax.

GUIs

While the console commands that are used to manipulate and configure netfilter are not terribly complicated, they can sometimes get very lengthy. As the length of the command line grows, the chances of an accidental error increase. Alternatively, you may not like working on the command line, in which case there are a wide variety of GUI and menu-driven interfaces available for netfilter. In most cases, these menu-drive interfaces use your input to create the appropriate iptables commands, and alleviate you having to know the various switches and options to use. There are a large number of GUI interfaces available to configure your netfilter firewall, which are listed in the following section in approximate order of ease of use. All else being equal, I have demonstrated the GUIs that are available on a wide variety of platforms over an equal quality choice that only works with one distribution. In general, simpler also means less full featured, so be aware that if you are trying to create a complex ruleset, some GUIs may not have the needed functionality.

Security Level Configuration

You can start the iptables GUI provided with Red Hat–based Linux distributions by navigating to **System | Administration | Security Level and Firewall**. You can also call the program directly by running *system-config-securitylevel* from a terminal window. While the interface looks nice, it is limited in what it can configure. Basically, all you can do with this GUI is permit or deny certain ports. Fedora Core 5 configures the *INPUT* and *FORWARD* chains to jump to a custom chain named *RH-Firewall-1-INPUT*. There is no ability to differentiate between ports permitted in the *INPUT* chain or the *FORWARD* chain, because all rules configured through the GUI are applied to this custom chain.

Some services are pre-defined for you. Placing a check next to **SSH** and clicking **OK** and then **Yes** to commit the changes, would create the following rule in the *RH-Firewall-1-INPUT* chain:

```
iptables -A RH-Firewall-1-INPUT -p tcp -m state --state NEW -m tcp --dport 22 -j
ACCEPT
```

By expanding **Other ports** on the **Firewall Options** tab, you can enter a custom port number (see Figure 2.10.)

Figure 2.10 Custom Ports

Click **Add**, and enter the desired port number in the dialog box. Use the drop-down menu to select **TCP** or **UDP** for the protocol and click **OK** (see Figure 2.11).

This creates a rule identical to the SSH rule. There are no other configuration options. While this interface is adequate for a home PC that isn't running any services, it probably will not be adequate for a corporate firewall. If you need to configure access based on the interface in use or need to configure any NAT rules, you will need to use a different GUI. While you probably won't be needing this particular GUI as a corporate firewall, it is still useful to be familiar with it if you are running any Linux systems as workstations.

Figure 2.11 Custom Port Dialog

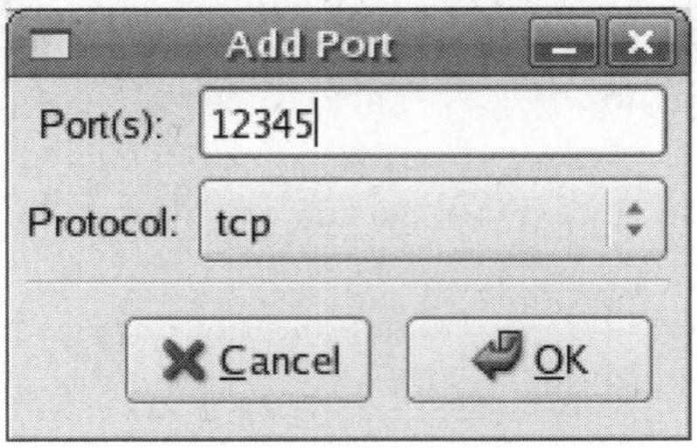

Lokkit

Lokkit is an ncurses-based menu for configuring your netfilter firewall. Lokkit is available for most major distributions and can be installed by default on some (such as Fedora Core 5). To start Lokkit, type **lokkit** in a terminal window. The first lokkit screen is shown in Figure 2.12.

Figure 2.12 Lokkit Main Screen

You can navigate the menus using the Tab key and the space bar to toggle the equivalent of radio buttons, such as the **Enable** and **Disabled** options shown here. If you select **Enabled** on this screen, the default ruleset is applied. To edit any custom settings, press **Tab** until the **Customize** button is highlighted and then press **Enter**. The customization screen is shown in Figure 2.13.

Lokkit does provide a little more flexibility than the Security Level Configuration GUI discussed previously; however, it is still limited. By selecting an interface in Trusted Devices, all traffic from that interface will be permitted. This would typically be used to select the inside interface and designate it as trusted. You do have the option of enabling *MASQUERADE*. The interface you select is the one that will NAT outbound traffic, therefore, you would generally select your *external* interface. Some pre-defined services are available, and you can enter your own service information in the "Other ports" section. Once you are satisfied with your choices, press **OK** and then **Enter**. This will take you back to the main screen, where you press **OK** and then **Enter** to apply the changes.

Figure 2.13 Lokkit Customization Screen

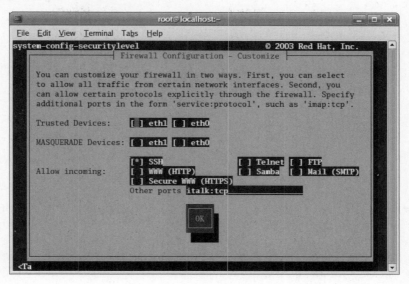

If you attempt to configure an interface for *MASQUERADE*, it must also be marked as trusted or Lokkit will generate an error. Bear in mind that although *MASQUERADE* is limited, it has enough flexibility to configure a firewall similar to a typical home firewall/router device. This makes Lokkit a handy little utility to have in your repertoire should you need to configure a simple firewall quickly. The value of this utility is also increased, because it is available for a wide number of Linux distributions.

Firestarter

Firestarter is a GUI front end for netfilter and iptables, and its goal is to make it simple for the average user to configure their firewall and protect themselves. Firestarter runs on many Linux distributions and the installation is supported by many automated package management systems (such as *yum*, *apt-get*, and *portage*). Firestarter is an excellent choice if your needs are relatively simple for your firewall configuration. To install it manually, downloaded it from www.fs-security.com/download.php. Once it is installed, the first time you start the GUI interface you will need to perform some initial configuration. Follow these steps to configure firestarter:

1. Start the Firestarter GUI. In Fedora Core 5 this is done by navigating to **Applications | System Tools | Firestarter**. This will start the Firewall wizard. Click **Forward** on the **Welcome to Firestarter** screen.

2. On the next screen, select your Internet-connected (i.e. external) network device from the "Detected device(s):" dropdown box (see Figure 2.14), and place a checkbox in the "IP address is assigned via DHCP" box. This is similar to the way a home router/firewall would be configured. When satisfied, click **Forward**.

Figure 2.14 Firestarter Network Device Setup

3. The next screen is the "Internet connection sharing setup" screen (see Figure 2.15), which is basically where you enable NAT. If you want to NAT all of the outbound packets to the external IP address, place a check in the "enable internet connection sharing" checkbox. When this checkbox is enabled, you can select the local area network device (i.e. the inside interface). If you only have two interfaces, it should be selected by default. When finished, press **Forward**.

Figure 2.15 Firestarter Internet Connection Sharing Setup

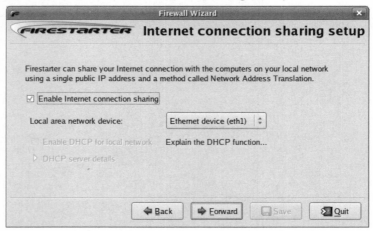

4. On the final screen, leave the "Start firewall now" box checked and click **Save**. This will install a service to start Firestarter each time the system boots up. Firestarter will also change the default action for the chains to *DENY*; therefore, you must explicitly configure any ports you want to permit through the firewall.

The main Firestarter GUI is shown in Figure 2.16. As you can see, it has a straightforward interface. The **Status** tab gives you high-level information such as sent and received data counters per interface, and a list of active connections. By clicking the **Stop Firewall** button, all of the iptables chains are flushed and the default action is changed to *ACCEPT*. This can be useful for troubleshooting issues to see if they are related to your firewall configuration.

Figure 2.16 Firestarter GUI

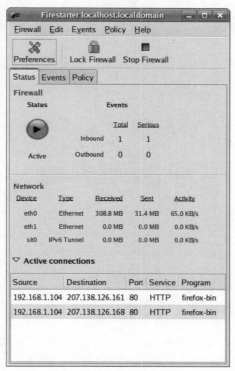

The "Events" tab lists recent blocked connection attempts. The "Policy" tab is where you configure certain rules to permit desired traffic (see Figure 2.17).

For example, if there was a Web server running on the Linux host, you could use the "Policy" tab to permit inbound connections to TCP port 80. The "Editing" dropdown box allows you to choose between inbound and outbound rules to edit. For the Web server example, we selected "Inbound traffic policy." The policy group you select when you click **Add Rule** determines where the policy is placed. The function of the various policy groups is outlined below.

Figure 2.17 Firestarter Inbound Policy

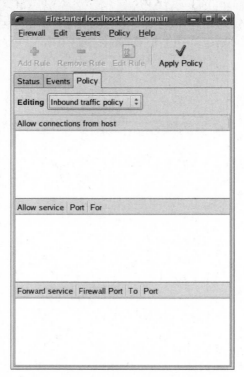

- **Allow Connections From Host** This is used to configure a given IP address, hostname, or network. When you enter the IP information and create a rule in this policy group, all traffic from the configured source is permitted.

- **Allow Service** The allow service policy group is used to permit individual services. You can configure the source to be anyone including a specific IP, or network, or all local area network (LAN) clients. The LAN clients option permits the service through the firewall with a source address that is on the same subnet as the inside network adapter.

- **Forward Service** This option is used only when you are NATing. This allows the firewall to forward a specific port or range of ports, so that a service hosted on an internal NAT'ed device can receive inbound connections from the external network.

The "Outbound traffic policy" window shows a different set of policy groups (see Figure 2.18). There are also the additional radio buttons to select "Permissive by default," "blacklist traffic," or "Restrictive by default, whitelist traffic." If you select the permissive option (the default), all outbound connections will be allowed and any rules you create will be *DENY* rules. This is the same default behavior of most home firewalls. If you select the restrictive configuration, the default target for the table is *DENY*, and any rules you create will be *PERMIT* rules.

Figure 2.18 Firestarter Outbound Policy

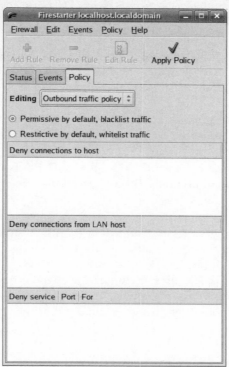

The function of the different policy groups toggle between "allow" and "deny," based on whether you select restrictive or permissive mode. The policy groups are outlined here:

- **Allow/Deny Connections To Host** This policy group is used to globally permit or deny outbound access to a given host, IP address, or network range. This policy uses the destination to match the rule. You can use this policy group in permissive mode to list certain Web sites you do not want anyone to have access to.

- **Allow/Deny Connection from LAN Host** This policy group is used to permit or deny all access from a particular host, IP address, or network range. This policy uses the source to match the rule.

- **Allow/Deny Service** This policy group permits or denies traffic based on its destination port and source. When you are using permissive mode, this policy group can be used to block all access to the bittorrent ports. The traffic source can be anyone; the firewall itself, LAN clients, or an arbitrary IP, hostname, or network range.

Configuring the policies will satisfy the bulk of what you need to accomplish, but there are some additional configuration options available by navigating to **Edit | Preferences**. Selecting **Interface | Events** allows you to configure some useful options. The "Skip redundant entries" checkbox only makes one event entry for sequential event entries. This helps prevent the event windows from being flooded by repetitive alerts. You also have the option of entering certain hosts or ports as being exempt from triggering the event log. After making your selections, click **Accept**.

Another preferences setting of note is under **Firewall | Network Settings**. This allows you to enable Internet connection sharing (the same as during the initial wizard), and enable the firewall host as a Dynamic Host Configuration Protocol (DHCP) server. This allows you to configure the Linux host similarly to a home firewall, which generally acts as a DHCP server in addition to perform NAT and act as a firewall. The ICMP filtering window also allows you to filter ICMP packets. By default, the permit and deny rules configured by Firestarter apply to TCP and UDP, but not ICMP. This screen allows you to permit the desired types of ICMP traffic. Generally speaking, it is better not to allow any ICMP from the Internet to your firewall or internal network unless absolutely necessary.

One final setting you want to configure is under **Firewall | Advanced Options**. In the broadcast traffic section, check both options under **Broadcast traffic**. In general, you should not permit broadcast traffic to go through your firewall, as doing so poses a security risk. You also want to check the option to "Block traffic from reserved addresses on public interfaces," which is a common filtering tactic. Because the "private" addresses outlined in RFC1918 should not be routed through the Internet, there is never a reason to receive traffic sourced from any of those addresses on your outside interface. If you do, it is almost always a hacker attempting to bypass a poorly configured firewall.

Short of any advanced packet mangling, there isn't much you can't accomplish using Firestarter as your configuration tool. If you need to implement a more advanced configuration, use an alternate tool, or generate the configuration using Firestarter and use those chains as a starting point to add your own more advanced options.

Easy Firewall Generator

Easy Firewall Generator is not a GUI per se, but it does help simplify your netfilter configuration and avoid the need to be familiar with the iptables syntax. By using the Web page at http://easyfwgen.morizot.net/gen/index.php, you can enter the relevant information and click the **Generate Firewall** button. As you select options, if additional information is needed click the **Generate Firewall** button and the page will refresh and provide the additional input fields. When all of the required information has been entered, the page will change to a text page that can be copied and pasted for iptables to read as a saved configuration. On Fedora Core 5 the iptables configuration is stored in /etc/sysconfig/iptables. Although this method requires you to replace the default iptables configuration file used by your distribution, it is fairly painless, and supports all of the same basic functionality as Firestarter.

Firewall Builder

Firewall Builder is the most complete GUI offering for managing netfilter firewalls with features and capabilities comparable to some commercial firewall products. As is almost always the case, this functionality and capability come at a price: as far as netfilter GUI's are concerned, Firewall Builder is not the easiest to configure and use. If you want or need it's superior management capabilities, however, the extra effort is well worth it. (Download firewall builder from www.fwbuilder.org/.) Firewall Builder manages netfilter firewalls as well as ipfilter, OpenBSD PF, and (commercially) Cisco PIX firewalls. Firewall Builder runs on many popular operating systems including Red Hat, Mandrake, Suse, FreeBSD, Mac OS X, and Windows XP.

Firewall Builder operates differently than all of the GUIs covered so far. It uses an object-based approach. Essentially, you must define an object to represent any entity that you want to use in the firewall rules. In most cases this means a source, a destination, and a service (port) at a minimum. Both the configuration and the GUI bear a strong resemblance to that of the Checkpoint Firewall GUI. Once the objects are defined, you can drag and drop them into the rules in order to permit or deny communications between the two. For this example we use a Windows XP host to run Firewall Builder and configure a Linux netfilter firewall.

1. Install Firewall Builder.

2. Start the GUI by navigating to **Start | Programs | Firewall Builder 2.1 | FWBuilder**, which opens the main Firewall Builder window. It is divided up into an objects tree (the left pane) and the dialog area (the right pane) (see Figure 2.19).

Figure 2.19 Firewall Builder

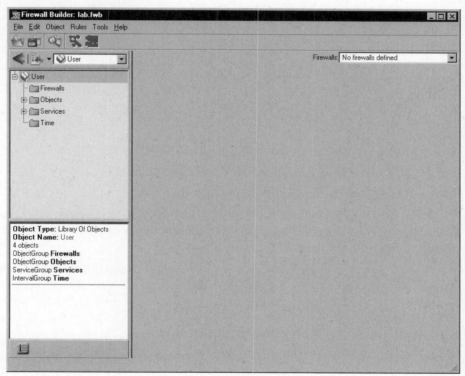

3. Initially, the dialog area will be empty. In order to add the first firewall (in this case a net-filter firewall) on the same host as you are running Firewall Builder, select **Firewalls** in the object tree.

4. Right-click and select **New Firewall**, which will open the New Firewall dialog box (see Figure 2.20).

Figure 2.20 FWBuilder New Firewall Wizard

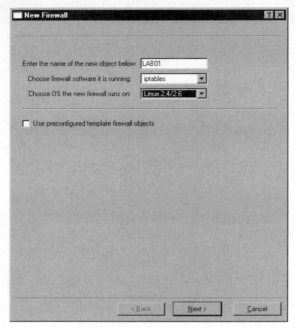

5. Enter the name for the new firewall (in this case LAB01).

6. For the firewall software, select **iptables**.

7. Choose **Linux 2.4/2.6** for the OS and click **Next**.

8. The next window allows you to configure the interfaces on the firewall. You can do so manually, or if the firewall is running SNMP, you can discover them via SNMP. We select **Configure interfaces manually** and click **Next**.

9. The manual interface configuration window is shown in Figure 2.21. Enter the relevant information for each network interface. The **name** must correspond to the actual interface name (same as if you entered ifconfig on the Linux host), such as *eth0*. The **Label** is a human friendly name for easy reference such as *OUTSIDE*. When you are done entering the information for a given interface click **Add**.

10. When you have entered the information for all interfaces (typically an *INSIDE* and *OUTSIDE*), click **Finish**.

11. You must designate one of the interfaces on the firewall as the management interface, typically the *INSIDE* interface. Do this by navigating to the firewall in the object tree. As you select each interface in the object tree, there is a "Management interface" checkbox in the dialog area. Check this box for the interface you want to use. This will be the interface that FWBuilder uses to connect and upload the firewall rules to. The interface properties are shown in Figure 2.22.

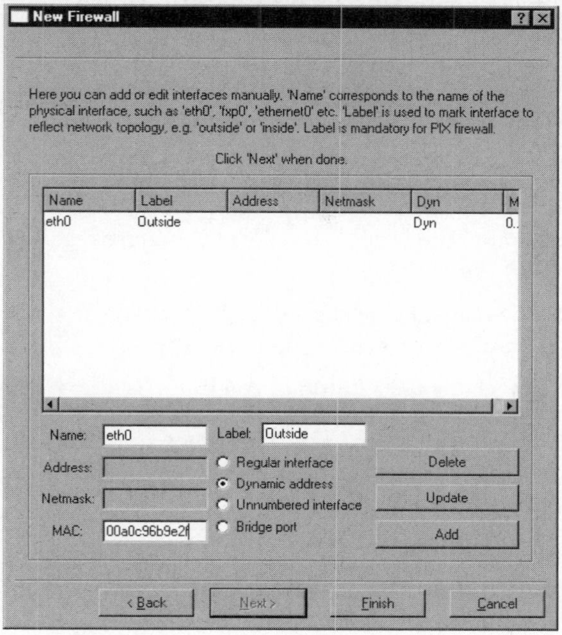

Figure 2.21 FWBuilder Manual Interface Configuration

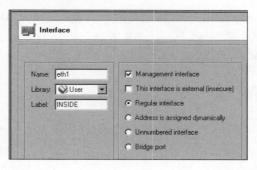

Figure 2.22 Management Interface

Now that you have the basic firewall defined, you need to define something for it to talk to. In this case, let's assume that 192.168.1.0/24 is your internal network, and you want to allow outbound Web browsing and access to an internal Web server (WEB1). For starters, you need to create an object to represent the internal network. Follow these steps to create the network object.

13.   Navigate to **Objects | Networks** in the object tree.

14.   Right-click **Networks** and select **New Network**.

15.   Enter **INTERNAL** for the name of the network, and use 192.168.1.0 for the Address field. Enter 255.255.255.0 for the Netmask and click **Apply**.

16. Let's go ahead and next create an internal Web server at 192.168.1.12. Right-click **Objects | Hosts** in the objects tree and select **New Host**.

17. Enter **WEB1** for the name of the object. Click the **Use preconfigured template host objects** check box and click **Next**.

18. Select **PC with one interface** and click **Finish**.

19. Expand the object tree to **User | Objects | Hosts | WEB1 | eth0 | WEB1**. Edit the IP address to be 192.168.1.12 and click **Apply**.

20. Next, define the appropriate services to allow Web browsing. Right-click **Services | TCP** and select **New Service**.

21. Enter **HTTP** for the name. Leave the source port ranges at zero, but change the destination port range to start and end at 80 and click **Apply**.

22. Repeat steps 20 and 21 for HTTPS on port 443 for secure Web pages.

This can be a lot of trouble; however, the real strength of an object-oriented approach is seen when it comes time to configure the rules. With all of the appropriate objects in place, let's define the rules to permit the inbound HTTP traffic.

23. In the top panel of the dialog area right-click and select **Insert Rule**.

24. Allow inbound HTTP to WEB1. Click on **WEB1** in the object tree and drag it to the destination cell for rule 0.

25. Now drag the **HTTP** and **HTTPS** service from the object pane to the Service cell in rule 0.

26. Right-click the big red dot in the **Action** column and select **Accept**. This allows the inbound Web traffic to access WEB1.

27. To allow outbound Internet access, create another rule by right-clicking on rule zero and selecting **Add Rule**.

28. Drag and drop **HTTP** and **HTTPS** from the object tree into the Service column of rule one.

29. Drag the Network object **INTERNAL** from the object tree to the **Source** column of the new rule.

30. Right-click on the **Action** column for rule 1 and change the action to **ACCEPT**. Your policy should look like the one shown in Figure 2.23.

31. Although our rules seem simple at the moment, let's apply them to see how things work. First, save your work by navigating to **File | Save** or **File | Save As**.

32. Next, right-click the **LAB01 Firewall** and select **Compile**.

33. When the "Select Firewalls for compilation" window comes up, **LAB01** should be checked. When satisfied with your selection, click **Next**. When the compilation is complete you should see "Success" in the "Progress" column. After verifying that the compilation was successful, click **Finish**.

Figure 2.23 Sample FWBuilder Policy

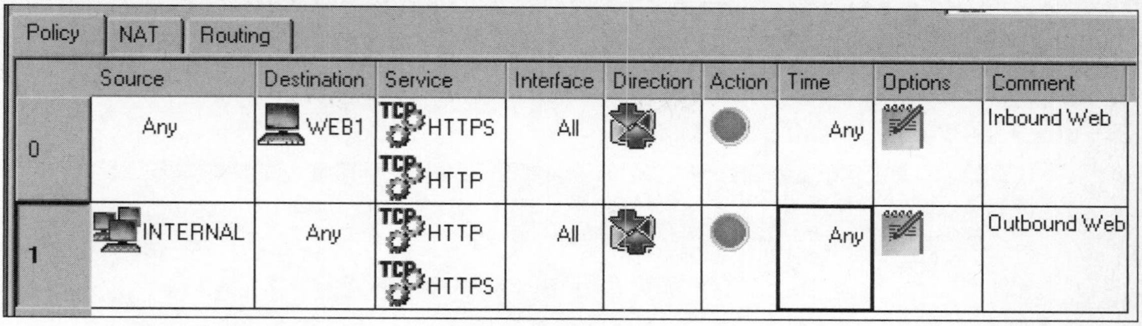

Tools & Traps...

Don't Block Yourself

Anyone who has spent any time configuring firewalls has learned the hard way to be very careful when configuring the rules. It is always a good idea to create the rules to PERMIT administrative access before any others. This is because as soon as you configure the default policies to DROP, your SSH connection will no longer be permitted unless you have it added to the access list. If you forget to do this, you could find that you no longer have remote access to your firewall after applying the policy. If that happens, you won't even be able to remotely connect to update the policy and change the ACLs.

The next step is to tell FWBuilder where to find the SSH executables, because this is how FWBuilder uploads the configuration to the firewalls. You need to have SSH working on both the firewall and the FWBuilder console (assuming they are on different systems).

34. Select Edit | Preferences from the menu.

35. Select the **SSH** tab and click the **Browse** button.

36. Navigate to the location of your desired SSH utility (e.g., *plink.exe*) and click **Open**. Note that if you are using Windows for the FWBuilder host, you cannot select *PuTTY.exe*; you must use the command-line PuTTY program, *plink.exe*.

37. After selecting the SSH executable, click **OK**.

38. Right-click the **LAB01** firewall in the object tree, and select **Install**.

39. Select the Firewalls you wish to install to, and click **Next**.

40. Enter the username and password for the SSH connection.

41. All other fields are optional; however, it is recommended that you check "Store a copy of the fwb on the firewall." When satisfied with your choices, click **Ok**.

After the upload completes, you will get a status of "Success" (see Figure 2.24). Checking your firewall (*iptables −L*) shows you the new rules that are listed.

Figure 2.24 Policy Install Success

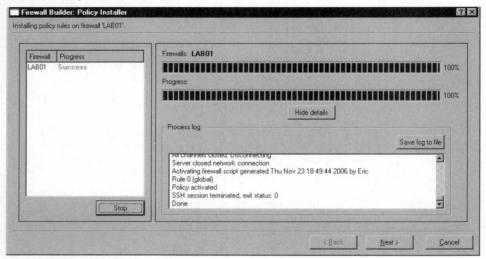

As you can probably see, once you have completed the up-front work of defining your objects, adding or modifying rules is simple. Additionally, unlike the other free GUI solutions, FWBuilder allows you to centrally and securely administer all of your (supported) firewalls from one location. When you use the aforementioned policy, Figure 2.25 shows a sample of the iptables rules that were generated.

Figure 2.25 FWBuilder Generated Chains

```
Chain FORWARD (policy DROP)
target     prot opt source              destination
ACCEPT     all  --  anywhere            anywhere             state RELATED,ESTABLISHED
RULE_0     tcp  --  anywhere            192.168.1.12         tcp multiport dports https,http state NEW
RULE_1     tcp  --  192.168.1.0/24      anywhere             tcp multiport dports http,https state NEW

Chain RULE_0 (2 references)
target     prot opt source              destination
LOG        all  --  anywhere            anywhere             LOG level info prefix 'RULE 0 -- ACCEPT '
ACCEPT     all  --  anywhere            anywhere

Chain RULE_1 (3 references)
target     prot opt source              destination
LOG        all  --  anywhere            anywhere             LOG level info prefix 'RULE 1 -- ACCEPT '
ACCEPT     all  --  anywhere            anywhere
```

Notice that the default chains have rules matching the rule you configured in FWBuilder, with a target of *RULE_<RULE NUMBER>*. These additional chains are used to configure the logging. There is also a rule at the beginning of all chains to *ACCEPT* traffic related to an established session. This is generally desirable but is still configurable. To remote this automatically generated rule, select the firewall in the object tree and click on **Firewall Settings** in the dialog area. There is a checkbox that is selected by default called "Accept ESTABLISHED and RELATED packets before the first rule." Although the FWBuilder policies you've configured can handle any basic rules you might need, there are still a few more bases to cover. If you need to NAT with your Linux firewall, configuring it with FWBuilder is easy. Follow these steps so that your Firewall will NAT all the traffic from the internal network to the DHCP address used on the outside interface. This configuration is also known as *source nat* because it is the source address that is being changed.

1. In the dialog area select the **NAT** tab.

2. Right-click and select **Insert Rule**. This will add a NAT rule number zero.

3. Drag your INTERNAL network object from the object tree to the **Original Src** column in the new NAT policy.

4. Drag the external interface on the firewall from the object tree to the "Translated Source" column in the NAT policy.

That's all there is to it. Save, compile, and install the new policy. Now traffic originating from the internal network will be NAT'ed to the IP on the external interface. Although this source NAT configuration will allow all your internal users to reach the internet, you will need to use *destination NAT* if Internet users need to reach an internal server. Because the internal server is using a private IP address (which is not routable on the Internet), you need to translate this destination to an IP address that the external users can reach. To configure packets destined for the firewall's single public IP address to an inside resource using destination NAT, follow these steps.

1. In the dialog select the NAT tab

2. Right click on the rule number zero of the existing NAT rule and select **Add Rule Below**.

3. Drag the firewall OUTSIDE interface into the Original Destination column of the new rule.

4. Drag the appropriate services (i.e. HTTP for web access) into the Original Service column of the new rule.

5. Drag the internal server into the translated destination column of the new rule.

Another nice feature is being able to create a time policy (e.g., if you only want the internal systems to be able to surf the Internet from noon to 1:00 P.M., you can easily make that adjustment.

1. In the object tree, right-click **Time**, and select **New Time Interval**.

2. In the "Name" field we'll call this rule **LUNCH**.

3. In the two time fields provided, enter a time for the rule to START and a time for the rule to STOP. In this case we will enter 12:00 and 13:00 and leave the date field as zeros. The day of the week can stay at -1, which means all days. When done, click **Apply**.

4. Drag the **LUNCH** time interval, form the object tree to the **Time** column of rule # 1.

Now, rule # 1 (which permits outbound Web surfing) will only be active from noon to 1:00 P.M. The ability to configure the rules to be active based on the time of day is a very powerful feature. If the organization is a strictly 8:00 A.M to 5:00 P.M type of place, you could configure the firewall to disable all access during non-business hours. Alternatively, certain non-business-related protocols (e.g., instant messenger, file sharing, and so on) could be enabled after the normal business day ends. While not the easiest of GUI to use, FWBuilder is definitely the most full featured, and the only one offering features you would expect to find in a commercial product.

Other GUIs

Although there are too many netfilter GUIs to cover them all extensively, I have tried to cover some of the best ones available. If none of the ones covered strike your fancy, or if you just like to experiment and see what else is out there, you might want to investigate some additional offerings. If you are running KDE look into Guarddog from www.simonzone.com/software/guarddog/#introduction, which is aimed at novice to intermediate users and offers the ability to define security policies based on logical groupings called network "zones." The Turtle Firewall Project (www.turtlefirewall.com/) allows you to administer your firewall host via a Web interface. While there is no substitute for a good understanding of the command-line configuration of iptables, for an uncomplicated firewall configuration many of these GUI's allow you to get your firewall up and running quickly and without having to read the iptables man page.

Smoothwall

Smoothwall (http://smoothwall.org/) is a firewall in it's own right, and is the site for SmoothWall Express. SmoothWall Express is a free, open source firewall solution. *Smoothwall.net* is the home of SmoothWall Limited, which produces several commercial security products including a version of the SmoothWall firewall. Smoothwall differs from the other solutions covered here, in that smoothwall is a dedicated firewall device. Other solutions using netfilter and optional GUIs to configure the firewall can be run on a workstation. You can still use the firewall system as a normal workstation, but it's not recommended. If you want to harden the firewall (as you should), you need to remove unneeded services and software from the system, and update all of the remaining software. Smoothwall takes a different approach in that all of this is done for you. When you install SmoothWall, it wipes out the filesystem and installs a secured version of Linux on the hard disk, along with the SmoothWall software. The SmoothWall firewall has no GUI on the system, only command-line access and administration via the Web management interface. SmoothWall is meant to be a firewall and nothing more.

With that in mind, there are several advantages to this approach. Foremost, you don't have to learn how to harden your Linux distribution so that it will be secure enough to use. Further, unlike installing Linux and then learning iptables syntax, with SmoothWall you don't need to know Linux. The installation menu walks you through configuring the minimum settings so that you can then use the Web interface to configure the firewall functionality. You don't need to know everything about Linux to get SmoothWall up and running (though it never hurts). The fact that the SmoothWall firewall is already stripped down and unneeded software and services are removed means that you can get the maximum performance out of an old computer without having to spend a lot of time trying to tweak a full (normal) Linux distribution.

Installing Smoothwall

The simplest way to install SmoothWall Express is by downloading the *.iso* image from http://smoothwall.org/get/. It is advisable to read along with the manuals located at http://smoothwall.org/docs/. The documentation provided with SmoothWall Express is exceptional among free products, and all of the installation screens are shown in the PDF installation guide. This installation method is used as we walk though installing SmoothWall Express.

1. After burning this image to a CD-ROM, boot the prospective firewall with the CD-ROM in the drive.

2. The boot screen will look typical of many Linux distributions. It will warn you that installing SmoothWall Express will delete all data on the hard drive. To continue with the installation, press **ENTER**.

3. The installation then shifts into a DOS-like GUI interface. Navigation is accomplished using the TAB, arrow, and ENTER keys. You will be prompted to insert the installation CD and press **OK**. This is done in case your system cannot boot from a CD-ROM and you used a boot floppy to begin the installation. Either way, ensure that the CD-ROM is (still) in the drive, highlight **OK**, and press **ENTER**.

4. You have to select **OK** twice before the hard disk will be repartitioned and all data lost.

5. When prompted, select **Probe** to allow the installation routine to see what network cards it can detect.

SmoothWall uses a concept of interface colors to denote their trust level, and you will begin seeing them referred to in that fashion during the installation process. For example, your inside interface is assumed to be the trusted traffic and is designated as the GREEN interface. Various dial-up or Indirect Defense Switched Networks (IDSNs) are designated as ORANGE interfaces. You can also have a combination of colors indicating your interface configuration. If you use an additional Ethernet interface as the untrusted (*OUTSIDE*) interface, in Smoothwall parlance that would be GREEN + RED.

After the files are installed successfully, you are given the opportunity to restore your configuration from floppy disks. This is useful if you are upgrading or migrating to new hardware. In this case, we select **OK**.

1. Select your keyboard layout (in my case "US," and select **OK**.

2. Select a hostname for the firewall (e.g., smoothwall) and select **OK**.

3. The next screen allows you to enter proxy server information in case you need to go through a proxy for the firewall to retrieve Web updates. If you are using a proxy, enter the appropriate information here; if not, select **OK**.

4. The next couple of screens allow you to enter configuration information for an ISDN or ADSL connection. The assumption of the installation process is that your *INSIDE* (trusted) interface will be an Ethernet interface, and the *OUTSIDE* (untrusted) interface will be either an Ethernet, ISDN, or ADSL. If you are using one of these, enter the appropriate information. If your *OUTSIDE* interface is a normal Ethernet interface (e.g., from a cable modem), select **DISABLE** for both the ISDN and Asymmetric Digital Subscriber Line (ADSL) configuration screens.

5. The next screen allows you to review and edit your network configuration. If you are using an Ethernet interface for both, you need to select **GREEN + RED** for the network configuration type. Check each menu option here and ensure that both interfaces have been

recognized, have a driver installed, and have IP address settings. Commonly, the RED inter-face uses DHCP and the GREEN uses a static IP address, so that internal hosts can con-figure the firewall as their default gateway out to the Internet.

6. When you are satisfied with all the settings, select **DONE**.

7. You will be asked if you want to enable the SmoothWall firewall to serve as a DHCP server. This is the same configuration as most home firewalls, acting as firewall, gateway, and DHCP server. If you do not already have a DHCP server in your network, enable it. Fill in the desired values for the various fields. Most of the settings are not mission critical, but one setting to take note of is the lease duration. Too long of a lease duration and you will slowly loose IP addresses from systems that did not get the changes to release the address properly prior to going offline (such as from a crash or power outage). If the lease time is too long, this IP address attrition can exhaust the DHCP scope and leave no address avail-able for other users. A 24-hour lease is not uncommon, and generally the larger the net-work the shorter the lease duration you will want. If you are unsure about DHCP, you can leave it disabled. The DHCP settings are easily configured later from the Web interface.

8. The next several screens allow you to enter the password for various accounts used by the firewall. Here are summaries of these accounts.

    ■ **Administrator** This is used for administering the firewall via the Web interface. This account is only for accessing the Web interface and cannot be used to login to the Linux OS on the firewall directly.

    ■ **root** This is a local Linux account that is used for command-line access on the firewall itself.

    ■ **setup** This is a local Linux account that is used to run the setup program, which auto-matically starts when you login as setup. The setup program allows you to configure some of the network settings if they need to be changed after the initial installation.

9. After you configure the final password, the CD-ROM will eject and the system will reboot. When the system comes back up, you can login directly via the console using the root account, or the preferred method is to login to the Web interface. The default Web interface is found at http://smoothwall:81 and the secure HTTP is found at https://smoothwall:441. Both the root and the setup account can also login via SSH, which is configured by default on port 222.

Configuring Smoothwall

When you first log into the smoothwall Web interface the screen will look like the one shown in Figure 2.26.

There is some information available before logging in, such as the number of users and average load on the firewall. As soon as you click on a menu item at the top you are prompted to authenti-cate with the Web admin user. By default, the account name is "admin." One of the first things you should do is enable SSH access, which is disabled by default. This allows you an additional way to manage the firewall if something goes wrong with the Web server or the firewall filters. You can enable SSH by clicking on the **Services** tab, and then selecting **Remote Access**. Next, place a check in the box next to SSH and click **Save**. You can verify what services are running by clicking the "About your smoothie" tab. There are three screens available under this tab. The *status* screen shows which services are running. The *advanced* screen shows more detailed information regarding memory usage, hard disk usage, network interface settings, and uptime. The *traffic graphs* screen shows input and output rates for all interfaces.

Figure 2.26 SmoothWall Web Interface

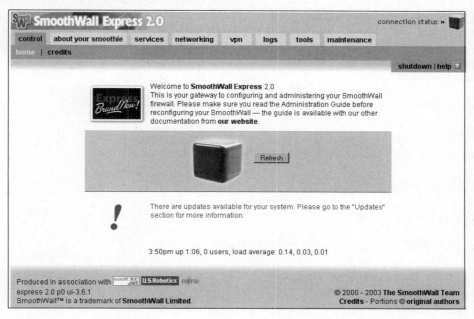

After enabling SSH, you should be able to connect on port 222. An example using *openssh* would be:

```
ssh <IP> -l root -p 222
```

Now that you have a backup way to get into the firewall, the next priority is to update the firewall. Although you don't have much of a configuration to warrant making a backup before applying the patches, it is still a good habit to get into. By selecting the **maintenance** tab and then the **backup** screen, you have a couple of options. The "Create backup floppy disk" button will write the configuration information directly to a floppy disk. Given the relatively unreliable nature of floppy disks, you should choose the "Create backup floppy image file" option. This creates and downloads an *.img* file to the system you are using for Web administration. You can store this file on a more reliable media, and then write the image to a physical floppy disk at a later date using a utility such as rawwrite. Once you have made a backup, you can safely apply the firewall updates.

Firewall updates are another area where the SmoothWall people have made things as painless as possible. Click on the **maintenance** tab and you will see two sections on the **updates** screen. The top section shows *installed* updates and the bottom one shows *available* updates. To update the firewall, go to http://smoothwall.org/get/. In the "Latest Updates and Patches" section there is a small link called **updates archive**. Click that link and on the following page, download all the available updates to your local system.

The bottom of the **Maintenance | Updates** page has a box to upload an update. Click **Browse** and select the first update, and then click **upload**. The firewall automatically installs the patch as it is uploaded and, when finished, the page will refresh and show the updated listed in the "Installed updates" section. Continue this process until all available updates have been completed. A partial list of the successfully installed updates can be seen in Figure 2.27.

Figure 2.27 SmoothWall Installed Updates

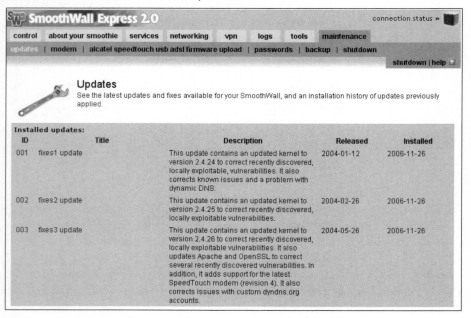

One final configuration option that should be a part of any firewall setup is providing the firewall with a good way to synchronize it's clock. Accurate time is important for many reasons, one of which is to make sure your logs have accurate time stamps. Without accurate time stamps, it will be more difficult, if not impossible, to reconstruct events later if there is an intrusion. You can configure the time source on the "Services" tab using the "time" screen. You should use the drop-down box to select the appropriate time zone. While SmoothWall does not give you the option to configure network time protocol (NTP) security, it does give you the option of using random public servers. In this fashion, even if it pulled time from one that was too far off (either accidentally or maliciously), the next time it is checked (a different server) would likely correct itself. To enable SmoothWall to retrieve the time from a public time server, check the **Enabled:** checkbox and then click **Save**.

With all of the basic administrative configuration out of the way, the actual rule configuration is next. SmoothWall relies heavily on the security level of the interfaces for access permissions. By default, all traffic will be blocked that enters on a RED interface and is destined for an address via a GREEN interface, unless it is specifically configured to be permitted. Similarly, traffic is blocked by default from an ORANGE interface to a GREEN interface. Traffic from a more secure interface to a less secure interface is permitted by default. This behavior is similar to several other commercial firewalls including the Cisco PIX/ASA. What all this means is that for your users to access the Internet, you don't need to configure anything at all.

On the other hand, suppose you wanted to permit inbound access to a Web server (GREEN interface) with an IP address of 192.168.1.63 from any host on the Internet (RED interface). You would configure this by selecting the **Networking** tab and the **Port Forwarding** screen (see Figure 2.28).

Figure 2.28 SmoothWall Port Forwarding

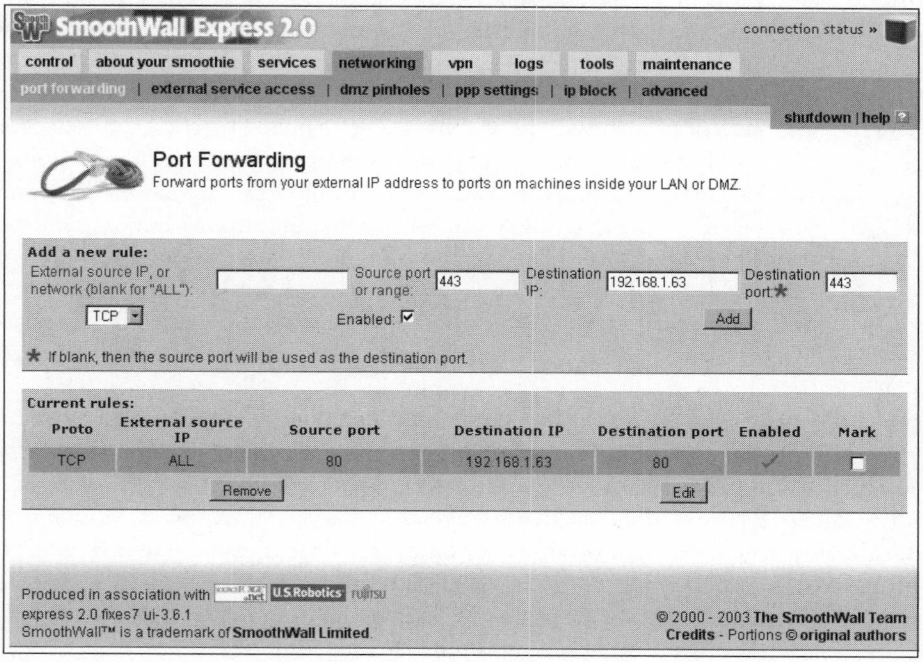

Leave the source IP blank (for ALL) and enter a source port of 80. For the destination IP, enter the internal server's IP of 192.168.1.63, and for the destination port, enter 80 for HTTP. When finished, click **Add**. If you need to permit HTTPS, you need to repeat the process with 443 as the destination port. By using SSH to connect to the firewall directly (smoothware use port 222 for SSH), you can list the netfilter rules using *iptables −L* and see where the HTTP and HTTPS rules were added.

```
Chain portfwf (1 references)
target      prot opt source        destination
ACCEPT      tcp  --  anywhere      192.168.1.63      state NEW tcp dpt:http
ACCEPT      tcp  --  anywhere      192.168.1.63      state NEW tcp dpt:https
```

If you have three interfaces in a one-legged DMZ design, the DMZ interface is labeled as ORANGE. If you need to permit access from the DMZ into the trusted (GREEN) network, the process is a little different. You would then navigate to the **networking | DMZ pinholes** screen. The interface is very similar to the port forwarding with the exception that there is no field to specify the source port.

At times, an internal system's permissions may allow it to communicate with a device outside the firewall (on the RED interface); however, you may wish to block the communications completely. If you do this, any access by the blocked site will fail, even attempts to respond to an internal trusted system's request. You can configure this on the "Networking" tab, using the "ip block" screen. Enter the source IP address or name to block, and click **Add** to save the rule. You also have the option to enable logging for the blocked attempts.

With the basic firewall rules and maintenance configured, there are a few "extras" that are nice to see in a free product. One of these is the built-in Intrusion Detection System (IDS). Because it uses Linux as its base operating system, it conveniently includes Snort IDS; all you have to do is enable it. Enable Snort by selecting the "Services" tab, and then the "Intrusion Detection System" screen. Place a check next to Snort and click **Save**. The Snort alerts and other logs can be viewed on the "logs" tab. There are several subscreens that include a drop-down box to select what subset of logs you want to see, such as SSH, SmoothWall (which will show your recently applied patches), and several more. The "Web proxy" screen is only useful if you are using the Web proxy feature of the firewall. The "firewall" page shows all blocked connections and allows you to filter by month and day. Lastly, the IDS screen shows events logged by the Snort IDS. Unfortunately, SmoothWall Express does not support remote logging natively, while the commercial offering does. It does, however, allow you to export the log files to a text file. See Chapters 4, 5, and 6 for more details on Snort.

Another nice option is the dynamic DNS support. There are various dynamic DNS services available that will allow you to use a consistent DNS name to refer to a system who's IP address is dynamic via DHCP. In order to do this, you typically must install a small program on the host system that will periodically contact the dynamic DNS server and alert them to your current IP address. The service then uses this information to update their DNS records so that people can locate the system via DNS. The SmoothWall firewall has the capability to perform these updates for you, to the major dynamic DNS providers. You can configure dynamic DNS support by selecting navigating to the **services | dynamic dns** page. Use the drop-down menu to select the dynamic DNS service you are using, fill in the rest of the information, and click **Add**. The firewall will then make the updates to the service and all of the hosts to IP mappings can be maintained in one place rather than having to install an agent on all of the systems that need dynamic DNS functionality.

SmoothWall Express is a very well put together firewall package. The documentation is very good, and the setup and management is straightforward and understandable with having to know anything about the underlying operating system. With all of the advanced features such as traffic graphs, intrusion detection, and respectable logging, it deserves a top spot on the list of contenders for "best free firewalls." If you want the efficiency of running your firewall on Linux without having to learn how to secure your Linux installation, give SmoothWall a try.

Configuring Windows Firewall

Although there is a plethora of commercial firewalls available to run on Windows, the field is a lot smaller when it comes to free offerings. Additionally, while there are several quality offerings for Windows as personal firewalls, there are not any free ones that are appropriate to protect your network perimeter. The built in *Windows Firewall* included with Windows XP and 2003 is very limited in its configuration options and is only appropriate as the personal firewall it was intended to be. The Windows Firewall included with Windows Vista is supposed to incorporate increased flexibility and control over the filtering rules, so that might be something to keep an eye on when it is released. Given this, configuring the Windows Firewall is covered in Chapter 3, along with other personal firewalls.

Providing Secure Remote Access

Sooner or later odds are good that you will either want or need the ability to work remotely. Providing remote access must be undertaken very cautiously, because, as soon as you allow an employee to connect to the corporate network, you have to some degree, extended your network boundary to their workstation. This means your network's security is now only as good as the security of the remote user's system or network. In many cases this borders on no security at all. That is why remote access must only be granted after careful consideration and planning. While the different types of remote access pose different levels of security risk, there are some planning and configuration steps that are common to all of them.

The first task is to determine what type of remote access is appropriate. With a virtual tunnel network (VPN), it is as if the remote workstation is on the corporate network. This generally provides the greatest level of functionality, but also poses the greatest risk. If the remote system is compromised, an attacker is effectively inside your corporate network. While there are steps you can take to mitigate these risks, they may be time- and effort-intensive. To plan, configure, and properly secure a VPN solution is the most involved choice of the various remote access solutions you could provide.

Another option is to provide remote desktop functionality. This would allow a remote user to see and use the desktop of a system at work. A remote desktop acts as if the user is at work, while a VPN acts as if the user's computer is at work. This type of solution is slightly easier to implement, because you can typically isolate the traffic that needs to be permitted through the firewall to a single TCP port. Many of the same risks exist, however, in that if an attacker manages to gain access to an internal desktop remotely, it is usually easy for them to move information out of the network or otherwise cause mischief. Another key consideration with this type of solution is that you need to have a computer at home and a computer at work. With the VPN option, you only need to use one system, so if the user has a laptop, it can be used while they work remotely.

The last and least functional option is that of a remote shell. Because most average users don't operate extensively (if at all) in a console (i.e., text only) environment, this type of remote access is generally most viable for network administration personnel. While it may be impossible for accountants to operate their accounting program without a GUI, many network tasks and most firewall administration tasks can be performed with only terminal access. Because the widely used Telnet protocol sends all data unencrypted, any sensitive tasks should only be performed using a secured protocol such as secure shell (SSH), or Telnet over a Secure Internet Protocol (IPsec) tunnel.

Providing VPN Access

A virtual private network (VPN) is exactly what it sounds like, the network connection you create is virtual, because you can use it over an otherwise public network. Basically, you take two endpoints for the VPN tunnel, and all traffic between these two endpoints will be encrypted so that the data being transmitted is private and unreadable to the systems in between. Different VPN solutions use different protocols and encryption algorithms to accomplish this level of privacy. VPNs tend to be protocol independent, at least to some degree, in that the VPN configuration is not on a per-port basis. Rather, once you have established the VPN tunnel, all applicable traffic will be routed across the tunnel, effectively extending the boundaries of your internal network to include the remote host.

One of your first considerations when planning to implement a VPN solution is the network design. Because the VPN tunnel needs two endpoints, one will be the remote workstation. The other will be a specially configured device for that purpose. This is generally called a VPN concentrator, because it acts as a common endpoint for multiple VPN tunnels. The remote systems will effectively be using the concentrator as a gateway into the internal network, as such the placement of the concentrator is important. In a highly secured environment, the concentrator is placed in a DMZ sandwiched between two firewalls, one firewall facing the Internet, and the other facing internally (see Figure 2.29). While this type of arrangement is the most secure, it takes more hardware to implement.

Figure 2.29 VPN Concentrator Design

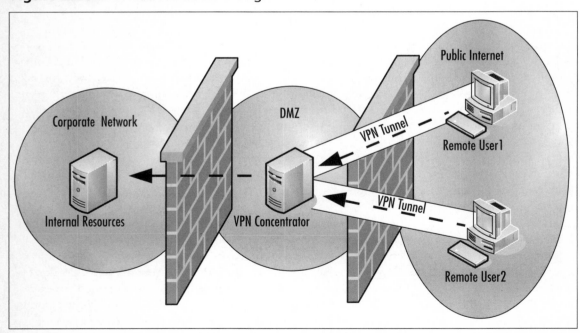

Another way to place the VPN concentrator inside a DMZ is to use an additional interface on the firewall as the DMZ in a "one-legged" configuration. This saves you having to implement an additional firewall, but still provides some isolation between the concentrator and the rest of the internal network. If an attacker compromised a remote host who was VPN'd into the concentrator or compromised the concentrator itself, they would still have a firewall between them and the internal network. The least preferable option it to place the concentrator inside the internal network. With this type of design, if the concentrator is compromised, the attacker would have full access to the internal network, with no firewalls to inhibit their activities. With any of these designs, you will have to permit the required ports through the firewall and forward them to your VPN concentrator.

Another consideration is the type of VPN protocol you want to use. IPSec is still the most widely deployed VPN technology for good reason. One is interoperability. As a widely used and tested standard, IPsec will work with virtually any modern firewall and operating system. The disadvantage of IPsec is that it can sometimes be difficult to configure properly, and there is zero margin for error on the configuration. Both ends have to use the same parameters for encryptions, hashing, and so forth, or the tunnel cannot be established. SSL is an increasingly popular choice for VPNs, largely because of it's simplicity to implement.

Once you have chosen a design and VPN technology, you need to consider the administrative ramifications of offering remote access. Some level of training will be required, at the very least so that they can sue the VPN software. You should educate the users on good security habits as well. A determination will also need to be made as to whether remote users are allowed to use their own personal computers, or if they must use a company-provided computer for remote access. The former option carries with it many risks. When a remote user connects their personal computer to the corporate network (via a VPN) they may have spyware, a virus, or any number or potentially damaging conditions present on their system. Due to the fact that you probably don't have any administrative access to their systems, you may have no way to secure the personal systems even if you wanted to. This is why most companies require that only corporate resources be allowed to connect to the company network. In the case of remote users, this typically means a company provided desktop, but I have also seen instances of older desktops being sent home for remote access.

A final consideration is one of hardware selection. Normal desktop productivity applications typically place very little strain on an even remotely modern processor. The same is not true when it comes to VPN connections. A single VPN connection requires little overhead and rarely impacts the remote user's system unless it is especially underpowered. For the VPN concentrator, however, it will handle the encryption and decryption of multiple connections, in addition to managing the volume of network data that will be accessed through it. For this reason, if you anticipate more than just a couple of VPN connections to be used simultaneously, you will want to test and evaluate your hardware needs.

Using Windows as a VPN Concentrator

For a simple VPN solution servicing a small number of users you can use a Windows 2000, XP, or 2003 system using native software. This has the advantage that you are not using any third-party software, so installation and support may be easier. Not only is the configuration reasonably simple, but it may be easier to sell to upper management, because it doesn't involve any non-Microsoft software being installed or relied on. The Microsoft VPN connection uses the point-to-point tunneling protocol (PPTP), which is not compatible with other types of VPNs such as IPSec-based or Secure Sockets Layer (SSL)-based VPNs. PPTP is a widely supported and relatively lightweight protocol. PPTP support can be found on Linux, MAC OS X, and Palm Personal Digital Assistants (PDAs). To configure a Windows host as a VPN endpoint using Windows 2000, follow these steps.

1.   Navigate to **Start | Control Panel | Network Connections**.

2. Click **Create New Connection**

3. On the welcome screen, click **Next**.

4. In the New Connection Type windows, select **Set up an advanced connection** and click **Next**.

5. In the Advanced Connections Options window, leave the default **Accept incoming connections** checked and click **Next**.

6. On the "Devices for incoming Connections" window, click **Next**. Any modems you have installed will be listed; however, for a network connection we can leave them unchecked.

7. On the next screen, select **Allow virtual private connections** and then click **Next**.

8. On the "User Permissions" window, place a check next to the user accounts you wish to be able to connect via VPN and then click **Next**.

9. On the networking software screen, highlight **Internet Protocol (TCP/IP)** and click **Properties** (see Figure 2.30).

Figure 2.30 Network Software

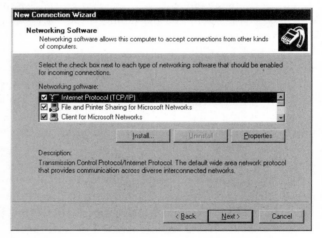

10. The Incoming TCP/IP Properties window is where you configure the most important settings for the VPN connection. The **Allow callers to access my local network** *must* be checked or the VPN connection won't work. For TCP/IP address assignment, you need to plan accordingly. If you leave the default selected, the remote systems will be assigned an IP address via DHCP as they connect.

11. When finished configuring the TCP/IP properties, click **OK**.

12. On the Networking Software window, click **Next**.

13. Click **Finish**.

After completing these steps the server should be ready to accept an incoming VPN connection. The next step is the client side of the configuration. We will walk through this configuration using a

Windows XP system, as the client, in order to make a VPN connection to the Windows XP VPN server.

1. Navigate to **Start | Control Panel | Network Connections**.
2. Click **Create New Connection**
3. On the welcome screen, click **Next**.
4. Select **Connect to the network at my workplace** and click **Next**.
5. Select **Virtual Private Network Connection** and click **Next**.
6. On the Connection Name window, choose a descriptive name for the connection and then click **Next**.
7. The next window is the VPN Server Selection screen. Enter an IP address or host name and click **Next**.
8. On the final screen you have the option of adding a shortcut for the connection to your desktop. Select the checkbox if you want to create the shortcut and then click **Finish**.

The shortcut that is created can be opened to initiate the VPN connection. You will be prompted to enter the login credentials to use for the VPN connection (see Figure 2.31).

Figure 2.31 Windows XP VPN Login

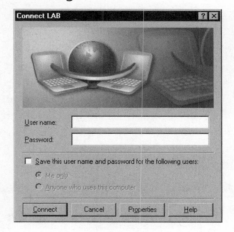

After entering your username and password, click **Connect**. If the connection is successful, you should see a pop-up in the system tray indicating that you are connected. Once connected, you can route traffic through the VPN server.

NOTE

In order for the connection to work, you must have a password for the account you are using to connect via VPN. If the account has no password, you will not be able to connect.

One final thing you may need to configure is the routing table on the client system. When you make the PPTP connection, a *default route* is added to the clients routing table after their existing default route. You can view the routing table on Windows using the **route print** command. The default route has 0.0.0.0 for the network destination. This means that any traffic destined for an IP address that the client doesn't know where to send it, will continue to go out the interface it was using before the PPTP connection was made. If you need to change this behavior so that all non-local traffic goes through the VPN tunnel, you can alter the routing tables with a simple batch file.

iPIG

iPig is a VPN solution provided by iOpus Software at www.iopus.com/ipig/. The client is freeware, and the server portion (the VPN concentrator) is offered as an unlimited commercial product (i.e., a five-user *iPig Server Express Edition*) for free. The five-user limit is for simultaneous connections to the VPN server. You can create more than five user accounts to use the VPN, but they cannot all use the server at the same time. Both the commercial and the free versions use AES256 for their encryption and run on Windows 2000, XP, and 2003. If you download the iPig client and do not install the iPig server, you can still use the client. In this configuration the client will connect to an iOpus-controlled server on the Internet. You are limited to 10MB of "free" bandwidth before you must pay for additional bandwidth. Instead, you should install your own server side component, which is the iPig Server Express Edition product. We walk through setting up the iPig server component first, then the client software.

Installing the iPig Server Express Edition

Download and install the iPig server software. There are no unusual options during the installation process. In typical fashion, the install begins with a welcome screen and then asks you to accept the License agreement. The next screens lets you choose the installation directory and start menu folders. When the installation is complete, you will get a window informing you that the server started successfully. You can configure the iPig server options by navigating to **Start | All Programs | iPig Server | iPig Server**. The main configuration screen is shown in Figure 2.32.

Figure 2.32 iPig Server Configuration

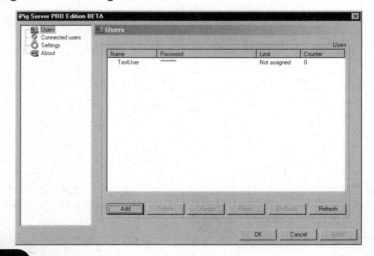

The first step is to define the VPN users.

1. Select **Users** in the left pane and then click **Add** in the right pane.

2. The Edit user window allows you to enter a username, a password, and a traffic limit if desired (see Figure 2.33). You can artificially throttle back the VPN users to make sure they do not consume too much of your Internet bandwidth and negatively impact Internet access for the local network users.

Figure 2.33 iPig Edit User

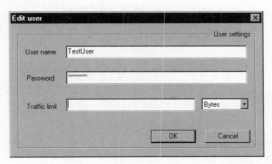

3. After entering the user information, click **OK**. Back at the main configuration window there are a few additional settings to configure. One option of note is under the "Settings" section in the left pane. If you select "Settings" you can then edit the Server port that is used to listen for incoming connections. Generally speaking, a non-default port is almost always better than using the defaults. You should also change the Log type from **None** to **Small** or, even better, **Full**, depending on how much VPN traffic you expect to see. The server log is located in the *\iPig\server\vpn_log.csv* file. The logging that is offered even in "Full" mode is pretty minimal, but it's better than nothing.

Installing the iPig VPN Client

Installing the client is equally as painless.

1. Download the client installer and run the installation for the client setup.

2. On the initial welcome screen, click **Next**, select the radio button to **accept the license agreement**, and then click **Next**.

3. Choose the installation folder and click **Next**.

4. Choose the start menu folder and click **Next**, and then click **Install** on the next screen. You will need to reboot the system when the installation completes.

5. Start the iPig client program by navigating to **Start | All Programs | iPig WLAN Security | iPig Client**.

Once the client is started, there are a couple of settings you must configure.

1. First, select **Advanced Settings** in the left pane (see Figure 2.34).

Figure 2.34 iPig Client Advanced Settings

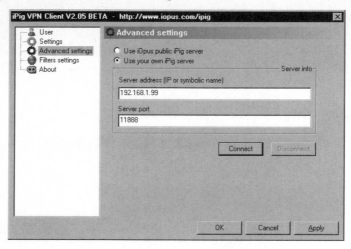

2. Select the radio button next to "Use your own iPig server," and enter the IP address and server port (11888 is the default port) and click **Apply**. Click **Connect** and select **User** in the left pane (see Figure 2.35).

Figure 2.35 iPig Client User Settings

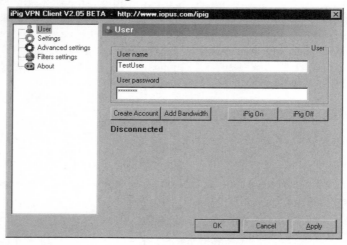

3. Enter the user name and password that matches one you defined in the iPig server.

4. When finished, click **iPig On**.

This is all that is needed to have the VPN tunnel up and working. However, there are some additional configuration options that would be advisable to configure.

In the Settings page, make sure you have **Log all Internet Access** checked. There is also a checkbox to encrypt UDP traffic. If you leave this unchecked, only TCP traffic will be encrypted. Depending on your needs, this may or may not be significant. One thing to consider is that if you encrypt UDP traffic, it will include DNS requests. Therefore, when the client requests an IP address to match a host name (e.g., www.syngress.com), the request is encrypted and sent to the iPig server, which then decrypts the request and sends it to its DNS server. In most cases, this shouldn't be an issue, but sometimes ISP's and others will configure their DNS servers to only answer queries when they come from their internal network.

Another option of note is the ability to configure encryption filters. The Filter settings window is shown in Figure 2.36.

Figure 2.36 iPig Client Filter Settings

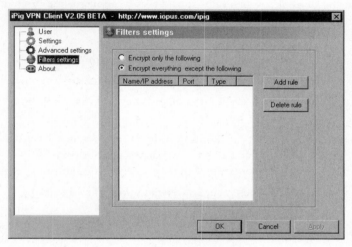

The two options at the top determine if this filter will act as an *inclusion list* or an *exclusion list*. If you select **Encrypt only the following**, only traffic matching the rules will be encrypted and everything else will be sent unencrypted as if the iPig VPN were not there. Alternatively, you can configure it to encrypt all traffic *except* those that match the filter rules. The latter option is probably more desirable, because it will allow you to send all data over the VPN except any applications you specify in the filters. The filters allow you to specify the name or IP address to match, as well as port number and protocol (UDP, TCP, or both).

The iPig VPN solution is extremely easy to set up, offering a quick and painless way to provide VPN connectivity to remote users. The limit of five connections to the iPig server is very reasonable and should be able to accommodate a small office. If you decide that the product meets your needs and you want to upgrade to the full, unlimited user version, the registration cost of $99 is very reasonable. Another offering in the "zero configuration" VPN space in LogMeIn Hamachi and available from www.hamachi.cc/. Their structure for the free version limits you to 16 systems in the VPN network and the documentation says that their "mediation" server is used to help clients find each other. It's not entirely clear if the initial authentication passes through Himachi-owned devices or not. As always, do your research. While iPig's limitations seem easier to work with, Hamachi might be worth investigating to see if it suits your needs.

OpenSSL VPN

There are many commercial VPN solutions using SSL to provide encryption. SSL is the same encryption protocol that is used for secure Web pages (*HTTPS://*) and as such it is a very well tested and widely understood protocol. There are not very many offerings for free SSL based VPNs, but OpenVPN is a very robust and active package. You can read about it and download it from http://openvpn.net. OpenVPN can be installed on Linux, Windows (2000 or newer), several versions of BSD, MAX OS X, and Solaris. We will be using Windows 2000 for the server, and Windows XP for the client, although the differences between using Windows and Linux should be minimal.

OpenVPN uses a single executable to serve as both the client and server components. Download the latest stable version from http://openvpn.net/download.html. You can download a *.ZIP* file or a Windows installation program (*.EXE*). The executable is the easiest to use, so that will be the installation method used in the examples. OpenVPN is natively a command-line program; however, there is a GUI available for download from *http://openvpn.se/*. Follow these steps to get OpenVPN installed and configured.

1. Start the installation program. Click **Next** on the welcome screen.

2. On the license agreement screen you must click **I Agree** to continue with the installation.

3. The next screen is the "Choose Components screen." Leave all components checked and click **Next**.

4. On the next screen, select your installation directory and click **Install**. During the installation you will receive a notice that the TAP driver has not been Windows certified. Click **Yes** (Windows 2000) or **Continue Anyway** to continue with the installation.

5. After the installation completes, click **Next** and then click **Finish**.

Configuring the OpenVPN Server

After installation, the next step is to edit the client configuration file and the server configuration file. You will first configure the server side. Pay strict attention when following the instructions as to whether you are working with the server configuration file or the client configuration file. Also note that your operating system has to be able to find any files it needs, so your configuration files either need to use the complete path for all file references, or you must have the appropriate directory in your system's search path. Sample configuration files can be found in the *OpenVPN\sample-config* directory.

1. Copy the *server.ovpn* file to the *OpenVPN\config* directory and rename it to something meaningful. For this example, we used *config\LAB_SERVER.ovpn*.

2. Open the server configuration file for editing with an American Standard Code for Information Interchange (ASCII) editor, such as Notepad.

3. There is a directive named port that specifies the port the server will listen on for inbound connections. The default port for the server is 1194. If you want to change the port and use something non-standard, edit the port number here.

4. Scroll down to the line containing *;dev-node*. You need to remove the *;* and enter the name of the virtual adapter that OpenVPN installed in place of the default "MyTap." You can

find this by going to a command prompt and entering **ipconfig /all**. One of the adapters will list "TAP-Win32 Adapter V8" as its description. The name of that adapter is often **Local Area Connection 2**, or something similar. Edit the line in the configuration file with the adapter name such as **dev-node Local Area Connection 2**.

5. Save your changes and then close the configuration file.

TIP

As a general rule, I always rename the network interfaces on my systems to make it easier to administer. When you are troubleshooting a connection or program it is far easier to understand which interface is which with a more meaningful name than Local Area Connection 1, Local Area Connection 2, and so on. To do this, navigate to your Network Connection, right-click any of the connections, and select **Rename**. You can use ipconfig to see the description, which usually tells you which one is which. In the preceding example, I renamed the OpenVPN virtual adapter to OpenVPN, so my configuration file would read **dev-node OpenVPN**.

At this point you can choose which type of authentication you want to implement. OpenVPN can support a wide variety of methods, including public key infrastructure (PKI), user/password, and even two-part authentication with the proper plug-ins. For simplicity, we use a simple user and password. You will need to create a server certificate and Certificate of Authenticity (CA) certificate. This must be done as part of the SSL encryption, and is required whether you use PKI or user/password authentication.

6. Open a command prompt prompt on the server and CD to the *\OpenVPN\easy-rsa* directory.

7. Enter the **init-config** command and press **Enter**. This creates the *vars.bat* file and the *openssl.cnf* files.

8. Edit the *vars.bat* file using a text editor such as *notepad.exe* or *write.exe*.

9. Edit the *HOME* variable to match your directory structure if you installed OpenVPN to a non-default directory location.

10. Edit the *KEY_COUNTRY*, *KEY_PROVINCE*, *KEY_CITY*, *KEY_ORG*, and *KEY_EMAIL* variables with their appropriate values. These are used to generate the key file.

11. Enter the following commands at the command prompt.

```
vars
clean-all
build-ca
```

When you run *build-ca* it will prompt you for some localized information. It should read the defaults from what you entered in the *vars.bat* file for any required fields.

Additional fields that were not in the *vars.bat* are optional. Pressing **ENTER** should accept each default value and fill in all of the required information. The only exception is the server's "common name," which you must enter. When the process completes there will be no special indication as to whether it was successful or not. You can verify the creation of the CA certificate by checking in the *OpenVPN\easy-rsa\keys* directory for a newly created *ca.crt* file.

12   Generate the required Diffie Hellman parameters by running *OpenVPN\easy-rsa\build-dh*.

13   Generate the server certificate by running *OpenVPN\easy-rsa\build-key-server server*. As with build-ca, there will be a series of questions you must answer. The questions that must be answered should pull information in from the vars.bat file and use it as the defaults Once again you will need to enter a common name in a series of prompts.

14   Add the following directives to the server configuration file (\OpenVPN\config\ LAB_SERVER.ovpn).

■   ***client-cert-not-required*** Tells the server not to expect the clients to present their own certificate.

■   ***username-as-common-name*** Tells the server to use the username the client provides as the unique identifier for the client, rather than the common name found in the client's certificate.

■   ***Auth-user-pass-verify <script> <via-file | via-env>*** tells OpenVPN how to authenticate users. This directive is required when not using certificates. The script is a file or program that authenticates the users. *Vie-file* or *via-end* tells OpenVPN to pass the username and password to the script as an environment variable or as a two-line file.

The default assumption for OpenVPN is that you will use PKI to authenticate all parties. If you want to use a user/password authentication mechanism, you are expected to configure OpenVPN so that it can pass the credentials out to a third-party process for verification. This modularity allows OpenVPN to support many different types of authentication. If you are running on Linux, there is a PAM module you can use. If you are running on Windows, there is no built-in way to verify the authentication. You can use any script you like. If the script produces an error code of zero, the authentication was successful; a one means it was not successful. This means there are many ways to verify the users, with only your imagination as a limitation.

To elaborate further, let's look at a simple example. Suppose all you want to do for verification is see if a directory is present on the VPN server with the same name as the user's name (not secure, but this is just an example of how the process works). You could create an "authentication" script called *C:\check.bat*. The line in the server configuration file would be *auth-user-pass-verify C:\check.bat via-env*. This will cause the OpenVPN server to call the batch file any time a user logs in. The batch file will have environment variables of *username* and *password*. The authentication script would only need the following line to check for the appropriate user directory:

```
IF EXIST C:\%username% EXIT
```

If the directory is present, an error level of zero would be returned to the OpenVPN Server and the user would be authenticated. For something more practical, we used a *psexec* utility, which is part of the pstools package. These are free tools available from Microsoft at www.microsoft.com/technet/sysinternals/Security/PsTools.mspx. The purpose of the tool is to allow you to remotely execute commands on Windows hosts. The key component we use allows you to authenticate, so if you try and run the command using the credentials the VPN client supplied, it will tell you if they are a legitimate user or not, based on their local Windows account. The *check.bat* file assumes all relevant files and utilities are in the system's path. *Check.bat* contains the following lines:

```
IF "%1"=="test" exit
psexec -l -u %username% -p %password% C:\check.bat test
```

The first line is checking the command line for an argument of test. The first time the OpenVPN Server calls check.bat, this argument will not be present so it will go to the next line. The next line will use psexec to run this same check.bat again. This will fail if the supplied credentials are not correct. If they are correct, check.bat (# 2) will be opened, this time with "test" as the first argument. When check.bat (# 2) sees "test" as the first argument, check.bat (# 2) will close. At this point, check.bat (# 1) has completed its assigned task and exits with an error code of zero, thus authenticating the VPN client. The psexec utility does allow you to specify the system to run the command on using \\<computername> format. When you omit the computername, as in this example, psexec will assume the account is local. In this case, the VPN server would need a local account to authenticate against.

1. Find the line with *Sever 10.8.0.0 255.255.255.0*. This line tells the VPN server to give out addresses to the clients from that network range. You will need to edit this to provide a range of IP addresses that fits your network topology and is not in use or conflicting with your own internal DHCP servers. If your DHCP assigned addresses from 192.168.1.100–192.168.1.200, you could use 192.168.1.64 255.255.255.224, which would assign clients to addresses 192.68.1.66–192.168.1.94, with one of the available IP addresses going to the VPN Server itself.

2. If there are any non-local subnets that the VPN clients need to access, you must update the clients routing table accordingly. There are two ways to accomplish this, and both use the *push* directive. One is by sending them a specific route in the format *push route 192.168.111.0 255.255.255.0*. This will modify the client's routing table and add a route to 192.168.111.0 with the VPN server as the next hop to reach that network. The other is using the *push "redirect-gateway"* directive. This will create a new default route in the client, so all traffic without a more specific route defined will go through the VPN server. The latter method is generally preferable as it is more secure. The increased security is because you will effectively disable normal Internet access from the remote client via it's own Internet link, thereby increasing the isolation between the corporate network and the rest of the Internet. The disadvantage is that when doing so, other non-work-related traffic will also traverse the corporate network, potentially consuming bandwidth.

3. When you are finished making your changes save them and close the configuration file.

Configuring the OpenVPN Client

The next step is to configure the client-side configuration file.

1. Copy the *client.ovpn* from the *\OpenVPN\sample-config* directory to the *\OpenVPN\config* directory and rename it. In this example it is named *LAB_CLIENT.ovpn*.

2. Open the new configuration file in notepad for editing.

3   Once again, edit the *dev-node* directive with the appropriate adapter name.

4   Edit the directive *remote my-server-1 1194*. Replace *my-server-1* with the hostname or IP address of the VPN server. The 1194 is the default port, which you can edit it if you want to use a different port number, which must match the port number you configured on the server "port" directive.

5   In the client configuration file, you can comment out the lines *cert client.crt* and *key client.key*.

6   Add the line *auth-user-pass* to the client configuration file. This instructs the client to prompt for a username and password.

7   You need to copy the *ca.crt* from the server to each client, and edit the directive to include the appropriate path. The server and all of the clients must have a copy of this file.

8   When you are finished making your changes save them and close the configuration file.

Once everything is configured, you can start the VPN server with the following **openvpn — config C:\openvpn\config\lab_server.ovpn** command. Obviously, you will need to make sure the path and name of the configuration files match your environment. If you do not have the file directories in the path, you will need to place an explicit path into the configuration files, using a double backslash for directories. For example, you would use *C:\\openvpn\\easy-rsa\\keys\\ca.crt* for the CA certificate path. Start the client with *openvpn —config C:\openvpn\config\lab_client.ovpn* or the equivalent for your directory path and file names.

Using PKI Certificates of Authentication

With this much complete, using CAs instead of a user/password is easy. Follow these steps to change the authentication mechanism from user/password to CAs.

1. In the server configuration file, comment out the following lines:

```
client-cert-not-required
username-as-common-name
auth-user-pass-verify C:\\check.bat via-env.
```

2. On the server, generate a key pair for each client that will connect to the VPN. In the *\OpenPVN\easy-rsa* directory run *build-key client1*, where *client1* is the name you want to use for the first client to connect. This is often the same as the users logon ID. When prompted, the common name should be unique for each client; and again, the login ID might be a good choice for the common name. When prompted, it is recommended that you create a password for the client certificate. If you do not, anyone who obtains the certificate files can access the VPN.

3. Move or copy the *client1.key* and *client1.crt* to the appropriate client host. The server does not need a copy of these files, but generally you would leave a copy on the server as a backup.

4. In the client configuration file comment out the *auth-user-pass* line.

5. Edit the *.cert* and *.key* directives that were commented out previously for password authentication. Configure both of these lines with the appropriate paths to the *.cert* and *.key* files you copied from the server. Remember to use double backslashes for the path.

After the VPN connection is established, there are a few helpful shortcuts you can use from within the terminal window.

- **F1 Conditional Restart** This is similar to a warm reboot of the VPN tunnel. This will reset the tunnel, but will not reset the virtual Network Interface Card (NIC) (TAP adapter).

- **F2 Show Connection Statistics** This will give you some basic input and output statistics. Sample output is shown with the time and date removed from each line to conserve space.

```
OpenVPN STATISTICS
Updated,Sun Nov 26 10:20:20 2006
TUN/TAP read bytes,240
TUN/TAP write bytes,240
TCP/UDP read bytes,4366
TCP/UDP write bytes,4109
Auth read bytes,272
pre-compress bytes,0
post-compress bytes,0
pre-decompress bytes,0
post-decompress bytes,0
TAP-WIN32 driver status,"State=AT?c Err=[(null)/0] #O=5 Tx=[4,0,0] Rx=[4,0,0]
IrpQ=[1,1,16] PktQ=[0,1,64]"
```

- **F3 Hard Restart** This reset will reset the virtual adapter.
- **F4 Exit** This will close the tunnel completely.

Configuring the OpenVPN GUI

Once the hard part is done (i.e., configuring the client-side and server-side OpenVPN configuration files and generating all the required keys) initiating the VPN tunnel is very simple. You could place the command line into a batch file or shortcut for your user's desktop. There is also a GUI interface available, though again, once you have everything running, the GUI may not be needed. This GUI interface can be downloaded from http://openvpn.se/index.html. The installation program is very straightforward, prompting for all of the normal parameters. The installer will install the base OpenVPN package in addition to the GUI components; therefore, you don't need to install both. You will be prompted to confirm the installation, because the virtual NIC driver is not Microsoft certified. You should remove the previous OpenVPN program (via Add/Remove programs) before installing the GUI version to the same directory. The uninstall will not remove your certificates, keys, or configuration files, and the install will not overwrite them.

After installing the GUI version, the virtual network adapter name will be reinstalled with a standard name (e.g., Local Network Adapter 2). If your configuration file refers to a more meaningful name, you will need to rename the adapter (again). There should be a new icon in the system tray. Right-click this and select **Connect**. If you have multiple configuration files present, you will be presented with a menu folder for each, and options to connect or edit each individually. You should see a progress window with the same messages as you saw in the console window. If it scrolls by too quickly and you want a second look, right-click the icon in the system tray and select **Show Status** (see Figure 2.37). After negotiation completes, a pop-up window will indicate a successful connection.

Figure 2.37 OpenVPN GUI Status Window

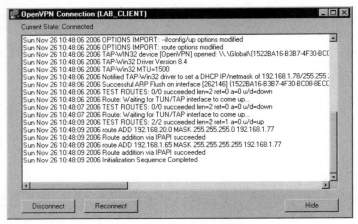

While OpenVPN is not a "zero configuration" VPN like iPig, it is very powerful and flexible. The capability to support such a wide variety of authentication methods is not offered by any other free VPN software at this time. What really sets OpenVPN apart is its enterprise class options and management features. As an example, add the line *management localhost 7505*. This directive will work in both the server and client configurations and will instruct OpenVPN to listen to the indicated port (7505 in this example) for management connections. This will allow you to remotely query the OpenVPN instance and execute some limited commands.

An additional feature that lends itself to corporate functionality is the *remote (remote <IP> <PORT>)* and *remote-random* directives on the OpenVPN client. While we used the remote directive to specify the OpenVPN server to connect to, you can define multiple servers in the configuration file and the client will attempt each one in turn. This will allow you to configure a backup VPN server for redundancy. The remote-random directive instructs the clients to randomly select from defined remotes. In this way, you can load balance across two or more OpenVPN servers in an active-active configuration.

There are many more features available for OpenVPN. If you are not discouraged by the configuration that is required, you will be hard pressed to find a more robust free VPN solution. A quick-start guide is available from the OpenVPN Web site at http://openvpn.net/howto.html#quick.

Providing a Remote Desktop

Some of the considerations for placing your remote desktop are similar to those of a VPN. The primary consideration (i.e., physical location for the desktop host) has very little flexibility. Because the remote users will be accessing the desktop virtually, the desktop needs access to all of the same things it normally has. Unless you have some systems you can dedicate to this task and place in a DMZ, this probably means the users will be coming in through the firewall and accessing their desktops that are sitting on the internal network. Because of this, you want to secure the connection as much as possible. This desktop will have a login prompt exposed to the Internet unless you take steps to prevent it. A personal firewall (covered in more detail in Chapter 3) can help mitigate this, as well as firewall rules on your Internet connection. Most home users will be using a dynamic IP address, so you will probably not be able to restrict the connection to the user's specific IP address. You can, however, restrict it to the block of IP addresses corresponding to the local ISP's dynamic range. It is better to only let your local geographic area be able to initiate a connection to the remote desktop than to the entire world.

There are people who scan the Internet looking for systems that are listening on ports commonly used for remote access. This is the primary reason you may want to consider using a non-standard port for your remote desktop solution. In the case of terminal services, the port is configured in the registry, and Microsoft does not recommend changing it; however, it can be changed. For third-party products such as Virtual Network Computing (VNC), changing the listening port is typically much simpler and advisable. Using a non-standard port does not guarantee the system will not be discovered and attacked. In fact, you can bet it will be, just less often than with a standard port. For this reason you must require and enforce a policy requiring very strong passwords for accounts with remote access privileges. If you're going to be exposing your internal network to the outside world, you should also implement an IDS if possible (see Chapters 4, 5, and 6 for details on deploying Snort).

Windows Terminal Services

Windows terminal services is a handy way to provide access to a remote desktop across a single TCP port using remote desktop protocol (RDP). The fact that terminal services only uses a single port (TCP 3389; however, you can configure the port to be any port), makes the firewall rules simple to configure. With Windows XP or Server 2003, the terminal services client and server will be installed by default. For Windows 2000, the terminal services component can be installed via the add/remove programs applet in the control panel. Another advantage of using the Windows terminal services is that the client portion can be installed on older systems, allowing them to use the newer hosts and software. The remote desktop client can be installed on Windows 95, 98, ME, and NT as well as all of the newer Windows operating systems.

To enable the remote desktop functionality on a Windows XP Professional or Windows 2003 system, follow these steps.

1. Right-click on the **My Computer** icon and select **Properties**
2. Select the **Remote** tab.
3. Check the box that says **Allow users to connect remotely to this computer**.
4. Click the **Select Remote Users** button (see Figure 2.38).

Figure 2.38 Enabling Windows Terminal Services

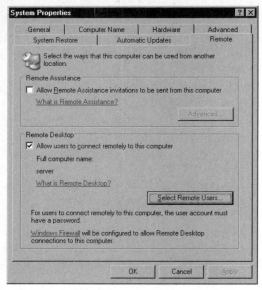

5. On the "Remote Desktop Users" screen, click **Add**

6. On the "Select Users" window, enter the name of any user accounts that should be able to connect remotely and click **OK**.

7. Click **OK** to close the "Remote Desktop Users" window.

8. Click **OK** to close the "System Properties" window.

If you are using a client host that has the remote desktop client already installed, navigate to **Start | Accessories | Communications | Remote Desktop Connection**. The "Remote Desktop Connection" window is shown in Figure 2.39.

Figure 2.39 Remote Desktop Connection

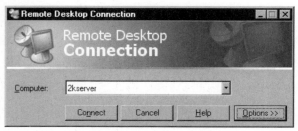

To connect to a remote desktop, enter the computer name or IP address in the "Computer" field and click **Connect**. If you click **Options** there are a wide variety of configurable parameters you can experiment with. Most of these settings are geared towards increasing the performance of the connection.

If you want to use terminal services on a Windows 2000 computer, you need to install it following these steps.

1. Navigate to **Start | Settings | Control Panel**.

2. Select **Add/Remove Programs**.

3. Click the **Add/Remove Windows Components** button.

4. Highlight **Terminal Services** and click **Details**.

5. In the "Terminal Services" window place a checkmark next to **Enable Terminal Services** and click **OK** (see Figure 2.40).

Figure 2.40 Installing Terminal Services

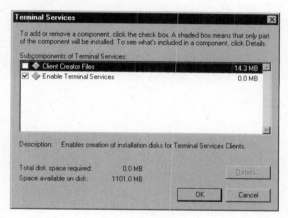

6. In the Windows Components Wizard, click **Next**

7. The Terminal Services Setup window will allow you to choose from **Remote Administration Mode** or **Application Server Mode**. Remote administration mode basically gives you a remote desktop, while application server mode allows you to share a single application. After selecting, click **Next**.

8. When the wizard completes, click **Finish**.

The simplicity of providing a complete desktop for remote users to access can be appealing, and the ability to do so without any third-party software can be a major factor when deciding which solution to use. The flexibility doesn't end there, however. If have a Windows server but need to access the server remotely from a Linux system, you can install rdesktop, which is an open source client capable of speaking RDP natively. After installing rdesktop (via whatever means you choose; *yum install rdesktop* works on fedora core 5), all it takes to connect to a terminal server at 192.168.1.90 is to enter the **rdesktop 192.168.1.90:3389** command at a console prompt. To make things even easier, you can install terminal server client (tsclient), which provides a single GUI interface for establishing client connections to several common types of terminal servers. You still must install a client program such as rdesktop, because tsclient is only a front end, it does not include the client software itself. The only function of tsclient is to save you the trouble of needing to know the command-line options needed to make the connection. The tsclient interface is shown in Figure 2.41.

Figure 2.41 tsclient

Given the variety of RDP clients available, you should be able to connect to a Windows terminal server from most any OS. And with the convenience of having a GUI interface to make the connection, it is an easy solution. You should not expose any RDP services to the general Internet because then your only protection will be the password to connect, and automated brute-force password crackers will eventually gain access. If you do need to allow any type of remote desktop functionality to an Internet-based source, you should filter traffic to the respective port so that only the trusted IP address is allowed to connect.

VNC

VNC computing and has been around for a long time. It has gone through a lot of changes and is now available under many names, each with their own focus. This resembles the situation with Linux distributions in that the number of options can sometimes make it difficult to know which one is the best choice. Some of the more prominent are RealVNC, TightVNC, UltraVNC, and more. TightVNC (www.tightvnc.com/) encrypts the password exchange when you initially logon, but the rest of the session is unencrypted. While you could use an encrypted tunnel to encapsulate the VNC session, the other alternatives include native encryption support. RealVPC Personal Edition (www.realvnc.com/) includes support for AES128 encryption, but is only available for Windows platforms. This leaves my current top choice as UltraVPN from http://ultravnc.sourceforge.net/. In addition to providing encryption plug-ins, the UltraVNC server will run on any Windows system (Windows 95 thru 2003) and allows you to connect to it from any system with a compatible browser. To install UltraVNC follow these steps.

1. Download the UltraVNC setup file. The setup program includes both the client (the viewer) and the server component.

2. Run the setup program.

3. Choose the language and click **OK**.

4. At the welcome screen, click **Next**.

5. Accept the license agreement and click **Next**.

6. Click **Next** on the information screen (after reading all of the text).

7. Choose the installation directory and click **Next**.

8. Select the components to install (the DSM Encryption plug-in should be checked), and click **Next**.

9. Choose a start menu folder and click **Next**.

10. Next is the "Additional Tasks" screen, which has some additional options. The more noteworthy are outlined in this section.

    - **Register UltraVNC Serer as System Service** This will cause the server component to be installed as a service. If you install this, the server will be started automatically. If you choose not to install the server as a service, the server will need to be started manually in order for someone to connect to the server. Requiring a manual start is more secure, but installing the server as a service might be a legitimate need in your environment.

    - **Start or Restart UltraVNC Service** This instructs the installation program to start the service during installation, or if it's already started, to stop and restart the service.

    - **Configure MS-Logon II** This is a relatively new option that allows an ACL to be configured that specifies who can have access to connect to the server, based on the Microsoft account information. If you select this option but do not configure the ACL, only the administrator group will have access. This may be the preferred way to configure it if you only plan on using the VPN connection for support purposes. It is recommended that you enable this for increased security and simplified administration.

    - **Configure Admin Properties** This option prompts you for the location of a file registry file (*.reg*) containing the administrative settings for the UltraVNC server. These settings control things such as what to do with disconnected sessions and what to do upon disconnect. This can make configuration more automated by exporting the *HKEY_LOCAL_MACHINE\SOFTWARE\ORL* key for use during the installation of subsequent hosts.

    - **Clean Old VNC Registry Keys** This option enables a house cleaning function to clear out old settings in the registry.

11. After making your selections, click **Next**.

12. Accept the defaults for any needed configuration files in the next couple of screens (such as the MS-Logon ACL file, if those options were checked) and then click **Install**.

13. Click **Next** on the information screen, and then click **Finish** on the next screen.

The server component should not be installed, but it still needs to be configured. Start up the UltraVNC server by navigating to **Start | Programs | UltraVNC | UltraVNC Server | Show Default Settings**. The properties page that opens is a little busy (see Figure 2.42).

Figure 2.42 UltraVNC Server

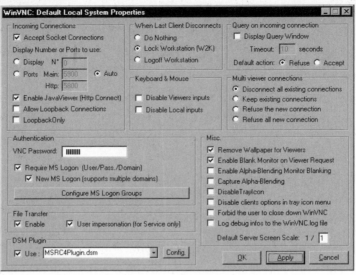

Most of these settings can be left at their defaults, but there are a few that are significant from a security perspective. The section labeled "When Last Client Disconnects" determines what happens after the viewer disconnects. Which setting is best will depend on your intended uses for UltraVNC. If you are going to use it primarily for technical support, there will probably be an authenticated user at the server when you disconnect, in which case you probably want **Do Nothing**. If, on the other hand, you plan on offering the server as a remote productivity tool, there may be no one present at the server end, in which case you likely want to **Lock Workstation**, or even better, **Logoff Workstation**. The "VNC Password" in the "Authentication" section is a default password to be used with no other password supplied. This must be configured or VNC will not accept any inbound connections.

In order to take advantage of the Microsoft user and groups, place a check next to "Require MS Logon," and preferably, "New MS Logon." After doing so, click on **Configure MS Logon Groups** and configure what access different groups will have to the VNC server. The "Security Editor" windows provide a high degree of granularity. The editor is shown in Figure 2.43.

You can configure each group or user to have different levels of access, including view only, which can be a good choice for presentations or other applications where you only want the viewer to be able to see what's occurring without the ability to interact with the server's desktop.

Perhaps the most significant portion of the configuration is the encryption plug-in, in the "DSM Plug-in" section of the window.

1. Place a checkmark next to **Use:** and select the appropriate plug-in from the drop-down box. More plug-ins are available from http://msrc4plugin.home.comcast.netndex.html. There are currently three different encryption plug-ins available:

    ■ **MSRC4Plugin** This plug-in provides RC4 128-bit encryption. There are two versions provided with the UltraVNC installation: *MSRC4Plugin.dsm* and *MSRC4Plugin_NoReg.dsm*. You should use the *MSRC4Plug-in_NoReg.dsm* plug-in.

Figure 2.43 UltraVNC Security Editor

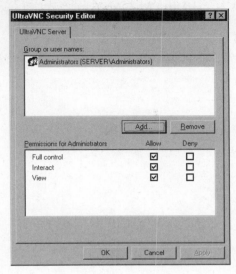

- **ARC4Plugin** This plug-in provides RC4 128-bit encryption and handles the pass-word slightly differently than the preceding one.

- **AESV2Plugin** This plug-in provides AES 128-bit encryption.

  The plug-in will not be available for selection in the drop-down box while it resides in the *UltraVNC*\ *plugin* directory. You must copy the *MSRC4Plugin_NoReg.dsm* plug-in to the main *UltraVNC*\ directory.

NOTE

The plug-in that comes with the installation is an older version than the one available from the plug-in site. The version that came with the install did not work for me. Using the latest plug-in resolved the issue. Also note that you need to use the same key on both the server and viewer, a fact that is not clearly spelled out in the documentation. It doesn't matter which system you generate it on, although the server probably makes more sense.

2. Select the *MSRC4Plugin_NoReg.dsm* in the dropdown box and click **Config**.

3. Click on **Gen Key** to create a server key. When finished, click **OK** to close the plug-in configuration window.

4. Click on **Apply** and then **OK** to close the Default properties window.

The VNC Server should now be started and running securely. The next step is starting up the UltraVNC viewer (the client), which is much easier to do.

1. Start the UltraVNC Viewer via the desktop icon (if applicable) or by navigating to **Start |
    Programs | UltraVNC | UltraVNC Viewer**. This will open the connection window
    (see Figure 2.44).

Figure 2.44 UltraVNC Viewer

2. Enter the host name or IP address in the VNC Server field. Follow this with two colons
    (::) and port number, or a single colon (:) and the display number. The Default port will be
    5901.

3. Place a check in the box next to **Use DMSPlug-in**.

4. Select the same exact plug-in in the drop-down box that you are using on the server. The
    plug-in files need to be the same version as well. Your key file should be the same one used
    on the server. The key file is not as "top secret" as you might think. Even if someone
    obtains the key file, they will still have to provide a username and password, and will be
    subject to the Windows account access you configured on the server.

Once you are connected, the status window will indicate that you are using encryption (see Figure
2.45). You can open the status window for an established connection by using the "Show Status
Window" button at the top of the viewer window (it has a large exclamation point on the button).

Figure 2.45 UltraVNC Viewer Status

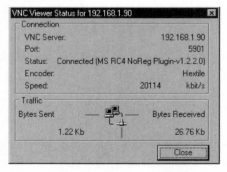

The status line will show the plug-in you are using (if any), thus indicating that you are using the MS RC4 plug-in, which in turn is a simple way to verify that you are successfully using encryption for your sessions.

Between using the native Windows Terminal Services and UltraVNC, you have a variety of options to provide you remote desktop access. Although Windows Terminal Services (also referred to by the Windows client/protocol name, Remote Desktop) is included and doesn't require additional software, a VNC solution is likely to offer more flexibility, and the server is supported on more platforms. VNC clients and servers are also available for virtually all Linux distributions. In fact, the default install of many includes one or both components. Fedora Core 5 installs the VNC server by default, while the client is an optional installation package. This widespread availability and support is one of the reasons VNC (in all it's variants) is such a widely used solution.

Using the X Window System

X window is the underlying management system for most Unix and Linux GUIs. It takes an entirely different architectural approach than a Microsoft Windows system, in that the X Window system is set up in a client-server architecture from the beginning, similar to VNC. When reading the X Window documentation, you will find that they user the terms server and client in the reverse of what would seem intuitive, meaning the server is where the display is being generated, not the remote machine you are connecting to. Most current implementations are based on the work of the *X.Org foundation* (http://x.org), which is the open source implementation of the X11 protocol. A closely related project is the XFree86 Project (www.xfree86.org), which is the open source version of the *X Window system* (which uses the X11 protocol). X11 is the protocol that is used to transfer information about the GUI between the server and the client. The end result of these design decisions is that much like Windows' built-in terminal server support, two Linux systems can remotely access each other via a GUI virtual desktop.

You can configure the X Window System to permit connections from remote systems without any third-party software. While this works, the evolution of desktop Window Managers and common software packages has rendered this method inefficient. A much more robust way to accomplish the same thing is using NX technology developed by *NoMachine*, which is a highly optimized process and protocol to make X sessions available remotely. NX is available for free (client and server) from www.nomachine.com/download.php. Commercial variations are also available. You can see the differences between versions, and thus see what the limitations of the free version are at www.nomachine.com/features.php. The big limitation is that the *NX Free Edition* limits you to only two concurrent connections. In most cases this won't be much of a limitation unless you are trying to use it as a full-blown terminal server solution rather than just a remote access mechanism. An open source version of the NX server is called FreeNX and is available from http://freenx.berlios.de/. FreeNX does not support relaying sounds to the client (while the NoMachine server does). This is the recommended server and the one used in the following examples.

To set up the FreeNX server, download and install FreeNX using whatever method is appropriate for your Linux distribution. For Fedora Core 5, I used *yum install freenx*. Yum (the package installer for Fedora Core 5) will automatically check for and install any dependencies. The aforementioned command also installed the core *nx* package, and *expect* as dependencies. In the case of Fedora Core 5, there is no need for any further installation. Depending on the distribution you are using, the installation may be more involved. Most of the major distributions should have packages available that make the installation relatively painless. You will need to have SSHD listening on port 22 in order for NX to work properly.

TIP

If you check the running services in an attempt to verify that the FreeNX server was installed successfully (via *chkconfig* or the like), you will not see it listed. This is because the server FreeNX server does not sit and listen on a port for an inbound connection like most services. Instead, when you login via SSH (this is why you need SSHD running on port 22), it logs you in as a special user (NX). That user's profile is configured such that it executes a process to start up the server and listen for the inbound connection.

With the server configured, the next step is to download and configure the client to make a connection. While there are alternate clients available, including some command-line clients, we will go with the original NoMachine client, which is installed on Windows XP for this exercise. Download the client and follow these steps to make a connection to the Linux FreeNX server:

1. Run the installation program. The installation is unremarkable, asking for all the standards prompts such as a license agreement, and choosing an installation directory, the option to create a desktop icon, and so on.

2. When you first run the NX Client for Windows shortcut, it will launch the NX Connection Wizard, because you have no sessions defined. The wizard will walk you through establishing a connection. On the first screen of the wizard click **Next**.

3. The next screen allows you to configure a name for the session. All of the connection settings will be saved under this name for future use. This window also asks for the host and port. Unless you have changed it, leave the port at the default of 22, and configure the appropriate host name or IP address in the host field. This screen is shown in Figure 2.46.

Figure 2.46 NX Client Wizard Session

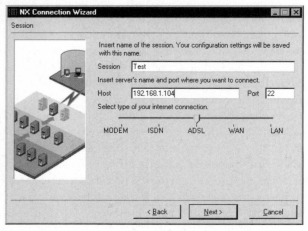

4. After entering the required information, click **Next**.

5. The Desktop setting window is next. Select the OS you will be connecting to, along with the window manager. In this case it was **Unix** and **GNOME**. This window also gives you the option of enabling SSL encryption of all traffic. Unless you have a reason not to have additional security, you should enable this option. If you do not enable encryption, all of the X11 data will be sent unencrypted, meaning that someone with a sniffer could capture and reconstruct everything sent between the client and the server. This screen is shown in Figure 2.47.

Figure 2.47 NX Client Wizard Desktop

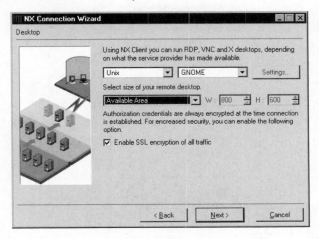

6. When you are satisfied with your settings, click **Next**.

7. The next screen of the wizard is the final one. The options are to **create shortcut on desktop**, and/or **show the advanced configuration dialog**. In order to enable SSL encryption for the connection, you will need to select the **show the advanced configuration dialog** checkbox and then click **Finish**.

8. The advanced configuration dialog is shown in Figure 2.48.

9. On the "General" tab in the "Server" section, click on **Key**. You must have a copy of the *client.id_dsa.key* file, which will be found on the server in either */etc/nxserver/* or */var/lib/nxserver/home/.ssh/*.

10. On the Key Management screen, click **Import**, and select the *client.id_dsa.key* file and then click **OK** followed by **Save**.

11. Finally, click **OK** to commit your settings for this session.

12. After completing the advanced configuration, you will see the client login window shown in Figure 2.49. Enter the appropriate login name and password, and click **Login**.

Figure 2.48 NX Client Advanced Dialog

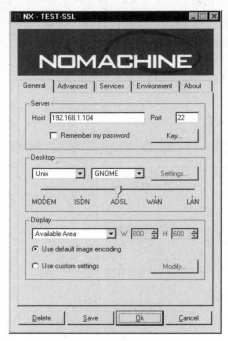

Figure 2.49 NC Client Login

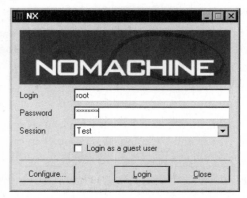

If you login as a user with administrative privileges, you will be given a warning (see Figure 2.50) that this is not best practices and that it would be more secure to use a non–administrator account. If you get this warning, you can click **Continue** to proceed with the connection anyway.

You will be prompted to verify the key fingerprint of the host you are connecting to, which can be done by clicking **Yes**. After a period of encryption and authentication negotiation, you should see the remote desktop. You will quickly notice that the desktop that is spawned is a "new" fresh desktop just for this login, not a view of an existing logged-in user's desktop. This default behavior is different than both Terminal Services and VNC, which both connect you to an existing session if one is present. While NX doesn't behave this way natively, there are some workarounds to try and modify this behavior. Hopefully, future releases will simplify this option and make it easier to configure as the current workarounds are not elegant.

Figure 2.50 NC Client Login Admin Warning

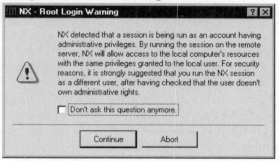

If you are in full screen mode such that you cannot see your real local desktop, there are some keyboard shortcuts available to accomplish some commonly needed tasks. These are outlined here.

- **CTR+ALT+F** Toggles full-screen mode.

- **CTRL+ALT+T** Shows the terminate/suspend dialog. If you terminate, the session is closed, while if you select suspend, you will be able to open the same session next time.

- **CTRL+ALT+M** Maximizes or minimizes the NX client window

- **CTRL+ALT+Mouse** Drags the desktop viewing area, so you can view different portions of the desktop. This is useful if the remote desktop has a higher resolution than your local resolution.

- **CTRL+ALT+Arrows CTRL+ALT+Keypad** – Will move the viewport by an incremental amount of pixels.

- **CTRL+ALT+S** It will activate "screen-scraping" mode, so all the GetImage originated by the clients will be forwarded to the real display. This will allow you to take a screenshot of the remote desktop, to your local clipboard. If you press the sequence again, nxagent will revert to the usual "fast" mode.

- **CTRL+ALT+E** Enables lazy image encoding for improved speed.

Providing a Remote Shell

Sometimes you need remote access to a system but all you need is command line access. Maybe you could use more, as in GUI access, but connecting via the command line might be faster if you just need to connect and check something quickly. The primary use where a command line only connection is most applicable is when you are doing scripted changes. For example, if you needed to connect to 3 dozen systems and change a value in a configuration file, this would actually take a significant amount of time to do manually via the GUI, and a batch file would not be able to handle the GUI interfaces anyway. In these instances what would be idea is a secure command line only remote access method. I mention secure expressly because a simple Telnet connection, while fast and efficient, includes no encryption, and all data during your session (including your login username and password) will be send in clear text across the network. For this reason you need a form of access that includes encryption such as Secure Shell.

Using Secure Shell

SSH (Secure Shell) requires both an SSH client and an SSH server component. SSH is the industry standard for remote command line access and most systems come with it as part of the default install. Windows systems of course are one of the few that do not. There are a variety of products available to bring SSH functionality to Windows, both commercial and free. One of the better known commercial SSH clients is SecureCRT (www.vandyke.com). Most of the free versions are based off of the OpenSSH (www.openssh.com) package. There is also a GUI front end for OpenSSH, called PuTTY. Cygwin (www.cygwin.com) is a port of many Unix tools for Windows and included in this package is an SSH server. To add even more options, SSHWindows is a free package that installs *only* the minimum components of the Cygwin package to use SSH, SCP, and SFTP. We will walk through setting up SSHWindows (on a Windows XP system). This package includes both the SSH client files and the SSH server files.

1. **Download** SSHWindows from http://sshwindows.sourceforge.net/ on the client *and* server

2. Unzip the file and run the setup utility. Answer the standard prompts and then click **Finish**

At this point the SSH client is ready to be used without the need for any additional configuration. Before you can use the SSH server however, you *must* create and edit the **\OpenSSH\etc\ passwd** and **\group** files.

1. If desired create a separate group on the system to hold users who will have access to SSH, and add the local user accounts to the group for anyone you wish to have access to connect to the SSH server.

2. At the console navigate to the directory where you installed \OpenSSH\bin\

3. Enter the following command on the server to specify which groups can connect via SSH mkgroup –l >> ..\etc\group. This will give all local (–l) groups permission to connect via SSH. You should open the group file and edit out the lines corresponding to any groups you do not wish to have access.

4. Enter the mkpasswd –l –u <accountname> >> ..\etc\passwd command on the server to specify a single account that is authorized to connect via SSH

   You must perform both these steps for SSH to work. If you do not specify the –u <*accountname*> all local users will be added to the passwd file.

5. Edit the *Banner.txt* file located in \etc\ to match the banner specified by your IP security policy.

   Once this is completed you can start and use the SSH server via the Services applet of the MMC or by entering **net start "openssh server"** at the command prompt. Here is an example of output from a successful SSH connection.

```
I:\OpenSSH\bin>ssh sshuser@192.168.1.101
*********** WARNING BANNER HERE ***********
sshuser@192.168.1.101's password:
Last login: Sat Jun 24 20:05:22 2006 from 192.168.1.99
Microsoft Windows 2000 [Version 5.00.2195]
(C) Copyright 1985-2000 Microsoft Corp.

C:\OpenSSH>ipconfig

Windows 2000 IP Configuration

Ethernet adapter Local Area Connection:

        Connection-specific DNS Suffix  . : rr.com
        IP Address. . . . . . . . . . . . : 192.168.1.101
        Subnet Mask . . . . . . . . . . . : 255.255.255.0
        Default Gateway . . . . . . . . . : 192.168.1.1
```

This is the sample output from sending a file to the bastion host (192.168.1.101) via SCP.

```
I:\Internet\OpenSSH\bin>scp sample.txt sshuser@192.168.1.101:/
*********** WARNING BANNER HERE ***********
sshuser@192.168.1.101's password:
Could not chdir to home directory /home/SSHuser: No such file or directory
sample.txt                                100% 1735    1.7KB/s   00:00
```

TIP

While the SSH port in SSHWindows uses standard CMD.exe syntax, the SCP command and SFTP command both use Unix style paths. Also of note is that unless it is configured differently, the SSH connection will assume that the directory you installed OpenSSH into is the starting root for client connections.

If you get an error of *segid: Invalid Argument*, this typically means that the permissions are incorrect in the passwd file. The logon account on Windows systems should be 544 instead of 514. The latest installation didn't seem to have this issue but it's not uncommon.

Using a Secure Shell GUI Client

In virtually all cases with a command line utility offering many options and configuration parameters, some one will come along and create a GUI front end to make things simpler. This is true with SSH as well. By far the most widely used front-end is PuTTY, which is available from www.chiark.greenend.

org.uk/~sgtatham/putty/. Setting it up is fast and simple because all you need to do is download the single PuTTY.exe file and it's "installed." When you run the EXE, the configuration window will look like the one shown in Figure 2.51.

Figure 2.51 PuTTY Configuration

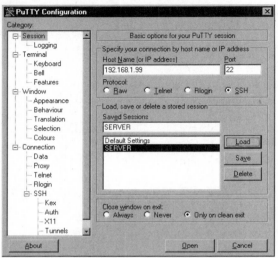

While there are a lot of options, a basic SSH session is easy to configure. Make sure that **SSH** is selected as the protocol, and enter the host name or IP address you wish to connect to in the appropriate field. You can enter a session name and click **Save** if you wish to save your settings for future use. When you are happy with your settings, click **Open** to initiate the session. If it is the first time to connect to that particular host you will be prompted to verify the server key by clicking **Yes** as shown in Figure 2.52.

Figure 2.52 PuTTY Server Key Verification

A console window will open and the configured logon banner will be displayed. You should then have access to the command prompt on the remote system. To restore the session settings, simply highlight the session name and click **Load**, followed by **Open** to connect.

There is a wide variety of options for providing free, secure remote access, probably more options than most people realize. Each option has its strengths and weaknesses, and in reality, what you already have in-house may dictate which server you use. Hopefully, the coverage of remote access clients and servers in this chapter, will allow you to make the most out of the resources you have available.

Summary

In this chapter, we examined a multitude of methods to secure your network perimeter and provide you, as the administrator, the access that is needed to administer the network. The Linux built-in fire-wall netfilter was covered extensively due to it's power and flexibility, not to mention availability, as a free stateful firewall. In addition to iptables, we looked at several GUI front ends that allow you to manage the netfilter firewall without knowing the iptables command line syntax. With your perimeter secured, the next step was to establish a secured doorway, so that you could sit at home and take care of the network. With command-line access via SSH, and Windows Terminal Services offering a remote desktop, FreeNX rounded out the offering by offering multiple remote desktop sessions from the same server.

Armed with this knowledge, there is no excuse to not have some type of firewall for protection on any and all unsecured connections. I say unsecured, not Internet intentionally, because any business partner, home user network, or the Internet are all considered untrusted, meaning you have no or incomplete administrative control over the security of the network you are connected to. Ultimately, you have no way to guarantee or enforce the proper security controls of an untrusted network. The sad fact is, if you have an Internet connection and don't have any type of firewall between a computer and the Internet, odds are very high that you have already been compromised. For other types of untrusted connections your odds may be better, but you're still gambling if you don't take steps to protect your network and systems.

Solutions Fast Track

Firewall Types

- In the networking sense, a firewall is basically any component (software or hardware) that restricts the flow of network traffic.

- Some firewalls are notoriously limited in capability, and others are extremely easy to use.

- To permit or deny traffic based on which network device is the sender or recipient and what ports are being used, you would use a packet-filtering firewall

Firewall Architectures

- The most securely configured firewall in existence will not provide much protection if the underlying network was not designed properly.

- A *screened subnet* is the simplest and most common firewall implementation. Most small businesses and homes use this type of firewall

- The one-legged demilitarized zone (DMZ) still has the advantage of cost, because you are building a DMZ using only a single firewall.

- The true DMZ is generally considered the most secure of firewall architectures. With this design, there is an external and internal firewall. Between the two is sandwiched any Internet accessible devices.

Implementing Firewalls

- netfilter is the built-in component that performs the firewall logic. iptables is the command-line interface used to configure the netfilter ACLs.

- Many GUI interfaces exist with widely varying degrees of functionality and complexity. My suggestion here is choose the simplest one that will do what you need it to do. In all likelihood the "right" one will change for you over time.

- SmoothWall sits in a class of its own, due to the fact that it turns a PC into a dedicated firewall appliance that is completely configurable without ever logging into the underlying Linux operating system.

Providing Secure Remote Access

- Your remote access options will depend most heavily on the platforms you have available to use for the remote access server. In most cases, the client used for remote access will run on virtually any OS.

- In conjunction with considering the available resources, you need to evaluate what your remote access needs really are. Is command line good enough? Do you need a remote GUI? Do you need to tap into existing sessions for a tech support type of functionality?

- For any remote access solution, remember to make sure you are using encryption if you plan on the session traversing an untrusted network, such as the Internet.

Frequently Asked Questions

The following Frequently Asked Questions, answered by the authors of this book, are designed to both measure your understanding of the concepts presented in this chapter and to assist you with real-life implementation of these concepts. To have your questions about this chapter answered by the author, browse to **www. syngress.com/solutions** and click on the **"Ask the Author"** form.

Q: How do I make the NX Client connect to an existing session?

A: Currently, the most oft used solution is to have the local user use an NX session (to localhost). That way, all of their activities are always within an NX session, making management (terminate, pause, resume) much simpler. Again, it's not elegant but it works adequately.

Q: I like the features of a particular flavor of VNC (or any remote access method) but it doesn't support encryption. What can I do to secure it?

A: One of the most common approaches is to use the SSH port-forwarding functionality. This is how many of the VNC variants are providing encryption behinds the scenes anyway.

## Chapter 3

Protecting Network Resources

Solutions in this chapter:

- **Performing Basic Hardening**
- **Hardening Windows Systems**
- **Hardening Linux Systems**
- **Hardening Infrastructure Devices**
- **Patching Systems**
- **Personal Firewalls**
- **Providing Anti-Virus and Anti-Spyware Protection**
- **Encrypting Sensitive Data**

- ☑ **Summary**
- ☑ **Solutions Fast Track**
- ☑ **Frequently Asked Questions**

Introduction

Chapter 2 focused on protecting the perimeter of your network, which typically means the Internet link, but it could include any link to the outside world, including connections to business partners and affiliates. This chapter focuses on how to secure the network-connected resources, such as servers and workstations. Many times an organization looks only at securing its perimeter, while leaving its interior network wide open and unprotected. This hard-exterior-soft-squishy-interior approach is surely better than no security, but it is not the best approach. The best approach is through *defense in depth*, which is the practice of applying security measures at all levels of the network. A solid defense-in-depth approach includes defenses at the outer perimeter—typically, firewalls and an intrusion detection system. It also includes defenses within the interior of the network, such as internal firewalls, network segmentation, and port-level access controls. Finally, at the core of the security onion are the actual network resources. You can protect these resources in a variety of ways, including via personal firewalls, antivirus software, antispyware software, data encryption, and automated security policy enforcement.

Performing Basic Hardening

All general-purpose operating systems will, by their very nature, come with weaker security settings than you might like. This characteristic is unavoidable, largely because the devices are general-purpose. To accommodate the wide variety of uses the system might fulfill, some sacrifices must be made when it comes to securing the system. This isn't necessarily true when it comes to special-purpose systems, which often come with highly secured and specially tailored configurations so that the system can be used only for its intended purpose. You, on the other hand, know exactly what you want systems to do, so you can customize the general-purpose installation to be more secure in your environment. Securing a system is also referred to as *hardening* the system, which means to make it harder for an attacker to compromise the system.

Regardless of what purpose the system serves, there are some common hardening steps that you should apply to all systems. There are high-level tasks, and as such, the specific implementation details are going to vary from system to system. These high-level hardening tasks have been outlined here. Any plan you develop to harden any network resource should address all of these issues in some fashion.

Defining Policy

You cannot possibly harden a system, at least not from an auditing perspective, if you do not have a definition and set of criteria for what constitutes "hardened," or secure. Because of this, any hardening process actually starts long before you ever configure anything on a device, with defining policies and standards. Your IT security team will clearly outline the objectives you are trying to meet. The related standards will provide measurable milestones to meet in pursuit of that objective. Your security standards are your yardstick for success and provide an objective measure of your progress. Although the words "make the server secure" imply certain objectives, they do not clearly define measurable tasks; therefore, proving that you have "made the server secure" would be difficult at best. As such, having some well-defined security standards will be to everyone's advantage.

The IT policies and standards your organization employs should accurately reflect your organization's specific needs. Many organizations will sell you an IT policy to use, or one to use as a shell for filling in your own specifics. Taking this approach of using a "canned" policy has many challenges. What constitutes an appropriate policy or standard for one organization may not adequately cover the needs of another organization. The business model, type of business, and a host of other factors all contribute to making a good policy fit your organization. You always will want your security policy and security standards to address some elements, as shown in the following list. Note that you need to represent each item in both policy *and* standards:

- **Classifying Data.** You must have some guidelines on the classification of data (public, confidential, secret, etc.) in order to define steps to secure the data. These classifications will drive subsequent standards, such as "confidential data must be secured on untrusted networks." Also, such policy needs to define when data needs to be classified, and explain the different levels of data classification.

- **Information Confidentiality.** This policy and standard should define how to keep data private. This will include encryption requirements and methods. You also need to define the requirements concerning authorization and authentication. Any password requirements would fall into this category. This will also include procedures for granting and revoking access to data, and who has the authority to do so.

- **Information Availability.** This covers when and where redundancy mechanisms are required. This should spell out what levels of redundancy are needed under what circumstances, such as redundant hardware, redundant Internet circuits, RAID arrays, server clusters, failover hot sites, spare hardware, and UPS requirements.

- **Physical Security.** These will address requirements concerning granting access, revoking access, monitoring, and types of access. These could include when and where badge readers are required, when keys should and should not be used, office locks, access by service personnel, and so on.

Generally speaking, the larger the organization, the larger the IT security documents will be. In some cases, you may get as specific as to have separate documents for "Physical Security for IT Datacenters" and "Physical Security for Retail Storefronts." In a very small organization, the entire IT security policy may be one document, and the entire set of IT security standards another document. Your IT policies are an instance of where "size doesn't matter," meaning that a large 100-page policy is not necessarily a "better" policy than a short, concise one. The key is that the policy fits your organization and addresses your needs.

Except in an emergency situation (where you have vulnerable devices in need of immediate hardening steps), defining the appropriate policies and standards should be the first step toward securing your network. You will not be able to create a proper IT security policy without understanding the business first. The creation of these policies cannot be done in a vacuum. I have seen more than one policy or standard that was written without input from the appropriate groups. Although you could point to it and say, "yes, we have a policy defined," the policy was constantly in need of revision, and there were innumerable exceptions. Remember, from an audit perspective, a high number of exceptions against a very granular policy are likely to look less favorable than very few exceptions against a more liberal policy.

Access Controls

Access to the devices will be one of the first issues to consider, regardless of what type of device it is. This will include hardening both the logical access and the physical access. When it comes to logical access, the simplest control to introduce is use of firewalls, whether separate firewalls or a built-in "personal" firewalls on the host in question. Some systems have their own mechanisms for implementing logical access controls in addition to simply filtering network packets. Where possible, using these additional methods helps provide defense in depth and increase security. You should address physical access as well. The universal truth is that if you have physical access to a system, you can have full access to the system. This is because if you have physical control of a system, generally the system has mechanisms that allow you to gain complete access to the system.

For example, if you have physical access to a server, you can boot it up under Linux, edit the raw data on the hard disk, and reset the administrator password. You can use encryption mechanisms to encrypt the entire hard disk, which will render this particular attack ineffective. In this scenario encryption is serving as a type of access control as part of your defense-in-depth strategy. These types of requirements are exactly the ones you would need to spell out within your policy and then implement them to secure your systems and your data. Your hardening steps should address all of these concerns.

Authentication

Authentication means to prove your identity. In the most common form, you do this using passwords. Recall that there are several different means to authenticate a user, including something they *have, are, know, or any combination of the three*. In the case of a password, this would mean using something the user knows (the password) to prove he is who he claims to be. When you hear the term *two-factor authentication*, this refers to using two out of the three mechanisms for proving someone's identity. Two-factor authentication most often takes the form of a token which randomly generates a key. This key (something you have), combined with a password or PIN (something you know), provides heightened authentication. One of your key goals of your hardening efforts is to strengthen the authentication process as much as possible. Your hardening steps will need to provide authentication as much as possible.

Authorization

Authorization means to define what you have access to do. Obviously, authorization cannot occur securely without authentication happening first. You cannot possibly know what Jill should be able to access until you have positively identified that the person in question is in fact Jill. Usually you control and harden authorization through tighter configuration of file-level security. It can also include access to systems—for instance, a restricted user who is not allowed to install software drivers or applications on his workstation. The objective is, of course, to provide as few privileges as possible, while still enabling the person to perform his assigned tasks. This concept is known as the *principle of least privilege*. It helps to determine the least amount of access a user requires in order to fulfill his assigned duties.

Auditing

Auditing is a part of the hardening process as well. A system with no audit trail is certainly less secure than one with an audit trail. While most of the security hardening you will perform to various network resources comprises preventive controls, an audit trail serves as a detective control. You should not only enable and configure the appropriate level of auditing but also take steps to protect the resultant audit logs. Remember to protect the logging process (by using a secured account to run it) and the logging configuration (typically using file-level access controls). You will need to safeguard the audit logs by implementing mechanisms to ensure log integrity and availability. If you cannot ensure the integrity of a log file, it may still be useful when it comes to troubleshooting a technology issue. The log file will be practically useless, however, if you need it to reconstruct the actions of a hacker or for use during legal proceedings.

Hardening Windows Systems

Windows systems have a reputation for being insecure out of the box. This reputation is certainly less justified than it once was. Microsoft has made a lot of progress toward a very difficult goal, which is to make its operating systems inherently more secure without diminishing the user's experience. After all, a secure system that is unusable isn't going to be of much value. Much like minimum password requirements, there is a point at which your efforts to increase security will actually backfire and will reduce your overall security level. Because of this, you should always maintain an effort to balance increased security measures with overall system usability and functionality. Again, doing this properly will require an in-depth understanding of the needs and processes of the organization.

The first thing to do in terms of hardening a system is to assess the *current* security posture of the device in question. Only after you know how the system is configured can you determine what you need to do next. Chapter 1 provided some good guidance on how to assess the current security posture of your network. This chapter will focus on the tools that you can use to configure security settings in an effort to harden your network resources.

General Hardening Steps

All the possible steps that you can take to secure a Windows host could fill (and have filled) entire volumes. The contents of this chapter should start you on your way with the basic hardening steps, and hopefully will point out a few tools you might not have known you had at your disposal. Be aware that in some cases, certain policies and standards may influence or affect other areas indirectly. For example, if you use biometric scanners for logon on all workstations, a "secure password" policy becomes practically moot. Under those circumstances, the password policy would end up applying only to special-purpose devices that were not able to take advantage of the biometric scanner. The exception, of course, is a requirement to use multifactor authentication, such as biometrics and a password. In this way, all of the hardening steps are interrelated and interdependent. A policy decision in one area can impact a policy in another area, and we see a similar relationship in the use of standards.

Most configurations on modern Microsoft systems are performed using the Microsoft Management Console, or MMC. The MMC has come standard on Windows systems since Windows 2000. Because we'll be relying on it so heavily in the following sections, let's get familiar with using

the MMC here. You can start by opening a new MMC console. Do this by navigating to **Start |
Run | mmc.exe**.

Figure 3.1 shows the blank console.

Figure 3.1 Empty MMC Console

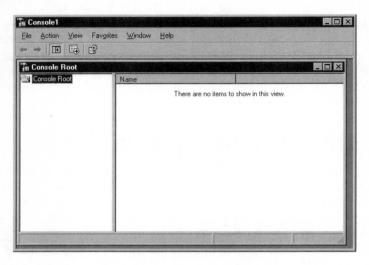

The MMC is not very exciting without some additional configuration. The various interfaces are
called *snap-ins*. The first time you open the MMC in this fashion it will have no snap-ins loaded. To
load the services snap-in, you would open the console and click **File | Add/Remove Snap-in**.
Then, in the Add/Remove Snap-in window, click the **Add** button. On **the Add Standalone Snap-
in** window (shown in Figure 3.2), select the desired snap-in—in this case, **Services**, and click the
Add button. Leave the default selection of **Local Computer** and click **Finish**. You can then close
the **Add Standalone Snap-in** window by clicking **Close**. Click **OK** on the **Add/Remove Snap-
in** window. If you peruse the fields of the services snap-in you will find that they are the same as
what you'd see if you had navigated to the stand-alone services snap-in via **Start | Run |
Services.msc** or **Start | Programs | Administrative Tools | Services**. For one-off configura-
tion tasks, the individual snap-ins might be easier to access, but an MMC console that includes all the
snap-ins you need in one place is very efficient.

When you close the MMC you will be asked whether you want to save your settings. If you
click **Yes**, you can choose a name and location for the .msc file. In this way, you can have access to an
MMC with your preferred snap-ins for future use. These saved configuration files are also portable, so
you could place the file on a pen drive or network share and use it on another system. This can be
handy for support personnel to have access to when working on other systems, especially since the
start menu shortcuts might not be available on all systems. Now that you understand the basic operation of the MMC, let's move on to some actual hardening steps.

Figure 3.2 Add Standalone Snap-in Screen

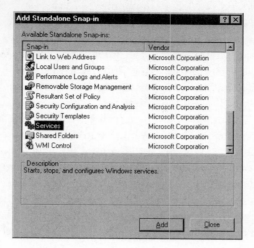

Users and Groups

One of the simplest ways to define access is by configuring the user and group accounts and the rights they have. Typically you can access the users and groups configuration via the **Control Panel** under **User Accounts**. You can also access the same information (in an easier-to-use format, at least in my opinion) within the MMC using the **Local Users and Groups** snap-in. If you try to use the **Local Users and Groups** snap-in on a domain controller, you will receive an error. You should instead use the **Active Directory Users and Computers** snap-in to manage your domain user and group accounts. There are a few common hardening steps you can perform with little effort, which are very effective from a security standpoint.

Most user and group administration will revolve around the Administrator account. On Windows, the Administrator account is a special account. Although the Administrator account is in the Administrator group, the uniqueness of the account goes far beyond that. Placing another user in the Administrator group will not give it the level of access and breadth of power that the Administrator account enjoys. Because of the privilege this account provides (similar to the root account on Linux), the Administrator account is the number-one target for attacks upon the Microsoft operating system. The name of this account is identical on every Microsoft Windows system, so everyone knows which account to attack. But we don't have to leave it that way. You cannot delete the Administrator account, but you can rename it to a more customized (and unknown) username.

A clever security technique is to rename the Administrator account. You can then create a new user account (with a username of *administrator*) with as little access as possible. This new Administrator account can have very thorough logging and auditing enabled for any actions this account performs. Using this method, all of your local technical support personnel will know about the renamed Administrator account and will not attempt to use it. Therefore, the only people attempting to use the Administrator account are likely to be up to no good, or at least such account activity would be highly suspicious. Renaming the Administrator account is as simple as right-clicking the account and selecting **Rename**. You might also want to remove the description for the newly named

Administrator account. In some environments, the accounts are renamed to very innocuous-looking names, such as Printing or Lockout. In other environments, I have seen random-looking account names, such as XHOU923744. You can decide what strategy you want to employ. Just make sure the people who need to know can figure out the appropriate account to use.

Creating a new, fake "administrator" account is simple. Just right-click **Users** in the tree view (the left pane of the MMC) and select **New User**. Enter **Administrator** for the account name. You could even enter **Built-in account for administering the computer/domain** in the description field. You can change the password to random characters, as no one should ever really be logging on using the new Administrator account anyway. If you really want to make life difficult for an attacker, you can configure the login script for the fake Administrator account to execute some type of notification program. If anyone does actually manage to log in as the new administrator, it can send an e-mail to the security team. I have also seen organizations in which the legitimate Administrator account (the renamed one) did the same. They did this because tech support personnel should never be using the local Administrator account. Instead, they should be using their own personal accounts or a separate account that possesses administrative access to the local workstations.

If you wanted, you could take this concept a step further. You could require that any administrative accounts are to be used for administrative activities only and that they are *not* to be used for day-to-day login, even by the administrators. In this scenario, an administrator would have his normal account, which would have the same access as any other user account, and also have a unique account to use when doing administrative tasks. This unique account would have the elevated privileges that are required. Although this approach might be considered extreme, it does provide increased separation, as well as a high-quality audit trail of what high-privilege accounts are being used for. Whenever possible shared accounts should not be used (including the local administrator's account) because, if something happens, having the audit trail tell you the local administrator account was used won't really mean much when any number of support staff have access to the administrator password.

You can add a special script to the fake Administrator account by double-clicking the account name and selecting **Properties**. Click on the **Profile** tab and enter the path to an appropriate file in the **Login Script** box. I have seen instances where the true Administrator account was also "trapped." When anyone logged in with either the "fake" or the real Administrator account, a batch file was run to collect a variety of system information, and then it was all e-mailed to the security team. A *net send* was also used to send an alert message to the entire security team. How elaborate you want to get when it comes to "trapping" the accounts is up to you.

Another simple step is to *disable* the guest account. In an environment where you have a domain controller you want all users to log in using their domain accounts anyway. This provides for much more meaningful auditing. The only common instances where a guest account serves a useful purpose would be when the environment is completely peer-to-peer and there are no domain controllers. Even then it would be preferable to have each person log in with a unique account, although doing so would require creating the account on all the workstations to which the person needed access. You can use *net user* to programmatically add a user account. By entering **net user newuser newpass /add** at a command prompt, you can add an account, called *newuser*, with a password of *newpass*. If you add **/domain** to the end and execute the command on a domain controller, it will add the account to the domain instead of adding it as a local account. If you use the same command without the */add* or */domain*, it will allow you to change the password for the account.

When it comes to account management, there is also an issue of education. It is desirable to use the actual Administrator account as little as possible. It is also desirable to perform day-to-day operations as a standard user instead of as a user with administrative access. This limits the possibility of a virus or other malware from being able to compromise the system. When the software in question attempts to modify the Registry or perform other actions to embed itself it would be met with inadequate privileges. Because spyware, malware, and viruses almost always require some type of elevated privileges to propagate, this mode of operation is much safer. In reality, most people know this is the recommended way to operate, but few people actually do it because of the inconvenience it can cause. Many programs are written poorly and require access only an administrator has, and still others truly require administrative access by their nature. People can quickly grow tired of not being able to run the software they want to, so they tend to revert back to just logging in as an administrative user for their day-to-day activities.

Some tools, when combined with education, can help make it easier to follow best practices and limit the use of Administrator accounts. The Windows NT 4 Resource Kit included a utility called *su.exe*. This program allows you to execute a command as the super user, even though you are logged in as another user. More modern Windows operating systems accomplish the same functionality using the runas.exe tool. Here is the help output for runas.exe:

```
RUNAS USAGE:

RUNAS [/profile] [/env] [/netonly] /user:<UserName> program

    /profile        if the user's profile needs to be loaded
    /env            to use current environment instead of user's.
    /netonly        use if the credentials specified are for remote access only.
    /user           <UserName> should be in form USER@DOMAIN or DOMAIN\USER
    program         command line for EXE.  See below for examples


Examples:
> runas /profile /user:mymachine\administrator cmd
> runas /profile /env /user:mydomain\admin "mmc %windir%\system32\dsa.msc"
> runas /env /user:user@domain.microsoft.com "notepad \"my file.txt\""
```

By using *runas*, a normal (nonprivileged) user could operate safely, but still have access to elevate his privileges quickly and conveniently in order to perform a specific task. The following command opens a command prompt as the user named *test*, on the *lab* machine:

```
runas /user:lab\test cmd
```

After executing the command, you will of course be asked to provide the password for the account you specified. This doesn't keep the administrative staff from knowing the password for an elevated account, but at least they can use it only when needed. You can start most programs in this fashion. The most common scenario where the *runas* command doesn't work properly is when multiple smaller executables must be started for a single application to function properly. You could even use *runas* to open the MMC with administrative access, to perform detailed administrative steps.

I have seen a normal user with administrative access on many occasions. The justification was that the user used some application which required administrative access. If you've ever tried to figure out what access the program truly needed in order to lock it down, this can be quite a chore. Microsoft provides a diagnostics tool to help you isolate the specific access that is required. Called the Microsoft Standard User Analyzer, the tool unfortunately will run only on Windows XP or newer machines. The program also needs the Microsoft Application Verifier (www.microsoft.com/ technet/prodtechnol/windows/appcompatibility/appverifier.mspx), which is an additional download. Still, it can be a very powerful tool for locking down a standard user who happens to use a software package that "requires admin." You run the analyzer, specify the application to run, as well as any parameters the target application needs, and then click **Launch**. Figure 3.3 shows the main output screen.

Figure 3.3 Microsoft Standard User Analyzer

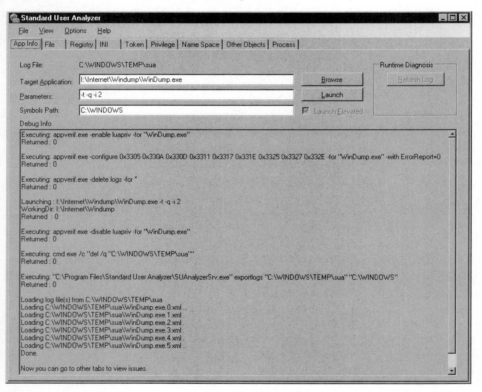

While the program is running, you will want to activate as many of its functions as possible. If you do not use a particular feature or menu function, the program may not fully exercise all the access rights it needs. When you are through testing the program, stop the program manually. This will cause the analyzer to complete its analysis and show the results. Each tab contains the elevated access that the program used. In the example shown in Figure 3.3, I was testing Windump, the Windows command-line sniffer. If you navigate to **View | Detailed Information**, the window will split into multiple panes showing more detailed fields explaining what type of access was requested. With the help of this tool, the odds are very good that you can have user access restricted to that of a standard user and simply grant elevated privileges where needed, rather than making the user account an Administrator account.

File-Level Access Controls

With all your accounts and groups organized and secured, the next step is to get more granular and look at file-level access controls. This is also the next logical step if you have used the Microsoft Standard User Analyzer and now need to modify some access within the file system. The standard way to access the file-level permission for a given directory or file is to right-click on the file or folder in Explorer and select **Properties**. Select the **Security** tab and you will be able to see the currently applied access for users and groups, as shown in Figure 3.4.

Figure 3.4 File-Level Security

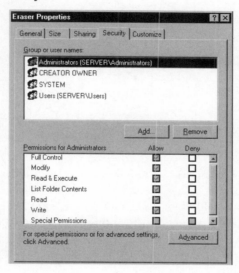

As you highlight each user or group in the top pane, the assigned rights will be displayed in the bottom pane.

! WARNING

Avoid the common mistake of clicking **Deny** when you do not want a particular user to have access to a file or directory. To remove access, you should instead remove the check in the **Allow** column. If the user is not granted access via the Allow column—either directly or as an inherited permission from a folder higher up—the user will not have any access. The Deny selection overrides any granted access that may be present. This particular error occurs most often when an administrator wants to remove access to a directory for the Everyone group. By clicking Deny, no one will have access, including authorized users.

By clicking the **Advanced** button you gain access to several tabs with some very powerful functionality. One of those is the **Permissions** tab, shown in Figure 3.5.

Figure 3.5 Windows Advanced Security Settings

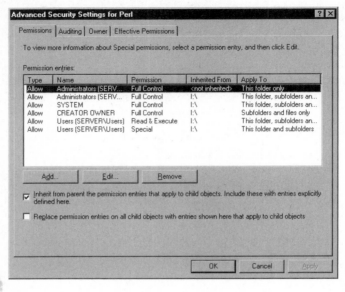

The **Permissions** tab allows you to control inheritance. With inheritance, if you grant access to a folder, it is assumed that you should have the same level of access to newly created files and folders underneath that folder. The new folders effectively inherit the same access control lists. The **Replace permission entries on all child objects with entries shown here that apply to child objects** checkbox allows you to do much the same thing with existing folders and files. The **Auditing** tab allows you to configure auditing on files or folders. The **Owner** tab can be very useful to an administrator. In cases where the administrator has been denied access to a file or folder (either directly or via membership in the **Everyone** group), the simple method to regain control over the file or folder is to go to a level above it, where the administrator *does* have access, and take ownership. You can do this by navigating to the **Owner** tab. The administrative user you are logged in as should already be entered in the **Name** field. Select the checkbox that says **Replace owner on subcontainers and objects** and click **OK**. As the new owner, you will always have access. You can then edit the permissions as needed to restore proper operation.

The **Effective Permissions** tab allows you to specify a particular group or account and generate a listing of what access users would have. This takes into account inheritance, group membership, and any explicitly defined permissions that may be present. To see the effective permissions for a user, click **Select**. On the next screen, you can enter the account name, or if you are unsure of the account name, you can click **Advanced**. This will take you to a third window that allows you to search for an account name. You can click the **Object types** button to limit the search to only users, groups, or built-in security principles, for example. The **Locations** button will allow you to choose on which system you want to search. After selecting your search criteria, you can click the **Find Now** button. With no search criteria defined, you will see a list of all accounts, groups, and built-in security principles for the local machine. Clicking one and then clicking **OK** will place the name in the **Select User or Group** window. You can then click **OK** to show the effective permissions. Figure 3.6 shows the **Effective Permissions** window. This is an effective way to know the result of all the various levels of filter and access controls. This is also one of the first places to check when a program or user action generates an access denied error when you don't want it to.

Figure 3.6 Windows Effective Permissions

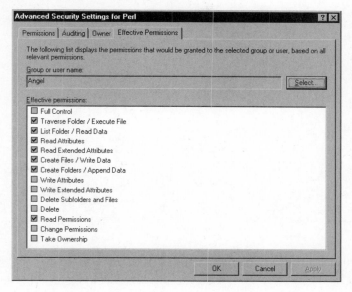

Sometimes you may be looking for a security issue and you want to look at all the directories, not specific directories or folders. The built-in security interfaces don't do a very good job of allowing you to do that. Some additional utilities do, however.

AccessEnum (www.microsoft.com/technet/sysinternals/Security/AccessEnum.mspx) is a GUI utility that you can use to quickly identify permissions that deviate from the norm. AccessEnum will run on Windows NT, 2000, XP, and 2003. It will scan the folder you specify and all subfolders and files, and list only the ones that deviate from their parent. In this way, you can quickly see which ones have had permissions changed or modified in some fashion. AccessEnum can also scan a portion of the Registry, looking for similar permission deviations. This is a big plus because the provided interfaces for working with Registry permissions are very cumbersome. Unfortunately, AccessEnum abbreviates the access types to just Read, Write, and Deny, so it's probably not an auditor's best friend, but it can help you spot things that look out of place.

Another handy utility is AccessChk (www.microsoft.com/technet/sysinternals/Security/AccessChk.mspx). This is a command-line program that will run on Windows 2000, XP, and 2003. AccessChk will also collapse the various permissions into a simplified read, write, and deny, but this program is still a very powerful tool for a security administrator. The following command will list the access for all files and folders at the root of the C: drive:

```
I:\Internet\Firefox>accesschk eric c:\
```

```
AccessChk v2.0 - Check account access of files, registry keys or services
Copyright (C) 2006 Mark Russinovich
Sysinternals - www.sysinternals.com


RW c:\i386\
RW c:\My Documents\
RW c:\MSDOS.SYS
RW c:\WINDOWS\
RW c:\IO.SYS
RW c:\Program Files\
RW c:\Windows Update Setup Files\
RW c:\boot.ini
RW c:\CONFIG.SYS
RW c:\AUTOEXEC.BAT
RW c:\ntldr
RW c:\ntdetect.com
RW c:\BOOTSECT.DOS
RW c:\Documents and Settings\
RW c:\System Volume Information\
RW c:\Recycled\
```

If you add the −s switch, it will recursively list all directories, and the −v switch will cause it to list all permissions that are present, instead of just R, W, and Deny. You could easily combine this utility with a little creative programming and create a batch file that could generate some very useful security reports, as shown here:

```
I:\Internet\Firefox>accesschk someuser I:\testfile.txt -v


AccessChk v2.0 - Check account access of files, registry keys or services
Copyright (C) 2006 Mark Russinovich
Sysinternals - www.sysinternals.com


R  I:\TestFile.txt
      FILE_EXECUTE
      FILE_LIST_DIRECTORY
      FILE_READ_ATTRIBUTES
      FILE_READ_DATA
      FILE_READ_EA
      FILE_TRAVERSE
      SYNCHRONIZE
      READ_CONTROL
```

AccessChk will also scan the Registry, and you can specify a service instead of a username for the reporting. Several other switches add to the functionality and flexibility. Running AccessChk without any parameters will induce the program to output its usage text.

Additional Steps

There are, of course, additional steps that you can take to harden a Windows system besides tightening users and groups, and file-level permissions. As you might expect, Microsoft has the inside track on securing Windows systems. You can read some very extensive hardening guides on the Microsoft Web site. Here is a list of some of the more noteworthy security documents available:

- **Windows Server 2003 Security Guide:** www.microsoft.com/technet/security/ prodtech/windowsserver2003/w2003hg/sgch00.mspx

- **Windows XP Security Guide:** www.microsoft.com/technet/security/prodtech/windowsxp/secwinxp/default.mspx

- Microsoft **Windows 2000 Security Hardening Guide:** www.microsoft.com/technet/security/prodtech/windows2000/win2khg/default.mspx

- The Microsoft **Windows NT 4.0 and Windows 98 Threat Mitigation Guide:** www.microsoft.com/technet/security/guidance/networksecurity/threatmi.mspx

Although the respective guides will go into great detail on hardening the operating system you are interested in, there are, of course, many more articles on the Internet and books on the subject. Essentially you can summarize all of the hardening steps in a few high-level tasks which are the same on any operating system, and most of them do not require additional software other than what is included with the operating system. The steps are as follows:

1. Remove unnecessary software.

2. Disable unneeded services/daemons.

3. Patch the operating system and any remaining software.

4. Configure user and group accounts to provide only the minimum required access.

5. Tighten operating system parameters (login requirements, timeouts, etc.).

6. Configure network access to permit only the minimum required connectivity (IP/ports).

Using Microsoft Group Policy Objects

If you find yourself wanting to lock down a particular security setting, such as removing user access to a directory, you could connect to each system and edit the security properties individually. While this would work, it's not a very efficient way of doing things. Of course, you can use the MMC to edit and control these settings individually, but you can also configure these settings and then have them applied to computers automatically. This collection of security settings is called a *group policy object (GPO)*. You can apply a GPO to the domain level, to individual organizational units (OUs), or to individual computers. Unless you have special security needs, such as for a high-risk host, you will configure most of your security policy to apply to all devices within the domain. If this is the case, the logical place to define your GPO is at the domain level. You could then address any high-security hosts by applying a more restrictive local policy (this policy should not include settings that conflict with the domain policy or else they will be overwritten) or placing the high-security hosts in a particular OU and apply an OU GPO. Here is a step-by-step example of how this would work.

1. Local policies are applied. These could be modified or just left at the default; it doesn't really matter if you will be updating them with the domain GPO anyway.

2. The domain GPO is applied to every device on the network (workstations and servers). This overwrites the local policy with settings you want applied to everyone. In effect, this acts as your security baseline.

3. The GPO for the server OU is applied to the servers (or other high-security hosts). These devices will still have the minimum security settings from the domain GPO, but in cases where you wanted to define a more strict security setting, the OU GPO will allow you to do so.

The nature of GPOs is that you will configure settings with the intent of overriding other settings. GPOs are applied in the following order: local, the site GPO, the Domain GPO, and each OU GPO working downward. Typically you configure the domain settings to intentionally override the local computer security settings. Because such behavior is intentional, you would apply GPOs locally, then work your way up the domain tree structure until you finally get to the default domain policy. In this way, each successive application of the GPO overrides the previous one, which also has the desired side effect that the local policies are of lowest priority. You can view the *default domain policy* by opening your MMC console. Add the **Active Directory Users and Computers** snap-in. Right-click the domain in question and select **Properties**. Click the **Group Policy** tab. Initially the window will contain only the **Default Domain Policy**. This represents the top level of the domain, and you can configure multiple policies here. Again, all settings you configure in the domain GPO will override any local settings.

If the default domain policy does not have that particular setting configured at all, the previous policy settings will remain in effect. Because the default domain policy contains all of your default settings, you do not want to edit it directly. Instead, click on **New**, give the new policy a name, and then click **Edit**. This will place the newly created policy below the domain policy. You can use the **Up** and **Down** buttons to shift positions of the highlighted policy. As you can see in Figure 3.7, the highest policy in the list will take priority (remember all of the GPOs in this list are domain GPOs). Because any newly created policies are intended to override the default domain policy, you probably want to click **Up** so that your policy takes precedence over the default policy. Figure 3.7 shows the **Group Policy** tab showing the default domain policy.

You can follow the same procedure to add a GPO to an OU (right-click **Properties | Group Policy**). In this fashion, you can assign very granular policies to all your resources. If you click **Edit**, you are presented with the same MMC console structure as that found within the **Local Computer Policy** snap-in. If you were to instead edit the Local Computer Policy settings, you would be configuring a local GPO, which would be overwritten in the event of conflicting settings with the domain GPO, or an OU GPO.

Figure 3.7 Domain GPOs

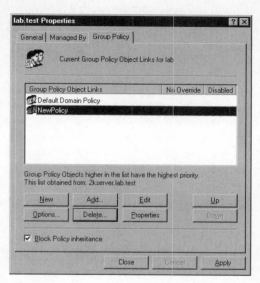

You may have noticed that within the Local Computer Policy snap-in there is no mechanism to export and import settings. This would imply that you have to configure any desired policies within Active Directory instead of doing so locally. Indeed, if you plan to apply the settings to all hosts, doing it within Active Directory may be a better way to do it, but there is actually a way to configure the desired settings and then export them for use on another machine's local GPO. You do this through either the GUI or the command line. The GUI is, of course, the MMC. You will need to add the **Security Configuration and Analysis** and, optionally, the **Security Templates** snap-ins to your console.

In order to import settings from another system, you have to have configured the desired settings at some point. To do this you use the Security Templates snap-in. A *template* is simply a preconfigured collection of settings. You can, of course, edit the templates to your taste, or create your own. The following is a brief summary of the templates included with Windows XP:

- **compatws.** Relaxes the default file and Registry permissions for the Users group.

- **hisecdc.** Provides further restrictions on LanManager authentication and further requirements for the encryption and signing of secure channel and SMB data above and beyond what is configured within the securedc template.

- **hisecws.** Provides further restrictions on LanManager authentication and further requirements for the encryption and signing of secure channel and SMB data above and beyond what is configured within the securews template.

- **rootsec.** Will reset the default permissions on the drive roots and propagate those permissions to child objects. Use with caution.

- **securedc.** A "secure domain controller" template that will configure tighter restrictions on domain account policies and additional restrictions on anonymous users.

- **securews.** A "secure workstation" template that will configure tighter restrictions on local account policies and additional restrictions on anonymous users.

- **setup security.** Holds the default settings and is usually a good place to start if you're not sure which template to use.

Figure 3.8 shows the Security Templates snap-in. If you want to create your own template, or make any changes to one of the default templates, you should make a copy and work from that one so that you always have the original if you need it. You can copy the **Setup Security** template by right-clicking and selecting **Save As**. You can edit the settings in the template by drilling down using the Security Templates snap-in. After making changes, be sure to save the template. Because these templates are simply ASCII files, you can open a template to use the settings on different computers. If you can edit the security settings and import and export them using the Security Templates snap-in, you might be wondering why you would need the Security Configuration and Analysis snap-in. You need it because there is no way to *apply* the templates using the Security Templates snap-in.

Figure 3.8 Security Templates MMC Snap-in

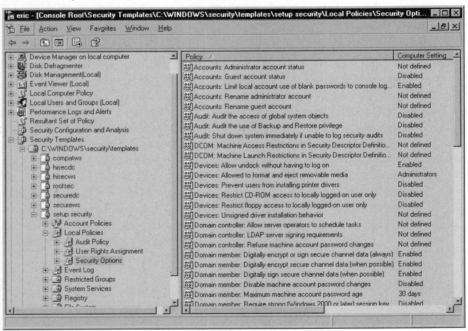

In order to apply the settings in a security template, right-click on the **Security Configuration and Analysis snap-in** and select **Open Database**. Since this is the first time you're configuring the settings, you will be creating a new database. Enter a meaningful name ending in .sdb and click **Open**. You will be prompted to import a template. This is where you can import the custom template you configured previously. Once you do this, you can apply your template by right-clicking the **Security Configuration and Analysis snap-in** again, and this time select **Import Template**. The various settings will populate within the snap-in. This provides you with yet another opportunity to edit the security settings. The settings are still not applied, however. The final step to commit the settings is to right-click again and select **Configure Computer Now**. All of the settings configured within the template will be applied. Depending on the number of nondefault settings this step could take a few minutes to complete.

Should the need arise, you also have the ability to create a template based on the current policy settings of the local system. You can do this using the Security Configuration and Analysis snap-in. Right-click the snap-in and select **Analyze Computer Now**. Choose a filename and path for the log file, or just accept the default and click **OK**. This will reveal several expandable items, all under Security Configuration and Analysis. These settings represent what is currently configured. To save these settings as a template, right-click and select **Export Template**. The most common reason to work from the current policy template and change it would be if you wanted to make incremental changes in a very controlled fashion. This would carry less risk of breaking something than applying any of the pregenerated templates if the system has undergone significant policy adjustments since it was originally installed.

Microsoft also provides a command-line utility called *secedit.exe* which you can use to import and export policy settings. In order to export a policy template using *secedit*, you must start by analyzing the current settings against a template. Using *secedit /analyze /db C:\export.sdb /cfg C:\test.inf* would instruct secedit to analyze the current local policy, using the test.inf template. The results will be stored in a database file called C:\export.sdb. To export the settings to an .inf file that you can import, you would use *secedit /analyze /db C:\export.sdb /cfg C:\test.inf*.

> **NOTE**
>
> If you try to export the setting and the file ends up being empty, you will be experiencing a known bug with secedit. The bug is caused because XP stores the security information in a different location than secedit is looking for it (secedit was originally developed for Windows 2000). A hotfix is available to fix the issue, and it's basically is just a newer version of seced.exe. See article ID 897327 for more information on the bug with secedit.

Account Lockout Policy

Now that you are familiar with GPOs and how to apply them, we will discuss a few policy settings that you may want to consider implementing, either at the domain level or with local GPOs. The account lockout policy \Computer Configuration\Windows Settings\Security Settings\Account Policy\Account Lockout Policy) allows you to configure the number of incorrect passwords that a user can enter before being locked out of an account, how long the account stays locked out, and how long before the lockout counter will reset. The following recommended settings will provide the most security an in average environment:

- **Account Lockout Duration** represents how long the account will stay locked out. Setting this to zero means that the account will stay locked out until an administrator manually unlocks it. This is the most secure option. However, even allowing the account to reset after as little as 10 minutes will serve to slow down a hacker who is attempting to brute force the password.

- **Account Lockout Threshold** represents how many invalid passwords a user can attempt before locking out the account. A setting of three invalid logon attempts is usually considered adequate. If the number is too low, a simple typo could result in an account being locked out. If this is set to 0 (insecure), the account will never be locked out.

- **Reset Account Lockout Counter After** determines how long before the invalid attempt counter is reset. The default setting of 30 minutes is usually adequate. A longer setting is considered more secure.

Figure 3.9 shows the account lockout policy setting and MMC console.

Figure 3.9 Account Lockout Policy

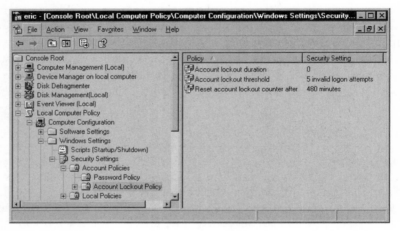

Audit Policy

Don't forget that the audit trail you configure can help you catch a hacker, and sometimes help you troubleshoot issues. Having extensive auditing of failed access attempts, for example, can sometimes help you isolate a rights issue that is keeping software from properly running.

User Rights Assignment

The list of configurable events under user rights assignments is extensive. These settings (Local Computer Policy\Computer Configuration\Windows Settings\Security Settings\Local Policies\User Rights Assignments) allow you to configure what users (including the accounts processes run as) can do. Many of these settings are used only in unusual circumstances to allow particular software to run. Rather than elaborate on all of the specific settings in this category, we will examine only the *most significant* configurable events and recommend the most secure settings for the majority of environments:

- **Access This Computer from the Network.** You can safely set this to Authenticated Users and remove all other access. You should make certain that ANONYMOUS LOGON is not in the allowed list. In some cases it is more secure to remove the ability to log on locally for normal users. For example, a nonadministrator account really has no reason to need to log on to your domain controller.

- **Act As Part of the Operating System.** No accounts should need this privilege. It allows a user to impersonate any other user on the system without authentication. This would pose a huge security risk, and it would render your other auditing events meaningless. If an application needs this type of access to function properly, it should use the LocalSystem account, which includes this access by default.

- **Bypass Traverse Checking.** This setting allows a user to navigate through directory trees even if the user does not have access to a directory. It does not allow the user to list the directory contents of a directory to which he does not have the appropriate rights. You should set this to Administrators Only.

- **Change the System Time.** While setting the time might not seem important at first glance, setting it incorrectly can create a huge security hole. If you do not set the time correctly, certain encryption systems such as IPSec will fail. Further, it becomes impossible to accurately correlate event logs, and critical transactions could fail, causing a denial of service for legitimate traffic. You should set this setting to Administrators Only.

- **Create Token Object.** This setting allows an account to create a token that can be used to gain access to any system resource. You should not need to set this right manually on any account. If you need this right, you should assign it to the LocalSystem account.

- **Debug Programs.** This right will allow a user to attach a debugger to a process which, in turn, will give the user access to many sensitive internal resources. You should assign this right with great care. Usually you will not need it on a production host anyway.

- **Deny Access to This Computer from the Network.** This should include the local Administrator account. There is no legitimate need for the local account to access the system over the network.

- **Deny Logon As Batch Job, and Deny Logon as Service.** You should set both of these to the local administrator. By doing this, you ensure that if the local Administrator account is compromised, the attacker will not be able to immediately install a service or batch job to further compromise system security.

Security Options

This group of settings is also extensive (Local Computer Policy\Computer Configuration\Windows Settings\Security Settings\Local Policies\Security Options) and offers important security settings that impact the entire system, instead of individual accounts. For most of these settings, the purpose and function will be fairly obvious, but a brief description should hopefully clear up any lingering doubts. The following list represents the settings that are the most important for securing your systems:

- **Do not display last username in logon screen.** You should set this to Enabled. By displaying the last user to log on, you are giving any attacker that can get to that logon screen a first clue as to what a viable account name to attack might be. This may not prevent attempts by attackers who have done some reconnaissance, but it will not provide 50 percent of the credentials to be available to the casual attacker.

- **Message text for users attempting to log on.** You will see this message when someone attempts to log on to the console directly (after entering **Ctrl + Alt + Delete**). This setting, also known as the *logon banner*, gives some legal protection against unauthorized access. Fill this in with a message stating that only authorized users should be accessing the system. Your organization's IT security staff and its legal department should work together to develop a suitable message. The purpose of this message is primarily to remove attackers' claims that they didn't know they were doing anything wrong.

- **Message title for users attempting to log on.** This is the title for the preceding message. Something suitably ominous such as **"Warning"** or **"Authorized Users Only"** should be adequate. Consult your legal department to be safe.

- **Number of previous logons to cache (in case domain controller is not available).** Because this is a stand-alone server, there should be no credentials to cache and you can set this to zero (which disables caching). Even if you are using domain authentication on your bastion host, the most secure setting is a setting of 0.

- **Rename Administrator account.** As mentioned earlier, the local Administrator account is the most popular user account for attack. Changing this account name to something other than the default can help prevent the success of some automated attacks, such as an automated password-cracking attack against the local Administrator account. You should avoid any obvious alternatives, such as "Admin" or "root."

- **Rename Guest account.** For the same reasons as the Administrator account, you should select this option as well. While the Guest account has few privileges, it can still provide a local logon account and act as a first step toward elevating an attacker's privileges. Code Red, for example, adds Guest to the local Administrators group. Since this account name is mentioned specifically in Code Red's payload, merely renaming this account would prevent such a group membership modification from succeeding.

TIP

While some of the policy settings will take effect immediately, some will take effect only after the system is rebooted. For this reason, you should immediately reboot after making any policy changes to ensure that the changes take effect.

Hardening Linux Systems

When you install a given Windows operating system (OS), you will always get the same basic installation for that version of OS, including the default security settings. Basically, all versions of Windows XP are the same out of the box, unless your have customized the installation yourself. With Linux, this isn't true. Some distributions you install are very secure as part of their default configuration and others are very insecure. At a high level, the hardening steps remain the same for Linux as they do for Windows, but some of them may be done for you to a greater or lesser extent. The following list represent the high-level hardening tasks that you would need to perform:

- Remove unnecessary software.

- Disable unneeded services/daemons.

- Patch the operating system and any remaining software.

- Configure user and group accounts to provide only the minimum required access.

- Tighten operating system parameters (login requirements, timeouts, etc.).

- Configure network access to permit only the minimum required connectivity (IP/ports).

These are the same steps you would perform to harden a Windows system. A special-purpose distribution, such as the Smoothwall firewall, performs most of these steps except for applying the latest patches performed as part of the basic installation. At the other end of the spectrum are distributions that emphasize user friendliness, such as Ubuntu or Red Hat. If a default install is performed with these types of distributions there will be a lot of hardening work left to do. As such, they may not represent the best choice in a high-security environment.

General Hardening Steps

Some of the most basic ways to implement logical access controls is through the use of users and groups (to establish authentication), and then to apply file-level access controls based on those identities. The basic procedures are the same for Linux as they are for Windows, but the commands are different, of course. We will walk through how to create users and groups, assign users to groups, and grant access to users and groups within the file system.

Users and Groups

Most Linux distributions that include a GUI will include a GUI interface for managing users and groups in addition to the normal command-line tools. If you have access to a GUI utility, that will probably be the easiest way to configure your users and groups. The only time the command line would be preferable would be if you need to make a large number of changes at one time. Using Fedora Core 5, you can navigate to **System | Administration | Users and Groups** to open the GUI interface for the User Manager, as shown in Figure 3.10.

The interface probably looks a little "busier" than the Windows interfaces, but managing users isn't too difficult. Let's start by looking at the GUI to see what information we have available. First, you can see that this system has several users created, including ones named *user*, *sguil*, and *snort*. You may notice that the root user is missing from the list. There are actually an additional 40 or so accounts, but you have to navigate to **Preferences** and remove the checkmark next to **Filter system users and groups** in order to see them in the list. The User ID was automatically generated for these accounts, incrementing them from 500 upward. The user ID is analogous to the username, in that it is a unique identifier for a user; however, the system will use the user ID to track file and directory permissions.

Figure 3.10 Linux GUI User Manager

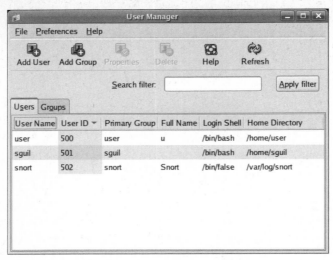

If you click **Add User** you are presented with a window offering all the standard fields, including User Name, Full Name, Password, and so on. This process is very straightforward and doesn't really need much explanation. After you create a user, you can highlight the user in the list and click **Properties**. The tabbed window shown in Figure 3.11 allows you to set various options, including an expiration time for the account, which can be valuable when you have temporary staff or other accounts you need for only a limited time.

Figure 3.11 Linux GUI User Properties

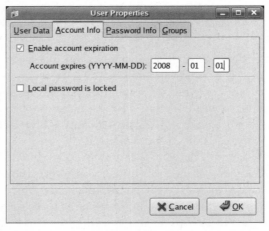

Other tabs allow you to change the password (User Data), configure password aging policies (Password Info), and assign users to groups (Groups). All of this may seem overly simplistic, but that's because a lot of things were done automatically by using the GUI. You may not always have the GUI available, and being able to quickly add a user from the command line can be a valuable ability. You can add a user via the command line with the *adduser* command. A simple example is *adduser test2*. This will create a new user named *test2*, and it will use the defaults for all the other required settings. In most cases, this will also create the user directory at /home/test2, though you can override this behavior with the *−M* switch. You can set a password for the new account using *passwd test2*, after which you will be prompted to enter the new password and then confirm the new password.

Every user account that you create must belong to at least one group. By default, a group will be created with the same name as the newly created user account. There is no "everyone" group, like there is in Windows, so if you need a global account to which to assign broad access rights you have two choices. You can create a group yourself and assign the required access to that group, or you can rely on the access that is granted when no other access has been explicitly defined. In my experience, one of the most difficult things about using Linux is that if you are not familiar with the various commands to use, finding them can be difficult. For this reason, I have compiled the following list of the various user/group administration commands dealing with user or group administration that are both most useful and most likely to be supported on a variety of Linux distributions:

- **adduser/useradd.** *adduser test* will add a user to the system named *test*.
- **chage.** Used to change the time the user's password will expire and various other parameters related to password aging.
- **chown.** Changes the owner of the file(s) to another user. Using *chown test file.txt* would change the owner of file.txt to the user *test*.
- **gpasswd.** Allows you to add or remove users from groups. Using *gpasswd −a test test2* would add the *test* user to the *test2* group. Using *−d* will delete a user from a group.
- **groupadd.** Creates a new group.
- **groupdel.** Deletes a group.
- **groups.** Prints all the groups a user is in.
- **id.** Prints the real and effective user id and group ids.
- **passwd.** Set a user's password. Use *passwd newuser* to set the *newuser's* password.
- **su.** Allows you to change the effective user and group of the current user. Entering *su testuser* would change the current user to *testuser*. If the current user is root, no password will be needed. The −m option will preserve the original user's environment variables instead of resetting them.
- **userdel.** Deletes a user account.
- **usermod.** Allows you to configure various settings for a given user account.

File-Level Access Controls

Linux file permissions are the source of a lot of frustration for those not familiar with Linux. The system, while elegantly simple, is not intuitive. To help sort it out, we will again start with the GUI interface. Open the GUI file manager for your distribution, right-click on a file, and select **Properties**. The window you see should look similar to the one shown in Figure 3.12.

Figure 3.12 Linux GUI File Permissions

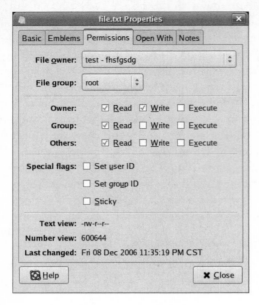

You can clearly see the file owner and the group to which the file belongs. The next section lists which permissions (read, write, and execute) the file owner, file group, and all others have to the file. The special flags section lists whether the set user ID, set group ID, or sticky bit is set. These bits are important, so we will discuss them in detail. The last section, with the text view and number view, displays the respective views for the file permissions listed above. We will explore those as well, but for now, just make note of them.

The set user ID and set group ID bits are also referred to as the *SUID* and *SGID* bits. In simple terms, the SUID bit causes a given file/application to run as the user who is the owner of the file, rather than the user who is executing the file. Most often this is used to allow a normal, nonprivileged user to run a script or process requiring root access. The first thing that comes to most people's minds is that this would be a big security risk. Well, like so many other things, it can be a big risk, but it can also increase security. An obvious example of a big security risk would be one where the application or script is interactive, or allows manipulation of other system parameters. Obviously, allowing an unprivileged user to run a file manager as the root user would be a big security risk. Many security scanners will report the number of SUID files which are also owned by root for exactly this reason. The following command would search the entire file system from the root for files that are owned by root, and have the SUID bit set:

```
find / -type f -perm /4000 -uid 0 -ls
```

Find is the utility that is doing the searching (see **man find** for more information). The *type –f* option says to look for normal files (instead of named pipes and other, more unusual options). The *–perm* option specifies that we are looking for the SUID bit being set. The *–uid* option specifies the owner as user ID 0, which is always root. Finally, *–ls* tells *find* to format the output such that all unusual characters are escaped. This is for your own protection in case any filenames are using non-printing characters that could cause problems within your terminal. You can use the same command with *−perm /2000* to list the SGID files belonging to the root group.

SUID can increase your security as well. Suppose you have a program or script that you want the user to run, to perform some administrative task automatically. If this program requires root permissions to function properly, you would have to give the user the root password, or run the program yourself. Instead, when you set the program SUID bit and make root the owner, the user could run the program without ever needing to know the root user password. Basically, whether SUID is an asset or a liability depends on the program to which it is attached. The SGID bit does the same thing, except the program is run as the owning group. All of the same security considerations apply for SGID as for SUID.

The sticky bit is much less interesting than it sounds. When set, it tells the operating system not to unload the executable from memory after a user closes it. In this fashion, the program (the sticky bit applies only to executable files) will now start faster. This can have some security implications, but in reality, is it not used much anymore and is mostly a holdover from when Linux was intended to serve as a multiuser operating system.

With those special bits out of the way, let's look at the basic file system permissions. You can list the files in a directory in long list format, including the detailed file permissions, using *ls −o*:

```
ls -o
total 116
drwxr-xr-x 5 root   4096 Dec  9 00:10 Desktop
-rw-r--r-- 1 test    164 Dec  8 23:32 file (copy).txt
-rwSr--r-- 1 test    164 Dec  8 23:32 file.txt
-rw-r--r-- 1 root  26225 Sep  9 14:37 install.log
-rw-r--r-- 1 root   3973 Sep  9 14:36 install.log.syslog
```

You'll notice that the file.txt file we looked at earlier is different from all the rest. The leftmost column contains the permissions for the file, and the series of dashes and letters corresponds to the grid of checkboxes in the GUI permissions tab. The breakdown of the permissions designations is as follows.

```
1222333444
```

1   This first character designates the object type. Usually the object is a directory (d), but other options are possible, such as a socket (s) or a named pipe (p). A directory will contain a *d* in the leftmost position.

222   The next three characters indicate the permissions granted to the owner of the object (*r* = read, *w* = write, *x* = execute). *x* is replaced with *S* when the SUID bit is set.

333   These characters represent the permissions granted to the group the object belongs to, using the same *rwx* notation. The *x* bit is replaced with an *s* when the SGID bit is set.

444   These last character indicate the permissions granted to users who are neither the object owner nor in the object's group. The *rwx* notation is the same. The *x* is replaced with a *t* when the sticky bit is set.

If you refer back to the file permissions in Figure 3.12, you will notice that the "number view" is listed. This is actually yet another way to represent file permissions. As you check or uncheck the various permissions, the number view will be updated and will display the new number view. If the pattern to the numbers is a little hard to sort out, here is how it works. The rightmost digit indicates the permission for "other" users. The next character to the left represents the permissions for the group, and the next one to the left represents the permissions for the object owner. Read access corresponds to a *4*, write corresponds to a *2*, and execute to a *1*. Each of these (*rwx*) is added together to indicate the access. Thus, read access by the owner, group, and other would be *444* for the rightmost numbers. Read and write access for all three would be *666*, and finally, *rwx* for all three would be represented numerically as *777*. You can use the *chmod* utility to change the permissions on a file from the command line, as shown here:

```
# ls file.txt -o
-r--r--r-- test 164 Dec  8 23:32 file.txt
# chmod 777 file.txt
# ls file.txt -o
-rwxrwxrwx test 164 Dec  8 23:32 file.txt
```

Administering Linux file permissions is not more difficult than doing so for a Windows file system, but there are a lot of utilities involved when administering from the command line. Understanding permissions will be essential to properly lock down users and restrict their access to only the minimum that is needed. For more advanced configuration suggestions, you might want to research the following commands related to disk usage quotas: *quota, quotaoff, quotaon, quotacheck, repquota*, and *edquota*. You also can enable process accounting using the *accton* command.

Using the Bastille Hardening Script

There are many settings to configure when it comes to hardening your Linux distribution, and all you have to do is miss one setting and a hacker can compromise the system. To help combat this, many people have developed semi-automated scripts to help harden a Linux system. These scripts basically just make a bunch of configuration changes automatically based on configuration selections that you would have otherwise had to make manually. One of the oldest hardening scripts, and thus one of the most mature and well developed, is the Bastille Linux script. It has evolved from a crude basic script to a well-refined hardening system with a GUI interface. Bastille currently supports Red Hat Enterprise Linux, Fedora Core, SuSE, Debian, Gentoo, Mandrake, and HP-UX, with a Mac OS X version in development. You can read and download Bastille from www.bastille-linux.org.

You can pass only three options to Bastille, each of which tells it to run in a different mode. If you use *bastille —report* it will generate a Web-based report of your current "hardness." The *–c* option will run the actual hardening script in a text-based mode, and *–x* will run it in a graphical mode, as shown in Figure 3.13.

All you have to do to use Bastille is start it up, and it will present a series of yes/no questions to which you must respond. Based on your answers, it will configure various security settings automatically. These settings include removing SUID bits from some programs, disabling insecure services (such as *rshell*, for example), changing user account expiration, and much more. The script does a good job of presenting you with reasonable defaults, providing the most secure option that will not overly impact normal usage of the system. When you are finished answering the questions, you will be prompted to choose whether to save the resulting Bastille configuration. Note that saving the configuration is *not* the same as applying it, as the next question is whether you want to *apply* the configuration.

Figure 3.13 Bastille Graphical Configuration

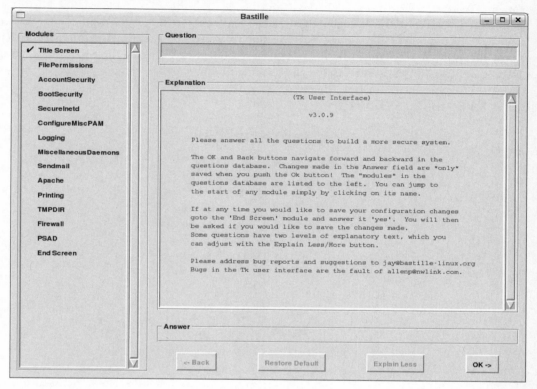

Bastille is a powerful tool that helps harden a default install. Depending on your selections, you can easily make a system too secure and unsuitable for use as an everyday workstation. A little experimentation, combined with reading the excellent explanations that Bastille provides, should help you create a very secure system with a minimal amount of effort.

Using SELinux

SELinux stands for *security-enhanced Linux*, and it was developed in partnership with the National Security Agency (NSA). It provides a higher level of security by enforcing mandatory access controls (MAC) through the kernel. *Mandatory access controls* are very different from the standard *discretionary access controls*. Most systems are said to use discretionary access controls because someone (the file owner, or the root/administrator user account) has discretion over who has access to what. Mandatory access control is based on the principle that a given role has predetermined access rights, and these are immutable. Basically, the only way to change access permissions is for the user to be assigned to a new role (called *contexts* in SELinux terminology). Because the enforcement is through the kernel, it can restrict the actions of *any* process, even a process run by the root user. As far as the underlying components of SELinux are concerned, there is no concept of a root user, only security policies and security contexts. SELinux is available for many Linux distributions (see which ones at http://selinux.sourceforge.net/distros/redhat.php3). SELinux is installed by default (though disabled) on Fedora Core 5. You can read the SELinux FAQ from the NSA at www.nsa.gov/selinux/info/faq.cfm for more information.

SELinux is a work in progress. Currently the setup and configuration can be rather complicated. You can enable SELinux on Fedora Core by navigating to **System | Administration | Security Level and Firewall**. On the **SELinux** tab, you enable SELinux by changing the **SELinux Setting** from Disabled to **Enforcing** *or* **Permissive** and clicking **OK**, as shown in Figure 3.14.

Figure 3.14 Enabling SELinux

SELinux uses the *xattr* labels within the file system to generate labels describing the security context of a file or directory which are persistent across reboots. These labels are not normally used; thus, when you enable SELinux, you will get the warning dialog shown in Figure 3.15. You must select **Yes** in order to enable SELinux. Then click **OK** on the **Security Level Configuration** window, and then reboot.

Figure 3.15 Relabel Warning Dialog

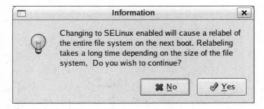

It is recommended that you select Permissive initially, in which case the system will generate logs based on the configured SELinux policy but will not actually restrict any activities. This allows you to see the impact of a policy without impacting productivity. You can then use the results of the log files to adjust your policy until it is usable. Once you are satisfied with the SELinux rules, you can enable enforcing mode, which will actually apply your configured policy. You can define your policies as targeted or strict. A *strict* policy applies to all processes and files on the system, and a *targeted* policy is applied to only specific files. Strict mode is very difficult to configure properly. Targeted is easier to configure and is the default policy type when SELinux is first enabled. You can check the status of SELinux by typing **sestatus**.

If you navigate back to the **Security Level Configuration** window, and then click to expand **Modify SELinux Policy** on the **SELinux** tab, you will be presented with a list of options to toggle various SELinux settings. These options represent only a limited set of preconfigured choices to toggle settings in the SELinux policy files. For any serious configuration, you will need to edit the files manually. You can also download a third-party SELinux policy editor from the SELinux Policy Editor Project (http://seedit.sourceforge.net/index.html). This package includes a simplified set of tools that is slightly less functional than the normal package. You can, however, switch between using one or the other.

You can see what actions the policy *would* have denied if it were enforced by reviewing the logs. You can find log messages from SELinux in /var/log/messages or /var/log/audit/audit.log. Enabling SELinux is not a project to be undertaken lightly. Implementing SELinux in a manner that is both useful and functional will likely require a good deal of investigation and research. It is recommended that you read the documentation on the Web site of your chosen distribution if SELinux is supported, as well as the documentation on the official SELinux Web site (www.nsa.gov/selinux).

Hardening Infrastructure Devices

Don't overlook hardening your infrastructure devices. Not all routers and switches have administrative capability, but many do. For those that do, referred to as *managed* devices, they usually allow you to control many aspects of the device, including redirecting traffic to ports of your choosing and basically enabling or disabling all traffic flow through the device. Given the often central role these devices fulfill in your network, control over one of them will often mean control over your entire business. For this reason, you should exercise the same care and due diligence in securing your infrastructure devices as you would your critical servers. The same high-level bullets for hardening host-based systems also apply to managed infrastructure devices.

Most managed devices will have a means to authenticate using a local account as well as a central authentication server, such as TACACS or RADIUS. Ensure that the accounts are secured and a high-quality password is used. Sometimes even routers and switches will have unneeded services installed by default. One common example is enabling an HTTP interface for managing the devices. While this can certainly be handy, often the Web interface opens up an entire category of potential security risks that would not otherwise be present. The highest level of security is achieved by disabling any services that are not needed. Conservative timeouts for abandoned sessions and a login warning banner are advisable security measures.

You will also need to update the software on the device. Given the criticality and potential scope of impact for these devices if an update causes a problem, these devices are rarely configured to update automatically. In most cases, this will be a manual process which you must incorporate into your patch management and change management processes. Pay extra attention to any device connected to the Internet as these are going to be attacked on a regular basis. You must secure them before you connect them to the Internet, or you will likely lose control of them in short order.

Patching Systems

Patching systems is an age-old chore that no one likes. Besides the time and labor involved, sometimes an update will actually do more harm than good, breaking some functionality or, in a worst-case scenario, rendering the system unusable and requiring a complete rebuild. While both the labor involved and the number of adverse reactions to patches have decreased as patching methodologies have matured, it is still not a fun task. In this section, we will look at ways to keep your systems patched with a minimal amount of effort.

Patching Windows Systems

Windows systems are known for breaking from updates. This is true to some degree with patches, but service packs (which are nothing more than several patches rolled into one) are almost legendary for breaking things. Microsoft has made the task of keeping your systems up-to-date nearly painless with Automatic Updates. Automatic Updates allows a system to download and install patches automatically as they are released. Now, given the fact that any patch runs a risk of causing undesirable side effects, you might question the safety of using Automatic Updates. This is a reasonable precaution. Keep in mind that millions of users are using Automatic Updates every day without incident (Automatic Updates is enabled automatically on Windows XP when SP2 is installed). The configuration options allowed within Automatic Updates can help lessen the risk of applying updates automatically.

Within the Control Panel you should have an Automatic Updates icon. Clicking it will open the Automatic Updates configuration window shown in Figure 3.16.

Figure 3.16 Windows Automatic Updates

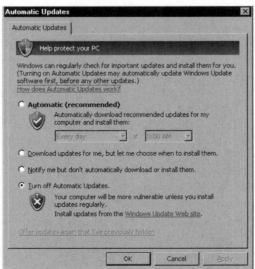

Each of the four options offers a different level of invasiveness on behalf of the Automatic Updates service. At the bottom, you can disable automatic updates completely. This offers the most control over the update process. Because you will need to apply any updates manually, this ensures that you will be on hand and that the updates won't catch you by surprise. The function of the other options is self-explanatory. While these options do offer some security, in many cases they do not provide enough control for some organizations.

Windows Server Update Services (WSUS) offers increased control over the update process, and some other advantages as well. You can read about WSUS at www.microsoft.com/windowsserver-system/updateservices/default.mspx. Basically, WSUS acts as an intermediary between the systems using Automatic Updates and the Windows Update server at Microsoft. You configure the internal hosts to use the WSUS server to retrieve updates, and the WSUS server will offer greater control over which updates are to be installed and when. WSUS is currently considered beta software and you must register in order to download the server component. Figure 3.17 depicts the WSUS update process.

Figure 3.17 WSUS Process

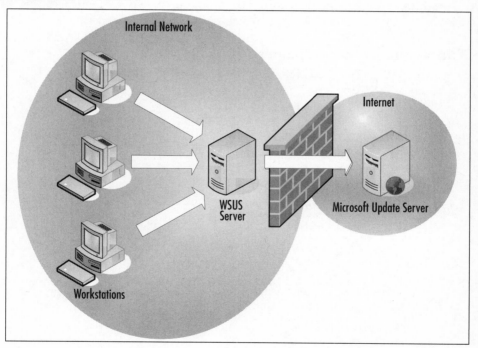

This solution offers more advantages than just control of the updates installed using Automatic Updates. You also can realize considerable bandwidth savings through the use of WSUS. If 20 machines download a 25MB update, you have to download 500 MB. If you are using only a T1 for your Internet connectivity, this will saturate the link for around 45 minutes solid. If you use the Internet for business reasons, this could be very inconvenient. Using WSUS, the WSUS server will download the 25MB update once, and all other systems will download the updates from the WSUS server without needing to use any Internet bandwidth at all. As tempting as WSUS may be, the server component will run only on Windows Server 2003 or newer. The client computers can be Windows 2000 (SP4) or newer.

Patching Linux Systems

The methods for patching your Linux distribution vary greatly from other distributions. In the case of Fedora Core 5, entering **yum update** without any program name specified will update all programs on the system, including the kernel. Of course, you can update individual programs using yum as well, by specifying the program name—**yum update tcpdump**, for example. You can cause yum to check the repositories and produce a list of all programs for which newer versions exist using the **yum check-update** command. Similar functionality is offered on Debian-based systems using the *apt-get* utility. Using **apt-get update** followed by **apt-get upgrade** will update all installed software. The upgrade option is used to tell *apt-get* to update its application listing database. You can install or update individual packages using **apt-get install tcpdump**. If you are using a GUI desktop environment, most likely a GUI interface will be provided. For Fedora Core 5, there is a GUI package manager at **Applications | System Tools | Software Updater** (shown in Figure 3.18). You can also install a GUI front end for yum, called *yumex* (which stands for yum extender).

Figure 3.18 Fedora Software Updater

Personal Firewalls

Personal firewall is a term that refers to firewalls that protect only the single host on which they reside. While many excellent personal firewalls are free versions of commercial software, you should read the license agreement for these firewalls carefully. In most cases, the free use extends only to home users and specifically excludes use in a business environment. One example is ZoneAlarm, from Zone Labs (www.zonelabs.com), which comes in a free version as well as a commercial offering. The free version offers great program control but is for nonbusiness use only. Kerio Personal Firewall (www.sun-belt-software.com/Kerio-Download.cfm) follows a similar business model, with the free version being for "personal use" only. For any freeware products you find, and there are several excellent ones, be sure to review the license agreement carefully to ensure that you can deploy it within your organization legally. If you are unsure, consult your organization's legal council to determine whether a given product license is suitable.

Windows Firewall

Although it hasn't been around for as long as the netfilter firewall (for Linux), the Windows firewall enjoys a similar advantage in that it is included with all modern Windows operating systems (Windows XP and Windows 2003). Because it is enabled by default, most users have some firewall protection in place even if they don't know it. While fairly ubiquitous, the Windows Firewall is very simple in its configuration and capability. It cannot perform any advanced packet manipulation and is really designed only to protect the host on which it is running. You can access your Windows Firewall by navigating to **Start | Settings | Control Panel | Windows Firewall**. The **General** tab has only three settings: an **On** setting, and **Off** setting, and a **Don't allow exceptions** option. If you select **Don't allow exceptions**, any selections you make on the **Exceptions** tab are simply ignored.

The **Exceptions** tab is where all the fun happens. The Windows Firewall operates as most personal firewalls do by default, which is to allow the local system to communicate outbound unhindered. The only traffic that is allowed inbound to the interface is reply traffic to sessions that were established outbound first. In this way, your surfing and other network access is unimpeded, but others cannot initiate a session to the protected system. This is usually perfectly adequate; however, if you happen to be running any type of server on the local machine, no one will be able to initiate a connection to the listening port. In other words, if you had a Web server running on the protected system, the Windows Firewall would block connection attempts to port 80. The **Exceptions** tab allows you to configure an exception to that normal behavior and allow a particular port in. Figure 3.19 shows the Exceptions tab.

One nice feature of the Windows Firewall is the ability to permit access based on the program that is running instead of on the port number. For the standard services, you probably know what port is needed, but sometimes a single application might need a large number of ports, or it may use a custom port and you're not sure which port it needs. In these cases, you can permit the application to open a listening port, and the firewall will allow inbound connections. To do this simply click **Add Program**, navigate to the program needing access, and then click **OK**. If you happen to know the port you need to open, this is easy as well. Click **Add Port**, and enter a reference name for the rule, such as **Web Server**. Then enter the port number—**80**, for example. As a final step, select whether to open the port for TCP or UDP connections using the radio buttons. Figure 3.20 shows the Add a Port window.

Figure 3.19 Windows Firewall Exceptions

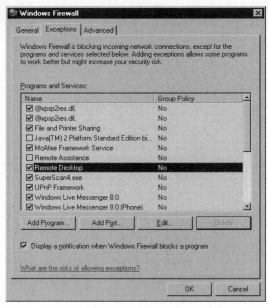

Figure 3.20 Windows Firewall Add a Port Window

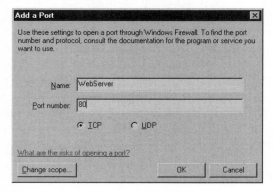

By clicking the **Change Scope** button, you can change the systems for which the port will be open. This allows you greater control over who will be able to connect to these ports. Your available options are Any Computer, My Network (meaning the subnet that the host is on), or a custom list of IP addresses. File sharing access would be a good example of when changing the scope from the default (Any) may be advisable. As long as your entire network is on the same subnet, there is no reason to leave the scope at Any. By setting it to My Network, you ensure that only local IP addresses can connect.

The Advanced tab (shown in Figure 3.21) has a few interesting settings of its own. Starting from the bottom of the window and moving upward, the setting with the simplest options is the **Restore Defaults** button. Of course, this will restore the default settings for the Windows Firewall, which is useful if the configuration is messed up and starting fresh is the easiest option. The next section is ICMP. By clicking the **Settings** button, you can configure a list of checkboxes, with each one corresponding to another type of ICMP packet. If you highlight a particular option a description will be displayed below. The descriptions are pretty helpful, and in most cases you shouldn't need to edit these unless you have some specific needs. The Security Logging section also has a **Settings** button. Clicking the **Settings** button will allow you to configure whether dropped packets and successful connections should be logged. You can also specify the path for the log file and enter a maximum log size.

Figure 3.21 Windows Firewall Advanced

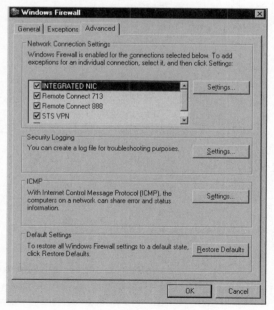

The top section, Network Connection Settings, allows you to select which interfaces will have the Windows Firewall enabled. In this way, it doesn't have to be an all-or-nothing proposition. You can specify that one network card has the Windows Firewall working and another one doesn't. This section also has a **Settings** button of its own. The **Settings** button applies only to the highlighted interface. This allows you to configure additional port exceptions on a per-interface basis. Clicking the **Settings** button will open an **Advanced Settings** window. From within the **Advanced Settings** window you can permit services, similar to the **Exceptions** tab, however these services apply only on the interface you highlighted when you clicked **Settings**. You can also use the **ICMP** tab to configure your ICMP permissions on a per-port basis.

When it comes to Windows-based systems, little administration is done from the command line. In most cases, GUI tools are used. If you need to script things, often for use in login scripts, command-line tools can be invaluable. Microsoft added Netsh firewall support as of Service Pack 2, which allows you to manipulate the Windows Firewall from the command line. To access the firewall context of Netsh, enter **netsh** and then **firewall** at the command prompt to use Netsh interactive mode. Your command prompt will change to **netsh firewall>**. You can view useful diagnostic information by entering **show state** or **show config**. You can display the same information without entering interactive mode by entering **netsh firewall show state** from a command prompt, as follows:

```
C:\>netsh firewall show state


Firewall status:
-------------------------------------------------------------
Profile                          = Standard
Operational mode                  = Disable
Exception mode                    = Enable
Multicast/broadcast response mode = Enable
Notification mode                 = Enable
Group policy version              = None
Remote admin mode                 = Disable


Ports currently open on all network interfaces:
Port    Protocol  Version  Program
-------------------------------------------------------------
137     UDP       IPv4     (null)
139     TCP       IPv4     (null)
138     UDP       IPv4     (null)
3389    TCP       IPv4     (null)
445     TCP       IPv4     (null)
```

Additional useful commands for scripting purposes might be **netsh firewall show allowedprogram**, **netsh firewall show logging**, and **netsh firewall show portopening**. All of these commands can provide valuable data, which you can use to scan systems programmatically for certain settings.

With the command-line utility, you can easily make many changes to the Windows Firewall configuration at one time using a batch file, or login script. This is advantageous in that making many changes via the GUI would be very time consuming, but making those changes via the command line could be done with a batch file very quickly. If you wanted to add an allowed program to the Windows Firewall, you would use the following command syntax to add a program, and then verify that it was added successfully:

```
C:\>netsh firewall add allowedprogram C:\program.exe appname ENABLE
Ok.


C:\>netsh firewall show allowedprogram

Allowed programs configuration for Domain profile:
Mode      Name / Program
------------------------------------------------------------------
Enable    Remote Assistance / C:\WINDOWS\system32\sessmgr.exe
Enable    AOL Instant Messenger / I:\Internet\AIM95\aim.exe


Allowed programs configuration for Standard profile:
Mode      Name / Program
------------------------------------------------------------------
Enable    Remote Assistance / C:\WINDOWS\system32\sessmgr.exe
Enable    AOL Instant Messenger / I:\Internet\AIM95\aim.exe
Enable    appname / C:\program.exe
```

You can also enable a particular port using any of the following syntax examples:

```
netsh firewall add portopening TCP 80 Webserver
netsh firewall add portopening UDP 80 Webserver
netsh firewall add portopening ALL 80 Webserver
```

As yet another means to configure and control the Windows Firewall, you can use GPOs. You can find the settings for the Windows Firewall in the MMC Group Policy Editor snap-in. Navigate to **/Computer Configuration/Administrative Templates/Network/Network Connections/ Windows Firewall/** to locate the appropriate settings.

The Windows Firewall can usually do an adequate job of protecting the local system. The Windows Firewall configuration allows you to configure global settings on the General and Exceptions tabs, and allows a higher degree of granularity using the Advanced tab. The Advanced tab allows you to configure many of the same settings as the global settings, but you can configure them on a per-interface basis. You also can configure these same settings from the command line using the Netsh utility. While I wouldn't recommend using the Windows Firewall as a perimeter firewall gateway, it can make an excellent personal firewall for your Windows-based network resources.

Tools & Traps...

What's in a Name?

The ability to specify access through the Windows Firewall based on the program name is pretty handy. By doing so, you don't need to figure out which port it needs, or whether the program needs to listen on a lot of ports or manage a large list of ports to allow through the firewall. This ease is not without its pitfalls, however. The access is based on the program name and nothing else. This means if the Windows Firewall is configured to allow inbound connections to *helphesk.exe*, and a user renames *badapp.exe* to *helpdesk.exe*, connections to *badapp will* be permitted through the firewall. This is why renaming an executable of the user's choosing is a popular method of bypassing Windows Firewall restrictions.

Netfilter Firewall

Netfilter is the firewall component that is included with the Linux kernel. Unless firewall support has been explicitly removed, netfilter should be present on all Linux distributions. Unlike the Windows Firewall, which is really suited only for use as a personal firewall, netfilter is just as capable of serving as a personal firewall as it is a dedicated firewall for your perimeter Internet connection. Detailed usage guidelines, including several recommended GUI interfaces for configuring netfilter, is discussed in detail in Chapter 2. All of the same configuration recommendations that were discussed when implementing netfilter as a perimeter firewall will apply when using it as a personal firewall.

Configuring TCP Wrappers

You can find similar functionality to the Windows Firewall's capability to permit access based on a program name in the Linux utility, TCP Wrappers. TCP Wrappers works in conjunction with the network-level filtering of a firewall. Whereas a firewall permits or denies traffic based on data contained in the IP header of the packet, TCP Wrappers filters access to services (by name) on the host on which the service is running. Only services that are compiled against the libwrap.a library can use TCP Wrappers. With TCP Wrappers enabled, attempts to access a given service will be compared against the /etc/hosts.allow file, and then the /etc/hosts.deny file. Rules are checked sequentially and processing of the rules files stops when a match is found. If a match is not found in either file, access will be granted. As an example, if you wanted to allow only connections from syngress.com to SSH on your bastion host while rejecting all other attempts, you would have the following two lines in your hosts.allow and hosts.deny files:

```
/etc/hosts.allow
sshd : .syngress.com
```

```
/etc/hosts.deny
sshd : ALL
```

While you would not want to rely on TCP Wrappers as your only means of protection, it does have the advantage that in the preceding example, access would be permitted to *sshd* regardless of the port on which it was listening. The two filter files accept several wildcards, such as *ALL, LOCAL, KNOWN, UNKNOWN,* and *PARANOID.* You can enable logging in the rule files as well, and configure the facility and severity of the log entry. With TCP Wrappers' limited functionality and syntax, you might wonder why you would ever use it over simply using netfilter. Because iptables works at the packet level, if you want to deny access to a particular process, such as HTTP, you must do it based on port number. So if you use netfilter to explicitly block connection attempts to port 80, and the user starts up the Web server and tells it to listen on port 8080, the connection will be allowed. With TCP Wrappers, you permit or deny access to a process. In this way, you can ensure that a given process will work only on the port you want it to work. This distinction could prove invaluable if you have a service which uses a large number of listening ports, or some type of service that is spawned as needed and the port number isn't always consistent, or if the packets are tunneled in another protocol, rendering identification via port numbers impossible.

Providing Antivirus and Antispyware Protection

Antivirus and antispyware efforts are a necessary evil in today's world. Having no protection from viruses and spyware will almost guarantee that you will fall victim to one or the other eventually. Almost everyone has a good feel for the risk a virus can pose, from just being a nuisance to rendering a system inoperable. Spyware, despite all the hype, often doesn't get the attention it deserves. I have seen many systems that have become so choked with spyware-consuming resources that they have slowed to a crawl and are no longer usable. Worse yet, some spyware is very difficult to remove, which translates into more lost time and effort just to clean the computer. In the end, it's definitely better not to let any spyware or viruses on a system in the first place than it is to have to deal with the hassle of trying to clean up the mess after the fact.

Antivirus Software

Antivirus software is required on all systems. Most computers these days come with antivirus software installed, typically with a limited duration of updates for the virus definitions (often as short as 30 days or, at best, a year). Unfortunately, many systems are never updated and continue running the out-of-date virus signatures. While an out-of-date antivirus program is still better than no antivirus program at all, it will not offer you much protection from the latest virus threats. Whichever antivirus methodology you use (Automatic Updates, live Web scans, manual updates), you will need to ensure that the signature files are maintained and remain current. Several of the best free antivirus programs have license agreements limiting their use to home or personal computers, specifically excluding a business environment. However, there are still some excellent free alternatives.

Clam AntiVirus

Clam AntiVirus (www.clamav.net) is an open source, free antivirus program with a lot of commercial-grade features. Clam was natively written for use on UNIX/Linux systems, but a Windows port also is available. Clam provides a command-line scanner for spot scans or scripted scanning. This is the primary way Clam was intended to be used. There is also an (experimental) on-access scanner, similar to what you'd find in most commercial products. It even includes a utility to update your signature files automatically. You can view the latest online documentation at www.clamav.net/doc/latest/html. Because Clam AntiVirus is one of the few antivirus solutions available without stipulation that it be used for "personal" use, I will discuss using it on both Linux and Windows systems.

Installing Clam AntiVirus on Linux

You should be able to download the needed files to install Clam AntiVirus from your standard repositories. If they are not available, you can download the base packages from www.clamav.net and install them manually. After installation, there is some configuration required. Follow these steps to get Clam AntiVirus running:

1.   Install the ClamAV package and any dependencies.

2.   You will need to create a ClamAV user and group. Typing the command **useradd −s /bin/false clamav** will create the ClamAV user and will set the user shell to */bin/false*. On Fedora Core 5 /home/clamav will be created automatically, but you will want to verify that this is true on your distribution. If the directory is not created automatically, you will need to create the directory manually.

You can now run the command-line scanner using the syntax *clamscan <target>*. As an example, *clamscan −r /home* would scan all the home directories and all subdirectories (*−r* specifies a recursive scan). Clamscan includes a large number of command-line options. The most significant ones are explained in the following list (you can enter **clamscan --help** for a more detailed explanation of the many command-line options):

-   **--infected.** This causes clamscan to list only infected files in its output.

-   **--bell.** This will cause a bell sound to be played if a virus is found.

-   **--recursive / -r.** This will cause clamscan to scan recursively—that is, to scan all subdirectories of the specified path.

-   **--move=<directory<.** You use this to specify that infected files be moved to a particular location. Typically the target directory is one that normal users have no access to, effectively placing the file in quarantine.

That's about all there is to the on-demand portion of Clam AntiVirus. As soon as you run any of the example commands, or any on-demand scan, clamscan will notify you that the definitions are out-of-date. You can see this error in the following example:

```
[root@localhost ~]# clamscan /input.txt
LibClamAV Warning: **************************************************
LibClamAV Warning: ***  The virus database is older than 7 days.  ***
```

```
LibClamAV Warning: ***           Please update it IMMEDIATELY!        ***
LibClamAV Warning: **************************************************
/input.txt: OK


----------- SCAN SUMMARY -----------
Known viruses: 75410
Engine version: 0.88.6
Scanned directories: 0
Scanned files: 1
Infected files: 0
Data scanned: 0.00 MB
Time: 3.023 sec (0 m 3 s)
[root@localhost ~]#
```

The next step would be to update the virus definition files. You do this using the *freshclam* updater (the clamav-update package in the Fedora repository). Follow these steps to get freshclam up and running.

1. Install the clamav-updater package.

2. Edit the /etc/freshclam.conf file. You may want to configure many settings. These are the settings which you *must* configure at a minimum in order to use freshclam:

   ■ Locate and edit the following line:

Example

   Either delete this line or add a # to the beginning of the line so that it will be a comment. This will prevent freshclam from running because it assumes you have not edited the example configuration file yet.

   ■ Locate and edit the following line:

```
#DatabaseMirror db.XY.clamav.net
```

   Remove the # to uncomment the line. Change *XY* to your two-letter country code.

3. Verify that the /var/log/freshclam.log file is writable by the owner and is owned by the *clamav* user.

4. Verify that the /var/lib/clamav/ directory is writable by the owner and is owned by the *clamav* user. This is the directory where the signature database files are stored.

TIP

Unless you use the —*user=* option to specify a different user for *clamav* to run as, it will run as the *clamav* user. This is true even if you are running the process as the root user. As soon as the *clamav* process starts, it drops from the running user to the *clamav* user. This explains why you may run the process as root but still receive a permissions error. In my case, with Fedora Core 5, the permissions were not set correctly for clamscan or freshclam to run and had to be edited.

You can run freshclam with no options and it will use the Internet to update the database definitions. You can automate the database update process in several ways. You could run the same command as the command line and schedule it with cron to run as frequently as you like. You could also run freshclam in database mode by adding the *−d* switch. If you are going to use database mode, the default is to connect and check for updates every two hours. You can edit this in the freshclam.conf file with the line reading *#Checks 24*. Uncomment this line to cause freshclam to check for updates every hour (i.e., 24 times per day).

This covers running on-demand scans. You gain a lot of protection by running these scans regularly in this fashion. You may want to evaluate the pros and cons of running an on-access scanner so that all files will be scanned as they are accessed. By scanning files as they are accessed, you may prevent the payload of an infected file from ever being triggered. With a nightly scan, an entire system could be infected by the time the nightly scan runs. You can configure clamav to run in this fashion; however, this additional protection comes at a price. By scanning every file as it is accessed, a small additional delay is incurred for each file. On a system that accesses a large number of files, this delay can bring the system to a grinding halt. Clamuko functionality (discussed shortly) is also not as stable as the base package, so even if the expected level of file access is low, you should evaluate whether an unexpected lockup is acceptable. The best bet is to run the on-access feature on a test system and evaluate the stability for yourself.

If you do want to enable on-access scanning, you can do so by installing Clamuko, which is a thread within the *clamd* daemon process. Unfortunately, Clamuko requires the use of Dazuko for the file access tracking. Dazuko is not available as a precompiled binary, and in order to install it you must recompile your kernel and incorporate Dazuko into the kernel as a kernel module. You should check your particular distribution, as a few have Dazuko support already integrated into their kernel. If you do not have Dazuko support already enabled, you will need to download the kernel source and the Dazuko source and recompile both, which is beyond the scope of this book.

Installing Clam AntiVirus on Windows

You can download the Windows port of Clam AntiVirus from several different locations (see www.clamav.net/binary.html). One of the most well-polished versions, which includes a GUI front end for performing various scanning tasks and right-click integration with Windows Explorer, is located at www.clamwin.com. It will run on Windows 98, ME, 2000, XP, and 2003. As a bonus, clamwin is available as a portable application (meaning you do not need to execute any type of installation, so you can run it from a USB drive) from http://portableapps.com. To install clamwin, download and run the setup utility. Follow the prompts, accepting the license agreement and choosing the installation folder. You can probably accept the defaults for the entire installation. At the end of the installation, it will automatically update the virus definitions (assuming you left that option checked). When it's finished, you should see a clamwin icon that looks like a target in the System Tray.

If you double-click on the icon in the System Tray or navigate to St**art | Programs | ClamWin Antivirus | Virus Scanner** you will open the main windows shown in Figure 3.22.

Figure 3.22 ClamWin

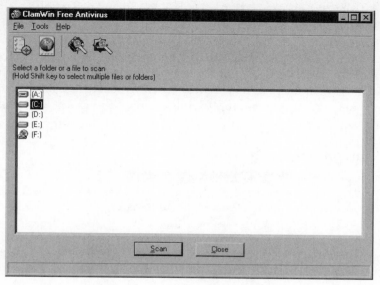

Remember that the Windows version has no support for on-access scanning. You must perform all scanning manually, although you can still run it from the command line, and thus script and schedule it. Scanning files is easy. Simply use the main window to select the file or folder you want to scan and click **Scan**. The four icons across the top, in order from left to right, are for accessing preferences, Web-based Virus Signature Updates, scan memory, and scanning files or folders (the same as the **Scan** button).

By clicking the **Preferences** button, you can open another window and configure many ClamWin options (as shown in Figure 3.23).

Figure 3.23 ClamWin Preferences

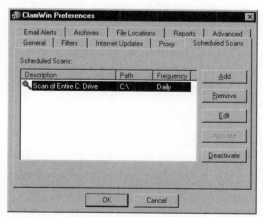

You probably will be most interested in the Internet Updates, Scheduled Scans, and Email Alerts tabs. Internet Updates allows you to specify when ClamWin should update itself, and how often. A daily update in the middle of the night is usually adequate. Click on the **Scheduled Scans** tab and you can add a scanning process to the scheduler. To do so, click **Add** to open the Scheduled Scan window shown in Figure 3.24. Set the **Scanning Frequency** and **Time**. Make sure that **Activate This schedule** is checked. Select a **Scan Folder** and, optionally, a **Description**, and click **OK**. I recommend a scan time when the machines will be on, but hopefully not in use, so that the scan does not slow down the system's responsiveness. If the systems are routinely left running all night, this shouldn't be an issue.

Figure 3.24 ClamWin Scheduled Scan

You can schedule e-mail alerts for when a virus is found, by using the **Email Alerts** tab. The configuration is straightforward. Enter the SMTP server name and, if required, your username and password. You can send a test e-mail using the button at the bottom. When you are finished configuring the preferences, click **OK** to accept the settings. You can view the reports ClamWin generates by navigating to **Tools | Display Reports** and then selecting the **Virus Database Update Report** or the **Scan Report**.

While ClamWin lacks on-access scanning, which *is* supported with virtually every commercial antivirus product, the integrated scheduling functionality and automated e-mail alerts are very nice features in a free product. The ClamWin virus signature database is updated several times a day, so you have the ability to keep your signatures updated without any manual configuration. If you are trying to keep your network secure without spending a lot of cash, you should definitely consider ClamWin.

Using Online Virus Scanners

Another option is to use any of several free online virus scanners. These are not as hands-off as installing a product is, because you need to go to the Web site and initiate a scan. This process will also require installation of various browser plug-ins to function. Although many Web sites offer free online scans, many actually require you to download software, which isn't really an "online" scan. Trend Micro offers a true online scan using HouseCall, from http://housecall.trendmicro.com. When you run the scan, HouseCall will allow you to choose between performing the scan using a Java-based application or via an ActiveX browser plug-in. Loading HouseCall will take some time. Once HouseCall is completely initialized, you can choose to scan the complete computer, or selected files and folders. If you select the entire computer, there are no other options to configure and the scan will commence. If you choose selected files and folders, you will be presented with a tree view to choose which folders to scan. After making your selection, click **Next**. One word of caution: Stick with reputable antivirus vendors' Web sites for online scans; otherwise, you could fall victim to a hacker posing as an online virus scanner.

Antispyware Software

Spyware can cause a lot more problems than most people realize. Even if a corporate firewall prevents the software from ever revealing any confidential information, the processes that are running can rob the system of valuable resources. Right off the top, these programs will consume processor cycles, and with enough of them, or with a poorly written program, the impact can be substantial. Also, the running spyware will consume some amount of memory. In addition to these resources, the spyware will consume *some* amount of disk space, though this is typically the least of your worries. All these are present even if the spyware in question is working perfectly. The truth is, this is rare. In most cases, the people installing the spyware don't care whether your system crashes, and these programs are rarely tested adequately. The source of many unexplained problems is often spyware. Luckily, many free antispyware utilities are available. Take note that the same licensing caveats that apply to antivirus software (and all free software, really) apply to antispyware software. In many instances, the default business model is to offer a feature-limited version for free, in an attempt to convince you to buy the commercial version. In most of these cases, the license agreement will expressly exclude installation in a business environment. Be sure to review the license carefully and ensure that you are using the software legally. When in doubt, consult your legal team.

Microsoft Windows Defender

Microsoft Windows Defender is a relatively new offering which will attempt to block and defend you from spyware and other malware. You can read about it and download Windows Defender from www.microsoft.com/athome/security/spyware/software/default.mspx. Unfortunately, Windows Defender will run on only Windows XP SP2 or Windows 2003 SP1. Windows Defender does include real-time protection, which few of the other "personal" antispyware products include. You can download and run the installation directly from the Microsoft Web site. During the installation, you will be asked whether you want to join the Microsoft SpyNet online community via the window shown in Figure 3.25.

A brief description is provided next to each choice. SpyNet is a system whereby the actions users take collectively form a profile of a given program to help determine whether it is malicious. Participating in this will mean that some nonuser-specific data will be sent back to Microsoft. If you don't want to send any data, the more conservative option is to select **Ask me later**. If you want to participate in SpyNet, select the top option. The option in the middle allows you to update your spyware signatures without joining SpyNet. After making your selection, click **Next**. Choose between a complete install and a custom one. If you're like me, you will almost always click **Custom**, just because you want to see what the options are. There really aren't any, other than choosing the installation directory. Click **Next** and then **Install**. When the installation is complete, you can click **Finish**. You should leave the checkbox selected to **Check for updated definitions and run a quick scan now**.

Figure 3.25 Microsoft SpyNet Community

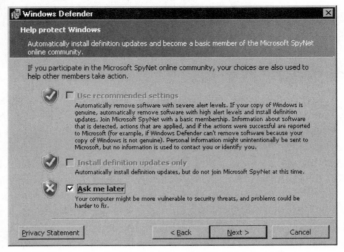

The main Windows Defender window will open (see Figure 3.26).

Figure 3.26 Windows Defender

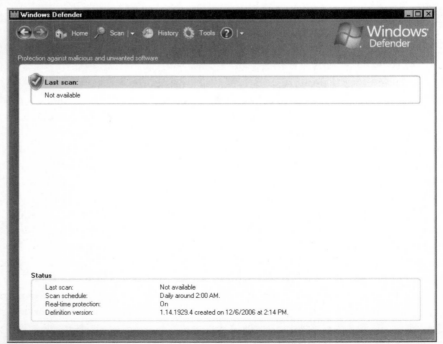

Windows Defender has some nice features. If you select **Tools** at the top, the window shows several icons for different functions. Selecting **Options** will allow you to configure the Windows Defender settings. The options are not exhaustive, but they are functional. You can choose to enable automatic scanning (enabled by default daily at 2 A.M.). You can also choose for the automatic scan to be a quick scan or a full scan. Most of the default selections will probably be appropriate for most users. Default Actions is a critical configuration area. This determines how invasive you want Windows Defender to be. You can choose available actions for detected items which are high-, medium-, or low-risk. Each one offers the same options: **Default action** (which is defined by Microsoft's signature database), **Ignore**, **Remove**, and **Quarantine**, as shown in Figure 3.27.

Figure 3.27 Windows Defender Options

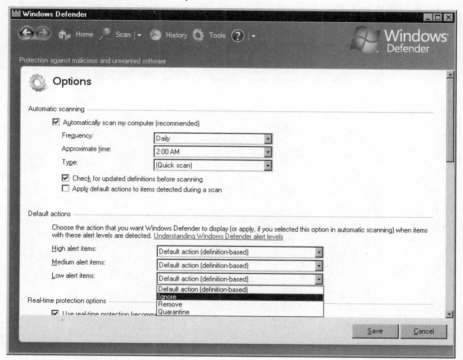

By allowing Microsoft to use the default action, you are trusting that the company will know what's best. If you want to ensure that nothing critical can be accidentally deleted you can change all actions to **Ignore**.

Another interesting window is under **Tools | Software Explorer**. This is a useful screen that will give you information on all running processes, just startup processes (the default view), programs using the network, or Winsock service providers. These can be very informative lists to see what is happening on your current system.

Microsoft Malicious Software Removal Tool

The Microsoft Malicious Software Removal Tool is a specialized utility designed to help you remove a specific subset of the most damaging viruses and worms. Because some of these software packages can be both very damaging to your system and very hard to remove, this too was designed to help. The goal of the Microsoft Windows Malicious Software Removal Tool is to remove the offending software while minimizing any lasting damage to existing files. This utility does not offer any type of ongoing protection; it is purely intended to help you clean up and recover after an infection has occurred. You can download and read about the tool at www.microsoft.com/security/malwareremove/default.mspx. To see a list of the malicious software that the tool checks for, refer to the knowledge base article located at http://support.microsoft.com/?kbid=890830.

Running the tool is easy. Just download the tool and run the downloaded executable. You will be prompted to choose the type of scan you want to run, as shown in Figure 3.28.

Figure 3.28 Microsoft Malicious Software Removal Tool

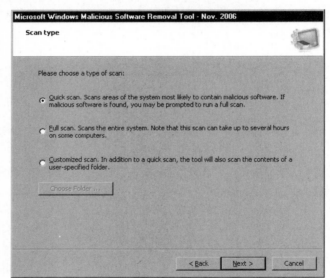

After making your selection, click **Next** and the scan will begin. A quick scan really is very quick, and the next window you see will be the **Scan Results** window. That's really all there is to it, unless the tool detects something, in which case you will be prompted to determine what action you want to take.

Encrypting Sensitive Data

Another way to protect your sensitive data is through encryption. In theory, even if logical controls are compromised and bypassed, an encryption mechanism can still keep data out of a hacker's hands. There are some critical caveats to employing any form of data encryption, whether for personal use or within an organization. You should never encrypt something without having a means to decrypt the data in an emergency. You typically would do this through a password escrow mechanism, whereby a central repository contains all the needed passwords to decrypt the data.

The objective is to ensure that the encryption does not become a liability. This can occur in a surprising number of ways. An employee who has the password for critical encrypted data could quit or become unreachable. A malicious employee could intentionally encrypt important data, or a criminal could even use your encryption mechanism to encrypt critical data and then offer the password up for ransom. If the encryption protocols and methods are truly secure, the data will be as unrecoverable for you as it would be for any other attacker. The requirement for a password recovery mechanism exists whether you are implementing encryption that is supported natively by the operating system, or in the form of third-party software. This warning is so important that many security experts advise *disabling* the native Windows encryption (encrypted file system, or EFS) if you do not implement a means (of which there are several) to recover encrypted data (see the next section for more information).

You should also consider the types of encryption you need. Encrypting single files is a convenient way to secure specific files on an as-needed basis. Another alternative is to create a normal file, which you can access as though it were an entire disk volume. The volume is integrated into your operating system and appears as another drive letter. Any files placed on this virtual disk will be encrypted automatically. This type of encryption can be useful for large numbers of frequently changing files. The native Windows encryption is a sort of hybrid solution, encrypting and decrypting data files automatically using your Windows credentials. You may not need to use all of these methods of encryption, or you may benefit from a combination of methods. Ultimately, one of the most common determining factors is ease of use. An encryption method that is easy to use will probably be used far more consistently than one that is hard to use. We will review some of these methods in the next section in order to help you make an informed decision.

EFS

Microsoft's EFS really shines when it comes to ease of use. Once you configure it, there are no additional passwords to remember (other than your Windows login credentials), and you don't need to manually encrypt or decrypt anything. EFS was introduced with Windows 2000, and you can implement it only on Windows 2000 or newer. With Windows 2000, a recovery policy was required in order to implement EFS. This allowed for an alternative means to recover encrypted data, in addition to the data being unencrypted by the original user who encrypted it. Without a recovery policy defined, EFS would simply not work. With Windows XP and 2003, this requirement was removed, meaning that if EFS is enabled and there is no recovery policy, a user could encrypt data that was not recoverable by the organization. In most cases IT policy is worded in such a way that any data the user might store belongs to the organization, and therefore, the organization has a right to ensure that the data is recoverable. Because the default data recovery agent is the domain administrator, the risk of data becoming unrecoverable is particularly high with stand-alone workstations.

Because EFS is enabled by default, it's easy to encrypt an individual file or folder. Select the file you want to encrypt, right-click it, and select **Properties**. Click **Advanced** and check the box next to **Encrypt contents to secure data**, as shown in Figure 3.29.

Figure 3.29 Windows EFS Encryption

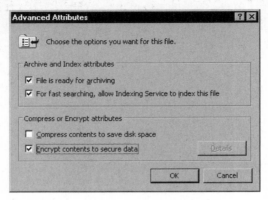

Afterward, click **OK,** and then **OK** again. You will receive an encryption warning, which alerts you that the folder the file resides in is not an encrypted folder. You will need to click **OK** to close the warning. Under these circumstances, you can edit the file and close it and it will remain encrypted, but if you use **Save As** and rename the file, it will no longer remain encrypted. This opens up the possibility that a user will either forget to encrypt the file after modifying it, or neglect it due to the inconvenience of doing it every time a filename is changed due to versioning or other factors. This is why it is recommended that you set entire folders as encrypted, instead of individual files. The process is the same, except you select a folder instead of an individual file. After you do this, all files placed in the folder will be encrypted, even ones moved or copied from other folders. This makes encryption painless to use.

A significant disadvantage to using EFS is that it does not support access to encrypted content based on group membership. This means that once a user encrypts the data, only that user can encrypt the data, or individual users manually given access on a per-file basis (Windows XP and newer only). This makes EFS unsuitable, or at least cumbersome, for files that are shared among a group of users. To configure additional users to access a specific encrypted file, open the **Advanced Properties** for the file and click **Details**. You can then click **Add** to add an individual user to be able to access that encrypted file.

TIP

Some applications will remove the certificate information associated with a file. This certificate information is used to allow multiple users to access the file. As a result, all the additional users that were granted access to the encrypted file individually are removed.

With Windows 2000, if the administrator changed the password for a user account, that user could still access all of his encrypted content. With Windows XP, that is no longer true. Instead, the user will lose all access to his previously encrypted files. The only way to retrace the encrypted data is to use the data recovery agent. Stand-alone XP workstations with no recovery policy defined (and thus, no data recovery agents defined) make it very easy to permanently lose access to your encrypted data. If you elect to disable EFS entirely, you can do so via local GPOs on individual computers. You can also disable EFS via the domain GPOs, though if the workstations are part of a domain, you could instead define the data recovery agent and thus eliminate the risk of lost data in the first place. You could even enable EFS for specific subsets of systems based on a GPO applied to an OU. To do so, navigate to \Computer Configuration\Windows Settings\Security Settings\Public Key Policies\Encrypting File System within the appropriate policy snap-in (local or domain). Right-click **Encrypting File System** and select **Properties**. You will see a single **General** tab, with a single checkbox. Uncheck the checkbox next to **Allow users to encrypt file using Encrypting File System**.

If you elect to use EFS, you must have a data recovery agent. Windows XP does not create one by default. The recovery policy defines the data recovery agent to be used. The recovery policy is inherited from the domain for machines that are members of a domain. For stand-alone machines, you must create the recovery policy and data recovery agent manually. To manually create the recovery policy and assign the data recovery agent on XP machines, follow these steps:

1. Using the credentials of the desired data recovery agent, enter **cipher /r:<filename>** to generate encryption keys. In this example, I generated the keys while logged in as the user Eric. You will be asked to provide a password and verify the password in order to complete the process. This will generate two files, named filename.cer and filename.pfx.

2. Navigate within the Local Computer Policy snap-in to \Computer Configuration\Windows Settings\Security Settings\Public Key Policies\Encrypting File System. Right-click **Encrypting File System** and select **Add Data Recovery Agent**.

3. Click **Next** on the welcome screen. On the **Select Recovery Agents** screen, click **Browse Folders**, select the .CER file you created previously, and click **Open**.

4. Click **Next**, and then **Finish**.

Now you can use this certificate to decrypt data on that local machine, regardless of which user account encrypted it. You can see that the data recovery agent's key was incorporated into the encrypted file by again viewing the **Encryption Details**, as shown in Figure 3.30.

You can see that the certificate we created earlier and configured in the recovery policy is now listed as the data recovery agent. To recover data using this certificate, follow these steps.

1. Right-click the file you want to decrypt (in my example, the file was created by a user named recovery1) and select **Properties**.

2. Click **Advanced** and then remove the checkmark next to **Encrypt contents to secure data**.

3. Click **OK** and **OK** again to close the **Properties** window.

Figure 3.30 Encryption Details with the Data Recovery Agent

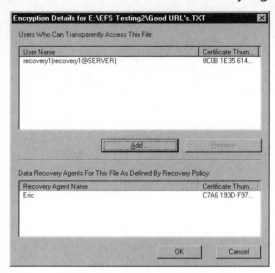

The files will no longer be encrypted. The designated recovery agent can also simply open the files in question directly, however they will remain encrypted when the data recovery agent closes them. The recovery agent will only have access to decrypt files encrypted *after* the policy was configured. If files were encrypted prior to defining the data recovery agent, you can update the encryption on all files using the *cipher /u* command. Note that this command will be able to update only the files you have access to. If you had three users with files that were encrypted prior to the data recovery agent being defined, all three would need to run the command to update their encryption keys with the data recovery agent information.

Cipher.exe also has several other uses. You can use it to encrypt a file or folder from the command line, or to display a listing of the encryption status of a directory and its contents. *Cipher* with no options will list the files and folders in the current directory and tell it which are encrypted. A *U* indicates that the file or folder is unencrypted, and an *E* indicates that it is encrypted:

```
E:\>cipher

 Listing E:\
 New files added to this directory will not be encrypted.

U Burned to CD
U Docs
U backup Files
E EFS_ERIC
E EFS_RECOVERY1
E EFS_RECOVERY2
```

To encrypt a file, use *cipher* with the */a* option. You can encrypt a directory with */a* (which will not mark the directory as encrypted) or */e* (which will mark the directory to be encrypted). To decrypt a directory, use the */d* option. To decrypt a file in a directory, you must use */d /a <filename>*, which will decrypt the specified file:

```
E:\>cipher /D EFS_RECOVERY1
 Decrypting directories in E:\
EFS_RECOVERY1 [OK]
1 directorie(s) within 1 directorie(s) were decrypted.
```

Here, I have included examples of encrypting and then decrypting a file, with a plain listing from *cipher* to illustrate the file's status, to clarify the use of the switches. I have removed blank lines to conserve space:

```
E:\EFS_RECOVERY1>cipher
 Listing E:\EFS_RECOVERY1\
 New files added to this directory will not be encrypted.
U test.TXT


E:\EFS_RECOVERY1>cipher /e /a test.txt
 Encrypting files in E:\EFS_RECOVERY1\
test.TXT            [OK]
1 file(s) [or directorie(s)] within 1 directorie(s) were encrypted.


Converting files from plaintext to ciphertext may leave sections of old
plaintext on the disk volume(s). It is recommended to use command
CIPHER /W:directory to clean up the disk after all converting is done.


E:\EFS_RECOVERY1>cipher
 Listing E:\EFS_RECOVERY1\
 New files added to this directory will not be encrypted.
E test.TXT


E:\EFS_RECOVERY1>cipher /d /a test.txt
 Decrypting files in E:\EFS_RECOVERY1\
test.TXT [OK]
1 file(s) [or directorie(s)] within 1 directorie(s) were decrypted.


E:\EFS_RECOVERY1>cipher
 Listing E:\EFS_RECOVERY1\
 New files added to this directory will not be encrypted.
U test.TXT
```

A final, very useful function you can get from *cipher* is the */w* option. You can use the */w* option to remove remnant data from "empty" portions of the hard disk. When you delete a file, only the pointer to the file in the file allocation table is really removed. The actual data from the file stays right where it was on the hard disk, until something else randomly comes along and needs that particular piece of disk real estate. The various programs designed to "undelete" files work by scanning the disk and finding the original data, and then rebuilding the file allocation table entry for it. The */w* option of *cipher* will intentionally overwrite all unallocated disk space to ensure that files cannot be undeleted. You can find additional information on the Encrypting File System at www.microsoft.com/technet/security/guidance/cryptographyetc/efs.mspx.

Summary

Many security solutions are available for protecting your network resources. You should perform basic hardening on all network resources, from workstations, to servers, to routers and switches. After basic hardening, regular patches and updates are required to ensure that you are running the most secure software possible. Personal firewalls can serve as your first line of defense, providing logical access control based on the contents of network packets. After the network is secured, your defenses turn inward, to protecting your assets from such things as viruses and spyware. Finally, we wrapped up with the last line of defense—file encryption—to protect sensitive data even if the system or encrypted files should fall into the wrong hands.

Solutions Fast Track

Performing Basic Hardening

- ☑ Have an IT security policy in place so that you have a concrete set of standards against which to measure. Having specific objectives in mind when you are hardening systems will increase the odds of you achieving those objectives.

- ☑ Requiring high-quality passwords is a balancing act between requiring a good password and making the requirements so difficult that the user ends up writing down the password in order to remember it.

Hardening Windows Systems

- ☑ Renaming the administer account and disabling the user account are simple and effective security measures.

- ☑ Utilizing GPOs is a means to provide centrally managed security configurations to all of your protected hosts.

Hardening Linux Systems

- ☑ Understand how file system permissions work in order to lock down access to only the minimum that is required.

- ☑ Employ TCP Wrappers to restrict network access based on applications (daemons) instead of based on network ports or IP addresses.

Hardening Infrastructure Devices

- ☑ You must perform the same high-level tasks for infrastructure devices as for any other workstation or server.

- ☑ Remember to disable the unneeded services that most managed infrastructure devices will enable by default.

Patching Systems

- ☑ Remember that a controlled patch management methodology does not mean applying all the patches the instant they are released. You should conduct proper research and testing before making any changes to a system's software.

- ☑ Most modern operating systems (Linux and Windows) include tools to automatically check for software updates online and apply them if desired.

Personal Firewalls

- ☑ Pay careful attention to the license agreements and make sure you are not using a great "personal" firewall illegally.

- ☑ Windows Firewall provides adequate controls for what types of access are permitted, but it only really is suitable as a personal firewall, not as a network perimeter firewall.

Providing Antivirus and Antispyware Protection

- ☑ Free antivirus and antispyware software often prohibit use in a business setting. Verify that the license agreement allows you to deploy the software in your environment.

- ☑ Both antivirus and antispyware software require regular patching with the current signature files in order to remain effective.

Encrypting Sensitive Data

- ☑ You should use EFS only if a data recovery agent has been configured and enforced via group policy. Using EFS without a data recovery agent runs the risk of permanently losing access to encrypted data if the original user who encrypted it becomes corrupt or unavailable.

☑ Consider carefully the ease of the encryption methods you choose. A high-quality encryption program that is hard to use probably will go unused.

Frequently Asked Questions

The following Frequently Asked Questions, answered by the authors of this book, are designed to both measure your understanding of the concepts presented in this chapter and to assist you with real-life implementation of these concepts. To have your questions about this chapter answered by the author, browse to **www.syngress.com/solutions** and click on the **"Ask the Author"** form.

Q: Is there any way to automate the live Web-based virus scans?

A: While you can do it, such a project would likely be very time-intensive. You could start with the set of tools called libwww, from www.idm.ru/content/view/9/8/lang.en. This includes tools for command-line HTTP tools for retrieving Web sites, and even sending input back. You could probably patch together a script that would perform the scan, though again, I don't recommend it unless you really need that functionality desperately.

Q: I haven't had a virus or any spyware before. Do I really need to worry about installing any software to protect myself?

A: First, I would encourage you to run some scanners. Many systems are infected with a virus or spyware without it causing enough of a problem for anyone to notice. Second, even the most well-informed users can sometimes make mistakes, and with no protection, it will take only one mistake to potentially bring your entire network to its knees. If you want to see how easy it is to fall victim, try this. Burn a CD-ROM and configure the autorun file to execute a program that will e-mail you when run. Do the same with an executable on the disk. Give the files interesting-sounding names, such as quotes, incomes, merchants, or discounts. When finished, leave the unlabeled CD-ROM lying around somewhere near your organization's building. Sit back and see how long it takes before you receive your e-mail. All it takes is one person getting curious and putting the disk in the drive.

Q: How can I disable the configuration of Windows Firewall so that my users can't turn it off?

A: You can read about the process of configuring Windows Firewall using GPOs in more detail here: www.microsoft.com/technet/security/smallbusiness/prodtech/windowsxp/fwgrppol.mspx. The appropriate settings are located in the policy under Computer Configuration\Administrative Templates\Network\Network Connections\Windows Firewall. When your configuration changes are completed, you can apply the policy by running gpupdate, rebooting the machine, or waiting for the default policy refresh to occur.

Q: What happens if I'm using EFS and copy an encrypted file to my USB drive? Will it remain encrypted, or does Windows decrypt it before copying it out?

A: It depends on a lot of factors. If the destination file system is not formatted as NTFS, the file will be decrypted and copied. If you are using Windows 2000 EFS, this decryption takes place transparently, so you may not be aware that the file was decrypted. With newer versions of Windows, you will receive a warning reminding you that the file will be decrypted. Without getting too long-winded, EFS behaves differently depending on (1.) whether you are doing a move or a copy operation; (2.) the way the destination file system is formatted; and (3.) what OS and directory access the destination operating system has.

Q: I'm a home user. Will Windows Firewall protect my host if I plug it in directly to my cable modem?

A: Placing your system directly on the Internet with no firewall at all ensures that the system will be compromised and used for some purposes you probably wouldn't approve of—possibly without you ever even knowing. Enabling Windows Firewall is a big improvement over no firewall and will offer some protection. A real firewall (even an inexpensive home model) offers additional security that Windows Firewall doesn't. This includes source NAT for one, which will help hide your machines real IP address and make directing attacks toward it more difficult. So will Windows Firewall protect you? Sure, to a degree, but remember defense in depth is the objective.

Q: How long should I wait before applying patches to my protected hosts?

A: This is really going to depend on your environment, and the requirements will likely be different for different resources within your environment. The development servers probably deserve a different patching schedule than the critical Web portal that makes the majority of company revenue. Another important determining factor will be the severity of the issue(s) the patch addresses. If the patch closes a remotely exploitable security hole, applying it will be more urgent than if the patch addresses a vulnerability that can only be exploited while someone is logged in to the machine locally.

## Chapter 4

Introducing Snort

Solutions in this chapter:

- How and IDS Works
- Where Snort Fits
- Snort System Requirements
- Exploring Snort's Features
- Using Snort on Your Network
- Snort and Your Network Architecture
- Pitfalls When Running Snort
- Security Considerations with Snort

- ☑ Summary
- ☑ Solutions Fast Track
- ☑ Frequently Asked Questions

Introduction

An IDS is the high-tech equivalent of a burglar alarm, one that is configured to monitor information gateways, hostile activities, and known intruders. An IDS is a specialized tool that knows how to parse and interpret network traffic and/or host activities. This data can range from network packet analysis to the contents of log files from routers, firewalls, and servers, local system logs and access calls, network flow data, and more. Furthermore, an IDS often stores a database of known attack signatures and can compare patterns of activity, traffic, or behavior it sees in the data it's monitoring against those signatures to recognize when a close match between a signature and current or recent behavior occurs. At that point, the IDS can issue alarms or alerts, take various kinds of automated actions ranging from shutting down Internet links or specific servers to launching back-traces, and make other active attempts to identify attackers and collect evidence of their nefarious activities.

By analogy, an IDS does for a network what an antivirus software package does for files that enter a system: it inspects the contents of network traffic to look for and deflect possible attacks, just as an antivirus software package inspects the contents of incoming files, e-mail attachments, active Web content, and so forth to look for *virus signatures* (patterns that match known malware) or for possible *malicious actions* (patterns of behavior that are at least suspicious, if not downright unacceptable).

To be more specific, intrusion detection means detecting unauthorized use of or attacks upon a system or network. An IDS is designed and used to detect such attacks or unauthorized use of systems, networks, and related resources, and then in many cases to deflect or deter them if possible. Like firewalls, IDSes can be software-based or can combine hardware and software in the form of preinstalled and preconfigured stand-alone IDS devices. IDS software may run on the same devices or servers where firewalls, proxies, or other boundary services operate, though separate IDS sensors and managers are more popular. Nevertheless, an IDS *not* running on the same device or server where the firewall or other services are installed will monitor those devices with particular closeness and care. Although such devices tend to be deployed at network peripheries, IDSes can detect and deal with insider attacks as well as external attacks, and are often very useful in detecting violations of corporate security policy and other internal threats.

You are likely to encounter several kinds of IDSes in the field. First, it is possible to distinguish IDSes by the kinds of activities, traffic, transactions, or systems they monitor. IDSes that monitor network links and backbones looking for attack signatures are called *network-based IDSes*, whereas those that operate on hosts and defend and monitor the operating and file systems for signs of intrusion and are called *host-based IDSes*. Groups of IDSes functioning as remote sensors and reporting to a central management station are known as distributed IDSes (DIDSes). A *gateway IDS* is a network IDS deployed at the gateway between your network and another network, monitoring the traffic passing in and out of your network at the transit point. IDSes that focus on understanding and parsing application-specific traffic with regard to the flow of application logic as well as the underlying protocols are often called *application IDSes*.

In practice, most commercial environments use some combination of network-, host-, and/or application-based IDSes to observe what is happening on the network while also monitoring key hosts and applications more closely. IDSes can also be distinguished by their differing approaches to event analysis. Some IDSes primarily use a technique called *signature detection*. This resembles the way many antivirus programs use virus signatures to recognize and block infected files, programs, or active Web content from entering a computer system, except that it uses a database of traffic or activity patterns related to known attacks, called *attack signatures*. Indeed, signature detection is the most widely used approach in commercial IDS technology today. Another approach is called *anomaly detection*. It uses rules or predefined concepts about "normal" and "abnormal" system activity (called *heuristics*) to distinguish anomalies from normal system behavior and to monitor, report, or block anomalies as they occur. Some anomaly detection IDSes implement user profiles. These profiles are baselines of normal activity and can be constructed using statistical sampling, rule-base approaches, or neural networks.

Hundreds of vendors offer various forms of commercial IDS implementations. Most effective solutions combine network- and host-based IDS implementations. Likewise, the majority of implementations are primarily signature-based, with only limited anomaly-based detection capabilities present in certain specific products or solutions. Finally, most modern IDSes include some limited automatic response capabilities, but these usually concentrate on automated traffic filtering, blocking, or disconnects as a last resort. Although some systems claim to be able to launch counterstrikes against attacks, best practices indicate that automated identification and back-trace facilities are the most useful aspects that such facilities provide and are therefore those most likely to be used.

IDSes are classified by their functionality and are loosely grouped into the following three main categories:

- Network-based intrusion detection system (NIDS)
- Host-based intrusion detection system (HIDS)
- Distributed intrusion detection system (DIDS)

How an IDS Works

We've already touched on this to some degree in our survey of the different kinds of IDSes out there, but let's take a look at exactly what makes an IDS tick. First, you have to understand what the IDS is watching. The particular kinds of data input will depend on the kind of IDS (indeed, what sorts of information an IDS watches is one of the hallmarks used to classify it), but in general there are three major divisions:

- Application-specific information such as correct application data flow
- Host-specific information such as system calls used, local log content, and file system permissions
- Network-specific information such as the contents of packets on the wire or hosts known to be attackers

A DIDS may watch any or all of these, depending on what kinds of IDSes its remote sensors are. The IDS can use a variety of techniques in order to gather this data, including packet sniffing (generally in promiscuous mode to capture as much network data as possible), log parsing for local system and application logs, system call watching in the kernel to regulate the acceptable behavior of local applications, and file system watching in order to detect attempted violation of permissions.

After the IDS has gathered the data, it uses several techniques to find intrusions and intrusion attempts. Much like firewalls, an IDS can adopt a known-good or a known-bad policy. With the former technique, the IDS is set to recognize good or allowed data, and to alert on anything else. Many of the anomaly detection engines embrace this model, triggering alerts when anything outside of a defined set of statistical parameters occurs. Some complex protocol models also operate on known-good policies, defining the kinds of traffic that the protocol allows and alerting on anything that breaks that mold. Language-based models for application logic also tend to be structured as known-good policies, alerting on anything not permitted in the predefined structure of acceptable language or application flow.

Known-bad policies are much simpler, as they do not require a comprehensive model of allowed input, and alert only on data or traffic known to be a problem. Most signature-based IDS engines work from a known-bad model, with an ever-expanding database of malicious attack signatures. Known-good and known-bad policies can work in conjunction within a single IDS deployment, using the known-bad signature detection and the known-good protocol anomaly detection in order to find more attacks.

Finally, we should consider what the IDS does when it finds an attempted attack. There are two general categories of response: passive response, which may generate alerts or log entries but does not interfere with or manipulate the network traffic, and active response, which may send reset packets to disrupt Transmission Control Protocol (TCP) connections, drop traffic if the IDS is inline, add the attacking host to block lists, or otherwise actively interact with the flow of dubious activity.

Having outlined these principles in the abstract, let's take a look at some real network-based attacks.

What Will an IDS Do for Me?

The strengths of IDSes are their capability to continuously watch packets on your network, understand them in binary, and alert you when something suspicious that matches a signature occurs. Unlike human security analysts, the speed of IDS detection allows alerting and response almost immediately, even if it's 3 A.M. and everyone's sleeping. (The alerting capability of IDSes can allow you to page people and wake them up, or, if you're deploying an IDS in inline mode or an intrusion prevention system [IPS], block the suspicious traffic, and potentially other traffic from the attacking host.) An IDS can allow you to read gigabytes of logs daily, looking for specific issues and violations. The potential enhancement of computing and analysis power is tremendous, and a well-tuned IDS will act as a force multiplier for a competent system/network administrator or security person, allowing them to monitor more data from more systems. By letting you know quickly when it looks like you are under attack, potential compromises may be prevented or minimized.

It is important to realize that any IDS is likely to create tremendous amounts of data no matter how well you tune it. Without tuning, most IDSes will create so much data and so many false positives that the analysis time may swamp response to the legitimate alerts in a sea of false alerts. A new IDS is almost like a new baby—it needs lots of care and feeding to be able to mature in a productive and healthy way. If you don't tune your IDS, you might as well not have it.

Another positive feature of an IDS is that it will allow the skilled analyst to find subtle trends in large amounts of data that might not otherwise be noticed. By allowing correlation between alerts and hosts, the IDS can show patterns that might not have been noticed through other means of network analysis. This is one example of how an IDS can supplement your other network defenses, working cooperatively to enact a defense-in-depth strategy.

What Won't an IDS Do for Me?

No IDS will replace the need for staffers knowledgeable about security. You'll need skilled analysts to go through those alerts that the IDS produces, determining which are real threats and which are false positives. Although the IDS can gather data from many devices on a network segment, they still won't understand the ramifications of threats to each machine, or the importance of every server on the network. You need clever, savvy people to take action on the information that the IDS provides.

In addition, no IDS will catch every single attack that occurs, or prevent people from trying to attack you. The limitations of any kind of IDS and the timing between the development of new attacks and the development of signatures or the ability to hide within acceptable parameters of an anomaly-based system make it exceedingly likely that there will be a small window in which 0-day attacks will not be detected by a given IDS. The Internet can be a cruel and hostile place, and although it's advisable to implement strong network defenses and prepare to be attacked, IDSes cannot psychically make people decide not to attack your network after all. In most cases, an IDS will not prevent attacks from succeeding automatically, as its function is primarily to detect and alert. There are some mechanisms that do address this problem—inline IDS, or IPS, for example—but in most cases, an IDS will not automatically defeat attacks for you. This is one of the reasons that an IDS should be seen as a complement to your other network defenses such as firewalls, antivirus software, and the like, rather than as a replacement for them.

Where Snort Fits

Snort is an open source network IDS capable of performing real-time traffic analysis and packet logging on Internet Protocol (IP) networks. Snort can perform protocol analysis and content searching/matching, and you can use it to detect a variety of attacks and probes, such as buffer overflows, stealth port scans, Common Gateway Interface (CGI) attacks, Server Message Block (SMB) probes, operating system fingerprinting attempts, and much more. Snort is rapidly becoming the tool of choice for intrusion detection.

You can configure Snort in three main modes: sniffer, packet logger, and network intrusion detection. Sniffer mode simply reads the packets off the network and displays them in a continuous stream on the console. Packet logger mode logs the packets to the disk. Network intrusion detection mode is the most complex and configurable, allowing Snort to analyze network traffic for matches against a user-defined ruleset and to perform one of several actions, based on what it sees.

In addition to the community signatures provided with Snort and the Sourcefire VDB signatures available for download to registered users, you can write your own signatures with Snort to suit the particular needs of your network. This capability adds immense customization and flexibility to the Snort engine, allowing you to suit the unique security needs of your own network. In addition, there are several online communities where leading-edge intrusion analysts and incident responders swap their newest Snort rules for detecting fresh exploits and recent viruses.

Snort's network pattern matching behavior has several immediately practical applications. For example, it allows the detection of hosts infected with viruses or worms that have distinctive network behavior. Because many modern worms spread by scanning the Internet and attacking hosts they deem vulnerable, signatures can be written either for this scanning behavior or for the exploit attempt itself. Although it is not the job of the IDS to clean up infected machines, it can help identify infected machines. In cases of massive virus infection, this identification capability can be immensely useful. In addition, watching for the same behavior after supposed virus cleanup can help to confirm that the cleanup was successful.

Snort also has signatures that match the network behavior of known network reconnaissance and exploit tools. Although for the most part, rule writers make an effort to match the signature of the exploit and not of a particular tool, sometimes it's helpful to be able to identify the tool scanning or attacking you. For example, there are rules that identify the SolarWinds scanner's tendency to embed its name in the payload of its scanning Internet Control Message Protocol (ICMP) packets, making for easy device identification. The vast majority of exploits that end up in popular tools such as Metasploit have signatures in the Snort rulebases, making them detectable by their network behavior.

Snort System Requirements

Before getting a system together, you need to know a few things. First, Snort data can take up a lot of disk space, and, second, you'll need to be able to monitor the system remotely. The Snort system we maintain is in our machine room (which is cold, and a hike downstairs).

Because we're lazy and don't want to hike downstairs, we would like to be able to maintain it remotely *and* securely. For Linux and UNIX systems, this means including Secure Shell (SSH) and Apache with Secure Sockets Layer (SSL). For Windows, this would mean Terminal Services (with limitation on which users and machines can connect and Internet Information Servers [IIS]).

Hardware

It's difficult to give hard-and-fast requirements on what you'll need to run Snort because the hardware requirements are tremendously variable depending on the amount of traffic on your network and how much of that you're trying to process and store. Busy enterprise networks with thousands of active servers are going to have much greater requirements than a poky home network with one client machine on it. However, we can provide general guidelines.

At a bare minimum level, Snort does not have any particular hardware requirements that your OS doesn't already require to run. Running any application with a faster processor usually makes the application work faster. However, your network connection and hard drive will limit the amount of data you can collect.

One of the most important things you'll need, especially if you're running Snort in NIDS mode, is a really big, reasonably fast hard drive. If you're storing your data as either syslog files or in a database, you'll need a lot of space to store all the data that the Snort's detection engine uses to check for rule violations. If your hard drive is too small, there is a good chance that you will be unable to write alerts to either your database or log files. For example, our current setup for a single high-traffic enterprise Snort sensor is a 100GB partition for /var (for those of you not familiar with Linux/UNIX systems, /var is where logs, including Snort data, are most likely to be stored). Some high-end deployments even use RAID arrays for storage.

You will need to have a network interface card (NIC) as fast or faster than the rest of your network to collect all the packets on your network. For example, if you are on a 100MB network, you will need a 100MB NIC to collect the correct amount of packets. Otherwise, you will miss packets and be unable to accurately collect alerts. A highly recommended hardware component for Snort is a second Ethernet interface. One of the interfaces is necessary for typical network connectivity (SSH,

Web services, and so forth), and the other interface is for Snorting. This sensing interface that does the "snorting" is your "Snort sensor." Having separate interfaces for sensor management and for network sniffing enhances security because it allows you to strongly restrict which machines are able to access the management interface without interfering with your promiscuous packet sniffing on the "snorting" interface.

Given the new improvements to the Snort engine, we also suggest not shorting your system on memory. Since Snort has a bigger memory footprint than earlier versions, it's useful to make sure that your sensors have enough RAM to handle the volume of traffic that you're getting. If you notice performance lag, it's worthwhile to make sure that your system is not swapping memory intensively.

Operating System

Snort was designed to be a lightweight network intrusion system. Currently, Snort can run on x86 systems Linux, FreeBSD, NetBSD, OpenBSD, and Windows. Other systems supported include Sparc Solaris, x86 Mac OS X, PowerPC Mac OS X and MkLinux, and PA-RISC HP-UX. In short, Snort will run on just about any modern OS.

> **NOTE**
>
> People can get into religious wars as to which OS is best, but *you* have to be the one to administer the system, so you pick the OS.

There is an ongoing argument regarding the best OS on which to run Snort. A while back, the ★BSDs had the better IP stack, but since Linux has gone to the 2.4 kernel, the IP stacks are comparable. Some of the authors prefer FreeBSD, but your preference might be different.

Other Software

Once you have the basic OS installed, you're ready to go. Make sure that you have the prerequisites before you install:

- autoconf and automake★
- gcc★
- lex and yacc (or the GNU implementations flex and bison, respectively)
- the latest libcap from tcpdump.org

> **NOTE**
>
> These are only necessary if you're compiling from source code. If you are using Linux RPMs or Debian packages or a Windows port installer, you do not need these. AND YOU SHOULD NOT HAVE THEM ON A PRODUCTION IDS SENSOR! Once you have

compiled and put Snort into place, all of the tools for compiling it should be removed from any sensor that you expect to put into your production environment.

You can also install the following optional software products:

- MySQL, Postgres, or Oracle (SQL databases)
- smbclient if using WinPopup messages
- Apache or another Web server
- PHP or Perl, if you have plug-ins that require them
- SSH for remote access (or Terminal Server with Windows)
- Apache with SSL capabilities for monitoring (or IIS for Windows)

There's more detail on installation in Chapter 5, "Installing Snort."

Exploring Snort's Features

In the Introduction, we provided you with a brief overview of Snort's most important features that make it very powerful: packet sniffing, packet logging, and intrusion detection. Before learning the details of Snort's features, you should understand Snort's architecture. Snort has several important components such as preprocessors and alert plug-ins, most of which can be further customized with plug-ins for your particular Snort implementation. These components enable Snort to manipulate a packet to make the contents more manageable by the detection engine and the alert system. Once the packet has been passed through the preprocessors, passed through the detection engine, and then sent through the alert system, it can be handled by whatever plug-ins you have chosen to handle alerting. It sounds complicated initially, but once you understand the architecture, Snort makes a lot more sense.

Snort's architecture consists of four basic components:

- The sniffer
- The preprocessor
- The detection engine
- The output

In its most basic form, Snort is a packet sniffer. However, it is designed to take packets and process them through the preprocessor, and then check those packets against a series of rules (through the detection engine).

Figure 4.1 offers a high-level view of the Snort architecture. In its simplest form, Snort's architecture is similar to a mechanical coin sorter.

1. It takes all the coins (packets from the network backbone).

2. Then it sends them through a chute to determine if they are coins and how they should roll (the preprocessor).

3. Next, it sorts the coins according to the coin type. This is for storage of quarters, nickels, dimes, and pennies (on the IDS this is the detection engine).

4. Finally, it is the administrator's task to decide what to do with the coins—usually you'll roll them and store them (logging and database storage).

Figure 4.1 Snort Architecture

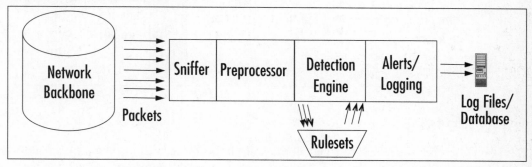

The preprocessor, the detection engine, and the alert components of Snort are all plug-ins. Plug-ins are programs that are written to conform to Snort's plug-in API. These programs used to be part of the core Snort code, but they were separated to make modifications to the core source code more reliable and easier to accomplish.

Packet Sniffer

A packet sniffer is a device (either hardware or software) used to tap into networks. It works in a similar fashion to a telephone wiretap, but it's used for data networks instead of voice networks. A network sniffer allows an application or a hardware device to eavesdrop on data network traffic. In the case of the Internet, this usually consists of IP traffic, but in local LANs and legacy networks, it can be other protocol suites, such as IPX and AppleTalk traffic.

Because IP traffic consists of many different higher-level protocols (including TCP, UDP, ICMP, routing protocols, and IPSec), many sniffers analyze the various network protocols to interpret the packets into something human-readable.

Packet sniffers have various uses:

■ Network analysis and troubleshooting

■ Performance analysis and benchmarking

■ Eavesdropping for clear-text passwords and other interesting tidbits of data

Encrypting your network traffic can prevent people from being able to sniff your packets into something readable. Like any network tool, packet sniffers can be used for good and evil.

As Marty Roesch said, he named the application because it does more than sniffing—it snorts. The sniffer needs to be set up to obtain as many packets as possible. As a sniffer, Snort can save the packets to be processed and viewed later as a packet logger. Figure 4.2 illustrates Snort's packet-sniffing ability.

Figure 4.2 Snort's Packet-Sniffing Functionality

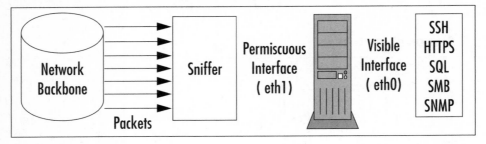

Preprocessor

At this point, our coin sorter has obtained all the coins it can (packets from the network) and is ready to send the packets through the chute. Before rolling the coins (the detection engine), the coin sorter needs to determine if they are coins, and if so, what sorts.

This is done through the preprocessors. A preprocessor takes the raw packets and checks them against certain plug-ins (like an RPC plug-in, an HTTP plug-in, and a port scanner plug-in). These plug-ins check for a certain type of behavior from the packet. Once the packet is determined to have a particular type of "behavior," it is then sent to the detection engine. From Figure 4.3, you can see how the preprocessor uses its plug-ins to check a packet. Snort supports many kinds of preprocessors and their attendant plug-ins, covering many commonly used protocols as well as larger-view protocol issues such as IP fragmentation handling, port scanning and flow control, and deep inspection of richly featured protocols (such as the HTTPinspect preprocessor handles).

This is an incredibly useful feature for an IDS because plug-ins can be enabled and disabled as they are needed at the preprocessor level, allocating computational resources and generating alerts at the level optimal for your network. For example, say that you're fed up with the constant rate of port scans of your network, and you don't want to see those alerts any more. In fact, you never want to hear about a port scan again. If that's the case, you can say you don't care about port scans coming into your network from the outside world and disable that plug-in while still continuing to use the others to examine other network threats. It's a modular configuration, rather than an all-or-nothing scenario.

Detection Engine

Once packets have been handled by all enabled preprocessors, they are handed off to the detection engine. The detection engine is the meat of the signature-based IDS in Snort. The detection engine takes the data that comes from the preprocessor and its plug-ins, and that data is checked through a set of rules. If the rules match the data in the packet, they are sent to the alert processor.

Figure 4.3 Snort's Preprocessor

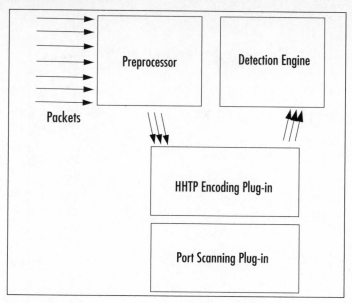

Earlier in this chapter, we described Snort as a signature-based IDS. The signature-based IDS function is accomplished by using various rulesets. The rulesets are grouped by category (Trojan horses, buffer overflows, access to various applications) and are updated regularly.

The rules themselves consist of two parts:

- **The rule header** The rule header is basically the action to take (log or alert), type of network packet (TCP, UDP, ICMP, and so forth), source and destination IP addresses, and ports

- **The rule option** The option is the content in the packet that should make the packet match the rule.

The detection engine and its rules are the largest portion (and steepest learning curve) of new information to learn and understand with Snort. Snort has a particular syntax that it uses with its rules. Rule syntax can involve the type of protocol, the content, the length, the header, and other various elements, including garbage characters for defining butter overflow rules.

Once you get it working and learn how to write Snort rules, you can fine-tune and customize Snort's IDS functionality. You can define rules that are particular to your environment and customize however you want.

The detection engine is the part of the coin sorter that actually rolls the coins based on the type. The most common American coins are the quarter, dime, nickel, and penny. However, you might get a coin that doesn't match, like the Kennedy half-dollar, and discard it. This is illustrated in Figure 4.4.

Figure 4.4 Snort's Detection Engine

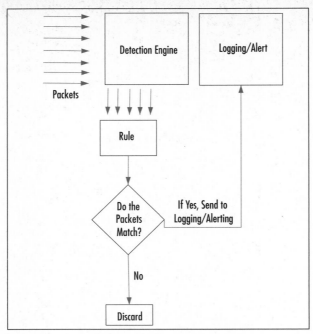

Alerting/Logging Component

After the Snort data goes through the detection engine, it needs to go out somewhere. If the data matches a rule in the detection engine, an alert is triggered. Alerts can be sent to a log file, through a network connection, through UNIX sockets or Windows Popup (SMB), or SNMP traps. The alerts can also be stored in an SQL database such as MySQL and Postgres.

You can also use additional tools with Snort, including various plug-ins for Perl, PHP, and Web servers to display the logs through a Web interface. Logs are stored in either text files (by default in /var/log/snort) or in a database such as MySQL and Postgres.

Like the detection engine and the preprocessor, the alert component uses plug-ins to send the alerts to databases and through networking protocols such as SNMP traps and WinPopup messages. See Figure 4.5 for an illustration of how this works.

Additionally, with syslog tools such as Swatch, Snort alerts can be sent via e-mail to notify a system administrator in real time so no one has to monitor the Snort output all day and night.

Table 4.1 lists a few examples of various useful third-party programs and tools.

Table 4.1 Useful Snort Add-Ons

Output Viewer	URL	Description
SnortSnarf	www.silicondefense.com/software/snortsnarf	A Snort analyzer by Silicon Defense used for diagnostics. The output is in HTML.
Snortplot.php	www.snort.org/dl/contrib/data_analysis/snortplot.pl	A Perl script that will graphically plot your attacks.
Swatch	http://swatch.sourceforge.net	A real-time syslog monitor that also provides real-time alerts via e-mail.
ACID	http://acidlab.sourceforge.net	The Analysis Console for Intrusion Databases. Provides logging analysis for Snort. Requires PHP, Apache, and the Snort database plug-in. Since this information is usually sensitive, it is strongly recommended that you encrypt this information by using mod_ssl with Apache or Apache-SSL. ACID is basically deprecated and not being developed further at this point; we strongly recommend you use BASE instead.
BASE	http://sourceforge.net/projects/secureideas/	A later Web front end for Snort based off the ACID codebase, the Basic Analysis and Security Engine is our current favorite way to query and analyze Snort alerts.
Demarc	www.demarc.com	A commercial application that provides an interface similar to ACID's. It also requires Perl, and it is also strongly recommended that you encrypt the Demarc sessions as well.
Razorback	www.intersectalliance.com/projects/RazorBack/index.html	A GNOME/X11-based real-time log analysis program for Linux.
Incident.pl	www.cse.fau.edu/~valankar/incident	A Perl script used for creating incident reports from a Snort log file.

Continued

Table 4.1 continued Useful Snort Add-Ons

Output Viewer	URL	Description
Loghog	http://sourceforge.net/projects/loghog	A proactive Snort log analyzer that takes the output and can e-mail alerts or block traffic by configuring IPTables rules.
Oinkmaster	www.algonet.se/~nitzer/oinkmaster	A tool used to keep your rules up-to-date.
SneakyMan	http://sneak.sourceforge.net	A GNOME-based Snort rules configurator.
SnortReport	www.circuitsmaximus.com/download.html	An add-on module that generates real-time intrusion detection reports.

Figure 4.5 Snort's Alerting Component.

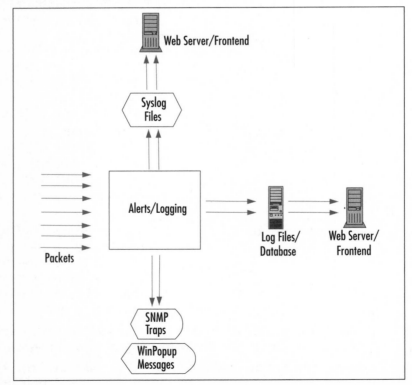

Using Snort on Your Network

Your IDS can use just one Snort system, or more than one if you need redundancy or coverage of multiple network segments. For example, it is possible to divide the task of network monitoring across multiple hosts. The chief benefit of dividing tasks within a segment is redundancy—if one element of the system goes down, the network can still be monitored and protected. However, for monitoring extremely large and busy networks, we advise you to place at least one sensor in every distinct segment so that you can capture all the local traffic, not just the traffic that's sent to the segments where your main sensors are.

The previously outlined network structure can be used for *passive monitoring* or *active monitoring*. Passive monitoring is simply the ability to listen to network traffic and log it. Active monitoring involves the ability to either:

- Monitor traffic and then send alerts concerning the traffic that is discovered
- Actually intercept and block this traffic

Snort is primarily used for active monitoring and alerting, though it will generally not intercept and block unless you are using Snort inline and configure it accordingly.

Don't intrusion detection applications also do signature-based and anomaly-based detection? Signature-based detection means that you predefine what an attack looks like and then configure your network monitoring software to look for that signature. Anomaly-based detection requires the IDS to actually listen to the network and gather evidence about "normal" traffic. Then, if any traffic occurs that seems different, the IDS will respond by, for example, sending out an alert to the network administrator. Snort's rule-based matching is an example of signature detection, and some of the alerts generated by the preprocessors are examples of anomaly-based detection.

After dealing with a postmortem on a compromised system, you'll be amazed at how helpful a Snort NIDS can be. On the flip side, it's also frustrating when your Snort system does not log a possible attack. Let's take a possible attack: the IMAP login overflow attack. In this case, an attacker tries a buffer overflow to cause a remote root exploit.

Snort can let you know that someone is sending an IMAP packet that contains the signature of an IMAP login overflow. Depending on how you have Snort set up, you can either monitor the output or you can be notified by e-mail. Great, now you can yank the Ethernet cable from the wall and look at the corpse and find some tools used to break into the system and what they plan on doing on your machine.

The rule for detecting this attack is:

```
alert tcp $EXTERNAL_NET any -> $HOME_NET 143 (msg:"IMAP login buffer \
    overflow attempt"; flow:established,to_server; content:"LOGIN";    \
    content:"{"; distance:0; nocase;                                   \
    byte_test:5,>,256,0,string,dec,relative; reference:bugtraq,6298;   \
    classtype:misc-attack; sid:1993; rev:1;)
```

This rule checks for any packet originating from the external network (defined by EXTERNAL_NET) to any system on the internal network (defined by HOME_NET) to port 143, which is the IMAP port. The *msg* variable defines what is sent to the Snort alert, and the rest of the information of the packet is content based. There are definitions on the type of attack (*misc-attack*), the SID number (1993), and the Bugtraq (www.securityfocus.com) reference on the attack *6298* (which you can find at www.securityfocus.com/bid/6298).

Then, there's the flip side: what happens when Snort does not detect an attack on your system? Take another UNIX system you have running. This one is running Apache with FrontPage extensions (gasp!). Someone finds a new overflow on FrontPage, writes a zero-day attack, and then he or she has your box. No IDS is perfect, and Snort will not catch attacks if there's no preprocessor code or signature written to cover them yet. This is one of the primary reasons why it's important to keep your rules as up-to-date as possible—you stand a greater chance of detecting attacks if you have the most recent rules. Because rules actively developed as new attacks show up on the Internet, Snort's detection capabilities continually improve in response to the evolution of new attacks.

Snort's Uses

Snort has three major uses:

- A packet sniffer
- A packet logger
- An NIDS

All the uses relate to each other in a way that builds on each other. However, it's easiest to put the packet sniffer and the packet logger together in the same category—basically, it's the same functionality. The difference is that with the logging functionality, you can save the packets into a file. Conversely, you can read the packet logs with Snort as well.

Using Snort as a Packet Sniffer and Logger

In its simplest form, Snort is a packet sniffer. That said, it's the easiest way to start. The command-line interface for packet sniffing is very easy to remember:

```
# snort -d -e -v
```

Note that the *-v* option is required. If you run Snort on a command line without any options, it looks for the configuration file (.snortrc) in your home directory. Snort configuration files are discussed in Chapter 5.

Table 4.2 lists Snort options and their function.

Table 4.2 Basic Snort Options for Packet Sniffing and Logging

Option	What It Does
-v	Put Snort in packet-sniffing mode (TCP headers only)
-d	Include all network layer headers (TCP, UDP, and ICMP)
-e	Include the data link layer headers

You cannot use options *–d* and *–e* together without also using the *–v* option. If you do, you get the same output if you use *snort* without any options:

```
florida:/usr/share/doc/snort-doc# snort -de
Log directory = /var/log/snort


Initializing Network Interface eth0
using config file /root/.snortrc
Parsing Rules file /root/.snortrc


+++++++++++++++++++++++++++++++++++++++++++++++++++++++
Initializing rule chains...
ERROR: Unable to open rules file: /root/.snortrc or /root//root/.snortrc
Fatal Error, Quitting..
```

Now, if you run snort with the *–v* option, you get this:

```
whiplash:~ root# snort -v
Running in packet dump mode


        --== Initializing Snort ==--
Initializing Output Plugins!
Verifying Preprocessor Configurations!
***
*** interface device lookup found: en0
***


Initializing Network Interface en0
OpenPcap() device en0 network lookup:
        en0: no IPv4 address assigned
Decoding Ethernet on interface en0


        --== Initialization Complete ==--


   ,,_     -*> Snort! <*-
  o"  )~    Version 2.6.0 (Build 59)
   ''''     By Martin Roesch & The Snort Team: http://www.snort.org/team.html
            (C) Copyright 1998-2006 Sourcefire Inc., et al.


01/22-20:27:44.272934 192.168.1.1:1901 -> 239.255.255.250:1900
UDP TTL:150 TOS:0x0 ID:0 IpLen:20 DgmLen:297
Len: 277
```

```
=+=+=+=+=+=+=+=+=+=+=+=+=+=+=+=+=+=+=+=+=+=+=+=+=+=+=+=+=+=+=+=+=+=+=+=+=+

01/22-20:27:44.273807 192.168.1.1:1901 -> 239.255.255.250:1900
UDP TTL:150 TOS:0x0 ID:1 IpLen:20 DgmLen:353
Len: 333
=+=+=+=+=+=+=+=+=+=+=+=+=+=+=+=+=+=+=+=+=+=+=+=+=+=+=+=+=+=+=+=+=+=+=+=+=+
[]
```

After a while, the text scrolls off your screen. Once you press Ctrl–C, you get an output summary that summarizes the packets that Snort picked up, by network type (TCP, UDP, ICMP, IPX), data link information (including ARP), wireless packets, and any packet fragments.

```
Snort analyzed 56 out of 56 packets, dropping 0(0.000%) packets
Breakdown by protocol:        Action Stats:
    TCP: 0        (0.000%)        ALERTS: 0
    UDP: 44       (78.571%)       LOGGED: 0
   ICMP: 0        (0.000%)        PASSED: 0
    ARP: 1        (1.786%)
  EAPOL: 0        (0.000%)
   IPv6: 0        (0.000%)
    IPX: 0        (0.000%)
  OTHER: 11       (19.643%)
DISCARD: 0        (0.000%)
===========================================================================
Wireless Stats:
Breakdown by type:
    Management Packets: 0    (0.000%)
    Control Packets:    0    (0.000%)
    Data Packets:       0    (0.000%)
===========================================================================
Fragmentation Stats:
Fragmented IP Packets: 0   (0.000%)
    Fragment Trackers: 0
   Rebuilt IP Packets: 0
   Frag elements used: 0
Discarded(incomplete): 0
   Discarded(timeout): 0
  Frag2 memory faults: 0
===========================================================================
TCP Stream Reassembly Stats:
    TCP Packets Used: 0      (0.000%)
    Stream Trackers:  0
```

```
        Stream flushes:    0
        Segments used:     0
        Stream4 Memory Faults: 0
================================================================================
Snort received signal 2, exiting
```

Because this isn't very useful for checking the data of the packets, you'll run snort with the −*dev* option to give you the most information:

```
whiplash:~ root# snort -dev
Running in packet dump mode


        --== Initializing Snort ==--
Initializing Output Plugins!
Verifying Preprocessor Configurations!
***
*** interface device lookup found: en0
***


Initializing Network Interface en0
OpenPcap() device en0 network lookup:
        en0: no IPv4 address assigned
Decoding Ethernet on interface en0


        --== Initialization Complete ==--


  ,,_      -*> Snort! <*-
  o"  )~   Version 2.6.0 (Build 59)
   ''''    By Martin Roesch & The Snort Team: http://www.snort.org/team.html
           (C) Copyright 1998-2006 Sourcefire Inc., et al.
01/22-20:28:16.732371 0:4:5A:F2:F7:84 -> 1:0:5E:7F:FF:FD type:0x800 len:0x5B
131.215.183.30:57535 -> 239.255.255.253:427 UDP TTL:254 TOS:0x0 ID:26121 IpLen:20
DgmLen:77
Len: 57
02 01 00 00 31 20 00 00 00 00 73 70 00 02 65 6E  ....1 ....sp..en
00 00 00 17 73 65 72 76 69 63 65 3A 64 69 72 65  ....service:dire
63 74 6F 72 79 2D 61 67 65 6E 74 00 00 00 00 00  ctory-agent.....
00                                               .

=+=+=+=+=+=+=+=+=+=+=+=+=+=+=+=+=+=+=+=+=+=+=+=+=+=+=+=+=+=+=+=+=+=+=+=+=+=+=+=+
```

```
01/22-20:28:18.354830 0:4:5A:F2:F7:84 -> 1:0:5E:0:0:2 type:0x800 len:0x3E
131.215.184.253:1985 -> 224.0.0.2:1985 UDP TTL:2 TOS:0x0 ID:0 IpLen:20 DgmLen:48
Len: 28
00 00 10 03 0A 78 01 00 63 69 73 63 6F 00 00 00   .....x..cisco...
83 D7 B8 FE                                        ....


=+=+=+=+=+=+=+=+=+=+=+=+=+=+=+=+=+=+=+=+=+=+=+=+=+=+=+=+=+=+=+=+=+=+=+=+=+=+
```

If you've used TCPDump before, you will see that Snort's output in this mode looks very similar. It looks very typical of a packet sniffer in general.

```
{date}-{time} {source-hw-address} -> {dest-hw-address} {type}
{length} {source-ip-address:port} -> {destination-ip-address:port} {protocol} {TTL}
{TOS} {ID} {IP-length} {datagram-length} {payload-length} {hex-dump} {ASCII-dump}
```

This is all great information that you're gathering, and Snort can collect it into a file as well as display it to standard output. Snort has built-in packet-logging mechanisms that you can use to collect the data as a file, sort it into directories, or store the data as a binary file.

To use the packet-logging features, the command format is simple:

```
# snort -dev -l {logging-directory} -h {home-subnet-slash-notation}
```

If you wanted to log the data into the directory /var/adm/snort/logs with the home subnet 10.1.0.0/24, you would use the following:

```
# snort -dev -l /var/adm/snort/logs -h 10.1.0.0/24
```

However, if you log the data in binary format, you don't need all the options. The binary format is also known as the TCPDump formatted data file. Several packet sniffers use the TCPDump data format, including Snort.

The binary format for Snort makes the packet collection much faster because Snort doesn't have to translate the data into a human-readable format immediately. You need only two options: the binary log file option *-L* and the binary option *-b*.

For binary packet logging, just run the following:

```
# snort -b -L {log-file}
```

For each log file, Snort appends a time stamp to the specified filename.

It's great that you're able to collect the data. Now, how do you read it? What you need to do is parse it back through Snort with filtering options. You also have the option to look at the data through TCPDump and Ethereal, as they use the same type of format for the data.

```
# snort [-d|e] -r {log-file} [tcp|udp|icmp]
```

The last item on the line is optional if you want to filter the packets based on packet type (for example, TCP). To take further advantage of Snort's packet-logging features, you can use Snort in conjunction with the Berkeley Packet Filter (BPF). The BPF allows packets to be filtered at the kernel level. This can optimize performance of network sniffers and loggers with marked improvements to performance. Because BPF filtering happens at a low level in the operating system, packets are eliminated from processing before they go through extensive processing at higher levels. To use Snort with a BPF filter, use the following syntax:

```
# snort -vd -r <file> <bpf_filter>
```

To help you find your feet, here are some examples of BPF filters. They are commonly used for ignoring packets and work with expressions (and, or, not).

If you want to ignore all traffic to one IP address:

```
# snort -vd -r <file> not host 10.1.1.254
```

If you want to ignore all traffic from the 10.1.1.0 network to destination port 80:

```
# snort -vd -r <file> src net 10.1.1 and dst port 80
```

If you want to ignore all traffic coming from host 10.1.1.20 on port 22:

```
# snort -vd -r <file> not host 10.1.1.20 and src port 22
```

For further information about BPF filters and their syntax, you can read the man page for tcp-dump, which uses the same syntax (www.hmug.org/man/8/tcpdump.html).

Using Snort as an NIDS

Now that you understand the basic options of Snort, you can see where the IDS comes into play. To make Snort an IDS, just add one thing to the packet-logging function: the configuration file.

```
# snort -dev -l /var/adm/snort/logs -h 10.1.0.0/24 -c /root/mysnort.conf
```

Your rules are in the configuration file, and they are what trigger the alerts.

Snort and Your Network Architecture

So how do you make Snort as useful as possible? You place your sensors as strategically as possible on your network, allowing them to see as much of the crucial network traffic as possible for your deployment. Where this is depends on several factors: how big your network is and how much money you can get your management to spend on Snort systems.

If you cannot get enough money to acquire enough Snort systems to achieve the optimal designs shown in Figure 4.6, you'll need to see what you can use from a practical sense. If you need to limit your spending, forego the system inside the router and just make sure you have the Snort systems inside the subnets you want to protect. In general, placing the sensors closer to your key assets will make it easier to see what those systems are sending and receiving. If you can't place sensors on all your subnets, choose wisely, and protect your most important machines with a sensor on their segments.

Many network administrators set up a screening router that acts as a poor-man's firewall and stops packets at the network level, usually by their well-known ports. The problem with this is that many packets can be rerouted through other ports.

However, if a packet does get past your screening router, it is useful to have an IDS sensor there to note the fact. The IDS sensor enables you to detect what you deem as attacks while enabling some filtering to hopefully catch some of the problems with the router. Figure 4.6 shows the IDS network architecture with a screening router.

Figure 4.6 An IDS Network Architecture with a Screening Router

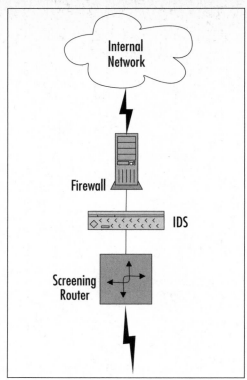

In this case, you would want to put an IDS system on the inside of your firewall and another in between your outside router and your firewall. Here, we're also assuming that your router is filtering some traffic through the access lists as well. You do not want your Snort system on the outside of your network because it will increase your false positive rate and leave your Snort system more vulnerable to attack (see Figure 4.7). Most important is the Snort system inside your firewall. This is the one you should monitor frequently for attacks. This system should trigger alerts only from potentially legitimate attacks and will produce many fewer false positives. However, the Snort system in between your router and your firewall will also provide you with useful information, especially for a postmortem if one of your systems does get compromised.

Many network architectures have a demilitarized zone (DMZ) for providing public services such as Web servers, FTP servers, and application servers. DMZs can also be used for an extranet (which is a semitrusted connection to another organization), but we'll stick to the public server DMZ architecture in this example. This is illustrated in Figure 4.8.

Figure 4.7 A Firewalled Network with Snort Systems

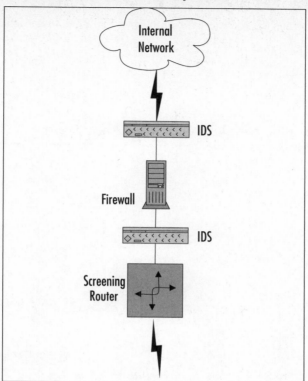

Figure 4.8 A Firewalled Network with a DMZ

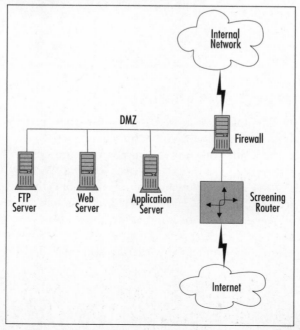

In this case, you would want three Snort systems: one inside the router, one inside the DMZ, and one inside the firewall. The reason for the additional IDS machine is because you have an additional subnet to defend. Therefore, a good rule of thumb for an optimal Snort deployment is:

- One inside the router
- One inside each subnet you want to protect

This is illustrated in Figure 4.9.

Figure 4.9 A Firewalled Network with a DMZ and Snort

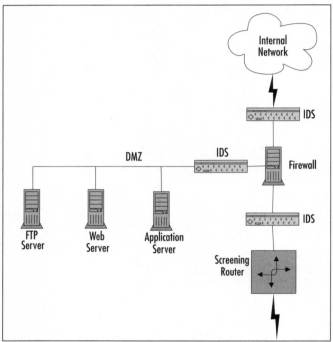

Snort and Switched Networks

Snort can be used on a switched network as well. Because switches are core infrastructure for most enterprises these days, monitoring them with Snort (or any other IDS) becomes more and more critical. Your switch can either be inside your router or inside your firewall.

A switch provides you with Layer 2 (Data Link layer on the OSI seven-layer model) configurability, including virtual LANs (VLANs), allowing you to subnet directly at the switch. Switches have also been used as overpriced routers. (You'll want to save your money if you're not using your switch's features.) In this case, you can connect the Snort system directly to the switch. The switch has a SPAN port (Switched Port Analyzer) port, which is where the Snort system will be connected. The Snort system then takes "copies" of all the packets to be analyzed, which are passed to it by the switch (see Figure 4.10).

Figure 4.10 A Switched Network

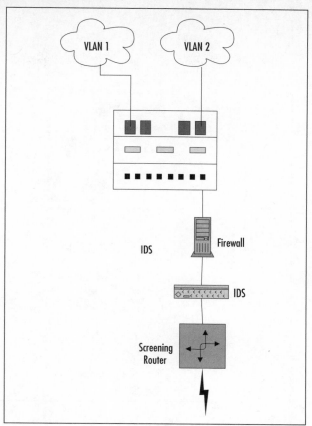

In this case, you'll have to decide which other ports on your switch you want to monitor with the SPAN port. You can monitor just one port, or you can forward all traffic from a VLAN or even all traffic from the switch to the SPAN port. If you take that last option, it is important to keep an eye on traffic levels and make sure that the SPAN port is not overwhelmed; a flooded SPAN port drops packets and can spike its processors. If you're trying to shove 10 ports running at 100Mb each through one port running at 100Mb, it won't work, and you might kill the performance of both your switch and your IDS (see Figure 4.11). We will discuss architecture and sensor placement in Chapter 6.

Figure 4.11 A Switched Network with Snort Systems

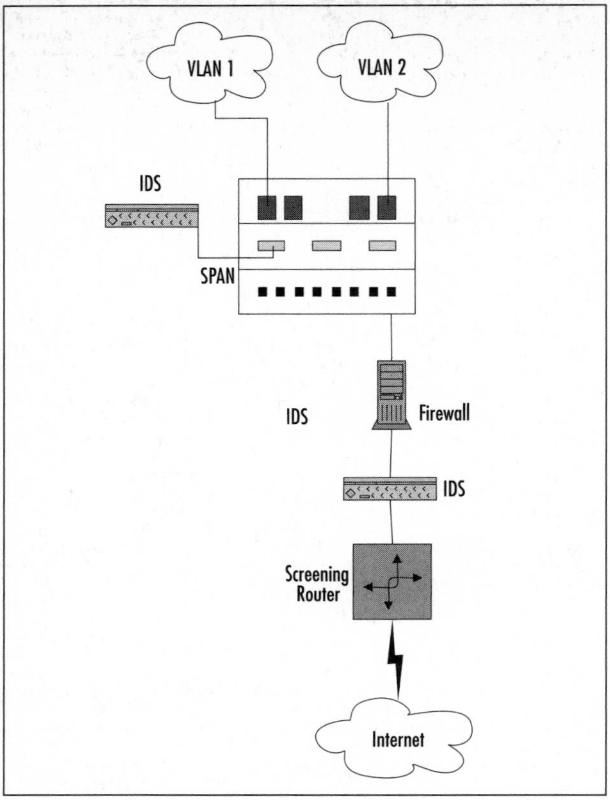

Pitfalls When Running Snort

Snort is a wonderful tool; however, like all tools, it has its pitfalls. Snort has three major pitfalls:

- Not picking up all the packets
- False positive alerts
- False negative alerts

Snort might not pick up all packets because of the speed of the network and the speed of the promiscuous interface. Snort's performance can also depend on the network stack implementation of the operating system. Ensure that your underlying infrastructure is as high end as possible to support your Snort deployment. In addition, to ensure optimal performance, it's a good idea to run some known attacks against the network segment that Snort is monitoring and ensure that it caught everything that it should have. Problems with dropped packets can lead to particular confusion with stream and flow reassembly, as well as missing critical network data.

False Alerts

False positives are when Snort gives you a warning when it shouldn't. Basically, a false positive is a false alarm. If you go with a default ruleset with Snort, then you will definitely get many false alarms. Why do IDSes behave this way? Well, it's better to get false alerts and whittle them down through tuning than it is to miss data that might have been a critical attack. So a new Snort installation can trigger a lot of alerts until you decide what is relevant to your network. The more open your network is, the more alarms you'll want to monitor.

On the opposite end, you can get false negatives. In other words, someone compromises a Snort-monitored system and your Snort system doesn't detect it. You might think that this doesn't happen, but when you get an e-mail from another system administrator describing a suspicious activity and your Snort system didn't pick it up, well, this is a very real scenario, and it usually happens with either out-of-date rulesets or brand-new attacks for which signatures have not yet been written. Make sure you keep your Snort rulesets up-to-date.

Upgrading Snort

Upgrading Snort can be quite painful for two reasons: the ruleset syntax may change, and the interface to the alert logs may change. We have found both to be obstacles when trying to upgrade Snort systems, and they can be quite a pain to deal with, particularly when you didn't want to have to do a forklift upgrade. If Snort changes its architecture to increase performance (as happened with the Snort 2.0 upgrade), you may experience a painful upgrade to any custom rulesets or alert interfaces in now-deprecated syntax and interfaces.

In addition, there are administrative foibles that may be encountered while creating rules, while reading logs, and while analyzing logs. When writing your own rules, make sure that they do what you think they're going to do, and test them to make sure that they alert you when they're supposed to. Rule syntax is tricky sometimes, and all it takes is one misplaced PCRE expression to cause either a whole lot of false positives or a whole lot of nothing. Having the rule in place won't help you much if the rule is incorrectly written. Similar attention should be paid when reading and analyzing logs—make sure that your security analysts understand the network and its context enough to be able to accurately identify when something is a false positive rather than a problem, and vice versa. We've seen unfortunate deployments where clueless analysts marked every noisy rule as a false positive and tuned it out, rather than figuring out what was triggering the rule and writing a targeted pass rule for allowed traffic. That sort of approach doesn't help anyone, and may negate much of the benefit of having an IDS in the first place.

Security Considerations with Snort

Even though you are using Snort to improve your security, making sure that your Snort system is as secure as possible will make the data more trustworthy. If someone breaks into your Snort system, there is no reason to trust the alerts that it sends, thereby making the system completely useless until after you wipe the disks and reinstall everything.

Snort Is Susceptible to Attacks

With that said, a typical Snort installation is subject to attacks, both in Snort itself and in the underlying OS. Why? You'll want to get in remotely (SSH), and you'll probably want to store the alerts in a database (MySQL or Postgres). In addition, you'll probably want to view the alerts with a spiffy interface that might require a Web server (Apache or IIS). Any listening service is a possible surface for attacks, and some driver attacks can even target a listening interface that isn't advertising any services in particular at all. This makes your Snort system just like any other application, so stay on top of security vulnerability announcements and OS security announcements for whatever platform you've chosen, just as you would for any other crucial network appliance.

Now, based on this information, you may have several ports open on your Snort system: SSH (port 22), HTTP (port 80), HTTPS (port 443), and possibly MySQL (port 3306) or Postgres (port 5432). Anyone with access to the network can use NMAP and port scan your sniffer directly on its nonpromiscuous interface. This is one of the major reasons that we advocate having a separate interface for management than for sniffing and for locking down the management interface to restrict access and services as tightly as possible. Reducing the potential attack surface will help keep your IDS secure.

This is something that needs to be addressed because all of the preceding applications have had quite a few serious security issues, historically. In addition to making sure that your applications are up-to-date, you need to make sure that your kernel is configured properly and that it also is up-to-date. You didn't think that running Snort allows you to disregard basic system administration practices; did you?

Notes from the Underground....

Snort Security Vulnerabilities

All applications end up with some discovered vulnerabilities eventually. Snort is no exception. Although Snort itself has had relatively few flaws, some of the vulnerabilities in recent years have been notable. The RPC preprocessor flaw of 2003 (http://xforce.iss.net/xforce/alerts/id/advise141) allowed denial of service or potential host compromise. The flaw in the Back Orifice handling in 2005 (www.osvdb.org/displayvuln.php?osvdb_id=20034) could be triggered by a single UDP packet, and the frag3 Preprocessor Packet Reassembly Vulnerability earlier this year (2006) could potentially allow malicious traffic to pass undetected (www.osvdb.org/displayvuln.php?osvdb_id=23501). Because of issues like these, it is critically important to pay attention to vulnerability research and announcement lists and to patch your systems as new software becomes available.

Securing Your Snort System

Even though your Snort implementation is locked down, your system itself might not be. Make sure you do the basics. There are some things you need to do without exception:

- **Turn off services you don't need** Services like Telnet, the Berkeley R services, FTP, NFS, and NIS should not be running on your system. In addition, make sure you don't have any of the useless services running; for example, echo, discard, and chargen.

- **Maintain system integrity** Tripwire is a freeware application that checks for those backdoors and Trojans you don't suspect. There are plenty of other freeware applications like Tripwire—AIDE and Samhain are two worth mentioning.

- **Firewall or TCP Wrap the services you do use** Services like SSH and MySQL should be TCP wrapped or firewalled because they have their own security holes as well, and access should be restricted to the smallest possible set of necessary users. For services that you can't TCP Wrap such as Apache, make sure you have them configured as securely as possible. IPTables is the latest version of the Linux firewall, and there are plenty of references on how to implement it.

- **Encrypt and use public key authentication as much as you can** You should enable public key authentication only for OpenSSH. Another thing you might want to consider doing for Apache for using it to view logs is to use Apache-SSL and use digital certificates for client-side authentication. This helps keep the obvious people out of your system through the usual compromisable channels.

- **Patch, patch, patch** We cannot stress this enough. Make sure you keep your patches and packages up-to-date as much as possible. Stay on top of applications you use and their security announcements—the same goes for any operating system you use. For FreeBSD/NetBSD/OpenBSD, make sure you keep your ports and packages up-to-date. For Red Hat Linux, make sure you stay on top of the updated RPMs. For those of you who are using Debian, you'll have the easiest time as long as you remember to run *apt-get update && apt-get upgrade* on a regular basis.

You can find more detail about securing your Snort system in Chapter 5.

> **NOTE**
>
> You can perform all these actions on your own, or you can use something handy like Bastille Linux (www.bastille-linux.org/) to do the majority of the necessary hardening for you.

Summary

This chapter provided practical knowledge of the open-source IDS called Snort, and how it can help you with your security concerns. You learned about the history of Snort, how the Snort architecture works, and system requirements.

Additionally, you learned about Snort's different uses, including using Snort as a packet sniffer, a packet logger, and an IDS. You also learned about some pitfalls with Snort, including false positives.

Finally, this chapter also touched on some security issues that you should consider when running a Snort system. It's critical to keep the system as secure as possible, especially as an active packet logger or IDS.

Solutions Fast Track

What Is Snort?

☑ Snort is a packet sniffer, a packet logger, and a network IDS.

☑ Snort runs on various operating systems and hardware platforms, including many UNIX systems and Windows. Hardware platforms include Intel-based systems, PA-RISC, PowerPC, and Sparc.

☑ We highly recommended having a large hard disk for data storage. Additionally, it is recommended to have two network interfaces on the system: one to run in promiscuous mode and the other for typical network connectivity (for example, SSH and HTTPS).

Exploring Snort's Features

☑ Snort's major components are the preprocessor, the detection engine, and the alert/logging components. All of Snort's components are implemented as plug-ins to increase flexibility.

☑ The preprocessor is used to take the packet data and process it before the data gets checked against the rules in the detection engine.

☑ The detection engine works by checking the data in each packet against a ruleset. Snort comes with a standard set of rules, but administrators can write their own as well.

☑ The alert/logging component takes the output of the data after it gets checked against the ruleset. The data can go straight into a log file in text or binary (TCPDump data) format. In addition, the data can be stored in SQL databases or be sent over the network through SNMP traps or WinPopup messages.

Using Snort on Your Network

☑ Snort can be used in various ways on your network. You can use it as a packet sniffer or as a packet logger in addition to for network intrusion detection.

☑ Snort can write packets in both text and binary mode. Binary mode is also known as TCPDump data format. This is not human readable, but it is a standard that Snort, TCPDump, and Ethereal all use to read and write network data. In addition to writing data, Snort can also filter the data to human-readable format from the binary format.

☑ Snort as an IDS needs to go on each of the private subnets you plan to monitor. It also helps to be able to place a Snort system behind the screening router as well.

Security Considerations with Snort

☑ Like any other application, Snort is subject to security vulnerabilities, including buffer overflows and DoS attacks.

☑ Snort should be upgraded on a regular basis to keep up-to-date with the latest signatures and the latest bug fixes with the application itself.

☑ In addition to securing the Snort application, you also need to secure the OS. This includes disabling unnecessary services, regularly applying patches, and proper configuration. It also includes encrypting sensitive traffic, such as login sessions with SSH and HTTP traffic with SSL.

Frequently Asked Questions

The following Frequently Asked Questions, answered by the authors of this book, are designed to both measure your understanding of the concepts presented in this chapter and to assist you with real-life implementation of these concepts. To have your questions about this chapter answered by the author, browse to **www.syngress.com/solutions** and click on the **"Ask the Author"** form.

Q: What OS can I run Snort on? Which one is best for performance?

A: Snort runs on many UNIX distributions, including Linux, FreeBSD, OpenBSD, NetBSD, Mac OS X, HP-UX, and Solaris. It also runs on Windows. The ★BSD distributions are known for the good implementations of the TCP/IP stack; however, Linux is comparable in kernel Version 2.4.x and higher.

Q: Why log the Snort data in binary format? What can I gain from this?

A: Snort's binary format is also known as the TCPDump data format. Logging the packets to binary format makes packet collection faster. It also means that later you can look through the data and filter it after collection instead of during. Logging in binary format saves time because Snort does not have to translate the data from binary to human-readable format on the fly.

Q: How does Snort use plug-ins?

A: Snort uses plug-ins in various ways. The preprocessor can take plug-ins to translate data such as HTTP data into a more readable format, or it can take plug-ins that check for patterns such as checking for port scans. The detection engine can take rulesets of various types, but it can also take plug-ins. The alerting/logging component is the most obvious place you'll see plug-ins. The plug-ins for alerting/logging include functionality for SQL databases, SNMP traps, and WinPopup messages.

Q: How do I keep my Snort system secure?

A: Keeping your Snort system secure is just a matter of good system administration. This includes proper configuration, disabling unnecessary services, regular updates, and encrypting sensitive data.

## Chapter 5

Installing Snort 2.6

Solutions in this chapter:

- Choosing the Right OS
- Hardware Platform Considerations
- Installing Snort
- Configuring Snort
- Testing Snort
- Maintaining Snort
- Updating Snort

☑ Summary

☑ Solutions Fast Track

☑ Frequently Asked Questions

Introduction

In this chapter, we?re going to be using our Snort sensor in a security server context, so we've got lots to consider with regard to our operating system choice. When choosing an operating system for your Snort sensor, you need to think about how the OS really affects the sensor in the long term. You need to be prepared to deal with patching, upgrading, and maintenance issues.

Choosing the Right OS

Our objective is pretty straightforward: build a solid Snort sensor that operates efficiently in any environment. We will be building a network security system; in particular, an IDS or IPS. As such, our system will be tasked with a variety of duties, including:

- Packet capture
- Packet analysis
- Writing data to disk
- Alerting
- Remediation or response

The operating system will be the tool with which you will solve your problems and perform the necessary work these duties require. The operating system will interact with many pieces of the system in order to accomplish its duties, and it must do so effectively and efficiently. To do this the operating system must rely on several critical components, including the following:

- CPUs
- Network interface cards (NICs)
- Disk drives
- RAM
- System bus

Snort will—for the most part—run on most operating systems (and of course, because you can get the source code, you can compile it for any OS you want if you are willing to spend a little time), but we should pay attention to the following additional areas which will allow us to begin closing in on the best operating system for our specific job:

- Performance
- Stability
- Security
- Support
- Cost

Performance

We define *performance* in terms of our end goal: to monitor and analyze *all* packets of interest traversing our network and, more important, to not drop *any* of those packets. The inherent dangers of dropped packets become evident in light of the various single-packet attacks, such as Witty.Worm and LAND attacks, and the potential devastating effects they can cause.

Let's assume that network packet capture and packet payload inspection will be our sensor's primary duties, while keeping in mind that logging, alerting, and bandwidth issues must also be considered.

How efficiently an operating system interacts with the CPU(s) will impact overall performance. In addition, how its network stack is implemented—and subsequently, how efficiently the stack, the NIC, and the NIC's device driver interact are also contributors to improved performance. Of the components mentioned earlier, the following sections will briefly cover the CPU and NIC as they pertain to operating system selection.

The Operating System and the CPU

Our operating system controls how our application interacts with our hardware, particularly the CPUs. It's worthwhile to explore the "behind the scenes" mechanisms operating systems employ to deal with this issue.

Of particular importance here is whether we are using a single processor, or dual-core or multiple processors. Different operating systems perform and behave differently depending on the number and type of CPUs present, understanding these differences will help you avoid performance bottlenecks that may be caused by Snort.. One way developers seek to improve application performance is through threaded programming. A *multithreaded program* enables the application to operate faster by exploiting concurrency in multiprocessor and dual-core processor systems, provided that this is supported by the operating system's thread implementation. *Concurrency* is defined as an application's capability to effectively utilize the number of CPUs available by simultaneously executing independent tasks. In order to achieve these benefits, the program must be multithreaded and the operating system must support multithreaded programs.

WARNING

It's important to note the difference between *threading*, which we'll define in terms of multithreaded applications, and *symmetric multiprocessing* (SMP), which is the execution of processes on multiple CPUs in parallel.

A particular operating system may or may not provide the best—or any—implementation of thread support for the given task at hand. Either an operating system's kernel provides support for multithreaded applications and thus allows for true concurrency to be realized, or its kernel does not support multithreaded applications in which an application's threads are multiplexed and cannot attain true concurrency.

We provide more information regarding this issue throughout this section. Read on for further explanation.

Usually an operating system creates a single process that has at least one thread with which an application is run. Some operating systems allow and support the capability for a single process to be composed of multiple threads. This is important because sometimes a single process needs to do multiple things at the same time (concurrently). Welcome threads and Symmetric Multi Processing.

Threads can be thought of as individual processes with special attributes that make them more efficient for today's more complex applications. The special attributes threads contain are shared process address space, global variables, registers, stack, state, and other process type information. In addition to sharing all of these resources, threads also maintain their own separate data as well. For instance, individual threads manage their own registers, stack, and state.

Threading is the mechanism by which applications divide a process into several parts, typically decomposed into independent units of work. SMP is the capability of an operating system to employ concurrency. For instance, consider that a graphical user interface must constantly refresh or redraw its screen while at the same time continue to be responsive to operations such as text input or servicing mouse clicks. Additional tasks that benefit from concurrency are computationally intensive applications such as those which perform complex matrix multiplication or intensive graphics rendering.

You can utilize the operating system, threads, multiple processors, and Snort in a single system to provide optimal performance, but you must pay further attention to the kernel's implementation of thread support to gauge how much, if any.

Although too exhaustive a topic to be covered in depth here, it is worth noting the common implementations of certain operating systems.

- **User-level thread.** A *user-level thread* is often referred to as an N:1 thread model because the implementation assigns each of the application's N number of threads onto a single kernel resource. This model is implemented entirely within an application and has no explicit support from the kernel. The kernel is completely unaware of the existence of threads. This implementation multiplexes user-space threads into a single execution context or process. Therefore, processes themselves compete against each other for the CPU; not threads within the process. This means user threads cannot truly realize parallelism or use of multiple CPUs.

- **Kernel-level thread.** A *kernel-level thread* employs a strict 1:1 model whereby each user thread maps directly to a kernel thread. The issue here is the potential overhead of the kernel creating and maintaining new threads, especially for applications that may use a lot of threads. However, the benefit is that the kernel can support individual threads within a given process, allowing a multithreaded application to truly exploit multiple CPUs.

- **Hybrid thread.** A *hybrid thread* strives to utilize the best methods found within the user-level and kernel-level implementations. A hybrid thread is often referred to as a two-level scheduler and employs an M:N model whereby M number of user threads map to N number of kernel threads. This implementation takes advantage of the speed and efficiency of user-level threads for thread creation, scheduling, and synchronization, and the capability of kernel-level threads to truly exploit multiple processors. Hybrid threads are typically multiplexed onto a pool of processes. The process pool size is determined by special algorithms in the scheduler/thread library that automatically adapts based on system characteristics such as the number of processors and number of threads.

NOTE

The key point is that threads are becoming commonplace and the majority of software applications today are being actively written to a threaded model. In addition, multiprocessor systems are becoming somewhat commonplace throughout the home, corporate America, and data centers by way of affordable and powerful new technologies and architectures, such as dual-core processors that offer a substantial increase in performance and a good return on investment.

So, the method in which the operating system interacts with the CPUs may be an area where you can realize performance gains. Although some applications cannot take explicit advantage of multiple processors, there are ways in which you can "help" these applications to exploit their use, provided your creative gene is up for it!

Table 5.1 lists some of the more popular thread implementations operating systems are using today.

Table 5.1 Popular Thread Implementations

Implementation	Type	Operating system
Native Posix Threads Library (NPTL)	Kernel-level threads—1:1	Linux
Scheduler Activation (SA)		
Kernel Scheduler Entities (KSE)	Hybrid threads—*M:N*	NetBSD 2.x and recent
Light Weight Kernel Threading (LWKT)		
Solaris Threads (LWP)		
FreeBSD 5.x and recent		
DragonFly BSD		
Solaris 9 and recent		
libc_r	User-level threads	FreeBSD 4.x and earlier
OpenBSD		

For additional information regarding these topics, visit the following Web sites:

- Linux NPTL: http://people.redhat.com/drepper/nptl-design.pdf

- FreeBSD KSE: www.freebsd.org/kse/index.html

- FreeBSD SMPng: www.freebsd.org/smp/index.html

- NetBSD Scheduler Activations (SA):
  http://people.freebsd.org/~deischen/docs/Scheduler.pdf

- Solaris LWP: www.sun.com/software/whitepapers/solaris9/multithread.pdf

- DragonFly BSD: www.dragonflybsd.org/goals/threads.cgi

At this point, we should note that Snort is *not* multithreaded and cannot explicitly take advantage of multiple CPUs by itself. Why isn't Snort multithreaded? Well, threaded programming has started to come into its own only within the past couple of years. Snort has been around for a while and has already been ported to several operating systems, and the effort involved in continuing to ensure that a multithreaded version of Snort would continue to be portable across its wide OS base would be too great. The decision was made to focus on maintaining Snort's current operating system support and adding features and functionality to it, instead of overhauling Snort to be a multithreaded application.

So, if Snort is not a multithreaded application, why mention threads? Because our Snort sensor will be performing a lot of tasks which could hinder overall performance, and it's essential that it be capable of performing optimally under any condition. Just because Snort isn't a multithreaded application doesn't mean it can't benefit from multiple processors. Noting the thread model implemented by our operating system candidate, we can now clearly define and implement our approach to attaining and sustaining sensor performance.

One way to take advantage of Snort on a multiprocessor system is to run multiple instances of Snort (ideally, one instance for each processor, assuming you have enough memory), each with its own Berkeley Packet Filter to direct traffic. With the support of process and interrupt request line (IRQ) affinity streamlined into the Linux 2.6 kernel, specific processes and IRQs can be strictly bound to particular CPUs. IRQ/CPU affinity provides the added benefit of keeping the top and bottom halves together and thereby reducing any cache misses. Additionally, you can take advantage of a multiprocessor system by employing Snort to perform the core IDS/IPS tasks of packet analysis and inspection, and use Barnyard as a separate process to perform the logging and output.

The Operating System and the NIC

Another important relationship to consider is that of the operating system and the NIC. Some NICs are better suited to the job of collecting packets off the wire than others are. The hardware and software (device driver) methods used to communicate between the NIC and the operating system are what make some NICs better suited for our sensor. These NICs also have advanced features for handling high-bandwidth networks and heavy sustained throughput, and certain operating systems can take advantage of these features better than others can. Let's clarify the definition of *network interface card* to mean the hardware device used to transfer data from the physical medium to the operating system/application. This allows for the inclusion of many specialty hardware devices such as those offered by Endace, Intel, Freescale, Sensory Networks, and numerous other hardware vendors specializing in high-bandwidth traffic capture. Although you can categorize these devices as NICs, they are better classified as hardware accelerators and network processors. These devices have advanced features such as zero copy transfer and on-chip processing. Compared with standard commodity NICs, and depending on the utilization of a given network, the specialty devices have a clear advantage but often come with a hefty price.

With today's increase in network bandwidth availability and throughput, the traditional methods that network card device drivers employed are no longer scalable—servicing an interrupt for each packet received on gigabit networks will suffocate the CPU and saturate the bus. FreeBSD's network stack had been superior in performance to Linux until recently, with the implementation of Linux's new network stack API, aptly named *NAPI*, which has been available since Linux kernel version 2.4.20. NAPI adapts to high-performance networks by disabling interrupts and switching to a polling-driven model for periods of sustained high throughput. That being said, the NIC must explicitly provide support for NAPI within its driver code.

Packet loss has become a primary concern for organizations which must satisfy the onslaught of compliance mandates required by state and federal law, but such performance requirements come at a price and typically require special/custom hardware to achieve such throughput.

Although we could probably tweak some kernel parameters to squeeze a few more ounces of performance out of our OS, it may not be the one best suited for the job on a number of other levels. So, as we can see, it's not really as simple as just using what you are told to use or what you are familiar with; it should be a compromise, with the compromise being toward increased sensor performance.

Stability

The stability of an operating system has a lot to do with how and where a system is and should be deployed. Let's face it; we're not going to use an operating system that reboots every two hours. This is where particular operating systems start to differentiate themselves. For instance, you wouldn't expect to find some of the relatively new Linux distros loaded up with sensitive data and placed on a production network (well you shouldn't, at least). The operating system's user community, and the support behind it, is a great place to turn to when trying to figure out whether the OS is suited for particular scenarios or duties.

Security

No matter how secure you believe your OS to be, it is critical that you closely monitor the security updates and patches for your OS. You can stay up-to-date by monitoring OS distro-specific mailing lists, or your distro's Web site. You also can use hardening tools such as Bastille (www.bastille-linux.org). Snort itself is susceptible to attack; it is a piece of software, just like any other application. You need to patch and update it regularly, just like you do your OS.

Because we are talking about an IDS, it seems appropriate to mention the security aspects of the operating system of choice. A commitment to security is a must on both the Linux distro end and the user's end. With that being said, security is a primary focus of Gentoo Linux and the Gentoo Linux Security Project, which is tasked with providing timely security information regarding potential security vulnerabilities in Gentoo Linux. In addition, package management is a vital component and many Linux distros make it extremely easy to manage, update, and upgrade your system. Gentoo uses the *portage tree* and *emerge* as the core of its packet management. The portage tree is similar to the ports collection on ★BSD and Debian's *apt-get*.

Support

Whether you get it from your commercial OS vendor, your IT support consultant, or the open source community, support should be a vital concern. If you're a one-man show within your organization's security department, you'd better have the necessary support available should you-know-what hit the fan. Your ability to quickly access information about the product you're using is critical. The open source community is pretty big, is available 24 hours a day, and best of all, is *free*.

Although it's not uncommon for organizations to standardize on commercial products purely for the support they get from a well-known brand, it's not always good to do so—and worse, it can be pricey.

Cost

Although cost may be an issue, it's certainly not recommended that you build your sensor from spare parts found under your desk. For the most part, it is very common for organizations to purchase highly optimized hardware to run their IDS sensors. It is a painstaking process to engineer a platform solely for the purpose of being a security-conscious sensor capable of effectively handling everything that an IDS is subject to: large numbers of packets at very high rates, deep packet inspection, computationally intensive operations, and so on.

If you potentially have a wide-scale Snort sensor deployment on your hands, cost will definitely be a factor sooner rather than later. Hardware cost, software licensing cost, support cost—all of these add up rather quickly, and can be pretty significant. You'll find that the majority of Snort sensors are deployed on Linux or BSD because these operating systems are free and do not require hefty licensing fees that commercially available operating systems charge. More often than not, even organizations that typically standardize on commercial operating systems such as Microsoft Windows or Sun Solaris will often deploy Snort on a Linux or BSD distribution.

Stripping It Down

No matter what OS you choose, the first things you need to do are strip out all the unnecessary pieces and harden the system to prevent your IDS from being compromised. Because we are going to focus on Linux, we will spend a little time talking about stripping Linux. After all, one of the biggest advantages of running this cutting-edge OS is that you can build it into anything you want, and better yet, you can fine-tune it to be some of the fastest-running software on the planet. This is one of the critical reasons why you should choose an OS with which you are familiar—you must know enough about it to effectively optimize and harden it.

- **Compiler options.** One of the first things we'll cover is the GCC compiler and its options, notably *CHOST*, *CFLAGS*, and *CXXFLAGS*. These are basically environment variables that the software building process uses to tell the compiler the type of optimizations with which the software will be built. Most of you know (and love) this process as *./configure && make*. Most Linux systems today are compiled for the i486 processor type, but many (such as Mandrake Linux) are compiled by default for i686. If your system is running an AMD Athlon, for example, it will perform better if the software running on it is compiled for that architecture.

- **Kernel tuning.** The Linux kernel is the core operating system upon which everything else in the system relies. Without the Linux kernel, there would be no Linux. Basically, the kernel stores information about supported devices that can be connected to the system and controls how they can interact with it. Although having more devices supported at the kernel level ensures that the system will be more automated when handling new devices (i.e., Plug and Play), it also adds to the software's overhead. Each device driver compiled into the running kernel, depending on whether it was compiled directly or added as a module, adds to its overall size. A good general rule of thumb is that the bigger the kernel gets, the slower it will be.

The most efficient *and secure* kernel is that which *only* has support for the devices that are physically connected to it. As we said previously, most distributions have room for improvement in terms of kernel efficiency. Why? The simple answer is that they ship with almost all devices supported by Linux and added to the system. One of the first steps you should take when building a high-performance Linux system is to enter your kernel configuration and remove *all* device driver support that you are not currently using. If you need to add a device, you can always compile it in later.

■ **Software and services.** Last, but definitely not least, is the area of software and system services. Another good Linux rule of thumb is to build the system with the smallest number of applications and libraries to get the job done. If you need more, you can add them later. This helps to eliminate conflicts down the road as well. Chalk it up to keeping your systems secure, organized, and clean. For example, there is absolutely no reason to have OpenOffice or XMMS (tools commonly used on Linux desktops) loaded on an IDS.

In terms of system services, it is good to maintain a similar mindset. Disable every service that you do not need to run on your system. For example, most modern Linux distributions come with GPM (the service that provides the capability to use a mouse on a command line) loaded and running by default. Although this may be right for some, it isn't right for us. Disable it. Unless you need it, there is no reason to have mouse support at the console either. The same rule might hold true for Apache (httpd) and other services. As we said, it all depends on your setup and particular needs.

■ **Additional items.** There are several other areas to look at when concentrating on overall system performance. For example, you can glean more performance out of the hard drive(s) and major file systems by using built-in tools such as hdparm. The file systems also have native performance-enhancing capabilities that you can call out in */etc/fstab* by way of options. For instance, Linux has the *noatime* option available for its file systems, which disables the "last accessed" time/date stamp functionality. In the case of files that receive heavy I/O, this option can reduce the overhead associated with time/date stamping considerably. Performance will increase as a result. This has obvious security implications if your sensor becomes compromised, but if your IDS sensor does become compromised you have bigger issues. See your file system's documentation for further details. *Virtual consoles* (the consoles that are available when using **Ctrl + Alt + F1** through **F6**; **F7** is usually reserved for X Windows) also consume system resources. Each available console uses RAM, regardless of whether the console is in use. You control these consoles via the */etc/inittab* file. Here is a sample file:

```
c1:1235:respawn:/sbin/agetty 38400 tty1 linux
c2:1235:respawn:/sbin/agetty 38400 tty2 linux
c3:1235:respawn:/sbin/agetty 38400 tty3 linux
c4:1235:respawn:/sbin/agetty 38400 tty4 linux
```

```
c5:1235:respawn:/sbin/agetty 38400 tty5 linux
c6:12345:respawn:/sbin/agetty 38400 tty6 linux
```

To disable virtual consoles, simply comment out the lines containing the consoles you will not need, or delete them entirely. You can add them back easily later if necessary. Usually, you need one or two consoles on a Linux system. Any more is simply overkill and a waste of resources. You'll be happy you did it.

Removing Nonessential Items

It's not a good idea to run an IDS with X Windows loaded; it just isn't necessary. When you install Linux, you are given the option of what to install. It's best to not include this component during the install, instead of trying to remove it after the fact. Bear in mind that your system will be far more efficient if it runs only the bare minimum it needs for Snort IDS.

It is recommended that you eliminate at least the following:

- The graphical base system
- Desktop environments
- Help and support documentation
- Office applications
- Games
- Multimedia
- Development tools[1]

Once you've removed these items, the system should be fairly slim, but if you have the time and ability, you should get even more granular with the system. Remove everything that is not crucial to your operation. For example, you can remove certain libraries, games, documentation, applications, and so forth to make the system as lean as possible. There's no need to have XMMS or Kaffeine on a machine that will most likely never have a user sit in front of it for these types of tasks.

Most major Linux distributors ship their products with an insane number of applications loaded by default; even if you don't see their categories selected in their respective Install/Remove Software applications, chances are they still have some residuals left on the drive. It will obviously take some serious time to filter through all of the packages (spanning five CDs), but if you have the time, it's well worth it.

Debian Linux

Now that we've pretty much beaten that horse to death, it's time to start talking about some real operating systems and distributions.

Debian is known for its adherence to the UNIX and free software philosophies, and for its abundance of options. The current release includes more than fifteen thousand software packages. Debian is also the basis for several other distributions, including Knoppix and Ubuntu. It is probably best known for its package management system, APT, and especially for its ease of use, its strict policies regarding the quality of its packages and releases, and its open development and testing process. Debian offers easy upgrades between releases without the need for rebooting, as well as easy, automated package installation and removal. The main advantages to apt-get are the speed at which it installs and the vast software arsenal at our disposal.

If there's anything to criticize Debian for, it's its slightly longer release cycles, which can lead to old and outdated packages. This criticism is countered to some degree by the existence of:

- **A backported packages repository.** These are updated package versions compiled in the stable environment.

- **Debian's testing branch.** This contains updated software that is more stable than its name might indicate. This branch can also become turbulent after a new release of the stable environment.

Another criticism is that some software and documentation are not available in the official Debian software repository because they do not satisfy the Debian Project's strict requirement of freeness. The project has deemed *nonfree* any documents that use the GNU Free Documentation License and contain sections that the author does not permit to be altered or removed. In such cases, you may obtain the software or documentation from third-party sources or from the auxiliary non-free section of Debian file servers. For example, the proprietary Adobe Acrobat Reader is not distributed by Debian, but other free PDF readers are, and you can download Acrobat Reader from Adobe and install it manually.

You'll find many production-class servers and even commercial solutions deployed on a Debian distro. It is extremely solid in terms of stability, security, and maintenance. Debian is an obvious excellent choice for use as a Snort sensor.

CentOS

The Community ENTerprise Operating System (CentOS) is built from publicly available, open source SRPMS provided by Red Hat. Its goal is to provide a free enterprise-class computing platform to anyone who wants to use it, and in that regard it is designed for people who need an enterprise-class OS without the cost or support of commercial Linux vendors. CentOS uses *yum* (Yellowdog Updater, Modified) for its update system and Red Hat Package Manager (RPM) for package management. Considering that CentOS is built from a very popular Linux distribution (Red Hat), it's a solid choice for use as a Snort sensor. Several projects out there today have standardized on the CentOS distro, including Asterisk@Home and SME Server.

For those familiar with working with and installing RPMs, CentOS should pose no problems to veterans or newbies when installing new packages. As noted earlier, CentOS does offer yum, which is an automatic updater and package installer/remover for RPM systems that automatically computes dependencies and figures out what things should occur to install packages. This makes it easier to maintain groups of machines without having to manually update each one using RPM.

The latest version of CentOS is 4.3. You can find more information at www.centos.org.

Gentoo

It seems that Gentoo has emerged as one of the more popular Linux distros among hardcore Linux users. It has support for tons of applications, is highly configurable, and has an excellent package system in *emerge*.

For those not familiar with Gentoo, the concept is simple: you're in control of what you want on your system. The most common way to install Gentoo is through the minimal install ISO. The minimal install image provides only the necessary pieces to get you into a minimal Gentoo environment and then relies on an Internet connection to install the rest of the distribution. The install is fairly straightforward, as long as you know your hardware and exactly what you are looking to do with your box.

What allows Gentoo to stand out among its Linux distro peers is its customizability. Gentoo uses the latest tested versions of the Linux kernel, userland utilities, and more than seven thousand programs in its portage tree.

That being said, Gentoo hasn't quite made it to the server room just yet. It's highly suited to desktop use and provides an excellent environment for those who love to tinker around with their operating systems. Gentoo's flexibility comes in terms of its install-from-source methodology. Gentoo's portage downloads the sources off a mirror site and compiles them for your system, automatically solving dependencies. Among the things that potentially keep Gentoo out of the server room are its relative newness, strong association with desktop use, and fairly lengthy installation process. Gentoo gives you the power and control you need to try out all kinds of things, but this may not be the best approach on a live production system. Gentoo's portage also allows for GCC optimization flags and "use flags," both of which have an influence on your system, and this flexibility makes Gentoo harder to troubleshoot. These kinds of settings in Gentoo allow you to really optimize your system, but if you're not careful, you could also seriously break it. Gentoo is evolving very quickly, but it may take some more time before it is considered for use on production servers; until then, more stable distributions will likely win out. Gentoo still provides a lot more fun and excitement on a box where you want to tinker and get to know your system. In Gentoo, you can emerge betas and Concurrent Versions System (CVS) versions, and recompile your packages with or without support for a feature. Gentoo is a great distro to learn about and play with Linux, but perhaps not as great for use as a production Snort sensor.

Let's see how easy and flexible Gentoo is by using *emerge* to install an application. Like *apt-get*, *emerge* will download the source code from the portage tree, check for any dependency issues and install any missing dependencies, compile the application, and then install the application into the running system. The thing to note here is that *emerge* compiles from source by default. You'll notice *emerge* is reminiscent of the FreeBSD ports tree.

Here we'll install MySQL and tell *emerge* to inform us of the packages/dependencies that we must install in order to successfully install MySQL on our system:

```
shell> emerge -p mysql

These are the packages that would be merged, in order:

Calculating dependencies... done!

[ebuild  N    ] dev-db/mysql-5.0.22  USE="berkdb perl ssl -big-tables -cluster -
debug -embedded -extraengine -latin1 -max-idx-128 -minimal -srvdir -static"

[ebuild  N    ] dev-perl/Net-Daemon-0.39  USE="perl -minimal"
```

```
[ebuild     U ] sys-devel/libperl-5.8.8-r1 [5.8.7]
[ebuild     U ] dev-lang/perl-5.8.8-r2 [5.8.7-r3]
[ebuild   N ] virtual/perl-Storable-2.15
[ebuild   N ] dev-perl/PlRPC-0.2018  USE="perl -minimal"
[ebuild   N ] dev-perl/DBI-1.51  USE="perl -minimal"
[ebuild   N ] dev-perl/DBD-mysql-3.0004  USE="perl -minimal"
[ebuild   N ] perl-core/Test-Harness-2.62  USE="perl -minimal"
[ebuild     U ] app-admin/perl-cleaner-1.04.1 [1.01]
[ebuild   N ] perl-core/PodParser-1.34  USE="perl -minimal"
```

Now that we know what the dependencies are, we can go ahead and install MySQL by using *emerge mysql.*

Gentoo's a great distro and is definitely worth a look. Its current stable version is 2006.0; you can find out more by visiting www.gentoo.org.

The BSDs

The BSD family of operating systems has a long tradition of stability and performance. There are four mainstream BSDs:

- FreeBSD
- NetBSD
- DragonFly BSD
- OpenBSD

Each BSD has its own niche. Usually the best methods in one are often adopted and implemented by the group. FreeBSD is generally known for its stability and maturity. NetBSD is generally known for its wide platform compatibility. DragonFly BSD is relatively new and is based on FreeBSD; DragonFly BSD branched from FreeBSD in 2003 with a radically different idea about how to approach SMP, concurrency, and basically the entire kernel subsystem. OpenBSD is known for its security and security-centric development processes.

OpenBSD

OpenBSD is often the operating system of choice for the pure fact that it has experienced only a single vulnerability within the past eight years. That's pretty impressive and makes a compelling case for selecting OpenBSD as the operating system of choice for a network intrusion detection system.

Furthermore, OpenBSD is largely known for its commitment to security in that its dedicated and experienced core team of developers run through all packages which ultimately are included in the base system, fixing or removing any potential security flaws, and then tightly integrate them so that they coexist and cooperate with the rest of the system in a nice, secure, symbiotic manner.

Although OpenBSD is only for those who are not fainthearted, its support community is fantastic; there is only slightly less documentation for Snort coupled with OpenBSD as there is for Linux and Snort. Although this may not be of major concern to most, it can be a sticking point with some security system administrators.

OpenBSD uses packages (precompiled binary packages) and ports (the same concept that FreeBSD uses) for its package management. Although the packages and ports collections do not undergo the same rigorous security audit as does the base system, every effort is used to ensure a rather high level of security.

Installing OpenBSD and Snort

Because OpenBSD is often the security analyst's OS of choice, let's explore this one a little further and put together a working Snort/OpenBSD sensor. OpenBSD is renowned for its attention to detail and security consciousness. It's also not the friendliest OS in terms of installation and supported user applications, but it's definitely a great choice for a security platform. The current release is OpenBSD 3.9, which was released May 1, 2006.

The easiest and preferred method of installation is via CD-ROM. OpenBSD encourages people to support the project by ordering the Official CD-ROM set, but you can always make your own. *cd39.iso* is the ISO image that you should use to create the bootable CD-ROM. It contains the widest selection of drivers, and is the recommended choice for booting from CD-ROM.

Before actually diving into the OpenBSD installation, we need to perform some due diligence and plan for what we want to end up with in terms of our Snort sensor. We'll need to verify that our current platform's hardware is supported by looking at the hardware compatibility page, our disk partitioning scheme, and network settings, and determine whether any windowing system will be used. Once we are able to answer these questions we can move along to the next step.

If you were not using the Official CD-ROM set, you'd have to burn your own CD using a tool such as *cdrecord*.

Now that we have our installation media ready we can start the installation process. Upon successful boot, you should see tons of text messages scrolling by. Don't worry if you can't read them all, as these messages are saved in */var/run/dmesg.boot* and you can view them by issuing the *dmesg* command.

You will then see the following:

```
rootdev=0x1100 rrootdev=0x2f00 rawdev=0x2f02
erase ^?, werase ^W, kill ^U, intr ^C, status ^T
(I)nstall, (U)pgrade or (S)hell? I
```

In our example, we will be performing an install. So, the next thing you should see is the install program's welcome message:

```
Welcome to the OpenBSD/i386 3.9 install program.


This program will help you install OpenBSD in a simple and rational way. At any
prompt except password prompts you can run a shell command by typing '!foo', or
escape to a shell by typing '!'. Default answers are shown in []'s and are selected
by pressing RETURN. At any time you can exit this program by pressing Control-C and
then RETURN, but quitting during an install can leave your system in an
inconsistent state.


Specify terminal type: [vt220] Enter
kbd(8) mapping? ('L' for list) [none] Enter
```

The next prompt advises us to back up our data before proceeding and tries to ensure this by requiring our interaction:

```
Proceed with install? [no] y
```

Now we move on to setting up the disks. This process requires two steps: first we define the OpenBSD slice, and then partitions are created out of this slice. OpenBSD will try to determine the hard disk(s), prompt for the disk to be used as the root disk, and ask whether the entire disk should be used. For our example, our disk is wd0 and the entire disk will be used:

```
Available disks are: wd0.
Which one is the root disk? (or done) [wd0] Enter
Do you want to use *all* of wd0 for OpenBSD? [no] yes
```

This will result in a standard Master Boot Record and partition table being written out to disk which consists of one partition equal to the size of the entire hard disk, set to the OpenBSD partition type and marked as the bootable partition. This is the typical choice for most production uses of OpenBSD.

The next step is to create the disk label, which is where we will create the file systems and swap space for our OpenBSD partition. Partitioning is well beyond the scope of this chapter; you can find more information in the OpenBSD installation docs. That being said, we will not spend too much time describing the setup of disk labels, but we should mention that OpenBSD requires that we create at least two partitions—namely, *a* and *b*—before the installation process continues. Partition *a* is used for the root (/) file system and *b* is used for swap. After we have created and written our disk labels, it's time to define our mount points and file system choices. Fortunately, we configured out mount points during the disk label process. The OpenBSD install at this point just verifies our selections and continues.

The next steps are pretty trivial, really. We now have to set our system's host name, configure networking, set the password for the root account, and choose which file sets to install. Once we've installed the base system, we can install Snort.

There are two ways to install Snort on OpenBSD: via package and via port. The OpenBSD ports tree is derived from FreeBSD and is essentially a set of makefiles for controlling every aspect of compiling and installing the application on the system. *Ports* are instructions for compiling source code, and *packages* are precompiled ports. It is worth noting that compiling an application from the ports tree does not install the "port" onto the system; rather, it creates a package. OpenBSD recommends installing prebuilt packages and considers packages to be the goal of their work, not the ports themselves.

To use the ports tree first you must install it. Once installed and configured, the ports tree is located in */usr/ports*. Now, you must simply find the appropriate subdirectory for the application in question and type *make*.

We'll use a prebuilt package of Snort. One of the best places to find prebuilt packages is via the OpenBSD Web site for the particular version of OpenBSD being used. For our example, we would look in www.openbsd.org/3.9_packages/i386.html for the application we wanted to install. Once we've found it, we can install it using *pkg_add*. Make sure you have root permissions before installing; alternatively, you can use *sudo*:

```
sudo pkg_add -v snort-2.4.3
```

It's always a good idea to use the −*v* flag to get as much verbose output during the install as possible for debugging purposes. During the install, you'll probably run into dependency issues, but OpenBSD has this all figured out. When installing packages (or even ports, for that matter), *pkg_add* is capable of handling dependency issues, and as such ensures that all dependencies are installed before continuing to the application at hand.

At this point, Snort should be installed. Surely we will need to address some tweaking and configuration, so read on to learn more about configuring and tuning our Snort sensor.

Windows

We've saved this one for last. Although we strongly recommend against using a Windows system as a Snort sensor, in some environments you may not have a choice. A Windows machine offers little or no capability to remove unnecessary services which (as we've already discussed) is essential for an IDS sensor. This fact may pose a performance and security risk from the standpoint of a system placed at a strategic location within a network and having extreme visibility to potentially malicious traffic.

See Chapter 6 for more details on installing and configuring Snort on a Windows Machine.

Bootable Snort Distros

A bootable CD can sometimes make life much easier for security analysts and systems administrators. Suppose you want to "try out" a certain Linux distro, but you don't want to go through the hassle of partitioning your drive and configuring your system to do it. Maybe your primary system has crashed and you're trying to get it back online, or maybe you want to perform some forensics operations. There are plenty of uses for bootable CDs.

Let's put this in terms of why it would be beneficial to have a bootable CD for our application of using and building a Snort sensor. Getting a Snort sensor up and running isn't an instantaneous process. We need to install core libraries and dependencies, along with any databases (MySQL, PostgreSQL) and graphical user interfaces (ACID, BASE), not to mention finding the necessary and appropriate hardware on which to deploy it. It could take a security analyst half a day—if not an entire day—to get a Snort sensor up and running.

This could prove handy for pen testing, if you're constrained by not being able to use your own equipment for fully disclosed tests; also, it's useful for red teaming and social engineering, where, by chance, you get access to the office/computer of an employee who is out to lunch or on vacation, or you score the big one: the data center.

The following bootable CDs may prove useful for a variety of situations:

- Knoppix-STD
- Auditor
- Arudius
- Hackin9
- Pentoo
- Trinux
- SENTINIX

- Plan-B
- Bootable Snort Project

The Network Security Toolkit As a Snort Sensor

The concept and attraction of a bootable Snort sensor is to provide someone who has little to no experience with Snort or Linux with a fully configured Snort IDS in minutes. It also provides experienced security analysts the ability to quickly deploy additional Snort sensors on their networks. However, its primary benefit is the speed with which such a CD provides a fully configured Snort; you can stand up and deploy a Snort sensor in mere minutes. A secondary benefit is the fact that all the dependencies and additional Snort niceties, such as MySQL and BASE, come preinstalled and preconfigured; it's just a matter of tuning such details as database name, and so on.

Let's look at using the Network Security Toolkit (NST) as a Snort sensor. To get started all you need to do is ensure that the target system meets some minimal system requirements, such as RAM and hard-disk capacity, and the capability to boot from the media (often CD or DVD). What you get is a fully functioning Linux system with some really useful software and tools for performing a variety of tasks.

Booting the System

Booting into the live system is really a trivial process. You are literally prompted the entire way through the boot and configuration process. The system presents you with a range of options, such as which base system/image to use and any additional device/application support required.

Configuring NST's Web User Interface

Assuming that you've started up NST using the default boot options and that it was assigned the address 192.168.20.15, you should be able to access the Web User Interface (WUI) by pointing your browser at https://192.168.20.15/nstwui. It's important to note use of *https* in the preceding URL, as secure access is the only access method permitted. To start the NST WUI, click the link labeled **NST WUI**. That's it.

Configuring Snort

One of the really cool things about bootable CDs is that they make it so easy to use and configure the available software. For instance, with NST, Snort can be up and running and fully configured in two steps. Using NST's WUI, you just locate the **Intrusion Detection** heading in the **Networking** table and click on the **Snort** link. You will be taken to the Snort configuration page, which is where you define the interface on which to listen, the rules file location, and any command-line options. At this point, you can start Snort by clicking the big gray button labeled **Start Snort**. That's all there is to it, really.

To find out more regarding bootable CDs, visit the following Web sites:

- http://networksecuritytoolkit.org
- http://santechsecurity.net

Hardware Platform Considerations

When evaluating hardware for your Snort sensor you must be very careful. The choices you make here are absolutely critical to the sensor's performance and stability. It's not uncommon to spend many weeks selecting and evaluating the necessary and correct hardware components for use in a Snort sensor. Fortunately, there are vendors from which you can purchase optimized hardware platforms for use in security contexts. In this section, we will briefly discuss the considerations you should take when building a Snort sensor. Just remember the bottom line: don't make compromises to the point where you end up with a minimally equipped Snort sensor.

When building/selecting your sensor, you should consider the following components:

- The CPU
- Memory
- The system bus
- The NIC
- Disk drives

The CPU

What can we really say here? The CPU is going to be put through its paces, especially when it comes to packet payload processing. You'll need to ensure that you have the fastest processor you can afford, while keeping in mind that you wouldn't want just any old processor responsible for certain tasks, such as extremely high-performance network segments. Remember, although the CPU is a critical component, it is only as good as the weakest component within the system.

Memory

If there's one thing you don't want to skimp on, it's memory, especially if your Snort sensor will be looking at large numbers of flows or very large address blocks. Next to the CPU itself, memory is one of the chief factors affecting overall system performance. Adding memory can often make more of a difference than getting a newer and/or faster CPU.

Let's briefly discuss how memory works in the grand scheme of things. The CPU contains several controllers that manage how information travels between it and the other components in the system. The memory controller is part of the CPU chipset and establishes the information flow between memory and the CPU. The memory bus goes from the memory controller to the system's memory sockets. Newer systems have a frontside bus (FSB) from the CPU to main memory, and a backside bus from the memory controller to level 2 (L2) cache. In order for data to be retrieved, the CPU must send a signal to the memory within the systems clock cycle which varies depending upon the speed of the memory and bus speed.

The speed of the system is often thought to be exclusively tied to the speed of the processor. This is mostly false as system performance is dramatically affected by the speed at which data can be transferred between system memory and the CPU. It is easy to see that the system bus and memory are critical system components when it comes to determining the overall speed and efficiency of the system – not just the CPU. This is true because all data that is to be processed by the CPU ultimately comes from memory. It's true that memory can be a more cost effective alternative to increasing system performance.

The system also contains a memory known as cache memory. cache memory is typically rather small, comprised usually of 1MB of high-speed memory, resides right next to the CPU and is tasked with delivering the most frequently accessed data to the CPU. It takes a fraction of the time, compared to normal memory, for the CPU to access the data in cache memory. The main concept behind cache memory is that the data most often needed by the CPU is often in cache memory 20 percent of the time. Cache memory tracks instructions, putting the most frequently used instruction at the top of the list. Once the cache is full, the least used instruction is dropped. Today most cache memory is incorporated into the CPU. It can also reside just outside the CPU. Cache that is closest to the CPU is labeled level 1 (L1) cache; the next closest is L2 cache, and so on. According to HowStuffWorks.com, here are some of the memory types:

- **SRAM.** Static random access memory uses multiple transistors, typically four to six, for each memory cell, but doesn't have a capacitor in each cell. It is used primarily for cache.

- **DRAM.** Dynamic random access memory has memory cells with a paired transistor and capacitor requiring constant refreshing.

- **FPM DRAM.** Fast page mode dynamic random access memory was the original form of DRAM. It waits through the entire process of locating a bit of data by column and row and then reading the bit before it starts on the next bit. Maximum transfer rate to L2 cache is approximately 176 MBps.

- **EDO DRAM.** Extended data-out dynamic random access memory does not wait for all of the processing of the first bit before continuing to the next one. As soon as the address of the first bit is located, EDO DRAM begins looking for the next bit. It is about 5 percent faster than FPM DRAM. Maximum transfer rate to L2 cache is approximately 264 MBps.

- **SDRAM.** Synchronous dynamic random access memory takes advantage of the burst mode concept to greatly improve performance. It does this by staying on the row containing the requested bit and moving rapidly through the columns, reading each bit as it goes. The idea is that most of the time the data the CPU needs will be in sequence. SDRAM is about 5 percent faster than EDO RAM and is the most common form in desktops today. Maximum transfer rate to L2 cache is approximately 528 MBps.

- **DDR SDRAM.** Double data rate synchronous dynamic random access memory is just like SDRAM, except that it has higher bandwidth, meaning greater speed. Maximum transfer rate to L2 cache is approximately 1,064 MBps (for 133 MHz DDR SDRAM).

Memory's Influence on System Performance

As stated above, memory can dramatically increase system performance. With too little memory, the system resorts to utilizing virtual memory where the system's hard disks are used to supplement memory. A system's hard disk is far slower than system memory and too much 'swapping' can cause the system to be slowed down significantly. In an average computer, it takes the CPU much less time to access RAM compared to accessing the hard drive. The CPU searches for instructions stored in memory. If those instructions are not stored in memory, they will have to be transferred from the hard disk to memory—such is the case of "loading" an application. So, a greater amount of memory means more instructions are able to fit into memory and, therefore, many larger programs can be run at once.

Virtual Memory

When a system does not have enough memory, virtual memory is used. As we mentioned above, virtual memory is a method that extends the system's available physical memory by utilizing the system's hard disk.

The most obvious and main drawback to virtual memory as compared to main memory is the performance degradation. Access times for hard drives are considerably slower than access times for main memory. We recommend that you take a very liberal approach to determining memory capacity, and even if a miscalculation creeps in, it's always better to make sure you have more than enough memory in your sensor.

The System Bus

For a long time now, most of our PCs have been stuck in a bandwidth quandary. We've been saddled with a 33 MHz/32-bit Peripheral Component Interconnect (PCI) bus for years. The entire bus can be completely used up with a measly 133 MB/second of throughput (1 MB = 1 megabyte = 8 megabits = 8 Mbits). In fact, the PCI bus often peaks at between 100 and 110 MB/second. That may sound like a lot, but consider this: hard drives nowadays often use the ATA-133 standard, which could potentially fill the entire PCI bus alone. Sure, you can't do it with a single drive, but use a couple of high-performance drives at once and you can come very close. Now add the bandwidth of FireWire, USB 2, and a 10/100/1000 PCI network card; if you are using Gigabit Ethernet, you can potentially fill the entire PCI bus with that alone.

PCI

Standard PCI is a parallel-based communications technology that employs a shared bus topology to allow for communication among the various devices present on the bus. Each PCI device (i.e., network card, sound card, RAID card, etc.) is attached to the same bus, which communicates with the CPU.

There are several devices attached to the bus—this means that there has to be a way for deciding which device gets access to the bus and at what time. When a device tales control of the bus, it becomes a Bus master.

The Southbridge routes traffic from the different I/O devices on the system (i.e., hard drives, USB ports, Ethernet ports, etc.) to the Northbridge, and then on to the CPU and/or memory. The Southbridge, Northbridge, and CPU combine to fill the host or root role, which runs the show by detecting and initializing the PCI devices as well as controlling the PCI bus by default.

The theoretical maximum amount of data exchanged between the processor and peripherals for standard PCI is 532 MB/second.

PCI-X

According to Wikipedia, "PCI-X is a revision to the PCI standard that doubles the clock speed from 66 MHz to 133 MHz, and hence the amount of data exchanged between the CPU and peripherals. PCI-X is also a parallel interface that is directly backward compatible with all but the oldest PCI devices. The theoretical maximum amount of data exchanged between the processor and peripherals for PCI-X is 1.06 GB/second." PCI-X is more fault tolerant than PCI and provides the ability to reinitialize a faulty card or take it offline before computer failure occurs.

Table 5.2 outlines the specifications of the different varieties of PCI-X available.

Table 5.2 PCI-X Specifications

Type	Bus width	Clock speed	Bandwidth
PCI-X 66	64 bits	66 MHZ	533 MB/second
PCI-X 133	64 bits	133 MHz	1.06 GB/second
PCI-X 266	64 bits	133 MHz, Double Data Rate	2.13 GB/second
PCI-X 533	64 bits	133 MHz, Quad Data Rate	4.26 GB/second

PCI-Express

PCI Express (PCIe) is an implementation of PCI that utilizes a much faster serial communications protocol and more efficient point-to-point bus physical bus architecture. A point-to-point topology essentially provides each device its own dedicated bus or link. The overall effect of this new topology is increased bandwidth.

You can equate increased bandwidth with increased system performance. You've no doubt long known that to get the most out of your processor you need to get as much information into it as possible, as quickly as possible. Chipset designers have consistently addressed this by increasing FSB speeds. The problem with this is that FSB speed increases the speed of transfer between the memory and CPU, but often you've got data that's coming from other sources that needs to get to the memory or CPU, such as drives, network traffic, and video. PCIe addresses this problem head-on by making it much faster and easier for data to get around the system.

The specification for PCIe defines link widths of x1, x2, x4, x8, x12, x16, and x32. A single lane is capable of transmitting 2.5 GB/second in each direction, simultaneously.

There are competing technologies to PCIe. Some of these technologies are InfiniBand, HyperTransport, and RapidIO.

Theoretical Peak Bandwidth

Typically when we talk of bus bandwidth we're really describing the bus's theoretical peak bandwidth. Let's dig in a little further and take a closer look at theoretical peak bandwidth.

For a 100MHz bus, it runs at 100 million clock cycles per second (100 MHz) and delivers 8 bytes on each clock cycle, its peak bandwidth is 800 million bytes per second (800 MB/second). For a 133MHz bus, it runs at 133 MHz and delivers 8 bytes per clock cycle, its bandwidth is 1,064 MB/second (or 1.064 GB/second).

Here's how we perform the calculation:

$8\ bytes\ *\ 100MHz\ =\ 800\ MB/s$

$8\ bytes\ *\ 133MHz\ =\ 1064\ MB/s$

Dual vs. Single Bus

It's worth making sure the motherboard you are using has dual PCI buses. For the most part, we will be deploying our Snort sensor on x86-ish boxes and not on more expensive, embedded systems with 140 GB/second capable switch fabric backplanes. In our Snort sensor, the NIC or NICs are going to have to handle a lot of packets. In order to deploy sensors that can adequately handle the sustained traffic rates of today's corporate networks, we're going to need to be able to handle extremely large numbers of packets and phenomenal sustained data transfer rates. To ensure that our NICs are doing their job effectively (handling packets and transferring those packets, via the bus, to the CPU for processing), we need to make sure that our NICs have their own dedicated bus to the CPU. We need an unencumbered, clean path between the NIC and the CPU. This is necessary because if we also have a RAID card, graphics card, or any other peripherals on the sensor, we need to ensure that any critical paths are clean and open; hence, having a separate bus for our NICs. The more devices that share the bus, the less bus bandwidth is available for each device.

The NIC

Because this component is directly responsible for seeing and getting the packets off the wire, it's highly recommended that you make sure you conduct the proper research before selecting a NIC.

Numerous NICs are available for a variety of purposes. Some are designed and geared for the typical user, others are geared for more advanced applications such as servers, and yet others are designed for more specialized applications to include guaranteed line-rate packet capture and the ability to support ATM, POS, and the like.

We're not going to dive deeply into the area of specialty cards, but they do warrant a few sentences. These cards are not your run-of-the-mill commodity NICs. These devices have some pretty extraordinary capabilities and are designed to offload the packet-capturing overhead found in most commodity NICs by removing the system's CPU from the entire process. They do this by eliminating the typical interrupt model of the normal packet reception of traditional NICs. Not only do these devices guarantee some pretty high throughput, but also they are capable of filtering, load balancing, and regular expression functionality, all at the hardware level. Although regular expression capabilities may have drawbacks—for instance, no support or limited support for pcre-based matches—due to the nature of regular expressions, it is currently too cost inefficient to implement such circuitry on these devices. In fact, these specialty devices may be worth their weight in gold due to their tremendous amount of processing which can help eliminate the unwanted traffic at the card level before it reaches the system's critical resources, such as memory and CPU. All of this high performance and functionality comes with a pretty steep price: the typical starting price is around $5,000.

Although most of us can only wish that our budgets included funds for such endeavors, all hope for high-performance network packet capture is not lost. There are ways to attain high performance on a system with a traditional NIC. On Linux there is NAPI, the new API mentioned earlier, which was a development task that was aimed at making the Linux networking subsystem more performance minded. The concept of NAPI is based on the fact that polling can effectively and significantly increase packet reception and throughput while decreasing the load on the CPU, especially on high-speed interfaces. NAPI works by using a combination of interrupts and polling. For instance, when new frames are received they are placed on the device's input queue; if new frames are received while the kernel is still processing frames on the queue, there is no need to issue interrupts. Only when the queue is empty are interrupts enabled again. In order for the advantageous aspects of NAPI to be available, the device and its driver must support it. NAPI is available in the current Linux 2.6 kernel and has been backported to the 2.4.20 kernel.

Polling has been around for a long time. Polling within the networking subsystem, however, is a rather new concept in Linux, but has been an option in FreeBSD for some time. Polling often causes many of us to cringe, but if we think about it, it's really rather beneficial when implemented properly for high-speed network interfaces.

Disk Drives

When it comes to disk drives, there are many aspects to consider. For instance, we mentioned earlier that optimal situations require dual buses in order to have unobstructed access from the peripheral to the CPU. Considering the load the sensor will or may be subject to—regardless of whether a database will be used, what type of logging is being used, and so on—selecting the optimal drive and drive strategy is key, an in depth discussion on this topic is beyond the scope of this chapter. We will cover only a limited subset of data that is directly related to a disk drive's performance on a Snort sensor.

The types of drives usually found in a Snort sensor are typically IDE, SATA, and SCSI. As such there are certain characteristics that should be considered when choosing a disk drive. One of the more important aspects of a drive to consider is the spindle speed; this is the actual speed at which the drive rotates/spins. Common spindle speeds for IDE, SATA, and SCSI range from 5,400RPM to 15,000RPM. Another important aspect to consider is the drive's capacity. This is important from a forensics and investigational point of view. Spindle speed and drive capacity are not mutually exclusive. More likely, spindle speed and drive capacity will be bound by the actual disk drive technology. It should be noted that when we talk about spindle speed we are really talking about a speed that can be achieved for only a very short period of time and under optimal conditions.

The bottom line comes down to choosing the drive(s) with the fastest spindle speed and as much capacity as is needed for the purpose of our Snort sensor's application/usage.

Installing Snort

Now we will explore how to actually install Snort using a few different operating systems. It is our preference and experience that Snort on Linux or BSD is the best choice and as such will be the focus of this section. We will, however, briefly cover the necessary steps for performing an install on a Windows-based system as well.

Before you can install Snort, you need to do a few things to prepare your environment for Snort. You need to meet a few dependencies even before you can install Snort to perform its basic capabilities. Depending on whether your sensor will function as an in-line device you must meet other specific dependencies as well.

Prework

Before you can install Snort, you need to perform a few preliminary steps. First you must make sure that you have installed all the necessary dependencies. Also, if you are going to be using a database, you need to ensure that the database and tables are set up properly. Lastly, you should know where your sensor is to be placed.

Installing pcap

Packet capturing is an essential capability of our Snort sensor. Operating systems can capture packets on a network in various ways, but here we will focus on using either libpcap or winpcap. Both act as high-level interfaces to the underlying operating system's packet capture facility. It's recommended that you install the latest version of libpcap or winpcap in order to take advantage of newer features, bug fixes, and optimizations.

Installing/Preparing Databases

Notes from the Underground…

Performance Issues with Writing Directly to a Database

Although we are about to describe how to install a database and configure Snort to write alerts directly to it, it is important to realize that this approach creates a very significant bottleneck for the Snort process. The better method is to have Snort write alerts and logs in the binary unified format and then use Barnyard on a separate system to load the data into a database. We'll talk more about Barnyard and configuring Snort to use it in Chapter 6.

Snort is capable of writing data to multiple databases—even simultaneously, although that's not recommended for performance reasons. Currently, Snort supports the following databases:

- PostgreSQL
- MySQL
- Any UNIX ODBC database
- Microsoft SQL Server
- Oracle

In this section, we will focus on installing and preparing a MySQL database for use on our Snort sensor, but the same principles apply to other supported databases.

The Snort distribution includes in the *schemas* directory the necessary schemas for each database listed previously. Let's look at how to set up the database on MySQL. Once we're sure that MySQL has been installed, we'll need to create the database for our Snort database schema. We can do this using mysqladmin or the mysql client.

First we'll use mysqladmin to create the database:

```
[moneypenny ~]$ mysqladmin –u root -p create snort
```

Now we need to create the user for our Snort database and set the appropriate grant privileges:

```
mysql> grant INSERT,SELECT on root.* to snort@localhost;
mysql> SET PASSWORD FOR snort@localhost=PASSWORD('a_secure_password');
mysql> grant CREATE, INSERT, SELECT, DELETE, UPDATE on snort.* to snort@localhost;
mysql> grant CREATE, INSERT, SELECT, DELETE, UPDATE on snort.* to snort;
```

Let's create the tables:

```
[moneypenny ~]$ mysql -u root -p < dir/to/snort/schemas/create_mysql snort
```

It's always wise to verify that the tables were created:

```
[moneypenny ~]$ mysqlshow -u snort -p snort
Enter password:
Database: snort
+------------------+
|      Tables      |
+------------------+
| data             |
| detail           |
| encoding         |
| event            |
| icmphdr          |
| iphdr            |
| opt              |
| reference        |
| reference_system |
| schema           |
| sensor           |
| sig_class        |
| sig_reference    |
| signature        |
| tcphdr           |
| udphdr           |
+------------------+
```

Now we'll need to make sure to update our *snort.conf* file to use MySQL. We'll need to uncomment and edit the following line in *snort.conf*:

```
# output database: log, mysql, user=snort password=<a_secure_passwd> dbname=snort
host=localhost
```

Time Synchronization (NTP)

We need to keep accurate time on the sensors without having to manually set the clocks. The easiest way to keep your sensors in sync is to use the Network Time Protocol (NTP). NTP is useful for ensuring coordinated timing between the Snort sensor and the server.

Edit the */etc/ntp.conf* file:

```
# is never used for synchronization, unless no other
# synchronization source is available. In case the local host is
# controlled by some external source, such as an external oscillator or
# another protocol, the prefer keyword would cause the local host to
# disregard all other synchronization sources, unless the kernel
# modifications are in use and declare an unsynchronized condition.
#
server myntpserver.com
#example 172.16.1.0 stratum 10
```

Next, start the ntpd daemon and make it run at startup:

```
# /etc/rc.d/init.d/ntpd start
# chkconfig ntpd on
```

Installing from Source

Some people want total control over their systems, to the point where they always compile their apps from source as opposed to installing binary packages that the distro may provide as part of its package management system. The biggest problem with binary-based distros is that you can end up with a whole bunch of packages that you don't need because they are installed as dependencies. Using something such as Gentoo and the BSDs can help you streamline the installation and prevent installation of unnecessary stuff. Compiling from source also has the added advantage that you can customize apps the way you want, instead of the way that the distro maintainer has stipulated.

Benefits and Costs

Compiling from source does have definite advantages which can make it worth the effort. The most significant benefits of compiling from source are:

- The level of control you have over your system
- Potential performance gains
- The ability to link with oddly placed or custom libraries

There is a price to pay in order to achieve these benefits. Namely, these are:

- Time
- Difficulty

Compiling from source certainly allows potential performance increases and provides far more control over the app itself. The amount of system control that compiling from source provides is undeniable, as are the methods of optimizing the app.

If you are adamant about compiling from source, we suggest that you analyze your system's specific purpose and install only the apps the sensor needs and uses for its immediate tasks. In our case, those tasks/apps are:

- Snort
- Packet capture (libpcap)
- Packet manipulation (libnet, libipq)
- Packet payload inspection (libpcre)
- Database (MySQL, Postgres)
- GNU C library (glibc)

If control and performance are what you are after, we suggest compiling from source only the apps/libraries that are crucial to and directly affect or interact with the Snort sensor.

RPM-based distros provide Source RPMs (SRPMs) that allow you to compile RPMs for your specific platforms, using your own compiler flag optimizations. That way, the dependencies and other package management features are still there. In addition, most SRPMs have patches and the most appropriate configure settings, though you can edit the SPEC file and override them. So, even though package builders may tend to build to the lowest common denominator, you can override and reinstall optimized versions of only the key packages you need via RPM.

Debian users can also benefit from being able to install from source and still enable the package management system to keep track of installed apps. These users can do this with CheckInstall.

Notes from the Underground…

Using CheckInstall to Manage Compiled from Source Software

CheckInstall is a wonderful piece of software for anyone running a Linux system. It allows you to take source code and a makefile and create an install package for Slackware, Debian, or RPM. This allows you to manage your custom-compiled software in the same fashion that you manage your prepackaged software. We strongly recommend that you check it out (http://asic-linux.com.mx/~izto/checkinstall).

Compile-Time Options

There are more advantages to compile-time options than just speed—for instance, compile-time options provide support for odd configure options and strange or custom libraries. If the processor being used in your sensor is different from the one used to compile a binary package, compiling from source will allow the binaries to be optimized for your system. Compiling apps just for the sheer sake of gaining a percentage or two more speed through obscure GCC options is not recommended, but commended. Typically, the performance gains of compiling an application from source vs. using a binary package are usually very small; somewhere in the order of a couple of percentage points.

Installing Binaries

On the other hand, there is the beauty and efficiency of binary packages and distros. A couple of us started with Gentoo, thinking that all the hardcore *CFLAGS* would make our machine much faster. They probably did—and even so probably by only a small percentage—but the amount of time we spent waiting for the apps to compile didn't seem to justify this minimal performance increase. For example, suppose you are running Gentoo or FreeBSD and you just got your system up and running, are browsing the Web, and see a PDF doc you want to read. Finding out that Adobe Acrobat Reader isn't installed and now requires compiling means you are left waiting a considerable amount of time while the compile and install run (much longer than for a binary package to be installed).

With binary packages you get a program which is compiled properly and integrates nicely with everything else on your system. Some people are concerned about the security of binary distributions, but as long as you are using a solid distro with solid security procedures, there should be minimal need for worry, at least on most systems for your environment.

Another thing to consider is whether the package (or the most recent version of the package) you want is not available in your distro's particular package format. If you have the experience, you can create the package yourself. In this case, it may be easier to install from source.

Notes from the Underground…

Potential Weaknesses in Precompiled Software Builds

It's *strongly* recommended that you know who and where you download your software from. An IDS is positioned at a key place on the network. If the IDS is vulnerable or is running infected code, it can wreak tremendous havoc on an unsuspecting organization. Therefore, it is critical to test each new version in a lab environment to provide a level of assurance in the software.

Apt-get

Let's look at how to use *apt-get* to install an application. To begin the installation, make sure you have root privileges and enter the following command:

```
apt-get install snort
```

You will see some output from *apt-get* informing you of any dependencies, recommended additional packages, as well as new packages that will be installed. Using *apt-get* is really simple, as the interface will walk you through the entire process painlessly.

When you've answered all the questions, the installation continues, including (provided there were no errors) the setup of all configuration files, path settings, documentation, and so forth.

At this stage, Snort should be running. You can easily determine this by running ps -A to see all of the processes running on the system.

RPM

To install Snort via RPM, open a console or terminal and enter the following command at the prompt:

```
rpm -Uvh snort-2.6.0-snort.i386.rpm
```

This will perform the complete installation for you. Notice the use of *–U* (upgrade) versus *–i* (install)—Snort will be installed either way. It's always a concern that if you use *–i*, the installer will not upgrade files properly (if there are any files to upgrade to newer versions), but if you use the *–U* flag, it will do a more thorough job of installing the software.

Now we will look at the SRPM as a means of a more solid installation. This is one of the more preferable methods used to install packages if you use RPM-based distributions such as CentOS, SUSE Linux, or Red Hat Linux, and the SRPMs are readily available to you. Usually sites such as www.freshrpms.net and www.rpmfind.net will have these available for most packages and almost all RPM-based distros.

RPM takes care of all the minute details involved in a recompile and rebuild. Let's start with the SRPM located in the */Snort-2.6.0/Linux/srpm* folder on the accompanying CD-ROM. It is the most current version of Snort and is ready for rebuilding into your system. Depending on the version of RPM you are using, the syntax can vary slightly. For RPM version 4.1 or higher enter **rpmbuild — rebuild snort-2.6.0-1snort.src.rpm**. For RPM versions earlier than 4.1 enter **rpm —rebuild snort-2.6.0-1snort.src.rpm**. This will prompt RPM to rebuild the file into a regular RPM specifically designed for your system.

Windows

Well, we finally made it to the Windows portion of our discussion. It's worth noting that Windows installation and configuration are far easier than *nix. We recommend that you install on Linux rather than Windows if you have the resources and knowledge to do so. The reasons are stability and pure speed. Linux is also far superior at performing network-related tasks.

Let's get started with the installation. First, we'll need to install the packet capture library for Windows, WinPcap. You can find it under the *Snort-2.6.0/Win32/winpcap3.0* directory. The installation is very simple and should go off without a hitch.

To install WinPcap you'll need to get it first. You can find it online at www.winpcap.org/install/default.htm. Download WinPcap and double-click on the resulting WinPcap.exe to begin the installation. The prompts and screens that follow are self-explanatory and should pose no difficulties to any user of any skill level.

You can find Snort binaries for Win32 systems at www.snort.org/dl/binaries/win32. Once you download Snort, double-click on the resulting .exe and away you go. See Chapter 6 for more details.

Hardening

Because we're going to working toward securing a network, it just makes sense to ensure that our IDS is locked down tight and is as secure as it can possibly be. We wouldn't want to have known vulnerable software or even unneeded software on this box, as that could lead to potential exploitation, which is not a good thing to have happen to a security device.

General Principles

As a general principle, it makes sense to take every possible precaution (within budget and reason) to ensure the security posture of the IDS itself. Also, many federal, state, and local mandates require that organizations employ certain measures constantly, including data retention, logging, and process accounting, so that they can take every reasonable measure to investigate security breaches.

Luckily for us, figuring out how to best harden and lock down our systems is no longer a black art. Numerous open source utilities as well as features are built into Linux and BSD to help us in our endeavor. Also, see Chapter 6 for more details on installing and configuring Snort on a Linux system.

Bastille Linux

Bastille Linux is an operating system hardening program, lead by Jay Beale. Bastille is also capable of evaluating your system's current state of hardening and can provide detailed reports about the settings for which it supports. Currently, Bastille supports numerous Linux distributions such as Red Hat (et al.), SUSE, Debian, Gentoo, Mandrake, and HP-UX. Support for Mac OS X is currently under development.

Bastille works by allowing the system administrator the ability to choose exactly to what level he or she wants to harden the system. Bastille operates in two modes: interactive and assessment. In interactive mode, Bastille walks the user through the entire hardening process by presenting a series of questions. Based on the answers the user provides, Bastille creates a hardened security policy and employs it within the system. In assessment mode, Bastille evaluates the current settings, provides information regarding available settings, and provides a detailed report outlining the system settings that it has hardened.

Bastille is a great program, and takes the approach of educating users on the principles of system hardening. It is reported that some organizations even mandate Bastille hardening sessions as part of mandatory training for newly hired system administrators. You can find more information on Bastille at www.bastille-linux.org.

AppArmor

AppArmor, which is developed by Novell for SUSE Linux, is a robust framework designed to provide security for user applications utilizing mandatory access control. AppArmor makes use of security policies called *profiles*, where individual applications along with their associated privileges are defined. AppArmor provides a number of default profiles and claims to be easy enough to use that it can be configured and deployed for even very complex applications in just a matter of hours.

AppArmor has a significant advantage over SELinux (discussed shortly), in that there is less system overhead (0-2%) as opposed to roughly 7% for SELinux and ease of policy creation For more information on AppArmor, visit www.novell.com/linux/security/apparmor and www.opensuse.org.

SysTrace

SysTrace enforces system call policies for applications by constraining the application's access to the system. The policy is generated interactively. Operations not covered by the policy raise an alarm, allowing a user to refine the currently configured policy. SysTrace is available for OpenBSD, NetBSD, and Linux.

SELinux

Security-Enhanced Linux (SELinux) was developed as a research project at the National Security Agency (NSA) and was designed to provide a flexible mandatory access control architecture within the Linux operating system.

SELinux enforces information separation based on requirements such as integrity and confidentiality. Mandatory access control policies in SELinux are used to confine applications and system servers to the minimum privilege level required to perform their tasks. SELinux's confinement mechanism is independent of traditional Linux access control mechanisms and it does not share the shortcomings of traditional Linux security mechanisms such as a dependence on setuid/setgid binaries.

You can find implementations of SELinux in the mainline Linux 2.6 kernel. For more information on SELinux, visit http://www.nsa.gov/selinux/code/.

LIDS

The Linux Intrusion Detection System (LIDS) was designed as an enhancement to the Linux kernel and implements numerous security features that are not natively included in the standard Linux kernel such as mandatory access control along with enhanced protection of files and processes. LIDS consists of a Linux kernel patch and a set of administrative tools aimed to help in securing Linux systems. LIDS currently supports kernels 2.6 and 2.4 and is released under GPL. For more information visit www.lids.org.

Configuring Snort

In order to make Snort do the stuff you want it to do, you need to give it some basic information. The configuration you choose is a direct representation of the capabilities you aim to squeeze out of Snort. As such, there are many configuration files to edit, preprocessor directives to tune, and event alerting and logging mechanisms to implement.

The snort.conf File

The Snort configuration file contains six basic sections:

- **Variable definitions.** This is where you define different variables that are used in Snort rules as well as for other purposes, such as specifying the location of rule files.

- **Configure dynamic loadable libraries.** You also can use these options on the command line.

- **Preprocessor configuration.** You use preprocessors to perform certain actions before a packet is operated by the main Snort detection engine.

- **Output module configuration.** Output modules control how Snort data will be logged.

- **Defining new action types.** If the predefined action types are not sufficient for your environment, you can define custom action types in the Snort configuration file.

- **Rules configuration and include files.** Although you can add any rules in the main *snort.conf* file, the convention is to use separate files for rules. These files are then included inside the main configuration file using the *include* keyword. This keyword will be discussed later in this chapter.

Although the configuration file provided with the distribution works, it's recommended that you modify it for your specific environment. A sample configuration file is presented later on.

Variables

Variables in Snort can be extremely useful. For example, variables can help to define an organization's IP space as a particular variable name. This way, when new rules are created, all you need to add to the rules is the variable. Moreover, variables help the performance and accuracy of the sensor and its backend storage; for instance, if the sensor had been placed in a tap off an organization's perimeter with no tuning. In that case, the sensor likely would be overloaded with alarms which would not be prevalent to the network, or would detect attacks coming from inside the network that were just normal traffic. Variables can also be of great use in custom signatures; for example, if you were looking for all traffic from a list of IPs, such as a *hot list*, which is a list of IP addresses or ranges that an organization wants to watch for traffic to or from (this could be a list of foreign countries, known virus hosting servers, or even a range of spyware/ad servers). Then, all the IPs/ranges could go in that list, so you would have to write only one or two rules to log all of those IPs. Not using variables could result in rules as long as or longer than the hot list. Another use of variables is in ports, such as all NetBIOS ports for Microsoft Windows communication. For example, when the welchia and blaster worms (see link) were prevalent, we used a group of ports that welchia could be used over to exploit a victim's machine. This way, we could monitor over five ports with one custom rule for any welchia attack/probe that tried to hit our network.

Using Variables in snort.conf and in Rules

Being able to define and use variables in the *snort.conf* file is a very convenient way to create rules. For example, you can define the variable *HOME_NET* in the configuration file:

```
var HOME_NET 192.168.20.0/24
```

Later you can use *HOME_NET* in your rules:

```
alert ip any any -> $HOME_NET any (ipopts: lsrr; msg: "Loose source routing
attempt"; sid: 1000001;)
```

Obviously, using variables makes it very convenient to adapt the configuration file and rules to any environment. For example, you don't need to modify all of your rules when you copy rules from one network to another; you need to modify only a single variable.

Command-Line Switches

When you invoke it from a command line, Snort has several runtime options that you can invoke via switches. These options control everything from logging, alerts, and scan modes to networking options and system settings. It is important to note that the command-line switches will override any conflicting configuration that is in the *config* file.

Here is a list of all the Snort 2.6 command-line options:

- **–A <alert>.** Set *<alert>* mode to **full**, **fast**, **console**, or **none**. **Full** mode does normal, classic Snort- style alerts to the alert file. **Fast** mode just writes the timestamp, message, IPs, and ports to the file. **None** turns off alerting. There is experimental support for UnixSock alerts that allows alerting to a separate process. Use the *unsock* argument to activate this feature.

- **–b.** Log packets in *tcpdump* format. All packets are logged in their native binary state to a *tcpdump*-formatted log file called *snort.log*. This option results in much faster program operation because it doesn?t have to spend time in the packet binary->text converters. Snort can keep up pretty well with 100 Mbps networks in *–b* mode.

- **–B <mask>.** Obfuscate IP addresses in alerts and packet dumps. All IP addresses belonging to the specified Classless Inter Domain Routing mask are obfuscated to protect the innocent and the guilty. This is useful when you want to publish or display packet dumps/traces/alerts to drive home a point but you want or need to hide the real address(es).

- **–c <rules>.** Use the *<cf>* rules file.

- **–C.** Dump the ASCII characters in packet payloads only; no hexdump.

- **–d.** Dump the application-layer data.

- **–D.** Run Snort in daemon mode. Alerts are sent to */var/log/snort/alert* unless otherwise specified.

- **–e.** Display/log the L2 packet header data.

- **–F <bpf>.** Read BPF filters from the *<bpf>* file. Handy for those of you running Snort as a SHADOW replacement or with a love of super-complex BPF filters.

- **–g <gname>.** Run Snort as group ID *<gname>* after initialization. As a security measure, this switch allows Snort to drop root privileges after its initialization phase has completed.

- **–G.** Ghetto backward-compatibility switch; prints cross-reference information in the 1.7 format. Available modes are basic and URL.

- **–h <hn>.** Set the "home network" to *<hn>*, which is a class C IP address similar to 192.168.1.0. If you use this switch, traffic coming from external networks will be formatted with the directional arrow of the packet dump pointing right for incoming external traffic, and left for outgoing internal traffic. Kind of silly, but it looks nice.

- **–i <if>.** Sniff on network interface *<if>*.

- **–I.** Add the interface name to alert printouts (first interface only).

- **–k <checksum mode>.** Set *<checksum mode>* to **all**, **noip**, **notcp**, **noudp**, **noicmp**, or **none**. Setting this switch modifies Snort's checksum verification subsystem to tune for maximum performance. For example, in many situations, Snort is behind a router or firewall that doesn't allow packets with bad checksums to pass, in which case it wouldn't make sense to have Snort re-verify checksums that have already been checked. Turning off specific checksum verification subsystems can improve performance by reducing the amount of time required to inspect a packet.

- **–K.** Logging mode. The default logging mode is now **pcap**. Other available options are **ASCII** and **NONE**.

- **–l <ld>.** Log packets to the *<ld>* directory. Sets up a hierarchical directory structure with the log directory as the base starting directory, and the IP address of the remote peer generating traffic as the directory in which packets from that address are stored. If you do not use the *–l* switch, the default logging directory is */var/log/snort*.

- **–L <file>.** Log to the *<file> tcpdump* file.

- **–m <umask>.** Set the umask for all of Snort's output files to the indicated mask.

- **–M.** Log messages?not alerts?to syslog.

- **–n <cnt>.** Exit after processing *<cnt>* packets.

- **–N.** Turn off logging. Alerts still function normally.

- **–o.** Change the order in which the rules are applied to packets. Instead of being applied in the standard Alert | Pass | Log order, this will apply them in Pass | Alert | Log order, allowing people to avoid having to make huge BPF command-line arguments to filter their alert rules.

- **–O.** Obfuscate the IP addresses during logging operations. This switch changes the IP addresses that are printed to the screen/log file to *xxx.xxx.xxx.xxx*. If the homenet address switch is set (*–h*), only addresses on the homenet will be obfuscated, and non–homenet IPs will be left visible. Perfect for posting to your favorite security mailing list!

- **–p.** Turn off promiscuous mode sniffing. Useful for places where promiscuous mode sniffing can screw up your host severely.

- **–P <snaplen>.** Set the snaplen of Snort to *<snaplen>*. This filters how much of each packet gets into Snort; the default is 1514.

- **–q.** Quiet. Don't show banner and status report.

- **–r <tf>.** Read the *tcpdump*-generated file, *<tf>*. This will cause Snort to read and process the file fed to it. This is useful if, for example, you have a bunch of Shadow files that you want to process for content, or even if you have a bunch of reassembled packet fragments that have been written into a *tcpdump*-formatted file.

- **–R <id>.** Include the *<id>* in the *snort_intf<id>.pid* filename. This is useful when you are listening on multiple interfaces.

- **–s.** Log alert messages to the syslog. On Linux boxes, they will appear in */var/log/secure*; */var/log/messages* on many other platforms. You can change the logging facility by using the syslog output plug-in, at which point you should not use the *–s* switch (command-line alert/log switches override any config file output variables).

- **–S <n=v>.** Set the variable name *n* to the value *v*. This is useful for setting the value of a defined variable name in a Snort rules file to a command-line-specified value. For example, if you define a *HOME_NET* variable name inside a Snort rules file, you can set this value from its predefined value at the command line.

- **–t <chroot>.** Changes Snort's root directory to *<chroot>* after initialization. Please note that all log/alert filenames are relevant to the *chroot* directory, if *chroot* is used.

- **–T.** Snort will start up in self-test mode, checking all the supplied command-line switches and rules files that are handed to it and indicating that everything is ready to proceed. This is a good switch to use if daemon mode is going to be used; it verifies that the Snort configuration that is about to be used is valid and won't fail at runtime.

- **–u <uname>.** Change the UID Snort runs under to *<uname>* after initialization.

- **–U.** Turn on UTC timestamps.

- **–v.** Be verbose. Prints packets out to the console. There is one big problem with verbose mode: it's still rather slow. If you are doing IDS work with Snort, don?t use the *–v* switch; you will drop packets (not many, but some).

- **–V.** Show the version number and exit.

- **–w.** Dump 802.11 management and control frames.

- **–X.** Dump the raw packet data starting at the link layer.

- **–y.** Turn on the year field in packet timestamps.

- **–Z <file>.** Set the performonitor preprocessor file path and name.

- **–z.** Set the assurance mode for Snort alerts. If the argument is set to **all**, all alerts come out of Snort as normal. If it is set to **est** and the stream4 preprocessor is performing stateful inspection (its default mode), alerts will be generated only for TCP packets that are part of an established session, greatly reducing the noise generated by tools such as stick and making Snort more useful in general.

- **–?.** Show the usage summary and exit.

Configuration Directives

Snort.conf –dynamic-* Options

The advantage of dynamic components is that developers can write their own modules without having to patch or modify Snort directly.

The new rules structure should make writing complex rules easier. Sourcefire has not determined whether it will completely replace the old style rule format in favor of the new format. Dynamic rules aren't just loaded by default; you have to tell Snort to load them. You can do that on a per-directory basis or on an individual basis. The same is true for dynamic preprocessors and dynamic engine objects. You can load the dynamic components from both the command line and snort.conf.

Ruletype

In Snort, rules start with actions. Current rule actions are:

- **Alert.** Generate an alert acc. to alert method, and then log the packet.
- **Log.** Generate a log entry.
- **Pass.** Ignore the packet.
- **Activate.** Alert and turn on dynamic rules.
- **Dynamic.** First must be activated by activate rule, and then act as a log rule.
- **Drop.** Make *iptables* drop the packet and log the packet.
- **Reject.** Make *iptables* drop the packet, log it, and then send an unreachable message if the protocol is the User Datagram Protocol (UDP).
- **Sdrop.** Make *iptables* drop the packet but do not log it.

The *ruletype* keyword allows for new actions to be created. For instance, the following rule creates a new action called *mytype*:

```
ruletype mytype
    {
            type alert
            output alert_syslog: LOG_AUTH
    }
```

This definition allows for the creation of the new action named *mytype* which generates alerts that are logged by syslog. It should be noted that in order for pass rules to work you need to modify the parsing order via the *–o* command-line option.

Plug-In Configuration

Configuring our plug-ins is a vital step of our process. The plug-ins are what give Snort the capability to do what it does best: identify malicious traffic and alert us of it.

Preprocessors

Preprocessors in Snort provide us with the ability to perform numerous useful activities. Such activities include stream reassembly (stream4, frag3), flow tracking (flow), detecting anomalous activity such as port scans (sfPortscan), and application-level inspection such as File Transfer Protocol (FTP), Telnet and Simple Mail Transfer Protocol (SMTP) inspection. Preprocessors are useful for performing some "prechecks" of packets before they reach the detection engine.

In the following subsections we will discuss the preprocessors currently available in Snort.

Flow

This preprocessor is where all of Snort's state-keeping mechanisms are to be kept. The flow preprocessor is based on the definition of a flow, which is considered a unique tuple consisting of the following elements:

- IP
- Source IP address
- Source port
- Destination IP address
- Destination port

Flow's configuration directives are as follows:

```
timeout [seconds] - sets the number of [seconds] that an unfinished
                    fragment will be kept around waiting for completion,
                    if this time expires the fragment will be flushed
memcap [bytes] - limit frag2 memory usage to [number] bytes
                 (default:  4194304)
min_ttl [number] - minimum ttl to accept
ttl_limit [number] - difference of ttl to accept without alerting
                     will cause false positives with router flap
```

Frag3

Frag3 is an IP fragmentation reassembly module which has the ability to model a user defined target and allow for the handling of fragmentation-type attacks. Frag3 also ensures the fragmentation model for the specified target is based on that targets TCP/IP stack. The frag3 preprocessor works in two steps:

1. Global initialization phase
2. Definition of defragmentation engines

The global configuration directive applies to frag3 in a macroscopic fashion: setting a memory cap, defining the maximum number of fragmentation tracking structures active at any given time, and the number of individual fragments that can be processed at once. For more information see the **frag3_global options** section of snort.conf. . .

After we configure the global options we continue to configure the frag3 engine. The engine is responsible for modeling the target and handling fragmentation attack detection. Configuring frag3's engine consists of setting expiry timeouts for fragmented packets, setting ttl hop limits and minimum accepted values, activating anomaly detection, a policy/model to apply to the fragmented packets, and a list of IP addresses to bind the engine to. For more information see the **frag3_engine options** section of snort.conf.. . .

Multiple frag3 engines can be configured and run in parallel. Multiple running frag3 engines is useful when you want to use specific policies for particular groups of IP addresses and also have a default fallback policy for all other traffic. For more information please refer to the *README.frag3* file in the *.doc* directory of the Snort tarball.

Stream4

Stream4 is a stateful stream reassembly and inspection module. Stream4 is made up of two configurable modules:

- Stateful analysis
- Stream reassembly

The stream4 stateful analysis/inspection module is most notably used for its ability to detect TCP state problems and port scans. The stateful analysis module is highly configurable and most likely requires the most tuning. For more information see the `stream4` sections in the Snort manual and snort.conf.

The stream4 reassembly module performs complete stream reassembly for TCP. It has the ability to handle both client side and server side streams as well as the ability to define which ports to perform reassembly on and a number of other useful reassembly directives. For more information see the **stream4** section in the Snort manual and also in snort.conf.

sfPortscan

This preprocessor is considered the successor to the portscan and flow-portscan preprocessors. sfPortscan was developed by Sourcefire as a comprehensive method for combating various scan techniques in use today. Basically, you tell this module which protocols you want to watch, along with the type of scan you are looking for and a sensitivity level. While sfPortscan provides enormous functionality, tuning it can be a rather difficult process.

You must use the flow preprocessor when using sfPortscan so that you can assign the associated direction of the flow to the connectionless protocols, such as UDP and ICMP. It's also recommended that you disable evasion alerts from within the stream4 preprocessor when using sfPortscan because it can cause multiple alerts to be generated for the same scan packets.

Notes from the Underground…

Idle Scanning

Idle scanning is a port scanning technique that utilizes a machine with a predictable IP-ID field in order to scan another remote machine without sending any packets from the original host. This technique is more thoroughly documented in a paper at http://www.insecure.org/nmap/idlescan.html and is also implemented by the nmap security scanner.

Output Plug-Ins

Here is a list of the preprocessors currently available in Snort:

- alert_syslog
- log_tcpdump
- database
- unified: alert_unified, log_unified
- log_unified
- alert_prelude

Included Files

Snort comes with a number of files essential to runtime configuration, as well as files necessary for performing the appropriate mappings between rules, subsystems, and classifications. The included files are essential in getting Snort up and running, but also require the necessary attention in order to provide the appropriate parameters for optimal sensor performance.

Rules Files

Unless you're going to be using Snort as a packet logger only, you're going to need some rules in order for Snort in IDS/IPS mode to work. By default, Snort no longer comes with rules. You are now required to at least register with Snort.org in order to be able to access VRT-certified rules. There are three levels of VRT rule sets:

- **Subscribers.** This level benefits from real-time rule updates as they become available.
- **Registered users.** This level gives you the ability to access rule updates five days after they've been released to subscribers.

- **Unregistered users.** This level gives you a static rule set at the time of each major Snort release.

The subscription service is not free and use of VRT rule sets is expressly prohibited for commercial use.

NOTE

Here's what Sourcefire says regarding VRT rule sets as a subscription service:
"Sourcefire VRT Certified Rules are the official rules of snort.org. Each rule has been rigorously tested against the same standards the VRT uses for Sourcefire customers."

Then there is the community rule set. This rule set contains rules submitted by members of the open source community. Although these rules are available as is, the VRT performs basic tests to ensure that new rules will not break Snort. These rules are distributed under the GPL and are freely available to all open source Snort users.

There are other ways to obtain rules. One of the best ways is through Bleeding Snort (www.bleedingsnort.com), which provides a comprehensive set of rules for Snort. The other way is to learn how rules work, read the FAQs provided with Snort, and begin writing your own.

Snort rules are essentially the heart of the system.

sid–msg.map

This file contains a mapping of alert messages to Snort rule IDs. The *sid-msg.map* file is used for post-processing/displaying events.

threshold.conf

This file is useful in helping to reduce the number of alerts for noisy rules, and to suppress rules for IPs or groups of IPs.

Thresholding options in this file basically help to limit the total number of times an event is logged during a given time interval. This file defines three types of thresholds:

- **Limit.** This type of threshold will alert only on the first N events that occur during a defined time interval and will ignore events for the remainder of the time interval.

- **Threshold.** This type of threshold generates an alert every N times we see this event during a defined time interval.

- **Both.** This type of threshold will generate an alert once during a defined time interval after seeing N occurrences of the event; additional events during the time interval are ignored.

This file also provides the ability to completely suppress rules based on IPs or groups of IPs.

gen-msg.map

This file provides the mapping of messages to the relevant Snort component that generated the alert. The following output is an example of how this works:

```
snort[3174]: [119:4:1] (http_inspect) BARE BYTE UNICODE ENCODING
```

If we look at the grouping *[119:4:1]* and associated text, this tells us what component fired the alert (*119 -> http_inspect*), the alerted (*4 -> BARE BYTE UNICODE ENCODING*), and a revision number. Preprocessors will have this number set to 1; rules will include their respective number.

classification.config

This file provides the ability to classify and prioritize Snort alerts. It's also totally customizable and allows you to define your own classifications and priorities. There are three priority levels by default: low (3), medium (2), and high (1). If, for instance, we decided that a particular classtype needs a higher priority, all we have to do is change the number associated with it. For example, if we want to change the priority level of the network-scan classtype, all we need to do is change the following:

```
config classification: network-scan,Detection of a Network Scan,3
```

to:

```
config classification: network-scan,Detection of a Network Scan,1
```

As stated earlier, we can also define our own classifications if the current types don't suit our needs. All we have to do is define the new classification in the classification.config file and assign a priority to it, like so:

```
config classification: newclasstype,Detected New Classification Type,2
```

It's worth mentioning that when editing this file and creating or changing classtypes, descriptions, or priorities that no spaces are to be introduced between the delimiting commas.

Now that we have defined a new classtype we can proceed to use it in new and existing rules. It's as easy as:

```
alert tcp $EXTERNAL_NET -> $HOME_NET any
(msg:"NEW CLASS TYPE interesting data found";content:"I am very interesting data";
flow:from_server,
established;classtype:newclasstype;)
reference.config
```

This file provides the URL to external Web sites where you can find further information about the specifics of what a particular rule is trying to do. In order to really understand how this file fits into the overall configuration and usage of Snort, an example is probably in order.

The following rule checks incorrect login attempts on the Telnet server port:

```
alert tcp $TELNET_SERVERS 23 -> $EXTERNAL_NET any (msg:"TELNET login incorrect";
content: graphics/ccc.gif"Login incorrect"; flow:from_server,established;
reference:arachnids,127; classtype:bad  unknown; sid: graphics/ccc.gif718; rev:6;)
```

Notice the use of the *reference* keyword used in this rule—in particular, *reference: arachnids, 127*. This provides a reference to a Web site where you can find more information about this vulnerability. The URLs for external Web sites are placed in the *reference.config* file in the Snort distribution. Using the information in this file, you can determine that the URL for more information about this rule is www.whitehats.com/info/IDS=127, where 127 is the ID used for searching the database at the arachnids Web site.

Thresholding and Suppression

Sometimes you will want to be able to control the frequency and volume of your alerts. Perhaps you are testing a new rule and are somewhat unsure of how it will interact with the network (probably not a good idea in the first place, but hey, this is real life). Thresholding and suppression give you this ability by allowing you to define attributes that control these particular aspects—for instance, if you're accustomed to seeing particular traffic for a specific group of systems but you don't want to be bothered with the flood of alerts every time the associated rule is fired. Refer to the previous section, which describes the *threshold.conf* file.

Testing Snort

Testing and tuning rules and sensors is one of the most, if not the most, important aspects of an IDS. Most testing should occur in a test lab or test environment of some kind. One part of Snort (new to the 2.1 version) is the use of a preprocessor called *perfmonitor*. This preprocessor is a great tool for determining sensor load, dropped packets, the number of connections, and the usual load on a network segment. Of greater benefit is to use perfmonitor combined with a graphing tool called perfmonitor-graph, located at http://people.su.se/~andreaso/perfmon-graph.

It does take some tweaking of the perfmon preprocessor to generate the snortstat data. Moreover, an ongoing issue with the perfmon preprocessor seems to be that it counts dropped packets as part of the starting and stopping of a Snort process. This issue hasn't been resolved as of this writing. However, one suggestion is to document every time the Snort process is stopped or started, and that time should match the time in the graph.

Tools & Traps...

Performance Monitoring

Perfmonitor-graph generates its graphics based on the Perl modules used by RRDtool (http://people.ee.ethz.ch/~oetiker/webtools/rrdtool). RRDtool is a great tool usually used by network operations staff. This tool takes log data from Cisco and other vendors' logs and provides graphs about things such as load, performance, users, and so forth. If you don't want to install the full RRDtool, you can just install the Perl libraries:

Continued

```
shell> make site-perl install
```
With this installed, the perfmonitor-graph functions will work and generate the graphics.

Perfmonitor-graph combs through the data logged by the Snort preprocessor and displays it in a generated HTML page. With some tweaking, this is a great way to make hourly/daily/weekly charts of trends in several metric-capable charts. This can prove invaluable in larger or government organizations where metrics control the budget.

When it comes to Snort rules, Turbo Snort Rules (www.turbosnortrules.org) is a great place to visit when looking to optimize your sensor's ruleset. Turbo Snort Rules provides speed/efficiency testing of your Snort rules as well as provides tips for making Snort run faster via optimized rulesets. Virtual machines are a hot topic these days. VMware (www.vmware.com) and Xen (http://www.xensource.com) are great virtualization software and prove invaluable to the budget constrained security analyst. It provides the ability to run multiple and disparate operating systems on the same machine at the same time. This is quite useful in gaining experience with other operating systems similar to the ones' in your production environment, and provides worry free testing and development environments for those of us who like to tinker and tweak our systems.

Testing within Organizations

Whether your security team is composed of one person or several 24/7 teams throughout the world, testing new rules and Snort builds should be the second most important role your team handles. The first is to document just about everything your team does, including testing and rule creation, removal, and maintenance. The scope of a security team's testing also may depend on the size of an organization, monetary backing, and time and materials. Several ways to test include using a test lab with live taps from the production network to a single laptop/desktop plugged into a network, or using Snort rule generation tools such as Snot and Sneeze. Snot and Sneeze are just two of the tools that take the contents of a rules file and generate traffic to trigger on the rules. A new and controversial toolset, Metasploit, is available to help organizations protect their networks (www.metasploit.com/projects/Framework).

Notes from the Underground...

Metasploit

The authors of this book are in no way encouraging readers to download or run this tool. Metasploit is a flexible set of the most current exploits that an IDS team could run in their test network to gather accurate signatures of attacks. One of the "features" of the Metasploit framework is its capability to modify almost any exploit in the database. This can be useful for detecting modified exploits on a production network, or writing signatures, looking deep within packets for telltale backdoor code.

Continued

The possibilities that this brings to an IDS team in terms of available accurate, understandable attack data are immense. Although all of these methods are great for testing, most organizations are going to have to choose some combination thereof.

Small Organizations

We consider "small" organizations as those without a dedicated IDS team or those that have an IDS team of up to five people, and not much monetary backing. As such, most of these teams use either open source tools or tools that are fairly inexpensive; for example, using a second-hand desktop/laptop or doubling up a workstation as a testing box.

Using a Single Box or Nonproduction Test Lab

One method that a person or small team could use to test new rules and versions of Snort before placing them in a production environment is to use a test lab with at least one attack machine, one victim machine, and a copy of an existing IDS sensor build. Understandably, this might be a lot for a small team to acquire, so a suggestion would be to find a single box. If one can't be found in the organization, usually a local electronics store will sell used or cheap machines. This box should be built with the same operating system as a team's production OS and have the same build of Snort. That way, when the team is testing rules or versions, if an exploit or bug occurs for the OS or, in the rare case, for Snort, the team can know it before it hits a production system. This method can be made easier if the team uses disk-imaging software, such as dd from the open source community or a commercial product such as Norton Ghost. This way, as the team's production systems change, they can just load the production image onto the test box to test against the most current production system.

If the team or person doesn't have the time or resources to run a dedicated test machine, one option is to use a virtual test lab. You can create a virtual test lab by adding a tool such as VMware or Virtual PC to a workstation on the network. This would provide a means to install a guest OS such as Linux or *BSD, which is most likely the OS of choice for a Snort sensor in a small security team. This small team could then test and run new rules or Snort builds against any traffic hitting the workstation, without having to use the production sensors. If this software is loaded on a standard Intel PC, with a little tuning, the image, in the case of VMware, could be placed on a laptop and taken to other sites for use as a temporary sensor when testing at new or remote sites.

Finally, another option for a smaller organization is for the security team to perform testing with its own workstation. As most organizations have a Microsoft Windows environment for their workstations, we will be using Windows as the OS of choice in this discussion. There are Snort builds for the Windows environment, known as win32 builds, which allow people to run Snort from a Windows machine. One piece of software, called EagleX and available from Eagle Software (www.eaglesoftware.com), does a nice job of installing Snort, the winpcap library needed to sniff traffic, the database server, and the Web server. This is all done with only local access to the resources, setting up a Snort sensor on the Windows workstation to log all information to a local MySQL database, and running the Analyst Console for Intrusion Detection (ACID), which is a Web-based front end for Snort. This is great for both new Snort users and a small staff to test rules and determine whether a Snort build or a rule is going to flood Snort and its front end.

Large Organizations

We consider "large" organizations as those with an IDS team of more than five people. These are teams who are usually given their own budget and cover a 24/7 operation or are geographically dispersed. In an environment such as this, a team should have a dedicated test lab to run exploit code and malware to determine signatures for detecting attacks and for testing new Snort builds and rules. This test lab would also ideally have a live-feed tap from the production network to test with accurate data and load of the rules and builds. Creating an image of the production sensor build would make the most sense for large security teams. This would greatly help the deployment time and processes of new sensors, and provide a means to quickly test rules in the current sensors.

Another option for a large organization is the consideration of port density on each point on a network where sensors are located. If, for example, at each tap/span of live data this is plugged into a small switch or hub, the production systems could be plugged into the switch/hub. Then, a spare box, perhaps of the same OS build as the production system, could be placed at points on the tap infrastructure most important to the organization. By placing an extra box at the span point, testing of a new rule or Snort build could be exposed to a real-time accurate load, giving the best picture for a sensor. We have found this to be good for use on points, such as the external tap used for testing and running intelligence rule tests such as strange traffic that normally wouldn't be getting through the firewall. Alternatively, you could place an extra box at the RAS/virtual private network remote access points, as nearly every IDS analyst who has monitored a RAS link into an organization knows that these are the points where you can see some of the earliest victims of viruses and worms, out-of-date security-patched machines, and strange traffic in general. If you placed an extra tap at each of these locations, you would get a highly accurate view of the new rules or Snort builds and how they would perform, without compromising the integrity of the production sensors.

Finally, another extremely useful method for large organizations to test Snort rules and builds is a full test lab. This is sometimes shared with other IT teams such as Operations for new infrastructure equipment or a help desk team for testing new user software. If all of these are present, this will help in demonstrating the effectiveness of an attack or virus. For example, if this lab is a disconnected network from the live network, when malware or exploits are found, they can be run in this environment to help the Computer Incident Response Team understand containment and countermeasures to use, and the IDS team can use this data to create and test signatures to determine infection and detect initial attacks and, possibly, other side effects of hostile traffic.

Maintaining Snort

Now that you have Snort up and running and optimized for our environment, how do you keep it up-to-date? Well, there are numerous aspects to consider. First, you'll need to make sure you're running the latest and greatest version of Snort.

Are You 0wned?

Latest Snort Versions

It's recommended to at least view the changelog of each new release of Snort, because even if it's organizational policy to not always use the most recent version of Snort, there may be fixes to potential bugs or exploits in any one of the components of Snort, such as the preprocessors.

Updating Rules

Updating your rules can make all the difference. For example, one of the authors once worked for a large government agency. We had been running Snort 2.0.*x*, although it hadn't changed much in the 2.0 revisions. We were hitting 99 percent accuracy for a Nimda exploited machine with the "http directory traversal" signature. Nimda was the name given to an attack that affected Microsoft Internet Information Server (IIS) Web servers. This attack was the first of its kind that could use multiple attack vectors to exploit systems. This attack could come in the form of a malformed Multipurpose Internet Mail Extensions attachment (*.eml*) that was automatically run by Microsoft Outlook and Outlook Express mail clients, infecting the victim machine by sending itself to all entries in the address book. This worm could also gain access to an unpatched Microsoft IIS Web server through a Unicode attack called *directory traversal*, which allowed attackers to run, view, and execute files otherwise unavailable remotely. Nimda could also infect machines that were infected with a backdoor program called *root.exe*, which was left by the CodeRed II worm. Both of these attacks would then place a *readme.eml* file in the root of every Web-accessible folder. Files with the extension *.eml* are a hidden Microsoft extension that is automatically run, which would create possibly thousands of victims from users just browsing to an infected IIS server. Once on the victim's machine, this attack would enable full access to the root C drive and enable the Guest account on the system.

We upgraded to the new Snort 2.0 release without checking the new rule set for any changes to that particular signature. Within minutes of turning on the new version and rule set, our number of alarms tripled. Our first reaction was that we were facing a level of infection that we hadn't accounted for previously. Then, while our junior analysts were running down the actual packets that were triggering, we started looking at the rule set and noticed that with this release of Snort the "http directory traversal" signature had been changed. The signature, "http directory traversal," was triggering on a payload of ../ instead of the old "Volume Name" in the payload. This seemingly minor change was causing major differences in the number of alarms we were receiving, as this payload in URLs is used for several high-traffic sites such as MSN.com, Yahoo.com, and Google.com. This URL is also used by several Web and application servers such as Cold Fusion, IIS, Jakarta-Tomcat, and Lotus Domino, to name a few. On a large enterprise network, the majority of your Web traffic is generated by several of the previously listed sites and servers. Upon realizing the change, we immediately dropped back to our old rule set and began a manual comparison through the entire new rule set for changes before running the new rule set on our production systems.

Please refer to Chapter 6 for a more thorough discussion of updating Snort rules.

How Can Updating Be Easy?

Many elements can help make rule updating easier—for example, using Snort's flexibility to use variables in its rules; or the "local" rules file, which you can use for per-sensor or per-incident rule generation; or placing rules in the deleted rules file for change control. For example, you can use a local rule to track a problem server or to assist operations staff with a problem server.

Updating Snort

Information security is under constant threat. Like most venues of security, IDS is a constantly changing environment that needs to be able to meet these changing threats. For example, when the antivirus industry receives new viruses and variations on current ones, it rallies together to add detection and removal tools and instructions, as the security industry does when a new threat faces networks through Web sites, mailing lists, and newsgroups. All of these methods will help an IDS team to stay abreast and sometimes ahead of threats to their networks and users.

Upgrading Snort

Assuming that you are actively involved in your Snort sensor deployment to include writing your own preprocessors, modifying existing core components to better suit your needs, or just have your Snort sensors to the point where they are highly tuned and optimized, what do you do about the newest Snort version that gets released? Well, not to worry. Several avenues are available in this situation. You can always make a patch out of your highly tuned Snort sensor and incorporate that into the newest version (in fact, you should always read the changelog of each new release). You also can start from a fresh compile of the new version and make the necessary modifications to get it up to speed.

Fortunately, upgrading Snort is not a difficult process. Its basic backward compatibility with previous versions of Snort is rarely broken. It's always a good thing to think in worst-case scenarios. So, just be sure to make backups of any data or configuration files that are critical to the sensor's operation. Most likely, newer versions of Snort either have added functionality (which you may not find useful in your deployment), or potential holes have been fixed, optimizations have been made to the core engines, or new features have been added.

When it comes down to the act of upgrading Snort, there's really no alternative other than installing the new binary or compiling the newest version from scratch.

Monitoring Your Snort Sensor

You can keep tabs on your Snort sensor in a number of ways. Aside from using Snort's local facilities, such as the perfmon performance monitor preprocessor and syslog, there are also numerous front-end user interfaces that can help provide much-needed insight into your sensor's performance, such as BASE, ACID, IDSCenter, and Sguil, to name a few.

Like most people, having multiple angles of view on a particular problem is a huge benefit. Although looking at a raw packet and some raw alerts is usually enough for the seasoned security analyst, having the ability to see a two- or three-dimensional graph of a Snort sensor's performance can prove invaluable to novice security analysts, as well as upper management.

Summary

We covered a lot of ground in this chapter. We talked about choosing the appropriate operating system for use on a Snort sensor. We also talked about the performance implications of the various components and subsystems of the physical sensor itself. We made important note of the fact that you should take every precaution to harden your Snort sensor to prevent it from being compromised, because it will be sitting at a critical point within your network.

Once we discussed all of the aspects regarding building a sensor, we talked about some real-world operating systems and discussed briefly the pros and cons of each. We then talked about the process of installing and configuring Snort. Integral to Snort installation and configuration is the underlying operating system's means for package management and how to install and keep a system up-to-date. We explored how to use *apt-get*, RPM, portage, and, of course, binaries.

After you install Snort, you have to make sure it is configured properly, so we talked about the files included in the Snort distribution that help Snort do its job. We also talked briefly about the various preprocessor and output plug-ins and their configuration directives. Once we had a highly tuned and effective Snort system up and running, we talked about testing and marinating Snort. Because Snort is an open source application and can benefit from many highly skilled developers contributing to it, it's always a good idea to have an upgrade/update strategy; each new release likely adds functionality and potentially fixes holes.

The concepts introduced and discussed in this chapter should be helpful to anyone wanting or needing to set up a highly tuned and optimized Snort IDS.

Solutions Fast Track

Choosing the Right OS

- ☑ The best operating system for a Snort IDS is one which meets the standards of the obstacles it will face in the network.

- ☑ Excessive tools and applications such as graphical desktop environments and development tools should not be part of a production IDS system.

- ☑ Operating system considerations for a large-scale deployment should include security concerns, hardware/software cost, the capability to strip the operating system of unnecessary parts, and remote management capabilities.

Hardware Platform Considerations

- ☑ The CPU is highly dependent upon other hardware components, such as RAM, and is only as powerful as the components that make up the entire system.

- ☑ High-bandwidth networks can bring a sensor to its knees. So, it's important to ensure that there is a dedicated bus between the NIC and the CPU.

- ☑ NAPI-compliant devices and drivers can add significant network performance boosts to Linux-based systems.

Installing Snort

- ☑ Installing Snort from source is the preferred method.

- ☑ Depending on how Snort will be used, you must meet various dependencies, such as libpcap for packet capture, libnet for packet modification, and libipq for inline use.

- ☑ Snort is available for a wide variety of systems, including Windows, Linux, BSD, and Solaris, to name a few.

Configuring Snort

- ☑ The preferred method of configuring snort is via *snort.conf*.

- ☑ To use many of the plug-ins available in Snort you must have a deep understanding of your network and the problem you are trying to solve.

- ☑ Command-line options are available and you can use them in conjunction with directives in *snort.conf*.

Testing Snort

- ☑ You should conduct thorough tests of Snort offline to ensure that any changes to rules, plug-ins, or any of Snort's core engines do not affect the overall functionality of the IDS.

- ☑ Organizations should employ the use of red teams of a select group of individuals whose responsibility is to try and defeat/evade the Snort sensor.

Maintaining and Updating Snort

- ☑ Each new release of Snort adds some level of functionality or fixes issues with previous releases.

- ☑ Open source tools are available for seamless maintenance and management of Snort rules.

Frequently Asked Questions

The following Frequently Asked Questions, answered by the authors of this book, are designed to both measure your understanding of the concepts presented in this chapter and to assist you with real-life implementation of these concepts. To have your questions about this chapter answered by the author, browse to **www. syngress.com/solutions** and click on the **"Ask the Author"** form.

Q: What operating systems does Snort support?

A: Snort will run on the various Linux distributions (Red Hat, CentOS, etc.) as well as on FreeBSD, NetBSD, OpenBSD, Solaris, HP-UX, Mac OS X, and Microsoft Windows.

Q: Does hardware choice really make that much of a difference?

A: Yes. Depending on various factors such as network throughput and the number of hosts on the network, the hardware comprising the Snort sensor is a big deal. Being able to successfully handle and process the data requires that all components be optimally tuned and in sync with one another.

Q: Is Snort free?

A: Well, yes, sort of. Snort is licensed under GPL v2. As long as you're not redistributing the VRT rules as part of a commercial product, Snort is free for you to use.

Q: I've been hearing a lot about network behavior anomaly detection lately. Does Snort do this?

A: Snort is a signature-based IDS by default, meaning it compares certain characteristics of known attack patterns against live network traffic. The beauty of Snort is in its modular design. You can configure Snort to perform a limited amount of anomaly detection through it preprocessors. Check out SPADE (www.bleedingsnort.com/cgi-bin/viewcvs.cgi/?cvsroot=SPADE) for more information about integrating anomaly detection into Snort.

Q: How can I get Snort?

A: Snort is available as downloadable binaries and a source tarball from www.snort.org. You can also retrieve Snort via the CVS tree.

---

[1] Remember, if you remove the development tools you will not be able to compile Snort or any other applications on the system. This is not a bad thing, but you will need to ensure that you have a precompiled install package for your OS for any applications you want on it. If you aren't able to download the packages you need, you can frequently create them yourself using freely available tools.

## Chapter 6

Configuring Snort and Add-Ons

Solutions in this chapter:

- **Placing your IDS**
- **Configuring Snort on a Windows System**
- **Configuring Snort on a Linux System**
- **Other Snort Add-Ons**
- **Demonstrating Effectiveness**

☑ **Summary**

☑ **Solutions Fast Track**

☑ **Frequently Asked Questions**

Placing Your NIDS

When it comes to implementing a network intrusion detection system (NIDS) like Snort, the single biggest factor in its effectiveness is its placement within the network. The value of the NIDS is in identifying malicious traffic and obviously it can't do that if it can't see the traffic. This means you want to place the NIDS in a location to maximize the data it will see. In smaller environments where there may be only one switch or hub, this is a pretty simple decision. Depending on your objectives, you may place it inline with the Internet connection only, so that you are inspecting traffic only to or from the Internet. In a larger installation, you will need to place multiple network cards in the NIDS so that it can inspect traffic from several chokepoints in your network.

Notes from the Underground…

Further Considerations

Remember that an IDS is also a target for a hacker just like any other system, and often even more so. As such, the IDS host system should be hardened and locked down as much as possible (See Chapter 5 for more details). In addition to being a target because it can alert administrators to their activities, the hacker might target the IDS system itself because it often contains logs with valuable information in it on various systems. The IDS also has the capability of capturing packets that match its rulebase, and these packet dumps can contain valuable data as well. Don't neglect securing your IDS or you may be creating a security liability instead of the asset you intended.

Be cognizant of the fact that if you do choose to install multiple network cards to monitor multiple segments that you have the potential to create an alternate data path that enables traffic to bypass a firewall. As part of your hardening of the Snort host, you must ensure that routing is not enabled so that Snort cannot forward traffic from one segment that it is monitoring to another. There are multiple approaches to protect against this happening. The simplest is to use a network *tap* instead of just plugging in a normal network card. A tap is a specially designed piece of hardware that will only listen to traffic but will not transmit. Because it is hardware, there is no possibility of hacking the configuration or making a mistake in the configuration and accidentally allowing routing. Unfortunately, network taps are not free. Disabling routing, ensuring the host has no static routes, and disabling any routing protocols is the free way to ensure that you don't create a path around a firewall. Figure 6.1 illustrates bypassing the firewalls using your IDS.

The first dotted line (data flow #1) represents the desired (secure) data flow. Traffic from outside can only terminate on a server in the DMZ, and traffic going into the internal network can only come from a server in the DMZ. With this configuration traffic from the Internet can never pass all the way through directly to a host on the internal network. The second data flow, #2, represents how an *incorrectly configured* IDS could be used to route traffic from the outside (untrusted) network, into the internal network.

Figure 6.1 Bypassing the Firewalls using the IDS

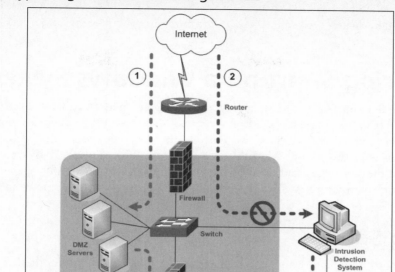

When it comes to placement of your IDS, you need to be aware of the difference between a switch and a hub. A hub operates by sending any traffic it receives on any port to every other port. Therefore, when using a hub, the IDS will see all the traffic passing through that hub, which is usually what you want for your IDS. A switch is more advanced than a hub, and most new devices are switches. A switch listens and learns what machines are connected to which port. It then uses this information to construct a forwarding table. After it has learned which port a given host is on, it will then only send traffic destined for that host to that specific port. This means that without any additional configuration, when you plug your IDS into a switch port, it isn't going to be seeing much traffic.

Luckily, there are some options for getting around this feature. Most enterprise switches have a port mirroring option. The terms used to describe this functionality varies from one manufacturer to another, Cisco calls it *Switched Port Analyzer* (SPAN). This enables you to configure a specific port such that it will see traffic from other designated ports (or all other ports) even though the traffic is destined for a different port. Typically, one port is configured to mirror all other ports and the IDS is attached to this port. On a Cisco 3750 switch with 24 ports you could configure mirroring by entering the following commands:

```
switch(config)# monitor session 1 source interface gig1/0/1 - gig1/0/23
switch(config)# monitor session 1 destination interface gig1/0/24
switch(config)# end
```

This setup is pretty straightforward. Line one specifies which ports to forward traffic from, and line two specifies which port the traffic should be mirrored to. You will need to refer to the user guide for your specific switch hardware to see if port mirroring is supported, and if it is, how to configure it.

Configuring Snort on a Windows System

From the start, the developers of Snort wanted it to be available on a wide variety of platforms. The current version will run on Linux, UNIX, Windows, and Macintosh OSX. There are some caveats to be aware of when running Snort on Windows. For one, the documentation is very *nix-centric. Many times what is referred to as the "default" behavior is not the default for Windows Snort. Chapter 5 detailed the advantages and disadvantages of running Snort on various operating systems. Here, we will provide you with more detail on deploying Snort on both a Windows and a Linux machine.

Installing Snort

Begin by browsing to http://snort.org/ and clicking on the **Get Snort** link on the left-hand side of the Web page. Click on **Binaries**, then **Win32**, and download the latest Installer file. When this is done, navigate to the file you downloaded and double-click it to start the install process.

1. You must click **I Agree** on the **License Agreement** window to proceed with the installation.

2. The next screen enables you to configure support for oracle or SQL server logging (see Figure 6.2). MySQL and ODBC are already supported by default. For a smaller installation the (first) default option will usually be adequate. After making your selection, click **Next**.

Figure 6.2 Snort Setup Logging Options

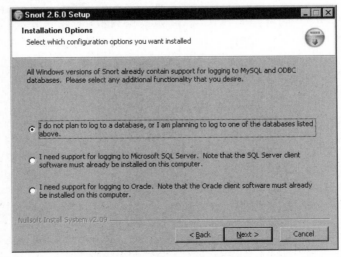

3. On the **Choose Components** screen shown in Figure 6.3, you should probably select the default, which is to install all components. The schemas are needed only if you plan to log to a database; however, the full install is only about 7 MB, so there isn't much space to be gained by trying to trim down the install. After making your selections, click **Next**.

Figure 6.3 Choose Components for Snort

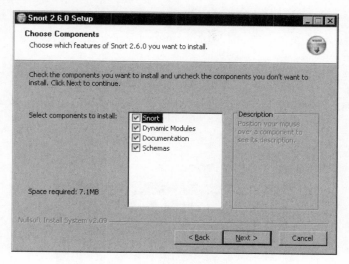

4. The next screen enables you to choose your installation location. The default is C:\snort. Remember, this server is a prime target for attackers and should be hardened as much as possible. As a general rule, non-default paths are almost always at least slightly more secure than default ones. After you've selected the installation path, click **Next**.

5. When the Installation has completed, click **Close**.

6. You will see a window, as shown in Figure 6.4, alerting you that Snort requires WinPcap to function and that it can be download from www.winpcap.org.

Figure 6.4 WinPcap Reminder

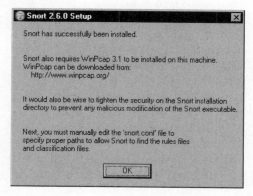

7. WinPcap is basically a Windows version of the UNIX libpcap API. This enables applications to interact with network packets directly, bypassing the Windows protocol stack. You will find WinPcap is required to run many networking tools on Windows. You will need to download WinPcap by clicking **Get WinPcap** on the left side of the Web page.

8. Save the setup file to a location of your choice and double-click it to begin the installation routine.

9. The first screen contains news and update information. Click **Next** to continue.

10. The next window is the License Agreement; you must click **I Agree** to continue the installation.

11. The install will complete. Click **Finish** to close the Installation Wizard.

Navigate to **Start | Control Panel | Network Connections | Local Area Connection**, right-click, and then choose **Properties**. You should see a new network driver in the properties list, as shown in Figure 6.5.

Figure 6.5 Local Area Connection Properties

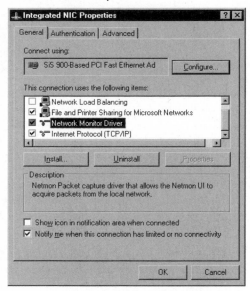

It would probably be a good idea to test the installation of WinPcap and the packet capture functionality before moving on to configuring Snort, that way if you need to troubleshoot Snort later, you can at least know WinPcap is working. The easiest way to test WinPcap is by starting up WinDump, which is a command-line packet sniffing utility for Windows that uses WinPcap. Windump can be downloaded from www.winpcap.org as well.

Configuring Snort Options

After you have verified that WinPcap is working, it's time to configure the various options that determine how Snort will behave using the Snort configuration file. The configuration file is excellently documented and very easy to use. The configuration file is divided up into six "steps" annotated within the comments. To get Snort working the way you want it to, follow these simple steps:

1. Start by opening the main Snort configuration file. By default it will be located at **C:\Snort\etc\snort.conf**. If you open it in Notepad it may not display properly, so WordPad would probably be a better choice.

2. Configure the HOME_NET variable, if desired, by removing the # from the line you need. (# is a comment indicator in the Snort configuration file.) The HOME_NET variable defines which networks are the "trusted" internal networks. This is used with the signatures to determine when the internal network is being attacked. By default, HOME_NET is set to any network with the *var HOME_NET any* line in the snort.conf. Setting this to accurately reflect your internal address space will reduce the number of false positive alerts you receive. A common example is *var HOME_NET 192.168.1.0/24*.

3. Configure the EXTERNAL_NET variable if desired. This is the network you expect attacks to come from. The recommended setting is to set this to everything *except* your HOME_NET using the following *var EXTERNAL_NET !$HOME_NET*. (Default: *var EXTERNAL_NET any*).

4. Next, define what servers are running specific services. For example, by setting HTTP_SERVERS to only specific servers, Snort will only watch for HTTP attacks targeted at those servers. If you wish to see attacks targeting servers that are not running the affected services, leave the defaults, which are to watch for attacks directed towards *any* internal servers. (Default: *var DNS_SERVERS $HOME_NET*). If you had a Web server running on 192.168.1.11 and 192.168.1.12, you could tell Snort to only look for HTTP attacks targeting that server by setting the following variable: *var HTTP_SERVERS [192.168.1.11/32,192.168.1.12/32]*.

5. If desired, configure the specific ports that services are available on. For an example, the default for HTTP is defined on the following line: *var HTTP_PORTS 80*. Similar to defining the servers in the preceding section, this will tell Snort to look only for attacks targeting specific ports. With the default configuration, Snort would ignore an HTTP attack to port 8080.

6. If you are interested in detecting the usage of AOL Instant Messenger (AIM), the various IP addresses of the AIM servers are defined in the snort.conf file. This is done because the IP addresses change frequently, and by using a variable, the rules don't have to be updated each time the IP address changes. If you don't wish to trigger based off AIM usage, don't worry about changing these IP addresses.

7. Configure the RULE_PATH variable, which tells Snort where to find the rules used for triggering events. This is one of the differences between Snort on Windows and Snort on other operating systems. Most operating systems will use a relative path, which is what is configured by default (*var RULE_PATH ../rules*), but on Windows you should use an absolute path. By default, the path would be *var RULE_PATH C:\snort\rules*.

8. The next section has some commented-out lines to disable certain detections of some infrequently seen types of traffic. Unless you are having some issues with those alerts or your IDS is very low on resources, it's probably fine to just leave those at the default (enabled) configuration.

9. The last few lines of the "step 1"section enable you to configure the detection engine for systems with limited resources. Unless you are having issues, you can leave this option alone.

10. After that the "step 2" and "step 3" sections of the configuration file to enable or disable specific functionality and detect particular types of attack, such as fragmentation attacks, stateful inspection, and stream reassembly options. (

11. The section labeled "Step #4" contains output options for Snort. There are several valuable options in this section. Uncomment **output alert_syslog: host=hostname, LOG_AUTH LOG_ALERT** and enter the hostname of your syslog server. LOG_AUTH is the facility to use, and LOG_ALERT is the priority for the alert. In my example I used the following command: *output alert_syslog: host=192.168.1.99, log_local7 log_notice*; this will log to the local7 facility as a notice. You also need to include the **–s** switch on the command line. If you don't have a syslog server to log to yet, just make note of the setting and come back to it when your syslog server is set up.

12. Edit the paths for the dynamically loaded libraries in section #2. Edit the lines as follows: **dynamicpreprocessor directory C:\snort\lib\snort_dynamicpreprocessor** and **dynamicengine C:\snort\lib\snort_dynamicengine\sf_engine.dll.** Note that for the preprocessor directory we are editing it for an absolute path (with no trailing slash). For the dynamicengine, we are altering the path from the default libsf_engine.so to the sf_engine.dll used in Windows.

13. Change *include classification.config* to an absolute path such as **include C:\snort\etc\classification.config**. Do the same for **include reference.config**.

14. The include section enables you to specify which rulesets are to be checked. Some rules are disabled by default, such as chat.rules, which is triggered by the use of various instant messaging clients. To enable or disable a given ruleset, simply add or remove a # at the beginning of the include line. This entry can be left as relative (that is, include $RULE_PATH/local.rules) because the RULE_PATH variable will be expanded to make it an absolute path.

15. After you are satisfied with your changes, save and close the configuration file.

16. The basic install does not include any rules. Go to **www.snort.org** and click **RULES** on the left side of the Web page. On the next page, click **DOWNLOAD RULES** on the far-right side of the page. Scroll down to **Sourcefire VRT Certified Rules – The Official Snort Ruleset (unregistered user release)** and click **Download** by the most current ruleset. The ruleset will be a compressed file so you will need a program to uncompress it; IZArc or FileZip are good options. There is also a selection of community-provided rules at the bottom of the page. If you are looking for something unusual, you might find it there without having to create the rule yourself.

17. Extract all files in the archive's signatures folder to **C:\snort\doc\signatures** and extract all files in the archive's rules folder to **C:\snort\rules**. This will take some time because there are currently about 3,700 rules.

You are now ready to start up Snort and see what it looks like in action. Go to a command prompt window and change your working directory to the \snort\bin directory, which is where the snort.exe is located. Type **snort −W** to list the available interfaces. In my case I get the output shown in Figure 6.6.

Figure 6.6 Snort Interface Listing

```
C:\Snort\bin>snort -W


  ,,_       -*> Snort! <*-
 o" )~    Version 2.6.0-ODBC-MySQL-FlexRESP-WIN32 (Build 57)
 ''''     By Martin Roesch & The Snort Team: http://www.snort.org/team.html
          (C) Copyright 1998-2006 Sourcefire Inc., et al.



Interface     Device      Description
-------------------------------------------
1  \Device\NPF_GenericDialupAdapter (Generic dialup adapter)
2  \Device\NPF_{F95B71A4-C943-40BA-9F65-CD73D4B20769} (Intel(R) PRO/100B PCI Adapter
(TX))
3  \Device\NPF_{A7F703C5-7567-49BC-B6C1-1A1F14614CAF} (SiS NIC SISNIC)
```

(Note: The line has been wrapped for Interface 2 to fit this page.)

When we start Snort, we can specify the interface to listen on using the −i switch. If you don't specify, it will use the first interface, which in my case won't see anything because it's a dial-up interface that is not in use. Use the −c option to tell Snort which configuration file to use. It can be useful to have multiple configuration files configured so that you can quickly switch configurations for special circumstances. You could prepare different configuration files to home in on certain issues, segments, or more in-depth logging. Another important option is −A, which tells Snort what type of alerts to generate. The options are fast, full, console, or none.

The following command example would start Snort listening on interface 3, with alerts going to the console only, using the configuration file at C:\snort\etc\snort.conf. The −K switch tells Snort what types of logs to generate. ASCII logs are easier for a human to read, but they take a little more time to log. If speed isn't a concern, the ASCII logs will probably be the easiest to read and analyze manually.

```
snort -A console -i 3 -c C:\snort\etc\snort.conf -l C:\snort\log -K ascii
```

You should see any triggered rules produce a message on the console. If you add the −s switch to the end of the line, it will tell snort to log to the syslog server you have configured in the snort.conf file; however, it will not also display on the snort console. If you want to create a rule for testing purposes to see what the results look like, create a test rule file, such as TESTING.rules, and place it in the rules folder (C:\snort\rules\ by default). In this file you could place the following line, which would trigger on any attempts to ping another system.

```
Alert icmp any any -> any any (msg:"TESTING rule"; sid:1000001;)
```

Edit the snort.conf to include your new rule by adding the following line: **include $RULE_PATH/TESTING.rules**. As a last step, edit the snort\stc\sid-msg.map file. This file provides a mapping between snort alert messages and alert IDs or numbers. Custom alerts should use an ID number of more than one million. Add the following line at the end of the file:

```
1000001
```

Placing the ID number is the minimum requirement for Snort not to output an error. You can certainly fill in all the other fields, following the existing message maps as a guideline. When this is done, you will need to stop and restart Snort. Here is the console output of a single ping and the reply:

```
08/10-18:22:19.823970  [**] [1:0:0] TESTING rule [**] [Priority: 0] {ICMP}
192.168.1.99 -> 192.168.1.1
08/10-18:22:20.284438  [**] [1:0:0] TESTING rule [**] [Priority: 0] {ICMP}
192.168.1.1 -> 192.168.1.99
```

You can also add your own custom rules to the local.rules file. When you open the file, you will find it is essentially empty, existing solely for you to place your custom rules in it. The local.rule is "included" in the snort.conf by default, so you will not need to add it there. You will, however, still need to edit the sid-msg.map file for any rules placed in local.rules. The aforementioned command example would display only to the console. For day-to-day operations you would probably want to use fast alerts in your log files, which look like the ones that are sent to the console with the *console* option.

```
snort –A fast –I 3 –c C:\snort\etc\snort.conf –l C:\snort\log –K ascii -s
```

Congratulations! You now have a working IDS. Packets will get logged by default to C:\snort\log\. A subdirectory will be created for each source IP that triggers an alert. In this subdirectory will be placed a log file named after the rule that was triggered. Additional instances of the same alert will be appended to the same file. Figure 6.7 shows an example of the log file C:\snort\log\192.168.1.99\ICMP_ECHO.ids:

Figure 6.7 ICMP Example Log

```
[**] TESTING rule [**]
08/10-20:25:51.282620 192.168.1.99 -> 192.168.1.107
ICMP TTL:128 TOS:0x0 ID:13266 IpLen:20 DgmLen:60
Type:8  Code:0  ID:512   Seq:28928  ECHO
61 62 63 64 65 66 67 68 69 6A 6B 6C 6D 6E 6F 70  abcdefghijklmnop
71 72 73 74 75 76 77 61 62 63 64 65 66 67 68 69  qrstuvwabcdefghi

=+=+=+=+=+=+=+=+=+=+=+=+=+=+=+=+=+=+=+=+=+=+=+=+=+=+=+=+=+=+=+=+=+
```

```
[**] TESTING rule [**]
08/10-20:25:52.282888 192.168.1.99 -> 192.168.1.107
ICMP TTL:128 TOS:0x0 ID:13274 IpLen:20 DgmLen:60
Type:8  Code:0  ID:512    Seq:29184   ECHO
61 62 63 64 65 66 67 68 69 6A 6B 6C 6D 6E 6F 70   abcdefghijklmnop
71 72 73 74 75 76 77 61 62 63 64 65 66 67 68 69   qrstuvwabcdefghi


=+=+=+=+=+=+=+=+=+=+=+=+=+=+=+=+=+=+=+=+=+=+=+=+=+=+=+=+=+=+=+=+=+=+=+
```

Take note that the output on the console (same as fast) are not the same as those logged in \log\. The logged packets also include the data portion of the ICMP ping (a through z repeated). The preceding configuration will log to the syslog server you specified in the snort.conf. In my case, the syslog server is Kiwi syslog. The incoming alerts for the ICMP test rule are shown in Figure 6.8.

Figure 6.8 Snort Sending Syslog Alerts to Kiwi Syslog

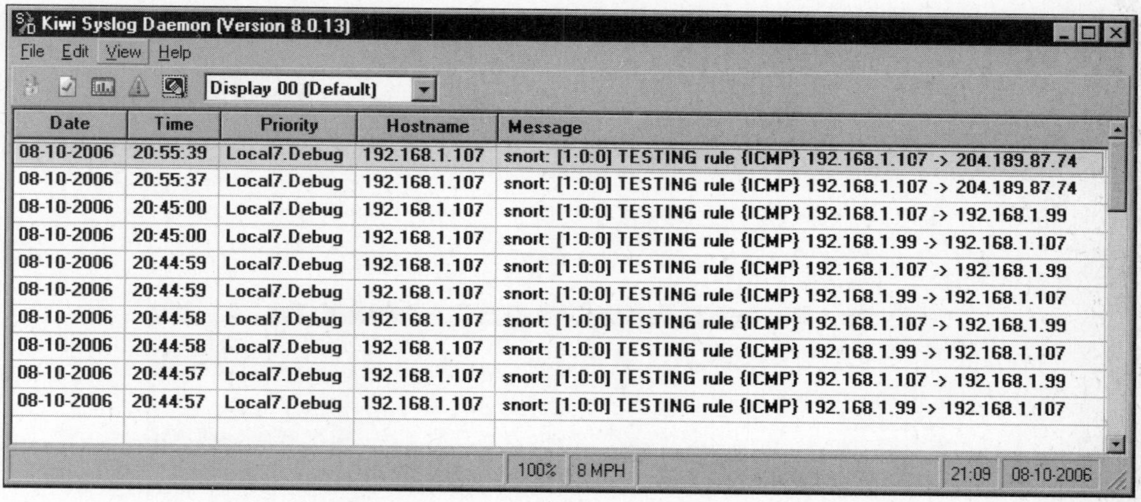

Using a Snort GUI Front End

Many times the command-line options for programs with lots of functionality can seem cryptic, opaque, or even overwhelming. At these times a GUI front end can make things a lot easier. Rather than know a certain command-line option and syntax, a check box can often be a lot easier to get right. Even an experienced admin can find these front ends easier to use than the command-line versions. While it's always going to be preferable to know the command-line operation *in addition* to being able to use a GUI, there is no need to memorize a lot of syntax if you don't have to. Although it is capable of "managing" the execution of Snort, IDS Policy Manager (IDSPM) is primarily geared toward managing and customizing the Snort rules.

Configuring IDS Policy Manager

IDS Policy Manager is available for download from www.activeworx.org/programs/idspm/index.htm. This program will run on Windows 2000 and Windows XP and provides a graphical interface for Snort rule management and configuring Snort itself via the Snort configuration file. Unlike IDScenter, IDSPM does not need to be installed on the sensor itself; in fact, one of the strengths of IDSPM is that it can manage multiple sensors remotely. IDS Policy Manager's primary strength is in its capability to manage the Snort rules, making this a must have for anyone who will be customizing and working with their rules extensively. IDSPM also supports the automated download of the newest Snort rules, using Oinkmaster. Setting up IDSPM can be accomplished by following these steps.

1. Download and run the installation program.

2. If you do not currently have the Microsoft .NET 2.0 framework installed you will be asked if you want to install it. The window that prompts you will refer to it as an optional component. In my case the product would not install until I had installed .NET V2, so I'm not sure how optional it really is. This shouldn't pose any issues unless you are running some other software that relies on older .NET features and is incompatible with the newer version.

3. Follow the installation prompts, accepting the license agreement and choosing the installation directory.

4. When you first run the software, you will see a pop-up window alerting you that your oinkcode is not set up; click **OK** to get past this message.

5. Next open the IDS Policy Manager shortcut. The opening screen is shown in Figure 6.9.

Figure 6.9 IDS Policy Manager

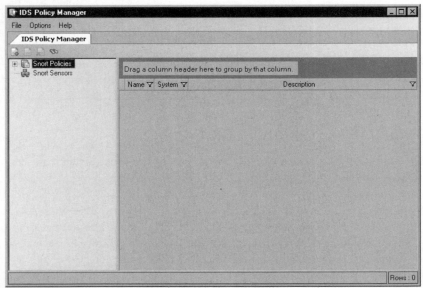

One of the first steps is to configure adding a sensor and then configure Oinkmaster. Add a sensor by right-clicking **Snort Sensors** and selecting **Add Sensor**. There are several tabs of information to fill out on the Sensor properties window shown in Figure 6.10.

Figure 6.10 IDSPM Add Sensor

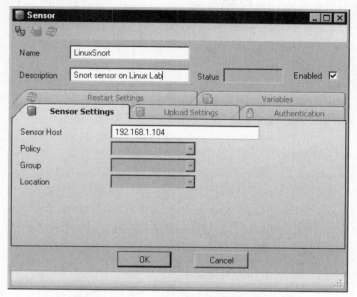

6. At a minimum, fill out the **Name** and a **Description** for the sensor.

7. Also enter the **IP address** or host name on the **Sensor Settings** tab.

8. On the **Authentication** tab, enter the **username** and **password** to use to connect to the sensor (IDSPM will use SSH to communicate with the sensor). You can also use PKI for authentication. If you select PKI in the **Authentication Mode** drop-down box, the password fields will then change to fields to indicate the location of your public and private key files.

9. On the **Upload Settings** tab, ensure that the Upload Directory is configured; by default it's **/etc/snort/rules**.

10. When you are finished filling out the information, click the small monitors in the upper-left corner of the window. This will test the SSH connection to the server. The first time it connects, you will get the standard choice of accepting the RSA key or not. Choose **Yes**. Afterwards a brief Test connectivity Log will be displayed. All these should have a result of OK. Click **OK** to continue.

11. Click **OK** to close the Sensor properties window.

    To configure the Oinkmaster portion of IDSPM, you will need to go to www.snort.org and register so that you can download the rules file. After registering, log onto the Snort Web site and click the link that says **User Preferences**. At the bottom of the page is a section titled Oink Code; click the **Get Code** button. Copy this code for use in the Oinkmaster configuration file.

12. Navigate to **Options | Settings**.

13. In the **Settings** pane on the left, select **Miscellaneous**.

14. You will need to paste the Oink Code you generated previously, so that Oinkmaster can download the latest Snort rules.

15. Use the drop-down boxes to select how often you wish to check for updates and how often to back up the rules database. After you are finished, click **OK**.

16. The next step is to create a policy. In this context, a policy is a definition of which rules to apply to a given sensor. Right-click **Snort Policies** and select **Add Policy**.

17. Provide a **name** and **description** for the policy. Use the drop-down box to select the Snort version. The **Initialize policy** check box should be checked, so that it will apply the new settings immediately.

18. Select the **Update Locations** tab shown in Figure 6.11. Click the "plus" to add a location.

19. Click the cell under **Update Location Name** and select the appropriate location. You can define alternate locations at **Options | Setting** under **Update Locations**. After selecting the update location, click **OK**.

Figure 6.11 IDSPM New Policy Locations

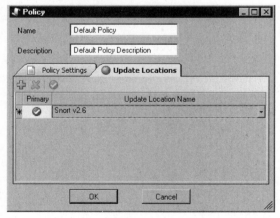

20. The **Initialize Policy** window will come up. This window enables you to pull your rules from a pre-defined location (in this case, the one called "Snort 2.6, which is a Web URL), a local file, or another HTTP address that has not been pre-defined. Select the proper location (or just leave the default) and click **Start**.

21. The next step is to edit the policies' various properties to match your environment.

NOTE

There is no mechanism to import your current Snort configuration into IDSPM. This means that if you have a working Snort configuration already, you will need to redefine it within IDSPM. After you start using IDSPM to manage your Snort sensors, you shouldn't ever need to edit the sensors' configuration directly and, in fact, doing so would cause your changes to be overwritten the next time you applied the configuration from IDSPM.

By clicking the plus next to Snort Policies, it should expand and show the newly created policy. By expanding the newly created policy, a number of property groups come into view, as shown in Figure 6.12. The primary one to configure is the **Variables** group. This is where you set the various variables in the configuration file so Snort knows what alerts to look out for.

Figure 6.12 IDSPM Variables

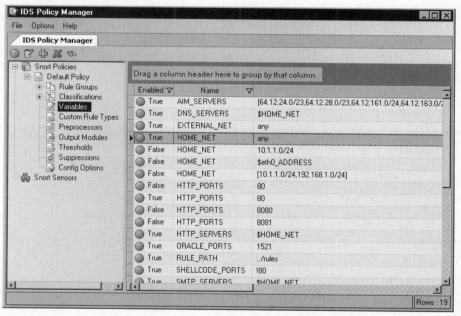

In the example you will see that there are multiples of many variables defined. This is done as a convenience to enable you to easily switch between them by right-clicking and selecting **Disable Item** or **Enable Item**. If, for example, you don't want HOME_NET to be any (the default), you will right-click the highlighted variable and select **Disable Item**. You could then double-click (or right-click and select **Edit Item**) the HOME_NET that is defined as 10.1.1.0/24 and edit it. After changing the value to 192.168.1.0/24, click **Save**. Lastly, right-click the newly defined HOME_NET and select **Enable Item**.

If you need to edit the output modules, such as if you wanted Snort to log to MySQL, you would select the **Output Modules** section. If you do want to use Snort to log to a MySQL database, select either of the output modules with a name of "database" and with "mysql" in the value column. There should be two available, and each is the same except one specifies the localhost for the DB user. After editing the value to match your user name, database name, and the MySQL password, click **Save**. After the rule value has been saved, right-click and select **Enable Item**.

To select which rule groups to apply, select **Rule Groups** in the left pane. Each category can be enabled or disabled. These settings correspond to commenting out the include statements in the snort.conf file. For example, to enable all the backdoor checks (over 500), right-click the row with "backdoor" in the name column and select **Enable Item**. By drilling down in the left column and selecting backdoor there, you can choose between individual rules to enable or disable in the right column. A very handy feature of IDSPM is the Find Rule function. With Rule Groups selected in the left pane, a small pair of binoculars will appear in the upper-left of the window; click this to open the **Find Rule** dialog. You can enter a **Rule ID** or **Rule Name** and then click **Search**. You don't have to know the entire name; you can enter a partial name and it will pull up a list of rules.

Perhaps the most compelling feature of IDSPM is the GUI interface for creating your own custom rules. Follow these steps to create your own custom rule.

1. Drill down into **Rule Groups** until you get to individual rules in the right pane (it doesn't matter which group you are in).

2. Click anywhere in the right pane and select **Add Item**. The Rule window is shown in Figure 6.13.

Figure 6.13 IDSPM Rule Editor

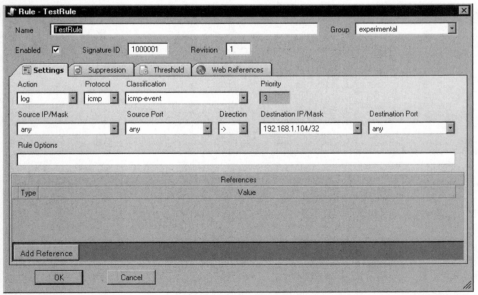

3. Start by entering a **Name** for the rule.

4. Select a **Group** for the rule to go into. This drop-down selection is why it doesn't matter which group you are in when you click Add Item. The **Local** group has been created specifically for the placement of custom rules.

5. The Settings tab is where you specify what triggers the rule. For example, if we wanted to create a rule that would trigger any time ICMP was sent to the Snort sensor (192.168.1.104), we could easily do so. For **Action**, use the drop-down box to select the desired action. Log will log the packet, while Alert will show an alert on the Snort console. We will select **Alert** for this exercise.

6. For **Protocol**, use the drop-down list to select **icmp**.

7. For **Classification**, use the drop-down list to select **icmp-event**.

8. In the **Destination IP/Mask** field, you can type 192.168.1.104/32.

9. Enter a unique **Signature ID** number. Any custom rules should have ID numbers over 1,000,000 (the first one million IDs are reserved).

10. Take note of the **Rule Options** field, but for now leave it blank.

11. Place a **Check** in the **Enabled** box at the top and click **OK**.

    The **Rule Options** field deserves a closer look. This is where you specify the bulk of the Snort rule logic. This is where the really interesting information is placed. There are currently four types of rule options: meta-data, payload, non-payload, and post-detection. Odds are good that the majority of what you might want to search for would be done using the payload option, which enables you to trigger based on defined strings being present (or absent) from the packet. While the rule options are behind the true power of Snort's custom rules, don't forget that there is a repository of user community rules available (from www.snort.org). Unless you are trying to match a rule based on very unusual characteristics, odds are good that the rule is already out there.

12. After you have finished all your customization, it's time to assign the new policy to your sensor and apply the policy. Select **Snort Sensors** in the left pane and then right-click and select **Edit item**, or double-click the sensor row in the right pane.

13. In the **Policy** drop-down box, select your new policy and click **OK**.

14. Now right-click the sensor and select **Upload policies to Sensors**.

15. The next window enables you to place a check next to each sensor you want to update. The status column will tell you if any rules applied to the selected sensor have been changed. If so, the status will read "Sensor needs to be updated." When satisfied with the selection, click **Start**.

16. After it is finished, click **Close**.

You will find that the **/etc/snort/rules/** directory contains a file called **local.rules**. The snort.conf file has an **include $RULE_PATH/local.rules** entry to enable the rules in this file. If you open this file, you can see our custom rule is there:

```
alert icmp any any -> 192.168.1.104/32 any (msg:"TestRule"; classtype:icmp-event;
sod:1000001; rev:1)
```

The resultant alert on the Snort console is also shown here.

```
12/01-12:16:41.236240 [**] [1:1000001:1] TestRule [**] [Classification: Generic ICMP
event] [Priority: 3] {ICMP} 192.168.1.99 -> 192.168.1.104
```

Configuring Snort on a Linux System

The process of installing Snort on a Linux system is very close to the process on a Windows system. The primary difference is that the default (relative) paths in the snort.conf file are much more likely to work without modification on the Linux system. You will need to download the latest version of Snort that is appropriate for your system. If you are using Fedora Core 5, this is as simple as typing *yum install snort*, or you could download and install the .rpm from snort.org.

Configuring Snort Options

The next step is to configure the various options that determine how Snort will behave using the Snort configuration file. The configuration file is excellently documented and very easy to use. To get Snort working the way you want it to, follow these simple steps.

1. Start by opening the main Snort configuration file. By default it will be located at /etc/snort/snort.conf.

2. Configure the HOME_NET variable, if desired, by removing the # from the line you need. # is a commend indicator in the Snort configuration file. The HOME_NET variable defines which networks are the "trusted" internal networks. This is used with the signatures to determine when the internal network is being attacked. By default, HOME_NET is set to *any* network with the *var HOME_NET any* line in the snort.conf. Setting this to accurately reflect your internal address space will reduce the number of false positive alerts you receive. A common example would be *var HOME_NET 192.168.1.0/24* or perhaps *var HOME_NET [192.168.1.0/24,192.168.2.0/24]*.

3. Configure the EXTERNAL_NET variable if desired. This is the network you expect attacks to come from. The recommendation is to set this to everything *except* your HOME_NET using the following: **var EXTERNAL_NET !$HOME_NET**. (Default: *var EXTERNAL_NET any*.)

4. Next, define what servers are running specific services. For example, by setting HTTP_SERVERS to only specific servers, Snort will only watch for HTTP attacks targeted at those servers. If you wish to see attacks targeting servers that are not running the affected services, leave the defaults, which are to watch for attacks directed towards *any* internal servers. (Default: *var DNS_SERVERS $HOME_NET*) If you had a Web server running on 192.168.1.11 and 192.168.1.12, you could tell Snort to only look for HTTP attacks targeting that server by setting the following variable: *var HTTP_SERVERS [192.168.1.11/32,192.168.1.12/32]*.

5. If desired, configure the specific ports that services are available on. For example, the default for HTTP is defined on the following line: *var HTTP_PORTS 80*. Similar to defining the servers in the preceding section, this will tell Snort to only look for attacks

targeting specific ports. With the default configuration, Snort would *ignore* an HTTP attack to port 8080. Again, this setting will help focus where Snort looks for different types of attacks to occur.

6. If you are interested in detecting the usage of AOL Instant Messenger (AIM), the various IP addresses of the AIM servers are defined in the snort.conf file. This is done because the IP addresses change frequently, and by using a variable, the rules don't have to be updated each time the IP address changes. If you don't wish to trigger based off AIM usage, don't worry about changing these IP addresses.

7. Download the Snort rules from http://snort.org/rules. Click **Download Rules** on the right-hand side of the page. On the **Download Rules** page, scroll down to the section labeled **Sourcefire VRT Certified Rules (unregistered user release)**. Download the latest ruleset.

8. Extract the rules (and /docs) to the location of your choice, typically /etc/snort/rules and /etc/snort/docs.

9. Configure the RULE_PATH variable, which tells Snort where to find the rules used for triggering events. You can use a relative path such as var RULE_PATH ../rules or an absolute path such as /etc/snort/rules.

10. The next section has some commented out lines to disable certain detections of some infrequently seen types of traffic. Unless you are having some issues with those alerts or your IDS is very low on resources, it's probably fine to just leave those at the default (enabled) configuration.

11. The next section enables you to configure the detection engine for systems with limited resources. Unless you are having issues, you can leave this option alone.

12. After that there are several sections of the configuration file to enable or disable specific functionality and detect particular types of attack, such as fragmentation attacks, stateful inspection, and stream reassembly options.

13. The section labeled Step #4 contains output options for Snort. Uncomment **output alert_syslog: LOG_AUTH LOG_ALERT** (the default). Despite what facility and severity you configure here, the snort alerts will be generated as auth.info. You also need to include the *–s* switch on the command line to enable syslog logging. If you don't have a syslog server to log to yet, just make note of the setting and come back to it when your syslog serer is set up.

- Using the preceding example of LOG_AUTH and LOG_ALERT, you would need the following in your syslog.conf file to log to a syslog server at 192.168.1.99:

```
auth. info            @managmentserverIP
```

- If you are using syslog-ng, you would need a logging destination defined, a filter that specifies what events to capture, and a log statement in the syslog-ng.conf file. An example of this configuration would be the following:

```
destination d_lab { udp ("192.168.1.99" port(514)); };
filter f_most { level(info..emerg); };
log { source(s_sys); filter(f_most); destination(d_lab); };
```

14. Edit the paths for the dynamically loaded libraries in section #2 to point to the proper path. Depending on your Linux distribution and installation method, these paths may not be the default. For example, on Fedora Core 5, using yum to install Snort, the settings would use the following paths: *dynamicpreprocessor directory /usr/lib/snort/dynamicpreprocessor* and *dynamicengine /usr/lib/snort/libsf_engine.so*. If you receive an error when you try to run Snort, along the lines of *Unknown rule type: dynamicpreprocessor directory* or *Unknown rule type: dynamicengine*, then your installation of Snort is not configured to use dynamically loaded processors. In this case, simply place a # in front of both of those lines to comment them out.

15. The last section (Step #6), contains various include statements that specify the rulesets to be checked. Some rules are disabled by default, such as chat.rules, which is triggered by the use of various instant messaging clients. To enable or disable a given ruleset, simply add or remove a # at the beginning of the include line. This entry can be left as a relative path (for example, include $RULE_PATH/local.rules) because the RULE_PATH variable will be expanded to make it an absolute path.

16. If you need any custom rules that are not included with the standard Snort release, you can download rules provided by the Snort community from the Rules page on the Snort Web site. If you are looking for something unusual, you might find it there without having to create the rule yourself.

You are now ready to start up Snort and see what it looks like in action. When you start Snort you can specify the interface to listen on using the *–i* switch such as *–i eth0*. If you don't specify, it will use the first interface. Use the *–c* option to tell Snort which configuration file to use. It can be useful to have multiple configuration files configured so you can quickly switch configurations for special circumstances. You could prepare different configuration files to home in on certain issues, segments, or more in-depth logging. Another important option is *–A*, which tells Snort what type of alerts to generate. The options are fast, full, console, or none.

The following command example would start Snort listening on the first interface (no *–i* used), with alerts going to the console only, using the configuration file at /etc/snort/snort.conf. The *–l* switch tells Snort where the logging directory is located. The *–K* switch tells Snort what types of logs to generate. ASCII logs are easier for a human to read, but they take a little more time to log. If speed isn't a concern, the ASCII logs will probably be the easiest to read and analyze.

```
snort -A console -c /etc/snort/snort.conf -l /etc/snort/log -K ascii
```

You should see any triggered rules produce a message on the console and logged to your syslog server. If you add the *–s* switch to the end of the line, it will tell snort to log to the syslog server you have configured in the snort.conf file; however, it will not also display on the snort console. If you want to create a rule for testing purposes to see what the results look like, create a test rule file, such as TESTING.rules, and place it in the rules folder (/etc/snort/rules, in this example). In this file you could place the following line, which would trigger on any attempts to ping another system.

```
Alert icmp any any -> any any (msg:"TEST rule";)
```

Edit the snort.conf to read your new rule by inserting the following statement towards the end of the file: **include $RULE_PATH/TESTING.rules**. .As a last step, edit the snort\stc\sid-msg.map file. This file provides a mapping between snort alert messages and alert IDs or numbers. Custom alerts should use an ID number of more than one million. Add the following line at the end of the file:

```
1000001
```

Placing the ID number is the minimum requirement for Snort not to output an error. You can certainly fill in all the other fields, following the existing message maps as a guideline. When this is done, you will need to stop and restart Snort. Here is a partial display of the console output of a single ping and the reply.

```
10/12-21:29:35.911089  [**] [1:0:0] TEST rule [**] [Priority: 0] {ICMP}
192.168.1.99 -> 192.168.1.103
08/10-18:22:20.284438  [**] [1:0:0] TEST rule [**] [Priority: 0] {ICMP}
192.168.1.103 -> 192.168.1.99
```

You can also add your own custom rules to the local.rules file. When you open the file, you will find it is essentially empty, existing solely for you to place your custom rules in it. The local.rule is "included" in the snort.conf by default, so you will not need to add it there. You will, however, still need to edit the sid-msg.map file for any rules placed in local.rules.

The *−A* option will alter the display of the alerts on the console, while the *−K* option controls how the alerts are logged to the log directory. You should experiment with the different display formats to find the one that provides adequate information with the minimal strain on the Snort host. For day-to-day operations you would probably want to use fast alerts in your log files, which look like the ones that are sent to the console with the *console* option. Available alert modes and logging formats are outlined here for handy reference.

- **−A console** Logs to the console in the following format:

```
10/12-21:29:35.911089  [**] [1:0:0] TEST rule [**] [Priority: 0] {ICMP}
192.168.1.99 -> 192.168.1.103
```

- **−A fast** Logs in the same *format* as console, but writes the alerts to a /snort/alert file with no output to the console.

- **−A full** Logs to the /snort/alert file in the following format:

```
[**] [1:0:0] TEST rule [**]
[Priority: 0]
10/12-21:38:53.741606 192.168.1.103 -> 192.168.1.99
ICMP TTL:64 TOS:0x0 ID:6350 IpLen:20 DgmLen:60
Type:0  Code:0  ID:512  Seq:7936  ECHO REPLY
```

- **–K pcap** This is the default mode if you don't specify an alternate format on the command line. This file will contain the alert packets in their entirety. You can open this file using a network sniffer such as Wireshark.

- **–K ascii** Will create a folder under /log for each IP address. Within that folder each rule will create a log file. The log entries will be the same format as the "full" alert format.

- **–K none** No log file will be created.

Congratulations! You now have a working IDS. Figure 6.14 shows the syslog alerts from the TESTING.rule in the Kiwi Syslog Daemon console.

Figure 6.14 Snort Alerts in Kiwi Syslog Daemon Console

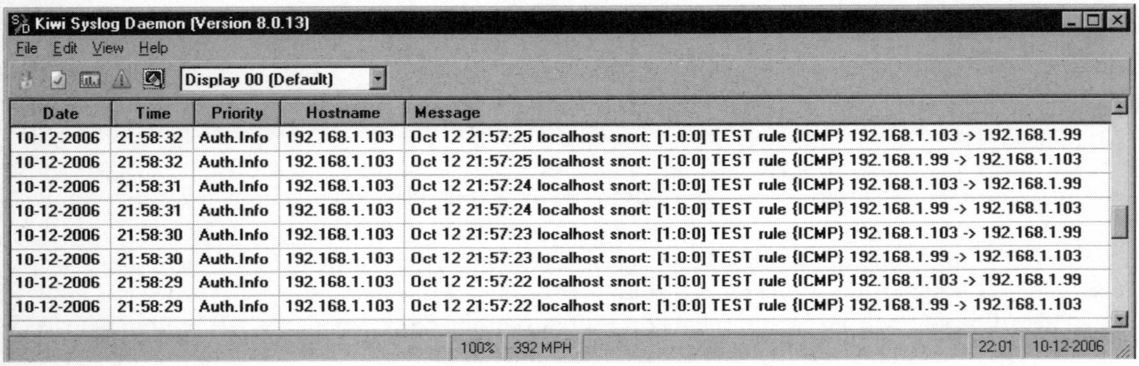

Using a GUI Front-End for Snort

Like the Windows version of Snort, some have felt the administration of Snort could be improved upon by implementing a more robust GUI interface. There are several Snort GUIs to choose from aimed at both the configuration of Snort, as well as the interpretation of the Snort alerts. Some really only offer buttons to configure options on the Snort command line, and offer very little additional functionality, while others bring some very powerful additional features to the table. We will discuss the operation of some of the better offerings in the next section.

Basic Analysis and Security Engine

Basic Analysis and Security Engine (BASE) is available for download from http://base.secureideas.net/about.php. The purpose of BASE is to provide a Web-based front end for analyzing the alerts generated by Snort. Base was derived from the ACID project (Analysis Console for Intrusion Databases). Whereas ACID is more of a general-purpose front end for viewing and search events, BASE is a Snort-specific utility. The instructions to configure BASE assume you have already installed and configured Snort. Snort must be installed with the *—with-mysql* switch because Snort does not support MySQL output by default. The Snort Web site has RPM packages with MySQL support already included for some operating systems. This is the list of dependencies for running BASE: httpd, Snort (with MySQL support), MySQL, php-gd, pcre, php-mysql, php-pdo, php-pear-Image-GraphViz, graphviz, and php-adodb. Follow these steps to get BASE up and running.

1. Download and install MySQL and BASE

2. Edit the /snort/snort.conf file. Uncomment and edit the following line:

```
output database: log, mysql, user=snort password=snortpass dbname=snort
host=localhost
```

3. The next few steps are related to setting up the MySQL database and settings. After installing MySQL, enter the MySQL commands by typing **mysql** on the command line. This will place you in an interactive command mode. All commands must have a ; at the end of the line. By default, the MySQL installation will not have a password set at all. You should add a default password with the following commands.

```
mysql

mysql> SET PASSWORD FOR root@localhost=PASSWORD('somepassword');
```

After you have assigned a password to the root account, simply entering mysql will not enable you to access the interactive command mode. After a password has been assigned, use **mysql −u <username> −p**. You will then be prompted to enter the password for the user you specified (typically root).

4. The next step is to create the Snort database.

```
mysql> create database snort;
```

5. You now need to give the Snort user permissions to add the needed tables to the Snort database. Use these commands:

```
mysql> grant INSERT,SELECT on root.* to snort@localhost;
```

6. You should not set the password for the Snort user to the same password you used in the Snort configuration file.

```
mysql> SET PASSWORD FOR snort@localhost=PASSWORD('snortpass');
```

7. The next step is to add some additional permissions for the Snort database using the following commands:

```
mysql> grant ALL on snort.* to snort@localhost;
mysql> grant ALL to snort;
mysql> exit
```

8. Now that the database has been created, you need to populate it with the tables Snort uses. Use the following command to create the tables:

```
mysql -u root -p < /etc/snort/schemas/create_mysql snort
```

When the command completes, it will not give any indication of its success; therefore, it will be necessary to manually verify that the tables were created.

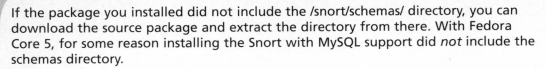

TIP

If the package you installed did not include the /snort/schemas/ directory, you can download the source package and extract the directory from there. With Fedora Core 5, for some reason installing the Snort with MySQL support did *not* include the schemas directory.

9. Verify the MySQL tables were created in the Snort database by entering the following commands. You should see output similar to that shown in the following example:

```
mysql -u root -p
show databases;
+----------+
| Database |
+----------+
| mysql    |
| snort    |
| test     |
+----------+
use snort;
show tables;
+------------------+
| Tables_in_snort  |
+------------------+
| data             |
| detail           |
| encoding         |
| event            |
| icmphdr          |
| iphdr            |
| opt              |
| reference        |
| reference_system |
| schema           |
| sensor           |
| sig_class        |
| sig_reference    |
| signature        |
| tcphdr           |
```

```
| udphdr            |
+-------------------+
exit
```

The list of databases is not significant, as long as the Snort database exists, of course. The table listing must be accurate. If any are missing, Snort will generate an error when you run it.

10. Install **php-gd** which is used to generate the graphs in BASE. On Fedora Core 5 you can just type **yum install php-gd**.

11. Install ADODB, which is a database abstraction library for PHP. On Fedora you can simply enter **yum install php-adodb**.

12. It's now time to configure BASE itself. Edit the **/usr/share/base-php4/base_conf.php** file to ensure that the following lines are configured with paths and settings appropriate for your configuration.

```
$BASE_urlpath = '/base';
$DBlib_path = '/usr/share/ododb';
$DBtype        = 'mysql';
$alert_dbname  = 'snort';
$alert_host    = 'localhost';
$alert_port    = '';
$alert_user    = 'snort';
$alert_password = 'snortpass';
```

You should not be able to access the BASE Web page at the following URL: **http://localhost/base/**.

Tools & Traps…

Troubleshooting Tips

■ You can enable debugging in BASE by editing the **/usr/share/base-php4/base-php4.conf** file.

```
$debug_mode = 2;
```

■ Use chkconfig to make sure that MySQL, Snort, and httpd are running.

```
Chkconfig --list | grep snort
Snortd      0:off   1:off   2:on    3:on    4:on    5:on    6:on
```

Continued

> If all entries say "off," then that service is configured not to start. Try **service snortd start.**
>
> - Httpd may need to be restarted for some configuration changes to take effect; when in doubt, restart it just to be safe: **service httpd restart.**
> - The httpd access log and error log can be found at /etc/httpd/logs.
> - You can control the logging level of the httpd by editing /etc/httpd/conf/httpd.conf.
>
> ```
> LogLevel debug
> ```
>
> - If you are having issues with the URLs not being found, the /etc/httpd/conf.d/base-php4.conf file tells the Web server to alias /base/ with the directory /usr/share/base-php4/.

The very first time you start up BASE, none of the database tables have been created. You will see something like the page shown in Figure 6.15.

Figure 6.15 BASE Setup

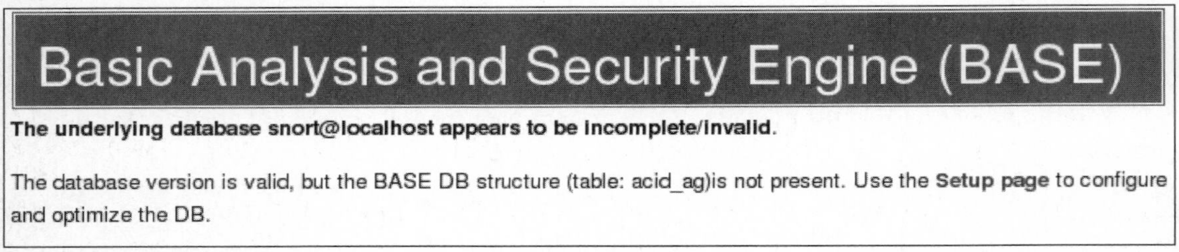

Basic Analysis and Security Engine (BASE)

The underlying database snort@localhost appears to be incomplete/invalid.

The database version is valid, but the BASE DB structure (table: acid_ag)is not present. Use the **Setup page** to configure and optimize the DB.

13. Click on the **Setup page** link.
14. Click the **Create BASE AG** button on the right-hand side. You see several success messages as shown in Figure 6.16.
15. Click the **Main Page** link. This should take you to the primary BASE interface as shown in Figure 6.17.

Figure 6.16 BASE Success

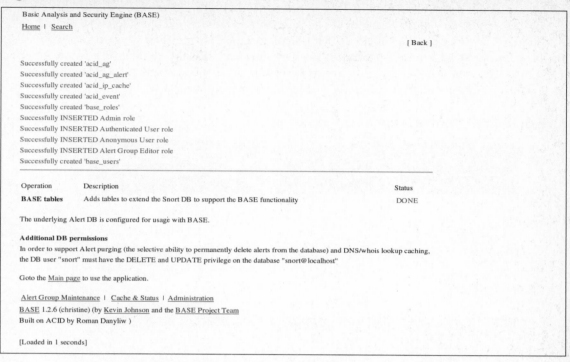

Basic Analysis and Security Engine (BASE)

Home | Search

[Back]

Successfully created 'acid_ag'
Successfully created 'acid_ag_alert'
Successfully created 'acid_ip_cache'
Successfully created 'acid_event'
Successfully created 'base_roles'
Successfully INSERTED Admin role
Successfully INSERTED Authenticated User role
Successfully INSERTED Anonymous User role
Successfully INSERTED Alert Group Editor role
Successfully created 'base_users'

Operation	Description	Status
BASE tables	Adds tables to extend the Snort DB to support the BASE functionality	DONE

The underlying Alert DB is configured for usage with BASE.

Additional DB permissions
In order to support Alert purging (the selective ability to permanently delete alerts from the database) and DNS/whois lookup caching, the DB user "snort" must have the DELETE and UPDATE privilege on the database "snort@localhost"

Goto the Main page to use the application.

Alert Group Maintenance | Cache & Status | Administration
BASE 1.2.6 (christine) (by Kevin Johnson and the BASE Project Team
Built on ACID by Roman Danyliw)

[Loaded in 1 seconds]

Figure 6.17 BASE Main Page

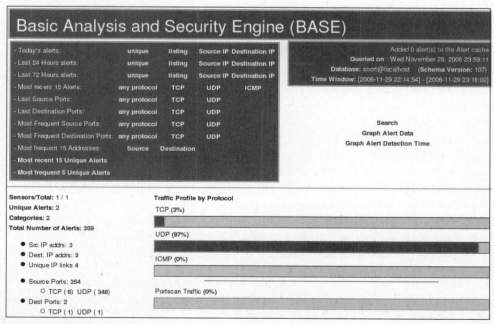

Basic Analysis and Security Engine (BASE)

- Today's alerts:	unique	listing	Source IP	Destination IP	
- Last 24 Hours alerts:	unique	listing	Source IP	Destination IP	
- Last 72 Hours alerts:	unique	listing	Source IP	Destination IP	
- Most recent 15 Alerts:	any protocol	TCP	UDP	ICMP	
- Last Source Ports:	any protocol	TCP	UDP		
- Last Destination Ports:	any protocol	TCP	UDP		
- Most Frequent Source Ports:	any protocol	TCP	UDP		
- Most Frequent Destination Ports:	any protocol	TCP	UDP		
- Most frequent 15 Addresses:	Source	Destination			
- Most recent 15 Unique Alerts					
- Most frequent 5 Unique Alerts					

Added 0 alert(s) to the Alert cache
Queried on : Wed November 29, 2006 23:59:11
Database: snort@localhost   (Schema Version: 107)
Time Window: [2006-11-29 22:14:54] - [2006-11-29 23:18:02]

Search
Graph Alert Data
Graph Alert Detection Time

Sensors/Total: 1 / 1
Unique Alerts: 2
Categories: 2
Total Number of Alerts: 359

- Src IP addrs: 3
- Dest. IP addrs: 3
- Unique IP links 4

- Source Ports: 354
  ○ TCP (6) UDP (348)
- Dest Ports: 2
  ○ TCP (1) UDP (1)

Traffic Profile by Protocol

TCP (3%)

UDP (97%)

ICMP (0%)

Portscan Traffic (0%)

Although this window may not be too flashy, there is a wealth of information you can discover. Most of the fields are actually links. By clicking to the right of **Today's alerts**, for example, you can get a sorted list of unique alerts, a listing of all alerts, or a list sorted by source IP address or destination IP address. The other headings along the left side offer similar functionality. Of particular note are the links for the **Most Frequent 15 addresses** by source address. This would enable you to quickly see which systems are *generating* the majority of your alerts. If you open that window (shown in Figure 6.18) there are several additional fields that are also hyperlinked.

Figure 6.18 BASE Most Frequent by Source IP

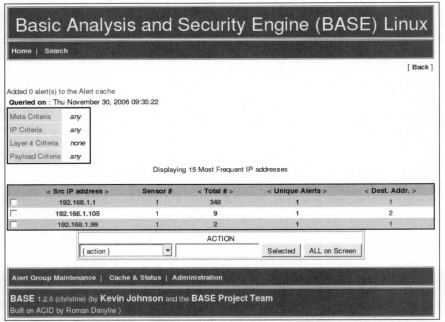

Note the field at the bottom labeled **ACTION**. This enables you to configure the *alert groups*. Alert groups are basically shortcuts to enable you to view a subset of alerts quickly, without having to navigate through the various menus to get there. For example, suppose you want to know anytime that 192.168.1.1 generates an alert. You can check the check box to the left of 192.168.1.1, and then use the {action} drop-down box to select Create AG (by Name**)**. In the action column, enter .1_ALERTS to use as the alert group name. Finally, click Selected.

The next screen enables you to enter a description for the newly created alert group. Enter a meaningful text description for the group and click Save Changes. The next screen will be a listing of all alerts from 192.168.1.1. This screen *is* the alert group. In the future, if you want to quickly see this group of alerts, you can click Alert Group Maintenance at the bottom of each page, and then click the alert group you want to view. In this way, any subset of alerts is only two clicks away, sort of like a shortcut straight to a particular set of filtering criteria.

Another feature of note is the Administration link at the bottom of each page. This will take you to a screen where you can configure users for BASE. There are four options on the administration screen: list users, create a user, list roles, and create a role. These screens enable you to create users and assign them to various roles. If you click List Roles, you can see the four predefined roles. If you want to assign a user in the administrator role, simple click Create a user. Enter the login name, a full name or description, and a password. Use the drop-down box to select a role and then click Submit Query. None of the settings here will take effect until you edit the base_conf.php file and change the value of $Use_Auth_System = 1;. A value of 0 (the default) means the authentication is disabled and everyone has full access to BASE. Only the admin role has access to the administration screen.

TIP

Remember the different logging options for Snort on the command line. Previously we used –*A console*, which would log Snort events to the Snort terminal. If you are going to be using a different front end for viewing Snort alerts, there isn't much value in also logging to the console. You can use –*A none* when starting Snort, which will cause Snort not to log anything to the Snort terminal, resulting in improved performance.

Other Snort Add-Ons

The number of Snort utilities and add-ons is impressive. Some of these address such key issues as keeping your Snort rulebase up to date, while others provide additional performance improvements such as faster logging. If you are looking for a particular feature or option, you should do some searching on the Internet, and you might find that the functionality you are looking for already exists. If you do find an add-in you are interested in using, remember to properly test it before deploying it in a production environment.

Using Oinkmaster

You may get tired of constantly having to update the Snort signature files. Because Snort is a signature-based IDS, having current signatures is vital. Without current signature files you could be unaware of intrusion attempts happening right in front of you. Although Snort itself does not include any means to automatically update the signature file, there is another utility that can help called Oinkmaster (http://oinkmaster.sourceforge.net/features.shtml). Oinkmaster is a Perl script that will update your Snort rules from the Snort Web site automatically. Because it uses Perl, Oinkmaster will run on a Linux or a Windows Snort host. The Oinkmaster Perl script can be scheduled to run and check for updates as often as you like. To get Snort rules downloads without having to wait until the next release of Snort, you have to register on the Snort Web site. You can register for free at https://snort.org/pub-bin/register.cgi. A password will be sent to the e-mail address you provide during registration. The configuration of Oinkmaster is outlined here.

1. After logging into the Snort Web site, click the link that says **User Preferences**.
2. At the bottom of the page is a section titled Oink Code; click the **Get Code** button.

3. **Copy** this code for use in the Oinkmaster configuration file.

4. Download the latest tar.gz from the Oinkmaster Web site.

5. Extract the folder in the archive to **/etc/oinkmaster**.

6. Edit the **oinkmaster.conf** file. Find the line that specified the URL for the current ruleset. (You can search for CURRENT.) Uncomment the line by removing the #, and then paste your oink code into the line in place of **<oinkcode>**.

```
url = http://www.snort.org/pub-bin/oinkmaster.cgi/<oinkcode>/snortrules-snapshot-
CURRENT.tar.gz
```

7. Start Oinkmaster with the following command:

```
oinkmaster.pl -C /etc/oinkmaster/oinkmaster.conf -o /etc/snort/rules
```

When it completes, Oinkmaster will tell you what rules were changed/updated. You can also specify the URL to retrieve the rules from the command line using the *–u <URL>* option. To configure the Oinkmaster script to run daily, use *crontab* with the following command:

```
crontab -u <user> -e
```

Enter the username you are running Oinkmaster as in place of <user>. This will open the crontab for that user. Adding the following line to the crontab will cause Oinkmaster to run each night at 2:00 A.M. If you prefer, there are also several GUI's available for configuring the cron daemon, such as gnome-schedule.

```
0 2 * * * oinkmaster.pl -C /etc/oinkmaster/oinkmaster.conf -o /etc/snort/rules
```

Now your Snort rules should stay up to date. Remember, if you change Snort versions, the URL to the appropriate rules may change, in which case you will need to update your oinkmaster.conf accordingly.

> **WARNING**
>
> Because the oinkmaster.conf file contains the path to update your Snort rules, if this file does not have secure access permissions on it, someone who could edit the file could render your IDS useless. With the ability to edit the configuration file, a malicious user could point the url to one of his choosing, with empty rule sets that will not trigger on anything, or even worse, rules that work perfectly except ignore the attacker's IP address. Make sure the oinkmaster.conf file is secured and only the account you are running Oinkmaster under has access to the file.

Additional Research

If the Snort utilities we have covered don't do everything you want them to do, there are other alternatives. Some of the utilities that are out there are more user friendly than others. Here are a few additional tools that are highly regarded and which may be helpful when running your Snort IDS. These include both Windows– and Linux-based tools.

- **ACID** ACID stands for Analysis Console for Intrusion Databases. You can download ACID from http://acidlab.sourceforge.net/. BASE was based off code from ACID, so the interfaces are strikingly similar. If you are only looking to use the Web front end for Snort logs, ACID probably doesn't buy you anything over BASE. If you plan to import data for additional non-Snort sources, however, ACID has the flexibility to do that.

- **Barnyard** Is available from http://sourceforge.net/project/showfiles.php?group_id=34732. It is basically a utility to offload the logging overhead from Snort. Using Barnyard, you configure Snort to log binary data (which is the fastest way to Snort to log, but not very human-readable) and Barnyard will then take the binary logs and convert them to human-friendly ASCII or import them into a database. For a small environment with low-alert volumes on the IDS, Barnyard is probably not needed. Snort will support logging to a MySQL database natively without using Barnyard.

- **Sguil** Sguil (http://sguil.sourceforge.net/) is pronounced "sgweel" and stands for Snort GUI for Lamerz. It is also referred to as the Analysis Console for Network Security Monitoring. The objective of sguil is to provide more than just a console to view Snort alerts, but to also give the analyst the capability to delve deeper into an alert, all the way to the captured packet, to facilitate investigation. Basically, sguil integrates multiple security tools into one interface for easy access. The sguil developers provide a demo sensor that you can connect to from the Web to see sguil in action. To use it, simply download and install the sguil client, and then connect to the sensor demo.sguil.net on port 7734. When prompted, you can enter any user name and password, and then select the sensor names "reset" in the console. Sguil is a powerful tool for investigating Snort alerts, but the configuration and setup is not for the faint of heart.

- **Snortsnarf** This is a log analyzer targeted specifically at analyzing Snort logs. You can download it from www.snort.org/dl/contrib/data_analysis/snortsnarf/.

Demonstrating Effectiveness

One of the age-old debates when it comes to network data collection is placement of the sensors. This applies to both IDS sensors and reporting sensors such as PRTG Traffic Grapher. The most common difference of opinion is whether you should place the sensor outside your external firewall or inside it. This is relevant because the data you see will be drastically different between the two. With the sensor placed outside your perimeter firewall, you will see all traffic directed at you from the Internet, including all the traffic your firewall is blocking. If the sensor is placed inside the perimeter firewall, you will only see the traffic that has managed to pass through your firewall.

Undeniably, the traffic of the most security relevance is the traffic that has managed to traverse your firewall and get into your internal network. These are the potential attacks, probes, and whatnot that need to be inspected and monitored closely to make sure the network is not compromised. If everything is configured properly, an IDS inside the perimeter should really see very little traffic, except perhaps triggers related to IT policy, such as file sharing or instant messaging protocols. So if all the data a security officer would find "interesting" is on the inside, you might wonder what value a sensor on the outside would bring.

The best value for placing a sensor outside is really one of public relations. The unfortunate fact is that when it comes to network security, if everything is done properly, no one ever sees much of anything. There are no flashing lights or alarms that say the network is functioning properly and securely. If you place an IDS on the outside of the perimeter, you can extract reports based on the traffic the IDS sees. These can be used to demonstrate to management in concrete terms what your security efforts are accomplishing. Saying "the network is running fine" is great, but probably doesn't have the impact that a one-page report with a pie chart would have. An executive summary of the attacks the sensor has seen could list some basic facts like "56,000 instances of code red worm were blocked, up 5% from last month," and so forth. With an old PC and a little up-front effort, these types of report would take very little effort to produce, but could reap huge rewards when it comes to public perception of network security.

When exposing *any* system to the Internet at large, remember it will be attacked. If your IDS is outside your perimeter firewall, there is nothing protecting the IDS except the IDS itself. This means the IDS will need to be hardened and secured as much as possible to ensure that it doesn't become a system for hackers to use. Under these circumstances, one of your best defenses would be for the IDS to use a network tap (not free) to ensure that it can only receive from the network and not transmit. There are various discussions on the Internet for making cables that can receive only. A little research will surely turn up some interesting designs to try. The success of these read-only cables will vary greatly depending on your system's network card and the switch or hub you are connected to. While this doesn't make the IDS sensor invulnerable to attacks or alleviate the need to harden it, this configuration will make it significantly harder to compromise.

Summary

Snort has the undisputed position as the lead open source IDS. As such, it enjoys several advantages. One advantage is the very large and diverse user base. This user base enables you to find a lot of help and information on the Internet for running, configuring, and customizing Snort. Although Snort may not enjoy the cohesive turnkey nature of a commercial package, you can assemble several utilities and tools to make Snort into an enterprise-class IDS. With no cost in software you can have an industry-standard IDS, with a large signature base and the ability to create your own custom signatures. You signatures can be automatically updated to keep them current, and you can use several GUI front ends to remotely configure and manage several Snort sensors at one central location. All this adds up to a lot of value and increased security, with no additional software cost.

Solutions Fast Track

Configuring an Intrusion Detection System

☑ Placement of the IDS will be key. If the IDS is not placed properly you will miss alerts and possibly think you are more secure than you really are.

☑ Remember that even with the proper physical placement, you need to have a hub in order for the IDS to be able to see traffic destined for other devices, or enable port mirroring if you are using a switch instead of a hub.

Configuring Snort on a Windows System

☑ Remember that every path in the snort.conf file needs to be an absolute path. A single incorrect path will prevent Snort from running properly.

☑ WinPcap will be required in order to use Snort on Windows. It is also required for many for using several other networking utilities on Window.

☑ IDScenter is aimed at configuring and running Snort itself (from the sensor), while IDS Policy Manager is used to centrally configure and manage Snort and Snort rules.

Configuring Snort on a Linux System

☑ You may want to consider a Snort alert front end such as BASE for viewing alerts.

☑ If your environment is primarily Windows, this will enable you to access the alerts from the Windows systems without having to view the Snort console on the Linux IDS host.

Other Snort Add-Ons

☑ A fully functioning IDS will not be of much value if no one is taking notice of the alerts it generates. An easy-to-use alert console can add a lot of value to your IDS in that it may increase the attention the alerts receive.

☑ I recommend using Oinkmaster to automatically keep your Snort signature files current.

Demonstrating Effectiveness

☑ One of the age-old debates when it comes to network data collection is placement of the sensors.

☑ The most common difference of opinion is whether you should place the sensor outside your external firewall or inside it.

☑ Undeniably, the traffic of the most security relevance is the traffic that has managed to traverse your firewall and get into your internal network. These are the potential attacks, probes, and whatnot that need to be inspected and monitored closely to make sure the network is not compromised.

Frequently Asked Questions

The following Frequently Asked Questions, answered by the authors of this book, are designed to both measure your understanding of the concepts presented in this chapter and to assist you with real-life implementation of these concepts. To have your questions about this chapter answered by the author, browse to **www.syngress.com/solutions** and click on the **"Ask the Author"** form.

Q: How do I configure Snort to send e-mail alerts?

A: You don't. Snort includes no native way to send e-mail alerts. This was an intentional decision because processing e-mail alerts would place an undue burden on the Snort process, possibly resulting in dropped packets and missed alerts. Instead, the simplest way to accomplish this is with a lag parsing tool, such as swatch.

Q: How do I turn Snort into an IPS instead of an IDS?

A: Snortsam (www.snortsam.net/) is designed to automatically adjust the rules on a firewall based on certain Snort alerts. It is a mature tool with relatively active development. Also check the user-contributed section of the Snort Web site for an assortment of utilities at www.snort.org/dl/contrib/patches/. Snort itself also has some limited capability to take actions, specifically when acting in "inline mode." Refer to the documentation at www.snort.org/docs/snort_htmanuals/htmanual_260/node7.html for more on Snort's native IPS support.

Q: How do I make a Snort rule to trigger for "X" application's traffic?

A: Start by searching online; you can usually find the rule already made for you. If not, the general procedure is to do a packet capture (with Wireshark, for example) and then review the packets. The tricky part is to identify something all the packets (or if not all, at least the initial packet) has in common. Some string that can uniquely identify that application's packet from any other's. Then you place this string in the rule using the payload option. See the online Snort manual for more information on rule option fields.

Q: How can I make my Snort sensor more secure?

A: There are many ways. First, configure a firewall on the sensor itself to protect itself. You would only filter traffic with a destination of the sensor, so that you don't accidentally filter the traffic you want to trigger alerts on. You can also have Snort listen on an interface without an IP address; this will make it a lot harder for an attacker to target the sensor. (See the main Snort FAQ for instructions on how to do this.)

## Chapter 7

Introducing Wireshark: Network Protocol Analyzer

Solutions in this chapter:

- **What is Wireshark?**

- **Supporting Programs**

- **Using Wireshark in Your Network Architecture**

- **Using Wireshark for Network Troubleshooting**

- **Using Wireshark for System Administration**

- **Using Wireshark for Security Administration**

- **Securing Wireshark**

- **Optimizing Wireshark**

- **Advanced Sniffing Techniques**

- **Securing Your Network from Sniffers**

Introduction

Wireshark is the best open-source network analyzer available. It is packed with features comparable to commercial network analyzers, and with a large, diverse collection of authors, new enhancements are continually developed. Wireshark is a stable and useful component for all network toolkits, and new features and bug fixes are always being developed. A lot of progress has been made since the early days of Wireshark (when it was still called Ethereal); the application now performs comparably (and in some regards) better than commercial sniffing software.

In this chapter, you will gain an understanding of what Wireshark is, what its features are, and how to use it for troubleshooting on your network architecture. Additionally, you will learn the history of Wireshark, how it came to be such a popular network analyzer, and why it remains a top pick for system and security administration. Along the way, we go over some tips for running Wireshark in a secure manner, optimizing it so that it runs advanced techniques smoothly.

What is Wireshark?

Wireshark is a network analyzer. It reads packets from the network, decodes them, and presents them in an easy-to-understand format. Some of the most important aspects of Wireshark is that it is open source, actively maintained, and free. The following are some of the other important aspects of Wireshark:

- It is distributed under the Gnu's Not UNIX (GNU) General Public License (GPL) open-source license.

- It works in promiscuous and non-promiscuous modes.

- It can capture data from the network or read from a capture file.

- It has an easy-to-read and configurable GUI.

- It has rich display filter capabilities.

- It supports tcpdump format capture filters. It has a feature that reconstructs a Transmission Control Protocol (TCP) session and displays it in American Standard Code for Information Interchange (ASCII), Extended Binary Coded Decimal Interchange Code (EBCDIC), hexadecimal (hex) dump, or C arrays.

- It is available in precompiled binaries and source code.

- It runs on over 20 platforms, including Uniplexed Information and Computing System (UNIX)-based operating systems (OSes) and Windows, and there are third-party packages available for Mac OS X.

- It supports over 750 protocols, and, because it is open source, new ones are contributed frequently.

- It can read capture files from over 25 different products.

- It can save capture files in a variety of formats (e.g., libpcap, Network Associates Sniffer, Microsoft Network Monitor (NetMon), and Sun snoop).

- It can capture data from a variety of media (e.g., Ethernet, Token-Ring, 802.11 Wireless, and so on).

- It includes a command-line version of the network analyzer called *tshark*.

- It includes a variety of supporting programs such as *editcap*, *mergecap*, and *text2pcap*.

- Output can be saved or printed as plaintext or PostScript.

History of Wireshark

Gerald Combs first developed Ethereal in 1997, because he was expanding his knowledge of networking and needed a tool for network troubleshooting. The first version (v0.2.0) was released in July 1998. A development team, including Gilbert Ramirez, Guy Harris, and Richard Sharpe, quickly formed to provide patches, enhancements, and additional dissectors. Dissectors are what allow Wireshark to decode individual protocols and present them in readable format. Since then, a large number of individuals have contributed specific protocol dissectors and other enhancements to Wireshark. You can view the list of authors at www.ethereal.com/introduction.html – authors. Because of the overwhelming development support and the large user base, Wireshark's capabilities and popularity continue to grow every day.

Notes From the Underground...

The GNU GPL

The GNU Project was originally developed in 1984 to provide a free UNIX-like OS. It is argued that Linux, the "OS" should be referred to as the "GNU/Linux" system because it uses the GNU utilities with a Linux kernel.

The GNU Project is run and sponsored by the Free Software Foundation (FSF). Richard Stallman wrote the GNU GPL in 1989, for the purpose of distributing programs released as part of the GNU Project. It is a copyleft (i.e., Copyleft—all rights reserved), free software license and is based on similar licenses that were used for early versions of GNU Editor Emacs (MACroS).

Copyleft is the application of copyright law to ensure public freedom to manipulate, improve, and redistribute a work of authorship and all derivative works. This means that the copyright holder grants an irrevocable license to all recipients of a copy, permitting the redistribution and sale of possibly further modified copies under the condition that all of those copies carry the same license and are made available in a form that facilitates modification. There are legal consequences to face if a licensee fails to distribute the work under the same license. If the licensee distributes copies of the work, the source code and modification must be made available.

The text of the GPL software license itself cannot be modified. You can copy and distribute it, but you cannot change the text of the GPL. You can modify the GPL

Continued

and make it your own license, but you cannot use the name "GPL." Other licenses created by the GNU project include the GNU Lesser GPL and the GNU Free Documentation License.

There remains an ongoing dispute about the GPL and whether or not non-GPL software can link to GPL libraries. Although derivative works of GPL code must abide by the license, it is not clear whether an executable that links to a GPL library is considered a derivative work. The FSF states that such executables are derivatives to the GPL work, but others in the software community disagree. To date, there have not been any court decisions to resolve this conflict.

Compatibility

As stated, Wireshark can read and process capture files from a number of different products, including other sniffers, routers, and network utilities. Because Wireshark uses the popular Promiscuous Capture Library (libpcap)-based capture format, it interfaces easily with other products that use libpcap. It also has the ability to read captures in a variety of other formats. Wireshark can automatically determine the type of file it is reading and can uncompress GNU Zip (gzip) files. The following list shows the products from which Wireshark can read capture files:

- Tcpdump
- Sun snoop and atmsnoop
- Microsoft NetMon
- Network Associates Sniffer (compressed or uncompressed) and Sniffer Pro
- Shomiti/Finisar Surveyor
- Novell LANalyzer
- Cinco Networks NetXRay
- AG Group/WildPackets EtherPeek/TokenPeek/AiroPeek
- RADCOM's wide area network (WAN)/local area network (LAN) analyzer
- Visual Networks' Visual UpTime
- Lucent/Ascend router debug output
- Toshiba's Integrated Services Digital Network (ISDN) routers dump output
- Cisco Secure intrusion detection systems (IDS) iplog
- AIX's iptrace
- HP-UX nettl
- ISDN4BSD project's i4btrace output
- Point-To-point Protocol Daemon (PPPD) logs (pppdump-format)

- VMS's TCPIPtrace utility

- DBS Etherwatch Virtual Memory System (VMS) utility

- CoSine L2 debug

- Accellent's 5Views LAN agent output

- Endace Measurement Systems' Electronic Remote Fill (ERF) capture format

- Linux Bluez Bluetooth stack "hcidump –w" traces

- Catapult DCT2000

- Network Instruments Observer version 9

- EyeSDN Universal Serial Bus (USB) S0 traces

Supported Protocols

When a network analyzer reads data from the network it needs to know how to interpret what it is seeing and then display the output in an easy-to-read format. This is known as *protocol decoding*. Often, the number of protocols a sniffer can read and display determines its strength, thus most commercial sniffers can support several hundred protocols. Wireshark is very competitive in this area, with its current support of over 750 protocols. New protocols are constantly being added by various contributors to the Wireshark project. Protocol decodes, also known as *dissectors*, can be added directly into the code or included as plug-ins. The following list shows the 752 protocols that are currently supported at the time of this writing:

3COMXNS, 3GPP2 A11, 802.11 MGT, 802.11 Radiotap, 802.3 Slow protocols, 9P, AAL1, AAL3/4, AARP, ACAP, ACN, ACSE, ACtrace, ADP, AFP, AFS (RX), AgentX, AH, AIM, AIM Administration, AIM Advertisements, AIM BOS, AIM Buddylist, AIM Chat, AIM ChatNav, AIM Directory, AIM E-mail, AIM Generic, AIM ICQ, AIM Invitation, AIM Location, AIM Messaging, AIM OFT, AIM Popup, AIM Signon, AIM SSI, AIM SST, AIM Stats, AIM Translate, AIM User Lookup, AJP13, ALC, ALCAP, AMR, ANS, ANSI BSMAP, ANSI DTAP, ANSI IS-637-A Teleservice, ANSI IS-637-A Transport, ANSI IS-683-A (OTA (Mobile)), ANSI IS-801 (Location Services (PLD)), ANSI MAP, AODV, AOE, ARCNET, Armagetronad, ARP/RARP, ARTNET, ASAP, ASF, ASN1, ASP, ATM, ATM LANE, ATP, ATSVC, Auto-RP, AVS WLANCAP, AX4000, BACapp, BACnet, Basic Format XID, BEEP, BER, BFD Control, BGP, BICC, BitTorrent, Boardwalk, BOFL, BOOTP/DHCP, BOOTPARAMS, BOSSVR, BROWSER, BSSAP, BSSGP, BUDB, BUTC, BVLC, CAMEL, CAST, CBAPDev, CCSDS, CCSRL, CDP, CDS_CLERK, cds_solicit, CDT, CFLOW, CGMP, CHDLC, CIGI, CIMD, CIP, CISCOWL-L2, CLDAP, CLEARCASE, CLNP, CLTP, CMIP, CMP, CMS, CONV, COPS, COSEVENTCOMM, CoSine, COSNAMING, COTP, CPFI, CPHA, cprpc_server, CRMF, CSM_ENCAPS, CUPS, DAAP, DAP, Data, dc, DCCP, DCE_DFS, dce_update, DCERPC, DCOM, DCP, DDP, DDTP, DEC_DNA, DEC_STP, DFS, DHCPFO, DHCPv6, DIAMETER, dicom, DIS, DISP, DISTCC, DLSw, DLT User A, DLT User B, DLT User C, DLT User D, DNP 3.0, DNS, DNSSERVER, DOCSIS, DOCSIS BPKM-ATTR, DOCSIS BPKM-REQ, DOCSIS BPKM-RSP, DOCSIS DSA-ACK, DOCSIS DSA-REQ, DOCSIS DSA-RSP, DOCSIS

DSC-ACK, DOCSIS DSC-REQ, DOCSIS DSC-RSP, DOCSIS DSD-REQ, DOCSIS DSD-RSP, DOCSIS INT-RNG-REQ, DOCSIS MAC MGMT, DOCSIS MAP, DOCSIS REG-ACK, DOCSIS REG-REQ, DOCSIS REG-RSP, DOCSIS RNG-REQ, DOCSIS RNG-RSP, DOCSIS TLVs, DOCSIS type29ucd, DOCSIS UCC-REQ, DOCSIS UCC-RSP, DOCSIS UCD, DOCSIS VSIF, DOP, DRSUAPI, DSI, DSP, DSSETUP, DTP, DTSPROVIDER, DTSSTIME_REQ, DUA, DVMRP, E.164, EAP, EAPOL, ECHO, EDONKEY, EDP, EFS, EIGRP, ENC, ENIP, ENRP, ENTTEC, EPM, EPMv4, ESIS, ESP, ESS, ETHERIC, ETHERIP, Ethernet, EVENTLOG, FC, FC ELS, FC FZS, FC-dNS, FC-FCS, FC-SB3, FC-SP, FC-SWILS, FC_CT, FCIP, FCP, FDDI, FIX, FLDB, FR, Frame, FRSAPI, FRSRPC, FTAM, FTBP, FTP, FTP-DATA, FTSERVER, FW-1, G.723, GIF image, giFT, GIOP, GMRP, GNM, GNUTELLA, GPRS NS, GPRS-LLC, GRE, Gryphon, GSM BSSMAP, GSM DTAP, GSM RP, GSM SMS, GSM SMS UD, GSM_MAP, GSM_SS, GSS-API, GTP, GVRP, H.223, H.225.0, H.235, H.245, H.261, H.263, H.263 data, H1, h221nonstd, H248, h450, HCLNFSD, HPEXT, HPSW, HSRP, HTTP, HyperSCSI, IAP, IAPP, IAX2, IB, ICAP, ICBAAccoCB, ICBAAccoCB2, ICBAAccoMgt, ICBAAccoMgt2, ICBAAccoServ, ICBAAccoServ2, ICBAAccoServSRT, ICBAAccoSync, ICBABrowse, ICBABrowse2, ICBAGErr, ICBAGErrEvent, ICBALDev, ICBALDev2, ICBAPDev, ICBAPDev2, ICBAPDevPC, ICBAPDevPCEvent, ICBAPersist, ICBAPersist2, ICBARTAuto, ICBARTAuto2, ICBAState, ICBAStateEvent, ICBASysProp, ICBATime, ICEP, ICL_RPC, ICMP, ICMPv6, ICP, ICQ, IDispatch, IDP, IEEE 802.11, IEEE802a, iFCP, IGAP, IGMP, IGRP, ILMI, IMAP, INAP, INITSHUTDOWN, IOXIDResolver, IP, IP/IEEE1394, IPComp, IPDC, IPFC, IPMI, IPP, IPv6, IPVS, IPX, IPX MSG, IPX RIP, IPX SAP, IPX WAN, IRC, IrCOMM, IRemUnknown, IRemUnknown2, IrLAP, IrLMP, ISAKMP, iSCSI, ISDN, ISIS, ISL, ISMP, iSNS, ISUP, isup_thin, ISystemActivator, itunes, IUA, IuUP, Jabber, JFIF (JPEG) image, Juniper, JXTA, JXTA Framing, JXTA Message, JXTA UDP, JXTA Welcome, K12xx, KADM5, KINK, KLM, Kpasswd, KRB4, KRB5, KRB5RPC, L2TP, LANMAN, LAPB, LAPBETHER, LAPD, Laplink, LDAP, LDP, Line-based text data, LLAP, llb, LLC, LLDP, LMI, LMP, Log, LogotypeCertExtn, LOOP, LPD, LSA, Lucent/Ascend, LWAPP, LWAPP-CNTL, LWAPP-L3, LWRES, M2PA, M2TP, M2UA, M3UA, MACC, Malformed packet, Manolito, MAP_DialoguePDU, MAPI, MDS Header, Media, MEGACO, message/http, Messenger, MGCP, MGMT, MIME multipart, MIPv6, MMS, MMSE, Mobile IP, Modbus/TCP, MOUNT, MPEG1, MPLS, MPLS Echo, MQ, MQ PCF, MRDISC, MS NLB, MS Proxy, MSDP, MSMMS, MSNIP, MSNMS, MSRP, MTP2, MTP3, MTP3MG, MySQL, NBAP, NBDS, NBIPX, NBNS, NBP, NBSS, NCP, NCS, NDMP, NDPS, NetBIOS, Netsync, nettl, NFS, NFSACL, NFSAUTH, NHRP, NIS+, NIS+ CB, NJACK, NLM, NLSP, NMAS, NMPI, NNTP, NORM, NS_CERT_EXTS, NSIP, NSPI, NTLMSSP, NTP, Null, NW_SERIAL, OAM AAL, OCSP, OLSR, OPSI, OSPF, P_MUL, PAGP, PAP, PARLAY, PCLI, PCNFSD, PER, PFLOG, PFLOG-OLD, PGM, PGSQL, PIM, PKCS-1, PKInit, PKIX Certificate, PKIX1EXPLICIT, PKIX1IMPLICIT, PKIXPROXY, PKIXQUALIFIED, PKIXTSP, PKTC, PN-DCP, PN-RT, PNIO, PNP, POP, Portmap, PPP, PPP BACP, PPP BAP, PPP CBCP, PPP CCP, PPP CDPCP, PPP CHAP, PPP Comp, PPP IPCP, PPP IPV6CP, PPP LCP, PPP MP, PPP MPLSCP, PPP OSICP, PPP PAP, PPP PPPMux, PPP PPPMuxCP, PPP VJ, PPP-HDLC, PPPoED, PPPoES, PPTP, PRES, Prism, PTP, PVFS, Q.2931, Q.931, Q.933, QLLC, QUAKE, QUAKE2, QUAKE3, QUAKEWORLD, R-STP, RADIUS, RANAP, Raw, Raw_SigComp, Raw_SIP, rdaclif, RDM, RDT, Redback, REMACT, REP_PROC, RIP, RIPng, RLM, Rlogin, RMCP, RMI, RMP, RNSAP, ROS, roverride, RPC, RPC_BROWSER, RPC_NETLOGON, RPL, rpriv, RQUOTA, RRAS, RS_ACCT, RS_ATTR, rs_attr_schema, RS_BIND, rs_misc, RS_PGO, RS_PLCY, rs_prop_acct, rs_prop_acl, rs_prop_attr, rs_prop_pgo, rs_prop_plcy, rs_pwd_mgmt,

RS_REPADM, RS_REPLIST, rs_repmgr, RS_UNIX, rsec_login, RSH, rss, RSTAT, RSVP, RSYNC, RTcfg, RTCP, RTmac, RTMP, RTP, RTP Event, RTPS, RTSE, RTSP, RUDP, RWALL, RX, SADMIND, SAMR, SAP, SCCP, SCCPMG, SCSI, SCTP, SDLC, SDP, SEBEK, SECIDMAP, Serialization, SES, sFlow, SGI MOUNT, Short frame, SIGCOMP, SIP, SIPFRAG, SIR, SKINNY, SLARP, SLiMP3, SLL, SM, SMB, SMB Mailslot, SMB Pipe, SMB2, SMB_NETLOGON, smil, SMPP, SMRSE, SMTP, SMUX, SNA, SNA XID, SNAETH, SNDCP, SNMP, Socks, SONMP, SoulSeek, SPNEGO, SPNEGO-KRB5, SPOOLSS, SPP, SPRAY, SPX, SRP, SRVLOC, SRVSVC, SSCF-NNI, SSCOP, SSH, SSL, SSS, STANAG 4406, STANAG 5066, STAT, STAT-CB, STP, STUN, SUA, SVCCTL, Symantec, Synergy, Syslog, T.38, TACACS, TACACS+, TALI, TANGO, TAPI, TCAP, TCP, TDMA, TDS, TEI_MANAGEMENT, TELNET, Teredo, TFTP, TIME, TIPC, TKN4Int, TNS, Token-Ring, TPCP, TPKT, TR MAC, TRKSVR, TSP, TTP, TUXEDO, TZSP, UBIKDISK, UBIKVOTE, UCP, UDP, UDPENCAP, UDPlite, UMA, Unreassembled fragmented packet, V.120, V5UA, Vines ARP, Vines Echo, Vines FRP, Vines ICP, Vines IP, Vines IPC, Vines LLC, Vines RTP, Vines SPP, VLAN, VNC, VRRP, VTP, WAP SIR, WBXML, WCCP, WCP, WHDLC, WHO, WINREG, WINS-Replication, WKSSVC, WLANCERTEXTN, WSP, WTLS, WTP, X.25, X.29, X11, X411, X420, X509AF, X509CE, X509IF, X509SAT, XDMCP, XML, XOT, XYPLEX, YHOO, YMSG, YPBIND, YPPASSWD, YPSERV, YPXFR ZEBRA, ZIP,

Wireshark's User Interface

Wireshark's GUI is configurable and easy to use. And like other network analyzers, Wireshark displays capture information in three main panes. Figure 7.1 shows what a typical Wireshark capture looks like. Each window is adjustable by clicking on the row of dots between the window panes and drag-ging up or down. The upper-most pane is the *summary* pane, which displays a one-line summary of the capture. Wireshark's default fields include:

- Packet number
- Time
- Source address
- Destination address
- Name and information about the highest-layer protocol.

These columns are easily configured, and new ones can be added under Preferences. You can also sort the columns in an ascending or descending order by field, and you can rearrange the panes.

> **NOTE**
>
> You will notice that the Windows Wireshark GUI resembles a UNIX application rather than a native Windows application. This is because Wireshark uses the GNU Image Manipulation Program (GIMP) Tool Kit (GTK) library to create the interface. So regardless of the OS you are running it on Wireshark will look the same.

The middle pane is the *protocol detail* pane, which provides the details (in a tree-like structure) of each layer contained in the captured packet. Clicking on various parts of the protocol tree highlights corresponding hex and ASCII output in the bottom pane, and the bottom pane displays the raw captured data in both hex and ASCII format. Clicking on various parts of this data highlights their corresponding fields in the protocol tree in the protocol view pane. Figure 7.1 shows the Wireshark interface and an example of a network synchronous (SYN) scan. Notice that highlighting the source MAC address in the middle protocol view pane automatically highlights that portion of the hexdump in the bottom data pane.

Figure 7.1 Wireshark's GUI

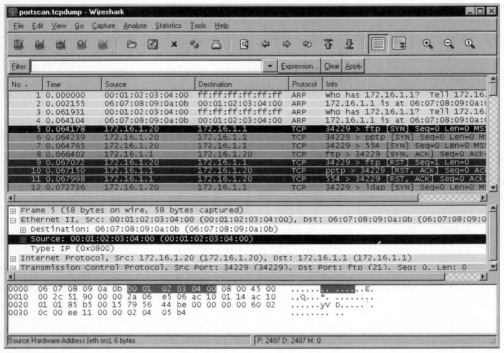

One of the best features of Wireshark is its ability to reassemble all of the packets in a TCP conversation and display the ASCII in an easy-to-read format. (It can also be viewed in EBCDIC, hexdump, and C arrays.) This data can then be saved or printed, and used to reconstruct a Web page Simple Mail Transfer Protocol (SMTP) or Telnet session. To reconstruct a Web page, follow the stream of the Hypertext Transfer Protocol (HTTP) session and save the output to a file. You should then be able to view the reconstructed Hypertext Markup Language (HTML) offline (without graphics) in a Web browser. Figure 7.2 shows the TCP stream output of a FTP session.

Figure 7.2 Follow the TCP Stream

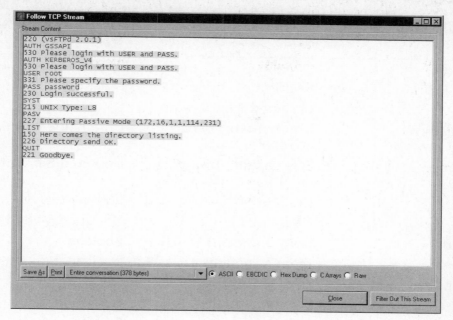

Filters

Filtering packets help you find a desired packet without sifting through all of them. Wireshark has the ability to use both *capture* and *display* filters. The capture filter syntax follows the same syntax that tcp-dump uses from the libpcap library. It is used on the command line or in the "Capture Filter" dialog box to capture certain types of traffic. Display filters provide a powerful syntax to sort traffic that is already captured. As the number of protocols grow, the number of protocol fields for display filters also grow. However, not all protocols currently supported by Wireshark have display filters. Also, some protocols provide display filter field names for some, but not all, of the fields. Hopefully, as the product matures and more users contribute to the development process, this will change. Table 7.1 shows an example of a supported protocol and its display filters:

Table 7.1 IP Display Filters

Internet Protocol (IP) Field	Name	Type
ip.addr	Source or Destination Address	IPv4 address
ip.checksum	Header checksum	Unsigned 16-bit integer
ip.checksum_bad	Bad Header checksum	Boolean
ip.dsfield	Differentiated Services field	Unsigned 8-bit integer

Continued

Table 7.1 continued IP Display Filters

Internet Protocol (IP) Field	Name	Type
ip.dsfield.ce		
ECN-CE, Explicit Congestion Notification: Congestion Experienced.		
	Unsigned 8-bit integer	
ip.dsfield.dscp	Differentiated Services Codepoint	Unsigned 8-bit integer
ip.dsfield.ect	ECN-Capable Transport (ECT)	Unsigned 8-bit integer
ip.dst	Destination	IPv4 address
ip.flags	Flags	Unsigned 8-bit integer
ip.flags.df	Don't fragment	Boolean
ip.flags.mf	More fragments	Boolean
ip.frag_offset	Fragment offset	Unsigned 16-bit integer
ip.fragment	IP Fragment	Frame number
ip.fragment.error	Defragmentation error	Frame number
ip.fragment.multipletails	Multiple tail fragments found	Boolean
ip.fragment.overlap	Fragment overlap	Boolean
ip.fragment.overlap. conflict	Conflicting data in fragment overlap	Boolean
ip.fragment. toolongfragment	Fragment too long	Boolean
ip.fragments	IP fragments	No value
ip.hdr_len	Header length	Unsigned 8-bit integer
ip.id	Identification	Unsigned 16-bit integer
ip.len	Total length	Unsigned 16-bit integer
ip.proto	Protocol	Unsigned 8-bit integer
ip.reassembled_in	Reassembled IP in frame	Frame number
ip.src	Source	IPv4 address
ip.tos	Type of service	Unsigned 8-bit integer
ip.tos.cost	Cost	Boolean
ip.tos.delay	Delay	Boolean
ip.tos.precedence	Precedence	Unsigned 8-bit integer
ip.tos.reliability	Reliability	Boolean

Continued

Table 7.1 continued IP Display Filters

Internet Protocol (IP) Field	Name	Type
ip.tos.throughput	Throughput	Boolean
ip.ttl	Time-to-live	Unsigned 8-bit integer
ip.version	Version	Unsigned 8-bit integer

Once a display filter is implemented, all of the packets that meet the requirements are displayed in the packet listing in the summary pane. These filters can be used to compare fields within a protocol against a value such as *ip.src == 192.168.1.1*, to compare fields such as *ip.src == ip.dst*, or to check the existence of specified fields or protocols. Filters are also used by statistical features and to colorize the packets. To create a simple filter to search for a certain protocol or field (e.g., you want to see all of the HTTP packets), type **http**. To see just HTTP request packets (e.g., *GET POST, HEAD*, and so on) type **http.request**. Filter fields can also be compared against values such as **http.request.method=="GET"** to see only HTTP GET requests. The comparison operators can be expressed using the following abbreviations and symbols:

- **Equal:** eq, ==
- **Not equal:** ne, !=
- **Greater than:** gt, >
- **Less Than:** lt, <
- **Greater than or equal to:** ge, >=
- **Less than or equal to:** le, <=

Three operators can be expressed by name. *Is Present* allows you to test for the existence of a field (e.g., in an Address Resolution Protocol [ARP] packet, the MAC address is present but not the TCP port). *Contains* allows you to search the data of a packet for a string or phrase. *Matches* uses a regular expression (*regex*) string for more powerful pattern matching.

As you can see, filters offer a great deal of flexibility when troubleshooting network problems.

NOTE

Wireshark supports many different types of media (e.g., Ethernet, Token Ring, Wireless, and asynchronous transfer mode [ATM]).

To ensure that you are using a compatible OS, go to the "Supported Capture Media" table at www.ethereal.com/media.html. As you will see, Linux supports nearly all media types, and Ethernet is supported on all OSes.

Notes From the Underground…

The Subversion System

Subversion (SVN) is a versioning system that allows developers to work on more than one same project simultaneously while keeping track of the changes made, who made them, and what versions were made. There are typically many versions of a project inside a SVN tree.

SVN and its predecessor Concurrent Versions Systems (CVS) are used for almost every open-source project (e.g., SourceForge [www.sourceforge.net] has CVS and SVN repositories for all of the projects it contains. Some projects allow Web-based access to SVN trees and most allow you to browse using a SVN client application.

Following are some helpful links for SVN:

- **SVN Command-line Client** The command-line client is available at www.SVN.tigris.orgwww or in package form from many Berkeley Software Distribution (BSD) and UNIX distributions.

- **TortoiseSVN** TortoiseSVN is a shell extension for Microsoft Windows that integrates with the file explorer available from www.tortoisesvn.tigris.org.

- **RapidSVN** RapidSVN is a cross-platform GUI for SVN that is available for Windows

- **Mac OS X and Linux** are available from www.rapidsvn.tigris.org.

- **Visual Studio .NET** Developers using Microsoft Visual Studio .NET can use a AnkhSVN (www.ankhsvn.tigris.org) a third-party integration tool for SVN.

The Wireshark SVN listing is maintained at www.ethereal.com/development.html. There are several ways to obtain the source code for Wireshark using SVN:

- **SVN Command Line** Used to anonymously download the development source.

- **Nighly Snapshots** Used to download gzipped tarballs containing nightly snapshots of the development source tree.

- **SVN Web Interface** You can download the source tree via the SVN Web Interface (http://anonsvn.wireshark.org/wireshark/trunk/) and view each file and the differences between each version file.

When using SVN versions of Wireshark or other open-source products, remember that they are considered beta code and may have bugs.

Great Resources

Some of the best resources for Wireshark information and support include e-mail distribution lists (see httwww.ethereal.com/lists for the appropriate form.

> **NOTE**
>
> When filling out the application, a password is sometimes e-mailed to you in clear-text. Make sure that you don't use the same password that you use for other accounts, because anyone sniffing network traffic can see the cleartext password when it is e-mailed.

- **Wireshark-announce** includes announcements of new releases, bug fixes, and general issues about Wireshark. All Wireshark users should subscribe to this list to remain current on important topics. This list tends to be low volume. To post a message, send an e-mail to www.ethereal-announce@ethereal.com.

- **Wireshark-users** includes general information and help using Wireshark. All Wireshark users should subscribe to this list to share ideas and make suggestions. It contains moderate traffic. To post a message, send an e-mail to www.ethereal-users@ethereal.com.

- **Wireshark-dev** includes developer-related information about the inner workings of Wireshark, and is intended for those interested in contributing to its development. This list receives a high volume of traffic per day. To post a message, send an e-mail to www.ethereal-dev@ethereal.com.

- **Wireshark-commits** includes developer-related information to monitor changes to the Wireshark source tree. It informs developers when changes are made and what the changes are. The SVN repository sends e-mails to this list every time code is committed to the Wireshark SVN repository; therefore, it receives a high volume of traffic. Users do not post directly to this list. Replies to messages on this list should be sent to www.wireshark-dev@wireshark.org.

When subscribing to mailing lists, you can choose to have your e-mail batched in a *daily digest*, which is a great way to cut down on the amount of traffic and messages on high-volume lists. However, you won't get any attachments that are included with the e-mails. All of the messages from the mailing lists are archived on the Wireshark Web site and other mirror sites. Messages are categorized by month, for as far back as 1998. When troubleshooting a problem, a good strategy is to search for someone else that has the answer. Another great source of information is the Wireshark User's Guide (by Richard Sharpe) located at www.wireshark.org/docs/wsug_html/. It is also available in many other formats including PDF at www.wireshark.org/docs. And, as always, the Wireshark Web page www.wireshark.org also has a lot of good information. The sample captures page (http://wiki.wireshark.org/SampleCaptures) contains packet traces of network traffic that can be downloaded and viewed with Wireshark.

The Wireshark Wiki page is another great resource, where anyone can add their own ideas and experiences with Wireshark. There are many examples of usage references and solutions for various challenging sniffing environments. If you have found a solution, feel free to add it to the wiki at http://wiki.wireshark.org.

Supporting Programs

Most people who are familiar with Wireshark use the Wireshark GUI. However, when Wireshark is installed, it also comes with several other support programs. The command-line version of Wireshark (called *tshark*) contains the following three programs to assist in manipulating capture files.

Tshark

Tshark is the command-line version of Wireshark, which can be used to capture live packets from the wire or to read saved capture files. By default, tshark prints the summary line information to the screen. This is the same information contained in the top pane of the Wireshark GUI. The following shows the default tshark output:

```
1.199008 192.168.100.132 -> 192.168.100.122 TCP 1320 > telnet [SYN] Seq=1102938967
Ack=0 Win=16384 Len=0

1.199246 192.168.100.132 -> 192.168.100.122 TCP 1320 > telnet [SYN] Seq=1102938967
Ack=0 Win=16384 Len=0

1.202244 192.168.100.122 -> 192.168.100.132 TCP telnet > 1320 [SYN

ACK] Seq=3275138168 Ack=1102938968 Win=49640 Len=0

1.202268 192.168.100.132 -> 192.168.100.122 TCP 1320 > telnet [ACK] Seq=1102938968
Ack=3275138169 Win=17520 Len=0

1.202349 192.168.100.132 -> 192.168.100.122 TCP 1320 > telnet [ACK] Seq=1102938968
Ack=3275138169 Win=17520 Len=0
```

The **–V** option causes tshark to print the protocol tree view like in the middle pane in the Wireshark GUI. This shows all of the protocols in the packet and includes the data portion at the end of the list. The following shows a more detailed protocol tree tshark output:

```
Frame 5 (74 bytes on wire
74 bytes captured)
    Arrival Time: Nov  2
2003 15:22:33.469934000
    Time delta from previous packet: 0.000216000 seconds
    Time relative to first packet: 1.349439000 seconds
    Frame Number: 5
    Packet Length: 74 bytes
    Capture Length: 74 bytes
Ethernet II
Src: 00:05:5d:ee:7e:53
Dst: 08:00:20:cf:5b:39
```

```
     Destination: 08:00:20:cf:5b:39 (SunMicro_cf:5b:39)
     Source: 00:05:5d:ee:7e:53 (D-Link_ee:7e:53)
     Type: IP (0x0800)
Internet Protocol
Src Addr: 192.168.100.132 (192.168.100.132)
Dst Addr: 192.168.100.122 (192.168.100.122)
     Version: 4
     Header length: 20 bytes
     Differentiated Services Field: 0x00 (DSCP 0x00: Default; ECN: 0x00)
          0000 00.. = Differentiated Services Codepoint: Default (0x00)
          .... ..0. = ECN-Capable Transport (ECT): 0
          .... ...0 = ECN-CE: 0
     Total Length: 60
     Identification: 0x160c (5644)
     Flags: 0x00
          .0.. = Don't fragment: Not set
          ..0. = More fragments: Not set
     Fragment offset: 0
     Time to live: 128
     Protocol: ICMP (0x01)
     Header checksum: 0xda65 (correct)
     Source: 192.168.100.132 (192.168.100.132)
     Destination: 192.168.100.122 (192.168.100.122)
Internet Control Message Protocol
     Type: 8 (Echo (ping) request)
     Code: 0
     Checksum: 0x3c5c (correct)
     Identifier: 0x0500
     Sequence number: 0c:00
     Data (32 bytes)
0000  61 62 63 64 65 66 67 68 69 6a 6b 6c 6d 6e 6f 70   abcdefghijklmnop
0010  71 72 73 74 75 76 77 61 62 63 64 65 66 67 68 69   qrstuvwabcdefghi
```

Finally, the **–x** command causes tshark to print a hexdump and an ASCII dump of the packet data with either the summary line or the protocol tree. The following shows the hex and ASCII output with the summary line:

```
  9.463261 192.168.100.122 -> 192.168.100.132 TELNET Telnet Data ...
0000  00 05 5d ee 7e 53 08 00 20 cf 5b 39 08 00 45 00   ..].~S.. .[9..E.
0010  00 9a c3 8a 40 00 3c 06 30 84 c0 a8 64 7a c0 a8   ....@.<.0...dz..
0020  64 84 00 17 05 29 cd 5d 7d 12 4c 1d ea 76 50 18   d....).]}.L..vP.
0030  c1 e8 47 ca 00 00 4c 61 73 74 20 6c 6f 67 69 6e   ..G...Last login
```

```
0040   3a 20 53 75 6e 20 4e 6f 76 20 20 32 20 31 35 3a      : Sun Nov  2 15:
0050   34 34 3a 34 35 20 66 72 6f 6d 20 31 39 32 2e 31      44:45 from 192.1
0060   36 38 2e 31 30 30 2e 31 33 32 0d 0a 53 75 6e 20      68.100.132..Sun
0070   4d 69 63 72 6f 73 79 73 74 65 6d 73 20 49 6e 63      Microsystems Inc
0080   2e 20 20 20 53 75 6e 4f 53 20 35 2e 39 20 20 20      .   SunOS 5.9
0090   20 20 20 20 20 47 65 6e 65 72 69 63 20 4d 61 79 20         Generic May
00a0   32 30 30 32 0d 0a 23 20                              2002..#
```

When using tshark to save packet data to a file, by default it outputs in the libpcap format. Tshark can read the same capture files and use the same display filters (also known as *read* filters) and capture filters as Wireshark. Tshark can also decode the same protocols as Wireshark. Basically, it has most of the powers of Wireshark (except those inherent to the GUI) in an easy-to-use command-line version.

Editcap

Editcap is used to remove packets from a file, and to translate the format of capture files. It is similar to the Save As feature, but better. Editcap can read all of the same types of files that Wireshark can, and writes to the libpcap format by default. Editcap can also write captures to standard and modified versions of:

- libpcap
- Sun snoop
- Novel LANalyzer
- Network Access Identifier (NAI) Sniffer
- Microsoft NetMon
- Visual Network traffic capture
- Accellent 5Views capture
- Network Instruments Observer version 9

Editcap has the ability to specify all or some of the packets to be translated. The following is an example of using editcap to translate the first five packets from a tshark libpcap capture file (called *capture*) to a Sun snoop output file (called *capture_snoop*):

```
C:\Program Files\Wireshark>editcap -r -v -F snoop capture capture_snoop 1-5
File capture is a libpcap (tcpdump
Wireshark
etc.) capture file.
Add_Selected: 1-5
Inclusive ... 1
5
Record: 1
```

```
Record: 2
Record: 3
Record: 4
Record: 5
```

Mergecap

Mergecap is used to combine multiple saved capture files into a single output file. Mergecap can read all of the same types of files that Wireshark can and writes to libpcap format by default. Mergecap can also write the output capture file to standard and modified versions of:

- libpcap
- Sun snoop
- Novel LANalyzer
- NAI Sniffer
- Microsoft NetMon
- Visual Network traffic capture
- Accellent 5Views capture
- Network Instruments Observer

By default, the packets from the input files are merged in chronological order based on each packet's timestamp. If the **–a** option is specified, packets are copied directly from each input file to the output file regardless of the timestamp. The following is an example of using mergecap to merge four capture files (*capture1*, *capture2*, *capture3*, and *capture4*) into a single Sun snoop output file called *merge_snoop* that will keep reading packets until the end of the last file is reached:

```
C:\Program Files\Wireshark>mergecap -v -F snoop -w merge_snoop capture1 capture2
capture3 capture4
mergecap: capture1 is type libpcap (tcpdump
Wireshark
etc.).
mergecap: capture2 is type libpcap (tcpdump
Wireshark
etc.).
mergecap: capture3 is type libpcap (tcpdump
Wireshark
etc.).
mergecap: capture4 is type libpcap (tcpdump
Wireshark
etc.).
mergecap: opened 4 of 4 input files
```

```
mergecap: selected frame_type Ethernet (ether)
Record: 1
Record: 2
Record: 3
Record: 4
Record: 5
Record: 6
Record: 7
Record: 8
Record: 9
Record: 10
output removed
```

Text2pcap

Text2pcap reads in ASCII hexdump captures and writes the data into a libpcap output file. It is capable of reading hexdumps containing multiple packets and building a capture file of multiple packets. Text2pcap can also read hexdumps of application-level data by inserting dummy Ethernet IP and User Datagram Protocol (UDP) or TCP headers. The user specifies which of these headers to add. This way Wireshark and other sniffers can read the full data. The following is an example of the type of hexdump that text2pcap recognizes:

```
0000  00 05 5d ee 7e 53 08 00 20 cf 5b 39 08 00 45 00    ..].~S.. .[9..E.
0010  00 9a 13 9e 40 00 3c 06 e0 70 c0 a8 64 7a c0 a8    ....@.<..p..dz..
0020  64 84 00 17 05 49 0e a9 91 43 8e d8 e3 6a 50 18    d....I...C...jP.
0030  c1 e8 ba 7b 00 00 4c 61 73 74 20 6c 6f 67 69 6e    ...{..Last login
0040  3a 20 53 75 6e 20 4e 6f 76 20 20 32 20 31 37 3a    : Sun Nov  2 17:
0050  30 36 3a 35 33 20 66 72 6f 6d 20 31 39 32 2e 31    06:53 from 192.1
0060  36 38 2e 31 30 30 2e 31 33 32 0d 0a 53 75 6e 20    68.100.132..Sun
0070  4d 69 63 72 6f 73 79 73 74 65 6d 73 20 49 6e 63    Microsystems Inc
0080  2e 20 20 20 53 75 6e 4f 53 20 35 2e 39 20 20 20    .   SunOS 5.9
0090  20 20 20 20 47 65 6e 65 72 69 63 20 4d 61 79 20        Generic May
00a0  32 30 30 32 0d 0a 23 20                            2002..#
```

The following is an example of using text2pcap to read the previously shown hexdump *hex_sample.txt* and output it to the *libpcap_output* file:

```
C:\Program Files\Wireshark>text2pcap hex_sample.txt libpcap_output
Input from: hex_sample.txt
Output to: libpcap_output
Wrote packet of 168 bytes at 0
Read 1 potential packets
wrote 1 packets
```

Using Wireshark in Your Network Architecture

This section looks at some of the network architecture and critical points of Wireshark. Network placement is critical for proper analysis and troubleshooting. Most importantly, make sure that you are on the proper network segment. When troubleshooting network issues, you may move between various wiring closets or even different buildings. For this reason, it is beneficial to run Wireshark on a laptop. It is also a good idea to keep a small hub and some network cables (crossover and straight-through) with your laptop for a troubleshooting toolkit. Figure 7.3 shows the incorrect placement of Wireshark if you want to capture communication between the external client and the server. The Wireshark laptop and the switch it is connected to will not see traffic destined for the server because it is routed to the server's switch.

Figure 7.3 Incorrect Wireshark Placement

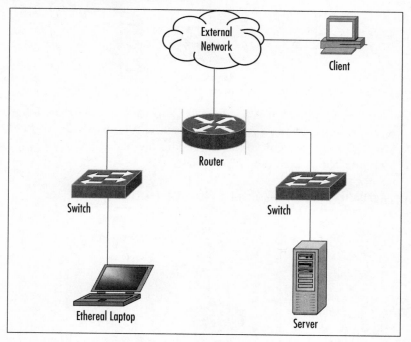

Figure 7.4 shows how to capture traffic from the external client to the server using *port spanning*. The Wireshark laptop must be connected to the same switch as the server. Next, port spanning is activated on the switch to mirror all traffic to and from the server's port to the port that Wireshark is plugged into. Using this method will not cause any disruption of traffic to and from the server.

Figure 7.4 Correct Wireshark Placement Using Port Spanning

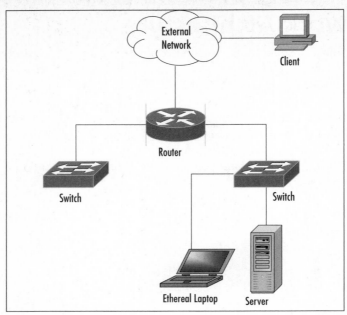

Figure 7.5 shows how to capture traffic from the external client to the server using a hub. Install a small hub between the server and the switch and connect the Wireshark laptop to it. Wireshark will then see all traffic going to and coming from the server. This method will temporarily disrupt traffic while the hub is being installed and the cables connected.

Figure 7.5 Correct Wireshark Placement Using a Hub

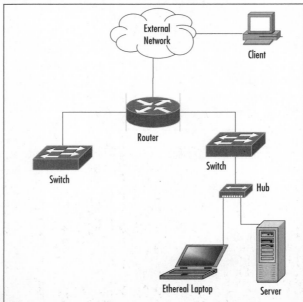

Figure 7.6 shows a network architecture that uses a permanent tap installed at the router. Some administrators use this method for a permanent connection point at critical areas. The Wireshark laptop then sees all traffic going to and from the server plus any other traffic on the segment. Using this method does not disrupt traffic to and from the server if the tap is permanently installed and the cables are already connected. Taps can also be portable and used like the hub in Figure 7.5.

Figure 7.6 Wireshark Placement With a Cable Tap

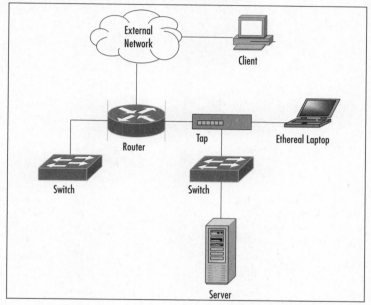

Most network architectures aren't as simple as those depicted in this section. However, these examples should give you a good idea of how to use Wireshark at various points in your network. Some architectures are complicated and can be fully meshed and include redundancy (see Figure 7.7). Also, network segments can branch out for several levels as your network is expanded to buildings and floors within buildings. You must have a good understanding of your network in order to make the most effective choices for sniffer placement.

Using Wireshark for Network Troubleshooting

Every network administrator has had the unpleasant experience of being called in the middle of the night to fix a network problem, which can often result in a surge of emotions (e.g., panic, urgency, and perhaps a sense of heroism). The key to successfully troubleshooting a problem is knowing how the network functions under normal conditions, which will allow you to quickly recognize unusual and abnormal operations. One way to know how your network normally functions is to use a sniffer at various points in the network. This will allow you to get a sense of the protocols that are running on your network, the devices on each segment, and the top talkers (computers that send and receive data most frequently).

Figure 7.7 Fully Meshed Network

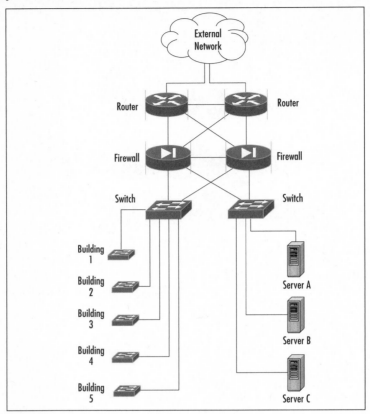

Once you have an idea of how your network functions you can develop a strategy for network troubleshooting. This way you can approach the problem methodically and resolve it with minimum disruption to customers. With troubleshooting, a few minutes spent evaluating the symptoms can save hours of time lost tracking down the wrong problem. A good approach to network troubleshooting involves the following seven steps:

1. Recognize the symptoms
2. Define the problem
3. Analyze the problem
4. Isolate the problem
5. Identify and test the cause of the problem
6. Solve the problem

7.   Verify that the problem has been solved

The first step to network troubleshooting is *recognizing* the symptoms. You can also learn about a network problem from another user network, where the management station alerts you of trouble (e.g., performance issues, connectivity issues, or other strange behaviors) accessing the network. Compare this behavior to normal network operation: Was a change made to the network or to a server right before the problem started? Did an automatic process such as a scheduled backup just begin? Is there a prescheduled maintenance window for this time period? Once you have answered these questions, the next step is to write a clear *definition* of the problem. Once the symptoms have been identified and the problem defined, the next step is to *analyze* the problem. You need to gather data for analysis and narrow down the location of the problem. Is it at the core of the network, a single building, or a remote office? Is the problem related to an entire network segment or a single computer? Can the problem be duplicated elsewhere on the network? You may need to test various parts of your network to narrow down the problem.

Now that you have analyzed and found the problem, you can move onto the next step of *isolating* the problem. There are many ways to do this, such as disconnect the computer that is causing problems, reboot a server, activate a firewall rule to stop some suspected abnormal traffic, or failover to a backup Internet connection.

The next step is to *identify* and *test* the cause of the problem. Now that you have a theory about the cause of the problem you need to test it. Your network analyzer can see what is going on behind the scenes. At this point, you may be researching the problem on the Internet, contacting various hardware or software vendors, or contacting your Internet Service Provider (ISP). You may also want to verify with www.cert.org or www.incidents.org that this is not a widespread issue. Once you have a resolution to the problem, you need to *implement* it. This could involve upgrading hardware or software, implementing a new firewall rule, reinstalling a compromised system, replacing failed hardware, or redesigning the segments of your network.

The last step of network troubleshooting is *verifying* that the problem has been resolved. Make sure that the fix for this problem did not create any new problems or that the problem you solved is not indicative of a deeper underlying problem. Part of this step of the process includes documenting the steps taken to resolve the problem, which will assist in future troubleshooting efforts. If you have not solved the problem, you must repeat the process from the beginning. The flowchart in Figure 7.8 depicts the network troubleshooting process:

NOTE

To be a successful network troubleshooter you need a strong understanding of network protocols. Understanding different protocols and their characteristics will help you recognize abnormal behavior as it occurs on your network.

Figure 7.8 Network Troubleshooting Methodology

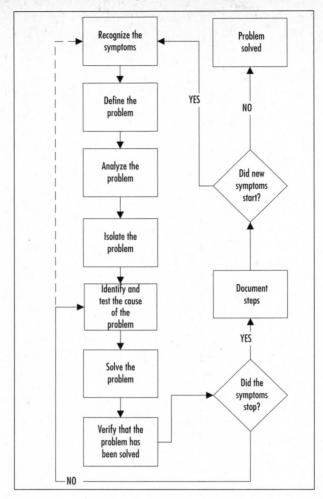

Using Wireshark for System Administration

System administrators are notorious for asking if there is something wrong with the network, and network administrators are notorious for saying the problem is within the system. In between this chasm of blame lies the truth waiting to be discovered by Wireshark.

Checking for Network Connectivity

At the heart of modern TCP/IP networks is Ethernet. Ethernet is a protocol that works without much fuss; however, there is a myriad of problems involving drivers, OSes, configurations, applications, network switches, and so forth, that may occur). The system administrator needs a tool that can detect whether the network is working from an OSI Layer 2 prospective or from an Ethernet prospective.

When a system administration problem occurs, the next step is to verify that the system is receiving the network packets. The most basic packet is the ARP packet.

The basics of the ARP are this: When a system needs to communicate with another system on the same subnet, and has an IP address for that system but not a MAC address, an ARP request is broadcast onto the Ethernet segment (e.g., a network with hosts 192.168.1.1 and 192.168.1.2 having MAC addresses 00:01:02:03:04:05 and 06:07:08:09:0a:0b) and issues the following command sequence through ARP:

```
00:01:02:03:04:05 to ff:ff:ff:ff:ff:ff Who has 192.168.1.2? Tell 192.168.1.1
06:07:08:09:0a:0b to 00:01:02:03:04:05 192.168.1.2 is at 06:07:08:09:0a:0b
```

Knowing that ARP traffic is a necessary precursor to normal network traffic, Ethereal can be used to check for the presence of this traffic on the network. There are several conditions of ARP that indicate specific problems. If there is no ARP traffic from the system on the network, either you are not capturing the traffic correctly or there are driver or OS issues preventing network communication. If the system is issuing ARP requests but there is no response from the host, it may not be on the network. Make sure that the system is on the correct LAN; it is no longer as easy as plugging into the correct network jack. If the system is receiving ARP requests and sending IP traffic out on the network, but not receiving a response that you have verified with your sniffer, there may be a firewall or driver issue with the system.

Checking for Application Network Availability

After verifying that you can see the network, the next step in troubleshooting is to check that systems on the network can connect to the application. Because most network applications are TCP-based, testing is confined to applications using that protocol. For this example, we use a Web server operating on port 80.

As previously discussed, the TCP protocol relies on a three-way handshake before exchanging any data. The handshake itself is indicative of problems with an application. Because Wireshark is qualified to dissect TCP packets, we can use it to locate application problems. Following are some of the scenarios you may encounter while troubleshooting application communication on a network.

Scenario 1: SYN no SYN+ACK

If your Wireshark capture shows that the client is sending a SYN packet, but no response is received from the server, the server is not processing the packet. It could be that a firewall between the two hosts is blocking the packet or that the server itself has a firewall running on it

Scenario 2: SYN immediate response RST

If your Wireshark capture shows that the server is responding with the reset (RST) flag, the destination server is receiving the packet but there is no application bound to that port. Make sure that your application is bound to the correct port on the correct IP address.

Scenario 3: SYN SYN+ACK ACK

Connection Closed

If your Wireshark capture shows that the TCP connection is established and that it immediately closes, the destination server may be rejecting the client's IP address due to security restrictions. On UNIX systems, check the *tcpwrappers* file at */etc/hosts.allow* and */etc/hosts.deny* and verify that you haven't inadvertently blocked communication.

Using Wireshark for Security Administration

"Is this protocol secure?" One of the most common tasks security administrators do, is verify the security of an arbitrary protocol. Wireshark is the ideal tool to use for this.

One of the most popular and useful Wireshark features is *packet reassembly*, which allows us to see the contents of exchanged data. For protocols such as Telnet and FTP, Wireshark clearly displays the username and password for the connection, without any reassembly. For unknown, custom, or otherwise obscure protocols, packet reassembly can be used. To use reassembly, capture the traffic through Wireshark or another tool and then load the capture file into Wireshark and right-click on any packet in the connection. Select the **Follow TCP Stream** option; a window will pop up with all of the communication that occurred in that session. It may help to select the ASCII option, and if the protocol is noisy you can select that sender, receiver, or *Entire Conversation* be displayed.

Detecting Internet Relay Chat Activity

Besides the policy implications of chat rooms, IRC is frequented by hackers and used as a command and control mechanism. IRC normally uses TCP port 6667. If you set Wireshark to detect traffic with destination port 6667, you will see IRC traffic that looks like the following:

```
Local client to IRC server
port 6667:
USER username localsystem.example.com irc.example.net :gaim

Remote IRC server to local client:
NOTICE AUTH :*** Looking up your hostname...

Local client to IRC server
port 6667:
NICK clever-nick-name

Remote IRC server to local client:
NOTICE AUTH :*** Checking ident
NOTICE AUTH :*** Found your hostname
```

At this point, you can be reasonably assured that you are seeing an IRC connection. Make sure that you know who is using it

Wireshark As a Network Intrusion Detection System

Although there are specialized open-source tools for Network Intrusion Detection Systems (NIDSes) such as Sourcefire's Snort (www.snort.org), if you had nothing except Wireshark to use as an IDS system, it would be able to alert you on any criteria. Consider the following Wireshark "rules" for intrusion detection:

- Database connections to your database from systems other than your Web servers
- Attempts to send e-mail to external e-mail servers on TCP port 25 from servers other than your e-mail relays
- Attempts to use Remote Desktop Connection (RDC) from outside your network or use Wireshark as a honeypot, listening for connections to an unused IP address.

Wireshark as a Detector for Proprietary Information Transmission

If your company marks its confidential and proprietary information with a consistent phrase, there is no reason why you cannot use Wireshark to detect the transmission of information. You could use Wireshark to capture all outbound traffic on a span port and then use Wireshark's *Find Packet* function. However, this could create a lot of traffic to sort through. To reduce the amount of traffic captured, you can use capture filters to exclude traffic where you don't expect proprietary information to be transferred through (e.g., DNS queries and internal network traffic).

Securing Ethereal

Although Wireshark is considered a security tool, it is not without its own occasional security issues. According to www.Securityfocus.com, between 2002 and 2006 there were 44 security advisories regarding Ethereal and Wireshark. Most of these were in obscure or rarely used protocol decoders. Still, there are a few things you can do to minimize the effects of any Wireshark bugs.

The primary step to running a more secure Wireshark installation is to update the software and the OS. Updates to Wireshark normally come out every few months and many people use binary versions of Wireshark that are easy to upgrade. The next step for securing Wireshark is to separate the capture process from the analysis process, and run both with the least amount of OS privilege that will work. Normally, all capture libraries require Local Administrator privilege access in Windows or root access in UNIX. Since many of the historical issues with Wireshark were in protocol decoders, if you run your analysis console as a non-privileged or non-root user, it may reduce the risk of security issues impeding your sniffing efforts. You can also use tshark or dumpcap (both included with Wireshark) to capture the network traffic to a file and then view the results later in Wireshark using a non-privileged account.

Optimizing Wireshark

Optimizing the system that you are running your sniffer on will go a long way towards speeding up Wireshark or any other sniffing application that you run. Your network card drivers and Wireshark will do their best to capture all the traffic that you throw at it, but to make sure that you are seeing the full picture of your network, some system-related issues should be considered.

Network Link Speed

Wireshark cannot capture packets any faster than the slowest point between you and the data you are sniffing. Careful attention must be paid so that the slowest link is not the one that Wireshark is on if the network is heavily loaded (e.g., if you are trying to sniff the connection between two computers that are exchanging data at 75 mbit/second, using a 10 mbit/second port span may cause you to not receive all of the data onto the sniffer.

Minimizing Wireshark Extras

Wireshark is an efficient packet sniffer, and not only due to its cost. While Ethereal has the capability to capture data efficiently, some of the more advanced options can slow it down.

In the "Capture Options" dialog box, the following options can slow down the capture: Update list of packets in real-time, Automatic scrolling in live capture, and any of the Name Resolution options. The "Enable network name" resolution option can particularly slow down the capture of a busy network, because DNS lookups need to be made for each source and destination. Using capture filters can speed up Wireshark if you know what type of packet data you are looking for. (Hint: If you separate the capture functions from the analysis functions of Wireshark, you may be able to capture more data.) Use tcpdump, tshark, or the specific tool for your OS, and use it to save the capture data to a file. After the capture is done, load the capture file into Wireshark.

CPU

A fast computer is not strictly necessary to run Wireshark, but tasks such as finding strings in large packet captures will complete faster with a speedier processor. The Wireshark application tries to be as optimized as possible, but faster processors allow more operations per second, which decreases the amount of time you spend waiting for it to process packets or to find certain bits of text in a packet capture.

Memory

The most effective way to make Wireshark run faster is to give it more random-access memory (RAM). This becomes especially important when working with captures that contain many packets. As with most applications, Wireshark needs memory to hold data. When an OS does not have enough memory to hold an application, the OS will *swap* memory from the RAM to the hard drive. The hard drive is much slower than the system memory, and moving data back and forth between the drive and RAM takes time. When Wireshark is short on memory, swapping will slow down the system and applications precipitously.

Advanced Sniffing Techniques

There are alternatives to using Wireshark with port spanning or using a network tap. Unfortunately, attackers can use these techniques to steal passwords and other data from your network.

Dsniff

Dsniff is a sniffing toolkit provided by Dug Song. Dsniff and many mirrors are available on Web site www.monkey.org/~dugsong/dsniff. Dsniff is most famous for its authentication (i.e., usernames and passwords) and sniffing capabilities. The current version of dsniff decodes authentication information for the following protocols:

- America Online (AOL) Instant Messenger (IM) (Citrix Winframe)
- CVS
- File Transfer Protocol (FTP)
- HTTP
- I Seek You (ICQ)
- IMAP
- IRC
- Lightweight Directory Access Protocol (LDAP)
- Remote Procedure Call (RPC) mount requests
- Napster
- Network News Transfer Protocol (NNTP)
- Oracle SQL*Net
- Open Shortest Path First (OSPF)
- PC Anywhere
- Post Office Protocol (POP)
- PostgreSQL
- Routing Information Protocol (RIP)
- Remote Login (rlogin)
- Windows NT plaintext Server Message Block (SMB)
- Network Associates Sniffer Pro (remote)
- Simple Network Management Protocol (SNMP)
- Socks
- Telnet
- X11
- RPC yppasswd

With today's switched networks and encrypted protocols, password sniffing doesn't always work as well as we want it to. Dsniff contains several redirect and man-in-the-middle (MITM) utilities to redirect the flow of traffic and decrypt sessions.

The first utility is *arpspoof* (formerly known as *arpredirect*), which is used by hosts to find the local router's Media Access Control (MAC) address. By spoofing ARP packets, you can convince other nearby computers that you are the router, which means that your machine has to forward the packets on to the legitimate router after receiving them; however, in the meantime, the dsniff password sniffer has a chance to process the packets. This runs well on local switched networks and cable-modem networks. However, this tool isn't completely foolproof; you are essentially trying to convince other machines of the local MAC address. As a result, traffic flows through your machine are sometimes intermittent. This technique is easily detected by network-based intrusion detection systems (IDSes). Sniffer Pro also has an expert diagnostic mode that will flag these as "duplicate IP addresses" (i.e., multiple machines claiming to have the IP address of the router).

The *dnsspoof* utility redirects traffic by spoofing responses from the local Domain Name System (DNS) server. When you go a Web site such as www.example.comht, your machine sends a request to your local DNS server asking for the IP address of www.example.com. This usually takes a while to resolve; however, DNS spoofs quickly send their own response. The victim takes the first response and ignores the second one. The spoofed response contains a different IP address than the legitimate response, usually the IP address of the attacker's machine. The attacker is probably using one of the other dsniff MITM utilities. The name MITM comes from cryptography, and describes the situation when somebody intercepts communications, alters it, and then forwards it. The dsniff utilities for these attacks are called *webmitm* for HTTP traffic (including Secure Sockets Layer [SSL]) and *sshmitm* (for Secure Shell [SSH]). Normally, SSH and SSL are thought to be secure encrypted protocols that cannot be sniffed. MITM utilities work by presenting their own encryption keys to the SSL/SSH clients. This allows them to decrypt the traffic sniff passwords and then reencrypt with the original server keys. In theory, you can protect yourself against this by checking the validity of the server certificate, but in practice, nobody does this. Dsniff can sniff passwords and other cleartext traffic.

The *mailsnarf* utility sniffs e-mails (e.g., the FBI's Carnivore), and reassembles them into an *mbox* format that can be read by most e-mail readers.

The *msgsnarf* utility sniffs messages from ICQ, IRC, Yahoo!, Messenger, and AOL IM.

The *filesnarf* utility sniffs files transferred via Network File System (NFS).

The *urlsnarf* utility saves all Universal Resource Locators (URLs) going across the wire.

The *webspy* utility sends those URLs to a Netscape Web browser in real time, essentially allowing you to watch in real-time what a victim sees on his or her Web browser.

The *macof* utility sends out a flood of MAC addresses, which is intended as another way of attacking Ethernet switches. Most switches have limited tables that can only hold 4,000 MAC addresses. When the switch overloads, it "fails open" and starts repeating every packet out every port, thereby allowing everyone's traffic to be sniffed.

The *tcpkill* utility kills TCP connections, and can be used as a Denial of Service (DoS) attack (e.g., you can configure it to kill every TCP connection your neighbor makes). It can also be integrated with tools like network-based IDSes to kill connections from hackers. The *tcpnice* utility is similar to tcpkill, but instead of killing connections, it slows them down (e.g., you could spoof Internet Control Message Protocol (ICMP) Source Quenches from your neighbor's cable modems so that you can get a higher percentage of bandwidth for your downloads).

Ettercap

Ettercap is similar to dsniff. It has many of the same capabilities (e.g., MITM attacks against SSL and SSH and password sniffing). It also has additional features for MITM attacks against normal TCP connections such as inserting commands into the stream. Ettercap was written by Alberto Ornaghi and Marco Valleri, and is available at http://ettercap.sourceforge.net.

MITM Attacks

The most effective defense against sniffing is using encrypted protocols such as SSL and SSH. However, the latest dsniff and Ettercap packages contain techniques for fooling encryption, known as a MITM attack. The same technique can be applied to encrypted protocols, when an attacker sets up a server that answers requests from clients (e.g., the server answers a request for https://www.amazon.com. A user contacting this machine will falsely believe they have established an encrypted session to Amazon.com. At the same time, the attacker contacts the real Amazon.com and pretends to be the user. The attacker plays both roles, decrypting the incoming data from the user and re-encrypting it for transmission to the original destination. In theory, encryption protocols have defenses against this. A server claiming to be Example.com needs to prove that it is indeed Example.com. In practice, most users ignore this. MITM attacks have proven very effective when used in the field.

Cracking

Tools such as dsniff and Ettercap capture unencrypted passwords and encrypted passwords. In theory, capturing encrypted passwords is useless. However, people sometimes choose weak passwords (e.g., words from the dictionary) and it only takes a few seconds for an attacker to go through a 100,000-word dictionary, comparing the encrypted form of each dictionary word against the encrypted password. If a match is found, the attacker has discovered the password. These password cracking programs already exist. Tools like dsniff and Ettercap simply output the encrypted passwords in a form that these tools can read.

Switch Tricks

A lot of people think that if they have a switched network it is impossible for an attacker to use a sniffer successfully to capture information. The following section discusses methods of successfully sniffing on a switched network.

ARP Spoofing

When attempting to monitor traffic on a switched network, you will run into a serious problem: The switch will limit the traffic that is passed over your section of the network. Switches keep an internal list of the MAC addresses of hosts that are on each port. Traffic is only sent to a port if the destination host is recorded as being present on that port. It is possible to overwrite the ARP cache on many OSes, which would allow you to associate your MAC address with the default gateway's IP address. This would cause all outgoing traffic from the target host to be transmitted to you. You would have to be sure to manually add an ARP table entry for the real default gateway, to ensure that the traffic will be sent to the real target and to ensure that you have IP forwarding enabled. Many cable modem networks are vulnerable to this type of attack, because the cable modem network is essentially an Ethernet network with cable modems acting as bridges. In short, there is no solution to this attack and new generations of cable modem networks will use alternate mechanisms to connect a user to the network. The dsniff sniffer (developed by Dug Song) includes a program named *arpspoof* (formerly *arpredirect*) for exactly this purpose. arpspoof redirects packets from a target host (or all hosts) on the LAN intended for another host on the LAN, by forging ARP replies. This is an extremely effective way of sniffing traffic on a switch.

MAC Flooding

To serve its purpose, a switch must keep a table of all MAC (Ethernet) addresses of the hosts that appear on each port. If a large number of addresses appear on a single port thereby filling the address table on the switch, the switch no longer has a record of which port the victim MAC address is connected to. This is the same situation as when a new machine first attaches to a switch and the switch must learn where that address is. Until it learns which port it is on, the switch must send copies of frames for that MAC address to all switch ports, a practice known as *flooding*.

The dsniff sniffer includes a program named *macof* that facilitates flooding a switch with random MAC addresses to accomplish this. macof floods the local network with random MAC addresses (causing some switches to fail open in repeating mode facilitating sniffing). A straight C port of the original Perl Net::RawIP macof program by Ian Vitek <ian.vitek@infosec.se>.—dsniff FAQ

Routing Games

One method to ensure that all traffic on a network passes through your host is to change the routing table of the host you wish to monitor. This may be possible by sending a fake route advertisement message via the RIP, declaring yourself as the default gateway. If successful, all traffic will be routed through your host. Make sure that you have enabled IP forwarding so that all outbound traffic from the host will pass through your host and onto the real network gateway. You may not receive return traffic unless you have the ability to modify the routing table on the default gateway in order to reroute all return traffic back to you.

Securing Your Network from Sniffers

At this point, you might be considering unplugging the network completely so that sniffers like Wireshark (or other more nefarious applications) cannot be used against you. Hold on to those wire cutters: there are other, more function-friendly ways to help secure your network from a determined eavesdropper.

Using Encryption

Fortunately for the state of network security, when used properly, encryption is the silver bullet that will render a packet sniffer useless. Using encryption (assuming its mechanism is valid) will thwart any attacker attempting to passively monitor your network.

Many existing network protocols have counterparts that rely on strong encryption and all-encompassing mechanisms (e.g., IPSec and OpenVPN) provide this for all protocols. Unfortunately, IP Security (IPSec) is not widely used on the Internet outside of large enterprise companies.

SSH

SSH is a cryptographically secure replacement for the standard UNIX Telnet rlogin, Remote Shell (RSH), and Remote Copy Protocol (RCP) commands. It consists of a client and server that use public key cryptography to provide session encryption. It also provides the ability to forward arbitrary TCP ports over an encrypted connection, which comes in handy for forwarding X11 Windows and other connections.

SSH has received wide acceptance as the secure mechanism to access a remote system interactively. SSH was conceived and initially developed by Finnish developer Tatu Ylönen. The original version of SSH turned into a commercial venture and, although the original version is still freely available, the license has become more restrictive. A public specification has been created, resulting in the development of a number of different versions of SSH-compliant client and server software that do not contain these restrictions (most significantly those that restrict commercial use). A free version of SSH-compatible software (OpenSSH) developed by the OpenBSD OS project, can be obtained from www.openssh.com. The new commercialized SSH can be purchased from SSH Communications Security (www.ssh.com) who have made the commercial version free to recognized universities. Mac OS X already contains OpenSSH software. PuTTY is a free alternative for the commercial SSH software for Windows. Originally developed for cleartext protocols such as Telnet, PuTTY is very popular among system administrators and can be downloaded at www.chiark.gree-nend.org.uk/~sgtatham/putty/.

SSL

SSL provides authentication and encryption services and can also be used as a virtual private network (VPN). From a sniffing perspective, SSL can be vulnerable to a MITM attack. An attacker can set up a transparent proxy between you and the Web server. This transparent proxy can be configured to decrypt the SSL connection, sniff it, and then re-encrypt it. When this happens, the user is prompted with a dialog box indicating that the SSL certificate was not issued by a trusted authority. The problem is, most users ignore the warnings and proceed anyway.

Pretty Good Protection and Secure/Multipurpose Internet Mail Extensions

Pretty Good Protection (PGP) and Secure/Multipurpose Internet Mail Extensions (S/MIME) are standards for encrypting e-mail. When used correctly, these standards prevent e-mail sniffers (e.g., dsniff and Carnivore) from being able to interpret intercepted e-mail. The sender and receiver must both use the software in order to encrypt and decrypt the communication. In the United States, the FBI has designed a Trojan horse called "Magic Lantern" that is designed to log keystrokes, hopefully capturing a user's passphrase. When the FBI gets a passphrase, they can decrypt the e-mail messages. In the United Kingdom, users are required by law to give their encryption keys to law enforcement when requested.

Switching

Network switches make it more difficult for attackers to monitor your network, but not by much. Switches are sometimes recommended as a solution to the sniffing problem; however, their real purpose is to improve network performance, not provide security. As explained in the "Advanced Sniffing Techniques" section, any attacker with the right tools can monitor a switched host if they are on the same switch or segment as that system.

Employing Detection Techniques

But what if you can't use encryption on your network for some reason? What do you do then? If this is the case then you must rely on detecting any network interface card (NIC) that may be operating in a manner that could be invoked by a sniffer.

Local Detection

Many OSes provide a mechanism to determine whether a network interface is running in promiscuous mode. This is usually represented by the type of status flag that is associated with each network interface and maintained in the kernel. This can be obtained by using the **ifconfig** command on UNIX-based systems.

The following example shows an interface on the Linux OS when it isn't in promiscuous mode:

```
eth0      Link encap:Ethernet   HWaddr 00:60:08:C5:93:6B
inet addr:10.0.0.21  Bcast:10.0.0.255  Mask:255.255.255.0
UP BROADCAST RUNNING MULTICAST  MTU:1500  Metric:1
RX packets:1492448 errors:2779 dropped:0 overruns:2779 frame:2779
TX packets:1282868 errors:0 dropped:0 overruns:0 carrier:0
collisions:10575 txqueuelen:100
Interrupt:10 Base address:0x300
```

Note that the attributes of this interface mention nothing about promiscuous mode. When the interface is placed into promiscuous mode (as shown next) the **PROMISC** keyword appears in the attributes section:

```
eth0      Link encap:Ethernet   HWaddr 00:60:08:C5:93:6B
inet addr:10.0.0.21  Bcast:10.0.0.255  Mask:255.255.255.0
UP BROADCAST RUNNING PROMISC MULTICAST  MTU:1500  Metric:1
RX packets:1492330 errors:2779 dropped:0 overruns:2779 frame:2779
TX packets:1282769 errors:0 dropped:0 overruns:0 carrier:0
collisions:10575 txqueuelen:100
Interrupt:10 Base address:0x300
```

It is important to note that if an attacker has compromised the security of the host on which you run this command, he or she can easily affect the output. An important part of an attacker's toolkit is a replacement **ifconfig** command that does not report interfaces in promiscuous mode.

Network Detection

There are a number of techniques of varying degrees of accuracy available to detect whether a host is monitoring a network for all traffic. There is no guaranteed method to detect the presence of a network sniffer.

DNS Lookups

Most programs that are written to monitor networks, perform reverse DNS lookups when they produce output that consists of the source and destination hosts involved in a network connection. In the process of performing this lookup, additional network traffic is generated; mainly the DNS query looking up the network address. It is possible to monitor the network for hosts that are performing a large number of address lookups alone; however, this may be coincidental and may not lead to a sniffing host. An easier way that would result in 100 percent accuracy would be to generate a false network connection from an address that has no business on the local network. You could then monitor the network for DNS queries that attempt to resolve the faked address giving away the sniffing host.

Latency

A second technique that can be used to detect a host that is monitoring the network is to detect latency variations in the host's response to network traffic (i.e., ping). Although this technique is prone to a number of errors (e.g., the host's latency being affected by normal operation) it can assist in determining whether a host is monitoring the network. The method that can be used is to probe the host initially and sample the response times. Next, a large amount of network traffic is generated that is specifically crafted to interest a host that is monitoring the network for authentication information. Finally, the latency of the host is sampled again to determine whether it has changed significantly.

Driver Bugs

Sometimes an OS driver bug assists in determining whether a host is running in promiscuous mode. In one case, CORE-SDI (an Argentine security research company) discovered a bug in a common Linux Ethernet driver. They found that when the host was running in promiscuous mode, the OS failed to perform Ethernet address checks to ensure that the packet was targeted toward one of its interfaces. Instead, this validation was performed at the IP level and the packet was accepted if it was destined to one of the host's interfaces. Normally, packets that do not correspond to a host's Ethernet address are dropped at the hardware level; however, in promiscuous mode this doesn't happen. You can determine whether the host was in promiscuous mode by sending an ICMP ping packet to it with a valid IP address and an invalid Ethernet address. If the host responds to this ping request, it is determined to be running in promiscuous mode.

NetMon

NetMon, available on Windows NT-based systems, has the ability to monitor who is actively running NetMon on a network. It also maintains a history of who has NetMon installed on their system. It only detects other copies of NetMon; therefore, if the attacker is using another sniffer, you must detect it using one of the previous methods discussed. Most network-based IDSes also detect these instances of NetMon.

Summary

In this chapter, we have given you a high-level overview of Wireshark and its various features and supporting programs. We covered the history of Wireshark, its compatibility with other sniffers, and its supported protocols. We took a brief look into the Wireshark GUI and the filter capabilities. We also covered the programs that come with Wireshark, that add additional functionality by manipulating capture files.

We explored several scenarios for using Wireshark in your network architecture. Spend time getting to know your network and the way it is connected. Knowing how your network is segmented will help with placing Wireshark to capture the information you need.

We also explored how Wireshark can be used by a wide range of people, including network system and security administrators. Wireshark can also be used by anyone on their own network. We touched on securing and optimizing Wireshark as part of your workflow. Although the application is robust and stable, there are some simple, cost-effective things you can do to improve your Wireshark experience.

Finally, we covered an example network troubleshooting methodology. It is good practice to use this methodology every time you troubleshoot a problem. Once again, spending time getting to know your network and the protocols running on it will help make troubleshooting a lot easier.

Solutions Fast Track

What is Wireshark?

☑ Wireshark is a free and feature-rich network analyzer that rivals commercial counterparts

☑ Wireshark can decode more than 750 protocols

☑ Wireshark is compatible with more than 25 other sniffers and capture utilities

☑ Display and capture filters can be used to sort through network traffic

☑ Wireshark mailing lists are a great resource for information and support

☑ Wireshark is free of charge and free to distribute, and you are free to modify it

Supporting Programs

☑ Wireshark installs with supporting programs (e.g., tshark)

☑ editcap

☑ mergecap

☑ and text2pcap

☑ Tshark is a command line version of Wireshark

☑ Editcap is used to remove packets from a file and to translate the format of capture files

☑ Mergecap is used to merge multiple capture files into one

☑ Text2pcap is used to translate ASCII hexdump captures into libpcap output files

Using Wireshark in Your Network Architecture

☑ The correct placement of Wireshark in your network architecture is critical to capture the data you need.

☑ Taps, hubs, and switches with port spanning enabled can all be used to connect Wireshark to your network.

☑ You can create a troubleshooting toolkit consisting of a small hub, a small network tap, and extra straight-through and crossover cables.

☑ Installing Wireshark on a laptop makes troubleshooting at various locations easier.

System and Security Troubleshooting

☑ Following a methodical troubleshooting process can minimize the time it takes to solve a problem.

☑ Identifying and testing the cause of a problem often involves research on the Internet or support calls to hardware or software vendors.

☑ Sometimes solving one problem could create another.

☑ Keeping detailed notes on how you solved a problem will assist in future troubleshooting efforts.

Securing and Optimizing Wireshark

☑ Capture packets using the appropriate security privileges; analyze packets with the least privilege possible.

☑ Update Wireshark when security vulnerabilities are found.

☑ Adding system memory will improve application responsiveness when analyzing large numbers of packets.

Advanced Sniffing Techniques

☑ MAC and ARP manipulation techniques can be used to sniff switched traffic without changing your physical network architecture.

☑ MITM attacks can be used to intercept traffic.

☑ Tools are available that sniff traffic and capture and crack passwords at the same time.

Securing Your Network from Sniffers

☑ If those hosts are also authenticated, host-to-host VPN encryption effectively hides data within packets from sniffers. Depending on the method used, the ports and protocols can also be hidden.

☑ Application-level encryption such as SSL also protects the data within the packets.

☑ Switched networks are slightly more difficult to sniff than networks using hubs.

Employing Detection Techniques

☑ Promiscuous mode interfaces on hosts may show the presence of a sniffer.

☑ You can detect the presence of some sniffers by their effects on the network such as extra DNS lookups, network latency, driver issues, and the applications themselves.

☑ No detection tool is effective in an organization without a strong policy that contains the guidelines for the appropriate use of sniffing technologies.

Frequently Asked Questions

The following Frequently Asked Questions, answered by the authors of this book, are designed to both measure your understanding of the concepts presented in this chapter and to assist you with real-life implementation of these concepts. To have your questions about this chapter answered by the author, browse to **www.syngress.com/solutions** and click on the **"Ask the Author"** form.

Q: Many open-source security tools have recently become commercialized. If the Wireshark team converted to a commercial product, would the open-source Wireshark still be free to use?

A: Wireshark was released using the GNU GPL; the source code will remain available and free for any version of software released using the GPL.

Q: With all the other commercial software out there that my company prefers, why should I use Wireshark?

A: Wireshark doesn't require you to decide on it; however, keep it in your toolkit in case you ever need it.

Q: I think I have found an intruder on my network and I would like to save my data. Can Wireshark help?

A: The best response is to use your company's predefined incident response plan. If your company doesn't have an incident response policy, the best time to create one is before you need one.

Q: How can I verify that the version of Wireshark I downloaded doesn't contain a virus or other unwanted software?

A: Downloading from a reputable place is a good start. However, no matter where you downloaded the software from, run **md5sum** and **sha1sum** against the file you downloaded. Check the results of those programs against the hashes in the SIGNATURE file in the Wireshark release directory. To verify that the hashes are correct, use GnuPG (www.gnupg.org) to verify that the hashes were signed correctly.

Q: How can I create packets for Wireshark to sniff?

A: Using the ping utility or going to a Web page will create traffic on your network. If you are looking for an example of a specific type of traffic, creating an environment where that traffic is likely to happen is the best bet. In other words, if you're looking to sniff Web traffic, create a Web server and use a Web browser. If your goal is to create specifically crafted packets, a Perl module named **Raw::IP** should do the trick and is downloadable from CPAN or www.ic.al.lg.ua/~ksv/index.shtml.

Q: How can I sniff all the traffic on my network if my switch doesn't support sniffing or is unmanaged?

A: One way or another you'll need to get into the network path. You can either run a sniffer on the host that sees the most traffic, replace the switch with a hub or another sniffable switch, or use ARP trickery such as dsniff.

Q: Is there a way to use Wireshark without installing it?

A: Using a bootable CD or DVD-ROM is a good option. After downloading and burning a bootable image such as Backtrack (www.remote-exploit.org) or Helix (www.e-fense.com/helix/), you can use Wireshark and other security tools without any installation. However, these bootable disks should not be used to violate your organization's security policies regarding the use of third-party software.

## Chapter 8

Getting and Installing Wireshark

Solutions in this chapter:

- Getting Wireshark
- Packet Capture Drivers
- Installing Wireshark on Windows
- Installing Wireshark on Linux
- Installing Wireshark on Mac OSX
- Installing Wireshark from Source

☑ Summary

☑ Solutions Fast Track

☑ Frequently Asked Questions

Introduction

In this chapter, we will cover all of the steps necessary to complete a functioning installation of the Wireshark network analyzer. Due to the overwhelming amount of Unix-based distributions available today, installation instructions can vary from distribution to distribution, and are beyond the scope of this chapter. For this reason, we will be focusing on information specific to installation on the Fedora Core 6 platform. We have chosen Fedora Core because it is the most commonly used Linux distribution in the world, and serves as a good starting point on which to base further installations. Most of what we cover here should apply to most other popular distributions without a large amount of modification. If the instructions do vary, however, the difference should be minimal. For the Windows side, we will be focusing on Windows XP, due to its common use. Lastly, we have included several installation options for Mac OSX.

For this chapter, we started with fresh installations of Fedora Core 6, Windows XP, and Mac OSX. We accepted the default installation parameters for each of the operating systems (OSs). These types of installations often install needless software, and leave many security vulnerabilities wide open. You should follow many best practices when installing new systems and also when subsequently applying operating system security procedures. These methods are beyond the scope of this book, but you should pick up a good reference for securing your particular operating system. Please make sure your operating system is current, patched, and secured. You will also need to verify that your networking is set up and functioning properly, or you might not be able to see any packets to analyze!

Let's take a moment to introduce you to the way we approached this chapter. When it comes to computers, networking, and security, some of you are beginners and some are pros. Based on the varying technical abilities of the target audience of this book, we tried to approach almost every subject as if we were learning it for the first time. Our only assumption was that you do have a basic understanding of the operating system and how to use it. For the beginners, we made the step-by-step instructions for each installation easy to find and read. This chapter will serve as an excellent *skimming* reference for the more experienced reader. The only time we will have a lengthier explanation with the procedures is when there is possibly some pitfall to watch for, or during description of certain side notes that might be helpful. We keep all of our longer descriptions and discussions *outside* of the chapter installation instructions. So, let's start installing Wireshark!

Getting Wireshark

Wireshark is readily available, in both source and binary form, for download from a variety of sources. The most authoritative source for downloads is the Wireshark download Web site at www.wireshark.org/download.html. This Web page contains a list of locations around the world where users can download binary distributions and ready-to-install packages for several platforms. It also contains the source code in zipped archive (tar.gz) format. Another source for obtaining Wireshark may be your OS CD-ROM. However, these tend to be older versions, and it is worth the time to download the latest versions. Several requirements and dependencies surround the proper installation of Wireshark. These requirements depend on a variety of factors, including the operating system platform and whether you are installing a precompiled binary, or compiling from source. We will address these issues for several platforms throughout this chapter.

The packages needed for installing Wireshark are available free of charge on the Internet at their respective Web sites. You may want to download the latest version of the software before beginning. Feel free to do so; just make sure to substitute package names when necessary. For example, if we reference the file wireshark–0.99.4.tar.gz and you have wireshark–0.99.5.tar.gz, use *your* filename because it's newer.

Platforms and System Requirements

So, on what operating system platforms can you install Wireshark? The following list shows a number of platforms that have readily available Wireshark binaries:

- Mac OSX
- Debian GNU/Linux
- FreeBSD
- Gentoo Linux
- HP-UX
- Mandriva Linux
- Windows
- NetBSD
- OpenPKG
- Red Hat Fedora/Enterprise Linux
- rPath Linux
- Sun Solaris/i386
- Sun Solaris/Sparc

This list is constantly expanding as developers *port* the Wireshark source to new platforms. If your operating system is not listed, and you are feeling brave, go ahead and download the source code and begin building it for your system!

NOTE

Several Wireshark binary packages are available through The Written Word at www.thewrittenword.com. The Written Word provides precompiled binaries of open-source software, specifically for AIX, HP-UX, IRIX, Red Hat Linux, Solaris, and Tru64 Unix. Releases can be purchased on a one-time basis, or as a subscription service.

Packet Capture Drivers

When a computer is placed on a network, the network card is responsible for receiving and transmitting data to other hosts. Network applications use methods, like sockets, to establish and maintain connections, while the underlying operating system handles the low-level details and provides protocol stacks for communications. Some programs, however, need direct access to handle the raw network data, without interference from protocol stacks. A packet capture driver provides exactly this; it has the ability capture raw network packets. Better than that, a packet capture driver can capture *all* data on a shared network architecture, regardless of the intended recipient. This is what allows a program like Wireshark to passively monitor network traffic.

Two very famous and widely used packet capture drivers are libpcap, and its Windows counterpart, WinPcap. Libpcap is a free, open-source packet capture library originally developed at the Lawrence Berkeley National Laboratory in California. It is now maintained by a variety of authors at www.tcpdump.org. Not only does libpcap allow data to be captured, it also provides a mechanism for filtering the data based on user specifications before passing it to the application. WinPcap is maintained by a group of developers at www.winpcap.org. It uses some of the code of libpcap as well as some newly added code. Many other programs use the libpcap and WinPcap libraries, including TCPDump, WinDump, Snort, Ettercap, Dsniff, Nmap, tcpflow, and TCPstat. Programs that use libpcap tend to be network monitors, protocol analyzers, traffic loggers, network intrusion detection systems, and various other security tools.

NOTE

TCPDump is another protocol analyzer, like Wireshark, that can be used to monitor network traffic. It is a command-line application that runs on Unix-based systems. The Windows version is called Windump.

Notes from the Underground...

Compression Utilities

As you are downloading software packages from the Internet, you will encounter numerous compression utilities. Many people are already familiar with the zip compression format used on both Windows and Unix systems. In this chapter, we discuss the tar format used for archiving files. The tar format does not provide compression. Instead, it merely packages files together into one single file. This single tar file will still take up the same amount of space, plus a little more, as the sum of all of the individual files. Tar files are typically compressed with other utilities such as gzip or bzip2.

Gzip is used to reduce the size of files, thus making it a great tool for compressing large packet captures. Gzip files are recognized by the .gz extension.

Continued

Wireshark can automatically uncompress and read Gzip compressed files, even if they don't have the .gz extension. Files can be compressed by typing the command **gzip** *filename*. Files can be *uncompressed* by using the commands **gzip –d** *filename* or **gunzip** *filename*.

Bzip2 is a newer file compression utility and is capable of greater compression ratios than gzip. Bzip2 files are recognized by the .bz2 extension. Files can be compressed by typing the command **bzip2** *filename*. Files can be *uncompressed* by using the commands **bzip2 –d** *filename* or **bunzip2** *filename*. At this time, Wireshark can not read bzip2 compressed files.

Installing libpcap

A lot of Linux systems already have libpcap preinstalled, including Fedora Core 6. However, this section addresses two methods of installing libpcap: the Red Hat Package Manager (RPM), and building from source—for those of you who may still need to install it. Once you install libpcap (or WinPcap), you won't have to do anything else with it unless you are a developer. Wireshark will use the libpcap libraries to passively capture network data. So let's get started installing libpcap!

NOTE

If you use Yellow dog Updater, Modified (YUM) to install Wireshark, it will install libpcap for you.

Installing libpcap Using the RPMs

Installing software from the RPM can be a very tricky process. See the "Notes from the Underground" sidebar in this chapter for more details on RPMs. Luckily, the libpcap installation poses no problems. Remember, there might be newer versions that have been released since the writing of this book; you can download the latest libpcap RPM from www.rpmfind.net. Make sure you are getting the proper RPM for your system. Before you begin, you will need to have root privileges to install an RPM. Make sure you are logged in as root, or switch to root by typing **su root**, pressing **Enter**, and typing the appropriate root password.

1. Install the libpcap RPM by typing **rpm –ivh libpcap-0.9.4-8.1.i386.rpm** and pressing **Enter**.

2. Verify the installation by typing **rpm –q libpcap** and pressing **Enter**. If you see libpcap-0.9.4–8.1 listed, it is installed!

The following output shows how to install the libpcap RPM and then verify it is installed:

```
[root@localhost]# rpm -ivh libpcap-0.9.4-8.1.i386.rpm
Preparing...              ######################################### [100%]
   1:libpcap              ######################################### [100%]
[root@localhost root]# rpm -q libpcap
libpcap-0.9.4-8.1
```

Not too bad! Now that you have libpcap installed, feel free to move on to the "Installing Wireshark on Linux" or "Installing Wireshark from Source" sections in this chapter.

Notes from the Underground…

A Word about RPMs

The Red Hat Package Manager (RPM) is a powerful package management system capable of installing, uninstalling, verifying, querying, and updating Linux software packages. Finding RPMs is relatively easy, and www.rpmfind.net has a well-designed search and download system. However, since RPMs tend to be contributed by various individuals, they are often times a version or two behind the current source-code release. They are created on systems with varying file structures and environments, which can lead to difficulties if your system does not match those parameters. Installing an RPM can sometimes be easier than compiling from source—provided there are no dependency problems.

The RPM system, while an excellent package management tool, is fraught with problems regarding dependencies. It understands and reports which specific files the package requires that you install, but is not yet capable of acquiring and installing the packages necessary to fulfill its requirements. If you are not familiar with the term, dependencies are packages and/or libraries required by other packages. The Red Hat Linux OS is built on dependencies, which you can visualize as an upside-down tree structure. At the top of the tree are your basic user-installed programs, such as Wireshark. Wireshark depends on libpcap to operate, and libpcap requires other libraries to function. This tree structure is nice, but it adds to the dependency problem. For example, you may want to install a new software package and receive an error stating that another library on the system needs to be updated first. OK, so you download that library and attempt to update it. But, now, that library has dependencies too that need to be updated! This can be a never-ending and stressful adventure.

You can get information about RPMs in several ways:

■ *rpm –q* (query) can be used to find out the version of a package installed?for example, *rpm –q wireshark*.

Continued

- *rpm –qa* (query all) can be used to show a very long list of all of the packages on the system. To make this list shorter, you can *pipe* the query into a *grep* to find what you are looking for: *rpm –qa | grep wireshark*.

- *rpm –ql* (query list) shows all of the files that were installed on the system with a particular package—for example, *rpm –ql wireshark*.

- *rpm –qf* (query file) can be used to find out which RPM a particular file belongs to—for example, *rpm –qf /usr/bin/wireshark*.

When using the RPM utility, you can install software three ways:

- *rpm –i* (install) installs a new RPM file, and leaves any previously installed versions alone.

- *rpm –u* (update) installs new software and removes any existing older versions.

- *rpm –f* (freshen) installs new software, but only if a previous version already exists. This is typically used for installing patches.

You can uninstall an RPM from your system by using the following:

- *rpm –e* (erase) removes an RPM from the system—for example, *rpm –e wireshark*.

Sometimes you can be successful by installing a package with the *—nodeps* option (notice it includes two hyphens). This causes the package to install regardless of the dependencies it calls for. This may, or may not, work, depending on whether the package you are installing really does need all of the dependencies to function.

Installing libpcap from the Source Files

Installing libpcap from the source *tarball* is a relatively simple process. A tarball is a single file that can contain many other files, like a zip file. The tar format by itself does not provide compression like the zip format does, so it is customary to compress the tar file with either gzip or bzip2. See the sidebar for more information on using the gzip and bzip2 compression utilities. We will be extracting the contents of the tar file as well as compiling the source code by following the common **configure | make | make install** format for building the package into the system. It is standard practice NOT to build software as root, but to change to root to do the *make install* step. Perform the following steps to install libpcap from the source files.

1. Unzip and extract the tarball by typing **tar –zxvf libpcap-0.9.5.tar.gz** and pressing **Enter**. This will create a new directory called **libpcap-0.9.5**. Notice the extracted output displayed on the screen.

2. Change directories by typing **cd libpcap-0.9.5** and pressing **Enter**.

3. Run the configure script by typing **./configure** and pressing **Enter**. The configure script will analyze your system to make sure that dependencies, environment variables, and other parameters are acceptable. Note the question-and-answer type of analysis displayed on the screen.

4. When the *configure* process is complete, and the command prompt is displayed, make sure there are no errors. If everything appears trouble-free, run the *make* utility simply by typing **make** and pressing **Enter**. This utility will compile the actual source code. The output of the compilation should appear on the screen.

5. The last step of the process is to distribute the executables and other files to their proper locations in the systems directories. Switch to the root user to perform this step. If the *make* utility completes without errors, type **sudo make install** and press **Enter**. Enter the password for root and press **Enter**. Once again, the output of this process should appear on the screen.

6. After the *make install* process completes, the command prompt will be displayed once again. If everything looks error free, you are done!

If at any time during the installation process you receive errors, you will need to investigate the problem and resolve it before continuing. Most of the time, dependency issues, software versions, or environment settings cause compiling errors. Compiling software from the source files offers the benefit of providing highly customized and optimized software for your system. Now that you have libpcap installed, move on to the "Installing Wireshark from Source" section where you can continue compiling Wireshark from the source code or choose one of the other processes.

NOTE

Let's take a moment to define the typical variables used for the tar command: *-z, -x, -v,* and *-f* options.

The *-z* option specifies that the file must be processed through the *gzip* filter. You can tell if an archive was created with gzip by the *.gz* extension. The *-z* option is only available in the GNU version of tar. If you are not using the GNU version, you will have to unzip the tar file with a command such as *gunzip* or *gzip –dc filename.tar.gz | tar xvf -.*

The *-x* option indicates you want the contents of the archive to be extracted. By default, this action will extract the contents into the current working directory unless otherwise specified.

The *-v* option stands for verbose, which means that tar will display all files it processes on the screen. This is a personal preference and is not critical to the extraction operation.

The *-f* option specifies the file that tar will process. For example, this could be libpcap-0.9.5.tar.gz. Sometimes it might be necessary to specify a full path if the file you want to work with is located in another directory.

NOTE

Some Linux distributions have software like libpcap and others preinstalled. It is worth the time and effort to install the latest versions of these packages. You will benefit from the increased stability, features, bug fixes, and speed of updated software.

Installing WinPcap

The Windows version of Wireshark now includes WinPcap, which you can choose to install as you are installing Wireshark. However, we wanted to include instructions for those of you who wish to install WinPcap separately. The latest WinPcap installation executable can be downloaded from www.winpcap.org. To install WinPcap, you need to have the right to install new drivers to your system, and you will need to be logged in as Administrator or have Administrator rights. Perform the following steps to install WinPcap 3.1 on a Windows XP system:

1. Download the WinPcap executable from www.winpcap.org.

2. Begin the installation process by double-clicking the installer, **WinPcap_3_1.exe**. The first screen is a general welcome screen for the installation wizard. Click **Next** to continue.

3. The next screen displays information on the WinPcap license. Once you have read and accepted the terms of the agreement, click **I Agree** to accept the license and continue.

4. The Setup Status window appears, showing the files being copied and displaying a progress bar. Once the installation is complete, click **Finish** to exit the setup.

NOTE

If you do not have WinPcap installed, you will be able to open saved capture files, but you won't be able to capture live network traffic.

WARNING

If you have an older version of WinPcap and would like to install a new one, you must uninstall the old version and reboot. This ensures the new version of WinPcap installs properly. At the time of this writing, version 3.1 was recommended.

NOTE

To make sure WinPcap is installed on your system, check by choosing **Start | Control Panel | Add or Remove Programs**. You should see WinPcap listed under the currently installed programs list.

WinPcap installs by default in C:\Program Files\WinPcap. If you need to uninstall WinPcap, use the provided uninstall executable located in this directory. See how easy that was! Now let's move on to the Wireshark installation.

Installing Wireshark on Windows

The latest Wireshark Windows executable can be downloaded from www.wireshark.org/download.html, and installs on a variety of Windows platforms. Note that you don't need Administrator rights to install Wireshark. Now that WinPcap is installed, perform the following to install Wireshark 0.99.4 on a Windows XP system.

1. Download the Wireshark executable from www.wireshark.org/download.html.

2. Begin the installation process by double-clicking the installer: **wireshark-setup-0.99.4.exe**. The first screen is a general welcome screen for the setup wizard. Click **Next** to continue.

3. The next screen is the Wireshark GNU General Public License Agreement. After reading and accepting the terms of the license, click **I Agree** to accept the license and continue.

4. The next screen allows you to choose which Wireshark components to install. The default components require 65.2MB of free space. Of course, you should have adequate free space for storing your capture files as well. Click **Next** to continue.

5. The screen that appears allows you to select shortcuts to create and associate file extensions with Wireshark. Click **Next** to continue.

6. The next screen allows you to choose the folder where you would like to install Wireshark. Accept the default of C:\Program Files\Wireshark and click **Next**.

7. The screen that next appears allows you to install WinPcap if it is not already installed. If you have not installed WinPcap already, you may choose to do so by clicking the Install WinPcap 3.1 box. Click **Install** to begin the installation process.

8. A screen showing the status of the installation process should appear. It gives line-by-line details of what is happening behind the scenes, as well as an overall progress bar. If Wireshark is installing WinPcap for you, you will need to click **Next** through the WinPcap installation screens and accept the WinPcap license agreement. Once the Wireshark installation is complete, click **Next** to continue.

9. All done! Wireshark is now installed and ready to go. It even puts a nice shortcut icon right on the desktop. You may click the boxes to run Wireshark and to show the Wireshark news file. Click **Finish** to close the dialog box. You can now double-click the Wireshark desktop icon to open the Wireshark network analyzer GUI.

NOTE

A nice feature of the completed installation box is the ability to save the installation log to a file. Simply right-click one of the lines in the box and a small window pops up that says "Copy Details To Clipboard." Select this option and paste the results into Notepad or your favorite text editor.

By default, Wireshark is installed in C:\Program Files\Wireshark. As you saw during the installation process, this can be changed. Several files are placed within the Wireshark directory, including the uninstall.exe file. You can use this executable to uninstall Wireshark if necessary. Other important files to note are the seven executables and their associated manual pages in HTML format: wireshark.exe, tshark.exe, capinfos.exe, dumpcap.exe, editcap.exe, mergecap.exe, and text2pcap.exe.

NOTE

If you are having trouble capturing packets with Wireshark, ensure that WinPcap is working properly by using Windump to try capturing packets. Windump can be downloaded from http://www.winpcap.org/windump/install/default.htm. The command *windump –D* will display a list of valid adapters that WinPcap is able to detect.

Installing Wireshark on Linux

In this section, we will cover the Yellow dog Updater, Modified (YUM) method of installing Wireshark. YUM is an open-source, command-line package management utility for RPM-compatible Linux systems. It is an automated method of installing, updating, and removing RPM packages. The next section will focus on building Wireshark from source. Each example performs the process of installing Wireshark 0.99.4 on Fedora Core 6. So let's get started installing Wireshark!

Installing Wireshark from the RPMs

Installing software from the RPMs can be a very tricky process because of dependencies. Luckily, YUM takes care of dependencies and does all the work for us. For example, you don't need to worry about installing libpcap because YUM downloads and installs it as part of the Wireshark package. The following step-by-step process can be used to install Wireshark on Fedora Core 6. Remember, newer versions may have been released since the writing of this book. Before beginning, you must have root privileges to install Wireshark. Make sure you are logged in as root, or switch to root by typing **su root**, pressing **Enter**, and typing the appropriate root password. Let's begin the Wireshark installation process:

1. Install the Wireshark package by typing **yum install wireshark-gnome** and pressing **Enter**.

That's it! YUM downloads Wireshark and its dependencies and installs them for you. Verify the installation by typing **wireshark** and pressing **Enter**. You should see the Wireshark GUI appear on your screen.

> **NOTE**
>
> When using YUM, you must install the wireshark-gnome package to get the
> Wireshark GUI.

The following output shows how to install the Wireshark RPMs and their dependencies using
YUM:

```
[root@localhost]# yum install wireshark-gnome
Loading "installonlyn" plugin
Setting up Install Process
Setting up repositories
Reading repository metadata in from local files
Parsing package install arguments
Resolving Dependencies
--> Populating transaction set with selected packages. Please wait.
---> Downloading header for wireshark-gnome to pack into transaction set.
wireshark-gnome-0.99.4-1. 100% |=========================| 4.9 kB    00:00
---> Package wireshark-gnome.i386 0:0.99.4-1.fc6 set to be updated
--> Running transaction check
--> Processing Dependency: libwiretap.so.0 for package: wireshark-gnome
--> Processing Dependency: wireshark = 0.99.4-1.fc6 for package: wireshark-gnome
--> Processing Dependency: libwireshark.so.0 for package: wireshark-gnome
--> Restarting Dependency Resolution with new changes.
--> Populating transaction set with selected packages. Please wait.
---> Downloading header for wireshark to pack into transaction set.
Wireshark-0.99.4-1.fc6.i3 100% |=========================| 27 kB    00:00
---> Package wireshark.i386 0:0.99.4-1.fc6 set to be updated
--> Running transaction check
Dependencies Resolved

=============================================================================
 Package              Arch        Version         Repository        Size
=============================================================================
Installing:
 wireshark-gnome      i386        0.99.4-1.fc6    updates           542 k
Installing for dependencies:
 wireshark            i386        0.99.4-1.fc6    updates           7.8 M
Transaction Summary
=============================================================================
Install      2 Package(s)
```

```
Update        0 Package(s)
Remove        0 Package(s)
Total download size: 8.4 M
Is this ok [y/N]: y
Downloading Packages:
(1/2): wireshark-gnome-0. 100% |=========================| 542 kB    00:03
(2/2): wireshark-0.99.4-1 100% |=========================| 7.8 MB    00:45
warning: rpmts_HdrFromFdno: Header V3 DSA signature: NOKEY, key ID 4f2a6fd2
Importing GPG key 0x4F2A6FD2 "Fedora Project <fedora@redhat.com>"
Is this ok [y/N]: y
Running Transaction Test
Finished Transaction Test
Transaction Test Succeeded
Running Transaction
  Installing: wireshark              ######################### [1/2]
  Installing: wireshark-gnome        ######################### [2/2]
Installed: wireshark-gnome.i386 0:0.99.4-1.fc6
Dependency Installed: wireshark.i386 0:0.99.4-1.fc6
Complete!
```

Installing Wireshark on Mac OSX

Installing Wireshark on Mac OSX from Source

Building Wireshark from the source code on Mac OSX is a lengthy, and sometimes tricky, process. However, many people prefer this method because of the control they have over the packages installed. We performed the source-code method of installing Wireshark on Mac OSX Tiger. If you have some free time and are feeling ambitious, you may try this method of installation; otherwise, use one of the ported methods such as DarwinPorts or Fink. If you downloaded newer versions of the software, make sure you change the names accordingly as you proceed through the installation steps.

1. Prepare your Mac by installing Xcode Tools, which is located on your Mac OSX CD. This installs the gcc compiler and other development tools needed to compile source code, such as the X11 environment. If you are running Tiger, find the **Xcode Tools** folder on the Mac OSX Install Disc 1. Double-click the **XcodeTools.mpkg** in this folder and follow the onscreen instructions to install **Xcode Tools**.

2. Install the X11 user environment, which is also located on your Mac OSX Install Disc 1. The package is located in **System | Installation | Packages | X11User.pkg**. Double-click the **X11User.pkg** and follow the onscreen instructions. This installs the X11 application in the Utilities folder.

3. Download the following packages and save them to your user folder, typically /Users/*user-name*:

   ■ **Pkg-config** pkgconfig.freedesktop.org

   ■ **Gettext** www.gnu.org/software/gettext

   ■ **Glib** www.gtk.org/download

   ■ **ATK** ftp.gtk.org/pub/gtk/v2.10/dependencies

   ■ **Libpng** libpng.sourceforge.net

   ■ **Libxml** ftp://xmlsoft.org/libxml2

   ■ **Freetype** freetype.sourceforge.net

   ■ **Fontconfig** fontconfig.org

   ■ **Cairo** ftp.gtk.org/pub/gtk/v2.10/dependencies

   ■ **Pango** www.gtk.org/download

   ■ **Jpgsrc** ftp.gtk.org/pub/gtk/v2.10/dependencies

   ■ **Tiff** ftp.gtk.org/pub/gtk/v2.10/dependencies

   ■ **GTK+** www.gtk.org/download

   ■ **Libpcap** www.tcpdump.org

   ■ **Wireshark** www.wireshark.org

4. Run the X11 application in the Utilities folder by double-clicking it. This will open an Xterminal window. By default, Xterminal should put you into the /Users/*username* directory and you should be able to see all of the packages you just downloaded by typing **ls** and pressing **Enter**.

5. Ensure that /usr/local/bin is in your $PATH. If not, add it by typing **PATH=$PATH:/usr/local/bin** and pressing **Enter**.

6. Extract pkg-config by typing **tar zxvf pkg-config-0.21.tar.gz** and pressing **Enter**. Next, change into the pkg-config directory by typing **cd pkgconfig-0.21** and pressing **Enter**. Run the configure script by typing **./configure** and pressing **Enter**. Compile the source code by typing **make** and pressing **Enter**. Next, install the files in their appropriate locations by typing **sudo make install** and pressing **Enter**. To install the software, you must enter the root password when prompted. When the software install is complete, change back to the original directory by typing **cd ..** and pressing **Enter**.

7. Extract gettext by typing **tar zxvf gettext-0.12.1.tar.gz** and pressing **Enter**. Next, change to the gettext directory by typing **cd gettext-0.12.1** and pressing **Enter**. Run the configure script by typing **./configure** and pressing **Enter**. Then, compile the source code by typing **make** and pressing **Enter**. Next, install the files in their appropriate locations by typing **sudo make install** and pressing **Enter**. To install the software, you must enter the root password when prompted. When the software install is complete, change back to the original directory by typing **cd ..** and pressing **Enter**.

8. Extract Glib by typing **tar zxvf glib-2.12.4.tar.gz** and pressing **Enter**. Next, change to the glib directory by typing **cd glib-2.12.4** and pressing **Enter**. Run the configure script by typing **./configure** and pressing **Enter**. Then, compile the source code by typing **make** and pressing **Enter**. Next, install the files in their appropriate locations by typing **sudo make install** and pressing **Enter**. To install the software, you must enter the root password when prompted. When the software install is complete, change back to the original directory by typing **cd ..** and pressing **Enter**.

9. Extract ATK by typing **tar zxvf atk-1.12.3.tar.gz** and pressing **Enter**. Next, change into the ATK directory by typing **cd atk-1.12.3** and pressing **Enter**. Run the configure script by typing **./configure** and pressing **Enter**. Then, compile the source code by typing **make** and pressing **Enter**. Next, install the files in their appropriate locations by typing **sudo make install** and pressing **Enter**. To install the software, enter the root password when prompted. When the software install is complete, change back to the original directory by typing **cd ..** and pressing **Enter**.

10. Extract libpng by typing **tar zxvf libpng-1.2.12.tar.gz** and pressing **Enter**. Next, change to the libpng directory by typing **cd libpng-1.2.12** and pressing **Enter**. Run the configure script by typing **./configure** and pressing **Enter**. Compile the source code by typing **make** and pressing **Enter**. Next, install the files in their appropriate locations by typing **sudo make install** and pressing **Enter**. To install the software, you must enter the root password when prompted. When the software install is complete, change back to the original directory by typing **cd ..** and pressing **Enter**.

11. Extract libxml by typing **tar zxvf libxml2-2.6.27.tar.gz** and pressing **Enter**. Next, change to the libxml directory by typing **cd libxml2-2.6.27** and pressing **Enter**. Run the configure script by typing **./configure** and pressing **Enter**. Compile the source code by typing **make** and pressing **Enter**. Next, install the files in their appropriate locations by typing **sudo make install** and pressing **Enter**. To install the software, you must enter the root password when prompted. When the software install is complete, change back to the original directory by typing **cd ..** and pressing **Enter**.

12. Extract Freetype by typing **tar zxvf freetype-2.2.1.tar.gz** and pressing **Enter**. Next, change to the freetype directory by typing **cd freetype-2.2.1** and pressing **Enter**. Run the configure script by typing **./configure** and pressing **Enter**. Then, compile the source code by typing **make** and pressing **Enter**. Next, install the files in their appropriate locations by typing **sudo make install** and pressing **Enter**. To install the software, you must enter the root password when prompted. When the software install is completed, change back to the original directory by typing **cd ..** and pressing **Enter**.

13. Extract Fontconfig by typing **tar zxvf fontconfig-2.4.1.tar.gz** and pressing **Enter**. Next, change to the fontconfig directory by typing **cd fontconfig-2.4.1** and pressing **Enter**. Run the configure script by typing **./configure** and pressing **Enter**. Then, compile the source code by typing **make** and pressing **Enter**. Next, install the files in their appropriate locations by typing **sudo make install** and pressing **Enter**. To install the software, you must enter the root password when prompted. When the software install is complete, change back to the original directory by typing **cd ..** and pressing **Enter**.

14. Extract Cairo by typing **tar zxvf cairo-1.2.4.tar.gz** and pressing **Enter**. Next, change to the cairo directory by typing **cd cairo-1.2.4** and pressing **Enter**. Run the configure script by typing **./configure** and pressing **Enter**. Then, compile the source code by typing **make** and pressing **Enter**. Next, install the files in their appropriate locations by typing **sudo make install** and pressing **Enter**. To install the software, enter the root password when prompted. When the software install is complete, change back to the original directory by typing **cd ..** and pressing **Enter**.

15. Extract Pango by typing **tar zxvf pango-1.14.7.tar.gz** and pressing **Enter**. Next, change to the pango directory by typing **cd pango-1.14.7** and pressing **Enter**. Run the configure script by typing **./configure** and pressing **Enter**. Compile the source code by typing **make** and pressing **Enter**. Next, install the files in their appropriate locations by typing **sudo make install** and pressing **Enter**. To install the software, enter the root password when prompted. When the software install is complete, change back to the original directory by typing **cd ..** and pressing **Enter**.

16. Extract jpgsrc by typing **tar zxvf jpgsrc.v6b.tar.gz** and pressing **Enter**. Next, change to the jpgsrc directory by typing **cd jpgsrc-6b** and pressing **Enter**. Run the configure script by typing **./configure** and pressing **Enter**. Then, compile the source code by typing **make** and pressing **Enter**. Next, install the files in their appropriate locations by typing **sudo make install** and pressing **Enter**. To install the software, enter the root password when prompted. When the software install is complete, change back to the original directory by typing **cd ..** and pressing **Enter**.

17. Extract tiff by typing **tar zxvf tiff-3.7.4.tar.gz** and pressing **Enter**. Next, change to the tiff directory by typing **cd tiff-3.7.4** and pressing **Enter**. Run the configure script by typing **./configure** and pressing **Enter**. Compile the source code by typing **make** and press **Enter**. Next, install the files in their appropriate locations by typing **sudo make install** and pressing **Enter**. To install the software, enter the root password when prompted. When the software install is complete, change back to the original directory by typing **cd ..** and pressing **Enter**.

18. Extract GTK+ by typing **tar zxvf gtk+-2.10.6.tar.gz** and pressing **Enter**. Next, change to the gtk+ directory by typing **cd gtk+-2.10.6** and pressing **Enter.** Run the configure script by typing **./configure** and pressing **Enter**. Compile the source code by typing **make** and pressing **Enter**. Next, install the files in their appropriate locations by typing **sudo make install** and pressing **Enter**. To install the software, enter the root password when prompted. When the software install is complete, change back to the original directory by typing **cd ..** and pressing **Enter**.

19. Extract libpcap by typing **tar zxvf libpcap-0.9.5.tar.gz** and pressing **Enter**. Next, change to the libpcap directory by typing **cd libpcap-0.9.5** and pressing **Enter**. Run the configure script by typing **./configure** and pressing **Enter**. Compile the source code by typing **make** and pressing **Enter**. Next, install the files in their appropriate locations by typing **sudo make install** and pressing **Enter**. To install the software, enter the root password when prompted. When the software install is complete, change back to the original directory by typing **cd ..** and pressing **Enter**.

20. Finally the moment we have been waiting for. Extract Wireshark by typing **tar zxvf wire-shark-0.99.4.tar.gz** and pressing **Enter**. Next, change to the wireshark directory by typing **cd wireshark-0.99.4** and pressing **Enter**. Run the configure script by typing **./configure** and pressing **Enter**. Then, compile the source code by typing **make** and pressing **Enter**. Next, install the files in their appropriate locations by typing **sudo make install** and pressing **Enter**. To install the software, enter the root password when prompted. When the software install is complete, change back to the original directory by typing **cd ..** and pressing **Enter**.

21. To run Wireshark, type **wireshark** and press **Enter**. The GUI should open.

Now you have successfully built Wireshark from the source code! Each time you wish to run Wireshark, make sure to run the X11 application and run Wireshark from the Xterminal window that opens. The Wireshark binary installs in /usr/local/bin, so if you don't have that directory in your permanent $PATH, you will need to add it. Once everything is installed, you may also remove the *.tar.gz files from your /User/*username* folder.

NOTE

SharkLauncher is a helpful tool that will launch the X11 environment and the Wireshark binary. It may be downloaded from sourceforge.net/projects/aquaethereal.

Installing Wireshark on Mac OSX Using DarwinPorts

DarwinPorts contains Unix-based software that has been modified to run on Mac OSX, known as *porting*. DarwinPorts automates the process of building third-party software for Mac OSX and other operating systems. It also tracks all dependency information for a given software tool. It knows what to build and install and in what order. After you download and install DarwinPorts, you can use it to easily install all kinds of other software—in our case, Wireshark.

1. Prepare your Mac by installing Xcode Tools, which is located on your Mac OSX CD. This will install the gcc compiler and other development tools needed to compile source code, such as the X11 environment. If you are running Tiger, find the **Xcode Tools** folder on the Mac OSX Install Disc 1. Double-click the **XcodeTools.mpkg** in this folder and follow the onscreen instructions to install **Xcode Tools**.

2. Install the X11 user environment located on your Mac OSX Install Disc 1 as well. The package is located in **System | Installation | Packages | X11User.pkg**. Double-click the **X11User.pkg** and follow the onscreen instructions. This installs the X11 application in the Utilities folder.

3. Download **DarwinPorts** from **macports.com**. Copy the file to the **/Users/*username*** folder.

4. Run the **X11** application in the **Utilities** folder by double-clicking it. This will open an Xterminal window. By default, Xterminal should put you into the **/Users/*username*** directory and you should be able to see the package you just downloaded by typing **ls** and pressing **Enter**.

5. Extract **DarwinPorts** by typing **tar zxvf DarwinPorts-1.3.2.tar.gz** and pressing **Enter**. Next, change into the DarwinPorts base directory by typing **cd DarwinPorts-1.3.2/base** and pressing **Enter**. Run the configure script by typing **./configure** and pressing **Enter**. Compile the source code by typing **make** and pressing **Enter**. Install the files in their appropriate locations by typing **sudo make install** and pressing **Enter**. To install the software, enter the root password when prompted. When the software install is complete, change back to the original directory by typing **cd ../..** and pressing **Enter**.

6. DarwinPorts installs the binary in the /opt/local/bin directory, so you may need to add that to your PATH by typing **PATH=$PATH:/opt/local/bin** and pressing **Enter**.

7. Update the ports to make sure they are current by typing **sudo port –d selfupdate** and pressing **Enter**.

8. Install Wireshark by typing **sudo port install wireshark** and pressing **Enter**. DarwinPorts will then start fetching and installing the appropriate software dependencies and the Wireshark binary.

9. Once the installation is complete, run Wireshark by typing **wireshark** and pressing **Enter**. The GUI will now open.

Now you have successfully installed Wireshark using DarwinPorts! Each time you wish to run Wireshark, make sure you run the X11 application and run Wireshark from the Xterminal window that opens. The Wireshark binary installs in /usr/local/bin, so if you don't have that directory in your permanent $PATH, you will need to add it. Once everything is installed, you may also remove the DarwinPorts-1.3.2.tar.gz file from your /User/*username* folder.

Installing Wireshark on Mac OSX Using Fink

The Fink Project modifies UNIX software so it compiles and runs on Mac OSX. This is known as *porting*. The distribution is then built with a package of the management tools **dpkg** and **apt-get**.

1. The first thing you need to do is prepare your Mac by installing Xcode Tools, which are located on your Mac OSX CD. This installs the gcc compiler and other development tools needed to compile source code, such as the X11 environment. If you are running Tiger, an **Xcode Tools** folder can be found on the Mac OSX Install Disc 1. Double-click the **XcodeTools.mpkg** in this folder and follow the onscreen instructions to install **Xcode Tools**.

2. Install the X11 user environment, which is located on your Mac OSX Install Disc 1 as well. The package can be found by choosing **System | Installation | Packages | X11User.pkg**. Double-click the **X11User.pkg** and follow the onscreen instructions. This installs the X11 application in the Utilities folder.

3. Download the Fink installer image from **fink.sourceforge.net**. Double-click the image to uncompress it, then double-click the **Fink pkg file** to launch the installer. Follow the onscreen instructions to walk through the Fink installer.

4. Open the **FinkCommander** file on the installer image and drag the **FinkCommander** binary to the **Applications** folder.

5. Double-click the **FinkCommand** application to open the GUI.

6. Perform an update by clicking the **Source** menu and choosing **Selfupdate-rsync**. This will ensure that all of the packages are current.

7. Now you are ready to install Wireshark. Scroll down through the list of packages and choose the **Wireshark** package. Click the icon in the upper-left corner of the window to install the binary package.

8. Once the installation is complete, you must open an Xterminal windows to run Wireshark. Run Wireshark by typing **wireshark** and pressing **Enter**. The GUI will open.

Now you have successfully installed Wireshark using Fink. Each time you wish to run Wireshark, make sure you run both the X11 application and Wireshark from the Xterminal window that opens. The Wireshark binary installs in /sw/bin, so if you don't have that directory in your permanent $PATH, you should add it.

Installing Wireshark from Source

Installing Wireshark from the source code is very beneficial in a number of ways. Not only will you have all of the source code, additional documentation, and miscellaneous files to peruse, you will also have the ability to control numerous aspects of the build process. Wireshark can be built from sources on both the Windows and Unix/Linux OS. We will only focus on the Unix-based build in this book, however. Building software from source will give you a better feel for how the whole process works and what goes on behind the scenes. What you will take away is a wealth of knowledge about the software package, programming, and operating system management.

The first thing we need to do to install Wireshark software from source code is install all of the required dependencies. Remember that we earlier stated we need certain files for Wireshark to operate smoothly and effectively? In addition to libpcap, Wireshark requires the following prerequisites: GTK+ and Glib. However, depending on your version of Unix/Linux you may also have the following additional prerequisites:

- **Pkg-config** pkgconfig.freedesktop.org
- **Gettext** www.gnu.org/software/gettext
- **ATK** ftp.gtk.org/pub/gtk/v2.10/dependencies
- **Libpng** libpng.sourceforge.net
- **Libxml** ftp://xmlsoft.org/libxml2
- **Freetype** freetype.sourceforge.net
- **Fontconfig** fontconfig.org

- **Cairo** ftp.gtk.org/pub/gtk/v2.10/dependencies
- **Pango** www.gtk.org/download
- **Jpgsrc** ftp.gtk.org/pub/gtk/v2.10/dependencies
- **Tiff** ftp.gtk.org/pub/gtk/v2.10/dependencies
- **Zlib** www.zlib.net

For more information on installing these packages, see the section "Installing Wireshark on Mac OSX from Source."

> **NOTE**
>
> As we stated previously, most installations follow the **configure | make | make install** format. However, in some instances, there may be other steps. Once the tar file has been extracted, there is usually an INSTALL text file included in the software subdirectory. Take a look at this file by typing **more INSTALL** to verify the installation process.

After the required dependencies are installed, we are ready to install Wireshark. There may be newer versions that have been released since the writing of this book, and you can download the latest versions from www.wireshark.org. Remember, it is standard practice NOT to build software as root, but to change to root to do the *make install* step.

1. Uncompress and extract the Wireshark tarball by typing **tar zxvf wireshark-0.99.4.tar.gz** and pressing **Enter**. This will create a new directory called **wireshark-0.99.4**.

2. Change to the wireshark directory by typing **cd wireshark-0.99.4** and pressing **Enter**.

3. Run the configure script by typing **./configure** and pressing **Enter**. At the end of the configure script output, you will see a summary of the options. These can be changed by using specific parameters with the configure script, something which is discussed in the section "Enabling and Disabling Features via *configure*."

4. When the *configure* process is complete and the command prompt is displayed, make sure there are no errors. If everything appears trouble-free, run the make utility simply by typing **make** and pressing **Enter**.

5. If the *make* utility completed without errors, type **su root** and press **Enter**. Enter the password for root and press **Enter**. Next, install the files in their appropriate locations by typing **make install** and pressing **Enter**. When the software install is completed, change back to the original directory by typing **cd ..** and pressing **Enter**.

6. After the *make install* process completes, the command prompt will be displayed once again. To run Wireshark, type **wireshark** and press **Enter**. The GUI will open.

Now you have successfully built Wireshark from the source code! The Wireshark binary installs in /usr/local/bin, so if you don't have that directory in your permanent $PATH, you must add it. Once everything is installed, you may also remove the *.tar.gz files.

> **NOTE**
>
> Other programs are listed in the configure output that you may not be familiar with. They are each very useful when you are developing for Wireshark. The idl2wrs program is used by developers to convert a CORBA Interface Definition Language (IDL) file to C source code for a Wireshark plug-in. The randpkt program is used to generate random packet capture files. It can generate different types of packets with a user-specified maximum byte count and the number of packets to create. Finally, the dftest program is a display filter compiler test program. It is used to display filter byte-code for debugging filter routines.

Once the installation is complete, the following programs should now be installed in /usr/local/bin: wireshark, tshark, editcap, mergecap, dumpcap, text2pcap, and idl2wrs. Plugins are installed in /usr/local/lib/wireshark/plugins/0.99.4. Some important resources to note are the files in the wireshark-0.99.4/doc directory. They contain several good README files about the inner workings of Wireshark. Several helpful README files can also be found in the wireshark-0.99.4 directory. Finally, the INSTALL and INSTALL.configure files located in the wireshark-0.99.4 directory are also a good resource.

> **NOTE**
>
> The *manuf* file is a text document, located in the /usr/local/share/wireshark directory, that contains a very large listing of well-known vendor MAC addresses. This can come in handy when troubleshooting network problems.

> **NOTE**
>
> The absolute latest version of Wireshark can be downloaded from the automated build section at www.wireshark.org/download/automated. This is the version of Wireshark that the developers are currently working on, so you must be aware that this is a beta version that may contain bugs.

Enabling and Disabling Features via *configure*

During the *configure* script portion of the build process, you can pass options to the installer to customize the application to your specific needs. The following options were harvested from the INSTALL file in the Wireshark tarball.

> **NOTE**
>
> Running *./configure --help* will give you information on the optional parameters, plus a whole lot more!

- **--sysconfdir=DIR** Wireshark installs a support file (manuf) in ${PREFIX}/etc by default, where ${PREFIX} comes from —prefix=DIR. If you do not specify any —*prefix* option, ${PREFIX} is "/usr/local". You can change the location of the manuf file with the —*sysconfdir* option.

- **--disable-usr-local** By default, *configure* will look in /usr/local/{include,lib} for additional header files and libraries. Using this switch keeps configure from looking there.

- **--disable-wireshark** By default, if *configure* finds the GTK+ libraries, the Makefile builds Wireshark, the GUI packet analyzer. You can disable the build of the GUI version of Wireshark with this switch.

- **--disable-gtk2** Build Glib/Gtk+ 1.2[.x]-based Wireshark.

- **--disable-tshark** By default, the line-mode packet analyzer, Tshark, is built. Use this switch to avoid building it.

- **--disable-editcap** By default, the capture-file editing program is built. Use this switch to avoid building it.

- **--disable-mergecap** By default, the capture-file merging program is built. Use this switch to avoid building it.

- **--disable-text2pcap** By default, the hex-dump-to-capture file conversion program is built. Use this switch to avoid building it.

- **--disable-idl2wrs** By default, the IDL-to-wireshark-dissector-source-code converter is built. Use this switch to avoid building it.

- **--enable-dftest** By default, the display-filter-compiler test program is not built. Use this switch to build it.

- **--enable-randpkt** By default, the program that creates random packet-capture files is not built. Use this switch to build it.

- **--without-pcap** If you choose to build a packet analyzer that can analyze capture files but cannot capture packets on its own, but you *do* have libpcap installed, or if you are trying to build Wireshark on a system that doesn't have libpcap installed (in which case you have no choice but to build a version that can analyze capture files but cannot capture packets on its own), use this option to avoid using libpcap.

- ■ **--with-pcap=DIR** Use this to tell Wireshark where you have libpcap installed (if it is installed in a nonstandard location).

- ■ **--without-zlib** By default, if *configure* finds zlib (a.k.a., libz), the wiretap library will be built so that it can read compressed capture files. If you have zlib but do not wish to build it into the wiretap library used by Wireshark, Tshark, and the capture-file utilities that come in this package, use this switch.

- ■ **--with-zlib=DIR** Use this to tell Wireshark where you have zlib installed, if it is installed in a nonstandard location.

- ■ **--disable-ipv6** If *configure* finds support for IPv6 name resolution on your system, the packet analyzers will make use of it. To avoid using IPv6 name resolution if you have the support for it, use this switch.

- ■ **--enable-setuid-install** Use this switch to install the packet analyzers as setuid. Installing Wireshark and Tshark as setuid root is dangerous. Repeat: IT'S DANGEROUS. Don't do it.

- ■ **--with-ssl=DIR** If your SNMP library requires the SSL library, and your SSL library is installed in a nonstandard location, you can specify where your SSL library is with this switch.

- ■ **--without-net-snmp** If configure finds a supported version of the Net SNMP library on your system, the SNMP dissector will be enhanced to use routines from that SNMP library. Employ this switch to avoid using the Net SNMP library even if you have it installed.

- ■ **--with-net-snmp=PATH** Tell the configure script where your net-snmp-config shell script that comes with the Net-SNMP package is located, if not in a standard location.

- ■ **--without-ucd-snmp** If configure finds a supported version of the UCD SNMP library on your system, the SNMP dissector will be enhanced to use routines from that SNMP library. Use this switch to avoid using the UCD SNMP library even if you have it installed.

- ■ **--with-ucd-snmp=DIR** Tell the configure script where your UCD SNMP library is located, if not in a standard location.

- ■ **--without-plugins** By default, if your system can support run-time loadable modules, the packet analyzers are built with support for plug-ins. Use this switch to build packet analyzers without plug-in support.

- ■ **--with-plugins=DIR** By default, plug-ins are installed in ${LIBDIR}/wireshark/plugins/${VERSION}. ${LIBDIR} can be set with *--libdir*, or they default to ${EPREFIX/lib}. ${EPREFIX} can be set with *--exec-prefix*, or iy can default to ${PREFIX}. ${VERSION} is the Wireshark version. Use this switch to change the location where plug-ins are installed.

Summary

In this chapter, we covered the basics of Wireshark installation, including RPM and source-code packages. We also covered complete installations of the libpcap and WinPcap libraries, as well as Wireshark for Windows, Mac OSX, and UNIX-based and Windows systems. We also learned how to install the necessary prerequisite software, and troubleshoot dependency issues.

As stated previously in this chapter, it is important to keep your Wireshark installation up-to-date. This includes the packet capture libraries, the supporting prerequisite software, and the Wireshark software itself. You should also visit the Wireshark site frequently to keep up on the latest announcements, as well as subscribe to some of the mailing lists. We also strongly recommend you keep your OS up-to-date as well, especially when it comes to security updates and patches. Computer security is an ever-changing technology, and it is necessary to keep up with things to avoid system compromises.

All of these parts will come together to form a solid network analysis system that will assist your network troubleshooting and security efforts for years to come.

Solutions Fast Track

Getting Wireshark

- ☑ Wireshark can be downloaded as binaries or source code.
- ☑ Wireshark binaries are available for a number of platforms.
- ☑ The packages you will need for installing Wireshark are available for free on the Internet at their respective Web sites.

Packet Capture Drivers

- ☑ Packet capture drivers are responsible for capturing the raw network packets.
- ☑ libpcap is a packet capture library for Unix systems; Windows uses WinPcap.
- ☑ Sometimes RPMs are a version or two behind the current source-code release.
- ☑ Wireshark must have libpcap (or WinPcap) installed to capture packets.
- ☑ Libpcap can be installed from a binary or source code.
- ☑ Uninstall older versions of WinPcap before installing newer ones.

Installing Wireshark on Windows

- ☑ Wireshark installs WinPcap for you if selected.
- ☑ Uninstall Wireshark by using the uninstall.exe program.

☑ Wireshark for Windows also installs tshark, editcap, mergcap, and text2pcap.

Installing Wireshark on Linux

☑ Yellow dog Updater, Modified (YUM) installs Wireshark and all its dependencies automatically.

☑ When using YUM, you must install the Wireshark-gnome package to get the Wireshark GUI.

☑ You may also install the individual Wireshark RPMs for your Linux system, but this can be a tricky process due to dependencies.

Installing Wireshark on Mac OSX

☑ You may install Wireshark on Mac OSX using DarwinPorts, Fink, or by compiling from source code.

☑ You must have Xcode Tools and the X11 user environment installed on your Mac OS to run Wireshark.

☑ DarwinPorts and Fink will install Wireshark and its dependencies for you automatically.

Installing Wireshark from Source

☑ Wireshark source-compiling prerequisites include libpcap, GTK+, and Glib.

☑ Source code installs are accomplished with the configure | make | make install process.

☑ Installing from source code gives you more control over the installation process.

☑ Installing from source gives you access to the source code and additional documentation.

☑ Wireshark installs by default in the /usr/local/bin directory.

☑ Many options to the configure script are available to customize your install.

Frequently Asked Questions

The following Frequently Asked Questions, answered by the authors of this book, are designed to both measure your understanding of the concepts presented in this chapter and to assist you with real-life implementation of these concepts. To have your questions about this chapter answered by the author, browse to **www.syngress.com/solutions** and click on the **"Ask the Author"** form.

Q: Can I mix methods of installation? For example, can I install libpcap with the RPM and then build Wireshark from source, or vice-versa?

A: Yes, you can, as long as your OS supports the methods you are trying to use. Depending on the method, you may have to adjust your $PATH variable for the install to find the necessary dependencies.

Q: What if I installed Wireshark and then later upgraded to GTK+2?

A: No problem, just re-run the *configure* script for Wireshark and then run *make* and *make install* again. Wireshark will automatically detect GTK+2 and use that version.

Q: A new version of Wireshark was released and I want to upgrade. How do I do that?

A: For Linux, you would use the *rpm –Uvh* command or *yum*. For Windows, simply run the new executable and it will upgrade your current version. For Mac OSX using DarwinPorts, you may use the *port upgrade wireshark* command. If you have compiled the code from source, you will need to perform the *configure | make | make install* process again for the new version

Q: A new version of WinPcap was released. How do I upgrade to it?

A: First, go to the directory with your current version of WinPcap (usually C:\Program Files\WinPcap) and run the uninstall.exe program. Reboot and proceed with installing the executable for the new version.

Q: I installed everything and it looks like it worked okay, but when I try to run Wireshark it says it can't find it?

A: Make sure the Wireshark directory is in the proper path—for example, */usr/local/bin*.

Q: Why do I have to install all this other stuff just to compile Wireshark?

A: Wireshark is a feature-rich, multifaceted software program. It relies on the details of some previously written libraries to take care of the low-level functions.

## Chapter 9

Using Wireshark

Solutions in this chapter:

- **Getting Started with Wireshark**

- **Exploring the Main Window**

- **Other Window Components**

- **Exploring the Menus**

- **Using Command-line Options**

☑ **Summary**

☑ **Solutions Fast Track**

☑ **Frequently Asked Questions**

Introduction

Wireshark provides insight into what is occurring on a network, which is useful when implementing protocols, debugging network applications, testing networks, and debugging live networks. In situations involving interaction with a network at a technical level, most problems can be resolved using Wireshark.

Wireshark is an excellent educational aid. Being able to see and analyze network traffic is very instructive. This chapter covers the main components of the Wireshark Graphical User Interface (GUI), including:

- Main window
- Menu bar
- Tool bar
- Summary window
- Protocol Tree window
- Data View window
- Filter bar
- Information field
- Display information

This chapter also covers the context-sensitive pop-up windows available in the Summary window, the Protocol Tree window, and the Data View window. It also explains the various dialog boxes that are launched by the menus and toolbars.

You will learn how to perform basic tasks in Wireshark (e.g., capturing network traffic, loading and saving capture files, performing basic filtering, printing packets) using the advanced tools provided by Wireshark. Examples have been provided to show you step-by-step how some of the less obvious areas of Wireshark work.

Getting Started with Wireshark

You can download binary packages for Wireshark from the Wireshark Web site at www.wireshark.com. If there are no binary packages available for your platform, or if they are not up-to-date, or if they are compiled without the options you need, you can download the source code from the Wireshark Web site and compile Wireshark using the following command:

```
wireshark
```

To launch Wireshark on Windows, select **Start | Programs | Wireshark | Wireshark**. The Main window of the Wireshark application will now be displayed.

Exploring the Main Window

It is important to define a common set of labels for the different components of the Main window. Figure 9.1 shows the Main window of Wireshark with its major components labeled.

Figure 9.1 Main Window

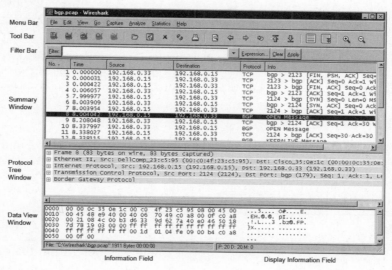

The Main window components are described in Table 9.1.

Table 9.1 Main Window Components

Window Component	Description
Menu Bar	A typical application menu bar containing drop-down menu items.
Tool Bar	Contains buttons for some commonly used functions of Wireshark. The Tool Bar icons have tool tips that are displayed when you pause the mouse pointer over them.
Filter Bar	Applies filters to the Summary window to restrict which packets in the capture are displayed, based on their attributes.
Summary Window	Provides a one-line summary for each packet in the capture.
Protocol Tree Window	Provides a detailed decode of the packet selected in the Summary window.

Continued

Table 9.1 continued Main Window Components

Window Component	Description
Data View Window	Provides a view of the raw data in the packet selected in the Summary window.
Information Field	A display area that provides information about the capture or field selected in the Protocol Tree window.
Display Information Field	A display area that provides information about the packet count in the current capture

Summary Window

The Summary window displays a summary of each packet (one per line) in a capture. One or more columns of summary data are displayed for each packet. Typical columns are shown in Table 9.2.

Table 9.2 Summary Window Columns

Column Name	Description
No.	The frame number within the capture.
Time	The time from the beginning of the capture to the time when the packet was captured (in seconds).
Source	This is the highest level source address, (frequently the Internet Protocol (IP) address); however, it can also be the Media Access Control (MAC) address for layer 2 Ethernet protocols, or other address types for other protocols (e.g., Internetwork Packet Exchange [IPX], Appletalk, and so forth). (See the Wireshark "Name Resolution" sidebar for a discussion of MAC addresses.)
Destination	The is the highest level destination address (frequently the IP destination address); however, it can also be the MAC address for layer 2 Ethernet protocols, or other address types for other protocols (IPX, Appletalk, and so forth).
Protocol	Typically the highest level protocol that is decoded. Examples include user-level protocols such as Hypertext Transfer Protocol (HTTP), File Transfer Protocol (FTP), and Simple Mail Transfer Protocol (SMTP).

Continued

Table 9.2 continued Summary Window Columns

Column Name	Description
Info	This field contains information that was determined by the highest level decode to be useful or informative as part of a summary for this packet.

The "Preferences" feature can be used to select which columns are displayed in the Summary window. Go to **Edit | Preferences** from the Menu bar.

The summary information for the packet selected in the Summary window in Figure 9.1, is shown in Table 9.3.

Table 9.3 Summary Window Column

Column Name	Value
No.	8
Time	8.004042 seconds since the capture started
Source	IP number *192.168.0.15*
Destination	IP number *192.168.0.33*
Protocol	Border Gateway Protocol (BGP)
Info	OPEN Message

We immediately see that this packet is carrying a message for opening a BGP session between 192.168.0.15 and 192.168.0.33. (More information on BGP is available in Request for Comment (RFC) 1771 at www.ietf.org/rfc/rfc1771.txt?number=1771.) Select packets in the Summary window by clicking on the row summarizing a given packet. The information for the selected packet is then displayed in the Protocol Tree window and the Data View window. Once you have selected a packet in the Summary window, you can use the Protocol Tree window to go into greater detail.

Protocol Tree Window

Conceptualize a packet as a tree of fields and subtrees. For each protocol, there is a tree node that can be expanded to provide the values in that protocol's fields. Within some protocols, there may be tree nodes summarizing more complicated data structures in the protocol. These tree nodes can be expanded to show those data structures. For any given node that has a subtree, you can expand its subtree to reveal more information, or collapse it to only show the summary. The Protocol Tree window allows you to examine the tree created by Wireshark from decoding a packet.

Now we'll examine the Protocol Tree window in the packet that was selected in the previous example (see Figure 9.2).

Figure 9.2 Protocol Tree Window Collapsed

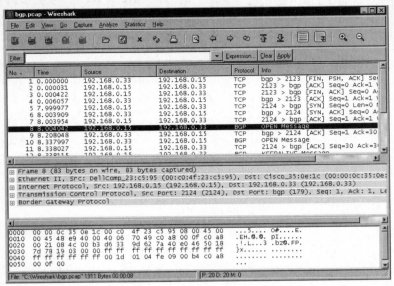

In the Protocol Tree window, each layer in the protocol stack for this packet contains a one-line summary of that layer (see Table 9.4).

Table 9.4 Protocol Layer Example

Layer	Protocol	Description
Packet Meta Data	Frame	83 bytes on wire, 83 bytes captured
Data Link (Layer 2/L2)	Ethernet II	Src Addr: 00:c0:4f:23:c5:95, Dst Addr: 00:00:0c:35:0e:1c
Network (Layer 3/L3)	IP	Src Addr: 192.168.0.15, Dst Addr: 192.168.0.33
Transport (Layer 4/L4)	Transmission Control Protocol (TCP)	Src Port: 2124, Dst Port: bgp(179), Seq: 2593706850, Ack …
Application Layer (Layer 7/L7)	BGP	

Each of these layers have plus (+) signs next to them, which indicate that there is a subtree that can be expanded to provide more information about that particular protocol.

In Figure 9.3, the BGP tree was expanded to reveal one OPEN message, and then the OPEN message was expanded to reveal the fields contained within.

Figure 9.3 Protocol Tree Window Expanded

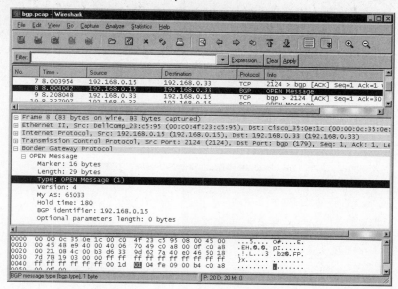

Selecting the Type field in the Protocol Tree window displayed the message, "BGP message type (*bgp.type*), 1byte." This indicates the long name of this field (BGP message type), the display filter field name used to identify this field for filtering and colorization (*bgp.type*), and the size of this field in the packet (1 byte).

Data View Window

The Data View window contains a series of rows that each begin with a four-digit number that represents the number of bytes in an octet. (An octet is comprised of either 8 bits, 1 byte, or 2 hexadecimal digits). The first octet in that row is offset from the beginning of the packet (see Figure 9.4). This offset is then followed by 16 two-character hexadecimal bytes. The last item in each row is a series of 16 American Standard Code for Information Interchange (ASCII) characters representing the same 16 bytes from the packet. Not all bytes can be displayed in ASCII. For those bytes, a period (.) is substituted as a placeholder.

When a field in the Protocol Tree window is selected, the bytes corresponding to that field are highlighted in the Data View window. In Figure 9.4. we selected the BGP Message Type field in the Protocol Tree window. In the Data View window, that byte is highlighted in the row with offset *0040* representing *0x40* hexadecimal or 64 bytes into the packet. The ninth byte in the row is highlighted, and has a value of *01* hexadecimal. In the ASCII representation, there is a period (.), because the value *0x01* is not represented in ASCII.

When you click on a hexadecimal byte or ASCII character in the Data View window, Wireshark highlights the field in the Protocol Tree window that corresponds to the selected byte and to all of the bytes in the Data View window associated with that Protocol field.

Figure 9.4 Data View Window

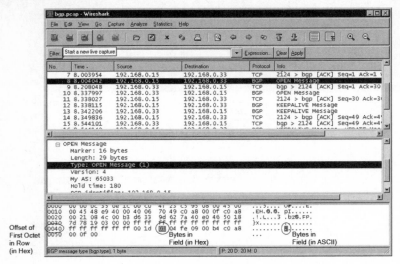

In Figure 9.5, we clicked on the beginning of row 0030 (note that the 48th byte [0030 or hexadecimal *0x30*] is the first byte of the 2-byte TCP Window Size field. As a result, the TCP Protocol Tree was automatically expanded and the Window Size field was highlighted. Additionally, the second byte (78 hexadecimal) in the 0030 row was also selected, because the TCP Window Size field is a 2-byte field.

This feature makes it easy to use the Protocol Tree window and the Data View window together, in order to obtain a solid grasp of the relationships between the fields in a protocol and the actual bits on the wire.

Figure 9.5 Data View Window Byte Selection

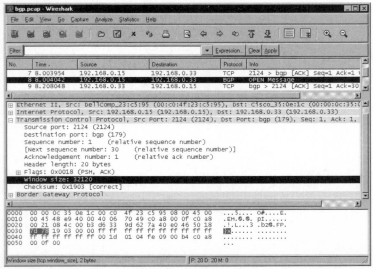

Other Window Components

The following are additional various components of the Wireshark window that you will find useful when examining packets.

Filter Bar

The Filter Bar (see Figure 9.6) allows you to enter a filter string that restricts which packets are displayed in the Summary window. Only packets that match the display filter string are displayed in the Summary window. A display filter string defines the conditions on a packet that may or may not match the packet (e.g., the display filter string *(ip.addr == 10.15.162.1 && bgp)* would match all packets with an IP address [source or destination] of *10.15.162.1* that are BGP protocol packets).

Figure 9.6 Filter Bar

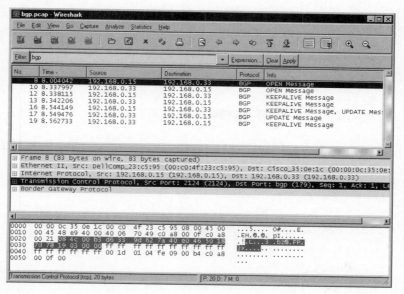

In Figure 9.6, a bgp filter has been applied. To apply a filter, enter the desired string into the Filter: text field and press **Enter** (or click the **Apply** button). Note that filter strings are case-sensitive; therefore, filter string BGP (uppercase) will not work. (Traditionally, filter string labels such as bgp are entirely in lowercase.) Also note that the Filter Bar text field has three different background colors, which indicate the status of the current filter. When the Filter Bar text field changes color, white indicates that there is no current filter, green indicates that a filter has valid syntax, and red indicates that the filter is incomplete or the syntax is invalid.

> **NOTE**
>
> Even though the Filter Bar text field is green (indicating a valid filter), it may not have been applied. When the field is red, Wireshark does not allow an invalid filter to be applied, and provides a warning message if you attempt to apply it.

Once the display filter string bgp is applied, only BGP packets are displayed in the Summary window. The No. column displays jumps between the frame numbers of the displayed packets, because there are packets in the capture that are being suppressed by the bgp filter string. Previously used filters can be easily recalled (see Figure 9.7).

Figure 9.7 Filter Bar Drop-down List

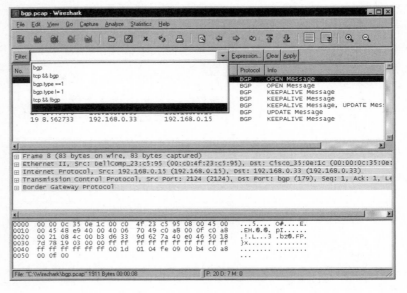

By clicking the drop-down arrow at the end of the Filter field, you can access a list of previously applied filters. To use one of these filters, select it from the list and press **Enter** or click the **Apply** button. To remove the currently displayed filter string and redisplay all packets, click the **Reset** button. If you click the **Filter:** button, the Display Filter dialog box will be displayed.

> **NOTE**
>
> To remove items from the Filter drop-down list, edit the *RECENT* file under the user's profile under *C:\Documents and Settings\<user>\Application Data\Wireshark*. Remove the appropriate lines from the most recent file located in the "Recent Display Filters" section.

Information Field

The Information field displays the name of the capture file, or information about the protocol field selected in the Protocol Tree window.

Display Information Field

The Display Information field displays the number of packets displayed in or filtered from the Summary window. *P* indicates the number of total packets, *D* indicates the total displayed packets, and *M* indicates the total marked packets.

Exploring the Menus

All of the functionality available within Wireshark is accessible from the Menu bar. In this section, we systematically explore that functionality and provide examples of its use.

File

The File menu provides access to loading, saving, and printing capture files (see Figure 9.8). The File menu options are defined in Table 9.5.

Figure 9.8 File Menu

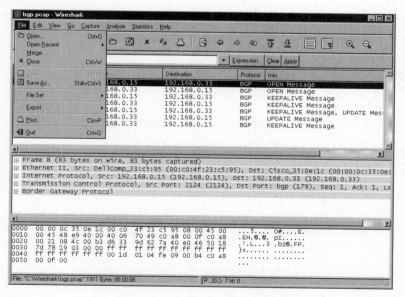

Table 9.5 File Menu Options

Menu Option	Description
Open…	Opens a capture file.
Open Recent	Displays the Open Recent submenu to open a capture file from a list of recently used capture files.
Merge file.	Merges one or more capture files with the current capture
Close	Closes the current capture file.
Save	Saves the current capture file.
Save As…	Saves the current capture file with a different filename/format.
File Set	Displays the File Set submenu for file set information and navigation
Export	Displays the Export submenu, allowing the portion of the packet highlighted in the Data View window to be exported as a hexadecimal dump.
Print…	Prints the current capture file.
Quit	Quits the Wireshark application.

Open

To open a file select **File | Open** (see Figure 9.9).

Figure 9.9 Open Dialog Box

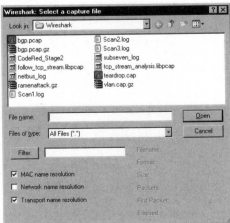

The Open dialog box provides normal mechanisms for navigation in selecting a file. Additionally, it provides a Filter: field where a Wireshark display filter string can be entered to filter out which packets are read from the capture file. Clicking the **Filter:** button opens the Display Filter dialog box (described in the "Analyze" section).

The Open dialog box also has checkboxes to enable name resolution for MAC addresses, network names, and transport names. To open a file, browse to the correct location and select the desired file, optionally provide a filter string, and enable or disable the name resolutions you want to use. Finally, click the **OK** button.

Notes from the Underground...

Wireshark Name Resolution

Wireshark provides three kinds of name resolution to make the numbers found in network protocols more comprehensible. You can choose to enable or disable MAC name resolution, network name resolution, and transport name resolution, when opening a file, starting a capture, or while a capture is running. It is useful to understand what the different name resolutions mean.

Every host on a LAN is identified by a 6-byte MAC address, which is used in Ethernet frames to provide source and destination addresses at the Data Link layer. MAC addresses are globally unique. To achieve this, the Institute of Electrical and Electronic Engineers (IEEE) assigns blocks of MAC addresses to manufacturers. The first 3 bytes of every MAC address designate the manufacturer who produced the device. When you select the **Enable MAC name resolution** checkbox in the Open dialog box, Wireshark resolves the first 3 bytes of the MAC address to a manufacturer and displays that information for each MAC address (e.g. the prefix *00:00:0c* has been assigned to Cisco Systems). When MAC address resolution is enabled, Wireshark displays the MAC address *00:00:0c:35:0e 1c* as *00:00:0c:35:0e:1c (Cisco_35:0e:1c)*.

Every node on an IP network has an IP address. When you select the **Enable network name resolution** checkbox, Wireshark performs a reverse Domain Name System (DNS) lookup when it encounters an IP address, to determine its associated domain name (e.g., www.syngress.com). Wireshark then displays this domain name with the IP address (e.g., IP address *66.35.250.150* can be resolved via reverse DNS to the domain name *slashdot.org* If network name resolution is enabled, Wireshark displays it as *slashdot.org (66.35.250.150)*.

Transport layer protocols like TCP and User Datagram Protocol (UDP) typically provide some form of multiplexing by allowing a source and destination port to be specified. As a result, two hosts can have multiple clearly delineated conversations at the same time, as long as they have unique source port and destination port pairs for each conversation. Many protocols that use TCP or UDP for their Transport layer have well-known ports that servers listen in on. When you select the **Enable transport name resolution** checkbox, Wireshark displays the name of the service that traditionally runs

Continued

over each port. This behavior can be seen in many of the examples in this chapter, where port 179 was labeled by the protocol that is known to run over that port: *bgp*. It's important to note that most ports have no protocols associated with them.

Save As

The Save As dialog box is displayed by selecting **File | Save As** (or by selecting **File | Save** for a capture that was previously saved). (See Figure 9.10.)

Figure 9.10 The Save As Dialog Box

The Save As dialog box allows you to perform normal tasks for saving a capture file in the desired location and with the desired name. You can save various subsets of the packets by selecting different radio options in the Packet Range section (e.g., only the packets that pass the currently active display filter) by enabling the **All packets** radio button while selecting the **Displayed** column radio button. To save only marked packets that pass the currently active display filter, select the **Marked Packets** radio button while selecting the **Displayed** column radio button.

Finally, save the file in one of the supported capture file formats (see Figure 9.11).

Print

The Print dialog box is displayed by selecting **File | Print** (see Figure 9.12).

Figure 9.11 File Formats

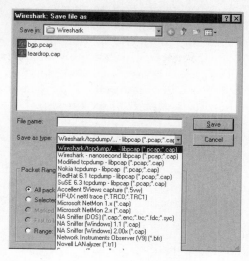

Figure 9.12 Print Dialog Box

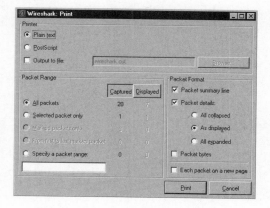

The Print dialog box helps answer the relevant questions regarding printing in Wireshark:

- How am I going to print?

- Which packets am I going to print?

- What information am I going to print for each packet?

The Printer section allows you to choose which packets you are going to print. You can choose your output format to be either Plaintext or Postscript. Once you have selected your output format, you may choose to print the output to a file by enabling the **Output to File:** checkbox and providing a filename in the **Output to File:** text box. If you do not choose to print to file, you can provide a command to be executed to print in the **Print command:** text box. This option is not available on Windows.

The Print Range section allows you to choose which packets you are going to print. You may choose to print only the packet currently selected in the Summary window, only packets that are marked in the Summary window, all packets displayed in the Summary window by the currently applied filter, or all packets captured. You can choose to print only the packet currently selected in the Summary window by selecting the **Selected packet only** radio button and the **Captured** column button. To print only the packets that have been marked in the Summary window, select the **Marked packets only** radio button and the **Captured** column button. To print all of the packets between the first and last marked packets, select the **From first to last marked packet** radio button and the **Captured** column button. If you want the current filter to apply, select the **Displayed** column button. By selecting the **Specify a packet range** radio button, Wireshark allows you to specify a packet range entered in a comma separated list (e.g., *1-12,15,17,17-19*). To print all packets displayed in the Summary window by the currently applied display filter, select the **All packets displayed** radio button and the **Displayed** column button. Printing all packets displayed or captured means that all of the packets that pass the currently applied filter will print. When you scroll up and down to a packet in the Summary window, it is considered to be "displayed" for the purposes of this print range option. You can print all packets in the capture by selecting the **All packets** radio button and the **Captured** column button.

The Packet Format section allows you to choose which information you want to print for each packet. If you do not enable the **Print packet details** checkbox, a one-line summary consisting of the columns currently being displayed in the Summary window, will be printed for each packet If the **Print packet details** checkbox is not selected, the result of just printing the selected packet (packet 8) would be:

```
No. Time       Source         Destination     Protocol Info
   8 8.004042  192.168.0.15   192.168.0.33    BGP      OPEN Message
```

The Packet Details section allows you to choose which details are printed for a packet when you enable the **Print packet details** checkbox. You may choose to print the protocol tree with all subtrees collapsed, with subtrees expanded in the Protocol Tree window, or with all subtrees in the protocol tree expanded. If you select the **All collapsed** option, the protocol tree prints with all subtrees collapsed. When printing only the selected packet, the output would look like:

```
Frame 8 (83 bytes on wire, 83 bytes captured)
Ethernet II, Src: 00:c0:4f:23:c5:95, Dst: 00:00:0c:35:0e:1c
Internet Protocol, Src Addr: 192.168.0.15 (192.168.0.15), Dst Addr: 192.168.0.33
(192.168.0.33)
Transmission Control Protocol, Src Port: 2124 (2124), Dst Port: bgp (179), Seq:
3593706850, Ack: 2051072070, Len: 29
Border Gateway Protocol
```

If you select the **As displayed** option, the protocol tree is printed with the subtrees that would be expanded in the Protocol Tree window if that packet was selected in the Summary window. Using this option to print only the selected packet would produce output like:

```
Frame 8 (83 bytes on wire, 83 bytes captured)
Ethernet II, Src: 00:c0:4f:23:c5:95, Dst: 00:00:0c:35:0e:1c
```

```
Internet Protocol, Src Addr: 192.168.0.15 (192.168.0.15), Dst Addr: 192.168.0.33
(192.168.0.33)
Transmission Control Protocol, Src Port: 2124 (2124), Dst Port: bgp (179), Seq:
3593706850, Ack: 2051072070, Len: 29
Border Gateway Protocol
    OPEN Message
        Marker: 16 bytes
        Length: 29 bytes
        Type: OPEN Message (1)
        Version: 4
        My AS: 65033
        Hold time: 180
        BGP identifier: 192.168.0.15
        Optional parameters length: 0 bytes
```

If you select the **All expanded** option, the protocol tree will be printed with all subtrees expanded. Printing just the selected packet would produce the output:

```
Frame 8 (83 bytes on wire, 83 bytes captured)
    Arrival Time: Mar 29, 2000 23:56:56.957322000
    Time delta from previous packet: 0.000088000 seconds
    Time since reference or first frame: 8.004042000 seconds
    Frame Number: 8
    Packet Length: 83 bytes
    Capture Length: 83 bytes
Ethernet II, Src: 00:c0:4f:23:c5:95, Dst: 00:00:0c:35:0e:1c
    Destination: 00:00:0c:35:0e:1c (Cisco_35:0e:1c)
    Source: 00:c0:4f:23:c5:95 (DellComp_23:c5:95)
    Type: IP (0x0800)
Internet Protocol, Src Addr: 192.168.0.15 (192.168.0.15), Dst Addr: 192.168.0.33
(192.168.0.33)
    Version: 4
    Header length: 20 bytes
    Differentiated Services Field: 0x00 (DSCP 0x00: Default; ECN: 0x00)
        0000 00.. = Differentiated Services Codepoint: Default (0x00)
        .... ..0. = ECN-Capable Transport (ECT): 0
        .... ...0 = ECN-CE: 0
    Total Length: 69
    Identification: 0x48e9 (18665)
    Flags: 0x04
        .1.. = Don't fragment: Set
        ..0. = More fragments: Not set
```

```
        Fragment offset: 0
        Time to live: 64
        Protocol: TCP (0x06)
        Header checksum: 0x7049 (correct)
        Source: 192.168.0.15 (192.168.0.15)
        Destination: 192.168.0.33 (192.168.0.33)
    Transmission Control Protocol, Src Port: 2124 (2124), Dst Port: bgp (179), Seq:
    3593706850, Ack: 2051072070, Len: 29
        Source port: 2124 (2124)
        Destination port: bgp (179)
        Sequence number: 3593706850
        Next sequence number: 3593706879
        Acknowledgement number: 2051072070
        Header length: 20 bytes
        Flags: 0x0018 (PSH, ACK)
            0... .... = Congestion Window Reduced (CWR): Not set
            .0.. .... = ECN-Echo: Not set
            ..0. .... = Urgent: Not set
            ...1 .... = Acknowledgment: Set
            .... 1... = Push: Set
            .... .0.. = Reset: Not set
            .... ..0. = Syn: Not set
            .... ...0 = Fin: Not set
        Window size: 32120
        Checksum: 0x1903 (correct)
    Border Gateway Protocol
        OPEN Message
            Marker: 16 bytes
            Length: 29 bytes
            Type: OPEN Message (1)
            Version: 4
            My AS: 65033
            Hold time: 180
            BGP identifier: 192.168.0.15
            Optional parameters length: 0 bytes
```

Regardless of the option you choose for expanding protocol tree subtrees, if you enable the **Packet bytes** checkbox, following the protocol tree for each packet will be a hexadecimal dump of that packet. Printing only the packet with the **All dissections collapsed** checkbox enabled and the **Packet bytes** checkbox enabled would produce this output:

```
Frame 8 (83 bytes on wire, 83 bytes captured)
```

```
Ethernet II, Src: 00:c0:4f:23:c5:95, Dst: 00:00:0c:35:0e:1c
Internet Protocol, Src Addr: 192.168.0.15 (192.168.0.15), Dst Addr: 192.168.0.33
(192.168.0.33)
Transmission Control Protocol, Src Port: 2124 (2124), Dst Port: bgp (179), Seq:
3593706850, Ack: 2051072070, Len: 29
Border Gateway Protocol


0000   00 00 0c 35 0e 1c 00 c0  4f 23 c5 95 08 00 45 00    ...5....O#....E.
0010   00 45 48 e9 40 00 40 06  70 49 c0 a8 00 0f c0 a8    .EH.@.@.pI......
0020   00 21 08 4c 00 b3 d6 33  9d 62 7a 40 e0 46 50 18    .!.L...3.bz@.FP.
0030   7d 78 19 03 00 00 ff ff  ff ff ff ff ff ff ff ff    }x..............
0040   ff ff ff ff ff ff 00 1d  01 04 fe 09 00 b4 c0 a8    ................
0050   00 0f 00                                            ...
```

If the **Each Packet on a new page** checkbox is selected, each new packet that is printed starts on a new page.

Edit

The Edit menu (see Figure 9.13) allows you to find and mark packets and set user preferences. Descriptions of the Edit menu options are given in Table 9.6.

Figure 9.13 Edit Menu

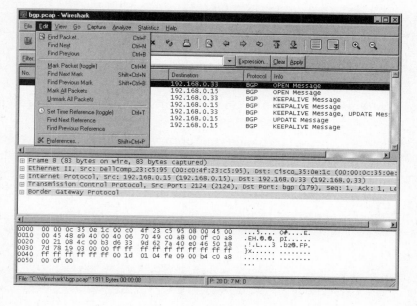

Table 9.6 Edit Menu Options

Menu Option	Description
Find Packet…	Searches for a packet using a display filter or by searching for a matching hexadecimal string or character string.
Find Next	Finds the next packet that matches the search defined in the Find Packet dialog box.
Find Previous	Finds the previous packet that matches the search defined in the Find Packet dialog box.
Mark Packet	Marks the packet currently selected in the Summary window. Marking provides a mechanism for manually selecting a packet or group of packets to be subsequently printed or saved.
Find Next Mark	Finds and highlights the next marked packet in the capture.
Find Previous Mark	Finds and highlights the previously marked packet in the capture.
Mark All Packets	Marks all packets that match the currently applied display filter.
Unmark All Packets	Unmarks all packets that match the currently applied display filter.
Set Time Reference (toggle)	Toggles the Time Reference flag for the currently selected packet.
Find Next Reference	Finds and highlights the next marked time reference packet in the capture.
Find Previous Reference	Finds and highlights the previous marked time reference packet in the capture.
Preferences…	Change user preferences, including preferences for packet decodes.

Find Packet

The Find Packet dialog box is displayed when you select **Edit | Find Packet…** (see Figure 9.14).

Figure 9.14 Find Packet Dialog Box

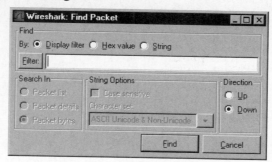

The Find Packet dialog box helps answer relevant questions regarding finding a packet in Wireshark:

■ What am I trying to find?

■ Which direction should I search in?

The **Filter:** text box allows you to define a search criterion by entering a string such as a display filter or hexadecimal or ASCII string. If you need assistance constructing a filter string, click the **Filter:** button to display the Display Filter dialog box.

The **Direction** section allows you to choose which direction you want to search in: *forward* from the packet currently selected in the Summary window, or *backward* from the packet currently selected in the Summary window.

The **Find Syntax** section allows you to define your search criteria. You can choose to search for packets that match a display filter string, a hexadecimal string, or a character string. If you select the **Display Filter** option, the string in the **Filter:** text box will be interpreted as a display filter string and you will search for matches to that display filter string. If you select the **Hex** option, the string in the **Filter:** text box will be interpreted as a hexadecimal string and will search for packets that contain that string.

If you select the **String** option, the string in the **Filter:** will be interpreted as a character string and you will search for packets that contain that character string.

The search for character strings is handled differently than the search for hexadecimal strings. Hexadecimal string searches attempt to search for a packet containing a particular sequence of bytes anywhere in the raw data of that packet. The search for character strings will not look for a packet that contains a string anywhere in the packet. Instead, you can use the **Search In** section to specify whether to look for the string in the **Packet data** left over after decoding all possible fields, look for the character string in the **Decoded packet** displayed in the Protocol Tree window, or look for the character string in the one-line **Packet summary** in the Summary window. If you select the **Packet data** option, Wireshark will search for the character string in the packet data. By packet data, we mean the data in the packet that is left over after decoding the protocol fields. Selecting the **Find Decoded packet** will cause Wireshark to search for the character string in the protocol field strings that are displayed in the Protocol Tree window. It does not matter if the subtree of the protocol tree containing the character string is collapsed or expanded. If you use the **Decoded packet** option, you must also use the **Character Set** drop-down list to select the character set for the character string you are trying to find. To make your character string search case-insensitive, enable the **Case Insensitive Search** checkbox.

Set Time Reference (toggle)

The **Set Time Reference (toggle)** menu option will toggle the time reference flag in the Summary window so that we may perform some time calculation based upon the marked packet. When the **Time** column in the Summary window is configured to display the time that has elapsed since the beginning of the capture, then the time displayed is the number of seconds since the beginning of the capture or the last time reference packet.

In Figure 9.15 below, we have set packets 5 and 10 as time reference packets. This is indicated by their **Time** column value (★REF★). Packets 1-4 are marked with the time since the beginning of the capture in which they were captured. Packets 6-9 are marked with the time since the time reference packet 5. Packets 11 and greater are marked with the time since the time reference packet 10.

Figure 9.15 Set Time Reference (toggle) Example

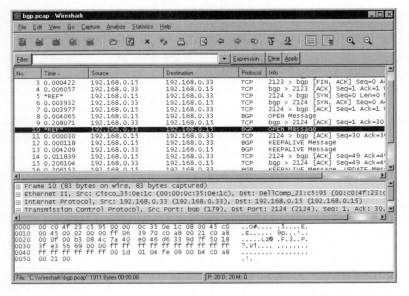

Preferences

The Preferences dialog box, shown in Figure 9.16, is displayed when you select **Edit | Preferences....**

Figure 9.16 Preferences Dialog Box

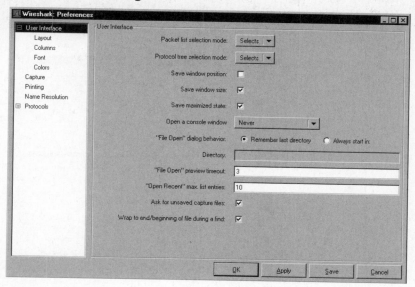

The Preferences dialog box allows you to set preferences for various subsystems of Wireshark, including setting preferences for decodes of various protocols. To edit preferences for an area of Wireshark, like **Columns** in Figure 9.16, select that area from the box on the left and change the settings displayed in the box on the right. It is strongly recommended that you browse through the protocol preferences for any protocol you use frequently, as protocol preferences can change the way a protocol is decoded or displayed.

When you have made your changes to Wireshark's preferences you can choose to apply them without closing the Preference dialog box by clicking the **Apply** button. To apply your settings and close the Preferences dialog box, click the **OK** button. To save your preferences for use in a different Wireshark session, click the **Save** button.

> **NOTE**
>
> The **Columns** preference, selected in Figure 9.18, is subtly broken in Wireshark. You can add, delete, or reorder columns in the Preferences dialog box, but your changes will not take effect unless you save them, then exit and restart Wireshark. As an upgrade to previous versions, this note is mentioned in the **Preferences** dialog box.

View

The **View** menu, shown in Figure 9.17, allows you to control GUI toolbar elements as well as how packets are displayed in the Summary window and the Protocol Tree window. You can also set up color filters to color the packets in the Summary window. The **View** menu options are described in Table 9.8.

Figure 9.17 View Menu

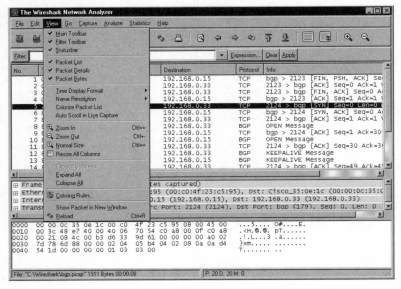

Table 9.8 View Menu Options

Menu Option	Description
Main Toolbar	Display or remove the Main Toolbar
Filter Toolbar	Display or remove the Filter Toolbar
Status Bar	Display or remove the Information Field and the Display Information Field
Packet List	Display or remove the Summary window
Packet Details	Display or remove the Protocol Tree window
Packet Bytes	Display or remove the Data View window
Time Display Format	A submenu for modifying the time displayed in the Summary window
Name Resolution	A submenu for selecting the name resolution options to perform during capture.
Colorize Packet List	Apply or remove the coloring defined in **Coloring Rules** to the Summary window
Auto Scroll in Live Capture	Sets the option to automatically scroll and update the Summary window list while capturing packets.

Continued

Table 9.8 continued View Menu Options

Menu Option	Description
Zoom In	Proportionally increases the font and column size in the Summary window
Zoom Out	Proportionally decreases the font and column size in the Summary window
Normal Size	Returns the Summary window font and column size to the default setting.
Resize All Columns	Automatically resizes column width in the Summary window to eliminate white space.
Expand Subtrees	Expands the entire selected subtree in the Protocol Tree window
Expand All	Expand all subtrees in the Protocol Tree window
Collapse All	Collapse all subtrees in the Protocol Tree window
Coloring Rules...	Create and edit color filters to colorize the packets in the Summary window that match a given display filter string.
Show Packet In New window	For the packet currently selected in the Summary window display it's Protocol Tree window and Data View window in a new window.
Reload	Reload the current capture file.

Time Display Information

For a given packet, you may choose to have the **Time** column in the Summary window display the **Time of day** when that packet was captured, **Date and time of day** when that packet was captured, **Seconds since beginning of capture** (or the last time reference packet) that packet was captured, or the **Seconds since the previous frame** that matched the current display filter.

Auto Scroll in Live Capture

In a live capture, you can choose to have old packets scroll up and out of view as new packets are captured and appended to the end of the Summary window. To do so, enable the **Automatic scrolling in live capture** menu option. This option is particularly helpful while performing a packet capture in which you need to watch for a particular even in real time.

Figure 9.18 Time of Day Display

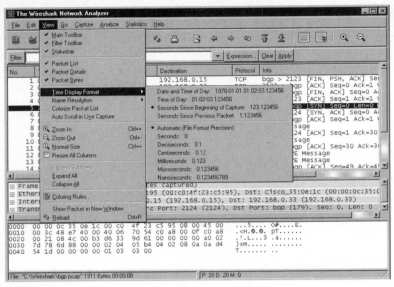

Apply Color Filters

The Apply Color Filters dialog box, shown in Figure 9.19, can be displayed by selecting **View | Coloring Rules...**.

Figure 9.19 Apply Color Filters Dialog Box

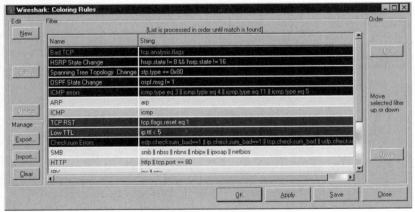

Wireshark has the ability to color packets in the Summary window that match a given display filter string, making patterns in the capture data more visible. This can be hugely useful when trying to follow request response protocols where variations in the order of requests or responses may be interesting. You can color such traffic into as many categories as you'd like and will be able to see at a glance what is going on from the Summary window instead of having to go through the Protocol Tree window for each packet.

To create a color filter click the **New** button in the Apply Color Filters dialog box. The Edit Color Filter dialog box will be displayed (Figure 9.20).

Figure 9.20 Edit Color Filter Dialog Box

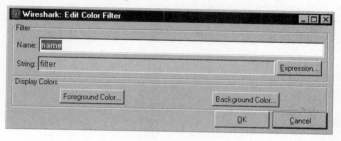

When the Edit Color Filter dialog box is first opened, the **Name** text box will have the string *name* in it, and the **String** field will contain the string *filter*. To create a color filter you should first fill in a name for it in the **Name** text box. Then, you should enter a filter string in the **String** text box. You may use the **Add Expression** button to display the Filter Expression dialog box to assist you in constructing a filter string. The Filter Expression dialog box is described in the section entitled "Analyze". Once you have a name and filter string you are happy with, you need to select the foreground and background color to colorize the packets matching your filter string. Click the **Background Color…** button to set the foreground color, as shown in Figure 9.21.

Figure 9.21 Background Color Dialog box

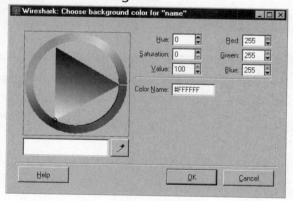

When you are happy with the color you have selected click the **OK** button. The Edit Color Filter dialog box (Figure 9.25) will be displayed.

Figure 9.22 Edit Color Filter

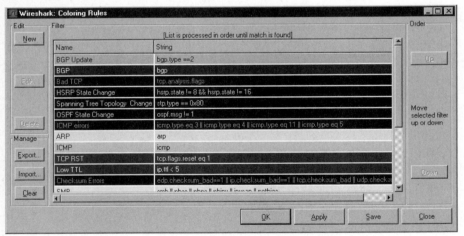

In Figure 9.22 we have created a filter named *BGP Update* with a filter string ***bgp.type == 2***. The name and filter string will be colored to match our background color choice. Click the **Foreground Color...** button to set the foreground color and proceed as you did with the background color. When you are happy with your name, filter string, and text coloring click the **OK** to close the Edit Color Filter dialog box.

Figure 9.23 shows the Apply Color Filters dialog box now populated with the new *BGP Update* entry and a *BGP* filter.

Figure 9.23 Apply Color Filters Dialog Box

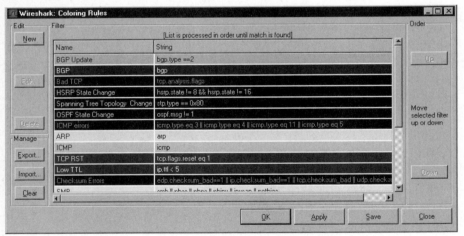

Click the **OK** button to apply the changes and close the dialog box. Click **Apply** to apply the changes and leave the dialog box open. If you wish to use your color filters with another Wireshark session, click **Save**.

If you click the **Revert** button, all coloring will be removed from the Summary window, the color filters will be removed from the **Filter** list, and the saved color file will be deleted. Use the **Export** or **Import** buttons to export your color filters to another file or import the color filters from a file of your choice. This is very useful for sharing color filters with coworkers or between different machines on which you have Wireshark installed. Notice the order of the color filters in the **Filter** list in Figure 9.23. For every packet in the Summary View the color filters strings will be tried in order until one is matched. At that point, its associated color will be applied. The filters in the

Filter list are applied from the top down, so the *BGP Update* color filter will be tried first. Only if the *BGP Update* color filter does not match a packet will Wireshark proceed to try the *BGP* color filter to that packet. An example of the application of these color filters can be seen in Figure 9.24.

Figure 9.24 Application of Color Filters

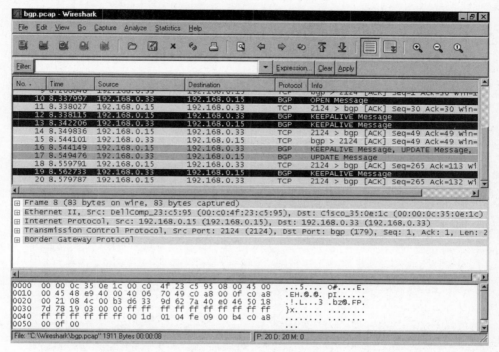

In Figure 9.24, the *BGP Update* messages (lines 16 and 17) are black text on light blue, not white text on dark blue, even though they would also match the white text on dark blue *BGP* color filter. This is because the black text on light blue *BGP Update* filter is applied first, and since it matches, no further color filter is tried.

Show Packet in New Window

You can display a packet's Protocol Tree window and Data View window in a new window by selecting a packet in the Summary window and selecting **View | Show Packet in New Window** (see Figure 9.25). This is useful when you would like to be able to see detailed information about more than one packet at once. Note that the title bar shows the same information as the summary line for this packet in the Summary window.

Figure 9.25 Show Packet in New Window

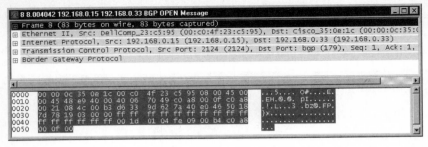

Go

The Go menu is shown in Figure 9.26, and the menu entries are explained in Table 9.9.

Figure 9.26 Go Menu

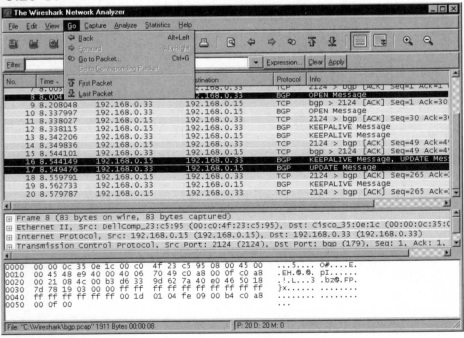

Table 9.9 Go Menu Options

Back	Moves to the previous packet displayed in the current capture.
Forward	Moves to the next packet displayed in the current capture.
Go To Packet...	Go to a packet by frame number.

Continued

Table 9.9 continued Go Menu Options

Go To Corresponding Packet	When a field that refers to another frame is selected in the Protocol Tree window, select the packet being referred to in the Summary window.
First Packet	Moves to the first displayed packet
Last Packet	Moves to the last displayed packet

Go To Packet

The Go To Packet dialog box, shown in Figure 9.27, can be displayed by selecting **Edit | Go To Packet Dialog**.

Figure 9.27 Go To Packet Dialog Box

Enter a packet number in the **Packet Number** text box and click **OK**. The packet with that packet number will be selected in the Summary window.

Capture

The **Capture** menu is shown in Figure 9.28, and the menu entries are explained in Table 9.10.

Table 9.10 Capture Menu Options

Menu Option	Description
Interfaces…	Opens the **Interfaces** dialog box
Options…	Opens the **Capture Options**
Start	Start a capture.
Stop	Stop a running packet capture.
Restart	Restart a stopped packet capture
Capture Filters…	Edit the capture filters.

Figure 9.28 Capture Menu

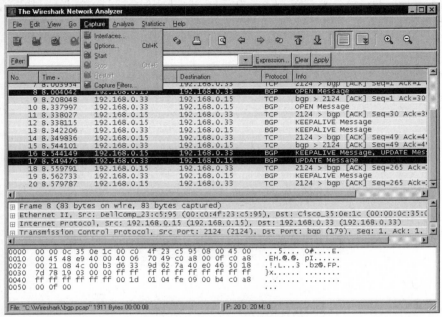

Capture Interfaces

The Capture Interfaces dialog box, shown in Figure 9.29, can be displayed by selecting **Capture | Interfaces…**.

Figure 9.29 Capture Interfaces Dialog

This dialog box gives us a wealth of information about the current interfaces in the system. With this dialog box we are presented a list and description of the current interfaces, the IP address assigned to each interface, the number of packets seen by the interface, and the rate at which they are seen (in packets per second). We are also presented with a number of options that can be performed on each interface.

NOTE

The packet count and packets per second displayed in the Capture Interfaces dialog box are not the total seen by the interfaces, but are the total count and rate seen by the interface from the time the Capture Interface dialog box was opened.

The **Capture** button immediately starts capturing packets in the selected interface with the options previously defined in the **Capture Options** dialog box. By utilizing the **Prepare** we are able to display the **Capture Options** dialog box to allow us to change options for the capture session before beginning to capture packets. Please refer to the Capture Options section later in this chapter for more information on the Capture Options dialog box.

If we need to know more information about the interface itself, we can select the **Details** button for the desired interface.

Notes from the Underground...

Where Did My Loopback Go?

You may notice in the screenshots for this section, there is no option for a loopback (or lo) interface, as these screen captures were taken under Windows. Due to the way Windows implements its loopback, it is not possible for us to capture traffic on the true loopback under Windows.

Wireshark relies on winpcap to provide an interface to the network devices on the system. Winpcap is only able to discover actual physical devices installed on the system through discovery of the actual network drivers. Unfortunately the Windows loopback adapter is not considered a physical device, and Windows does not install drivers. As a result, winpcap is unable to bind to non-existent drivers to capture the loopback traffic.

It is possible to install a loopback adapter under Windows, but again it is not a true loopback adapter, and does not get an address assigned out of the 127.0.0.0 subnet. Microsoft designed the special loopback adapter to provide a dummy interface for certain applications that require a network interface to function, and that may be installed in instances where a real network adapter is not needed, for example in a standalone demo system.

In the Interface Details dialog box, we are presented with five tabs that provide extremely detailed information about the selected interface, as queried from the underlying system driver. This information can prove invaluable in determining capabilities of the selected interface, as well some vital statistics including packet counts and driver information

Figure 9.30 Capture Interfaces Details

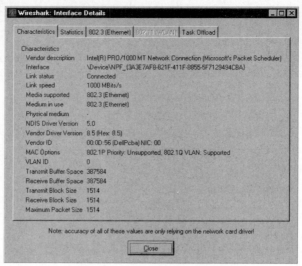

Capture Options

The Capture Options dialog box, shown in Figure 9.31, can be displayed by selecting **Capture |
Start…**.

Figure 9.31 Capture Options Dialog

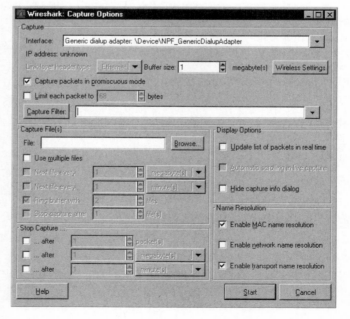

This dialog box helps answer basic questions about capturing data:

- What traffic am I capturing?
- Where am I saving it?
- How am I displaying it?
- When do I stop capturing?

The **Capture** section allows you to choose which traffic you are capturing. When choosing what traffic to capture ask:

- Which interface am I capturing from?
- How much of each packet am I capturing?
- Which packets arriving at the interface am I capturing?

The **Interface** drop-down list allows you to choose the interface you want to capture from. You can choose from the interfaces listed in the drop-down list, or you can enter one manually into the text box. If both libpcap and the interface you select support multiple link layers for that interface, you can choose the link layer header type to capture using the **Link-layer header type:** selector.

The Limit Each Packet To field lets you choose to capture a piece of an entire packet. When the **Limit each packet to** checkbox is enabled and a number is provided in the **Limit each packet to** text box, only the first number of bytes are captured from each packet. Be aware that if you choose to capture less than the full packet, Wireshark may mark your packets as fragments.

The **Capture packets in promiscuous mode** checkbox and the **Filter:** text box allow you to choose which packets arriving at the interface will be captured. If you enable the **Capture packets in promiscuous mode** checkbox, Wireshark puts the interface into promiscuous mode before capturing data. Normally, an interface only passes on the operating system packets that are destined for the MAC address of the interfaces. When an interface is in promiscuous mode, it passes on all packets arriving at the interface to the operating system. So, if you choose not to capture in promiscuous mode, you will only capture packets addressed to or being sent by the interface on which you are capturing. If you choose to capture in promiscuous mode you will capture all packets arriving at the interface. Entering a tcpdump-style capture filter in the **Filter** text box will cause Wireshark to only capture packets matching that capture filter. When you click on the **Filter** button, the Edit Capture Filter List dialog box will be displayed to allow you to choose among previously defined capture filters. (See the section entitled "Edit Capture Filter List" for more details.)

Notes from the Underground...

Promiscuous Mode Detection

There are many instances in which you may want to perform packet captures with Wireshark in promiscuous mode, or go undetected using an Integrated Data Store (IDS)/Intrusion Prevention System (IPS). Promiscuous mode captures all of the traffic seen by an interface, as well as traffic for other devices.

Assume that an attacker has installed Wireshark on a computer that is attached to your network, and is actively capturing traffic on your network in promiscuous mode with Network Name Resolution enabled. You monitor the uplink for this particular network segment with your installation of Wireshark, so that you can detect the attacker. If a user on the same network segment as the attacker opens a Web browser and directs it to the www.syngress.com Web site, both the attacker's installation and your installation will capture the request to DNS. (In this instance, you were able to detect the malicious individual, because Network Name Resolution was enabled in the attacker's copy of Wireshark.) Under normal circumstances, you should only see one DNS request for the www.syngress.com domain; however, because the attacker's copy of Wireshark has Network Name Resolution enabled, his or her copy attempts to resolve the www.syngress.com domain. As a result, there is a second DNS lookup for www.syngress.com that did not originate from the original computer.

With this information, you can discern that there is a computer on this network segment that is capturing packets in promiscuous mode.

The Capture File(s) section allows you to choose where to save a capture. If this section is left blank, Wireshark saves the capture to a temporary file until it is saved by selecting **File | SaveAs**. If you enter a filename in the **File** text box, Wireshark saves the capture to that file. Clicking the **File** button opens the Save As dialog box. If the **Use ring buffer** checkbox is enabled, you can save your capture to a ring buffer.

The **Display options** section allows you to choose how you are going to display packets as they are captured. By default, Wireshark does not update the list of packets in the Summary window during capture; only once the capture is stopped. If the **Update list of packets in real time** checkbox is enabled, Wireshark updates the Summary window as soon as a packet is captured and processed. By default, when Wireshark updates the Summary window during live capture, new packets are appended to the end of the Summary window. Consequently, the Summary window does not reveal new packets. To enable the Summary window to display the most recent packets, enable the **Automatic scrolling in live capture** checkbox. If you decide that you want automatic scrolling once a capture has started, select **View | Options** to disable this feature.

The **Capture limits** section allows you to choose when to stop capturing. You can manually stop a capture by selecting **Capture | Stop**; however, sometimes it's convenient to set conditions under which a capture will automatically stop. There are three types of automatic limits to a capture that are supported by Wireshark:

- Capture a specified number of packets.
- Capture a specified number of kilobytes of traffic.
- Capture for a specified number of seconds.

Wireshark allows you to set up any combination of these three limits simultaneously (i.e., it is possible to limit the number of packets, kilobytes, and seconds at the same time. Whenever one of the limits is satisfied, the capture stops.

When you enable the **Stop capture after… packet(s) captured** checkbox and enter a number of packets in the **Stop capture after… packet(s) captured** text box, the capture stops when it has reached the specified number of packets. When you enable the **Stop capture after… kilobyte(s) captured** checkbox and enter a number of kilobytes in the **Stop capture after… kilobytes(s) captured** text box, the capture stops once it has reached the specified number of kilobytes. When you enable the **Stop capture after… seconds(s)** checkbox and enter a number of packets in the **Stop capture after… seconds(s)** text box, the capture stops when the specified number of seconds have elapsed since the beginning of the capture. The **Name resolution** section allows you to choose the name resolution options for the capture.

When you have specified your capture choices via the Capture Options dialog box, start the capture by clicking the **OK** button. The **Capture Dialog** dialog box will be displayed (see Figure 9.32).

Figure 9.32 Capture Dialog Box

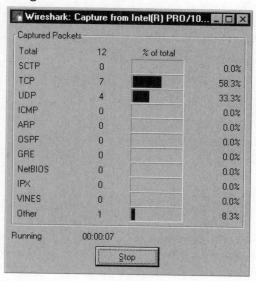

The Capture dialog box displays the number of packets of the various protocols that have been captured, and the percentage of all captured traffic consisting of those protocols. In Figure 9.32, a total of 12 packets have been captured, of which seven (58.3 percent) are TCP packets, four (33.3 percent) are UDP packets, and one (8.3 percent) is an Other (miscellaneous) packet. The capture can be stopped at any time by clicking the **Stop** button.

Ring Buffer Captures

There are applications where it makes sense to capture network traffic to a series of smaller files. At times, you may want to limit the number of small files and delete the oldest when starting a new one. This structure is called a *ring buffer*, because conceptually the data fills up a buffer and loops back to the beginning when it reaches the end.

There are certain questions that must be answered regarding ring buffer files:

- How many capture files in the ring buffer?
- What are the capture files named?
- When do I rotate to the next capture file?

To enable ring buffer captures, access the Capture Options dialog box and enable the **Use ring buffer** checkbox. The appearance of the Capture Options dialog box changes (see Figure 9.33).

Figure 9.33 Capture Options Dialog Box - Use Ring Buffer Selected

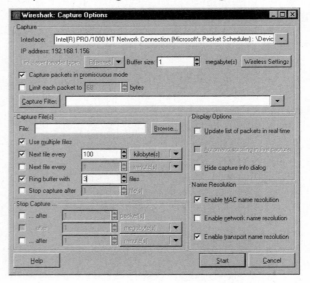

The **Rotate capture file every... second(s)** checkbox becomes available and the **Stop capture after... kilobytes captured** checkbox is renamed **Rotate capture file very... kilobyte(s)** and becomes unavailable.

The **Number of files** text box allows you to choose how many files are in the ring buffer. If you choose zero, the number of ring buffer files is assumed to be infinite (i.e., no old files are deleted to make room for new files).

The **File** text box provides the base name for the filenames in the capture ring buffer. The base name is broken up into a prefix and a suffix. The filename of a ring buffer capture file is *prefix_NNNNN_YYYYMMDDhhmmss.suffix*, where *NNNNN* is a 5-digit 0-padded count indicating the sequence number of the ring buffer file; *YYYY* is a 4-digit year; *MM* is the 2-digit 0-padded month; *DD* is a 2-digit zero-padded date; *hh* is a 3-digit 0-padded hour; *mm* is a 2-digit 0-padded minute; and *ss* is a 2–digit 0–padded second. (e.g., if the *foo.bar.libpcap* file is the fifth capture file in the ring buffer created at *23:21:01* on January 8, 2004, it would be named *foo.bar_00005_20040108232101.libpcap*). It is important to note that the sequence numbers in the filenames increase monotonically. If a ring buffer contains three files, when the fourth capture file is started it has sequence number 00004, and the file with sequence number *00001* is deleted. The sequence numbers are not recycled as you loop through the ring.

The **Rotate capture file every… kilobyte(s)** text box and the optional **Rotate capture file every… second(s)** text box allow you to choose when the capture files are rotated. Provide a kilobyte limit to the size of a capture file in the ring buffer, by entering a number (or accepting the default value) in the **Rotate capture file every… kilobyte(s)** text box. When a capture file reaches the number of kilobytes you have specified, a new capture file is created to store any new packets, and the oldest capture file in the ring buffer is deleted if the new capture file exceeds the limit specified in the **Number of files** text box. If you enable the **Rotate capture file every… second(s)** checkbox and enter a number of seconds in the **Rotate capture file every… second(s)** text box, if a capture file is open for that number of seconds, a new capture file is created to store any new packets captured. The oldest capture file in the ring buffer may then be deleted if the new capture file exceeds the limit specified in the **Number of files** text box.

NOTE

The **Use ring buffer** checkbox and the **Update list of packets in real time** checkbox are incompatible; therefore, Wireshark will not enable **Use ring buffer** if the **Update list of packets in real time** is already enabled. However, Wireshark will allow you to select **Update list of packets in real time** if **Use ring buffer** has *already been selected*. When this occurs, the **Use Ring buffer** checkbox is automatically (and without warning) disabled, which, in turn, causes the **Rotate capture file every… kilobyte(s)** checkbox to revert to **Stop capture after… kilobyte(s)**.

Tools & Traps…

Handling Large Captures

Eventually, everyone encounters a problem that involves enormous amounts of network data to analyze. Maybe it's an intermittent problem that happens every couple of days, where you need to see the message exchange that led up to the problem, or maybe it's a problem on a fairly active network. Whatever the reason, the issue of capturing and analyzing large captures is common. As captures become larger, Wireshark uses up memory; thus, filtering and finding packets takes a long time.

In these situations, it is best to use Tshark (the console-based version of Wireshark) to do the actual capture and initial processing of the data. To capture from an interface *<interface>* to a file *<savefile>*, use this command:

Continued

```
tshark -i <interface> -w <savefile>
```

If you have a limited amount of space and/or want to limit the size of your capture files, you can use the ring buffer functionality with Tshark to capture from interface *<interface>* to *<num_capture_files>* capture files with a maximum size each *<filesize>* and a base filename *<savefile>* by executing the following at the command line:

```
tshark -i <interface> -w <savefile> -b <num_capture_files> -a
filesize:<filesize>
```

Once you have captured the data you need, you can use Tshark to reduce the capture to a more manageable size. To use a display filter string *<filter string>* to filter a capture file *<savefile>* and save the results to a new capture file *<newsavefile>*, execute the following at the command line:

```
tshark -r <savefile> -w <newsavefile> -R <filter string>
```

If you need to extract all packets from the capture file that were captured between Jan 8, 2004 22:00 and Jan 8, 2004 23:00, execute the following command:

```
tshark -r <savefile> -w <newsavefile> -R '(frame.time >= "Jan 8, 2004
22:00:00.00" ) && (frame.time <= "Jan 8, 2004 23:00:00.00")'
```

Once you have reduced the data down to a size where Wireshark's performance is workable, open the Capture file in Wireshark to perform more involved analysis.

Edit Capture Filter List

The Edit Capture Filter List dialog box is displayed by selecting **Capture | Capture Filters...** (see Figure 9.34).

Figure 9.34 Edit Capture Filter List Dialog Box

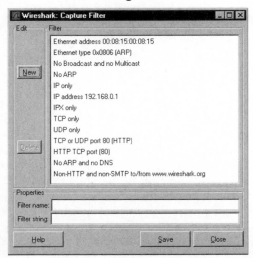

This dialog box allows you to create new tcpdump-style capture filters and save them for later use. To create a new capture filter, provide a name for your filter in the **Filter name** text box, provide a tcpdump-style capture filter string in the **Filter string** text box, and then click the **New** button (see Figure 9.35).

Figure 9.35 Edit Capture Filter List Dialog Box

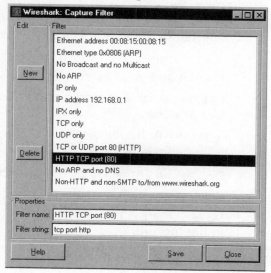

You can select an existing capture filter from the **Capture Filters** list to create a new capture filter, change an existing filter, or delete a filter. To change an existing capture filter, select it from the **Capture Filters** list and double-click on its name in the **Filter name** text box, and/or change its tcpdump-style capture filter string in the **Filter string** text box and then click **Save**. To create a new capture filter, enter a new Filter name and a new Filter string in the appropriate fields and select **New**.

You can delete a capture filter by selecting it from the **Capture Filters** list and clicking the **Delete** button. If you want your list of capture filters to be available in a subsequent Wireshark session, click the **Save** button to save them to disk.

Analyze

The Analyze Menu is shown in Figure 9.36, and its options are explained in Table 9.11.

Table 9.11 Analyze Menu Options

Menu Option	Description
Display Filters...	Edits the display filters.

Continued

Table 9.11 continued Analyze Menu Options

Menu Option	Description
Apply as Filter	A submenu for preparing and automatically applying a display filter based on any field selected in the Protocol Tree window.
Prepare a Filter	A submenu for preparing a display filter based on any field selected in the Protocol Tree window.
Firewall ACL Rules	
Enabled Protocols…	Enables and disables the decoding of individual protocols.
Decode As…	Specifies decoding certain packets as being part of a particular protocol.
User Specified Decodes	Reports which user-specified decodes are currently in force.
Follow TCP Stream	Displays an entire TCP stream at once.
Follow SSL Stream	Displays an entire SSL stream at once.
Expert Info	Displays a summary of the capture file.
Expert Info Composite	Displays statistics in a Protocol Tree view for the protocols in the capture.

Figure 9.36 Analyze Menu

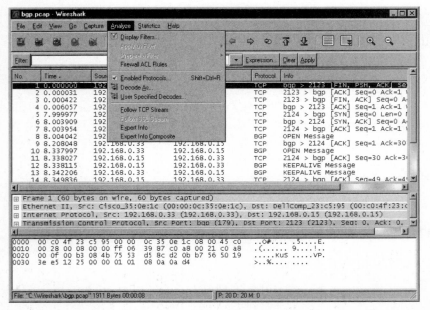

Edit Display Filter List

The Edit Display Filter List dialog box can be displayed by selecting **Analyze | Display Filter…** (see Figure 9.37).

Figure 9.37 Edit Display Filter List Dialog Box

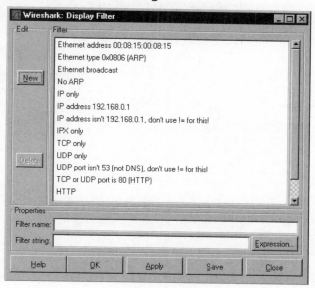

This dialog box is designed to help you construct a filter string. To create a new filter string, click the **Add Expression** button. The Filter Expression dialog box is displayed (see Figure 9.38).

Figure 9.38 Filter Expression Dialog Box

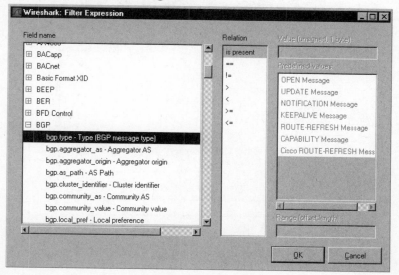

Select the protocol you want for your filter expression and expand it to show which of its fields can be filtered. Select the desired filter field. When you pick a relation other than **is present**, the Filter Expression dialog box changes to show your options for that field (see Figure 9.39).

Figure 9.39 Filter Expression Dialog – Equality

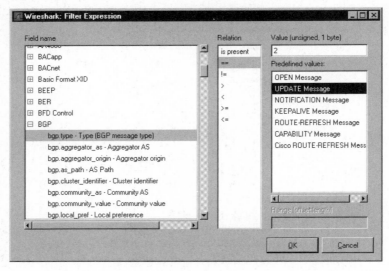

In this case, we have chosen the equality (==) relation. Choose the value you want to match and click the **Accept** button, which will insert the filter expression you just constructed into the **Filter string:** text box (see Figure 9.40).

Figure 9.40 Edit Display Filter List Dialog Box - Filter String

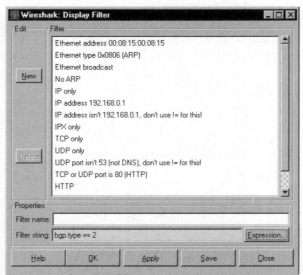

If you want to save the filter string you have just created, type a name in the **Filter name** text box and click the **New** button. The filter string will be added to the Display Filters List dialog box (see Figure 9.41).

Figure 9.41 Edit Display Filter List Dialog Box - Filter Name

Select an existing display filter from the list and choose to either change, delete, or copy it. To change an existing display filter, select it from the list, change its name in the **Filter name** text box (or change its display filter string in the **Filter string** text box), and click the **Change** button. To copy an existing display filter, select it from the list and click the **Copy** button. Save the list by clicking the **Save** Button.

When you have accessed the Edit Display Filter List dialog box from the filter bar, click **OK** to apply the filter and close the dialog box. Use the **Apply** button to apply the filter and leave the dialog box open (see Figure 9.42).

"Apply as Filter" and "Prepare a Filter" Submenus

The Apply as Filter and Prepare a Filter submenus have the same options and behave in the same way with one exception: the Prepare a Filter submenu items prepare a display filter string and place it in the **Filter** text box. The Apply as Filter submenu items prepare a display filter string, place it in the **Filter** text box, and apply it to the capture. Because of their close similarity, we will only discuss the Apply as Filter submenu.

The Apply as Filter submenu becomes available when a field in the Protocol Tree window is selected with an associated filter name that can be used in a display filter string (see Figure 9.43).

Figure 9.42 Display Filter Dialog Box - OK and Apply Buttons

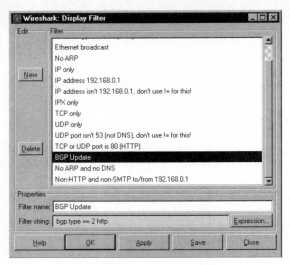

Figure 9.43 Apply as Filter Submenu

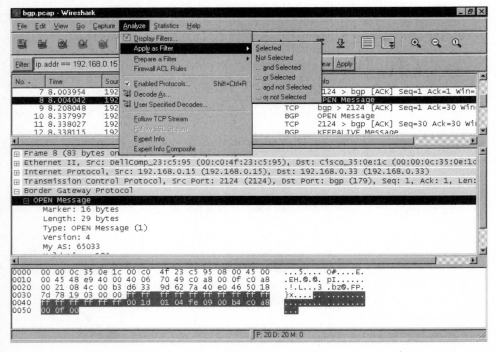

In Table 9.12, the filter string has been put into the **Filter:** text box for each of the **Apply as Filter** submenu options (see Figure 9.43). Note that the *ip.addr == 192.168.0.15* filter changes the

initial behavior of **And Selected**, **Or Selected**, **And Not Selected**, and **Or Not Selected** (see Table 9.12).

Table 9.12 Apply as Filter Submenu Option Examples

Menu Option	Display Filter String
Selected	bgp.type == 1
Not Selected	!(bgp.type == 1)
And Selected	(ip.addr == 192.168.0.15) && (bgp.type == 1)
Or Selected	(ip.addr == 192.168.0.15) || (bgp.type == 1)
And Not Selected	(ip.addr == 192.168.0.15) && !(bgp.type == 1)
Or Not Selected	(ip.addr == 192.168.0.15) || !(bgp.type == 1)

Enabled Protocols

The Enabled Protocols dialog box is displayed by selecting **Analyze | Enabled Protocols...** (see Figure 9.44).

Figure 9.44 Enabled Protocols Dialog Box

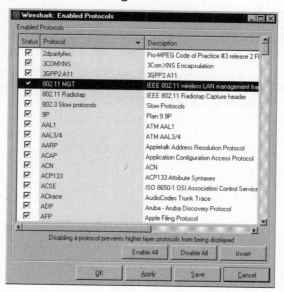

This dialog box allows you to enable or disable the decoding of one or more protocols. This can be done by clicking the Status column to toggle the status between *Enabled* and *Disabled*. Additionally, you can enable all protocols by clicking the **Enable All** button, disable all protocols by clicking the **Disable All** button, or enable all disabled protocols and disable all enabled protocols by clicking the **Invert** button. These settings can be applied to all Wireshark sessions by clicking the **Save** button.

Decode As

To force the decode of a packet as a particular protocol, select it in the Summary window and then select **Analyze | Decode As...**. The Decode As dialog box will be displayed (see Figure 9.45).

Figure 9.45 Decode As Dialog Box - Link Tab

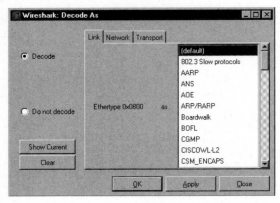

When Wireshark is decoding a packet, it uses *magic numbers* in each protocol to decide which dissector to use to decode subsequent parts of the packet. Magic numbers are values that specify a higher-level protocol (e.g., Ethertype *0x0800* specifies that an Ethernet packet contains an IP packet; IP protocol 6 specifies that an IP packet contains a TCP payload; TCP port 179 specifies that a TCP packet is carrying a BGP payload). There are occasions when you want to override Wireshark's choices of how to decode subsequent parts of a packet based on the magic numbers. The most common examples involve TCP ports; Wireshark frequently decides which dissector to call for a TCP packet, based on the source or destination port. You may be running a protocol over a non-standard port (e.g., running HTTP over port 7000). The **Decode As** feature allows you to tell Wireshark about these non-standard cases.

Wireshark allows you to force decodes based on the magic numbers in the Link, Network, and Transport layers. For the transport layer, you have the option of decoding based on source, destination, or both (see Figure 9.46).

To force a particular decode, you need to answer these questions:

■ After which layer do I want to start forcing my custom decode?

■ Which magic number do I want to key off of to determine whether to decode a packet with my custom decode?

■ Which protocol do I want the remaining traffic in the packet decoded as?

Figure 9.46 Decode As Dialog Box - Transport Tab

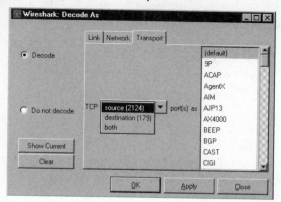

To choose the layer where you want to start forcing your custom decode, select the appropriate tab (Link, Network, or Transport), and choose which magic numbers to pick for the Transport layer (by source port, destination port, or both). Then, select from the list of protocols as to how you want the remaining traffic in the packet decoded.

Click the **Show Current** button to open the **Decode As: Show** dialog box, in order to see which decodes are currently being forced.

Decode As: Show

The **Decode As: Show** dialog box can also be displayed by selecting **Analyze | User Specified Decodes** from the menu bar (see Figure 9.47).

Figure 9.47 Decode As: Show

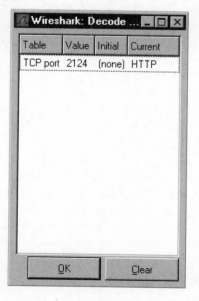

This dialog box displays the decodes specified through the **Decode As** dialog box (one per line). The Table column shows the magic number of the alternate decode (in this case, the TCP port). The Port column shows the magic number of the alternate decode (in this case 179). The Initial column shows the dissector that would normally be used to decode the payload of a packet with this magic number and magic number type (in this case, BGP). And, finally, the Current column shows the dissector currently being used to decode the payload of packets having this magic number and magic number type (in this case HTTP).

Follow TCP Stream and Follow SSL Stream

The Follow TCP Stream and Follow SSL Stream windows have the same options and behave in the same way with one exception; the Follow TCP Stream window follows any TCP stream, while the Follow SSL Stream only follows the selected Secure Sockets Layer (SSL) stream. Because of their close similarity, we will only discuss the Follow TCP Stream submenu.

The Follow TCP Stream window can be displayed by selecting a TCP packet in the Summary window and then selecting Analyze | Follow TCP Stream from the menu bar (see Figure 9.48).

Figure 9.48 Follow TCP Stream Window

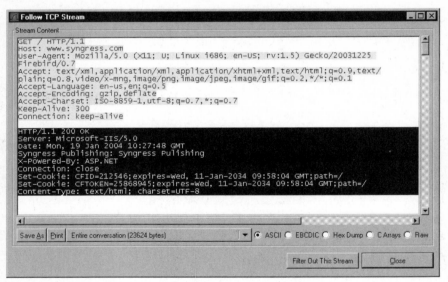

In this example, a TCP packet that was part of an HTTP conversation with the Web server for www.syngress.com, is shown. By default, one side of the conversation is shown in red (the upper portion), and the other portion is shown in blue (the lower portion). For readability purposes, the side of the conversation that is usually highlighted blue is shown as white text on a dark blue background. By scrolling down in this window, you can see all of the data exchanged during this TCP conversation. Click the Entire conversation selector to choose between displaying the entire conversation or one of the directions (see Figure 9.49).

Figure 9.49 Follow TCP Stream: Direction Selector

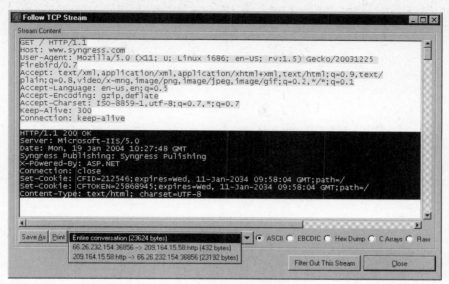

Clicking the Save As button brings up a Save As dialog box where you can save the stream contents as a text file. Clicking the Print button prints the capture as text. (Note that there is no dialog box associated with the Print button.) The Filter out this stream button appends the necessary filter string to the one in the filter bar and closes the Contents of the TCP Stream window. This can be useful when going through a large capture. As you look at the possible TCP streams of interest one by one and exclude them from the Summary window, you are left with only the unconsidered data.

You also have the option of choosing how the TCP stream is presented. In Figure 9.49, the **ASCII** option is selected. By choosing the **EBCDIC** option, you can cause the stream to be presented with Extended Binary Coded Decimal Interchange Code (EBCDIC). If you choose the **Hex Dump** option, there will be a hexadecimal dump of the TCP stream. And, if you choose the **C Arrays** option, the TCP stream will appear as a series of C arrays.

Expert Info and Expert Info Composite

The Expert Info and Expert Info Composite menu options provide identical information in similar layouts. Both options provide a breakdown of the current capture, and display summary information about current conversations, errors, and warnings that can be derived from the traffic patterns. These options are a great method to use to begin troubleshooting traffic-related issues, as they provide some simple error-related information without having to analyze each packet by hand.

Statistics

The Statistics Menu provides a variety of specialized tools to analyze network traffic (see Figure 9.50). These statistics are reported for certain protocol features. Many of the tools in the Statistics Menu are specialized and beyond the scope of this book; however, we will discuss some of the more generalized items, including graphing. The menu items are described in Table 9.13

Figure 9.50 Statistics Menu

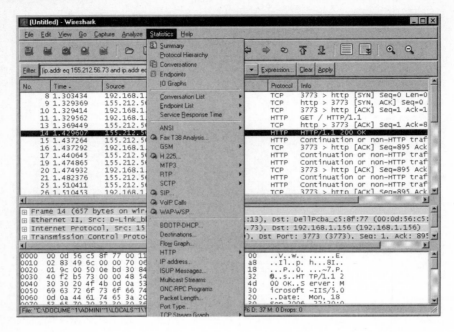

Table 9.13 Statistics Menu Options

Menu Option	Description
Summary	Provides basic statistics about the current capture.
Protocol Hierarchy	Displays a hierarchical breakdown of the protocols in the current capture
Conversations	Provides basic information on all of the conversations in the current capture.
Endpoints	Provides basic information on all endpoint counts in the current capture.
IO Graphs	Displays basic time sequence graphs.
Conversation List	A submenu for displaying conversation counts and basic statistics for 13 different layer 2 and layer 3 protocols and transport methods
Endpoint List	A submenu for displaying endpoint counts and basic statistics for 12 different layer 2 and layer 3 protocols and transport methods
Service Response Time	A submenu for displaying the service response time for 11 different protocols.

Continued

Table 9.13 continued Statistics Menu Options

Menu Option	Description
ANSI	A submenu for displaying breakdown counts of three different American National Standards Institute (ANSI) protocols.
Fax T38 Analysis...	Displays basic information on Fax T.38. This feature is currently implemented in the Voice Over Internet Protocol (VoiP) Calls menu.
GSM	A submenu for displaying breakdown counts for GSM ANSI protocols.
H.225...	Displays counts of H.225 messages.
MTP3	A submenu for displaying basic MTP3 count A submenu.
RTP	A submenu for displaying Real-Time Protocol (RTP) stream sessions and analysis of selected RTP streams.
SCTP	A submenu for analyzing and providing statistics on Stream Control Transmission Protocol (SCTP) associations.
SIP	Provides basic analysis of Session Initiation Protocol (SIP) code volumes.
VoiP Calls	Displays session information on Voice over Internet Protocol (VoiP) calls.
WAP-WSP...	Provides basic analysis of WAP-WSP.
BOOTP-DHCP...	Displays a count of Dynamic Host Configuration Protocol (DHCP) and Bootstrap Protocol (BOOTP) messages broken down by message type.
Destinations...	Provides a hierarchical view of all conversations in the current capture.
Flow Graph...	Provides a detailed graphical display of protocol flow information.
HTTP	A submenu for displaying HTTP request information.
IP Address...	Provides a hierarchical view of all IP conversations in the current capture.
ISUP Messages...	Displays a count of ISUP message types for the current captures.
Multicast Streams	Displays a detailed breakdown of multicast streams, and allow for Summary window filter preparation.
ONC-RPC Programs	Provides summary information on Open Network Computing (ONC)-Remote Procedure Call (RPC) conversations.

Continued

Table 9.13 continued Statistics Menu Options

Menu Option	Description
Packet Length...	Calculates packet length statistics by ranges for the current capture.
Port Type...	Provides a hierarchical view of all port usage for conversations in the current capture.
TCP Streams Graph	A submenu for calculating and displaying robust graphs.

Summary

The Summary dialog box can be displayed by selecting **Statistics | Summary** from the menu bar (see Figure 9.51).

Figure 9.51 Summary Dialog Box

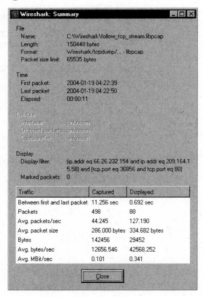

This Summary dialog box provides information about the capture file, basic statistics about the capture data, and basic information about the capture.

Protocol Hierarchy

The Protocol Hierarchy dialog box can be displayed by selecting **Statistics | Protocol Hierarchy** from the menu bar (see Figure 9.52).

Figure 9.52 Protocol Hierarchy Statistics Dialog Box

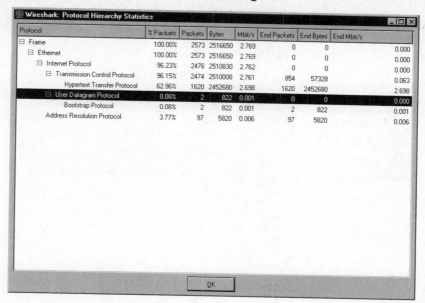

This dialog box provides a tree representation of protocols and statistics associated with them. Table 9.14 provides a description of what each columns means.

Table 9.14 Protocol Hierarchy Statistics Columns

Column	Description
Protocol	The protocol on which statistics are being reported. The protocol may have subitems on the tree representing the protocols it contains (e.g., the IP contains TCP and UDP).
% Packets	Percentage of all packets in the capture that are of this protocol.
Packets	The number of packets in the capture that are of this protocol.
Bytes	The number of bytes in this capture containing this protocol.
End Packets	The number of packets for which this protocol is the last protocol in the decode (e.g., a TCP Synchronous [SYN] packet containing no data would be an end packet for TCP and counted in TCP's end packets count).
End Bytes	The number of bytes for which this protocol is the last protocol in the decode.

TCP Stream Graph Submenu

The **TCP Stream Analysis** submenucan be displayed by selecting a TCP packet in the Summary window and selecting **Statistics | TCP Stream Graph** from the menu bar (see Figure 9.53). the **TCP Stream Graph** submenu options are shown in Table 9.15.

Figure 9.53 TCP Stream Graph Submenu

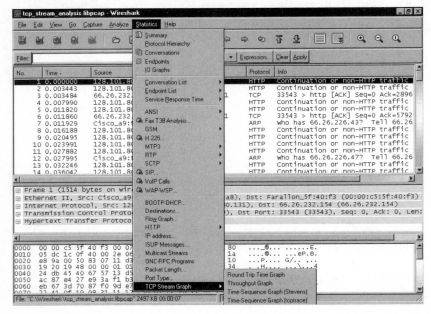

Table 9.15 TCP Stream Graph Submenu Options

Menu Option	Description
Round Trip Time Graph	Displays a graph of the round trip time (RTT) vs. the sequence number.
Throughput Graph	Displays a graph of throughput vs. time.
Time-Sequence Graph (Stevens)	Displays a time-sequence graph in the style used by W. Richard Stevens' TCP/IP Illustrated book.
Time-Sequence Graph (tcptrace)	Displays a time-sequence graph in the style used by the tcptrace program, which can be found at www.tcptrace.org/.

RTT Graph

The RTT graph shows the RTT vs. the sequence number (see Figure 9.54).

Figure 9.54 RTT Graph

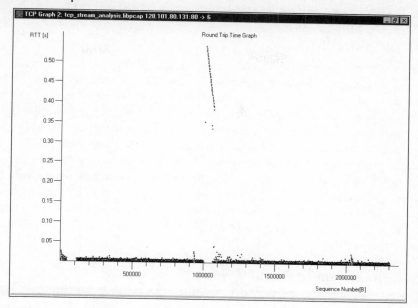

You can see the RTT spike around sequence number 1000000, which is roughly the same sequence number where you will see discontinuity in the time-sequence graphs.

Throughput Graph

The throughput graph shows the throughput of the TCP stream vs. time (see Figure 9.55).

Figure 9.55 Throughput Graph

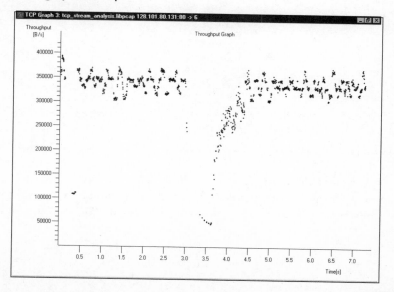

In Figure 9.58, the throughput fell off dramatically during the retransmit sequence seen in the time-sequence graphs.

Time-sequence Graph (Stevens)

The time-sequence graph (Stevens) produces a simple graph of TCP sequence numbers vs. time for the TCP stream containing the packet that was selected in the Summary window. The first derivative of this graph is the TCP traffic throughput. In an ideal situation where there is a constant throughput, the graph would be a straight rising line with its slope equaling the throughput. Unfortunately, things are seldom ideal, and you can learn a lot about where the source of throughput issues are coming from by looking at the time-sequence graph. In Figure 9.56, there is a graph showing a throughput problem. You can reproduce this graph by selecting the first packet of the *tcp_stream_analysis.libpcap* capture file, and selecting **Statistics | TCP Stream Graph | Time-Sequence Graph (Stevens)**. The captured file used in this graph is a classic example of TCP retransmit and the kind of issues you use the TCP Stream Analysis tool to debug. The full network capture can be found on the accompanying CD, and has been added to the collection of network captures on the Ethereal Web site.

Figure 9.56 Time-sequence Graph (Stevens)

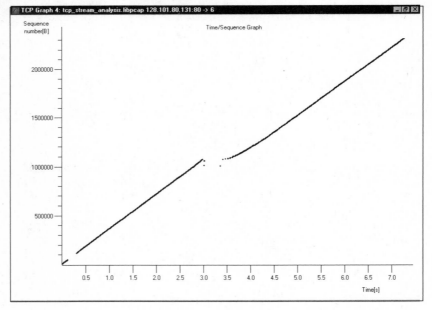

After about 0.3 seconds, the traffic has an even slope (constant throughput) for approximately 3 seconds, when there is a major disruption, as shown by the discontinuity in the graph. This gap suggests TCP retransmissions. The Steven's style time-sequence graph is simple, but you can see where the problems are.

Time-Sequence Graph (tcptrace)

The time-sequence graph (tcptrace) is also primarily a graph of TCP sequence numbers vs. time. Unlike the Stevens' style time-sequence graph, however, it conveys a lot more information about the TCP stream. Figure 9.57 shows that the tcptrace style time-sequence graph of this stream looks very similar to the Stevens' style time-sequence graph.

Figure 9.57 Time-sequence Graph (tcptrace)

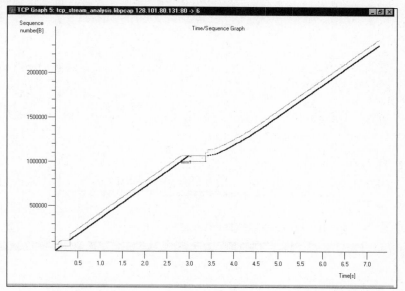

Explaining the elements shown in the tcptrace style time-sequence graph is easy using some of the graph manipulation tools that are available in all of the TCP stream analysis graphs. You can magnify a portion of the graph by pressing **Ctrl+right-click** on the graph (see Figure 9.58).

The box in the middle of the graph in Figure 9.58 is magnifying the region of discontinuity where packet loss has occurred. To get an even better view of it, use the zoom feature. Clicking on the graph with the middle mouse button allows you to zoom in on the part of the graph you are clicking on. Pressing **Shift+middle-click** zooms out. Whether you have zoomed in or out, clicking and dragging with the right mouse button on the graph allows you to move around in the zoomed graph. A zoom-in on the region of discontinuity in Figure 9.58, is shown in Figure 9.59.

Figure 9.58 Time-sequence Graph (tcptrace) – Magnify

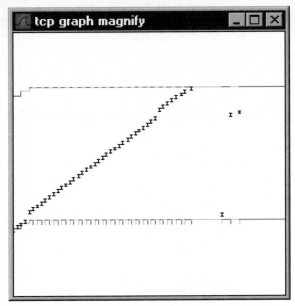

Figure 9.59 Time-sequence Graph (tcptrace) – Zoom

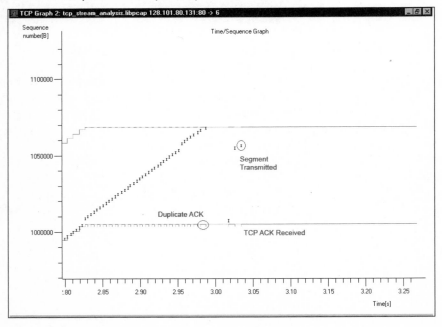

Figure 9.59 is a zoom-in on the section of the graph right before the discontinuity. The beginning of the discontinuity can be seen on the far right of the graph. There are the different elements

of the tcptrace style time-sequence graph. The lower line represents the sequence number of the last Acknowledgement (ACK) (TCP acknowledgement) seen. The top line represents the TCP window and consists of the sequence number of the last observed TCP ACK plus the previously seen TCP window size. The hash marks on the lower line represent duplicate ACKs, and the "I" bars represent transmitted segments.

Figure 9.59 is the same graph as Figure 9.60, but with different annotations to magnify what went wrong for this TCP stream. The capture behind this graph was taken from the receiver of a large transmission over TCP. Therefore, we only see the segments that we are receiving from the far end. What is seen in this graph is that early on the receiver missed two segments. The receiver continued to ACK the last segment received, and to receive subsequent segments until the segments received filled the TCP window. A couple of other segments were lost along the way. Finally, we receive the second missed segment, the third missed segment, and then the fourth missed segment. However, because the first missed segment has not yet turned up, the receiver continues sending the same duplicate ACK.

Figure 9.60 Time-sequence Graph(tcptrace) – Diagnosis

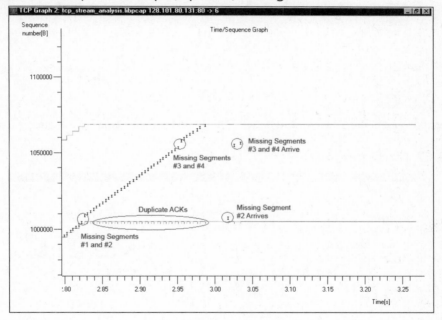

Figure 9.61 shows how this logjam is resolved.

In Figure 9.61, you can see the missing segment (presumed to be a retransmit) arrive. At this point, an ACK is transmitted acknowledging the last received segment, the TCP window increases, and the receiver begins to receive segments again.

Figure 9.61 Time-sequence Graph (tcptrace) - Zoom in on Retransmit

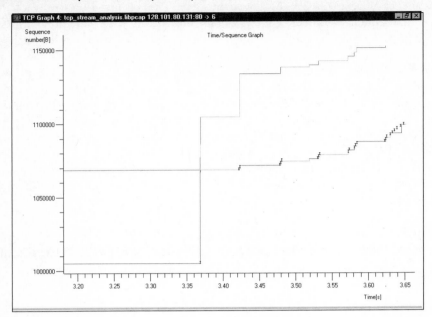

Throughput Graph

The throughput graph shows the throughput of the TCP stream vs. time (see Figure 9.62).

Figure 9.62 Throughput Graph

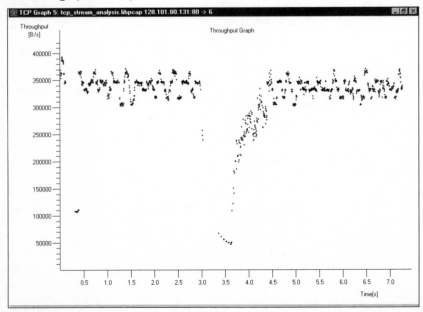

As seen in Figure 9.62, the throughput fell off dramatically during the retransmit sequence seen in the time-sequence graphs.

Graph Control

Throughout this section, we refer to any window containing a TCP stream analysis graph as a *graph window*. The term graph window refers to a Stevens' or tcptrace style time-sequence graph, a throughput graph, or an RTT graph. Whenever a graph window is created, a Graph Control dialog box is also created (see Figure 9.63).

Figure 9.63 Graph Control Dialog Box: Zoom Tab

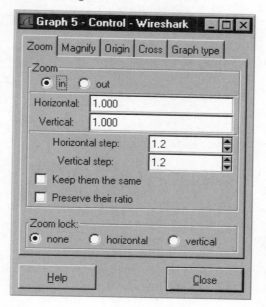

Notice that the number on the dialog box (*1*) matches the number on the graph window in Figure 9.59 (*1*). In the event that multiple graph windows are opened, you can use the index number to associate a Graph Control dialog box with its graph window.

The **Zoom** tab allows you to set the parameters related to the zoom functionality of the graph function (see Figure 9.63). The **Horizontal** and **Vertical** text boxes show the amount of zoom currently employed in the graph window.

The **Horizontal step** and **Vertical step** text boxes allow you to set the horizontal and vertical zoom factors applied to the graph when you press **Shift+middle-click** in the graph window. If you enable the **Keep them the same** checkbox, whenever you change either the horizontal step or the vertical step, the other will be changed to the same value. The **Preserve their ratio** checkbox causes the ratio between the horizontal step and the vertical step to be preserved. If the horizontal step is 1.2 and the vertical step is 2.4, when you change the horizontal step to 1.3, the vertical step will automatically change to 2.6.

The **Zoom lock** section allows you to lock the horizontal or vertical steps so that zoom is not applied to them. If the **horizontal** option is enabled, no matter what the value is for the horizontal step, zooming will not change the horizontal scale. If the **vertical** option is enabled, no matter what the value is for a vertical step, zooming will not change the vertical scale.

The **Magnify** tab allows you to control the parameters associated with the magnify functionality (see Figure 9.64).

Figure 9.64 Graph Control Dialog Box - Magnify Tab

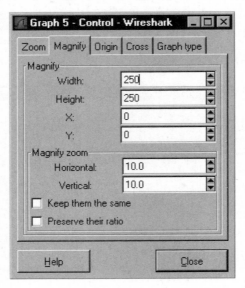

The **Width** and **Height** text boxes allow you to set the width and height of the magnification box that is displayed when you press **Ctrl+right–click** in the graph window. The **X:** and **Y:** text boxes allow you to set the x and y offset of the magnification box from the location of the mouse pointer. This can be useful for offsetting the magnification box to where it won't occlude the graph. The **Horizontal:** and **Vertical:** text boxes allow you to set the zoom factor used to blow up the graph in the magnification box. The **Keep them the same** checkbox causes the horizontal and vertical zoom factors to change in accordance with one another, and the **Preserve their ratio** checkbox causes the ratio between the horizontal and vertical zoom factors to remain constant.

The **Origin** tab allows you to change the various origins of the graph (see Figure 9.65).

The **Time origin** section allows you to choose the zero of time for your graph. If you select the **beginning of this TCP connection** option, you establish the beginning of the TCP connection as being graphed as your zero of time. If you select the **beginning of capture** option, you establish the beginning of the capture as your zero of time.

The **Sequence number origin** section allows you to choose whether your actual TCP sequence numbers or the relative TCP sequence numbers (the TCP sequence numbers minus your initial TCP sequence number) are shown on the graph. It is often convenient to use the relative sequence number, because it gives you an idea of how much data has been transmitted. If you select the **initial sequence number** option, the relative TCP sequence numbers will be used. If you select the **0 (=absolute)** option, the actual TCP sequence numbers will be used in the graph.

Figure 9.65 Graph Control Dialog Box - Origin Tab

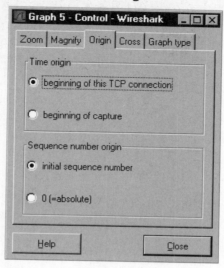

The **Cross** tab allows you to control whether crosshairs follow the mouse pointer in the graph window (see Figure 9.66).

Figure 9.66 Graph Control Dialog Box - Cross Tab

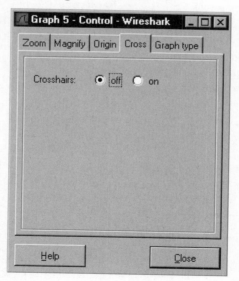

If you select the **off** radio button, there will be no crosshairs following the mouse pointer in the graph window. If you select the **on** option, there will be crosshairs following the mouse pointer in the graph window.

Once the graph window is displayed, use the **Graph type** tab to change which type of graph is being displayed (see Figure 9.67).

Figure 9.67 Graph Control Dialog Box - Graph Type Tab

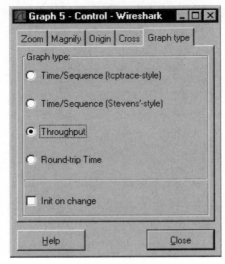

If you select the **Time/Sequence (tcptrace-style)** option, the Time-sequence (tcptrace-style) window will be displayed. If you select the **Time/Sequence (**Stevens'-style**)** option, the time-sequence (Stevens'-style) window will be displayed. If you select the **Throughput** option, the throughput graph window will be displayed. If you select the **Round-trip Time** option, the RTT graph window will be displayed.

By default, if you have applied a zoom to the graph window for one graph type, it will persist if you change graph types. If the **Init on change** checkbox is enabled, each time you change graph types the zoom will be reset.

Help

The **Help** menu is shown in Figure 9.68, and the **Help** options are explained in Table 9.16.

Table 9.16 Help Menu Options

Menu Option	Description
Contents	Displays the contents for the Wireshark online help.
Supported Protocols	Displays a list of the supported protocols and the display filter fields they provide.
Manual Pages	A submenu for accessing traditional UNIX-style manual pages for Wireshark, Wireshark filters, and command line utilities.

Continued

Table 9.16 continued Help Menu Options

Menu Option	Description
Wireshark Online	A submenu for accessing online Wireshark resources.
About Wireshark	Displays information about Wireshark version and compile information.

Figure 9.68 Help Menu

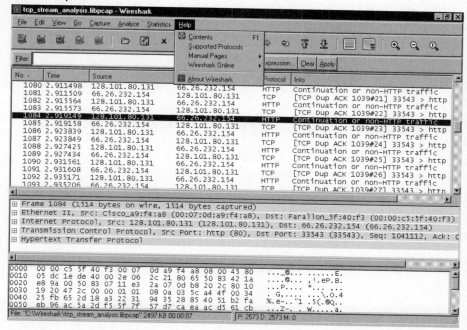

Contents

The Contents dialog box can be displayed by selecting **Help | Contents** from the menu bar (see Figure 9.69).

This dialog box provides an overview of Wireshark information, including Getting Started, Capturing, Capture Filters, Display Filters, and answers to Frequently Asked Questions (FAQs).

Figure 9.69 Help Contents Dialog Box

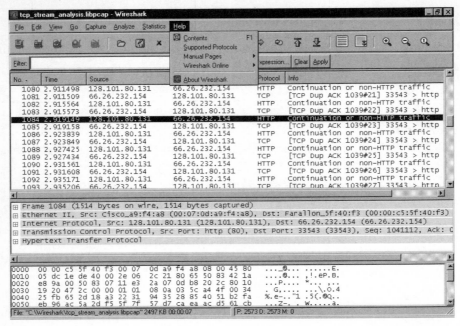

Supported Protocols

The Supported Protocols dialog box can be displayed by selecting **Help | Supported Protocols** from the menu bar (see Figure 9.70).

Figure 9.70 Supported Protocols Dialog Box

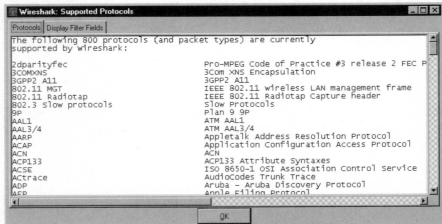

This dialog box provides a list of the protocols supported by the current version of Wireshark, and a list of the display filter fields provided in the current version of Wireshark.

Manual Pages Submenu

The Manual Pages submenu can be displayed by selecting **Help | Manual Pages** from the menu bar (see Figure 9.71). The Manual Pages submenu options are described in Table 9.17.

Figure 9.71 Manual Pages Submenu

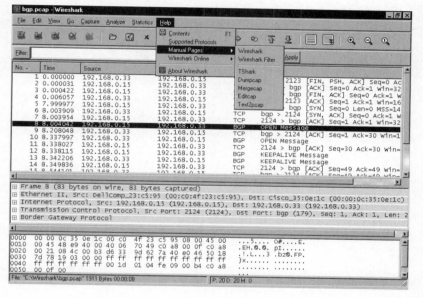

Table 9.17 Manual Pages Submenu Options

Menu Option	Description
Wireshark	Opens the manual page (manpage) for Wireshark.
Wireshark Filter	Opens the manpage for creating Wireshark filters.
TShark	Opens the manpage for TShark, the command-line version of Wireshark.
Dumpcap	Opens the manpage for Dumpcap, a command-line packet capture utility.
Mergecap	Opens the manpage for Mergecap, a command-line utility for merging two or more libpcap capture files
Editcap	Opens the manpage for Mergecap, a command-line utility for editing and translating libpcap files.
Text2pcap	Opens the manpage for text2pcap, a command-line utility for generating capture files from a text hexdump of packets

All of the Manual Pages submenu options display a Hypertext Markup Language (HTML)-formatted UNIX-style manpage with the default system Web browser. All of the command-line tools support libpcap files, (as indicated by the manpages), which is the default format used by Wireshark.

Wireshark Online Submenu

The Wireshark Online submenu can be displayed by selecting **Help | Wireshark Online** from the menu bar (see Figure 9.72). The Wireshark Online submenu options are described in Table 9.18.

Figure 9.72 Wireshark Online Submenu

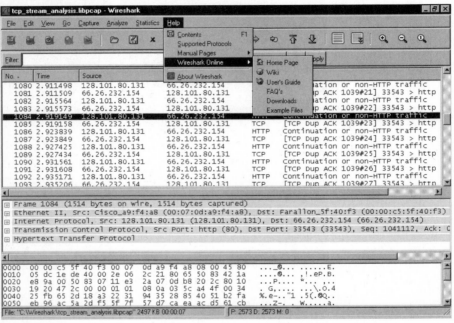

Table 9.18 Wireshark Online Options

Menu Option	Description
Home Page	Opens the Wireshark homepage, www.wireshark.org.
Wiki	Opens the Wireshark Wiki, http://wiki.wireshark.org.
User's Guide	Opens the online Wireshark User's Guide.
FAQ's	Opens the FAQ section of the Wireshark Web site.
Downloads	Opens the Downloads section of the Wireshark Web site .
Example Files	Opens the Sample captures section of the Wireshark Wiki. Here you can find the *bgp.pcap.gz* capture used in this chapter, as well as other real-world captures.

The Wireshark Online Options submenu provides instant access to more online content than we can cover in this book. The items and information available online are a great supplement to this book.

About Wireshark

The About Wireshark dialog box can be displayed by selecting **Help | About Plugins** from the menu bar (see Figure 9.73).

Figure 9.73 About Wireshark Dialog Box

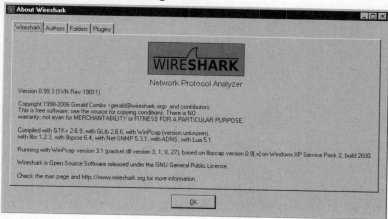

This dialog box contains information about the version of Wireshark you are running and the options it was compiled with. This information is important to know when you report a bug to the Wireshark developers.

Pop-up Menus

Wireshark has context-sensitive pop-up menus to assist you in performing tasks. None of these menus provide any additional functionality beyond what is available through the menu bar, but they are easier and quicker to use in some circumstances.

Summary Window Pop-up Menu

The Summary window pop-up menu can be displayed by right-clicking on the Summary window (see Figure 9.74).

Table 9.19 indicates where to find more information in this chapter on the Summary window pop-up menu options.

Figure 9.74 Summary Window Pop-up Menu

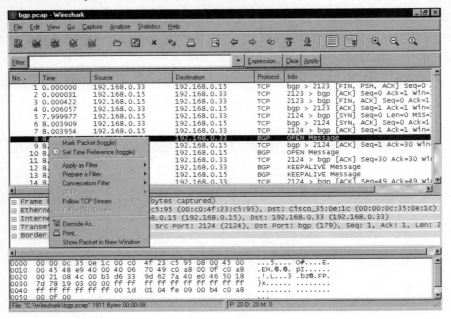

Table 9.19 Summary Window Pop-up Menu References

Menu Option	Reference
Mark Packet (toggle)	See "Edit: Mark Packet"
Set Time Reference (toggle)	See "Edit: Time Reference"
Apply as Filter	See "Analyze: Apply as Filter"
Prepare a Filter	See "Analyze: Prepare a Filter"
Conversation Filter	Opens the Conversation Filter submenu for filtering based on Ethernet, IP, TCP, UDP or PN-CBA Server
SCTP Submenu	Opens the SCTP submenu for following SCTP streams for Public Switched Telephone Network (PSTN) over IP
Follow TCP Stream	See "Analyze: Follow TCP Stream"
Follow SSL Stream	See "Analyze: Follow SSL Stream"
Decode As…	See "Analyze: Decode As"
Print…	See "File: Print"
Show Packet in New Window	See "View: Show Packet in New Window"

Protocol Tree Window Pop-up Menu

The Protocol Tree pop-up menu can be displayed by right-clicking on the Protocol Tree window (see Figure 9.75).

Figure 9.75 Protocol Tree Window Pop-up Menu

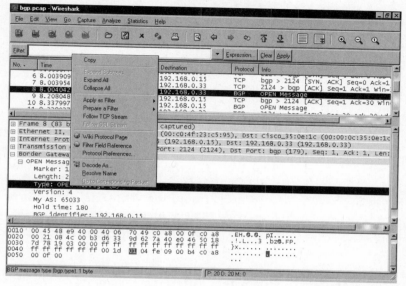

Table 9.20 includes descriptions for some items and indicates where to find more information in this chapter for other items.

Table 9.20 Protocol Tree Window Pop-up Menu References/Descriptions

Menu Option	Reference/Description
Copy clipboard	Copies the contents of the selected line to the
Expand Subtrees	See "View: Expand Subtrees"
Expand All	See "View: Expand All"
Collapse All	See "View: Collapse All"
Apply as Filter	See "Analyze: Apply as Filter"
Prepare a Filter	See "Analyze: Prepare a Filter"
Follow TCP Stream	See "Analyze: Follow TCP Stream"
Follow SSL Stream	See "Analyze: Follow SSL Stream"

Table 9.20 continued Protocol Tree Window Pop-up Menu
References/Descriptions

Menu Option	Reference/Description
Wiki Protocol Page	Opens the Wireshark Wiki at http://wiki.wireshark.org with the default system Web browser to the page for the selected protocol in the tree.
Filter Field Reference	Opens the Wireshark Documentation Web site on creating filters for the selected protocol with the default system Web browser.
Protocol Preferences	See "Edit: Preferences"
Decode As...	See "Analyze: Decode As"
Resolve Name	Forces resolution of all names for this packet. See the Wireshark Name Resolution sidebar for more information about Wireshark name resolution. Note that this option is only available if all name resolution is disabled.
Go to Corresponding Packet	See "Edit: Go To Corresponding Packet"

Data View Window Pop-up Menu

The Data View window pop-up menu can be displayed by right-clicking in the Data View window (see Figure 9.76).

Figure 9.76 Data View Window Pop-up Menu

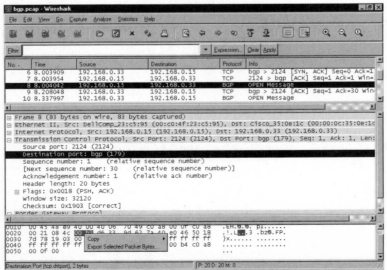

Table 9.22 indicates where to find more information in this chapter on the Data View window pop-up menu options.

Table 9.22 Data View Window Pop-up Menu References

Menu Option	Reference
Copy Submenu	Displays the Copy submenu in order to copy the entire contents of the decoded packet, as either the entire data block or just the ASCII reproducible characters.
Export Selected Packet Bytes	Allows the currently selected bytes to be exported in raw data format.

Using Command-line Options

Wireshark supports a large number of command-line options. This section documents some of the most commonly used options.

Capture and File Options

The most commonly used Wireshark options are those related to captures and files. Table 9.23 lists some of the most common command-line options related to these tasks.

Table 9.23 Capture and File Command Line Options

Command Line Option	Description
-i <interface>	Sets the name of the interface used for live captures to <interface>.
-k	Starts capture immediately; requires the –i option.
-a <test>:<value>	Sets an autostop condition for the capture. <test> may be one of duration or filesize. If the <test> is duration, <value> must be the number of seconds the capture should run before it stops. If <test> is the filesize, <value> is the number of kilobytes that should be captured before the capture stops.
-c <count>	Sets the number of packets to read before stopping the capture. After <count> packets have been read the capture stops.
-r <filename>	Reads the capture saved in <filename>.
-w <filename>	Writes the capture to <filename>.
-b <count>	Enables the use of <count> files in a ring buffer for captures. A maximum capture size must be specified with the –a filesize:<value> option.

To capture on interface *eth0* immediately and write the results to a ring buffer with three files of maximum size *100* kilobytes with base filename *foo.bar.libpcap*, execute the following at the command line:

```
Wireshark -i eth0 -k -w foo.bar.libpcap -b 3 -a filesize:100
```

Filter Options

Wireshark also allows you to specify filter information from the command line. Table 9.24 lists some of the most commonly used filter-related command-line options.

Table 9.24 Filter Command Line Options

Command Line Option	Description
-f <capture filter >	Set the tcpdump style capture filter string to <filter string>.
-R <display filter>	Only applicable when reading a capture from a file with the –r option. Applies the display filter <display filter> to all packets in the capture file and discards those that do not match.

To extract all packets from capture file *bgp.pcap.gz* with *bgp.type == 2*, execute the following at the command line:

```
Wireshark -r bgp.pcap.gz -R "bgp.type == 2"
```

Other Options

Other commonly used options are shown in Table 9.25.

Table 9.25 Other Command-line Options

Command Line Option	Description
-N <flags>	Turns on name resolution. Depending on which letters follow –N, various names will be resolved by Wireshark. n will cause network name resolution to be turned on, t will enable transport name resolution, m will enable MAC address resolution, and C will enable asynchronous DNS lookups for network name resolution.
-v	Prints the Wireshark version information.
-h	Prints Wireshark's help information.

Summary

In this chapter, you learned about the major components of the Wireshark GUI. You also learned about the major functionality of the Wireshark application and how to access it.

You should now be able to perform network captures, open saved network captures, and print captures. You are also equipped to use display filters to filter the packets displayed in the Summary window, color the packets in the Summary window for easier readability, or find a packet in the capture with particular characteristics.

We've shown you how to navigate the protocol tree in the Protocol Tree window to examine the contents of a packet, and to use the Protocol Tree fields to prepare new display filter strings.

Finally, we showed you how to force a packet or group of packets to be decoded by a particular dissector. You also learned how to enable and disable decoding of particular protocols, and should have some understanding of how to use some of the more commonly used tools in Wireshark to gain better visibility into TCP Streams.

Solutions Fast Track

Getting started with Wireshark

- ☑ Binary Wireshark packages for Windows, Linux, and various UNIX programs can be downloaded from www.wireshark.org.
- ☑ Source code can be downloaded and compiled from www.wireshark.org
- ☑ ary packages available don't meet your needs.
- ☑ Wireshark can be launched by typing **wireshark** at the command line.

Exploring the Main Windows

- ☑ The Summary window provides a one-line summary for each packet.
- ☑ The Protocol Tree window provides a detailed decode of the packet selected in the Summary window.
- ☑ The Data View window provides the hexadecimal dump of a packet's actual bytes.

Other Window Components

- ☑ The filter bar provides a quick mechanism for filtering the packets displayed in the Summary window.
- ☑ Clicking the filter bar's **Filter:** button displays the Display Filter dialog box to help you construct a display filter string.

☑ The **Information** field shows the display filter field name of the field selected in the Protocol Tree window.

Exploring the Menus

☑ Most preferences can be set in the Preferences dialog box.

☑ There are context-sensitive pop-up menus available by right-clicking on the Summary window, Protocol Tree window, or Data View window.

☑ Packets in the Summary window can be color-coded for easy reading using the Apply Color Filters dialog box.

Using Command–line Options

☑ Wireshark can apply display filters to packets read from a file with the −R flag, discarding packets that don't match the filter.

☑ Wireshark uses −r to indicate a file to read from and −w to indicate a file to write to.

☑ Wireshark can be made to start capturing from an interface immediately on startup by using the −i and k options.

Frequently Asked Questions

The following Frequently Asked Questions, answered by the authors of this book, are designed to both measure your understanding of the concepts presented in this chapter and to assist you with real-life implementation of these concepts. To have your questions about this chapter answered by the author, browse to **www. syngress.com/solutions** and click on the **"Ask the Author"** form.

Q: Why is Wireshark so slow displaying data during capture? It seems to lock up.

A: Your version of Wireshark may have been compiled without the Asynchronous DNS (ADNS) library. If so, Wireshark is stopping to do a DNS lookup for the source and destination IP address in each packet it decodes. It can take a long time for DNS queries to time out if they fail, and during this time, Wireshark may lock up while waiting for those failures. To solve this problem, get a version of Wireshark with ADNS compiled in. To work around this problem, deselect **Enable Network Name Resolution** in the Capture Options dialog box when starting a capture, or in the File dialog box when opening a capture file.

Q: Why is it that when I select some fields in the Protocol Tree window I don't see the field name in the Information field? How can I filter on the field if I can't find out its name?

A: Wireshark has been developed over many years by a team of volunteer programmers. Many different people have written the dissectors, which decode the protocols in Wireshark, at many different times. Not all dissector authors associated a filterable field with each field they display in the Protocol Tree. You will not be able to filter on such fields. If such filtering is important to you for a particular protocol, you are encouraged to alter the source code for that dissector to include the capacity, and submit it to the Wireshark team for inclusion.

Q: Why do I sometimes see an IP address or a TCP/UDP port number or a MAC address twice, once in parenthesis and once not?

A: When name resolution is turned off for an address type, or when no name is found for a given address, Wireshark inserts the actual address into the place where the name would have gone. As a result, the place where you would have seen the name with the address in parentheses (or vice versa) will show two copies of the address.

Q: I need more complicated capture filtering than tcpdump-style capture filters provide. Can I use Wireshark's display filters to restrict what I capture?

A: The short answer is no. Wireshark will not allow you to use display filters to filter on capture. However, there is a workaround to achieve this. While Wireshark will not allow you to use display filters on capture, Tshark will. To capture from an interface *<interface>* to a file *<savefile>* filtering with a display filter string *<filter string>* execute the following at the command line:

```
tshark –i <interface> -w <savefile> -R <filter string>
```

Tshark will capture from *<interface>* and only save to *<savefile>* those packets that match *<filter string>*. In many cases, display filter strings will not be as fast as the tcpdump-style capture filters.

Q: Does Wireshark really capture all the traffic arriving at an interface when capturing in promiscuous mode?

A: That depends. Wireshark gets whatever is captured by libpcap. Sometimes, due to a high load on the system you are capturing from, or just due to trying to capture from too-high bandwidth an interface, packets may be lost for a number of reasons, including being dropped by the kernel.

Q: Why am I seeing packets that aren't addressed to or being sent by my local interface even though I've turned off capturing in promiscuous mode?

A: There may be other applications running (e.g., Snort) on the system you are capturing from that have put the interface into promiscuous mode. Whether Wireshark or some other application puts the interface in promiscuous mode, if the interface is in promiscuous mode, you will see all traffic that arrives at it, not just the traffic addressed to or sent from the interface.

## Chapter 10

Network Reporting and Troubleshooting with other Tools

Solutions in this chapter:

- **Reporting on Bandwidth Usage and Other Metrics**
- **Collecting Data for Analysis**
- **Understanding SNMP**
- **Troubleshooting Network Problems**

☑ **Summary**

☑ **Solutions Fast Track**

☑ **Frequently Asked Questions**

Introduction

It is an unfortunate fact of life that network security is only glamorous to geeks. For everyone else, seeing an IDS purr away, or watching swatch grind through gigabytes of log messages is pretty dull, and more importantly, meaningless. There will inevitably be occasions where you need to demonstrate the state of your network to a less-technical audience. In some cases you need to justify a recent expense, in other cases you may need to provide support for a proposed expense. It is at these times that some useful tools to help turn the bits and bytes into graphs can go a long way. We covered Wireshark extensively in Chapters 7, 8, and 9. So in this chapter, we will focus on additional tools for data analysis and network troubleshooting.

Reporting on Bandwidth Usage and Other Metrics

If you've ever been in a position to request approval to upgrade your Internet bandwidth, one of the first questions that often comes up is, "What are we using the bandwidth for now?" You don't want to have to admit you don't have any idea. In these cases, some type of reporting mechanism on network traffic would come in really handy. Or maybe the Internet responsiveness is slow because your Internet connection is being saturated and you want to know what it's being used for. A report based on the protocols and ports being used would do the job nicely. There are administrative uses for traffic statistics, but where does security fit in? Maybe the entire network has come to a crawl and you need to know why… fast. There are a lot of ways to determine the cause, but a nice graph showing that a particular workstation is generating all the traffic could help. If your reports clearly showed a particular workstation is uploading large amounts of data over a file sharing network, there could definitely be security implications. When it comes down to it, there are a number of metrics that could be useful for administering and securing your network.

There are many commercial products to provide various levels of insight into your network data flows. There are also a large number of products, both commercial and free, to collect more-focused pieces of data (such as Web server statistics). The following list provides a brief summary of some of the best general-purpose free offerings, with additional instructions on how to install and configure the products provided later in the chapter.

- **Multi Router Traffic Grapher (MRTG)** When it comes to generic network statistics using free software, MRTG is one of the most widely used. You can download it for free from http://oss.oetiker.ch/mrtg/. It will run on Unix/Linux, Windows, or Netware systems and is incorporated into many third-party applications. It derives its figures and graphs from simple network management protocol (SNMP) information, so you will need to support SNMP on your devices to use MRTG or figure out some other means to get MRTG the data it needs. We will discuss SNMP concepts in more detail in the next section, so feel free to jump ahead if you are not comfortable with SNMP. MRTG uses perl (www.perl.org) on the back end for the real work, which is freely available and easy to install.

- **MZL & Novatech TrafficStatistic** TrafficStatistic (www.trafficstatistic.com) works a little differently than MRTG does; it gathers its data by sniffing all the network traffic. Much like an IDS, for traffic analyzers that work this way, placement within the network will be crucial to collecting the data you want to see. In a small environment, this should not be too difficult. TrafficStatistic offers only very minimal reporting data, consisting of total throughput (in, out, and combined) and a top-10 talkers (in, out, combined), and top-10 protocols (in, out, combined). If you need anything more than that, you can pay for additional *plug-ins*. Some of the plug-ins are pretty affordable. You can download the free version from www.trafficstatistic.com/pages/basemodules.html. TrafficStatistic might be a good option if you want something that's very easy to install and get running and only provides the most basic of reporting data.

- ■ **PRTG Traffic Grapher** This is probably the best free offering available at the time of this writing based on functionality and ease of use. You can download the free version from www.paessler.com/download/prtg. PRTG Traffic Grapher is one of the move versatile offerings and can extract statistical data from the NetFlow protocol, SNMP, and traffic sniffing. The setup is pretty painless and the graphs are well constructed by default. The limitation for the free version is that you can collect data from only three sensors, which is generous and will probably be plenty for a small environment.

- ■ **ntop** Ntop (www.ntop.org) is a very powerful Web-based utility to analyze network traffic. You can run ntop on FreeBSD, Linux, Solaris, SGI IRIX, AIX, and Microsoft Windows systems. Ntop does not natively include alarm and notification mechanisms, its sole purpose is the collection and reporting of traffic statistics, which it does very well. The level of detail offered by ntop exceeds that of any other utility reviewed here. Ntop is also completely free, with no restrictions or limitations.

Collecting Data for Analysis

As we discuss the various offerings for data analysis, a key consideration is how these products collect their data. The methods that are used will have a significant impact not only for what metrics are available for analysis, but also the analysis host's placement within the network and resource requirements. What follows is a brief explanation of what data-collection methods are most common, along with some of their strengths and weaknesses.

Sniffing data is one of the simplest methods of collecting data. Without any special configuration, sniffing the data means listening to all network traffic as it passes through the segment the host system is connected to. This technique is typically the most robust because in sniffing the traffic, the host has the capability to see every single packet. What is done with all this data is up to the analysis engine, but the focus here is that you are not grabbing select pieces of information, you are collecting all the data, and then sorting through it. This method will be more processor intensive than most other methods, especially if there is a high volume of traffic.

This method also requires precise placement of the host that will be collecting data, because it has no way to see the data unless it passes through the segment the host is on. Because of this, the physical location of the data-collection system will likely be dictated by the network topology and location of traffic you wish to analyze. Besides resource requirements, the biggest drawback to this method is that it will collect data at the network level, with no regard for product-specific metrics. Although some analysis platforms can attempt to remedy this and perform analysis on some higher-level information contained in the packet, you will not be able to get the same level of upper-layer information as you will with the other methods.

SNMP is a protocol that is designed specifically to accommodate the management of network-enabled devices. Although this management can include making changes, in a data analysis context, SNMP is really only used to retrieve information. When used this way, a network host requests certain information from the SNMP-enabled device, which then sends the desired metrics in response. Alternatively, the SNMP device can be configured to send the metrics as a sort of alarm when they surpass a configured threshold. The information collected is limited in that it is very focused. You can only ask a device for the specific statistics that it supports. While sniffing collects network layer data, SNMP can collect higher-layer, product-specific data that sniffing would not easily be able to gather. An example of product-specific counters is the *currentAnonymousUsers* and *currentNonAnonymousUsers* values from an IIS 6 server. Attempting to build in the logic for a sniffer to track each connection to the IIS server and monitor if that connection used authentication would be very burdensome. Instead, SNMP can provide these metrics directly from the IIS server, which is already tracking these things.

SNMP can also be a chatty protocol in a large environment, contributing to network congestion. In a small environment this may not be an issue, but it's something to be aware of. The primary benefit that SNMP has going for it is that you do not need to place your data collector in the path of the data. You can place the system anywhere and then it will reach out and poll the devices (using a *Get*) for the desired data points. You can also configure an SNMP-enabled device to send the metrics to a collector when they reach a preconfigured threshold (via a TRAP). SNMP and sniffing provide different information, which enables the two to complement each other's capabilities. Both SNMP and sniffing will require forethought and planning to implement mainly due to the fact that they each collect their statistics differently.

NetFlow is a specially designed protocol for collecting network traffic statistics. NetFlow is primarily supported on Cisco devices, but some other manufactures implement similar technologies, which exhibit varying levels of interoperability. NetFlow is similar in behavior to SNMP traps in that once a NetFlow-enabled device has been configured, it will then send traffic statistics back to the data collector. The difference is that while SNMP targets very specific metrics that must be supported by the SNMP device, NetFlow targets a very small subset of network traffic data. NetFlow gathers information based on source and destination IP address, source and destination port number, the protocol being used, the type of service settings, and the device interface. These metrics lend themselves to gathering data on bandwidth utilization and network top talkers. This may sound like just what the doctor ordered; however, NetFlow is not supported on all devices, particularly the more economical models. This may mean that NetFlow is a less viable option for data collection in a small networking environment. If you do have network devices that can support it, a little research would be advisable to see if you can take advantage of NetFlow data. You can read more about NetFlow from here: www.cisco.com/en/US/products/ps6601/products_ios_protocol_group_home.html.

> **NOTE**
>
> RMON stands for *remote monitoring*, which is yet another network management protocol. RMON is a relatively new standard, described in RFC1757, which uses SNMP for its underlying functionality and an extensive set of new MIB objects for its data collection. Because it uses SNMP, RMON is vendor neutral, and RMON also takes steps to reduce network traffic where possible. While RMON support on enterprise class network analysis devices is good, it is virtually non-existent on free network analysis solutions.

Understanding SNMP

As you can see from the brief summaries above, a lot of network devices rely on SNMP to gather information. This makes good sense, because SNMP is one of the most widely used architectures for managing systems in a centralized fashion. Some basic vocabulary you should be familiar with includes the *Management Information Base*, or MIB. The MIB is basically a hierarchical tree-like structure, serving as a catalog of settings that can be read or changed on the target system. The MIB consists of some portions that will be the same across all devices that support SNMP, and other portions that can be defined by individual vendors. Any specific object in the MIB can be referred to by its *Object Identifier* or OID, which is a numerical map to find the object in the MIB. As an example, the first highest level object in the MIB could be referred to as 1 and each of 3 objects one level lower would be 1.1, 1.2, and 1.3. This pattern is continued, and due to the large number of objects, a typical OID would be 1.3.6.1.2.1.2.2.1.14.1. In addition to using the numerical form to reference an OID, each subtree also has a corresponding name. Using the previous example, 1.3.6.1 could also be referenced with .iso.org.dod.internet. The full named form is used less often but you may encounter it. A *managed device* can be almost any network device that runs an *agent* that can translate device-specific management information into an SNMP-compatible format. The *Network Management Station* is the device doing the managing, and can be referred to by many names depending on where you are reading.

The basic operations the management station can perform on the MIB objects are *Get* and *Set*. There are some variations such as *GetNext*, or *GetBulk*, but suffice it to say that what it all boils down to is using a *Get* to read a value in the MIB, and using *Set* to set the value. In the case of graphing network throughput all we are doing is a *Get* for relevant MIB objects. An example would be .1.3.6.1.2.1.2.2.1.14, which is interface inbound errors. Another key feature of SNMP management is the *Trap*. While the *Get* or *Set* are initiated by the management station, acting as the client to the managed device, the *Trap* is initiated by the managed device. An SNMP trap is basically an alert of some preconfigured condition, much like the notifications available in PRTG Traffic Grapher. Traps are sent from the managed device to the management station that was specified as a sort of alarm.

If all this seems a bit confusing, don't be alarmed. If you follow the examples below, a little hands on should help clear things up. There are also several free tools to browse a device MIB. Using one of these will probably be useful for understanding what the OIDs mean and how they are used. I would suggest using *GetIf* from www.wtcs.org/snmp4tpc/. It is a free MIB browser that is pretty easy to use. Once you get it installed, simply enter an IP address or host name in the **Host name** field, ensure that you have a read community string entered, and then click **Start**. I would recommend only entering a read community string to prevent you from accidentally being able to change any settings on the target device. If *GetIf* populates the various fields, then it is connected via SNMP. Click the **MBrowser** tab and look around. By expanding the plus symbols next to **iso | org | dod | internet,** you can browse to the desired OID. After you select the desired OID, click **Start** (to send a *Get)* and query the value. Try to locate 1.3.6.1.2.1.2.2.1.5 to see the network interface speed, for example.

One final consideration concerning SNMP is that it is considered a "chatty" protocol. This is due to the process of querying multiple OIDS and receiving the responses. If you have a large SNMP infrastructure, and you are reading or writing a lot of SNMP MIB objects, the network traffic that can be generated can be significant. In a small environment, the SNMP traffic should be minimal, but it is a consideration to keep in mind.

Tools & Traps...

SNMP Security

Be aware that SNMP has been around for a long time and as such there are three major versions. SNMP version one and version two have some considerable security flaws. The foremost is that they send their data unencrypted, which could include a whole host of data you would rather not be viewable by just anyone. A second consideration is that the limited authentication capabilities rely on a community string only to determine not only who can read the SNMP data, but who can set the SNMP values, effectively granting access to configure the SNMP-enabled device.

SNMP version three mitigates many of these issues; however, it is not widely supported at this time. While SNMP v3 is often supported on the more prominent enterprise class platforms, support using free tools is practically non-existent. Given these facts, the best way to secure SNMP traffic is with a combination of access lists (where applicable) and some form of encryption, such as IPsec for example.

Configuring Multi Router Traffic Grapher

To get started using Multi Router Traffic Grapher (MRTG) you will need to download the appropriate version for your operating system from http://oss.oetiker.ch/mrtg/. Another version, which is packaged with a few useful SNMP tools, is available from www.openxtra.co.uk/products/mrtg-xtra.php. MRTG also requires Perl to function. Perl is a versatile scripting language that is in wide use. Perl is very rich in features and has modules to accomplish a variety of useful tasks. You can download ActivePerl from www.activestate.com/store/freedownload.aspx?prdGuid=81fbce82-6bd5-49bc-a915-08d58c2648ca. After you have both of these downloaded, follow these steps to configure them.

1. Run the installation file for Perl.

2. Choose the target installation directory.

3. When prompted, allow the Installation Wizard to add Perl to the PATH environment variable and create the Perl file extension association. This way your Perl scripts can be executed without having to explicitly provide the full path to the Perl executable.

4. Uncompress the MRTG Zip file to a directory of your choosing.

5. From the \mrtg-2.14.7\bin\ directory, run **perl mrtg**. It won't really do anything yet, because we still need to create the configuration file. This test is just to establish that Perl is in the PATH and can execute mrtg.

6. From the \mrtg-2.14.7\bin\ directory, enter the following command: **perl cfgmaker <SNMP STRING>@<SNMP DEVICE IP> —global "WorkDir: C:\www**

webroot" --output mrtg.cfg. This will create an initial configuration file. You can always use a different working directory. The working directory is where MRTG will place the HTML files, so it is typically in the directory structure of a Web server. If everything works properly, you will receive no output on the command line, but an mrtg.cfg file will have been generated in the \bin\ directory.

If you get an error it probably means the community string is incorrect or the SNMP security settings are not enabling MRTG to connect. In either of those cases you can follow these steps to adjust the SNMP security settings on Windows XP.

1. To edit the SNMP properties on a Windows XP system, open the Services plug-in (**Start | Run | services.msc**).

2. Locate the SNMP service and double-click it. Click the **Security** tab.

3. Ensure that the SNMP community strings are set correctly.

4. If you do not wish to restrict which machines can use SNMP to communicate with the SNMP device, select the **Accept SNMP packets from any host** radio button. Otherwise, ensure that the system running MRTG is listed in the **Accept SNMP packets from these hosts** section and click **OK**.

At this point you should have the mrtg file successfully created using *cfgmaker*. This file is only the starting point and will still require some manual editing before it's really ready to use.

1. You can now run MRTG using the following command from the \bin directory: **perl mrtg mrtg.cfg**. The first time you run the command you will get some warnings about missing log files. This is normal the first time it is run.

2. Several files will be generated, the primary one being an HTML file beginning with the target host's name/IP address. If you open this in a browser it will show the *bytes in* and *bytes out* traffic statistics.

A sample of the MRTG HTML output is shown in Figure 10.1.

By scheduling MRTG to run regularly, you can build a history of data points that are used to populate the graphs. MRTG can be run in *daemon* mode. In this mode, once you start MRTG it will not exit; it will stay running and continue to collect data. To do this requires two steps. First, edit the configuration file and add the line **RunAsDaemon: Yes** in the **Global Properties** section. Second, start MRTG using the following command from a command prompt: **start /b perl mrtg mrtg.cfg**. Yet another way to accumulate the needed data is to run MRTG as a Windows service using the *SRVANY.exe* and *INSTSRV.exe* Microsoft utilities. Given the wide range of options, there should be a way to execute MRTG that suits your environment.

MRTG has the benefit that there are no limitations on the number of systems you can collect data from. Although throughput is the default metric, if you know the OID of the metric you wish to monitor, MRTG can collect and record historical data for that as well. Some good examples might be disk space, CPU utilization, network errors, and available memory. As an example of specifying the target OID, here is a target specification:

```
Target[RTR]: 1.3.6.1.2.1.2.2.1.14.1&1.3.6.1.2.1.2.2.1.20.1:pass@192.168.1.25
```

Figure 10.1 MRTG HTML Output

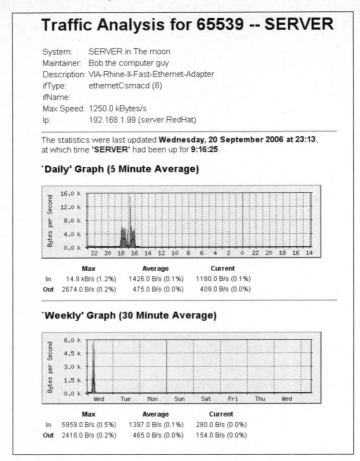

The OID format is *<OID for first line in graph>&<OID for second line in graph>*. In this example, you would be specifying a target device at IP address 192.168.1.25, using the SNMP community string of "pass." The OID to read would be 1.3.6.1.2.1.2.2.1.14.1 (input error counts) for one line on the graph, and 1.3.6.1.2.1.2.2.1.20.1 (output error counts) for the other line. The last number is the interface number. So the input error count on interface #2 would be 1.3.6.1.2.1.2.2.1.14.2. The label in the brackets (in this example "RTR") would be displayed on the graph page as a device name.

As you can see, getting simple throughput graphs in an HTML page using MRTG is pretty painless. With a little work, you can configure MRTG to graph a wide range of useful information. I would highly recommend doing some reading on the MRTG page with third-party documentation (http://oss.oetiker.ch/mrtg/3party.en.html). This page has many articles describing how to use MRTG in various circumstances. There are also links to many graphical utilities to help you manage your configuration files. For increased granularity in your graphs (as small as one-minute intervals) and more aesthetic graphs, check out RRDtool at http://oss.oetiker.ch/rrdtool/.

Configuring MZL & Novatech TrafficStatistic

While TrafficStatistic isn't the most full-featured solution available, it is very easy to get running. TrafficStatistic collects its information from network sniffing only, so you will need to place the host that is running TrafficStatistic in a location where it can see the network traffic you want to report on. Follow these steps to get TrafficStatistic running on an appropriately located host.

1. Download and run the installation file from www.trafficstatistic.com.

2. During the setup, take note of the HTTPSrv Service port (Default 7777) and the RunCPM Service Port (7778), altering them if desired. Other than that, you can simply accept the defaults.

3. When the setup completes, allow it to Start the IP capture service, HTTP server service, and run the GUI monitor.

4. If you have more than one network adapter listed in the Adapters pane, you will need to right-click the adapter you wish to collect data from and select Configuration.

5. Ensure that **Listen** is checked and click **OK**. You have the option of specifying billing periods at this time as well. These are targeted for ISPs and other providers who need statistics for certain billing periods to charge back to customers, but you could also configure them for your own reporting purposes. By default, the billing period will be from the current date with no end date.

6. After you click **OK** you will be prompted to verify your adapter selection. Click **Yes** to confirm your choice.

You should not be collecting data on the selected interface. The window should show several links in its default state. Click **Create report**, and then select **Usage Development**. In the next window, select the network interface you want to report on, and then click **OK**. The resultant report is shown below in Figure 10.2.

If you are reporting on addresses that are not "private" addresses as defined in RFC1918, you might find you aren't really interested in traffic that is local to your network, and a top-talker list that is not using Internet bandwidth may not be useful. In this case you have the capability to define the local address and tell TrafficStatistic not to use them in the reports it generates. This list doesn't truly have to be "local," but it does enable you to configure TrafficStatistic to *not* report on certain addresses. This could be handy if there are certain hosts that are high traffic as part of normal behavior and you want to exclude them from the reports altogether. To configure the list of local addresses and exclude them from the reports, follow these steps:

1. Ensure that you have the proper network interface selected in the Adapters pane.

2. Right-click the adapter and select **Configuration**.

3. Check the box labeled **Exclude traffic between local addresses**.

4. Click the button labeled **Edit LAL** (which stands fro *local address list*).

5. Click the **Add Host, Add Range**, or **Add Net** button and enter the appropriate information.

6. When finished, click **OK** and **OK** again to completely finalize your changes.

Figure 10.2 MZL & Novatech TrafficStatistic Report

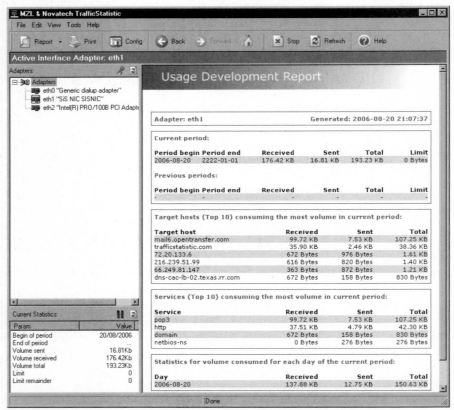

Note that these changes will not retroactively affect current data that has been collected.

The business model that is used by the makers of the MZL & Novatech TrafficStatistic is to provide the basic monitor for free. If you want additional functionality, you can buy add-on plug-ins.
The price of plug-ins varies greatly. The "Multi Optional Report" plug-in provides more-granular
bandwidth reports that enable you to actually drill down and see what ports a particular host was
using to generate the network traffic; it costs 50 Euro (approximately $66). If MZL & Novatech
TrafficStatistic provides adequate reporting for your needs, and you have a spare machine you can
place appropriately to sniff the network traffic, this might be a good fit.

Configuring PRTG Traffic Grapher

PRTG Traffic Grapher is, at this time, one of the best freeware options available. The same download is both the freeware version and a full-featured, time-limited trial version. PRTG is the only offering that supports data collection via sniffing, SNMP, and NetFlow. The graphs PRTG produces are very functional and a Web interface is provided that enables you to drill down into the data without having to be on the PRTG server or having to have any software installed. This means that if you want to collect data via sniffing, you don't have to worry about providing remote access to the PRTG server; you can access the reports via any Web browser. Follow these steps to get PRTG up and running.

1. Download the setup file from www.paessler.com/download/prtg and run it.

2. Click **Yes** to confirm that you wish to install the freeware/trial version.

3. Click **Next**.

4. Select the **I accept the agreement** radio button to accept the license terms, and then click **Next**.

5. Select the installation directory, and then click **Next**.

6. On the **Select Components** screen you can select the defaults and then click **Next**.

7. Choose if you wish for the Web interface to be enabled or not. If you *do* want the Web interface enabled, you can leave it at the defaults. The *PRTG Watchdog* service is a process that will monitor and restart the PRTG process if it terminates unexpectedly. You should leave this option enabled unless you have a specific reason not to. When satisfied with your selection, click **Next**.

8. Click **Finish** to complete the installation and start PRTG.

   When you first run PRTG it will present you with a window where you can choose which version to install. The freeware edition (limited to three sensors), a trial edition (which will work for 30 days), or you can purchase the commercial edition. This window is shown in Figure 10.3. You also have the option of comparing the various versions. In this example we're looking at the freeware edition, so select the corresponding radio button (which should be the freeware version by default), click **Next**, and then **Finish**.

Figure 10.3 Version Activation Screen

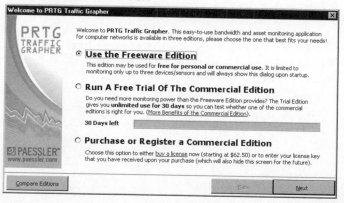

9.   During the next step you will see an empty window, with a button in the center that says **Click here to add your first sensor!** Click this button.

10.   Click **Next**

11.   Choose which data collection method you wish to use. In this context a sensor can be any of several data collection devices, including a router supporting NetFlow, a PC sniffing traffic, or any device that will support SNMP (including Windows systems). For this example I am using a PC that will sniff the network traffic. If your network infrastructure devices don't support SNMP data collection or NetFlow data, this may be your only option anyway. A final option is to make this installation a latency monitoring system. In this mode, the system will use pings to monitor the round trip time between this host and various other hosts on the network. After making your selection, click **Next**.

12.   On the next screen, enter the name of the sensor or leave the default value.

13.   Place a check next to the interface you wish to use and click **Next**.

14.   On the next screen you have the option of excluding certain traffic. I would suggest leaving the default of **Monitor all traffic**. The filters can be edited later if desired. Click **Next**.

15.   On the next screen you have the option of choosing what protocols to monitor (called channels). You can also define your own by clicking **Edit Port Filter Library**. For now, just click **Select All** and then **Next**. We will demonstrate creating your own "channel" shortly.

16.   On the next screen you can choose a grouping for you to add sensors under (with a limit of three sensors this grouping probably isn't that critical, but if you had hundreds of devices it would be very useful). You can also select the scanning interval. Unless you have reason to do otherwise, simply leave the defaults in place and click **Finish**.

The main PRTG Traffic Grapher console is shown in Figure 10.4. There are three panes. The leftmost is called Views and enables you to select between different layouts and to display different data. The middle one, Sensors, enables you to select different sensors to see their data. The rightmost pane is **View: <description>**, and will change depending on what you select in the Views pane on the far left. While the same installation file is used for Windows XP and Windows 2000, once installed, the interfaces have slight differences. The differences are very minor and these instructions should work for either version.

If you double-click on a given graph you will get an enlarged view that you can also use to edit the graph colors, units, and several other options. By default, the Web interface will be available on the IP of the machine you installed PRTG on, using port 8080. In this case you can open a browser to http://192.168.1.104:8080. The browser interface is shown in Figure 10.5 below.

Figure 10.4 PRTG Traffic Grapher Application

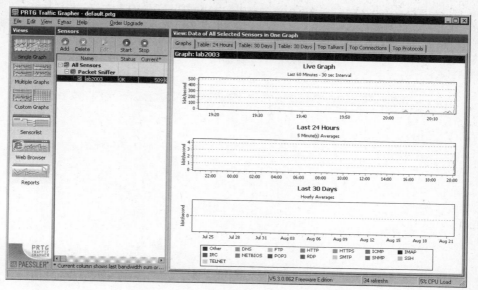

Figure 10.5 PRTG Web Interface

You should now be collecting data, which should be visible in the graphs. You might wish to customize a few features though. If you wish to disable, or modify the Web interface (and many other settings) navigate to **Extras | Options**. In the left pane, select **Web Server** as shown in Figure 10.6. Uncheck **Enable Internal Webserver** if you wish to disable the Web interface completely. If you plan on leaving the Web server enabled, you should place a check next to **Write webserver access logfile**. You should also change the **Website Access Control** to **Limited Access**. Because the sensor data and reports could contain confidential information, the default of unlimited access to the Web interface is not secure.

Figure 10.6 Options (Web Server) Screen

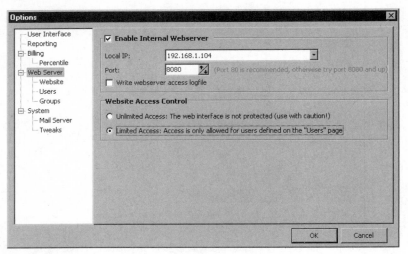

After configuring the **Web Server** options, select **Web Server | Users** in the left pane. The default configuration will be to permit the PRTG administrator only. Note that this is not the local machine's administrator account; this account is specific to PRTG. This might be all you need, but if you need to permit additional accounts click **Add** and enter the account information followed by **OK**.

Assuming you will want to send e-mail alerts, you will need to configure the mail server options within PRTG. Do this by navigating to **Extras | Options | System | Mail Server**. Enter the IP address or hostname for the SMTP server. Also enter an e-mail address, which will be the alert e-mail's "from" address. If SMTP authentication is needed you can enter the username and password in this window as well. Once you are satisfied with your selection click **OK** to accept the changes.

Now let's suppose you have some custom applications, or even just some applications you want to specifically target in the reporting. Any protocols/ports that do not have a channel defined will fall in to the "other" channel. This could be applications that were designed in-house using a non-standard protocol/port number, or a more common application that PRTG doesn't have defined yet, such as syslog. You can add to the list of "channels" and define your own by following these steps.

1. Navigate to **Extras | Channel Library**. The Channel Library window is shown in Figure 10.7

Figure 10.7 Channel Library

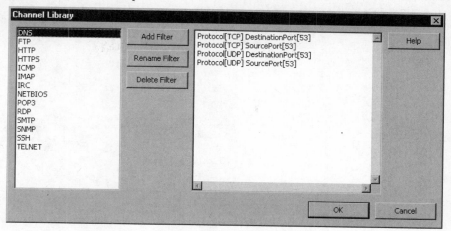

2. To add a specific graph entity for UDP-based syslog messages, for example, click **Add Filter**.

3. Enter a name for the channel, such as UDP_SYSLOG, for example, and click **OK**. The window will go back to the way it was, but the new channel name will appear in the list on the left. To edit the rules of the channel, select the channel to edit in the left pane, and then click in the right pane.

4. Enter **Protocol[UDP] DestinationPort[514]** and click **OK**. This adds the channel to the PRTG console but not to a specific sensor yet.

TIP

Remember that the "channels" use port numbers to identify an application. The reliability of this identification depends on the application using a consistent port. There is nothing stopping someone from running a Web server on TCP23 instead of port TCP80, in which case it will show up in the graphs as Telnet traffic. Other applications, like instant messengers and file sharing applications in particular, will use a wide range of ports in an attempt to find one that will get through corporate firewalls. Creating a filter to identify these based solely on port numbers will be unreliable at best.

5. Ensure that the proper sensor is selected in the **Sensors** pane and navigate to **Edit | Edit**. You'll notice the next window is titled **Edit Sensor**.

6. Select **Channels** in the left pane and click **Add** as shown in Figure 10.8.

Figure 10.8 Edit Sensor

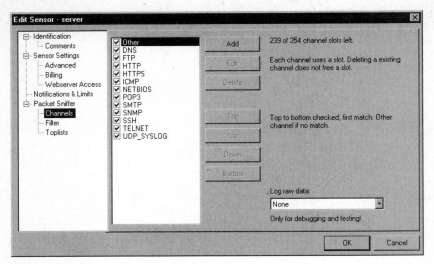

7. Select the new channel in the left pane and click **OK**.

8. Use the **Top, Up, Down, and Bottom** buttons to place the channel in the order you desire. The channel matches work much like a firewall access control list in that PRTG will stop processing the list as soon as it finds a match. If there is no match it will categorize the traffic as "Other."

9. Click **OK** again to close the **Edit Sensor** window.

You should now have a new channel displayed in the legend on the **Graph** tab. You are limited to only 254 channel definitions, though this limitation isn't likely to pose much of an issue in a smaller environment. You should now have PRTG collecting data via sniffing. You can view the graphs from the Web page or the PRTG console. You also have defined any additional ports you want PRTG to recognize as a specific application as its own "channel." The final configuration options I will discuss are that of configuring the alerts. Odds are good you won't be able to sit and stare at the graphs all day and all night, so setting up some notifications might be one way to save time and energy, not to mention make you look like you have "network ESP" to your manager. To configure notifications and limits, navigate to **Edit | Edit** and select the **Notifications & Limits** tab. This tab provides the following options:

- **Error Notification** This will be triggered only if a sensor reports an error. Be aware that if there is a connectivity outage to the sensor, the sensor cannot report the error until connectivity is restored.

- **Threshold Notification** This is used to set specific upper *or* lower limits on a per-channel basis. An *optional* time span can be configured from seconds to days. If you do not specify a time span, the event will trigger as soon as the threshold is exceeded.

- **Volume Notification** This is similar to the threshold notification, except the volume is defined as an upper threshold and a minimum time span of one hour is required.

- **Limit Line** The limit line only serves to add a line to the 30-day graph. This could be useful, for example, to set the limit to 75 megabits on a 100-megabit network (75%) as a warning of when your infrastructure is reaching capacity.

All the notifications have several options that can occur when triggered. You can choose to send an e-mail, perform an HTTP *Get* request, execute a program/batch file, and change color of the graph background for each trigger. You can also combine multiple notification methods for a single trigger, such as changing the color of the graph background *and* sending an e-mail. Given that PRTG includes a fully functional notification system, this really makes PRTG stand out among its peers as one of the best free network reporting tools available. As an example, let's assume you have a single T1 line at work (1.5 megabits per second) and you want to send an e-mail if traffic levels for FTP exceed 1 megabit per second. Follow these steps to configure the notification.

1. Select the desired sensor in the **Sensors** pane; then right-click and select **Edit**.
2. Select **Notifications & Limits** in the left pane.
3. Click the **Add Threshold Notification** button.
4. Choose a name, such as 1Mb_FTP.
5. In the **Channel** drop-down box, select **FTP**.
6. In the **Threshold** section, select **over, 1, megabit** per **second**.
7. Under **Notification** in the left pane, select **Email**.
8. Place a check next to **Send Email**.
9. In the **Address** field, enter the e-mail address of the e-mail recipient.
10. Select the e-mail template you wish to use and click **OK**.
11. In the **Edit Sensor** window, click **OK** to accept the changes.

With the capability to execute an external program based on thresholds and volumes, the possibilities are near limitless. If you wanted to integrate your PRTG alerts into a syslog infrastructure, you could use the EXE notification method to execute a batch file that uses a command-line utility to generate a syslog message. I hope that I have demonstrated what a powerful and full-featured product PRTG is. There is very little functionality that is unavailable in the free product, and a limitation of three sensors will likely pose little problem to a smaller organization. The graphing and reporting capabilities are exceptionally robust for a free product.

Configuring ntop

Ntop will run on many operating systems and while the initial setup will vary, once you have ntop installed, the configuration and usage is primarily via a Web interface, so the data will be presented in a uniform manner regardless of the underlying operating system. The ntop Web site offers multiple versions of the package for download. For Windows, they offer the source files, in which case you must compile them yourself, and they offer a pre-compiled binary distribution. The downside is that they have chosen to limit the pre-compiled version to capturing only the first 2000 packets, which makes it fairly useless to most people. This limitation does not exist in the Linux versions or the Windows source files. If compiling the source code is not a task your relish, you can download and install a precompiled version (meaning no 2000 packet capture limit!) of ntop from www.openxtra.co.uk, whose tagline is "network management for all." They have made available precompiled files for many popular packages including Ethereal, MRTG, Net-SNMP, ntop, Windump, and NMap. Follow these steps to install and configure the ntop package from OPENXTRA on a Windows host.

1. Download the installation file and execute the file.

2. Click **Next** on the welcome screen.

3. Accept the license agreement and click **Next**.

4. Enter a user name and organization if desired, choose whether the start menu entries will be made for all users or only the user who is running the Setup Wizard, and then click **Next**.

5. Choose which components to install (the defaults are recommended) and the installation target directory and click **Next**.

6. When the installation is complete, click **Finish**.

After the installation is finished, you should have a new icon in the system tray called **OPENXTRA Commander**. Double-click this icon to open the OPENXTRA Commander. If the **NTop Service** plug-in is not started, click **Start** in the **Action** column to start it. Once it is started, click the **Launch** action for the NTop plug-in, which will open your browser. If all is well, you will already be collecting some impressive data. If you have more than one *network interface card* (NIC) in the host, you may need to select the proper NIC. Do this by selecting **Admin | Configure | Startup Options** in the menu listing at the top of the page. You will notice that some menu entries have a small padlock icon in them; these are the Web pages that require a password to access. The default credentials for the XTRA package is user = admin, password = admin. The top of the page will contain a listing of your network interfaces. You *can* collect data from more than one interface if desired. If you change the selected interface, you will need to use the OPENXTRA Commander to stop and restart the Ntop Service.

The ntop FAQ can be a little hard to find; it's located at www.ntopsupport.com/faq.html. Because ntop is focused only on displaying data in a format that is easy to drill down into, there is very little to configure once you have it working properly. There is a host of information on the various screens. Any of the options under Summary can be useful. If you navigate to **IP | Local | Ports Used** you will see a screen similar to the one shown in Figure 10.9. This is just one of the many screens full of data that ntop provides; to include screen prints of all the available graphs and tables would require an inordinate number of pages.

Many of the elements on the ntop pages are actually hyperlinked to additional pages so that you can drill down and obtain more and more detailed information. Despite ntop's lack of native support for alarms and other active actions, you can perform several useful functions with a little customization. For example, the OPENXTRA Commander can be used to provide some handy links. By adding an appropriately configured .INI file to \OPENXTRA\Common\Plugins\, you can add entries to the Commander menu. For example, the following contents placed in an INI file would open Notepad.

```
[APPLICATION]
NAME=Notepad
DESCRIPTION=Launch notepad
ACTIONDESCRIPTION=Start
VERSION=1.0.0
COPYRIGHT=ESS
COMMAND=notepad
COMMANDARG=
```

Figure 10.9 ntop IP Ports Used

TCP/UDP: Local Protocol Usage

Reporting on actual traffic for 4 host(s) on 5 service port(s)

Service		Clients	Servers
domain	53	• server ⚑	
http	80	• server ⚑	
netbios-ns	137	• server ⚑ • a-desk • 192.168.1.1 ⇔⚑ • 192.168.1.111	• server ⚑ • a-desk • 192.168.1.1 ⇔⚑ • 192.168.1.111
netbios-dgm	138	• a-desk • 192.168.1.111	• a-desk • 192.168.1.111
netbios-ssn	139	• 192.168.1.111	• a-desk

The color of the host link indicates how recently the host was FIRST seen

0 to 5 minutes   5 to 15 minutes   15 to 30 minutes   30 to 60 minutes   60+ minutes

If you change the plug-in options, you will need to navigate to **View | Plug-ins | Reload Plug-ins** before your changes will take effect. There are also a few perl scripts available in \OPENXTRA\NTopWin32\www\perl\. Any of these can be executed with **perl <scriptname>** from the command line. Below is a short summary of the provided perl scripts.

- **dumpFlat.pl** This returns a flat listing of all the host data in ntop for the current time slice in a perl-like format, and loops every minute (by default) generating current data. See below for usage information.

- **mapper.pl** This script will use a host IP address to return a GIF flag of their location. This is what is used to generate the flag labels in various reports within ntop.

- **remoteClient.pl** This returns a perl-like listing of all the host data in ntop for the current time slice. See below for usage information.

Having the ability to pull this raw data opens up a host of possibilities. As a simple example, let's suppose you wanted to produce a listing of all the hostnames that ntop currently knew about.

Dumpflat.pl is configured by default to loop and dump the output on one-minute intervals. Remoteclient.pl is configured for a perl-like output, which isn't conducive to parsing in a DOS window. Copy the remoteClient.pl and rename it to raw.pl. Edit raw.pl and find the line that says

```
$URL = "http://".$ntopHost.":".$ntopPort."/dumpData.html?language=perl";
```

and change it to read

```
$URL = "http://".$ntopHost.":".$ntopPort."/dumpData.html?language=text";
```

Now executing **perl raw.pl** will produce the raw data held in memory by ntop. This output is easily parsable because each host it knows about has all of its data on one line. Now the following command would parse the output from raw.pl and print the fourth field (the hostname) to the screen for each line.

```
FOR /F "tokens=1-4 delims=|" %a in ('perl raw.pl') do @echo %d
```

You could also use find.exe (perl raw.pl | find "192.168.1.99") to pull out a line of data containing a known hostname or IP address. Once you have the raw data at your disposal you can perform a wide variety of parsing options on it.

In all likelihood, you will need to alter the list of defined port numbers. This serves two purposes in that it gives you greater insight into the applications being used on the network and reduces the amount of data that gets lumped into "other." Changes to the port list will affect the output of all screens under the **IP** menu option. The "create your own custom port definitions" follow these steps.

1. Create an application port list file in the **\OPENXTRA\NTopWin32\etc** directory, such as **portlist.txt**.

2. Enter the applications you wish to be displayed in portlist.txt file. The following list can be placed in the portlist.txt. The format is *name that will appear in ntop=port or portname, as defined by the OS, or a port range*. The first three sections are what ntop will use if no portlist file is specified.

```
## Default ntop portlist ##
FTP=ftp|ftp-data
HTTP=http|www|https|3128
DNS=name|domain
Telnet=telnet|login
NBios-IP=netbios-ns|netbios-dgm|netbios-ssn
Mail=pop-2|pop-3|pop3|kpop|smtp|imap|imap2
DHCP-BOOTP=67-68
SNMP=snmp|snmp-trap
NNTP=nntp
NFS=mount|pcnfs|bwnfs|nfsd|nfsd-status
X11=6000-6010
SSH=22


## Default ntop Peer-to-Peer portlist ##
```

```
Gnutella=6346|6347|6348
Kazaa=1214
WinMX=6699|7730
DirectConnect=0          Dummy port as this is a pure P2P protocol
eDonkey=4661-4665


## Default ntop Instant Messenger ports ##
Messenger=1863|5000|5001|5190-5193


## Extra ports ##
Syslog=514
PCAnywhere=5631
SQL=1433
```

TIP

The Web page will display the application names in the same order as they are defined in the portlist.txt file. This means you should list the port definitions you want to see first earlier in the portlist file to keep from having to scroll the Web page to see them.

3. After you have your portlist file created, navigate to **Admin | Configure | Startup Options**.

4. Select the **IP Preferences** hyperlink.

5. In the field **TCP/UDP Protocols To Monitor**, specify the full path to the portlist.txt file.

6. Stop and restart the ntop process for the changes to take effect.

You can restrict additional ntop pages. If you want a person to have to supply the user name and password to view *any* ntop pages, you can configure this by navigating to **Admin | Configure | Protect URLs**. Click **Add URL** at the bottom and then click the **Add URL** button without filling anything into the field. This will password protect all ntop pages.

Ntop stores all of its active data in RAM, so if the system is reset, you lose all your data. There is a mechanism to store the data to disk. Be forewarned that logging all the data to disk can consume a large amount of disk space, so it will require careful monitoring. Ntop stores the data in RRD files (round-robin database). You can configure the RRD plug-in by navigating to **Plugins | Round-Robin Databases | Describe**. The active column should say Yes; if it says No, click **No** to toggle it to active. To help you decide which reporting tools to focus your energies on, Table 10.1 highlights the various features of the utilities we discussed.

Table 10.1 Reporting Tool Features

Reporting Utility Features			
	MRTG	MZL & Novatech TrafficStatistics	PRTG	ntop
SNMP	✓		✓	
Sniffing		✓	✓	✓
Netflow			✓	✓
Linux	✓			✓
Windows	✓	✓	✓	✓
Limitations	Only two lines per graph	No Report Customization	3 Sensor Limit	Data only
Notes	Supported on Netware			

Enabling SNMP On Windows Hosts

All that's a lot to digest, so let's enable the SNMP agent on a Windows system and see what it can do for us. To enable the SNMP agent on Windows XP, follow these steps.

1. Navigate to Start | Settings | Control Panel.

2. Open **Add or Remove Programs**

3. Select **Add/Remote Windows Components** on the left side of the window.

4. Highlight **Management and Monitoring Tools**, but do not check it.

5. Click **Details**.

6. Place a check next to **Simple Network Management Protocol** and click **OK**.

7. Click **Next** and then click **Finish**

Next you need to configure some specific SNMP settings on the Windows host. Do this by following these steps.

1. Click **Start | Run** and enter **services.msc** to open the services snap-in.

2. Double-click the **SNMP Service** entry in the right pane.

3. Select the **Agent** tab.

4. Enter the **Contact** information and the **Location** information. These are used as identifiers for the system when viewed from the management console.

5. Open your MMC.

6. Select **Computer Management** in the left pane.

7. Expand this to **Computer Management | Services and Applications | Services**.

8. In the **Service** section, place a check next to the types of SNMP MIBs you want to use.

9. Select the **Traps** tab.

10. In the **Community name** drop-down list, enter a community name, also called a *community string*, and then click **Add to list**. A community string is very much like a password and serves to limit who can use SNMP on a given device.

11. In the **Trap Destinations** section, click **Add** and enter the system you want to send traps to. This would be the SNMP management console. To use a previous example, this could be the IP address of the system running PRTG Traffic Grapher.

12. Select the **Security** tab.

13. Highlight the default community name of **public** and click **Remove**. If you leave public as a READ ONLY community, anyone will be able to read the SNMP data of your system. The default on most systems is "public" with read-only access and "private" with full control. As is always the case, you don't want to use the defaults when it comes to passwords.

14. Click **Add** and enter a **Read Only Community Name**, and click **Add** again.

15. Repeat this process and add a community name with read/write access.

16. Select the radio button next to **Accept SNMP packets from these hosts** and click **Add**.

17. Enter an IP address or host name and click **Add**. In this example I entered the same IP as my PRTG management console.

18. Click **Apply** and **OK**.

Your Windows system is now ready to be managed using SNMP; all you need is a management console. In this case we can add it as an additional sensor to our PRTG system (remember the freeware version has a limit of three sensors). To add the Windows host to your PRTG console, follow these steps.

1. Open the PRTG application.

2. In the **Sensors** pane, highlight **All Sensors**.

3. Right-click and select **Add Sensor**. This will start the Add Sensor Wizard.

4. Click **Next**.

5. Select **SNMP** as your data acquisition type and click **Next**.

6. The default selection of **Standard Traffic Sensor** will enable you to see how much bandwidth is being used by the Windows system inbound and outbound. The **SNMP Helper Sensor** will enable you to view some more-detailed Windows-specific counters. For basic monitoring select **Standard Traffic Sensor** and click **Next**.

7. In the **Device Selection window**, enter a name for the sensor and the IP address. Choose your SNMP version (choose the highest one your device will support). Enter the community string to use for that sensor, and then click **Next**. It will connect to the sensor and enable you to select which interface to monitor.

8. Place a check next to the appropriate interface.

9. Choose which values to monitor (Bandwidth is the default) and click **Next**.

10. This final screen enables you to choose a group for the sensor listing and configure the scanning interval. The defaults are probably okay, so simply click **Finish**.

You should see a new set of graphs, with bandwidth in and bandwidth out, for the newly added sensor. To add a sensor that uses the SNMP helper freeware, the steps are mostly the same. The only significant difference is that you need to run the Paessler SNMP Helper Setup.exe file on the system to be monitored. This setup file can be found in the same directory that PRTG was installed in. The setup file has no real configuration options and is very easy to install.

After installing the SNMP helper, proceed with adding the sensor following the steps above, with the following changes. When you select the type of SNMP to use, simply select **SNMP Helper Sensor**, choose the **SNMP Helper Freeware** in the drop-down box, and then click **Next**. The PRTG console will connect to the agent and present you with a list of all the possible values you can monitor. After making your selections, click **Next**.

Enabling SNMP on Linux Hosts

If you want to collect data using SNMP from a Linux host, the first step is to see if the SNMP daemon (snmpd) is already installed. You can enter *chkconfig —list snmpd*, which will list the snmp daemon *if* it is installed, and indicate which run levels it is configured to start in. If the daemon is not installed, it can be installed using whatever method is appropriate for your distribution. On Fedora Core 5, for example, all it takes is *yum install net-snmp*. The daemons and some utilities are included in the net-snmp package. There is also the *net-snmp-utils* package, which includes utilities aimed more at using SNMP, such as MIB browsers and such, but does not include the daemon.

After you have snmpd installed, it needs to be configured. We will discuss two ways to configure snmpd. The current version of the daemon is very robust, which has the side effect of including a very complicated configuration file located at /etc/snmp/snmpd.conf. The simplest way to get SNMP up and running to just collect data, is to save the sample snmpd.conf file under a new name and create your own. The new snmpd.conf can contain only the single line *rocommunity labcommunitystring*. In this example, the read-only community string would be set to *labcommunitystring*. Obviously, you should select a secure password of your own. This type of configuration file is quick and easy but not overly secure.

You could also use the netfilter firewall and/or tcpwrappers to restrict SNMP access based on the IP address of the communicating system. Another option is to use the access control built into the SNMP daemon. To configure the snmpd access control, you will need to edit the snmpd.conf file. Granting access to the SNMP MIB requires four basic steps, which are all done in the configuration file. The example below includes a variety of configuration settings to hopefully provide a good idea of the possibilities. Add the following lines to the configuration file.

```
##       sec.name    source          community
## -------------------------------------------------------
com2sec  local       localhost       snmplocalstring
com2sec  internal    10.0.0.0/8      snmpcommunitystring
com2sec  admin_net   192.168.1.0/24  snmpadminstring
```

These lines serve to map a *community name* to a *security name*, thus the com2sec directive. The security name is just a name to use to reference the access you are granting. You can use whatever name you like. The source is the hosts that will use that access profile. You can also use a source of *default*, which will mean any IP address. The community is the community string to be used for that access. Note that there is no differentiation made between a read-only community string and a read-write community string. This is because the access that the security name will have will be defined later in the configuration file.

```
##         Access.group.name    sec.model         sec.name
## --------------------------------------------------------
group      Full_Group           v1                local
group      RO_Group             v2c               internal
group      Full_Group           any               admin_net
```

The next section maps a *security name* into a *group name* using the *group* directive. In this case, we mapped both the local security name and the admin_net security name to the same group (Full_Group). The sec.model determines which version of SNMP (1 or 2) will be used/allowed. Using version 3 requires a different configuration altogether.

```
##    MIB.view.name    incl/excl  MIB.subtree      mask
## --------------------------------------------------------
view all-mibs          included    .1
view limited           included    .1.3.6.1.2.1.2
```

This section defines a *view*, which basically defines a portion of the MIB tree. The *all-mibs* view includes the entire MIB tree, while the *limited* view includes only the .1.3.6.1.2.1.2 section, which are the network interfaces and related metrics. You can configure a given view's MIB subtree to be *included* or *excluded*. By excluding, you can omit certain sensitive portions of the MIB tree. You can use the MIB tree name instead of the number if desired. In the example used above, you could use *included .1.3.6.1.2.1.2* or you could instead use this command: *included .iso.org.dod.internet.mgmt.mib-2.interfaces*. The mask is an *optional* bit mask on the MIB tree that specifies which bits to match for the indicated access. The default (without the mask) is to match only the bits that are indicated in the view. You would most commonly use the mask to match a particular row or rows in a table. So in this example, the all-mibs view has access to .1 and everything under it.

```
##  MIB.group.name context sec.model sec.level prefix read    write notif
## ----------------------------------------------------------------------
access  Full_Group ""        any       noauth    0      all-mibs none  none
access  RO_Group   ""        any       noauth    0      limited  none  none
```

The final section is where you define access for a *group name* to a *view*. The context is optional and *no context*, "" is the default. For SNMP v1 or v2, the sec.level needs to be *noauth*. Under the read and write column, you define the view. The notify column is where you would specify the capability to send traps, except the notify view is not currently implemented.

After making your changes, you will need to restart the snmpd for the changes to take effect. So what does all this accomplish? The MIB is accessible form the localhost using the snmplocalstring as the community string, which will provide read access to the entire MIOB tree. Users from the 10.0.0.0/8 networks, which are assumed to be the bulk of the user base, can access the MIB using the snmpcommunitystring community string, and they will have read-only access to the network interface subtree only. Hosts on the 192.168.1.0/24 subnet, a network management subnet for example, can use the snmpadminstring community string to gain read-only access to the entire MIB tree.

After all this configuring you might be wondering what the difference is between one version of SNMP and another. As the protocol has matured, it has gone through several changes, the majority of which revolve around security. The basic differences between one version and another are highlighted for your reference.

- **SNMP v1** Included only basic functionality and sent SNMP data using clear text.

- **SNMP v2** Mostly introduced security features, including a two new branches of the MIB tree, 1.3.6.1.5 (security) and 1.3.6.1.6 (SNMPv2). Introduced the *GetBulk* operation, used for requesting large amounts of data in a single request. SNMP v2 also sends information using clear text.

- **SNMPv3** Introduced the *digest authentication protocol*, which is used for data *integrity*, ensuring that the message that was sent is the same one that is received using MD5. Introduced the *symmetric privacy protocol* to ensure data *confidentiality* using Data Encryption Standard (DES) encryption. Note that DES is not generally considered secure by modern standards and was replaced with triple DES (3DES), and, more recently, with *Advanced Encryption Standard* (AES). Introduced the *User-based Security Model* (USM) and the *View-based Access Control Model* (VACM).

Troubleshooting Network Problems from the Command Line

Inevitably, sooner or later, something will go wrong on your network. In most cases you can troubleshoot the problem using standard resources such as the error message and syslog logs. There will be those rare times, however, where the standard information sources just aren't giving you enough information to really know what is going on. In those cases, a network sniffer may be your only option. A sniffer will basically look at all the traffic at the network layer in its raw form and collect it. This means you can see the data the way your network card sees it, which is very different from the final product looks to the application. Different sniffers provide varying levels of sophistication and features. In Chapters 7, 8, and 9 we covered Wireshark, which is the most popular open source sniffer with a graphical user interface (GUI).

The primary difference between a commercial sniffer and a free one will be in remote management, and in some cases advanced analysis options. In many cases the sniffer will require special drivers to be installed in order to sniff traffic. The sniffer's role is mostly to simply display the data it collects. It is up to the human user to interpret the data and determine what it means in the big picture.

Using a Command-Line Sniffer

A command-line sniffer has less to process and will place less of a load on the system you are running it on. Sometimes you might be in a situation where you only have console (command-line) access and can't use a GUI tool. At these times a command-line sniffer might be able to provide the sneak peek into the network traffic you're looking for. I will briefly explain the use of a few command-line sniffers. One of them will require the WinPcap drivers, the other does not if you are using it on a Windows 2000 or newer operating system, and the last is a Linux command-line sniffer.

Windump

Many Linux systems have tcpdump installed by default. Because tcpdump is so common (at least on non-Windows systems), it has been ported to Windows and is called WinDump. WinDump requires WinPcap in order to work. WinDump can be downloaded from www.winpcap.org/windump/install/. There is no setup file; the .EXE you download is the entire package. Simply download it and place the file in a directory of your choosing. The manual for WinDump is pretty much the same as for tcpdump, and is located at www.winpcap.org/windump/docs/manual.htm. Although there are far too many options to explain them all in detail, here are a few that will get you started.

Windump −*D* lists the interfaces WinDump can see to capture on. *Windump* −*i 2* listens on interface number 2. You could restrict the output to show traffic only to or from the host named lab2003 by entering *windump* −*i 2 host lab2003*. Although the command-line syntax is relatively intuitive, there are a lot of options. The manual is very good, with some useful examples at the bottom. If we wanted to see traffic to or from host lab2003, with a source of destination port of 23 (used for Telnet), we could enter *windump* −*I 2* −*host lab2003 and tcp port 23*. I opened a Telnet session with lab2003 and the partial output is shown below in Figure 10.15. Note: I removed the timestamps so that every line would not wrap to the next line.

Figure 10.10 Windump of Telnet Session

```
windump: listening on \Device\NPF_{C428C1BF-C15A-460B-90D6-3A6F5DF68F22}
IP server.RedHat.2714 > LAB2003.23: S 639728410:639728410(0) win 16384 <mss
1460,nop,nop,sackOK>
IP LAB2003.23 > server.RedHat.2714: S 1106948603:1106948603(0) ack 639728411 win
16384 <mss 1460,nop,nop,sackOK>
IP server.RedHat.2714 > LAB2003.23: . ack 1 win 17520
IP LAB2003.23 > server.RedHat.2714: P 1:22(21) ack 1 win 17520
IP server.RedHat.2714 > LAB2003.23: P 1:4(3) ack 22 win 17499
IP LAB2003.23 > server.RedHat.2714: P 22:30(8) ack 4 win 17517
IP server.RedHat.2714 > LAB2003.23: P 4:28(24) ack 30 win 17491
IP LAB2003.23 > server.RedHat.2714: P 30:65(35) ack 28 win 17493
IP server.RedHat.2714 > LAB2003.23: P 28:31(3) ack 65 win 17456
IP LAB2003.23 > server.RedHat.2714: . ack 31 win 17490
IP server.RedHat.2714 > LAB2003.23: P 31:88(57) ack 65 win 17456
```

```
IP LAB2003.23 > server.RedHat.2714: P 65:228(163) ack 88 win 17433

IP server.RedHat.2714 > LAB2003.23: P 88:133(45) ack 228 win 17293

IP LAB2003.23 > server.RedHat.2714: . ack 133 win 17388

IP server.RedHat.2714 > LAB2003.23: P 133:319(186) ack 228 win 17293

IP LAB2003.23 > server.RedHat.2714: P 228:419(191) ack 319 win 17202

IP server.RedHat.2714 > LAB2003.23: . ack 419 win 17102

IP server.RedHat.2714 > LAB2003.23: P 319:320(1) ack 419 win 17102
```

One obvious thing you will notice is that by default WinDump shows only the high-level header information, not any of the packet data. To display this data, you will need to use the −*X* or −*XX* switch. By default, WinDump will display only a certain amount of the data portion of the packet; this is determined by the "snap length." This is set using the −*s* option on the command line and will default to 68 bytes if it is not set manually. WinDump's extensive filtering options make it a good tool for those times when you need very specific information. You can restrict the output using a number of parameters and end up with a very specific capture of the network traffic.

ngSniff

ngSniff is a little less robust than WinDump/tcpdump, but can be very handy to have in your network toolkit. The primary asset of ngSniff is that if you are using Windows 2000, Windows XP, or Windows Server 2003, you don't need to install any drivers to start capturing traffic. This makes it a much more attractive candidate when you need some quick insight into what is occurring on the network but don't want to run any setup programs or alter the drivers. If you type *ngSniff* with no options, it will show you the help screen and all the options ngSniff accepts. *ngSniff −list-interfaces* will list the available interfaces. To limit sniffing to only traffic to or from lab2003, you can enter *ngSniff −interface 0 −only-host lab2003*. A sample capture of an SNMP message from 192.168.1.104 to 192.168.1.99 is shown below.

```
IP HEADER 192.168.1.104 -> 192.168.1.99

-----------------------------------------

 IP->version: 4

 IP->ihl: 5

 IP->tos: 0

 IP->tot_len: 77

 IP->id: 20699

 IP->frag_off: 0

 IP->ttl: 128

 IP->protocol: 17

 IP->checksum: 13275


UDP HEADER

----------

 UDP->sport: 4337
```

```
UDP->dport: 161
UDP->ulen: 57
UDP->checksum: 48040


----- Begin of data dump -----
30 2f 02 01 00 04 09 74 65 73 74 77 72 69 74 65    0/.....testwrite
a0 1f 02 03 00 ee 18 02 01 00 02 01 00 30 12 30    .............0.0
10 06 0c 2b 06 01 04 01 cb 00 01 01 02 03 00 05    ...+...........
00                                                 .
----- End of data dump -----
```

With the capability to quickly have a sniffer up without requiring any installation, ngSniff should have a place in your networking toolkit. I have seen it used on production systems where installing anything would have not been desirable during business hours, but we could run ngSniff from a USB pen drive and see what was happening with the application and resolve the issue very quickly. If you would like a basic GUI sniffer that does not require any installation (on Windows 2000 or newer systems), you can also try SmartSniff from www.nirsoft.net/utils/smsniff.html or IP Sniffer (part of IP Tools package) from http://erwan.l.free.fr/.

Tcpdump

Tcpdump is native to Linux and does not run on Windows systems. Tcpdump is installed by default on a large number of Linux/UNIX systems. Because tcpdump is so widely used, there is a wealth of support information and articles on the Internet on how to use tcpdump. The syntax and usage is nearly identical to that of WinDump, which we have already discussed, so what I will do here is demonstrate how to install tcpdump on a Linux system if you find it isn't already installed.

In order to install the tcpdump package, obtain or locate the appropriate package file for your distribution. Different distributions may have packages specific to their configuration, or a given distribution may not support the newest version of a piece of software. Then enter the following command to install tcpdump (for this example it is version 3.9.4-1):

```
rpm -i tcpdump-3.9.4-1.i586.rpm
```

If the installation is successful, you should see output similar to the following:

```
Preparing...            ########################################### [100%]
   1: tcpdump-3.9.4-1    ########################################### [100%]
```

To uninstall the package you must use the package name, which is not the same as the name of the RPM file. To uninstall tcpdump 3.9.4-1, enter the following command, using the *-e* switch for *erase*:

```
rpm -e tcpdump-3.9.4-1
```

We hope that by this point you have some idea of the troubleshooting power a sniffer can provide. You might wonder why you wouldn't just put Wireshark on every system in case a troubleshooting issue comes up. Consider that if a hacker manages to gain access to one of your systems; a network sniffer can be an indispensable information-gathering tool for the hacker. If you provide a pre-installed and configured sniffer for the hacker to use, you might make the hacker's job a lot easier. On top of that, installing additional software on production systems is generally something you want to minimize if at all possible. Although the WinPcap driver install has been very dependable for a while now (which wasn't always the case), installing network drivers always carries the risk of disrupting network communications if something goes wrong. These are two very compelling reasons for using ngSniff or a comparable GUI-based sniffer that does not need to be installed on the system. In most cases these sniffers that use Windows raw sockets can be run from a pen drive or from a CD-ROM, or even run from a mapped network drive. Table 10.2 compares the features of four different sniffers.

Table 10.2 Sniffer Features

Sniffer Features				
	Wireshark	**Windump**	**TCPDump**	**NGSniff**
GUI Interface	✓			
Command Line	✓	✓	✓	✓
Special Drivers	✓	✓		
Windows	✓	✓		✓
Linux	✓		✓	
Notes	Most analysis options			No Install Needed

Additional Troubleshooting Tools

Because there are so many interdependencies that are involved in making a network-based application work properly, there is no single tool to isolate and identify problems. Expensive suites of software and data collection probes attempt to make the process as automated as possible, but in most cases the key tool is the human operator. Based on the symptoms of the problem, or lacking a specific symptom, starting at the bottom and working your way up, the human performing the troubleshooting has to systematically use process of elimination to try to identify the problematic component, and then take steps to remedy the issue. In most cases you will not need more than the basic troubleshooting tools available with any modern operating system, such as ping, traceroute, and various commands specific to the operating system. On some occasions, some specialized software can make the task of troubleshooting much easier. A couple of my favorites are explained here.

Netcat

Netcat has often been described as the "Swiss army knife" of troubleshooting tools. This is because its function is so elegantly simple that it has many uses. In essence, it establishes a communications session between two systems. You can enter *nc −l −p 2222* to tell system one to listen on port 2222. On system two, the command *nc 192.168.1.10 2222* would connect to system 1 (assuming the IP address is 192.168.1.10) on port 2222. After the connection is established, anything typed at the console of either system is sent to the stdout of the other system. Although both ends of the session can be the netcat executable, they don't have to be. In addition to providing a command line based method for transferring data, netcat enables you to test connectivity over arbitrary ports. By entering *nc <IP Address> 23*, you can connect to a system to verify that Telnet is listening and available. In fact, if you use the –*t* switch, netcat will negotiate the Telnet specifics. Although Telnet is often used in exactly the same way to test connectivity to arbitrary ports (telnet <IP> <port>), netcat is more versatile in that it enables you to connect via TCP (the default) or UDP.

There are additional functions netcat offers to aid the network troubleshooter. Netcat can be configured to create a hex dump of the session (via the –*o file* option). It can also be configured to execute a program when a connection is made (potentially unsafe if not used carefully), or to restart itself in listen mode after a session is terminated. Netcat can be downloaded from http://netcat.sourceforge.net/; the last update was in January of 2004. A Windows version (1.1) can be downloaded from www.vulnwatch.org/netcat/. Finally, a derivative project that adds twofish encryption is known as cryptcat and is available from http://farm9.org/Cryptcat/, with versions for both Linux and Windows. There is also a very similar utility called socat, which is being actively developed. Socat is very close to netcat in function but features additional capabilities. Socat can be downloaded from www.dest-unreach.org/socat/.

Tracetcp

Oftentimes, the ability to know the path that network traffic is traversing is key to troubleshooting connectivity issues. In most cases you can determine this by using the traceroute utility (tracert on Windows systems). When you execute the traceroute command ICMP (Internet Control Message Protocol) is used to transmit packets to the destination with a Time to Live (TTL) value of 1, and this increases for each hop. The way it works when everything goes smoothly, is each hop has to reduce the TTL by one; and when it becomes zero the packet is dropped and a message is sent to the receiver. The problem that often arises is that ICMP is often partially or completely filtered out by intervening routers of firewalls. In this case, you need a way to accomplish the same thing with a protocol that has a higher chance of success.

In these cases, a TCP traceroute can be a life saver. It will effectively do the same thing, by manipulating the TTL values, but it uses a TCP packet and allows a user-configurable port, which almost every firewall and router will allow if it is a well-chosen port. As an example, if you picked a popular Web site and tried a trace route, you may get several instances of "request timed out," which indicates that the hop is not responding. In most cases this means that ICMP is being filtered by a firewall. If you instead use a TCP-based traceroute utility and specify a destination port of 80, you may get better results. A good TCP-based traceroute utility for Windows is tracetcp from http://tracetcp.sourceforge.net/. For Linux, a very robust utility is LFT, which stands for "layer four traceroute," which can be downloaded from http://pwhois.org/lft/.

Netstat

You can use the netstat utility on Windows or Linux to see a list of network connections. The –*l* option (on Linux) will list only the listening ports for that system. On Windows, the same functionality is provided by using the –*a* option (-*a* works on Linux as well) to list all connections. From a troubleshooting perspective, there may be times when you want to verify that a service is listening on the proper port, or identify what service is listening on a given port. While older versions of netstat cannot show you this, modern Windows systems provide the −b option, which will list the process associated with a given listening port.

```
C:\>netstat -a -b

Active Connections

  Proto  Local Address        Foreign Address      State         PID
  TCP    server:4122          localhost:4123       ESTABLISHED   1988
  [firefox.exe]
```

If you are running an older version of Windows, or running Linux, there are utilities to show this. For the command line on Windows NT, XP, or 2000, fport from www.foundstone.com/resources/proddesc/fport.htm is very handy. The abbreviated output is shown here.

```
I:\Internet\fport>fport
FPort v2.0 - TCP/IP Process to Port Mapper
Copyright 2000 by Foundstone, Inc.
http://www.foundstone.com

Pid   Process         Port  Proto Path
1988  firefox     ->  4123  TCP   I:\Internet\Firefox\firefox.exe
```

For a Windows GUI, tcpview is very powerful and can be downloaded from Microsoft at www.microsoft.com/technet/sysinternals/utilities/TcpView.mspx. Tcpview also has a command-line version called tcpvcon. In the Linux world, you can see which processes are using which ports with the lsof (list open files) utility. Although the utility can be rather complex, a quick and simple way is:

```
lsof | grep LISTEN
syslog-ng 1555     root      6u     IPv4     4463        TCP *:7140 (LISTEN)
```

This will indicate that the syslog-ng process is listening for inbound connections on TCP port 7140.

Summary

As you can see, there are many powerful and free solutions for network reporting and troubleshooting available. Never underestimate the power of a visual aid, be it a graph, a pie chart, or whatever. A simple graph can get the point across far more quickly than a page full of numbers. Armed with the relevant data presented in an easy-to-understand format you can demonstrate the need for more Internet bandwidth. You could also demonstrate how the use of Internet streaming music is consuming all the bandwidth, and that with a policy change, a bandwidth upgrade *is not* needed. Depending on your specific policies, you could generate reports for whichever protocols are of interest to you. You could run a sniffer to try to collect and graph statistics on your own, but having free software that will do it for you is a real time saver. Far and away I would recommend PRTG and ntop as the best free solutions for tracking usage statistics.

If, despite your best efforts, problems do arise, there are powerful and free packet sniffing solutions available to help you troubleshoot problems at the network level. Once you have an understanding of the merits of the different products, you can select a sniffing tool that is right for the job. You can quickly see what is happening at the network packet level, and in some cases identify problems that would be virtually impossible to troubleshoot any other way.

Solutions Fast Track

Reporting on Bandwidth Usage and Other Metrics

☑ Remember that with any data collection system (that is, sensor), placement is key to ensure that the system can see the proper data to analyze.

☑ The type of data collection methods (sniffing, NetFlow, SNMP) you have available to you will have a huge impact on collector placement and on which tools you use.

☑ SNMP can be enabled on almost any modern operating system and collect and monitor assorted usage data, including product-specific metrics.

Collecting Data for Analysis

☑ Collecting data via sniffing will require that the collector sit inline with the traffic to be analyzed.

☑ Collecting data via SNMP enables you to place the collector independently from the devices to be monitored; however, you will only be able to gather data that is specifically supported by the sensor's MIB.

☑ Remember that SNMP creates its own network traffic, thus using up bandwidth.

☑ NetFlow is more focused than sniffing or SNMP, providing information focused on traffic flows and session information. The downside is that NetFlow is not supported on all devices.

Understanding SNMP

☑ Different devices often support different versions of SNMP, and each version has different security capabilities. These considerations could be important depending on how you plan to implement an SNMP infrastructure. SNMP version 3 is the preferred (i.e. most secure) version to use.

Troubleshooting Network Problems

☑ One of your first steps is to determine which sniffer is appropriate for the task. Consider factors such as: Do you need a GUI? How much filtering will you need to do? Is installing a driver acceptable or desirable?

☑ There is no shortcut to becoming skilled at interpreting the results of a packet capture. It requires in-depth knowledge of the underlying network protocols, but with some basic understanding you can often find a packet sniffer useful in troubleshooting problems.

Frequently Asked Questions

The following Frequently Asked Questions, answered by the authors of this book, are designed to both measure your understanding of the concepts presented in this chapter and to assist you with real-life implementation of these concepts. To have your questions about this chapter answered by the author, browse to **www. syngress.com/solutions** and click on the **"Ask the Author"** form.

Q: Is there any advantage to using tcpdump over WinDump or vice versa?

A: Not much, the syntax is almost identical, so functionally, it probably doesn't matter. The only factor that would tip the scales in favor of one or the other would be that if you are sniffing a very high-volume network, the Linux system using tcpdump will likely have better performance than a Windows system using WinDump, so you would run less risk of dropping packets. If speed isn't an issue, go with whichever underlying operating system you are most comfortable with.

Q: How do I make ntop do "x"?

A: For starters, do some searching online; odds are good there is documentation out there already. There are also several mailing lists available to discuss ntop and its use. For general ntop use, refer to http://listmanager.unipi.it/mailman/listinfo/ntop. For development issues, refer to http://list-manager.unipi.it/mailman/listinfo/ntop-dev. Because ntop uses perl on the back end, with a little perl programming you can make it do almost anything you want, and much like a batch file, perl has the capability to call external programs. This means you could easily create a script to regularly check the ntop data and execute a certain program (like send a syslog message or e-mail) when certain thresholds are crossed.

Q: The graphs from MRTG seem very basic, is there any way to modify their appearance?

A: You can edit some of the images used to create the graphs. The most popular method is to configure MRTG to use RRDtool (which stands for Round Robin Database tool) from http://oss.oetiker.ch/rrdtool/. This will enable the data collected by MRTG to be stored more efficiently. MRTG supports RRDtool with little additional configuration. A document on configuring MRTG to work with RRDtool can be found at http://oss.oetiker.ch/mrtg/doc/mrtg-rrd.en.html. After you have your data in the RRD database, you can use one of the other third-party scripts to generate the HTML graphs, such as the *14all* script from http://my14all.sourceforge.net/.

## Chapter 11

Wireless Monitoring and Intrusion Detection

Solutions in this chapter:

- **Designing for Detection**
- **Defensive Monitoring Considerations**
- **Intrusion Detection Strategies**
- **Conducting Vulnerability Assessments**
- **Incident Response and Handling**
- **Conducting Site Surveys for Rogue Access Points**

- ☑ Summary
- ☑ Solutions Fast Track
- ☑ Frequently Asked Questions

Introduction

Network monitoring and intrusion detection have become an integral part of network security. The monitoring of your network becomes even more important when introducing wireless access, because you have added a new, openly available entry point into your network. Security guards patrol your building at night. Even a small business, if intent on retaining control of its assets, has some form of security system in place—as should your network. Monitoring and intrusion detection are your security patrol, and become the eyes and ears of your network, alerting you to potential vulnerabilities, and intrusion attempts. Designing secure wireless networks will rely on many of the standard security tools and techniques but will also utilize some new tools.

In this chapter, you'll learn about the planning and deployment issues that must be addressed early on in order to make monitoring and intrusion detection most effective when the system is fully operational.

You'll also learn how to take advantage of current intrusion principles, tools, and techniques in order to maximize security of your wireless network. Specialized wireless tools such as NetStumbler and AirSnort will also be used to provide a better overall picture of your wireless security.

Intrusion Prevention (IP) systems may offer an additional layer to detection. We'll discuss the pros and cons of their use, and their relationship to conventional intrusion detection. You'll also learn how to respond to incidents and intrusions on a wireless network, as well as conduct site surveys to identify the existence of rogue Access Points (APs).

Designing for Detection

In this section, we will discuss how to design a wireless network with an emphasis on monitoring, focusing on the choice of equipment, physical layout and radio interference. The decision-making involved in the design, deployment, and installation of a wireless local area network (WLAN), combined with the choice of product vendor, can play a key role in later efforts to monitor the network for intrusions. *Designing for detection* occurs when you build a network with monitoring and intrusion detection principles in mind from the start. For example, when a bank is built, many of the security features, such as the vault security modules, closed circuit cameras, and the alarm are part of the initial design. Retrofitting these into a building would be much more expensive and difficult than including them in the beginning. The same idea is true with a network. Designing your network for detection, having made the decisions about monitoring strategies and the infrastructure to support them, will save you time and money in the long run.

Knowledge of your building's layout and physical obstacles will strengthen your ability to identify red herrings. Additionally, understanding sources of radio interference and having an idea of the limits of your network signal can also help avoid potential headaches from false alarms and misleading responses when patrolling the network for intruders. Keeping these points in mind, laying out your wireless network for the most appropriate detection should be no problem.

Starting with a Closed Network

The choice of vendor for your wireless gear can dramatically alter the visible footprint of your wireless network. After an Access Point is installed, it will begin emitting broadcasts, announcing, among other things, its Service Set Identifier (SSID). This is a very useful function for clients to be able to connect to your network. It makes discovery and initial client configuration very easy, and quick. The ease of contact, however, has some security implications. The easily available nature of the network is not only available for your intended users, but for anyone else with a wireless card. The easier any system is to find, the easier it is to exploit.

In order to counteract some of the troubles with openly available and easily discoverable wireless networks, some vendors have developed a system known as closed network. With closed network functionality enabled, the wireless AP no longer broadcasts its SSID to the world; rather it waits for a client to connect with the proper SSID and channel settings. This certainly makes the network more difficult to find, as programs such as NetStumbler and dstumbler will not see it. The network is now much more secure, because it is much more difficult for an attacker to compromise a network he or she can't see. The potential disadvantage, however, is that clients must now know the SSID and settings of your network in advance in order to connect. This process can be difficult for some users, as card configuration will be required. From a security standpoint, however, a closed network system is the ideal foundation from which to begin designing a more secure wireless network solution. A closed network-capable AP is recommended for all but those who wish to have an openly available wireless network (in such a scenario, security concerns are generally not primary).

Ruling Out Environmental Obstacles

Another important design consideration is the physical layout. A knowledge of the obstacles you are designing around is vital for determining the number of APs that will be required to provide adequate coverage for your wireless network. Many installations have suffered from administrators failing to take notice of trees, indoor waterfalls, and even the layout and construction materials of the building. Features such as large indoor fountains and even translucent glass walls can be a barrier to proper signal path. Fixing a broken network is much more of a burden than making sure everything is set up properly from the beginning. Before starting, learn as much as you can about the building in which you're planning to deploy. If the building is concrete with a steel frame, the 802.11 signal will be much more limited than if it were passing through a wood/drywall frame building. When placing the initial 802.11 AP, design from the inside-out. Place the AP toward the center of your user base and take advantage of the fact that the signal will radiate outwards. The goal of this placement is to provide the best quality of signal to your users, while limiting the amount and strength of the signal that passes outside of your walls. Remember, potential attackers will be looking for a signal from your network, and the weaker the signal is when it leaves your premises, the less likely an attacker can safely snoop on your network. Safely, in this case, means that an attacker doesn't need to worry about being seen in an unusual place with a laptop. For example, an attacker sitting in your lobby with a wireless card is suspicious, but, someone sipping coffee in a coffee shop with their laptop isn't. Of course, signal strength alone isn't a security measure, but is part of a whole secure security package you will want to have built into your wireless network.

The second physical consideration that should be kept in mind when designing a wireless network is the building floor plan. Using the inside-out method of AP placement, place the AP as far from possible from external windows and doors. If the building layout is a square, with cubicles in all directions, place the AP in the center. If the building is a set of long corridors and rooms, then it will be best to experiment with placement. Try putting the APs at different locations, and then scout the location with NetStumbler or other tools to determine where the signal is strongest, and whether or not it can be seen from outside of your facility. We'll talk more about using NetStumbler and other site evaluation tools a bit later.

Another consideration should be your neighbors. In most environments, there will be other companies or businesses operating nearby. Either from the floors above, below, or right next door, your signal may be visible. If you have competitors, this may be something which you wish to avoid, because they will be able to join your network, and potentially exploit it. Close proximity means that an attacker could easily and discreetly begin deciphering your wireless encryption keys. Proper placement and testing of your APs before deployment can help you gain a better understanding of your availability to those around you.

WARNING

Remember that good design requires patience and testing. Avoid at all costs the temptation to design around obstacles simply by throwing more APs at the situation, or increasing the signal strength. While providing more signal and availability, this potentially dangerous scenario adds more points of entry to your network, and can increase your chance of compromise.

Ruling Out Interference

Thought should also be given to whether or not there are external or internal sources of radio interference present in your building. Potential problems can come from microwave ovens, 2.4GHz wireless phones, wireless video security monitors, and other 802.11b wireless networks. If these are present in large numbers in your environment, it may be necessary to do some experimentation with AP placement and settings to see which combination will provide the most available access. We'll discuss interference in more detail in the next section, but be aware that these devices may create holes, or weaken your range. Having properly identified these sources and potential problems can help you diagnose future problems, and realize that an outage may not necessarily be an attacker but rather a hungry employee warming lunch.

Defensive Monitoring Considerations

Monitoring wireless networks for intrusion attempts requires attention to some newer details, which many security administrators have not encountered in the past. The use of radio for networking introduces new territory for security administrators to consider. Issues such as signal strength, distortion by buildings and fixtures, interferences from local and remote sources, and the mobility of users are some of these new monitoring challenges not found in the wired world. Any attempt to develop an intrusion detection regime must take into account these new concepts. Security administrators must make themselves familiar with radio technology and the direct impact the environment will have on networks using these technologies.

Security monitoring is something that should be built into your initial wireless installation. Many devices have logging capabilities and these should be fully utilized in order to provide the most comprehensive overall picture possible of what is happening on your network. Firewalls, routers, internal Web servers, Dynamic Host Configuration Protocol (DHCP) servers, and even some wireless APs will provide log files, which should be stored and reviewed frequently. Simply collecting the logs isn't enough; they should be thoroughly reviewed by security administrators. This is something that should be built into every security procedures guide, but is often overlooked. A firewall log is worthless if it's never reviewed! Having numerous methods and devices in place to review traffic and usage on your network will provide critical insight into any type of attack, either potential or realized.

Availability and Connectivity

Obviously the most important things in building and operating a wireless network are availability and connectivity. A wireless network that users cannot connect to, while very secure, is completely useless. Interference, signal strength and denial of service (DoS) attacks can all dramatically affect your availability. In the past, for an attacker to perform a denial of service attack against your internal network, they would have needed to gain access to it, not always a trivial task. Now, however, an attacker with a grudge against your organization needs only to know that a wireless network is present in order to attack. We'll discuss the possibilities of denial of service attacks later in this section. Even if the network has been designed securely, simply the fact that the network is radio-based means these issues must be considered.

Interference and Noise

Identifying potential sources of interference during the design phase can help you identify potentially malicious sources of interference within your environment once you undertake your monitoring activities.

For example, during one wireless deployment, we were experiencing a major denial of service in one group. Users in one group were either unable to connect to the AP at all, or suffered from diminished bandwidth. It was suspected there was a potentially malicious source of activity somewhere, but after reviewing our initial design notes about the installation, we remembered a kitchen near these users. At the time of deployment, there was no known source of interference in the kitchen, but upon investigating further, we discovered the group had just installed a new commercial grade, high wattage microwave oven. As you can see, when deploying a wireless network, it's important to explore all possible solutions of interference before suspecting foul play. If your organization uses noncellular wireless phones, or any other type of wireless devices, be certain you check whether or not they are operating in the 2.4GHz spectrum. While some devices like telephones won't spark a complete outage, they can cause intermittent problems with connections. Other devices like wireless video monitors can cause serious conflicts, and should be avoided at all costs. Identified potential problems early can be very useful when monitoring for interference and noise in your wireless network environment.

It should be noted that some administrators may have few, if any, problems with microwave ovens, phones, or other wireless devices, and tests have been performed on the World Wide Web supporting this. A simple Web search for microwave ovens and 802.11b will give you plenty of information. However, do realize that while some have had few problems, this is no guarantee you will be similarly blessed. Instead, be thorough. Having an idea of potential problems can save you time identifying later connectivity issues.

As mentioned earlier, knowledge of your neighbors is a good idea when building a wireless network. If you are both running a wireless network with similar settings, you will be competing on the same space with your networks, which is sure to cause interference problems. Given this, it's best to monitor what your neighbors are doing at all times to avoid such problems. Notice that conflicts of this kind are generally inadvert. Nevertheless, similar situations can be used to create a denial of service, which we'll discuss later.

Signal Strength

From a monitoring standpoint, signal strength is one of the more critical factors to consider. First, it is important to monitor your signal regularly in order to know the extent to which it is available. Multiple APs will require multiple investigations in order to gain a complete picture of what a site looks like externally. Site auditing discovery tools should be used to see how far your signal is traveling. It will travel much farther than most manufacturer claims, so prepare to be surprised. If the signal is adequate for your usage, and you'd like to attempt to limit it, some APs will allow you to fine-tune the signal strength. If your AP supports this feature, experiment with it to provide the best balance between internal and external availability.

Whether you can fine-tune your signal strength or not, during initial design you should have noted points externally where the signal was available. Special attention should have been paid to problematic areas, such as cafes, roadways or parking lots. These areas are problematic because it is difficult, or impossible to determine whether or not an attacker is looking at your wireless network specifically. When monitoring, those areas should be routinely investigated for potential problems. If you are facing an intrusion, knowledge of places like these, with accessibility to your network could help lead you to your attacker.

Detecting a Denial of Service

Monitoring the wireless network for potential denial of service attacks should be part of your security regime. Surveying the network, checking for decreases in signal strength, unauthorized APs, and unknown Media Access Control (MAC) addresses, are all ways to be proactive about denial of service.

Denial of service attacks can be incredibly destructive. Often times, however, their severity is overlooked because a DoS attack doesn't directly put classified data at risk. While this attitude may be acceptable at certain organizations, at others it can cost a tremendous amount of money both in lack of employee productivity and lost customer revenue. One only needs to look back at the DoS attacks conducted in February 2000 against several major E-commerce companies to realize the threat from such attacks.

On an Internet level, this type of attack can be devastating, but at the wireless networking level, they may not be as severe. The largest possible loss could come from lost employee productivity. The availability of a wired alternative can help mitigate the risks from a wireless DoS, but as networking moves toward the future, and away from wires, this may become less of a possibility.

As mentioned earlier, the radio-based nature of 802.11b makes it more susceptible to denial of service. In the wired world, an attacker generally needed access to your internal network in order to cause a DoS outage. Since many wireless installations offer instant access into this network, it can be much easier for an attacker to get in and start shutting things down. There are two main ways an attacker can conduct a DoS against your wireless LAN. The first method would be fairly traditional. They would connect to the network, and simply start blasting packets to any of your internal machines—perhaps your DNS servers or one of your routers. Either scenario is likely to cause connectivity outages on the network. A second method of denying service to wireless LANs wouldn't even require a wireless LAN card, but rather just a knowledge of how the technology works. An attacker with a device known to cause interference could place it in the path of your wireless network. This is a very crude, but potentially effective method of performing a DoS attack. A third way to conduct a DoS against a wireless LAN is similar to the scenario we've just discussed, but requires a wireless AP. In this scenario, an attacker would configure a wireless AP to mimic the settings on your AP, but not connect the AP to the network. Therefore, users connecting to this AP would not be able to communicate on the LAN. And, if this AP were placed in an area with many of your users, since their cards are generally configured to connect to the strongest signal, the settings would match, making detection potentially difficult. A good way to save yourself from this scenario is to identify the MAC addresses of all your wireless APs, and then routinely do surveys for any nonmatching APs. This type of situation closely mirrors what we will discuss later when talking about rogue APs.

Monitoring for Performance

Keeping an eye on the performance of your network is always a good idea. Knowing your typical baseline usage, the types of traffic that travel on your network, as well as the odd traffic patterns that might occur will not only help you keep an eye on capacity, but clue you in to potential intrusions. This type of monitoring is generally part of a good security regime in the wired world, but should be adopted to cover traffic on your wireless network as well.

Knowing the Baseline

Knowing the baseline usage that your network generally sees can help you identify potential problems. Over time, you should be watching the network to get an idea of how busy it gets throughout the day. Monitoring baseline performance will give you a good idea of your current capacity, and help provide you with a valuable picture of how your network generally operates. Let's say, for example, your network generally sees its peak usage at 9AM at which point it generally sees a load of 45 percent. Then, in monitoring your performance logs you notice usage peaks at 3AM with much higher bandwidth consumed—you have an anomaly that should be investigated. Additionally, if, when monitoring, you find that massive amounts of bandwidth are being consumed, and you only have four or five users with minimal usage needs, this should be a red flag as well. A common attack motive for intruders is to gain access to bandwidth.

Monitoring Tools of the Trade

There are many performance-monitoring tools, with diverse prices and levels of functionality. Commercially available tools such as Hewlett-Packard's OpenView have great amounts of market share. OpenView can be configured to watch just about any aspect of your network, your servers, bandwidth, and even traffic usage patters. It is a very powerful tool that is also customizable and can be made to monitor just about anything imaginable. Being a solution designed for enterprise type organizations, it does come with a hefty price tag, but is generally considered one of the best monitoring tools available. There are some downsides to OpenView, however. It isn't security friendly, in that it requires the use of the User Datagram Protocol (UDP), which is something that is sometimes not allowed through firewalls due to the fact that it is a connectionless protocol. Connectionless protocols do not allow firewalls to verify that all transmissions are requested by the initiating party. In other words, there is no connection handshake like with the Transport Control Protocol (TCP). OpenView also has some problems working in a Network Address Translation (NAT) environment. Implementing OpenView into a secure environment can also be a real challenge, and may require some security requirement sacrifices. Proceed with caution.

If you are looking for something with a lower price tag, and potentially easier integration, SNIPS (formerly known as NOCOL) is an excellent monitoring package. It is very flexible in what it can do, but one particularly useful function is that it can be used to watch your Ethernet bandwidth. Watching bandwidth, as mentioned earlier, is a good idea because it can help you spot potential excess usage. SNIPS can also be configured to generate alarms when bandwidth reaches a certain level above what is considered normal use in your environment. Notification of this kind could alert you early to network intrusion, and when combined with specially designed detection software can be a very powerful combination. The screenshot in Figure 11.1 shows the different alert levels SNIPS features, and how they are sorted.

Figure 11.1 SNIPS: A Freely Available Monitoring Package

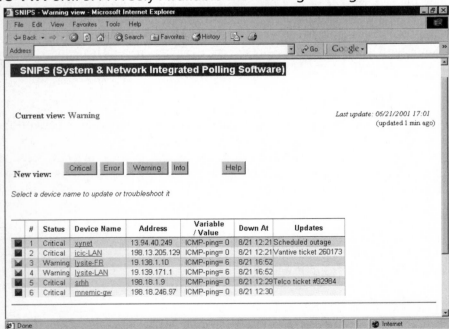

Another excellent tool for watching bandwidth on your network is called EtherApe. It provides an excellent graphical view of what bandwidth is being consumed, and where. With breakdowns by IP or MAC address, and protocol classifications, it is one tool that should be explored. It is freely available at http://etherape.sourceforge.net. For example, if you were detecting great slowdowns on your network, and you needed to quickly see what was consuming your resources, start EtherApe. It listens to your network and identifies traffic, protocols, and network load. Additionally, it traces the source and destination of the traffic, and provides a nice visual picture of the network. It's a great tool for identifying problems with the network, and can assist in explaining bandwidth and traffic issues to nontechnical people. Figure 11.2 shows EtherApe in action, illustrating how the traffic is displayed, graphically. The hosts are presented in a ring, with connections shown as lines drawn between them. The more intense the traffic, the larger the connection lines. Traffic can also be sorted by color, which makes it instantly easier to distinguish between types.

Figure 11.2 EtherApe for Linux

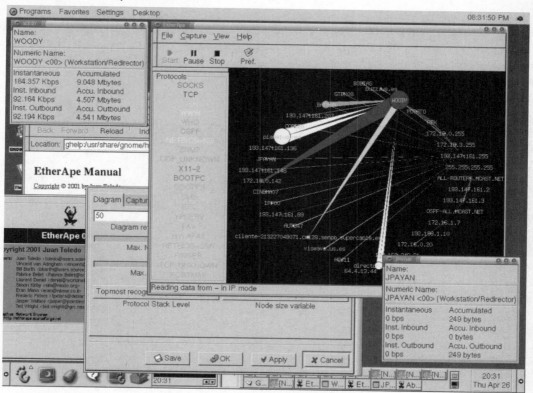

Intrusion Detection Strategies

Until now, we've primarily discussed monitoring in how it relates to intrusion detection, but there's more to an overall intrusion detection installation than monitoring alone. Monitoring can help you spot problems in your network, as well as identify performance problems, but watching every second of traffic that passes through your network, manually searching for attacks, would be impossible. This is why we need specialized network intrusion detection software. This software inspects all network traffic, looking for potential attacks and intrusions by comparing it to a predefined list of attack strings, known as signatures. In this section, we will look at different intrusion detection strategies and the role monitoring plays. We'll learn about different strategies designed for wireless networks, which must take into account the nature of the attacks unique to the medium. These include a lack of centralized control, lack of a defined perimeter, the susceptibility to hijacking and spoofing, the use of rogue APs, and a number of other features that intrusion detection systems were not designed to accommodate. Only a combination of factors we've discussed earlier, such as good initial design and monitoring, can be combined with traditional intrusion detection software to provide an overall effective package.

Integrated Security Monitoring

As discussed earlier, having monitoring built in to your network will help the security process evolve seamlessly. Take advantage of built-in logging-on network devices such as firewalls, DHCP servers, routers, and even certain wireless APs. Information gathered from these sources can help make sense of alerts generated from other intrusion detection sources, and will help augment data collected for incidents. Additionally, these logs should help you to manually spot unauthorized traffic and MAC addresses on your network.

Tools & Traps…

Beware of the Auto-responding Tools!

When designing your intrusion detection system, you will likely come across a breed of tools, sometimes known as Intrusion Prevention Systems. These systems are designed to automatically respond to incidents. One popular package is called PortSentry. It will, upon detection of a port scan, launch a script to react. Common reactions include dropping the route to the host that has scanned you, or adding firewall rules to block it. While this does provide instant protection from the host that's scanning you, and might seem like a great idea at first, it creates a very dangerous denial of service potential. Using a technique known as IP spoofing, an attacker who realizes PortSentry is being used can send bogus packets that appear to be valid port scans to your host. Your host will, of course, see the scan and react, thinking the address that its coming from is something important to you, such as your DNS server, or your upstream router. Now, network connectivity to your host is seriously limited. If you do decide to use auto-responsive tools, make sure you are careful to set them up in ways that can't be used against you.

Watching for Unauthorized Traffic and Protocols

As a security or network administrator, it is generally a good idea to continuously monitor the traffic passing over your network. It can give you an idea of the network load, and more importantly, you can get an idea of what kinds of protocols are commonly used. For most corporate networks, you are likely to see SMTP (e-mail), DNS lookups, Telnet or SSH, and, of course, Web traffic. There is also a good chance if you are using Hewlett-Packard printers, there will be JetDirect traffic on port 9100. If you have Microsoft products such as Exchange server, look for traffic on a number of other ports, with connections to or from your mail servers. After several sample viewings of network traffic, you should start to notice some patterns as to what is considered normal usage. It is from these samples that you can start looking for other unknown and possibly problematic traffic. IRC, Gnutella, or heavy FTP traffic can be a sign that your network is being used maliciously. If this is the case, you should be able to track the traffic back to its source, and try to identify who is using the offending piece of software. There are many Gnutella clients today, and it has become the most heavily used peer-to-peer networking system available. It is advised you become familiar with a few Gnutella clients, so they can be quickly identified and dealt with. BearShare, Gnotella, and LimeWire are some of the more popular ones. LimeWire, shown in Figure 11.3, provides an easy-to-use interface for Gnutella and offers lots of information about clients. Another point of caution about peer-to-peer client software should be the fact that it is often bundled with spyware—software which shares information about the user and their computer, often without their knowledge.

Figure 11.3 LimeWire: A Popular Gnutella Peer-to-peer File Sharing Program

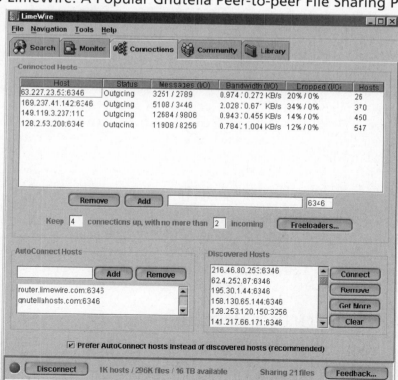

Within your security policy, you should have defined which types of applications are not considered acceptable for use in your environment. It is advisable to ban peer-to-peer networking software like Napster, Gnutella, and Kazaa. Constant monitoring is essential because the list grows larger each day and current policies may not prohibit the latest peer-to-peer software. Aside from possibly wasting company bandwidth, these tools allow others on the Internet to view and transfer files from a shared directory. It is very easy to misconfigure this software to share an entire hard drive. If shared, any other user on the peer-to-peer network would potentially have access to password files, e-mail files, or anything else that resides on the hard disk. This is more common than one would expect. Try a search on a peer-to-peer network for a sensitive file name like archive.pst, and you might be surprised by what you find.

Internet Relay Chat (IRC) traffic can also be a sign that something fishy is happening on your network. There are legitimate uses for IRC on an internal network. It makes a great team meeting forum for large groups separated by distances, or for those who require a common real-time chat forum. It should be kept in mind though that attackers commonly use IRC to share information or illegally copied software. If you are using IRC on your network, make sure you have a listing of your authorized IRC servers, and inspect IRC traffic to insure it is originating from one of those hosts. Anything else should be treated as suspect. If you aren't using IRC on your network, any IRC traffic (generally found on TCP port 6666 or 6667) should be treated as suspect.

A good way to automate this kind of scanning is generally available in intrusion detection packages. Snort, the freely available IDS has a signature file that identifies Gnutella, Napster, IRC, and other such types of traffic. Network Flight Recorder has similar filters, and supports a filter writing language that is incredibly flexible in its applications. We'll discuss some of the IDS packages a bit later in this chapter.

Unauthorized MAC Addresses

MAC address filtering is a great idea for wireless networks. It will only allow wireless cards with specified MAC addresses to communicate on the network. Some APs have this capability built in, but if yours doesn't, DHCP software can often be configured to do the same. This could be a major headache for a large organization, because there could simply be too many users to keep track of all of the MAC addresses. One possible way around this is to agree upon the same vendor for all of your wireless products. Each wireless card vendor has an assigned OUI or organizationally unique identifier, which makes up the first part of an Ethernet card's MAC address. So, if you chose Lucent wireless cards, you could immediately identify anything that wasn't a Lucent card just by noting the first part of the MAC address. This type of system could be likened to a company uniform. If everyone wore orange shirts to work, someone with a blue shirt would be easily spotted. This is not foolproof, however. An attacker with the same brand of wireless card would slide thorough unnoticed. In a more complicated vein, it is possible for attackers to spoof their MAC addresses, meaning they can override the wireless network card's MAC address. A system based solely on vendor OUIs alone wouldn't provide much protection, but it can make some intrusions much easier to identify.

Popular Monitoring Products

The number of available intrusion detection packages has increased dramatically in the past few years. There are two main types of intrusion detection software: host-based and network-based. Host-based intrusion detection is generally founded on the idea of monitoring a system for changes to its file system. It doesn't generally inspect network traffic. For that functionality, you'll need a network intrusion detection system (IDS), which looks specifically at network traffic, and will be our focus for this section.

Signature files are what most Intrusion Detection Systems use to identify attacks. Therefore, an IDS is generally only as good as its signature files. Using just a small snippet from an attack, the IDS compares packets from captured traffic to the signature file, searching for the specified attack string. If there's a match, an alert is triggered. This is why it's important to have control and flexibility with your signature files. When spotting new attacks, time is always of the essence. New attacks occur daily, and the ability to add your own signature files to your IDS sensor can save you the wait for a vendor to release a new signature file. Another thing to keep in mind with signature files is that, if they are written too generically, false alarms will become the norm. The downfall of any IDS system, false alarms can desensitize administrators to warnings, thus allowing attacks to sneak through—a perfect real-life example of "crying wolf."

Of all of the commercially available IDS products, one of the most flexible and adaptable is Network Flight Recorder, from NFR Security. Its sensors are run from a CD-ROM based on an OpenBSD kernel. Its greatest flexibility comes with the specially developed N-Code system for filter writing. N-Code can be used to grab any type of packet and dissect it to the most minimal of levels, then log the output. This is particularly useful when searching for attack strings, but can also be used to identify unknown network protocols, or to learn how certain software communicates over the network. Having the ability to write your own filters can be very helpful as well. For example, if your company has a specially developed piece of software, and you would like to identify its usage and make sure it isn't being utilized outside your network, a filter could be written to identify traffic from that specific program—a task which would be impossible with a hard-coded signature file system. Another excellent use of N-Code is in developing custom attack signatures. We'll discuss why having custom signatures can be important in the next section. NFR also supports the use of multiple sensors distributed throughout an environment, with a central logging and management server. Configurations and N-Code additions are done via a GUI, through a Windows-based program. Changes are centrally done, then pushed out to all remote sensors, eliminating the need to manually update each remote machine. This can be a huge timesaver in big environments.

A free alternative to NFR is a program called Snort, which is an excellent and freely available tool (downloadable from www.snort.org). Snort is a powerful and lightweight IDS sensor that also makes a great packet sniffer. Using a signature file or rule set (essentially a text file with certain parameters to watch the traffic it is inspecting), it generates alerts to a text file or database. We'll take a more in-depth look at writing rules in the next section. Snort has a large community of developers, so it is continually being updated to stay current with the latest changes in security. It is also now more able to deal with tools like Stick and Snot, which were designed to fool IDS sensors. One potential downside to Snort, however, is that because it is freeware, the group that writes it does not offer technical support. For home or small business use this might not be a problem, but for larger companies who require support when using Snort, a company called Silicon Defense offers commercial support and also sells a hardware, ready-to-go Snort sensor.

Signatures

It isn't uncommon for a sophisticated attacker to know the signature files of common IDS sensors, and use that knowledge to confuse the system. For a very simplistic example of this, let's say a particular attack contains the string "Hacked by hAx0r." A default filter might therefore search specifically for the string "hAx0r." Countering, an attacker with knowledge of the default signature files could send benign packets to your network containing only the string "hAx0r." This technically wouldn't be an attack, but it could fool the IDS. By sending a large series of packets all with "hAx0r" in them, the sensor could become overwhelmed, generating alerts for each packet, and causing a flurry of activity. An attacker could use this to their advantage in one of two ways. They could either swamp the IDS with so many packets it can't log them any more, or they could swamp it with alerts in order to hide a real attack. Either strategy spells trouble.

A custom signature could be defined to look for "by hAx0r," therefore defeating this type of attack strategy. Again, this scenario is a very simplistic example of custom signature writing. In reality, there is much more in the way of actual analysis of attacks and attack strings that must be done. Simple signatures can be very easy to write or modify, but the more complex the attack, the more difficult it is to write the signature. The best way to learn how to write signatures is to investigate already written ones included with the system. In the case of NFR, there are many N–Code examples that ship with the software, and many more can be found on the Web. A comprehensive N–Code guide is also available, which gives a detailed explanation of all the features and abilities of N–Code.

Snort, on the other hand, as we earlier described, just uses a text file with rules. A sample rule file for snort looks like this:

```
alert tcp $HOME_NET 21 -> !$HOME_NET any (msg:"FTP-bad-login";flags:PA;
    content:"530 Login incorrect";)
alert tcp !$HOME_NET any -> $HOME_NET 21 (msg:"FTP-shosts";flags:PA;
    content:".shosts";)
alert tcp !$HOME_NET any -> $HOME_NET 21 (msg:"FTP-user-root";flags:PA;
    content:"user root |0d|";)
alert tcp !$HOME_NET any -> $HOME_NET 21 (msg:"FTP-user-warez";flags:PA;
    content:"user warez |0d|";)
alert tcp !$HOME_NET any -> $HOME_NET 21 (msg:"IDS213 - FTP-Password
    Retrieval"; content:"passwd"; flags: AP;)
alert icmp !$HOME_NET any -> $HOME_NET any (msg:"IDS118 - MISC-
    Traceroute ICMP";ttl:1;itype:8;)
```

From this example, the format is easily readable. To create a simple signature, one only needs to specify the port number, an alert string, which is written to the file, and a search string, which is compared to the packets being inspected. As an example, we'll write a rule to search for Xmas tree scans, or a port-scan where strange packets are sent with the FIN, PSH, and URG TCP flags set. Most port scanning software, like Nmap will perform these scans. To begin, we can run some test Xmas tree scans just to watch what happens. Using a packet sniffer like Snort or Ethereal, we can see exactly which flags are set in our scan. Once we have that information gathered, the next step is to actually write the rule. So, our sample rule looks like this:

```
alert tcp !$HOME_NET any -> $HOME_NET any (msg:"SCAN
    FullXMASScan";flags: FPU;)
```

All alert rules start with the word "alert." The next three fields tell Snort to look for Transmission Control Protocol (TCP) packets coming from outside of our network on any port. The other side of the arrow specifies the destination of the traffic. In this case, it is set to anything defined as our home network, on any port. Next, we set our message, which is logged to the alerts file. It's generally a good idea to make the message as descriptive as possible, so you know what you're logging. The final two parts of the rule are where we fill in the information gathered from our sniffer. We know that the TCP flags were set to FPU, so we enter that in the flags field. This way, from start to finish the rule reads "make an alert if there is any TCP packet that comes from outside of our network, on any port, to anywhere on our home network, on any port with the flags FPU." Try reading through some of the rules listed previously and see if they begin to make sense. The first rule would read "Make an alert if anything on our network tries to connect to an FTP server outside of our network, and fails." Snort rules are fairly straightforward to read and write. For more complex rules, and a better definition of all the features that can be included with Snort rule writing, see the Snort project's home page.

Damage & Defense…

Keep Your Signatures Up to Date!

Most IDS sensors work by comparing traffic to a predefined list of signatures. When a match is found, an alert is triggered. This system has worked well in the past, but a new type of tool has been developed to mimic authentic signatures. One common tool is called Stick, and can be used to generate thousands of "attacks" per second, all from spoofed IP addresses. An attacker could use this to cause a denial of service to your IDS sensors, or to provide cover for his or her specific attack to your network. Some IDS vendors claim to now be able to distinguish between these fake attacks and real ones. Nevertheless, proceed with caution. And don't forget to update your signatures often!

Conducting Vulnerability Assessments

In this chapter, we'll cover the basics of a wireless vulnerability assessment. Being aware of changes in your network is one of the keys to detecting problems. Performing this kind of an assessment on a wireless network will be a fairly new exercise for most administrators. There are a number of new challenges that will arise from a radio transmission-based network, such as the mobility of clients and the lack of network boundaries.

When beginning a wireless vulnerability assessment, it's important to identify the extent of the network signal. This is where tools like NetStumbler, and the ORiNOCO client software will be very handy, because they will alert you to the presence of wireless connectivity. A good place to start the assessment is near the wireless AP. Start the monitoring software and then slowly walk away from the AP, checking the signal strength and availability as you move. Check out the entire perimeter of your area to make note of signal strength, taking special notice of the strong and weak points. Once you have a good idea about the signal internally, try connecting to your network from outside your facility. Parking lots, sidewalks, any nearby cafes, and even floors above and below yours should be investigated to analyze the extent of your signal. Anyplace where the signal is seen should be noted as a potential trouble area, and scrutinized in the future. If your signal is available far outside your premises, it might be a good idea to rethink the locations of your APs. If you can see your network, so can an attacker. Try to lower the signal strength of your AP by either moving it or making adjustments to its software, if possible. If limiting signal strength isn't an option, more emphasis should be placed on constant monitoring, as well as looking into other security devices.

If you have a signal from your network, externally, you'll now want to look at the visibility of your network resources from your wireless network. A good security design would isolate the wireless AP from the rest of the network, treating it as an untrusted device. However, more often than not, the AP is placed on the network with everything else, giving attackers full view of all resources. Generally, the first step an attacker takes is to gain an IP address. This is generally done via DHCP, which works by assigning an IP address to anyone who asks. Once an IP address has been handed out, the attacker becomes part of the network. They can now start looking around on the network just joined. In conducting a vulnerability assessment, become the attacker, and follow these steps to try to discover network resources. The next step is to perform a ping scan, or a connectivity test for the network, to see what else on the network is alive and responding to pings. Using Nmap, one of the best scanning tools available, a ping scan is performed like this:

```
# nmap -sP 10.10.0.1-15

Starting nmap V. 2.54BETA7 ( www.insecure.org/nmap/ )
Host  (10.10.0.1) appears to be up.
Host  (10.10.0.5) appears to be up.
Nmap run completed — 15 IP addresses (2 hosts up) scanned
    in 1 second
#
```

With this scan, we've checked all the hosts from 10.10.0.1 through 10.10.0.15 to see if they respond to a ping. From this, we gain a list of available hosts, which is essentially a Yellow Page listing of potentially vulnerable machines. In this case, .1 and .5 answered. This means they are currently active on the network. The next step is to see what the machines are, and what they run, so an exploit can be found to compromise them. An OS detection can also be done with Nmap like this:

```
# nmap -sS -O 10.10.0.1

Starting nmap V. 2.54BETA7 ( www.insecure.org/nmap/ )
Interesting ports on  (10.10.0.1):
```

```
(The 1530 ports scanned but not shown below are in state:
    closed)
Port        State        Service
22/tcp      open         ssh
25/tcp      open         smtp
53/tcp      open         domain
110/tcp     open         pop-3


TCP Sequence Prediction: Class=random positive increments
                         Difficulty=71574 (Worthy
                            challenge)
Remote operating system guess: OpenBSD 2.6-2.7


Nmap run completed — 1 IP address (1 host up) scanned in
    34 seconds
#
```

With this information, we now know that there is a machine with OpenBSD v2.6 or 2.7, running the services listed. We could now go and look for possible remote exploits that would allow us to gain access to this machine. If this were a real attack, this machine could have been compromised, giving the attacker a foothold into your wired network, and access to the rest of your network as well.

Snooping is another angle to consider when performing your vulnerability assessment. It can be every bit as dangerous as the outright compromising of machines. If confidential data or internal company secrets are being sent via wireless connection, it is possible for an attacker to capture that data. While 802.11b does support the Wired Equivalent Privacy (WEP) encryption scheme, it has been cracked, and can be unlocked via AirSnort or WEPcrack. These programs use the WEP weakness described by Scott Fluhrer, Itsik Mantin, and Adi Shamir in their paper "Weaknesses in the Key Scheduling Algorithm of RC4," which can be found at numerous Internet sites by searching for either the authors' or the paper's name. WEP does make it more difficult for an attacker to steal your secrets by adding one more obstacle: time. In some cases, it could take up to a week for an attacker to break your encryption. However, the busier the network, the faster the key will be discovered. To insure the best data privacy protection, have all wireless users connect to the internal network through a virtual private network (VPN) tunnel.

There are many opportunities for an attacker to gain access to a wireless network, simply because of their radio-based nature. After performing a vulnerability analysis, you should be able to spot some potential weaknesses in your security infrastructure. With these weakness identified, you can develop a plan of action to either strengthen your defenses, or increase your monitoring. Both are recommended.

Incident Response and Handling

Incidents happen. If your company has a network connection, there will eventually be some sort of incident. Therefore, an incident response and handling procedure is a critical component when it comes to protecting your network. This policy should be the definitive guide on how to handle any and all security incidents on your network. It should be clearly written and easy to understand, with steps on how to determine the level of severity of any incident. Let's take, for example, wireless intrusion attempts on two different networks, one without a good incident response policy, and one with more thorough policies in place.

Imagine one company without a formal security policy. As the company's network was built, the emphasis was placed on superior deployment, speed, and availability. While the network matured, and wireless access was added, there was little done in the way of documentation—they simply didn't afford it the time. There was still no security policy in place after adding wireless access, and no particular plans for how to handle an incident. Several weeks after deploying their companywide wireless network, the network administrators began to receive complaints of poor performance across the network. They investigated, based on what the various network administrators deemed necessary at that time. It was eventually concluded that perhaps one of the wireless Access Points was not functioning properly, and so they replaced it. After several more weeks, law enforcement officials visited the company—it seemed that a number of denial of service attacks had been originating from the company's network. Having had no formal security policy or incident handling process, the company was unable to cooperate with the officials, and could not produce any substantial evidence. Without this evidence, investigators could not locate the culprit. Not only was the company unable to help with the investigation, they had no idea they had even been attacked, nor did they know to what extent their internal data had been compromised. This left them with many more hours of work, rebuilding their network and servers, than if they had taken the time at the beginning to create a security and incident handling policy.

Next, imagine another company, one that attempted to balance performance and security considerations, and noticed some suspicious activity on their network from within their internal network. Through routine monitoring, the administrators detected some unusual traffic on the network. So, when their IDS sent an alarm message, they were ready to investigate. Within their security policy, guidelines as to how to handle the incidents were clearly detailed. The administrators had forms and checklists already prepared, so they were immediately able to start sleuthing. Using a number of steps outlined in their policy, they were able to determine that the traffic was coming from one of their wireless APs. They found this to be strange, as policy dictated that all APs were to have been configured with WEP. Further investigation found that this particular AP was mistakenly configured to allow non-WEP encrypted traffic.

In this case, having a good policy in place, the administrators were quickly able to track down the problem's source, and determine the cause. They were then able to systematically identify and reconfigure the problem Access Point.

Having an incident response policy is one thing, but the additional complexity posed by a wireless network introduces new challenges with forensics and information gathering. Let's investigate some of those new challenges, and consider some suggestions on how to contend with them.

Policies and Procedures

Wireless networking makes it easy for anyone to poke a gaping hole in any network, despite security measures. Simply putting a wireless AP on the internal network of the most secure network in the world would instantly bypass all security, and could make it vulnerable to anyone with a $100 wireless access card. It is for that reason that a provision to ban the unauthorized placement of any kind of wireless device should be drafted into a company's policy. This should be made to cover not just wireless APs, but the cards themselves. A user connected to your internal network could potentially be connected to an insecure wireless network, and bridging between the two interfaces on that machine would be very simple. The consequences of this to your network could be detrimental. Enforcing this policy can be difficult, however, as some popular laptop makers, such as Toshiba, have imbedded wireless access cards in their new notebooks. It should be considered a very severe infraction to place a wireless AP on the network—possibly one of the most severe—due to the level of risk involved. Having a wireless access card should also be treated seriously. Though this poses less of a risk than the AP, it should still be classified accordingly. Excellent sample policies are available on the SANS Web site at www.sans.org/newlook/resources/policies/policies.htm.

Reactive Measures

Knowing how to react to an incident is always a question of balance. On one hand, it would be tempting to close everything down and pull the plug on the whole network. That would certainly give you ample time to investigate the incident without further risk of compromise, but it would make your systems unavailable to your users. Some balance must be reached. When dealing with a wireless network compromise, it might be a good idea to disable wireless access until you can identify the entry point for the intrusion. Since wireless access is more of a luxury than a crucial business need, this may be possible. Of course, in organizations where wireless is critical, this isn't feasible. In either case, the WEP keys should be immediately changed, and if WEP isn't enabled, it should be. This will lock out the attacker for a limited time, hopefully giving you more of an opportunity to deal properly with the intrusion. In a secure and well-designed network, the scenario of a user joining a wireless network and immediately compromising it isn't as likely because more safeguards are in effect. If your network has been compromised through its wireless network, it's probably time to take some additional security measures.

While your network has been locked down, or at least had new keys installed, make sure to gather evidence of the intrusion. If the attacker was just passively listening to the network, there will be little evidence available, and not much taken as a result. However, if there were compromises into other network machines, it is critical to follow your company security policy guidelines to properly document the intrusion and preserve the evidence for the proper authorities. As mentioned in the introduction, covering how to handle evidence collection and performing forensics on a hacked machine is a book of its own!

Reporting

A wireless intrusion should be reported in the same manner as any other type of intrusion or incident. In most cases though, a wireless intrusion can be more severe, and difficult to document. Reporting a serious intrusion is a key part of maintaining a responsible approach to security. This is where a complete logging and monitoring system with IDS will be very useful. Having gathered and examined all log files from security devices; try to gain an understanding of the severity of the intrusion. Were any of the machines successfully attacked? From where were the attacks originating? If you suspect a machine was compromised, shut it down immediately, running as few commands as possible. Unless you really know what you are doing, and are familiar with computer forensics, the evidence should be turned over to investigators or forensics experts. The reason for this is that attackers will generally install a rootkit or backdoor system in a machine. These often feature booby traps, which can run and destroy critical information on the server. The primary places for booby traps like these are in the shutdown scripts, so it is possible you will have to unplug the machine, rather than use a script to power it down. Once that has been done, it's best to make two copies of the infected machine's disk for evidence purposes. If the authorities have been notified and will be handling the case, they will ask for the evidence, which should now be properly preserved for further forensics and investigation.

Cleanup

Cleaning up after an incident can pose a huge challenge to an organization. Once the level and extent of the intrusion has been determined, and the proper evidence gathered, one can begin rebuilding network resources. Generally, servers can be rebuilt from tape backup, but in some cases it may be necessary to start again from scratch. This is the type of decision that should be made after determining the extent of the intrusion. It is critical that when restoring from tape, you don't restore a tape of the system, post-intrusion—the same problems and intrusion will still exist. Some administrators feel there is no need to rebuild an infected machine, but simply to patch the security hole that allowed the intrusion. This is a particularly bad idea, because of the problem we mentioned with backdoors. The most advisable solution is to begin from scratch, or a known-to-be-safe backup. From there, the machines should be updated with the latest verified patches from the vendor.

Assuming the compromise did come from a wireless source, the wireless network should be re-examined. It may be difficult to determine exactly which AP was used for the compromise, but if you have an AP in a location that makes it easily accessible externally, you should probably consider moving it.

Prevention

As we've emphasized throughout this chapter, the best way to prevent an attack to your wireless network is to be secure from the start. This means designing a secure installation, maintaining firewalls and server logs, and continually patrolling your network for possible points of attack.

A secure wireless network is one which takes as many precautions as possible. Combining a properly secured AP with a firewall will provide a minimum level of security. Several steps that can be taken to help secure the network are adding a VPN to provide data privacy protection to your network. This is a critical step for organizations that require their data not be captured or altered in transmission. Isolation of network APs by a firewall is another often-overlooked step which should be implemented. Finally, simply making sure that WEP is enabled and enforced in all of your wireless APs can be just enough of a deterrent to save you from an intrusion. This may sound like quite a bit of extra work, which it is, but in order to remain secure, precautions must be taken.

Conducting Site Surveys for Rogue Access Points

Even if you don't have a wireless network installed, it's a good idea to perform scans of your area for wireless traffic. The low cost and ease of setup makes installing unauthorized or rogue APs very appealing. Whether installed by well-intentioned users of your own network, or by malicious outsiders, making sure you routinely patrol for any wireless activity on your network is a sound idea.

In this section, we'll discuss some strategies for surveying your network and tracking down rogue wireless APs. Using tools like the ORiNOCO Client Manager and NetStumbler we'll describe how to locate unauthorized wireless access at your network site, and instruct you in how to see your network as an attacker would.

The Rogue Placement

There are really quite a few scenarios in which a rogue AP could be placed on the network. In this section, we'll take a look at two scenarios, one done without any bad intentions, and one placed by an attacker hoping to gain access to a network.

The Well-intentioned Employee

The first situation involves a well-meaning employee. This person has been looking at advertisements at computer shops that feature low cost wireless network equipment, and having just purchased a wireless networking installation for home, wants to bring that convenience to work. Believing that having a wireless network available for the other employees will provide a great service, this employee goes to the shop and brings back the $150 wireless AP on sale that particular week. After carefully following the instructions from the manufacturer, the AP is made available, and the user announces the availability of the AP to fellow employees. Wanting the configuration to be as simple as possible, the well-intentioned employee has configured the AP not to require a preconfigured SSID string, allowing anyone to connect to it. This now provides the freedom to other department employees to roam about freely with their wireless cards. Note that none of this was done with authorization, because the user had no idea of the security implications involved. As we've discussed earlier, this now provides an open point of entry to anyone within range of the signal.

Scenarios such as this demonstrate the need to educate users as to the dangers of adding wireless APs to the network. Visual demonstrations or real-world examples assist in providing powerful explanations detailing the repercussions of this kind of security breach. It should also be made known that there exists within the company security policy a provision banning any kind of wireless networking.

The Social Engineer

A determined attacker will stop at nothing to compromise a network, and the availability and low cost of wireless networking equipment has made this task slightly easier. In this scenario, an attacker who has either taken a position at your company as a nightly custodian or has managed to "social engineer" their way into your office space will place a rogue AP.

One often-overlooked possibility for intrusion comes from an attacker posing as a nightly custodian, or one that has officially obtained that position. Night custodial staff often have unsupervised access to many areas of an office space, and as such are in the position to place a rogue wireless AP. Given time to survey the surroundings and find an inconspicuous location for an AP, this type of attacker can establish an entry point into your network for later access. In this kind of situation, an attacker may try to disguise their AP both physically, and from the network side. If there are other wireless APs present in your environment, the attacker may choose to use the same vendor, and SSID naming schema, making it all the more necessary to keep listings of the MAC addresses of all your authorized wireless APs. Another possibility is that an attacker will enable WEP encryption on their AP, ensuring that only they are able to access it at a later date. Attackers often tend to feel very territorial towards their targets.

A similar scenario to this involves a technique known as social engineering. This generally involves representing oneself as someone else. A good way to social engineer a situation is to first know some inside information about the organization which you are targeting. If it's a large company, they may have a published org-chart which will have important names that the social engineer can quote from to seem legitimate. Other sources for names include the company's Web site and press releases. In one example, during a vulnerability assessment for a fairly large firm, we were generally unable to find easy access to the network, so we employed a social engineering tactic. Posing as a vendor replacing hardware, we were able to gain access to the Accounting department and were able to place an AP in the most suitable location we could find: a VP's hard-wall office, overlooking the parking garage across the street. With this AP in place, we were successfully able to demonstrate both the need for education about the dangers of social engineering, and the need for tightened security on the company's internal network.

Tracking Rogue Access Points

If after conducting a vulnerability assessment or site audit, you've spotted an AP that should not be present, it's time to begin tracking it down. It may be that your assessment found quite a few APs, in fact. In a city office environment this is to be expected, don't worry. There's a better than average chance that many organizations around yours are using wireless access, and their APs are showing up on your scan. Nevertheless, they should all be investigated. A clever attacker could give their AP on your network the name of a neighboring business.

Investigating APs can be a tricky proposition. Perhaps the first step is to try to rule out all those who aren't likely to be in your location. This can be done with signal testing tools like NetStumbler, or LinkManager from ORiNOCO. Signals that appear to be weak are less likely to be coming from your direct area. For example, let's say we're looking for an AP called buzzoff that turned up on our NetStumbler site survey.

In Figure 11.4, we can see on our NetStumbler screen that two APs have been spotted. The AP called covechannel has a pretty weak signal, when it's even visible, so it's probably not nearby, though we may want to check it again later. Instead, we'll look at buzzoff, because it's showing a very strong signal. A very useful tool for investigating signal strength is the ORiNOCO Site Monitor, which comes bundled with the ORiNOCO Client Manager. Bringing up the client manager software and clicking on the **Advanced** tab will reveal the Site Monitor option. In this example, the Site Monitor software reveals that the signal for buzzoff is still fairly weak.

Figure 11.4 Network Stumbler: We've Found a Few Interesting APs

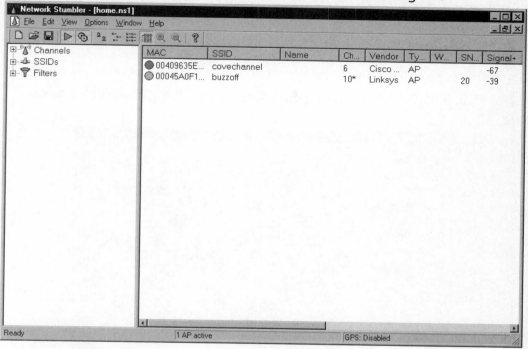

Figure 11.5 ORiNOCO Site Monitor: Looks Like We're Not too Close Yet

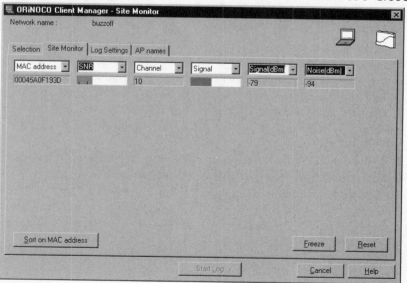

From the information we've seen in Figure 11.5, it looks like we're still a bit far from the AP. The signal isn't all that strong, and that's not terribly surprising since we've just started looking. Now we need to find this AP. The signal is strong enough to assume that it's probably somewhere nearby, so we'll start walking around until we get a stronger signal. At this point, finding the AP becomes a lot like the children's game, "Hot and Cold." When we move out of range, the AP's signal becomes weaker or "cold," so we move back in until the signal strengthens. This process can be time-consuming and slow, but with patience you'll be able to close in on the signal (as seen in Figure 11.6).

Figure 11.6 ORiNOCO Site Monitor: A Much Stronger Signal—We're Almost There

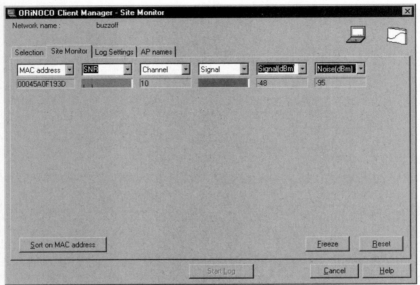

With a signal this strong, we're very close to the AP. At this point, it's time for the grunt work of the physical search. Knowing where all the LAN jacks are is helpful, because the AP will be plugged into one. It wouldn't be much of a threat otherwise. So, by systematically checking all possible LAN connections, we are able to locate this rogue AP sitting on top of an employee's computer. In this particular instance, it appears we have found an AP that falls under the "well-intentioned employee" scenario. Though, since we don't know for sure that it was the employee who placed it there, the AP should be handled very carefully.

With the AP found, it would also be advisable to conduct more audits of system machines to see if there were any break-ins during the time the rogue AP was available. To do this, refer to the monitoring section earlier, and start watching traffic patterns on your network to see if anything out of the ordinary pops up. Another good area to watch is the CPU load average on machines around the network. A machine with an extraordinarily high load could be easily explained, but it could also be a warning sign.

Summary

In this chapter, we've introduced some of the concepts of intrusion detection and monitoring, and discussed how they pertain to wireless networking. Beginning with the initial design for a wireless network, we've focused on the fact that security is a process that requires planning and activity, rather than just a product shrink-wrapped at the computer store. Through proper investigation of our site, we can build a wireless network in which we are aware of potential problems before they occur. Examples of this are noting potential sources of interference, and knowing which physical structures may be a barrier to the network.

After designing the network, we discussed the importance of monitoring. Using a combination of software designed for monitoring and the logs from our security devices, we can gain a valuable picture of how the network is supposed to look, and from there deduce potential problems as they occur. Knowing that the network is under a much heavier load can be a sign of an intrusion. Along with monitoring, dedicated intrusion detection software should be used in order to watch for specific attacks to the network. The software, using signature files that can be customized to look for specific attacks, will generate alerts when it finds a signature match in the traffic.

From there, we moved on to discussing how to conduct a vulnerability assessment. This is important to do regularly because it can help you learn to see your wireless network as an attacker does, hopefully before they do. Spotting problems early on can save time and money that would be wasted dealing with an intrusion.

Intrusions do happen, and adding a wireless network without proper security definitely increases that risk. That is why it is critical to have a security policy in place that not only prohibits the use of unauthorized wireless equipment, but also educates users to the dangers of doing so. Updating the security policy to handle wireless issues is key to maintaining a secure network in today's environment. However, should an intrusion occur through the wireless network, we discussed a few strategies on how to deal with the incident itself, and then how to contend with the cleanup afterward. We didn't delve into the realm of the actual computer forensics, however. That is a very complex and involved field of security, and is definitely a book of its own. Should you be interested in learning more about forensics, there are a number of excellent manuals available on the Internet that deal specifically with the forensics of Unix and Windows systems.

Lastly, we dealt with rogue Access Points (APs), possibly one of the greatest new threats to network security. Rogue APs can be placed by an attacker seeking access to your network, or placed by a well-meaning employee, trying to provide a new service. Either way, they offer attackers a direct and anonymous line into the heart of your network. After conducting a routine site audit, in our example, we discovered a rogue AP and tracked it down using a combination of the ORiNOCO Site Monitor and the NetStumbler tool. Once it was found, we handled it very carefully, in order to uncover where it came from, and why.

Intrusion detection and monitoring are one of the key building blocks in designing a secure network. Being familiar with the operations of your network, and knowing how to spot problems can be a huge benefit when an attack occurs. Proper intrusion detection software, monitored by a conscious administrator, as well as a combination of other security devices such as virtual private networks (VPNs) and firewalls, can be the key to maintaining a secure and functional wireless network.

Solutions Fast Track

Designing for Detection

☑ Get the right equipment from the start. Make sure all of the features you need, or will need, are available from the start.

☑ Know your environment. Identify potential physical barriers and possible sources of interference.

☑ If possible, integrate security monitoring and intrusion detection in your network from its inception.

Defensive Monitoring Considerations

☑ Define your wireless network boundaries, and monitor to know if they're being exceeded.

☑ Limit signal strength to contain your network.

☑ Make a list of all authorized wireless Access Points (APs) in your environment. Knowing what's there can help you immediately identify rogue APs.

Intrusion Detection Strategies

☑ Watch for unauthorized traffic on your network. Odd traffic can be a warning sign.

☑ Choose an intrusion detection software that best suits the needs of your environment. Make sure it supports customizable and updateable signatures.

☑ Keep your signature files current. Whether modifying them yourself, or downloading updates from the manufacturer, make sure this step isn't forgotten.

Conducting Vulnerability Assessments

☑ Use tools like NetStumbler and various client software to measure the strength of your 802.11b signal.

☑ Identify weaknesses in your wireless and wired security infrastructure.

☑ Use the findings to know where to fortify your defenses.

☑ Increase monitoring of potential trouble spots.

Incident Response and Handling

☑ If you already have a standard incident response policy, make updates to it to reflect new potential wireless incidents.

☑ Great incident response policy templates can be found on the Internet.

☑ While updating the policy for wireless activity, take the opportunity to review the policy in its entirety, and make changes where necessary to stay current. An out-of-date incident response policy can be as damaging as not having one at all.

Conducting Site Surveys for Rogue Access Points

☑ The threat is real, so be prepared. Have a notebook computer handy to use specifically for scanning networks.

☑ Conduct walkthroughs of your premises regularly, even if you don't have a wireless network.

☑ Keep a list of all authorized APs. Remember, Rogue APs aren't necessarily only placed by attackers. A well-meaning employee can install APs as well.

Frequently Asked Questions

The following Frequently Asked Questions, answered by the authors of this book, are designed to both measure your understanding of the concepts presented in this chapter and to assist you with real-life implementation of these concepts. To have your questions about this chapter answered by the author, browse to **www.syngress.com/solutions** and click on the **"Ask the Author"** form.

Q: I already have a wireless network installed, without any of the monitoring or intrusion detection you've mentioned. What can I do from here?

A: It's never too late to start. If you already have a network in place, start from the design phase anyway, and follow the steps we've listed. Adding to a currently in-production wireless network doesn't have to be difficult.

Q: I don't really think I know enough about security to perform a proper vulnerability assessment. What should I do?

A: You can always try. That's the best way to learn. However, until you're more comfortable, consider hiring an outside security vendor to perform a network vulnerability analysis for you. Even if you do know what you're doing, a second set of eyes on something can always be beneficial.

Q: I've bought an IDS system that says it is host-based. How can I make it start seeing the network traffic like you described in this chapter?

A: You can't. Host-based intrusion detection software is very different from network IDS. It mainly looks at the file system of the server on which it is installed, notices any changes to that system, and generates an alert from there. To watch the traffic, you need to look specifically for a network-based intrusion detection system.

Q: I can see a ton of APs from my office. How can I tell if any of them are on my network?

A: The first way would be to check the signal strength. If you're getting a faint signal that only appears intermittently, chances are it's not in your area. If you detect a strong signal, you can attempt to join the network and see if it assigns you an address from your network. Additionally, you could look at some of the traffic on the network to determine if it's yours, but that may introduce some legality questions, and is definitely not advised.

Q: I've found a rogue AP on my network. Now what?

A: First, start by determining who placed it. Was it an employee or an outside party? If it appears to be the work of an employee, question them about it to find out how long it has been present. The longer it has been around, the more likely an intrusion has taken place. In the case of it being put there by an attacker, handle it very carefully, and if necessary, be prepared to hand it over to the authorities. Also, consider having a professional system audit to see if any machines have been compromised.

Index